For Your Freedom a...

Lynne Olson and Stanley Cloud are co-authors of *The Murrow Boys*, a group biography of the American radio correspondents whom Edward R. Murrow hired before and during World War II to create CBS News. Olson is also the author of *Freedom's Daughters: The Unsung Heroines of the Civil Rights Movement from 1830 to 1970*. They are married to each other and live in Washington, D.C.

'Irksome as it is to read of Britain as a traitor and a coward, please swallow the pill and do so, because this is a tremendous story, grippingly told... As it was, the Poles, heroic, romantic, suffered the usual result of a clash between heart and politics. Their version deserves to be heard as widely as possible, since, as with the Holocaust, only knowledge gained by relatively honest minds can begin to expunge the shame of great historical wrongs.' *Spectator*

'A superb book... A moving tribute, as well as an indictment of Allied indifference' *Oxford Times*

'The Polish airmen who had escaped their savaged country in 1939 made a major contribution to the Royal Air Force's victory in the Battle of Britain in 1940. 303 Squadron, which they formed, was the most successful of all RAF units in shooting down German aircraft, attempting to bomb Britain into surrender. Their subsequent treatment by the British government including its refusal to let the survivors march in the Victory Parade of 1946, in craven deference to Stalin, was one of the most shameful episodes of the Cold War.' Sir John Keegan

'Olson and Cloud use the pilots' story as the centrepiece of an impassioned, riveting account of Poland's betrayal by Britain and the United States.' *Newsweek*

'Compelling reading... A passionately written, carefully researched piece of work – a fine tribute to a nation that, defying both Stalin and Hitler, refused to die.' *Catholic Herald*

'This book presents us with one of the most disgraceful ethical horrors of World War II – how, believing the need to support Stalin at all costs, we discredited, and later neglected, our oldest, bravest, and most trustworthy ally in order to conceal the truth of a revolting crime.' Robert Conquest

'This book will have you daydreaming about dogfights for weeks.' *Front*

'A gripping account of personal gallantry and of political treachery. On a par with the recent best-sellers about the fighting men of World War II.' Zbigniew Brzezinski

'Exciting and compelling, a fine story too rarely told, a tribute to the Polish fighting spirit, and a well-written war history about a distant but very good neighbor.' Alan Furst

Also by Lynne Olson and Stanley Cloud
The Murrow Boys

Also by Lynne Olson
Freedom's Daughters

FOR YOUR FREEDOM AND OURS

THE KOŚCIUSZKO SQUADRON:
FORGOTTEN HEROES
OF WORLD WAR II

LYNNE OLSON & STANLEY CLOUD

arrow books

Published in the United Kingdom in 2004 by Arrow Books

7 9 10 8 6

First published in the United Kingdom in 2003 by William Heinemann

First published in the US, under the title *A Question of Honor*, by Alfred A. Knopf, a division of Random House, Inc.

Arrow Books
The Random House Group Limited
20 Vauxhall Bridge Road, London, SW1V 2SA

Random House Australia (Pty) Limited
20 Alfred Street, Milsons Point, Sydney,
New South Wales 2061, Australia

Random House New Zealand Limited
18 Poland Road, Glenfield
Auckland 10, New Zealand

Random House (Pty) Limited
Isle of Houghton, Corner of Boundary Road & Carse O'Gowrie,
Houghton 2198, South Africa

The Random House Group Limited Reg. No. 954009

www.randomhouse.co.uk

A CIP catalogue record for this book
is available from the British Library

Papers used by Random House are natural, recyclable products made from wood grown in sustainable forests. The manufacturing processes conform to the environmental regulations of the country of origin

ISBN 9780099428121 (from Jan 2007)
ISBN 0099428121

Printed and bound in Great Britain by
Bookmarque Ltd, Croydon, Surrey

For the people of Poland

There is one helpful guide, namely, for a nation to keep its word and to act in accordance with its treaty obligations to allies. This guide is called honour.

—Winston Churchill

Contents

A Few Words About the Polish Language

To non-Polish eyes, written Polish, with its agglomerations of consonants, can seem daunting. It isn't quite as bad as it looks. The common combination **sz**, for example, is simply pronounced "sh." And **cz** is "ch." Joined as the startling but also very common **szcz**, the pronunciation, predictably, is "sh-ch" as in the Russian name KhruSHCHev, or the English words "freSH CHeese." Otherwise, with a few exceptions, those letters in the thirty-two-letter Polish alphabet that have English equivalents are pronounced more or less the same as in English, albeit somewhat more softly (**a**, for instance, is pronounced as in "waft."). As for the exceptions and extra letters, here is an abbreviated and somewhat simplified pronunciation guide:

- **Ą** or **ą** (as opposed to the **a** with no tail) stands for a somewhat nasal "awn" sound, as in "awning."
- **c** is "ts" as in "cats" (the Polish spelling of "tsar" is thus **car**).
- **ć** is "ch" as in "church" (only a Pole can tell the difference between the "ch" of **ć** and the "ch" of **cz**).
- **ch** is a guttural "kh" sound, as in the Scottish "loch."
- **Ę** or **ę** is a somewhat nasal "en," except before a **b** or **p**, when it becomes "em."
- **i** is "ee" as in "feet."
- **j** is a "y" sound, as in "yellow."
- **Ł** or **ł** is pronounced like the "w" in "warm."
- **Ń** or **ń** is a soft "n" that often sounds almost like "ing" with the "g" nearly silent.

- **Ó** or **ó** is "oo" as in "soot" (*not* "oo" as in "boot").
- **Ś** or **ś** is "sh" (again, the difference between this and the "sh" of **sz** is discernible only to Poles).
- **W** is "v" (thus, in Polish, Warsaw, which is spelled **Warszawa,** is pronounced "var-SHA-va"). At the end of a word, **w** is pronounced as an "f."
- **Ż** or **ż** is a "zh" sound like the "s" in "leisure" or the "j" in "soup du jour."

In Polish, virtually all multisyllabic words are accented on the penultimate syllable. For that reason, "Katyn," which seems to be more a Ukranian word than a Polish one, is pronounced "KA-tyn" in Polish and "ka-TYN" in Ukranian and Russian.

Here is the correct pronunciation of a few of the other words and names that appear in this book:

- **Władisław** is "vwa-DIS-waf."
- **Lwów** is "lvuf."
- **Kraków** is "KRAK-uf."
- **Gdańsk** is "gdainsk."
- **Poznań** is "POZ-nine."
- **Sejm** is "seim."
- **Lech Wałęsa** is "lekh va-WEN-sa."
- **Dęblin** is "DEM-blin."
- **Wojciech Jaruzelski** is "VOI-tsiekh yar-u-ZEL-ski."
- And, most important for our purposes, **Kościuszko** is "kosh-TSYUSH-ko" or, if that's a little awkward, just "kosh-TYUSH-ko" will do.

One final note: The family names of Polish women often have endings different from those of their husbands or male relatives. In most cases, a female's name ends in **a** ("ah") or **owa** ("ova"). Thus, Zdzisław Krasnodębski's wife is Wanda Krasnodębska.

THE FIVE

Mirosław Ferić
(mee-RO-swaf FEH-reech)

Witold Łokuciewski
(VEE-told wo-ku-TSIEV-ski)

Zdzisław Krasnodębski
(ZDEE-swaf kras-no-DEMP-ski)

Jan Zumbach
(yan TZUM-bach)

Witold Urbanowicz
(VEE-told oor-ba-NO-veech)

FOR YOUR FREEDOM AND OURS

Prologue

THEY MARCHED, twelve abreast and in perfect step, through the heart of bomb-pocked London. American troops, who were in a place of honor at the head of the nine-mile parade, were followed—in a kaleidoscope of uniforms, flags, and martial music—by Czechs and Norwegians, Chinese and Dutch, French and Iranians, Belgians and Australians, Canadians and South Africans. There were Sikhs in turbans, high-stepping Greek *evzoni* in pom-pommed shoes and white pleated skirts, Arabs in fezzes and *kaffiyehs*, grenadiers from Luxembourg, gunners from Brazil. And at the end of the parade, in a crowd-pleasing, Union Jack–waving climax, came at least 10,000 men and women from the armed forces and civilian services of His Britannic Majesty, King George VI.

Nearly a year earlier, the most terrible war in the history of the world—six years of fire, devastation, and unimaginable death—had finally ended. At the time there had been wild, spontaneous celebrations in cities all over the globe. But on this grey and damp June day in 1946, Britain and its invited guests, representing more than thirty victorious Allied nations, joined in formal commemoration of their collective victory and of those, living and dead, who had contributed to it. As church bells pealed and bagpipes skirled, veterans of Tobruk, the Battle of Britain, Guadalcanal, Midway, Normandy, the Ardennes, Monte Cassino, Arnhem, and scores of less famous fights were cheered and applauded by more than 2 million onlookers, many waving flags and tooting toy trumpets. The marchers snapped off salutes as they passed the reviewing platform on the Mall, where the king, his queen, and their two daughters stood. Prime Minister Clement Attlee was alongside the royal family, but the attention of many was focused on Attlee's predecessor, Winston Churchill, who had led and inspired Britain through the final five years of the war.

As the Victory Parade's last contingents marched by, a thunderous roar was heard overhead. The crowds stared up at the leaden sky, transfixed, as a massive armada of aircraft—bombers, fighters, flying boats, transports—approached from the east at nearly rooftop level. Leading the fly-past was a single, camouflaged fighter—a Hawker Hurricane, looking small and insignificant compared to the lumbering giants that flew in its wake. The Hurricane's pride of place, however, was unchallenged. If it had not been for this sturdy little single-seater and its more celebrated cousin, the Spitfire, the Victory Parade and the triumph it celebrated might never have occurred. In the summer and fall of 1940, RAF pilots had flown Hurricanes and Spitfires against Adolf Hitler's Luftwaffe and had won the Battle of Britain. In so doing, they changed the course of the war and the very nature of history.

Standing along the parade route that day was a tall, slender, fair-haired man with the difficult name of Witold Urbanowicz. As he watched the Hurricane flash by overhead, a flood of memories returned to him. He had been up there in a Hurricane during the Battle of Britain. He had gazed down on this city when it was blazing with fire. His squadron had become a legend of the battle. On the first day of the London Blitz—Hitler's attempt to bomb the British civilian population into submission—Urbanowicz's squadron was credited with shooting down no fewer than fourteen German aircraft, a Royal Air Force record.

Setting records had already become a habit for 303 Squadron—or the "Kościuszko Squadron," as it was also known. In its first eight days of combat, the squadron destroyed nearly forty enemy planes. By the Battle of Britain's end, it was credited with downing more German aircraft than any other squadron attached to the RAF. Nine of its pilots, including Urbanowicz, were formally designated as aces. Writing in *Collier's* three years after the battle, an American fighter pilot described 303 as "the best sky fighters I saw anywhere."

Yet, despite its accomplishments in the war, none of 303's pilots took part in the fly-past. None marched in the parade. For they were all Polish—and Poles who had fought under British command were deliberately and specifically barred from the celebration by the British government, for fear of offending Joseph Stalin. A week earlier, ten members of Parliament had written a letter of protest against the exclusion. "Ethiopians will be there," the letter declared. "Mexicans will be there. The Fiji Medical Corps, the Labuan Police and the Seychelles Pioneer Corps will [march]—and rightly, too. But the Poles will not be there. Have we lost not only our sense of perspective, but our sense of gratitude as well?"

———————

ON A JUNE day six years earlier, Winston Churchill had risen in the House of Commons to declare: "The battle of France is over. I expect that the battle of Britain is about to begin." From the first, the new prime minister, who had been in office barely a month, made clear that Britain would not follow France into ignominy: there would be no British capitulation to Germany. "We shall fight on the beaches," Churchill famously said. "We shall fight on the landing grounds, we shall fight in the fields and in the streets, we shall fight in the hills. We shall never surrender."

The courage and character that Churchill pledged for Britain had already been demonstrated by Poland. It was the first country to experience the terror of the Nazi *Blitzkrieg*, the first to fight back, the first to say—and mean—"We shall *never* surrender." Poland fell in October 1939, but its government and military refused then, and refused for the rest of the war, to capitulate. In a remarkable odyssey, scores of thousands of Polish pilots, soldiers, and sailors escaped Poland—some on foot; some in cars, trucks, and buses; some in airplanes; some in ships and submarines. They made their various ways first to France, thence to Britain to continue the fight. For the first full year of the war, Poland, whose government-in-exile operated from London, was Britain's most important declared ally.

When dozens of Polish fighter pilots, including 303 Squadron, took to the air during the Battle of Britain, the RAF already had lost hundreds of its own fliers, replaced in many cases by neophytes who barely knew how to fly, much less fight. The contribution of the combat-hardened Poles, especially the men of 303, was vital. Indeed, many believe it was decisive. "If Poland had not stood with us in those days...the candle of freedom might have been snuffed out," Queen Elizabeth remarked in 1996.

In all, some 17,000 Polish airmen fought alongside the RAF during the war. But the pilots and air crews were not the only Poles to play an important part in the conflict. The small Polish navy participated in several important operations. Polish infantry and airborne units fought in Norway, North Africa, Italy, France, Belgium, and Germany. By the war's end, Poland was the fourth largest contributor to the Allied effort in Europe, after the Soviet Union, the United States, and Britain and its Commonwealth. "If it had been given to me to choose the soldiers I would like to command," said Field Marshal Harold Alexander, commander of the Allied forces in North Africa and Italy, "I would have chosen the Poles."

Perhaps as significant as its role in combat was Poland's contribution to the Allies' greatest intelligence coup—deciphering the German military codes generated by the Enigma machine. Only Churchill and a handful of other British officials knew at the time of the Victory Parade that Polish cryptographers had provided the initial breakthrough for cracking Enigma—with incalculable importance to the outcome of the war.

And what did the Poles want in return? "We wanted Poland back," said Witold Urbanowicz. Throughout the war, Winston Churchill, moved by the Poles' valor, grateful for their help, and horrified by the Nazis' unprecedented savagery in their homeland, promised they would get it. "We shall conquer together or we shall die together," Churchill vowed to the Polish prime minister, General Władysław Sikorski, after the fall of France. Meeting Polish troops as they arrived in England in June 1940, British war secretary Anthony Eden declared: "We shall not abandon your sacred cause and shall continue this war until your beloved country be returned to her faithful sons."

Yet, as the great long line of marchers proceeded down the Mall on that June morning in 1946, and as the crowds cheered and basked in the postwar world's rebirth of freedom, proud Poland remained in the shadows. Despite Eden's pledge, its "sacred cause" *had* been abandoned by its two closest allies, Britain and the United States. One occupier, Hitler, had been replaced by another, Joseph Stalin. And on that gala day, Polish war heroes like Urbanowicz and his fellow 303 pilots—once called "the Glamor Boys of England"—were forced to stand on London sidewalks and watch.

One young Polish pilot looked on in silence while the parade passed. Then he turned to walk away. An old woman standing next to him looked at him quizzically. "Why are you crying, young man?" she asked.

PART ONE

———

EXODUS

CHAPTER ONE

Into the Air

THE NIGHT before the barnstormers came to Jan Zumbach's hometown, he was so excited he couldn't sleep. No flying machine had set down in little Brodnica before, and thirteen-year-old Jan, in the spring of 1928, had never laid eyes on one of those aviators he had heard and read so much about. When the sun finally rose the next morning, Jan and his family proceeded to the large meadow outside of town. It was National Defense Week in ever threatened, ever patriotic Poland, and nearly all the men, women, and children in Brodnica were on hand for the celebration. Flags were flying, tents had been erected for local officials and honored guests, a military band was working its way through its repertoire of polkas, marches, waltzes, and mazurkas, with a little opera thrown in for variety's sake. On the edge of the meadow, behind a cordon of uniformed soldiers, sat two gleaming Polish-built Potez 25 biplanes. Just looking at them made Jan all the more eager for the band to desist and the show to begin.

At long last, the bandleader laid down his baton. The crowd hushed. Jan and the other youngsters pressed forward as far as they could. The pilots, four of them, adjusted their leather helmets, pulled down their goggles, and climbed into their twin, open-cockpit two-seaters. With cool and practiced waves to the spellbound audience, they started off in a white blast of exhaust and a tractorlike roar. The propwash whipped off men's hats and fluttered women's skirts. Wingtip-to-wingtip, the two planes bounced over the meadow, then lifted and soared, taking Jan's heart with them as they climbed. Seconds later, still in close formation, they swooped low over the crowd.

Jan was one of the few who did not hurl himself facedown on the grass. Transfixed, he watched as the planes climbed again, looped-the-loop, then plunged into twin, heart-stopping nosedives. When they were what seemed only a few feet from the hard earth, they pulled up and were gone, vanished over the eastern horizon. In their place were silence and a gentle late-spring breeze. Then, while the crowd still gaped and began to wonder if the show was over, the Potez 25s exploded out of the west in a gut-wrenching, tree-level grand finale that had the men cheering at the top of their lungs and the women nervously fanning themselves.

And it was there and then, in that meadow, at that instant, that young Jan Zumbach, hovering somewhere between laughter and tears, "swore by all the saints that I must, I would, be a pilot."

At just about this same time, in a town called Ostrów Wielkopolski, 100 or so miles southwest of Brodnica, thirteen-year-old Mirosław Ferić was haunting the local *aeroklub,* watching planes take off and land, waiting impatiently for the day when *he* would be in the cockpit. Mika Ferić had always enjoyed testing gravity's limits. From an early age, he liked to teeter—arms outstretched like a tightrope walker's—on the narrow iron railing around the fourth-floor balcony of his family's apartment. Sometimes, he would swing by one arm from the same railing, terrifying his mother as she worked in her little garden, thirty or forty feet below. Mika, the mischievous ringleader of a group of neighborhood boys, was always the one to come up with daredevil games somewhere above ground level—scaling the red-tile roofs of other buildings in the apartment complex, or leaping to the ground from the garden sheds in back. "He was absolutely fearless," said Edward Idzior, Mika's closest childhood chum.

Budding aviators like Jan Zumbach and Mika Ferić (and more than a few girls) were everywhere in Poland in those days. Indeed, by the late 1920s, the mere idea of flying, of a perfect escape from the mundane realities of life, was captivating young minds and souls all over the globe. Charles Lindbergh's nonstop, transatlantic solo flight from Long Island to Paris in 1927 epitomized the romanticism and excitement of aviation. But other countries had lesser Lindberghs. Two years before the Lone Eagle landed at Orly, for instance, a young Polish military pilot named Bolesław Orliński flew solo (with several stops) from Warsaw to Tokyo—a distance of about 4,000 miles. Orliński's feat didn't come close to matching Lindbergh's, but he and others like him were local heroes all the same.

The fascination of young Poles with airplanes and flying was to have significant implications for the Polish military, for Polish society in general, and, in World War II, for the world. Historically, Poland's most dashing figures had come from the cavalry. During the sixteenth and seventeenth centuries, when Poland was a great power, mounted warriors were the key to its military might. Foreign armies, from the Turks to the Teutonic Knights, envied and feared the Polish cavalry. Of particular renown were the *Husaria,* who rode caparisoned steeds into battle and wore plumed helmets, jewel-encrusted breastplates, and large arcs of eagle feathers that seemed to rise, winglike, out of their backs. (The feather-covered steel frames were actually attached to their saddles.) In their day, the *Husaria* were the equivalent of Hitler's Panzer units: heavily armed, highly mobile, intended to crush enemy defenses in lightning charges. In one famous seventeenth-century battle, a Polish force of 3,500, including some 2,500 *Husaria,* crushed a Swedish army of 11,000.

To generations of young people, Poland *was* the *Husaria.* But to those who came of age after World War I—when the country was finally freed from more than a century of subjugation by the Germans, Austrians, and Russians—the cavalry had become a relic. The sons and daughters of a reborn nation were looking for new, more modern heroes. They found them in the air.

That the romance of flying attracted women as well as men made aviation all the more appealing to the men. In 1928, Witold Urbanowicz was a promising young military cadet from a modestly well-off family who was headed, as was expected of him, into the cavalry. One day, he and several classmates were at a restaurant near the Warsaw aerodrome. Sitting on the restaurant terrace, they watched as a Polish Air Force plane performed complicated, low-altitude maneuvers overhead. Witold and his companions could not help noticing that the pilot and his aerobatics had the full and admiring attention of a group of attractive young women at a nearby table. One of the women cast a jaundiced eye Urbanowicz's way. "You can't *do* such things on a horse!" she observed. It wasn't long before Urbanowicz decided to forget the cavalry and throw in his lot with the air force.

Unlike the cavalry, regarded by wealthy landowners and their sons as their private domain, aviation, in the more egalitarian Polish society of the 1920s, was open to just about anyone. Government-sponsored *aeroklubs* had been established all over the country, offering gliders, airplanes, and free lessons to those who wanted to fly. Among the teenagers who took advantage of the opportunity was Jadwiga Piłsudska, the pretty teenage daughter of Poland's chief of state, Marshal Józef Piłsudski. A cavalryman, Piłsudski did not approve of his daughter's soaring ambition, and he was not the only parent who felt that way. The mothers of Zumbach, Ferić, and countless other would-be pilots were similarly appalled.

When Zumbach first announced his aerial plans, his mother, the widow of a wealthy landowner, exploded. Aviators were drunkards and madmen! Jan's duty was to help his brothers manage their late father's large estate. "Yet, try as she might, my mother lost her battle to make me forget about flying," Zumbach reported. "She never stood a chance." At nineteen, he forged her signature on papers authorizing him to enlist in the military. After a few months of training in the infantry, he was accepted into the Polish Air Force academy at Dęblin. Mika Ferić's mother, a teacher whose Croatian husband had abandoned the family, was similarly horrified at her son's fascination with flying, and, as with Mrs. Zumbach, the first she heard of her son's application to Dęblin was after he had been accepted.

DĘBLIN SITS on a flat, grassy plain about 70 miles south of Warsaw, rimmed in the far distance by the low Bobrowniki Hills. The academy's headquarters is an eighteenth-century manor house that Tsar Nicholas I seized in 1825 after exiling the nobleman-owner to Siberia for plotting a Polish rebellion against Russia. Five years later, the tsar gave the white-columned house to a Russian general who had suppressed yet another uprising against the Russian occupiers. When Poland regained its independence in 1918, the new government turned the house and its magnificent lawns and gardens over to the air force.

With so many young Poles interested in aviation, Dęblin had a wealth of applicants in the 1920s and 1930s. By 1936, the year Zumbach and Ferić entered the school, more than 6,000 young men were competing for only 90 places. The new cadets came from every level of society. Landowners' sons joined the sons of peasants, teachers, miners, and artists. As soon as they arrived, these young men who represented Poland's future found themselves immersed in Poland's past. They dined in the 200-year-old manor house, with its parquet floors and crystal chandeliers, and received instruction in the art of being a gentleman as well as in the art of flying. They were taught that an officer, gentleman, and pilot always brings flowers when calling on a lady and always kisses the lady's hand—just so—on arrival and departure. An officer, gentleman, and pilot did not gamble, drink to excess, boast, or issue IOUs. At glittering formal balls in the academy's ballroom, the cadets practiced what they learned. They waltzed and danced the mazurka with fashionable young ladies. They kissed the women's hands and spoke of gentlemanly things. "Remember," the Cadet's Code declared, "that you are a worthy successor of the *Husaria* and of the pioneers of Polish aviation. Remember to be chivalrous always and everywhere."

Dęblin graduates appear to have taken most of their social training to heart—even if some did cut corners on the code's more puritanical aspects. Although discipline at the academy was famously strict, many cadets managed to become as well known for their off-duty escapades and for thumbing their noses at military authority as for their flying skills. To show off for girlfriends, cadet pilots were known to fly under bridges and between church spires, and if, while airborne, they happened to spot any stuffy, self-important cavalry officers riding through the countryside, they might buzz them to spook their mounts.

Prominent among the hell-raisers at Dęblin in the late 1930s were Zumbach, Ferić, and Witold Łokuciewski, a former cavalry officer with the dark, boyish good looks of a movie star and the raffish attitude of a born gambler. Łokuciewski, who came from an old landed family in eastern Poland, had been one of those cavalrymen whose horses were deliberately panicked by low-flying planes from Dęblin. But instead of cursing the pilots, as others did, Łokuciewski (who wasn't particularly fond of horses to begin with) dreamed of shedding his equine, earthbound existence and taking to the sky. When he got the chance to go to Dęblin, he grabbed it.

Known as "the Three Musketeers" during World War II, Zumbach, Ferić, and Łokuciewski were in almost constant trouble during their days as cadets. Class standing was based in part on a cadet's personal conduct and his willingness to follow orders. In the class of 1938, Łokuciewski finished next to last, Ferić eighth from last, and Zumbach thirty-eighth from last. According to a Polish Air Force historian, while "the Three Musketeers" were at Dęblin their main interests were "wine, women, song—and only then study."

But, oh, how they could fly! They not only survived their Dęblin training—which was as grueling and difficult as any flight training on earth—they excelled at it. After rigorous classroom courses in aerodynamics, navigation, physics, and mechanics, they learned to operate a variety of aircraft. But the primitive, open-cockpit trainers they flew tended to be old and were prone to malfunction—all of which, in a kind of aeronautical Darwinism, made better pilots of those who managed to survive. Of necessity, staying alert, using one's eyes, and improvisation were important parts of a Polish pilot's training. "We were trained to scan the sky, to look everywhere, not just in front of us," said one Polish flier. "At one time, I could turn my head almost a hundred and eighty degrees—really! a hundred and eighty!—watching for the enemy." American and British pilots who later flew with the Poles testified that they seemed to see the sky—the whole sky—better than anyone else.

Polish pilots also learned to be daring. In one exercise, Jan Zumbach was ordered to fly in a close, wing-to-wing formation with another aircraft, then to turn back and head directly at a third plane—nose-to-nose, at full speed. He was not to veer off until it was just short of too late. Following orders, Zumbach barreled toward the other plane. He waited . . . and waited . . . until he thought he could see the other pilot's eyes. Only then did he swerve—another tenth of a second, he believed, and they would have collided. After he landed, proud of his coolness under pressure, he was confronted by his commanding officer, who snapped: "Zumbach, you turned too damn *soon*!"

After Dęblin, the cadets were sent to air force squadrons throughout the country for more intense instruction. Zumbach and Ferić were told to report to the Kościuszko Squadron in Warsaw, a choice assignment. In the romantic, daredevil world of the Polish Air Force, the Kościuszko Squadron was unique. It had been formed in 1919 by a group of American pilots, come to Poland to volunteer in a nasty little war that the newly independent Poles were having with newly created Soviet Russia. Among the Yank volunteers were a former Harvard law student, a star football player from Lehigh, and a graduate of Yale.

The man who brought them all to Poland was a twenty-eight-year-old war hero with a thick Southern drawl named Merian C. Cooper.

CHAPTER TWO

"This Race Which Would Not Die"

THE SON OF a prominent Florida lawyer, Merian Cooper had been bewitched by Poland for as long as he could remember. Growing up in Jacksonville at the turn of the century, he had listened to stories about the friendship between his great-great-grandfather, Colonel John Cooper, and Kazimierz Pułaski, a Polish hero of the American Revolution. The tales of Poland's glorious but tragic past, told to Colonel Cooper by Pułaski, were passed down to later generations of the Cooper family. There was no more eager audience than young Merian.

SET ON A vast plain in Central Europe, Poland is protected on the north by the Baltic Sea and on the south by the Carpathian Mountains, with little natural protection to the east and west. Linguistically, the country is Slavic, but its culture, religion, and economics have long linked it to the West—at first mainly to Italy and France, later to Great Britain and America. For more than 200 years, from the fifteenth to the mid-seventeenth centuries, the Poles were a great European power with a mighty army. They had combined with Lithuania to form a vast multilingual and multiethnic commonwealth that eventually covered nearly a third of Europe, including Byelorussia and much of the Ukraine.

From the fourteenth century to the Age of Reason, Poland was probably continental Europe's most progressive country and certainly its most tolerant. Although predominantly Roman Catholic, Poland offered unrestricted religious freedom to anyone living within its boundaries, including hundreds of thousands of Jews, who had been welcomed there when other European nations were persecuting them. By the seventeenth century, more than four fifths of the world's Jews lived in Poland, mostly in separate, self-governing communities. There were times of animosity and tension between Christians and Jews, but in general, Polish Jews were able to live for several centuries in relative peace (and, for some, prosperity).

Among the Polish people's most striking characteristics is their devotion to personal freedom, rooted in a conviction that the state exists to serve the individual, rather than the reverse. By the late 1500s, when rigid autocracy still reigned in the rest of Europe, Poland had emerged as a limited parliamentary democracy, offering many of its citizens an unparalleled degree of constitutional, intellectual, and religious liberty. Poland's kings were elected and their powers limited by the *szlachta*, the country's gentry (a uniquely Polish institution of high- and lowborn, wealthy and poor, landed and landless).* Later, as the Bill of Rights was being tacked onto the U.S. Constitution, Poland produced a written constitution of its own—the first in Europe and only the second in the world.

By then, however, the Polish commonwealth had already disintegrated. Corruption, rural poverty and ignorance, as well as a reluctance to adapt Polish governmental and social structures to the requirements of modern life, all took their toll. Meanwhile, as Poland slowly lost its ability to shape its own destiny, powerful absolutist states were growing up around it. Poles were increasingly scorned and ridiculed by these hostile and aggressive neighbors, who now felt more or less free to paw over Polish territory at will.

Between the last half of the eighteenth century and 1989, Poland was essentially naked to its enemies. The most prominent and persistent of these were the Russians, Austrians, and Germans in all their various geopolitical guises—Russia, the Soviet Union, Austria, the Austro-Hungarian Empire, Prussia, and the unified Germany of Bismarck,

---

* By requiring that an act of the parliament, or *Sejm*, be passed unanimously in order to become law—the so-called *liberum veto*—the *szlachta* struck a blow for the power of the individual over the state, but the requirement predictably hog-tied the government and in time contributed to Poland's decline.

Kaiser Wilhelm, and Adolf Hitler. In 1772, Russia, Prussia, and Austria combined to partition Poland, dividing large parts of the commonwealth's territory among themselves and gradually replacing Polish governance with their own. This was the beginning of one of the darkest periods in Polish history. The Poles rose up repeatedly against their oppressors—particularly the Russians—and repeatedly were crushed.

Yet, through it all, they somehow managed to retain their sense of themselves, their language, their culture, their patriotic zeal, their progressive instincts—and to take heart from news of uprisings and revolutions elsewhere. Beginning in the eighteenth century, the Polish slogan, "For Your Freedom and Ours," implying Polish unity with all lovers of liberty, became a virtual creed. In the late 1770s, more than a hundred Poles crossed the Atlantic to fight with the American colonists in their struggle against the British crown. Among those who made the journey were two officers who would take their place in both the American and Polish pantheons: Kazimierz Pułaski and Tadeusz Kościuszko.

YOUNG MERIAN COOPER knew a great deal about Pułaski: How this brilliant cavalry officer had been sent into exile in 1776, after helping lead one of his country's many failed uprisings against its occupiers. How Pułaski arrived in Paris and met Benjamin Franklin, America's minister to France, who was trying to recruit Europeans into George Washington's Continental Army. How Franklin had written to Washington, urging him to make room in the army for this young Polish officer, "famous throughout Europe for his bravery and conduct in the defence of the liberties of his country." How the Continental Congress in 1777 authorized a brigadier's commission for Pułaski and charged him with organizing, equipping, and commanding America's first cavalry unit.

Resplendent in his hussar's uniform with its plumed helmet and yards of glittering gold braid, the fiery Pułaski stood out like a peacock against the grey of much of Washington's bedraggled army. Expert in guerrilla warfare and an excellent organizer, he transformed a motley bunch of colonial horsemen into "the Pułaski Legion"—a disciplined cavalry that covered Washington's many tactical retreats, spied on and harried advancing British columns, slowed their pursuit, and time and again saved the Continental Army from destruction.

Colonel John Cooper was among Pułaski's senior officers (along with thirteen Poles) and soon became his close friend. In the Battle of Savannah in 1779, Cooper and Pułaski were riding side by side during a charge when Pułaski was cut down by British grapeshot. According to family lore, Colonel Cooper personally carried his mortally wounded friend from the battlefield to the *Wasp,* an American warship anchored in the Savannah River estuary. Two days later, as the *Wasp* was making for Charleston, Pułaski died in Cooper's arms and was buried at sea.

While Merian Cooper was most enthralled by the stories about his great-great-grandfather and Pułaski, he was also well aware of the key role played in the Revolution by Pułaski's quiet and unassuming compatriot, Tadeusz Kościuszko. Kościuszko did not cut the same dashing figure as Pułaski, the Marquis de Lafayette, Baron von Steuben, and some of the other foreign officers in Washington's army. He did not lead troops into battle until late in the war, and then only briefly, during the fight for Charleston. What he did do was design and build fortifications, and he did it so brilliantly that he was given much of the credit for the American victory that proved to be the turning point of the Revolution.

An engineer whose specialty was defensive warfare, Kościuszko arrived in Philadelphia in 1776 and was made a colonel in Washington's army. The following year, he used the lovely, rolling New York countryside near Saratoga to create a killing field: a series of ingenious wood and earthen defenses that lured the British army into a position where it could be surrounded and defeated by a considerably smaller force. The resultant American victory at Saratoga helped change the course of the war, giving new confidence to Washington's army, and bringing France officially into the conflict on the American side. Afterward, General Horatio Gates, commander of the American forces at Saratoga, sought to deflect those who considered him to have been the hero of the battle. "Let us be honest...," he wrote. "The great tacticians of the campaign were the hills and forests which a young Polish Engineer was skillful enough to select for my encampment."

In 1778, Kościuszko oversaw the construction of fortifications at West Point, on the high western bank of the Hudson River, a spot that Washington had called "the key to America." Kościuszko's impregnable fortress, which made the Hudson River impassable to British troops, protected the Hudson Valley and the rest of upstate New York from attack for the remainder of the war.

George Washington, who well understood the importance of Kościuszko's contributions to the Revolution, was one of the Pole's particular admirers. Unlike some of Washington's other officers, the handsome, soft-spoken Kościuszko seemed without ego or overweening ambition. He even declined a promotion to brigadier for his work at West Point. In private correspondence, Washington frequently found reasons to extol Kościuszko and his deeds, in the process employing wonderfully creative spellings of the Pole's tongue-twisting name. (Washington, who had trouble enough with the spelling of many English words, variously spelled the foreigner's name as "Cosdusko," "Koshiosko," "Kosciousko," "Kosciuisco," and "Cosieski.") Kościuszko's manifold services to the American cause were formally heralded in 1783, when the Continental Congress granted him U.S. citizenship, a pension, title to various tracts of land, and the rank of brigadier general.

The next year, Kościuszko decided to return home and use the battlefield experience and strategic and tactical knowledge he had gained in America to renew the fight for freedom in Poland. He found, however, that his fellow countrymen were already preparing for rebellion. The partial partition of Poland twelve years earlier had only whetted the Polish appetite for independence.

On May 3, 1791, the *Sejm* (parliament) adopted a written constitution, modeled in part on the U.S. Constitution, that instituted sweeping social and political reforms. This act of Polish insolence could hardly fail to capture the attention of Catherine the Great, the autocratic Russian tsarina. Catherine did not think much of democratic impulses anywhere, and certainly not in what she regarded as her Slavic backyard. She promptly ordered the Russian army to put a stop to all this idealistic nonsense. The Poles' own army, with Kościuszko among its top commanders, fought bravely but was hopelessly overmatched and soon defeated. With repressive order thus reestablished, Catherine wasted no time in canceling the Polish constitution and joining with her Prussian and Austrian partners to impose a second and more severe partition. When their work was finished in 1793, all that was left of Poland was an 80,000-square-mile area around Warsaw and Lublin, with a puppet king and a resident Russian garrison.

Undaunted, Kościuszko set out almost immediately to organize a new revolt. In 1794, he led a popular-front army of 6,000 soldiers, among them many peasants armed with scythes and pitchforks, that won several early and impressive victories over the Russians. (Polish uprisings in the eighteenth and nineteenth centuries tended to be aimed primarily eastward, at the Russians, the harshest of Poland's three main oppressors.) His early success emboldened Kościuszko to issue a startling new manifesto of freedom calling for, among other things, property rights for peasants and the abolition of both the monarchy and serfdom. Kościuszko's manifesto, coming so soon after the second partition and after the revolutions in America and France, caused considerable distress among Europe's monarchists, particularly those in Moscow, Berlin, and Vienna.

A combined Russian-Prussian-Austrian force was hastily assembled and ordered to crush this latest example of Polish impudence. At the climactic Battle of Maciejowice, Kościuszko, wearing the white cloak and red, four-cornered hat of a peasant, was gravely wounded—slashed across the head with a saber, bayoneted three times as he lay on the ground, his leg shattered by a cannonball. The general survived, but his army was defeated, and Catherine ordered that "my poor beast of a Kostiushka," as she dismissively referred to him, be thrown into a Russian prison. Without Kościuszko, the Polish army was leaderless, and the uprising lacked intellectual cohesion. The Russians advanced on Warsaw and, after a horrific bloodbath, overran it. Poland lay utterly prostrate.

Vowing to rid themselves of this troublesome nation once and forever, the victors ordered the third partition in twenty-three years. This time there were to be no half-measures: in 1795, Poland was simply erased from the map of Europe. Declared a Prussian state document: "It is the wish of [the] King, who is supported by the Empress of Russia, that from this day henceforth the word Poland never be used in any official document or spoken in any government circle. In our several portions, every effort must be made to stamp out the language [and] the history...." It would be another century and a quarter before an independent Poland would emerge from behind this imperial shroud.

When Catherine the Great died in 1796, her son, Paul, the new tsar, who seems to have detested his mother even more than he detested the Poles, ordered Kościuszko released and sent into exile. Thus barred

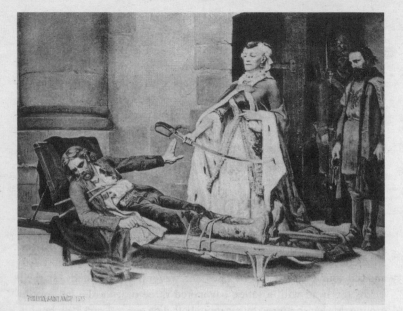

A gravely wounded Tadeusz Kościuszko, tied to a litter and in captivity after leading an unsuccessful rebellion against the Russians in 1794, rebuffs the disdainful offer of a sword by Tsarina Catherine the Great. (Library of Congress)

from returning home, the Polish general, whose wounds had never been treated properly by the Russians and who was unable to sit upright or walk unaided, returned to America for a visit, then moved to France and finally to Switzerland. All the while, he continued to work for Polish independence.

Shortly before his death of typhoid fever in 1817, Kościuszko wrote out his will. In it, this ardent champion of personal liberty freed all the serfs on his Polish estates. In a separate, earlier will disposing of his assets in America, he ordered that the property be sold and the proceeds be used to free and educate "in my name" as many American slaves as possible. He appointed his close friend Thomas Jefferson as executor and suggested that the proceeds from the sale of land be used to free some of Jefferson's own slaves at Monticello. In a tribute to Kościuszko after his death, Jefferson declared him to have been "as pure a son of liberty as I have ever known." Be that as it may, Kościuszko's directives regarding slaves were never carried out by Jefferson or anyone else.*

As the United States, having won its independence, embarked on an era of vigorous expansion, Poland faded into—and out of—memory. Throughout the world, there was sympathy for its plight, outrage toward the nations that had consumed it, and admiration for the heroics of Kościuszko and his followers. A Kościuszko craze swept English Romantic literary circles: Coleridge, Keats, and Byron were just a few of the literary figures who wrote paeans to Kościuszko in the early nineteenth century. Prominent American writers, including James Fenimore Cooper and Ralph Waldo Emerson, would also be swept up in outpourings of pro-Polish sentiment, and Edgar Allan Poe would go so far as to volunteer to fight with the Poles in their 1831 uprising against the Russians.

Yet, in spite of all the high-flown talk by foreign poets and politicians, nothing concrete was ever done to help this Central European country with its Western European mentality. No nation sent arms or financial aid; none marched to Poland's rescue. As Edmund Burke, who championed the Polish cause in the British House of Commons, acknowledged, "Poland might be, in fact, considered...a country on the moon" as far as England and the rest of the West were concerned. With no fear of challenge, Poland's two most ruthless occupiers, Russia and Prussia (which in 1871 became part of the German Empire), were free over the next 120 years to do their best to obliterate everything Polish. The Polish flag, national anthem, coat of arms, and other emblems of nationhood were branded as illegal and subversive. Russian troops confiscated the royal throne, and Prussian forces melted down the crown jewels. The singing of patriotic Polish songs was treason.

In an attempt to justify their actions, Russians and Germans promoted a highly distorted view of Polish history—one that has profoundly shaped Poland's international image ever since. Wiped out were the centuries of Poland's power and international prominence, its

---

* Jefferson, seventy-five at the time, pleaded that he was too old to take on the duties of executor. Some historians have speculated that he had qualms about freeing slaves. In any case, after a decades-long court fight, Kościuszko's estate went to his descendants in Poland.

religious tolerance, its traditions of freedom and independence. Russian and German propagandists peddled a cartoon image of the Poles that has lasted into the twenty-first century: a hopelessly romantic, ignorant, and impractical people—gallant but emotional; expert at drinking, fighting, and dying bravely but congenitally unable to govern themselves. As the oppressors explained it, they were not persecuting this chaotic country, merely imposing some much-needed order and discipline.

Seen from the Poles' perspective, however, the occupying powers were a tyranny to be resisted at all costs and at every turn. Regardless of which sector of their fragmented country they happened to occupy—the Russian, the German, or the Austrian—Poles clung stubbornly to their national identity and harbored thoughts of rebellion. In the first half of the nineteenth century, the advent of the Romantic movement in the arts struck a particularly responsive chord, serving to enhance the Poles' sense of loss and to renew their hope that Poland might someday regain its lost glory. In 1831, and again in 1863, thousands of Poles rose up against Russia. Both times, the insurrections were brutally quashed. Many rebels were tortured and executed. Others were sentenced to life at hard labor, then chained together and forced to march to Siberia. Yet Polish nationalism endured.

———

THE STORIES OF Poland's courage, struggle, and tragic failures were powerful stuff for young Merian Cooper, at home in Florida. By the time he reached adolescence, he was like a gun loaded and ready to fire. He wanted not only to defend America against all enemies, foreign and domestic, but also—somehow, somewhere, sometime—to repay what he saw as America's 150-year-old debt to Poland.

Like countless other youngsters, he had been captivated by the idea of flight from the day he heard that the Wright Brothers' creaky aeroplane had flown 120 feet from Kitty Hawk's windy Kill Devil Hills. In 1915, World War I having begun in Europe, the twenty-three-year-old Cooper enlisted in the Army Signal Corps, which in those days incorporated the fledgling U.S. aviation service. He could barely contain his excitement when he won his wings and a commission as a first lieutenant. In 1917, after the United States entered the war, he received orders for France. On his arrival, he wrote to his father: "I am the happiest I have been.... I am at the front at last."

The American squadron to which Cooper was assigned consisted of seven dilapidated De Havilland biplanes, dubbed "flying coffins" by the pilots. On September 26, 1918, the squadron was sent on a bombing raid over the Argonne Forest in support of a massive French offensive against the Hindenburg Line. Twenty-odd German fighters intercepted the Americans. During a furious dogfight, Cooper's De Havilland was raked by machine-gun fire, and the engine burst into flames. His "observer," Lieutenant Edmund Leonard, who acted as the pilot's gunner and eyes in combat, was shot in the neck. As the De Havilland began slowly spiraling to earth, Cooper, his face and hands fearfully burned, unbuckled his safety belt and clambered out of the now-blazing cockpit onto the wing. To jump meant certain death—military pilots didn't carry parachutes in those days—but Cooper, in agony, didn't care. "The only thing in the world that I wanted to do," he wrote, "was to get out of that pain."

Certain that his observer was dead, he was preparing to leap when he saw Leonard's eyes flicker open. Cooper struggled back into the cockpit, revved the engine, and, using his unburned knees and elbows to manipulate the stick, sent his plane—its cloth-covered, wooden frame by now riddled by more than sixty bullet holes—into a steep dive. His hope was that the wind created by the dive would extinguish the engine fire. It did. A few hundred feet above the ground, Cooper pulled out, then crash-landed in a large, grassy field. Moments later, one of the German planes landed nearby. True to the chivalric code that governed the early days of aerial combat, the Luftwaffe pilot saluted his gravely wounded enemies, took them captive, and summoned medical assistance for them.*

Cooper and Leonard spent the remaining weeks of the war in German prison hospitals, where they received good care and, being young, healed quickly. When the armistice was announced, Cooper felt that he had been "cheated." Released from the hospital, the husky, sandy-haired pilot was in no mood to return home and settle down. Marguerite Harrison, an American journalist who met him in Warsaw not long after the

---

* After the war, Cooper's superiors recommended him for the Distinguished Service Cross (DSC), citing his "extraordinary heroism and personal bravery." But Cooper thought others in his squadron deserved the medal more and refused to accept it.

war, found Cooper to be "stubborn as a mule, moody, quick-tempered," a man of "immense vitality [whose] body seemed strung on steel springs." What Cooper wanted was more combat. He would soon get his wish—in Poland.

———————

WHEN WORLD WAR I erupted, with Germany and Russia on opposite sides, the Poles saw an opportunity to break free. They received further encouragement in March 1918, a year after the Russian Revolution, when the new Soviet regime signed the Brest-Litovsk Treaty with Germany and the other Central Powers. Under the treaty, the Soviets agreed not only to end their participation in the war but to relinquish all tsarist claims on Poland and several other countries. Eight months later, Germany was defeated, Russia had a civil war on its hands, and the victorious Allies were sitting down to redraw the map of Europe.

This was precisely what the Poles had been waiting for. Thanks in no small measure to backroom politicking by the famed Polish pianist, composer, and statesman Ignacy Paderewski, U.S. president Woodrow Wilson was persuaded to support the cause of Polish independence. On January 8, 1918, Wilson appeared before a joint session of Congress to announce U.S. war aims, which became known as the Fourteen Points. Wilson's penultimate point called for the resurrection of a self-governing Poland with "a free and secure access to the sea" and whose "political and economic independence and territorial integrity should be guaranteed by international covenant." Wilson persuaded the other Allies to ratify Poland's rebirth, and on November 11, 1918, as the armistice to end the war was signed in France, Poland's new head of state, Marshal Józef Piłsudski, arrived in Warsaw to begin the process of restoring his country.

An awesome amount of rebuilding was needed. During the preceding century, the partitioning powers had looted and laid waste to Poland's industrial base, stripping factories of everything, down to machinery belts and cables. If that wasn't bad enough, Polish territory had served as the main battleground of World War I's eastern front, and Poland had been rendered a wasteland. Nearly half a million of its people were dead and at least a third of the survivors were starving. Agricultural lands were burned black. There were epidemics of typhoid and other diseases. Yet, for all the destruction and chaos they faced, Poles were delirious with joy at being free again.

On May 3, 1919, they celebrated their independence with their first national Constitution Day. (The date was chosen because Poland's first written constitution had been adopted on May 3, 1791.) In dirty, dilapidated Warsaw, red-and-white Polish flags flew over public buildings whose Russian inscriptions and double-headed Russian eagles had only recently been chiseled off. Throughout the city, there were empty pedestals, from which statues of tsars and famous Russian generals had been toppled. In cafés and restaurants, orchestras played the Polish national anthem and other patriotic songs. Crowds of Varsovians shouted "Long live Poland!" and danced in the streets. An American diplomat who observed the revelry wrote later: "Rarely had I experienced such unbridled enthusiasm on the part of a people as ... on May 3, 1919."

Not that the Treaty of Versailles, which imposed severe sanctions on defeated Germany, was entirely to the Poles' liking. For one thing, the Allied mapmakers did not give them back as much of their historic territory as they thought they deserved. For another, while the Allies were free to work their will on both Germany and Poland in regard to Poland's western frontier, their power was limited where the eastern boundaries with Russia were concerned. The Soviet Union, having quit the war in 1917, was not a party to the Versailles Treaty and did not feel bound by it. Complicating matters further, none of the Allies had diplomatic relations with Moscow. Indeed, both Britain and the United States had sent troops and employed harsh economic sanctions in 1918, at the time of the Brest-Litovsk Treaty, and in support of anti-Bolshevik forces during the Russian civil war of 1919–20.

In the midst of all this postwar turmoil, the Polish and Soviet governments separately decided to take matters into their own hands and resolve the issue of the eastern borderlands—Lithuania, Byelorussia, eastern Galicia, the Ukraine—by force of arms. The disputed territory had once been part of the Polish-Lithuanian Commonwealth, but most of it had been seized by tsarist Russia during the partitions. Particularly crucial to the Poles were Lithuania and eastern Galicia (on the western edge of the Ukraine). The main cities in both areas—Wilno in Lithuania and Lwów in eastern Galicia—were important centers of Polish culture, populated predominantly by Poles. In addition, many of

Poland's most celebrated political, military, and literary figures, including Kościuszko, the famous poet Adam Mickiewicz, the Radziwiłł family, and Piłsudski himself, were of Lithuanian birth.

Polish and Soviet troops quickly moved into position to support their countries' territorial claims. In January 1919, elements of the Red Army invaded Lithuania, captured Wilno, and moved on to occupy nearly all of Byelorussia. The conquest of Wilno, Piłsudski's hometown, was particularly galling to the Polish leader, who sent his forces to chase the Russian troops out. Exhausted and already stretched thin by their civil war, Soviet troops offered little resistance. In April, Poland occupied Wilno, then Minsk, the Byelorussian capital, which was also populated mostly by Poles.

Over the next year, the Poles watched with growing apprehension as the revolutionary "Red" Bolsheviks, having defeated the counterrevolutionary "Whites" in the Russian civil war, began to reinforce their forces in the Ukraine. Convinced that the Bolshevik leader, Vladimir Ilyich Lenin, was preparing an attack on Poland, Piłsudski decided that his only option was to launch a preemptive assault of his own. In late April 1920, Polish forces marched into the Ukraine and on May 7 captured Kiev, its principal city.

That summer, Lenin launched a massive counteroffensive, sending a large Red Army contingent, under the command of General Mikhail Tukachevsky, plus a Cossack cavalry unit under General Semyon Budenny, crashing into the Ukraine. The Russian army had little trouble routing the Poles, who retreated back to their homeland. Should the Russians pursue? Yes, Lenin decided, rejecting the advice of Joseph Stalin and his other lieutenants. Lenin ordered his troops to invade Poland and to capture and occupy Warsaw. For his part, Stalin foresaw only disaster. Warning that the Poles would be much more stubborn fighters in defending their own country than they were in the Ukraine, Stalin declared: "It is easier to saddle a cow than to establish communism in Poland."

For Lenin, however, the Soviet offensive provided an opportunity "to probe Europe with the bayonets of the Red Army." It would be the Soviet Union's first penetration into Europe proper, the first attempt to export the Bolshevik Revolution by force. Less than two years after regaining its independence, Poland was in mortal danger of losing it again. The Soviet Politburo had already appointed a puppet government—the Provisional Polish Revolutionary Committee—to take political control in Warsaw once the Polish army was defeated. The committee—headed by Felix Dzerzhinsky, a Pole by birth and the feared head of the Soviet secret police—waited aboard a special train in eastern Poland for its summons to the capital.

Not for the first, or last, time in a crisis, Polish appeals to the West for arms and troops went unheeded. The Allies' only assistance came in the form of a proposal for the establishment of a temporary boundary and armistice. Called the Curzon Line, after Britain's foreign secretary at the time, the proposed boundary would take on considerably more significance during World War II when Stalin used it to justify his demands for eastern Poland. At this juncture, however, the Bolsheviks flatly rejected the line, and Poland was on its own.

It was at this juncture, too, that Merian Cooper entered the picture. In 1919, Cooper, still in the U.S. Army, had been dispatched by the American Relief Administration, a government agency headed by Herbert Hoover, to deliver food to the starving populace of Lwów. In his time there, Cooper's long-held admiration for Poland and the Poles—"this race which would not die," as he put it in a letter to his father—only deepened. "There is," he later wrote, "romance to the word 'Poland' that attaches itself to scarcely any other country."

When the war with the Soviets broke out, Cooper traveled to the Polish capital to offer his services as a pilot in the fledgling Polish Air Force. He told Marshal Piłsudski that he "wanted to act in Poland as Kościuszko and Pułaski had acted in my own country." Reluctant at first to accept foreigners in his armed forces, Piłsudski finally agreed. Certainly, where the Polish Air Force was concerned, he needed all the help he could get. There was a shortage of everything—pilots, mechanics, ground crews, airfields, not to mention planes. The Poles had acquired an assortment of several hundred old aircraft (Austrian, German, Italian, British, French) that had been left on Polish soil after World War I. As many as possible were put back into service, but it was, at best, a patchwork air force.

Once Cooper received Piłsudski's approval, he returned to Paris, resigned his commission, and set to work trying to persuade other American pilots to join him in Poland. At a little sidewalk café in Paris, he recruited his first volunteer, a tall, lean army major from Mississippi with the improbable name of Cedric Errol Fauntleroy. A friend of

Cooper's, Fauntleroy had flown in France with Eddie Rickenbacker's famous "Hat in the Ring" squadron. He had grown up on a small plantation near Natchez, Mississippi, where his incorrigibly romantic mother had given him the first and middle names of the golden-haired protagonist of *Little Lord Fauntleroy** and read him poems by Byron and others celebrating the heroics of Tadeusz Kościuszko.

Cooper soon rounded up six other volunteers. (By the end of the Soviet-Polish War, there would be seventeen.) Although the whole thing had been Cooper's idea, Fauntleroy, who outranked everyone else and had more flying experience, was given command. One of the other pilots, Elliott Chess, designed an insignia, which was carefully painted on each of the planes of the newly christened Kościuszko Squadron. It featured the red, four-cornered military cap that Kościuszko wore in the uprising of 1794, plus two crossed scythes, representing the Polish peasants who had followed him into battle. These two symbols were superimposed on a background of red, white, and blue stars and stripes representing the U.S. flag. The insignia would continue to be used by the Polish Air Force for as long as the Kościuszko Squadron existed.

When the Yank volunteer pilots finally reached the front in eastern Galicia, they found themselves engaged in a far different kind of war than the one they had witnessed in France. The standoff in the trenches had given way to a series of rapid advances and retreats by both sides. As the Red Army began to march with alarming speed toward the heart of Poland, the air force was called on to help stop the advance. Using air tactics developed in World War I, Americans and Poles strafed and bombed Russian troops, Russian-occupied railway stations, and Russian trains. The Kościuszko Squadron and three Polish squadrons were given the especially difficult assignment of preventing General Budenny's Cossack cavalry from capturing Lwów. The Cossacks, with their black astrakhan hats, their slashing sabers, their fine horsemanship, and their propensity to plunder, rape, and murder, inspired terror wherever they went.

Flying mission after mission, from well before dawn to well after dusk, the American and Polish pilots turned the tables on the Cossacks. From an altitude of about 600 feet, the pilots would drop bombs by hand

---

* Fauntleroy was widely regarded as a tough guy, mostly because, as one friend put it, "With Cedric Errol Fauntleroy as a name, he had to learn to use his fists."

Merian Cooper (left) and Cedric Fauntleroy, American founders of the Kościuszko Squadron. Note the squadron emblem, featuring a stylized American flag and Polish cap and scythes, symbolizing the Kościuszko rebellion against the Russians. (L. Tom Perry Special Collections, Brigham Young University)

on Cossack columns, then dive in to strafe them with dual machine guns, pulling out only a scant dozen feet or so from the ground. Once they had caused a column to scatter, the pilots would pursue the fleeing Cossacks and try to pick them off as they returned fire. Not infrequently, the planes that managed to get back to their field were riddled with bullet holes. According to one Polish General Staff report, the Kościuszko Squadron was particularly good at producing "panic and chaos in the units of the enemy." General Antoni Listowski, the commander of the Polish southern front, wrote: "The American aviators, although exhausted by work, fight like madmen. Without their assistance, we would have gone to the devil a long time ago."

By the end of August, Lwów had been saved from attack and Budenny's cavalry forced to retreat. The Kościuszko Squadron and the other squadrons that took part in the fighting on the southern front were given most of the credit. Meanwhile, to the northwest, Tukachevsky's massive army had advanced to the outskirts of Warsaw, only to be routed by Piłsudski's forces in a spectacular counterattack. During the battle, which became known as "the Miracle on the Vistula," more than 100,000 Red Army troops were captured. Those who weren't captured or killed ran for the east in headlong retreat.

Lenin's first military adventure on foreign soil had ended in a humiliating defeat at the hands of Russia's rebellious former colony. In the peace negotiations that culminated in the Treaty of Riga, the Soviets managed to retain control of a large part of the Ukraine but ceded to Poland most of the other disputed territories, including the cities of Wilno and Lwów. According to the British historian A. J. P. Taylor, the Soviet-Polish War "largely determined the course of European history for the next twenty years or more. . . . Unavowedly and almost unconsciously, Soviet leaders abandoned the cause of international revolution." For the remaining four years of his life, Lenin never forgot the shame of being defeated by Poland. More important, neither did Joseph Stalin.

For Stalin, the mortification was personal. He had been the political commissar attached to Red Army forces in the south and had the final say in their operations. During the last days of the war, Budenny's cavalry had been ordered by Moscow to abandon its advance on Lwów and head north to support Tukachevsky's march on Warsaw. Stalin countermanded the order and told Budenny to proceed against Lwów. When the divided Soviet armies were both defeated, Stalin was threatened with a court-martial. In the end, the trial was not held. But Stalin never forgot the problems the Poles had caused him. Nineteen years later, he exacted his revenge.

In the late summer of 1920, as the Poles cheered their victory and the preservation of their independence, the founder of the Kościuszko Squadron was missing from the celebrations. A month before the end of the war, Merian Cooper had disappeared behind enemy lines and been given up for dead. For months, there was no word of his fate.

One day, Marguerite Harrison, the young American woman who had met Cooper earlier in Warsaw and who was now working with the Red Cross in Moscow, was handed a note smuggled out of a Soviet prison camp. It was from a man named Frank Mosher, who identified himself as an American pilot captured by the Bolsheviks. He was, he wrote, ill and nearly starving. Harrison sent food and clothing into the camp for Mosher, along with a letter. A few days later, she received another clandestine note. "My name is not Mosher," it said. "I am Merian C. Cooper of Jacksonville and I met you in Poland. Don't you remember dancing with me at a ball in the Hotel Bristol in Warsaw?"

He was calling himself Frank Mosher, Cooper explained, because, when his plane was shot down, he had been wearing a secondhand undershirt he had received from the Red Cross. The undershirt had Mosher's name written on it. Having been told that the Cossacks summarily shot all enemy officers and wearing nothing at the time of his capture to indicate his rank or his connection to the Kościuszko Squadron, Cooper passed himself off as a corporal to his interrogators (one of whom he believed to have been Stalin himself). In his note, he

Merian Cooper in Riga, Latvia, after his escape from a Russian prison camp in 1921. (L. Tom Perry Special Collections, Brigham Young University)

begged Harrison to keep his identity a secret but to let his parents know he was still alive.

Although his contact with Harrison might have been a first step toward release, Cooper was not willing to wait until the Russians decided what to do with him. Assigned to a prison detail that was hacking ice from railroad tracks outside Moscow, he and two Polish prisoners managed one day to make a run for it. They eluded their pursuers, and traversed 400 miles of flat, frozen landscape until they finally reached safety in Latvia. In May 1921, Cooper arrived back in Warsaw, just in time for a joyous reunion with his surviving Kościuszko Squadron comrades, then about to return to the United States. Before their departure, Józef Piłsudski himself presented the Americans with the *Virtuti Militari,* Poland's highest military award. When they headed home, they left behind in Lwów the graves of three of their comrades.

A monument erected by the Poles marked the graves. On it was an inscription: "They died so that we can live free."

CHAPTER THREE

Poland "Will Fight"

T HE POLES' SUCCESSFUL defense of their newly gained freedom did not mean they could relax. Germany and the Soviet Union, having lost Poland, spent much of the next nineteen years scheming to get it back. "Poland's existence is intolerable and incompatible with Germany's vital interests. She must disappear and will disappear.... A return to the frontiers of 1914 [i.e., with no Poland at all] should be the basis of agreement between Russia and Germany," the German army's commander in chief, Hans von Seeckt, wrote in 1922. Meanwhile, in the Kremlin, Lenin was observing that an independent Poland was likely to be a major irritant to any self-respecting German government. In such a situation, Lenin wrote, the Soviet Union "may safely count on Germany, as the Germans hate Poland and will at any time make common cause with us in order to strangle her. . . . Germany wants revenge, and we want revolution. For the moment our aims are the same."

When Adolf Hitler became chancellor of Germany in 1933, many Poles were already deeply concerned about their future. For Hitler, though, it was first things first. In 1936, having repudiated the Versailles Treaty, reintroduced conscription, and partially rebuilt the Luftwaffe and Wehrmacht, he sent German troops into the demilitarized Rhineland along the French border. In response, France and England, the only two Western European countries capable of halting the Nazi advance, watched and dithered. Both countries, still suffering the economic and social wounds of World War I, seemed to think that with a little luck and appeasement, Hitler might just go away.

In Britain, two years before Neville Chamberlain picked up his umbrella and set off to negotiate "peace in our time" with Hitler, his Tory predecessor, Stanley Baldwin, had placed the British government firmly in favor of appeasement. Such naysayers as existed then—Winston Churchill was, of course, the most prominent of them—were for the most part ignored by the rest of the country. The future prime minister Harold Macmillan, a member of Parliament at the time, recalled that "Hitler was always regarded by British politicians as if he were a brilliant but temperamental genius who could be soothed by kindness or upset by hard words." Most of the British press felt the same way. So did more than a few members of Britain's ruling class—including the reigning monarch, Edward VIII—who not only favored appeasement but were active admirers of Germany in general and Hitler in particular.

The mood began to change significantly only after Hitler had grabbed Austria and after Chamberlain and France's Premier Edouard Daladier had all but handed him Czechoslovakia at the Munich Conference. When Nazi troops finally marched into Prague in March 1939 and thus sealed Czechoslovakia's fate, Chamberlain did an abrupt about-face and pledged that Britain would form a close protective alliance with Hitler's next victim. The problem was that the next victim was likely to be Poland, and British officials were at best lukewarm about making common cause with the Warsaw government.

In British eyes, the Poles were insufficiently grateful for the help the Western Allies had given them in resurrecting their country after World War I. The British government, believing that the Poles should have been satisfied with the territory granted them by the Allies at the Paris peace conference, had strongly opposed Poland's fight to reclaim its eastern borderlands during the Soviet-Polish War of 1919–20. "The Poles have completely alienated the sympathies of the Cabinet by their levity, incompetence, and folly," Lord Curzon, the British foreign secretary, huffed at the time. Comparing Britain to a doctor trying to help his patient, Curzon added: "The patient must be loyal, helpful and obedient. Poland has none of these qualities." The British (and, for that matter, the French) were further incensed at attempts by Poland's chief of state, Józef Piłsudski, and his overbearing foreign minister, Józef Beck, to keep both the Soviet Union and Germany at bay through twin, doomed nonaggression treaties in 1932 and 1934.

In March 1939, Hitler demanded that Germany be ceded the Baltic port of Danzig, which the Treaty of Versailles had declared a "free city." Under the treaty, Poland had been awarded a narrow strip of German territory, the so-called Polish Corridor, to give the Poles access to the Baltic. In his March ultimatum, Hitler also demanded that a German highway and railway be allowed to cross the Polish Corridor and enter East Prussia. By this time, Piłsudski had died, and Beck, who was one of the "colonels" now governing Poland, rejected Hitler's demands. "Peace is a valuable and desirable thing," he told the *Sejm*. Nevertheless, he added with typical Polish chivalry and obstinacy: "We in Poland do not recognize the concept of peace at any price. There is only one thing in the life of men, nations, and states which is without price, and this is honor...." Poland, he said, "will fight."

Anthony Drexel Biddle, the U.S. ambassador to Poland, later wrote of the Polish government's behavior during this period: "While Poland ... was at first motivated by the desire to protect her own interests, she also hoped to instill in other states a spirit of resistance against Germany's boa-constrictor appetite.... Poland felt that were Hitler ever to be stopped, this was the time to do it." It seemed for a while that this approach was working. On March 31, Prime Minister Chamberlain stood before the House of Commons and declared: "In the event of any action which clearly threatened Polish independence and which the Polish Government ... considered it vital to resist with their national forces, His Majesty's Government would feel themselves bound at once to lend the Polish Government all the support in their power." France, he added, had authorized him to make the same guarantee on its behalf.

The pledge would have been remarkable for any British prime minister of that period—all the more so for one who had so recently been an advocate of appeasement. No British government in history had ever promised military support to a nation in Central or Eastern Europe. Even more astonishing, Chamberlain's new policy in effect yielded to Poland the power to decide whether or not Britain would go to war. A month later, France agreed to launch, within two weeks of general mobilization, a broad offensive with the "bulk of its forces" against any country that attacked Poland. In later talks with Polish military officials, General Sir Edmund Ironside, the chief of Britain's armed forces, promised that, in the event of a German invasion of Poland, the Royal Air Force would begin an immediate assault against Germany. If non-

military targets in Poland were bombed, Ironside added, British bombers would do the same to German nonmilitary targets. Thus reassured
by both the British and the French, the Poles were exuberant. "This
time, at least, we face our destiny...united, sword in hand, and with
Allies!" exulted Edward Raczyński, the Polish ambassador to Britain.

The ambassador would soon learn otherwise. Through that spring
and early summer, as Poland prepared for war, Britain and France
were having second thoughts. A *New York Times* correspondent in Paris
reported that London and Paris were now privately warning the Poles
not to rile Hitler. Britain also seemed increasingly reluctant to provide money or matériel to the Poles for their own defense. As the crisis
intensified, negotiations to extend loans and arms credits dragged on
without resolution. Hugh Dalton, a leading Labour member of Parliament, expressed his and others' concern about the impasse. "Surely the
whole purpose of these negotiations is to arm Poland, and arm her
quickly," Dalton declared in a House of Commons debate on July 31. "Is
it, perhaps, feared that if the Poles get too many arms too quickly, they
will get above themselves?...[Is there] some sinister and unrevealed
purpose to try to keep Poland weak and irresolute?" Finally, in August,
Britain, having ruled out any kind of direct loan, granted Poland £8
million in export credits, with the stipulation that they be used only in
trade with Britain.

In retrospect at least, His Majesty's Government seems to have been
guilty of a profound lack of gratitude. For, less than a month earlier,
Poland had presented both Britain and France with a gift of incalculable value. That July, while the aid negotiations were continuing, top
British and French codebreakers, who had been trying long and fruit-
lessly to crack Germany's cipher system, were summoned to a meeting
in a nondescript, heavily guarded building in a forest outside Warsaw.
There, they were shown a small black machine, resembling a type-
writer, with keys that rotated a cluster of three-inch wheels. It was a
precise replica of Germany's Enigma cipher machine. With it, unbeknownst to the British and French, the Poles had been reading German
military and political communications for six years. And they had built
two more machines just like it—one for the British and one for the
French.

From the day in 1918 that Poland regained its independence, it had
given top priority to intelligence gathering and codebreaking, specifi-

cally aiming at its historical enemies, the Germans and the Russians. Soviet codes were broken as early as 1920, and the Poles were thus able, among other things, to pinpoint the positions of the Red Army units that threatened Warsaw during the 1919–20 war. Early in the next decade, three young Polish mathematicians managed to decipher Germany's Enigma system—a feat that German cryptographers had sworn, with mathematical and Teutonic precision, would take 900 million years to accomplish. Armed with data provided by the mathematicians, the Polish cipher bureau built its own Enigma decoding machine and began reading German messages.

By the late 1930s, Germany had added new complexity to its ciphers, preventing the Poles from reading many—but not all—messages. Even so, the Enigma machines they presented to the British and French during that fateful July meeting outside Warsaw provided the foundation upon which the British built their own legendary codebreaking system, called Ultra. Many years after the war, Gordon Welchman, one of Ultra's top cryptographers, remarked that the system "would never have gotten off the ground if we had not learned from the Poles, in the nick of time, the details both of the...Enigma machine, and of the operating procedures that were in use."

ONE OF THE most popular books in Poland in the summer of 1939 was Margaret Mitchell's *Gone with the Wind*. Mitchell's descriptions of a society destroyed by war bore a melancholy fascination for a people who already knew quite a lot about war's destructiveness and who feared they were about to learn more. In a memoir of the period, the Polish writer Rulka Langer recalled thinking about *Gone with the Wind* as she watched her children play at the family's country house during those last golden days of summer and peace. "Somehow," she wrote, "I considered it prophetic." Her sense of impending loss could only have been intensified by the knowledge that there was now in Poland so much to *be* lost.

In the twenty-one years since the Poles reclaimed their independence, they had struggled to unify, rebuild, and modernize their nation. To a considerable extent they had succeeded. Two weeks after independence in 1918—and two years before the United States ratified the

Nineteenth Amendment—Poland granted women the right to vote. By the early 1930s, illiteracy had been reduced by more than half, an ambitious land reform program had been established, and the economic, legal, and educational systems had been reformed. As the power of feudal landholders diminished, an urban middle class finally began to emerge.

Interwar Poland was hardly a Western-style democracy: although Marshal Piłsudski rejected fascism and totalitarianism, his regime was unquestionably authoritarian, responsible for the arrest and imprisonment of a number of political opponents. Nonetheless, opposition parties were allowed to mount vigorous campaigns against the government, and the courts, trade unions, and press had considerable freedom. Artists, scholars, and intellectuals were an influential part of the urban elite.

Nowhere was the transformation of the country more apparent than in Warsaw, whose symbol was a mermaid with a sword in one hand and a shield in the other, over the motto *Contemnit procellas* ("It defies the storms"). Long the center of Polish culture and politics, Warsaw had become grey and bedraggled during the long years of Russian occupation. Now, with a population of 1.3 million, the city, perched on the banks of the Vistula River, was vibrant and cosmopolitan once again. Its potholed streets had been repaired, its cracked and crumbling walls patched and painted. Lovely old neoclassical palaces and churches were being refurbished, even as many new, modern office buildings were added to the skyline. In the *Stare Miasto* (Old Town), for centuries the focal point of the city's rich and diverse culture, artisans meticulously restored the brightly colored, intricately detailed façades. "Old Town," wrote a prominent Varsovian poet, "you're tearing the pall of mourning from your walls."

Every evening at twilight, throngs promenaded along Aleje Ujazdowskie, the city's most beautiful boulevard, lined with closely spaced and pruned beeches fifty feet high. The many parks, sidewalk cafés, and cabarets were crowded. So were the more than twenty-five legitimate theaters, whose productions that summer included plays by Molière, Shakespeare, and George Bernard Shaw, as well as the latest avant-garde Polish playwrights. A popular posting for foreign diplomats, Warsaw was known as "the Paris of the East," a label of which the Francophile Poles were especially proud.

The mayor of Warsaw, Stefan Starzyński, directed and symbolized this great surge of change and reform. The city was Starzyński's passion. Since taking office in 1934, he had fought graft and corruption in the municipal government and had modernized Warsaw's utility and transportation systems. He encouraged and sometimes personally supervised the construction and remodeling of hundreds of buildings. Most important in the minds of many Poles, with their celebrated love of flowers, he did everything he could to transform Warsaw into a garden. Thanks to the mayor's citywide planting campaigns, there were profusions of lilacs, roses, geraniums, and pansies in parks and squares, along sidewalks, in restaurant gardens, in apartment window boxes, in planters hanging under glass-globed streetlamps.

Yet Poland as a whole still faced many severe problems in the 1930s. The worldwide Great Depression struck many parts of the country with particular fury. Poverty, unemployment, and corruption soared. The national government under the junta of colonels that succeeded Piłsudski had become increasingly authoritarian and intolerant. The powers of the *Sejm* were curtailed, and strikes and demonstrations against the government were suppressed with increasing force. As people competed for jobs and food, especially in the countryside, tension increased among Poland's many ethnic and political groups.

Anti-Semitism in this once most tolerant of European nations became far more overt, notably in rural areas and among increasingly influential political right-wingers. Jews were widely blamed for the shriveling economy and accused of profiting from it, although a majority of Poland's 3 million Jews were poor even by Polish standards. Outbursts of anti-Semitic violence occurred in some cities and towns. The right-wing National Democratic Party, led by Piłsudski's leading political rival, Roman Dmowski, began to advocate anti-Semitic policies and "Poland for the Poles." Because Polish Jews were disproportionately involved in leftist organizations, they were widely seen (to some extent fairly) as pro-Soviet and hence (unfairly) as that most despised of Polish types: pro-Russian. There were official and unofficial anti-Jewish propaganda campaigns, particulary after Piłsudski, who resisted anti-Semitism, died in 1935 and the junta took over. University admissions quotas were established for Jews, and bullyboy students frequently forced their Jewish classmates to stand during lectures or to sit in segregated areas.

At the same time, a great many Poles were appalled by these campaigns and spoke out against them. Even after the Nazis invaded and decreed the death penalty for anyone helping Jews (Poland was the only German-occupied country on which that edict was imposed), many thousands of Poles tried to shield their Jewish neighbors and friends. The Polish resistance movement set up an organization, called *Żegota*, with the specific purpose of aiding Jews, the only underground movement in an occupied country to institutionalize the effort.

By the late 1930s, there were signs that the Polish economy was beginning to grow again and reason to hope that the social devastation of the Depression might begin to ease. Raymond Leslie Buell, president of the Foreign Policy Association in the United States, visited Poland in 1938 and wrote: "Even admitting the defects in Poland's social structure and the unrepresentative nature of its government, spiritually it formed part of the West. Its difficulties after [World War I] in bringing about unity and reconstruction were greater than those of any other state; and its achievements during the past twenty-five years have been little less than remarkable...." Also in 1938, former U.S. president Herbert Hoover, who had administered the relief program for Poland after World War I, revisited the country and found vast, positive changes: "Here...was a nation transformed, regenerated. The standards of living were improving. New homes and factories had risen in every city. Transportation and communication were advancing. Education had become universal."

Neither Hitler nor Stalin shared these views. For them, as for most German and Russian rulers in the past, Poland was a backward country that had no right even to exist. This became evident when all the frenetic diplomatic maneuvers during the summer of 1939 culminated in the signing of the infamous Ribbentrop-Molotov nonaggression pact. News of the treaty came as a shock to many governments (and Communist Party members) the world over, but it was a particular blow to the British and French. They had been trying, off and on, for months to persuade Stalin to join them in an alliance for the protection of Poland. The Poles, of course, regarded those efforts as naive, and Stalin must have agreed. The only thing France and Britain could offer him was

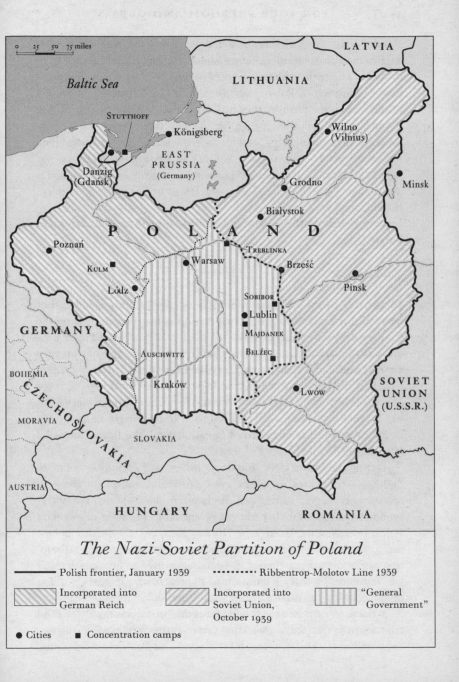

The Nazi-Soviet Partition of Poland

Polish frontier, January 1939   Ribbentrop-Molotov Line 1939

Incorporated into German Reich

Incorporated into Soviet Union, October 1939

"General Government"

● Cities   ■ Concentration camps

almost certain war with Germany in defense of a longtime enemy that he, like most Russian rulers before him, hated and wanted erased from the map. Hitler, in contrast, secretly offered Stalin a new German-Russian partition of Poland, by which both the Germans and Soviets would recover the territory they had lost in the aftermath of World War I. And as icing on this bitter cake, Stalin could take revenge for the personal embarrassment that Soviet losses in the war of 1919–20 caused him.

On August 22, 1939, the day before the nonaggression treaty was signed, Hitler told his generals: "The wholesale destruction of Poland is the objective. Speed is the chief thing. Pursuit until there is complete annihilation."

Very shortly, the Poles would have little time for novels about past wars.

———

AS AUGUST DREW to a close, there was an edge of tension and excitement in thriving, bustling Warsaw—but no panic. People tried on the gas masks the government had issued them and crisscrossed their windows with masking tape. Wireless loudspeakers boomed out practice air-raid warnings. When Starzyński called for volunteers to dig zigzag trenches, thousands turned out with picks and shovels, among them opera singers, rabbis, clerks, and artists. Meanwhile, foreign journalists, like scavengers sensing a kill, flocked to Warsaw, congregating nightly in the cavernous bar of the city's grandest hotel, the Bristol, owned a few years earlier by Ignacy Paderewski.

During the warm, clear August nights, crowds of military officers, diplomats, politicians, socialites, spies, mistresses, and prostitutes—all of them exchanging stories and the latest rumors—joined the correspondents in the hotel's bar and restaurant. At a late-night supper with Polish friends at the Bristol, Sir Howard Kennard, the British ambassador, was heard to lament that Hitler's rise had taken all the satisfaction out of diplomacy. "Being an ambassador used to be a gentleman's job," he said. "Now it's a question of fighting with gangsters. . . . You might as well try to make a deal with Al Capone."

What most surprised the foreigners at the Bristol was the Poles' calm confidence in the face of escalating German pressure. CBS correspondent William L. Shirer wrote in his diary: "The Poles are a delightful, utterly romantic people, and I have had much good food and drink and music with them. But they are horribly unrealistic." And *New York Times* reporter Walter Duranty wrote: "For good or ill—call it insouciance or boasting, as you please—I found no trace of defeatism anywhere in Poland. To hear the people talk, one might think that Poland, not Germany, was the great industrial colossus."

The Polish military did manage to take certain defensive precautions. On August 27, for example, the air force moved its combat planes to a nationwide network of secret, improvised airfields in rural cow pastures. Nevertheless, many Poles, perhaps most, seemed genuinely to believe that if the Germans attacked, Poland—with French and British assistance, of course—would defeat them. The Poles were confident that France, believed at the time to possess the world's most powerful army, and Britain, with its air force and renowned navy, would live up to their treaty obligations. Would Hitler dare invade in the face of so powerful an alliance? Even many Europeans outside Poland thought not.

———

THE KOŚCIUSZKO SQUADRON, now under the command of Major Zdzisław Krasnodębski, had been posted to one of the cow-pasture airfields, this one not far from Warsaw. The squadron was one of five assigned to the Warsaw Pursuit Brigade, which was charged with the Polish capital's defense. The thirty-five-year-old Krasnodębski had been with the Kościuszko Squadron since his graduation from Dęblin ten years earlier. He called the assignment "my dream come true." As a cadet, he had been enthralled with the squadron's unique history and traditions (including its annual flight to Lwów on May 30—Memorial Day in the United States—to lay a wreath at the tomb of those founding Yank pilots who had been killed during the Soviet-Polish War). As commander of this storied unit, Krasnodębski regarded himself not just as its leader but as the keeper of its eternal flame.

The son of a nobleman with estates in eastern Poland, Krasnodębski had been raised to join the cavalry but, like so many others, decided to become a pilot instead. He was given command of the Kościuszko Squadron, officially designated as 111 Squadron, in 1935. Three years later a second squadron, designated 112, was added to his command. His pilots called the reserved, broodingly handsome Krasnodębski "the King" for his regal bearing (the effect of which was somehow amplified, they said, by his five-foot-five-inch stature) and out of respect for his no-nonsense approach to his job. According to one of his pilots, Krasnodębski was "not an automaton or a walking book of rules." He could, however, be forceful when necessary—as it frequently was with such hard-drinking, hell-raising nonconformists as Jan Zumbach, Witold Łokuciewski, and Mirosław Ferić under his authority.

Krasnodębski himself was married and quite settled. The rowdiest he ever became was when he burst into song at squadron dances after a couple of vodkas. If his wife, Wanda, happened to be around at those times, she would slip an arm around his waist and whisper, "Haven't you had a bit too much to drink, Zdzichu?" Wanda, blond and petite, was the love of Krasnodębski's life. They had met while she was still in high school and he was a cadet at Dęblin. Four years after his graduation, they were married. They lived in an apartment in Warsaw's outskirts, next to the airfield where the 111 and 112 squadrons were based. When Krasnodębski received orders to move his men and planes outside the city, he assured Wanda that he would soon be back.

At their grassy, makeshift field, the cocky young fighter pilots had little to do during those final days of August but wait and watch the cows and horses graze. Most of them expected a German attack, but—steeped as they were in tales of Polish heroism and eager as they were to join their country's pantheon—they actually looked forward to going up against the Luftwaffe. In a diary he began during this period, Mirosław Ferić noted that his failure to pay enough attention to his date at a club one night earlier had led to a reproach from a fellow pilot. "Too bad," Ferić wrote in his diary. "But I'm husbanding all my strength for war." Another pilot recalled: "Like most of us, I believed in happy endings. We wanted to fight, it excited us, and we wanted it to happen fast. We didn't believe that something bad could really happen...."

With supreme confidence in their flying skill, Ferić and his hot-to-fly-and-fight comrades were quite unconcerned about the qualitative and quantitative inferiority of their equipment. Germany had at its disposal some 1,500 bombers and 1,100 advanced, combat-ready fighters; prominent among the latter were the ultramodern Me-109, then the fastest plane in the world, and the long-range Me-110. In comparison,

*Mirosław Ferić in Polish Air Force
uniform before the war. (Polish Institute
and Sikorski Museum)*

Poland had only about 390 planes fit for action, about 150 of which were fighters. They were Polish P-11s and P-7s, both slow, old, and obsolete. Built in the late 1920s and early 1930s, the gull-winged monoplanes had once been among Europe's most advanced. But time and technology had quickly outstripped them, and the Polish aircraft industry, hampered by the Depression and underdevelopment, had been unable to keep pace. The Polish fighters' undercarriages weren't retractable, and their open cockpits often filled with smoke when a pilot fired the two side-mounted machine guns. Nor was that the worst of it. The mechanisms that synchronized the firing of the machine guns with the rotation of the propellers had a nasty tendency to malfunction, with the result that pilots sometimes shot off their own props in midair. "Pitiful," William Shirer had written in his diary after attending a Polish Air Force exercise in early August; the planes, he observed, were "dreadfully obsolete."

Poland's air combat doctrine was even more so. The country's top military commanders (like those in France, England, and the United States, but unlike the Germans) had paid scant attention to the development of new wartime uses for military aircraft. Their thinking was still mired back in World War I, when airplanes were used primarily in support of ground forces. Only when war was imminent did the Polish high command begin to understand how archaic this approach was. In 1939, they scrambled to buy fighters and light bombers from France and England. But those countries were now in the process of modernizing their own air forces and had few planes to spare. In the end, they reluctantly agreed to do what they could, but they informed the Poles that deliveries could not possibly begin until mid-September at the earliest.

———————

IN DĘBLIN, meanwhile, Captain Witold Urbanowicz was brooding. Anyone with eyes could see that Germany was about to attack, and anyone with brains could understand that Poland was vulnerable, especially given the military leadership's high-button-shoe approach to modern warfare. Yet here Urbanowicz was, moldering away in this training academy backwater. He was a gifted flying instructor, and very fond of his cadets, but, damn it, he was first of all a combat *fighter* pilot! When war came, he wanted to be in it, not baby-sitting a bunch of kids. Urbanowicz's problem was that he had been too vocal in his criticisms of his superiors. A man of awesome stubbornness combined with what he regarded as refined tastes and sensibilities, he refused to kowtow— especially if what he saw as Poland's interests were at stake.

He had inherited this fierce, uncompromising patriotism from his paternal grandfather. The elder Urbanowicz had been conscripted twice into the Russian cavalry and forced to serve a total of fourteen years as a member of the tsar's personal guard in St. Petersburg. When he was finally allowed to return home, he joined in a series of anti-Russian conspiracies in eastern Poland, taking his grandson with him in a horse-drawn sleigh as he distributed anti-tsarist literature to nearby Polish landowners in the dead of winter. Young Witold's job was to shoot at the wolves that came stealing out of the darkness of the woods to attack the horses.

In 1936, Urbanowicz had been Krasnodębski's second in command with the Kościuszko Squadron when it was temporarily transferred to a base near the Polish-Russian frontier. The pilots' orders were to chase away any Soviet reconnaissance planes that might happen to wander over the long-disputed area. One day, one of them did just that, refusing

Dęblin flight instructor Witold Urbanowicz leads a group of Polish Air Force cadets in a skiing exercise before the war. (Jacek Kutzner)

to turn back in spite of repeated warnings that he had entered Polish airspace. Incensed, Urbanowicz moved in and shot the Russian down. Confronted later by Krasnodębski, Urbanowicz insisted that he had only returned fire, an uncheckable assertion. Krasnodębski managed to hush up the potentially explosive affair, and Urbanowicz was quietly content with the results of his little undeclared war. "Right afterward," he said, "the Russians stopped photographing our fortifications along the eastern border."

On another occasion during that same tour with the Kościuszko Squadron, he attended an international competition of sport aircraft at the Warsaw field where the squadron was permanently stationed. When a guard caught three Germans sneaking into a restricted area near the hangars, Urbanowicz, as second in command, investigated. One of the Germans, he discovered, was none other than Willy Messerschmitt, designer of the Luftwaffe's best fighter planes. Ignoring Messerschmitt's demands that he be released immediately, Urbanowicz ordered him to lie facedown on the grass and told the guard to keep his rifle pointed at the German's back. And there the prince of German aircraft designers lay, cursing Urbanowicz and the guard, until German authorities arrived to collect him. "You *must* be more diplomatic, Witold!" Krasnodębski barked. Urbanowicz was still bitter when he spoke about the incident years later: Krasnodębski "was wrong, and I was right—as he found out during the war, when he was shot down *twice* by Messerschmitts."

It was this sort of attitude that finally caused Urbanowicz to be packed off to flight instructor duty at Dęblin. There he spent his idle hours brooding about the coming war and his own sidelined status. He recalled the time, earlier in 1939, when he had gone on leave to Nazified Vienna. After a day of sightseeing, he returned to his hotel room to discover that it had been searched, presumably by the Gestapo. Later, in a nightclub, a table full of Luftwaffe pilots, mistaking the blond, blue-eyed, and mufti-clad Urbanowicz for one of their own people, offered to buy him a drink. He refused. The police were called and demanded to see his papers. "I am a Polish airman," Urbanowicz proudly and brashly informed them. The German pilots were amused. "We will meet again, in the sky over Poland," one of them said. Urbanowicz leveled a cold eye at him and replied, "I hope so." Now he wondered whether that hope had been in vain.

———

ON AUGUST 29, Polish foreign minister Beck ordered a mobilization of the army, then rescinded the order under pressure from the British and French. London and Paris, unaware that Germany had been fully mobilized for more than two weeks and eager to avoid giving offense to Hitler, had asked the Poles to wait another twenty-four hours. Beck, keen to demonstrate Poland's trustworthiness as an ally, agreed.

On paper anyway, the Polish army seemed fairly formidable. It was the fourth largest in Europe, with a peacetime strength of 300,000 men, plus 2 million trained reserves. There were thirty-nine infantry divisions, ten cavalry brigades, three mountain brigades, and two armored brigades. This compared more or less favorably with a German army of just under 2 million men in thirty-nine infantry divisions, six Panzer divisions, three mountain divisions, four "light" divisions, and one cavalry brigade. But the Polish numbers masked major deficiencies in both the quality and quantity of equipment and arms. Moreover, the Poles—once again, like their major allies and unlike the Germans—were woefully out-of-date in their appreciation of the importance of tanks as attack weapons. Polish tanks, in keeping with their support status, were small, slow, light, and inadequately armored. They amounted to little more than mobile machine guns. The army also lacked heavy artillery and modern communications and transportation systems.

CBS's William Shirer, well aware of Germany's vastly superior armaments, concluded that the Poles, "valiant and headstrong as they were," would be unable to withstand the German onslaught for long. Poland "no doubt outmatched Germany in its horse cavalry," he remarked. "But did its High Command intend to commit horses against tanks?" In fact, Polish leaders did believe that the country's legendary cavalry would play a major role in fending off a German invasion by mounting rapid thrusts over the country's largely roadless plains. No longer relying solely on saber and lance charges, the cavalry operated as highly mobile infantry and was armed with machine guns and antitank rifles.

But even if Polish forces had been fully mobilized and had possessed the most modern equipment, they still would have faced staggering odds. They had to defend a border more than 1,750 miles long, with no natural defense lines, and surrounded on three sides by the Wehrmacht. Poland's unfavorable strategic position led the French to suggest that, in the event of a German invasion, it simply give up its western provinces without a fight and make its stand behind the three major rivers in the center of the country. The suggestion was impossible for the Poles to accept. It would have meant abandoning the nation's largest cities, along with most of its population and industrial resources. No, the Polish high command decided, the army would resist as long as possible at the borders, waiting for Britain and France to launch their promised counterattack on Germany from out of the west.

DAWN HAD JUST broken on September 1, 1939, when Witold Urbanowicz took off from the Dęblin airfield, followed by one of his cadets. Time for another damned dogfight lesson by the instructor his students called "the Englishman" for his air of refinement and good breeding. The two P-7s flew in formation in the pale first light, until Urbanowicz gave the signal to begin simulated combat. As he banked into a turn, Urbanowicz saw a stream of what appeared to be tracer and incendiary bullets flash past his plane. A few seconds later, more bullets. Who had put live ammunition in the kid's guns? And an even greater mystery: how in the hell had this mere cadet managed to get *him*, Witold Urbanowicz, in his sights? Furious, he signaled the cadet to land immediately. As Urbanowicz was taxiing toward the hangar, another plane slipped in front of his and rolled to a stop. A fellow instructor jumped out and ran over.

"You're alive, Witold?" he exclaimed. "You're not hit?"

Urbanowicz grew even angrier. "What the hell's going on?" he shouted.

"You should go to church and light a candle," his friend said. "You were just attacked by a Messerschmitt!"

———————

WAR HAD COME to Poland yet again, but this time it came with unimaginable speed and fury. In the day's predawn dark, nearly 2 million German troops, spearheaded by hundreds of planes and tanks, had smashed into the country from the north, south, and west. By midday, armored Panzers were slicing through the heart of the Polish countryside—not, as Polish doctrine had it, in support of infantry but *preceding* the infantry, each tank a murderous attack weapon in its own right. This was warfare as never before. This was *Blitzkrieg,* "lightning war." As the motorized infantry and armor crushed opposition on the ground, clouds of screaming Luftwaffe dive-bombers and fighters blasted and strafed airfields, cities, towns, bridges, roads, and railway junctions choked with reserve soldiers on their way to join their woefully undermanned units.

In the first wave of the attack, eighty bombers and fighters swept toward Warsaw. The Kościuszko Squadron and three other fighter squadrons swarmed up to meet them. In the short but fierce dogfights that followed, the dreamy Poles finally came face-to-face with reality. German planes—faster, more maneuverable, better armed, capable of flying at higher altitudes—swooped down, guns blazing, on the vastly outclassed Polish relics. Pursuing even a German bomber, a Polish pilot said, was like a man on foot trying to catch a racing car.

But the Polish pilots were far better than their planes. They discovered that they had a chance—barely—against the Luftwaffe if they could climb above the German bombers and dive down on them, or if they could attack head-on, firing their guns at very close range. They had done this over and over again in training. Now they were faced with doing it in a desperately real war. They hurled themselves at the attackers, and, in moments, the clear late-summer sky was a great swirling tangle of planes and smoke. The initial raid on beautiful Warsaw was not prevented, but it was significantly weakened. The Germans lost six bombers, the Poles only three fighters.

But the Luftwaffe was relentless, sending wave after wave of bombers against Warsaw. For the Poles flying in defense of the city, the next few days became a blur of weariness. They would no sooner return from one sortie than they would be sent out on another. In the end, their task was impossible. Not only were the German planes of crushingly superior quality, there were far more of them: nearly 1,400 were already being used in Poland, and 1,000 more were waiting in reserve. The Luftwaffe enjoyed a four-to-one advantage in the overall number of planes, and a nine-to-one advantage when it came to fighters.

The odds against a Polish victory were brought home to Mirosław Ferić on the third day of combat, when a Messerschmitt 110 riddled his P-11 with bullets and literally shot the control stick out of his hands. As his plane arced into a nosedive, Ferić tried to bail out but was pinned back by the mounting G-force. In a "powerless fury," he cursed aloud and prayed as forests and green fields spiraled up to meet him. Then the plane rolled some more, and he dropped free—but at such a low altitude that his parachute barely had time to open before he landed in a forest. Battered and badly bruised, his back wrenched, he gathered up his parachute and, bent at the waist like an old woman, slowly made his way to a dirt road. There, he paused a moment to look up and watch as other Polish pilots tried to beat the odds.

Within five days, Germany was able to bomb targets at will. Polish warplanes—those that remained—still occasionally counterattacked, but to little real effect. Wrote a bitter Ferić in his diary: "The lovely Polish autumn [is] coming. Damn and blast its loveliness." From the air, he and his comrades surveyed a devastated landscape whose further devastation they were now powerless to prevent. The Warsaw Pursuit Brigade had destroyed no fewer than thirty-four German aircraft and damaged another twenty-nine; the Kościuszko Squadron alone accounted for eight kills. But the brigade had lost thirty-six of its own outclassed planes, two thirds of its original strength. Not all of them had been destroyed in combat: several had to be abandoned because of lack of spare parts.

With their nation on the brink of utter defeat, Ferić and the others in the brigade were beside themselves with frustration and fury. Their own inability to prevent Poland's devastation was a terrible blow, and for those who still clung to the chivalrous ideals of the Polish cavalry, the arrogance and brutishness of the German invaders, the terror of *Blitzkrieg,* only added to their rage. "Each of us was taught at home and in school to rely on basic ethical principles, and later to apply them to combat, as well," remarked Urbanowicz. "We were taught that these principles were inviolable."

It didn't take long for them to learn otherwise. In the first days of the war, when Stanisław Skalski, a Dęblin classmate of Łokuciewski and Ferić, shot down a German reconnaissance plane near Torun, he immediately landed beside the crashed plane and treated the injuries of the startled Luftwaffe pilot and observer. On September 3, Krasnodębski and 112 Squadron were locked in a series of fierce dogfights when a Messerschmitt 110 scored a direct hit on Krasnodębski's plane. His cockpit in flames, the Polish commander bailed out. Gliding down helplessly under his parachute, he saw the Messerschmitt turn and head straight for him, machine guns stuttering. As Krasnodębski braced himself for death, a Polish plane attacked the Messerschmitt at top speed and sent it fleeing. Krasnodębski escaped with only slight burns. Many other parachuting Polish fliers, not as fortunate, were picked off like targets in a shooting gallery. Those who landed safely were often strafed on the ground by German fighters.

The Poles were learning just how out of step with the twentieth century they were. (In time, some of them, having learned that lesson, would employ similar tactics against the Germans.) World War II was not going to be a chivalrous enterprise. On the first day of the war, Hitler had promised: "I will not war against women and children. I have ordered my air force to restrict itself to attacks on military objectives." But in a secret message to his military commanders, he authorized killing "without pity or mercy all men, women and children of Polish

A young Polish girl grieves over her sister, killed by a Stuka dive-bomber in early September 1939 while the two girls were picking potatoes in a field outside Warsaw. (Hulton Archive)

descent or language. Only in this way can we obtain the living space we need." The Führer commanded his men: "Close your hearts to pity! Act brutally!... The war is to be a war of annihilation."

With the Polish Air Force at a hopeless disadvantage, the Luftwaffe ranged freely over the country in those early September days, bringing terror and death to people in its path. "Everything around us reeked of barbarity," Urbanowicz recalled. The Germans machine-gunned women and girls picking potatoes in a field. They bombed churches and maternity hospitals. They strafed toddlers being herded to safety after the bombing of their nursery school. During one raid, they dived low over a Warsaw cemetery and machine-gunned mourners attending funerals for victims of previous raids.

In the town of Sulejów, German bombers set the town center ablaze, and as its residents ran toward the nearby woods, Ju-87 Stukas, with nerve-shattering sirens attached to their undercarriages, screamed down on them. "People were falling, people were on fire," said a survivor. "That night the sky was red from the burning town."

All of Poland, it seemed, was now on fire.

CHAPTER FOUR

"We Are Waiting . . ."

Like the poles, General Adrian Carton de Wiart, head of the British military mission to Poland, was no stranger to the ravages of war. During World War I, he had lost a hand at Ypres, had been shot in the head and ankle on the Somme, and through the hip at Passchendaele. But nothing prepared him for the wholesale murder he witnessed in Poland in September 1939. "I saw," he wrote, "the very face of war change—its glory shorn, no longer the soldier setting forth into battle, but the women and children being buried under it."

Yet General Carton de Wiart's colleagues and superiors at Whitehall and the officials at the Quai d'Orsay were still dithering. Britain, under its treaty with Poland, was to respond to a Nazi invasion by making war on Germany "at once" and with "all the support and assistance in its power." France had a similar obligation. The suddenness of Hitler's attack caught Poland's putative allies by surprise, however. They were neither ready nor willing to act. Indeed, Prime Minister Chamberlain never had any *intention* of acting. From the outset, Chamberlain assumed that his signature on the treaty would be enough to deter Hitler. When it failed to do that, Chamberlain and his French counterpart, Edouard Daladier, desperately tried to nudge the Führer back to the negotiating table. They still believed, against all evidence and their own experience, that better results could be achieved by talking than by honoring agreements and going to war. At this late date, their way of getting tough with Hitler was to set a new deadline for his response to their call for more talks.

On Saturday, September 2, Chamberlain announced the last-ditch negotiating scheme to the packed floor and galleries of a stunned House of Commons. "I had never seen the Commons so stirred, so profoundly moved, as it was that afternoon," recalled Brigadier General Edward Spears, a leading Tory MP. "It was dawning upon even the most uncritical of the Government's supporters that Great Britain's honour, of which we were the collective guardians, was in danger."

One of the angriest members was sixty-six-year-old Leo Amery, a former First Lord of the Admiralty. An old, close friend of Chamberlain's, Amery was a fellow Tory, whose constituency was in the prime minister's hometown of Birmingham. "For two whole days," Amery later wrote, "the… Poles had been bombed and massacred, and we were still considering within what time limit Hitler should be invited to tell us whether he felt like relinquishing his prey!… Was all this havering the prelude to another Munich?" To Amery, it seemed that just about everyone, regardless of party, was seeking the easy way out. When Arthur Greenwood, Labour's deputy leader, rose to respond to Chamberlain, the short, bespectacled Amery shot up on the government side of the chamber and urged Greenwood to eschew partisanship and "speak for England!"

Greenwood did. "I am gravely disturbed," he declared, staring at Chamberlain. "An act of aggression took place thirty-eight hours ago. The moment that act… took place, one of the most important treaties of modern times automatically came into operation.… I wonder how long we are prepared to vacillate at a time when Britain and all that Britain stands for—and human civilization—are in peril."

Amery and Greenwood were not alone in their opposition to Chamberlain. Indeed, they were not even the leading opponents. That distinction belonged to a sixty-four-year-old, plump, balding Tory with a taste for cigars and good brandy named Winston Spencer Churchill. Late on the night of the parliamentary debate, as thunder and lightning cracked the air above his apartment near Westminster, a distraught Churchill put in a call to Edward Raczyński, the Polish ambassador to Britain. "I hope…," he sputtered, "I *hope* that Britain will keep its…" Churchill could not continue. His voice caught, and he began to weep.

In Paris, Daladier and Foreign Minister Georges Bonnet were deluged with cables from the French ambassador in Warsaw, reporting the incessant German bombing of Polish civilians and urging immediate action. "The time has passed for accommodation," the ambassador declared. Still, the French leaders, like their British counterparts, equivocated to the point that Juliusz Łukasiewicz, the Polish ambassador to France, exploded at Bonnet in a meeting: "It isn't right! You know it isn't right! A treaty is a treaty and must be respected!...Do you realize that every hour that you delay the attack on Germany means...death to thousands of Polish men, women and children?" The chain-smoking foreign minister replied with almost equal fury: "Do you then want the women and children of Paris to be massacred?"

Emotions continued to run high as the horror of what was being done became clearer. By September 3, even Neville Chamberlain could see the futility of his policy. Exactly fifty-three hours after the Führer launched his *Blitzkrieg* against Poland, the British government at last declared war on Germany. Six hours after that, the French government did the same.

World War II had begun.

In Warsaw, there was silence at first when the radio announced Britain's declaration of war. Then pandemonium erupted. Residents rushed out of their homes into the rubble-filled streets, weeping and shouting, singing and cheering. Car horns blared. People kissed their neighbors and friends and danced along the sidewalks. By early afternoon, more than 100,000 Varsovians, drunk with joy, had gathered in front of the British Embassy on Aleje Ujadowskie. Waving improvised Union Jacks, they sang the Polish national anthem and tried to sing "God Save the King." "Of course no one knew it," Rulka Langer wrote, "but we all tried our best." When Britain's ambassador, Sir Howard Kennard, and Józef Beck appeared on the embassy balcony, a roar went up from the immense crowd. The tumult grew after Kennard shouted: "Long live Poland! We will fight side by side against aggression and injustice!" The ambassador and Beck were showered with flowers. Soon the balcony was knee-deep in them.

When news of the French declaration of war reached the Polish capital a few hours later, throngs of people similarly marched to the French Embassy, carrying still more flowers, singing the *Marseillaise* and shouting "*Vive la France!*" Exultant students seized the French military attaché as he attempted to enter the embassy. Playfully, they threw the poor man into the air and caught him before he hit the ground. Women grabbed the policemen assigned to hold back the surging crowds and danced with them.

During those few hours on September 3, the Poles felt that they were not alone. For centuries, they had regarded themselves as intrinsically linked to the West, even if virtually no one else did. Their geographical separation from France and other Western countries had not dampened their admiration for all things Western. For the Poles, "the West is...a land beyond the rainbow, the lost paradise," the British historian Norman Davies has observed. And now, finally, Poland's Western friends were coming to its defense. Those were to be, another historian wrote, the "last hours of unrestrained rejoicing and happiness" that the people of Poland would know for half a century.

But there was no rejoicing in Britain and France. The first day of war, a British novelist, Margery Allingham, wrote to friends, was marked by "no band, no cheering, no noise; only this breathless feeling of mingled relief and intolerable grief." In France, banner headlines screamed the words: "*C'est la Guerre!*" But the headlines "didn't really translate into 'War!'" observed CBS's Paris correspondent, Eric Sevareid. "It was still just '*C'est la Guerre*,' which you flipped off your tongue every day like 'The first hundred years are the hardest, chum,' or 'It never rains but it pours.'" The French, Sevareid continued, went to war with the unshakable "conviction that no human body, no single face, was expendable for any cause."

On September 4, the *New York Times* confidently predicted that "within a day or two," British and French troops would be locked in combat with the Germans. The accuracy of that prediction would depend upon one's definition of combat. The British and French governments immediately declared their "firm desire" to spare Germany's civilian population and historical monuments. Despite General Ironside's pledge to the Poles a few months earlier, the British and French armed forces were ordered to attack only "military objectives in the narrowest sense of the word." That Germany was massacring thousands of Polish civilians, bombing and burning Polish cities and towns, devastating Polish productivity, and pulverizing Polish historical monuments was to be kept as quiet as possible for fear of rousing the public. Said Leo Amery of Neville Chamberlain: "Loathing war passionately, he was determined to wage as little of it as possible."

While Ambassador Kennard's dispatches from Warsaw became increasingly urgent in tone, Parliament, the BBC, and the British press were by turns misled and pressured by the government to minimize the nature of the crisis. In one of his cables, Kennard reported that "machine gunning of civilians is a daily occurrence." A young officer with the British military mission in Poland, who had stood on the roof of the British Embassy in Warsaw and witnessed German planes gunning down women and children, made his way back to London to deliver a firsthand report. He pleaded with his superiors to help the Poles. Yet the government informed Parliament that the Germans were bombing only Polish military targets.

Clare Hollingworth, a *Daily Telegraph* correspondent in Poland, saw the strafing of dozens of civilian Poles as they—and she—fled from the pursuing Luftwaffe on rural roads. But when she told British diplomats what she had seen, they informed her that it would do no good to send the news on, because almost all accounts of the killings were being suppressed. Enraged at "this tacit bargain to let our allies suffer without reprisal, so long as London's skin keeps safe," she fired off three cables to her home office recounting what was happening. When she returned to London, she learned that none of the cables had been received.

At a meeting of the War Cabinet on September 4, Sir Cyril Newall, the British air chief of staff, opposed any attempt by the RAF to assist Poland. British planes, he declared, must be held in reserve to protect against attacks on France or Britain. His comment caused Winston Churchill, now a member of the Conservative government as First Lord of the Admiralty, to wonder aloud if the cabinet shouldn't be more concerned about the attack of the moment on Poland. Churchill urged that the French army and the RAF immediately assault the Siegfried Line, a string of German fortifications facing France. Other members of the cabinet agreed an attack was "a vital necessity." Indeed, the consensus was that it would be "dishonorable" *not* to attack.

Still, nothing was done, save for a few token patrols in the general direction of the Siegfried Line, a few reconnaissance flights over Germany, and the dropping of millions of propaganda leaflets informing the German people that they did "not have the means to sustain protracted warfare" and were "on the verge of bankruptcy." The leaflets soon became something of a laughingstock in Britain: Mollie Panter-Downes, the London correspondent for *The New Yorker,* referred to them as "the Leaflet-of-the-Month Club for the Third Reich." At the same time, a joke made the rounds about an RAF pilot who was scolded by his commander for not untying a bundle of pamphlets before throwing it out of his plane. "What are you trying to do," went the punch line, "—kill someone?"

In Parliament, Edward Spears and a number of like-minded colleagues were horrified at the Chamberlain government's timidity. It was "ignominious," Spears told Kingsley Wood, head of the Air Ministry, "to stage a confetti war against an utterly ruthless enemy who [is] destroying a whole nation. We were covering ourselves with ridicule by organizing this kind of carnival. It was as futile as reading a lesson on deportment to a homicidal maniac at the height of his frenzy." Leo Amery told Spears about his own encounter with Wood. When Amery suggested that the RAF drop incendiary bombs on Germany's Black Forest, then being used as a munitions storage area, Wood looked at him with horror. "Are you aware it is private property?" he asked. "Why, you'll be asking me to bomb [the Ruhr] next!"

Left to fight alone, albeit with the glimmering hope of French and British assistance, the Poles struggled to resist the German whirlwind. Pounded by the Luftwaffe, beset by Panzers, the troops fell back toward the southeastern part of the country. Their idea was to regroup on a much narrower front and then, with their allies, mount a counterattack. The German assault had caused a general breakdown of the Polish army's centralized communication and supply systems, exacerbated on September 7 when General Edward Smigły-Rydz, the army's chief of staff, inexplicably decided to flee Warsaw with the rest of the government and move his headquarters eastward. Much of the country was now without a government, and much of the military without a high command. "Smigły-Rydz will never be forgiven by the vast majority of Poles for his decision to desert his army…," noted Adrian Carton de Wiart, who had worked closely with the commanding general. "[I]t had never occurred to me he would throw aside his responsibilities in a hysterical rush to save his own skin. His behavior was in direct contradiction to everything that I knew about the Poles.…"

The day before the exodus began, the Kościuszko Squadron and the rest of the Warsaw Pursuit Brigade, now down to only nineteen operational aircraft and running low on fuel and spare parts, were ordered to withdraw to a base near Lublin, in southeast Poland. The order came as a staggering blow. It meant that Warsaw would be left without air cover, its residents at the mercy of the Luftwaffe. As Mirosław Ferić flew south with the other pilots, the smell and heat of war were everywhere. "There was so much destruction," he later wrote in his diary, "and we were so powerless." On the way to Lublin, he flew over Dęblin, and his eyes filled with tears when he saw how badly hit it was. The airfields were pitted with bomb craters; several of the buildings where he had spent so much time as a cadet were gutted. It was, he observed, "a sight of utter misery."

In Lublin, the brigade encountered still more confusion. There were no orders, no ground crews, no fuel, and no communication with headquarters. Siphoning gasoline from cars and trucks, the crippled squadrons resumed limited operations. In two days, they shot down three more Luftwaffe planes. Ferić and his comrades tried to convince themselves that they soon would be ordered to take part in a powerful counterattack. "Despite the rapid retreat of our forces, we refused to contemplate total defeat," he wrote. Then they were ordered to move farther east.

One of the Kościuszko Squadron's pilots, meanwhile, was trying desperately to rejoin it. When the war broke out, Jan Zumbach, who as a boy had been dazzled by an air show, was convalescing in the south of Poland with a compound leg fracture suffered almost five months earlier in a flying accident. As soon as he heard about the German invasion, he hobbled on crutches to the local station and caught a train for Warsaw. The train was strafed and bombed by the Germans twice during the trip, but Zumbach managed to arrive safely. He learned that his squadron was somewhere at the front, although no one seemed to know exactly where. In that case, Zumbach said, why not give him a small plane and let him fly liaison missions between army divisions whose communications had been cut? When his superiors looked doubtfully at his crutches, he burst out: "I don't fly with my legs! All I need is head, hands and feet, and they're all intact!" They gave him the plane.

Zumbach's situation—a Polish military man trying to join the fight in any way he could—was mirrored in all the services, all over the country. At the air force school in Dęblin, Witold Urbanowicz received orders to lead fifty of his cadets east to Romania, where British planes supposedly were waiting for them. They were then to return to combat inside Poland. The cadets came perilously close to mutiny when told of the plan. "They wanted to fight," Urbanowicz recalled, "and I kept explaining to them that I understood their desire to grab a gun and have a go at the enemy, but that they would make lousy infantrymen. They were worth much more in the air…. My job was to take them to where they could again climb into the cockpit of a fighter plane."

The truth was that Urbanowicz was even more frustrated than his cadets. In the opening days of the war, he and five other Dęblin instructors formed a makeshift fighter squadron of their own and tried to protect the school and its airfields from German bombers. In several dogfights, they pushed their old P-7 trainers to the limit. But those "miserable machines," as Urbanowicz called them, were not very effective against the Luftwaffe and did not prevent the school from being heavily bombed. After his own P-7 was destroyed on the ground, Urbanowicz begged his superiors in Warsaw to let him rejoin the Kościuszko Squadron. He was told that it had already been evacuated to Lublin. Besides, at this point what the squadron needed most was more planes, not more pilots. Urbanowicz was ordered to forget the squadron and get his cadets safely to Romania.

Dejected, he returned to the rubble at Dęblin and, realizing he would have to travel light, gave his radio and several new silk shirts to the woman who cleaned the officers' quarters and his formal evening clothes to the doorman. With that, Urbanowicz collected the cadets, found a bus, and, together, they started down a dusty road, fifty-one more refugees in a swelling river of refugees, all heading east.

———

POLAND WAS CHAOS. The army, having little left but courage and grit, refused to admit defeat. Soldiers fell back, regrouped on their own, fought on as best they could against a form of unrelenting warfare no one had ever seen before. On September 10, eight Polish army divisions launched a counterattack across the Bzura River, west of Warsaw. For three days, they drove the German Eighth Army back and captured more than 1,500 prisoners from one division alone. Of the Polish troops he faced, a German officer remarked: "They did not come forward with their heads down like men in a heavy rain—and most attacking infantry come on like that—but they advanced with their heads held high, like swimmers breasting the waves. They did not falter." Nazi propaganda notwithstanding, a professional German officer such as General Heinz Guderian, architect of the Panzer *Blitzkrieg,* saw something remarkable in the Poles. Even in defeat, Guderian said, they were "a tough and courageous enemy."

In Berlin, where the propaganda adhered better, Polish resistance to the invasion was regarded as a mere annoyance, an unacceptable affront to Teutonic inevitability. "We must have an orderly war, a correct war!" a government spokesman complained at a briefing for foreign correspondents based in the German capital. The journalists burst into derisive laughter. "A 'correct war' indeed!" John Raleigh of the *Chicago Tribune* wrote later. "With Polish villages going up in flames...."

In spite of the flames, the Bzura counteroffensive had put the Germans on the defensive—for the moment—and Polish garrisons in Warsaw and Lwów were continuing to hold out. If the Poles could keep fighting until September 17, when France's treaty obligations required a retaliatory assault against Germany, a far more ambitious counterattack might be mounted. The Germans had thrown most of their armored, motorized, and air forces into the invasion. The Siegfried Line fortresses along the French-German border were thus vulnerable to an assault from the west. "Nothing had been prepared except the attack on Poland," Field Marshal Alfred Jodl, chief of the German General Staff, acknowledged after the war. "The forces stationed [in the west] were so weak that we could not man all the pillboxes at one time...."

Then, on September 17, the Soviet Union invaded Poland while, treaty or no treaty, France did nothing. Poland was doomed.

THE 1939 TREATY between Germany and the Soviet Union was far more than a simple nonaggression pact. It was a blueprint for the destruction of a nation. The secret terms of the treaty gave Stalin carte blanche to invade Poland from the east after Germany had invaded from the west. On September 17, the Soviets, having watched the German aggression for more than two weeks, now joined in. As so often in the past, Germans and Russians were partners in a rape of Poland.

The Soviet campaign was remarkably easy and cost-free. In a matter of days, the Red Army occupied most of eastern Poland, including the cities of Lwów and Wilno—both of which the Soviets had lost in the

1919–20 war. In all, the Soviets occupied an area of more than 77,000 square miles, containing some 13 million people, one third of whom were Polish, one third Ukrainian, and the rest Jews, Byelorussians, and other ethnic groups. More than 230,000 Polish troops were captured, while fewer than 1,000 Soviet soldiers were lost. In effect, the vast territory that Stalin won was his reward for giving Hitler free rein. As the *New York Times* editorialized a day after the surprise Soviet attack on Poland: "Germany having killed the prey, Soviet Russia will seize that part of the carcass that Germany cannot use. It will play the noble role of hyena to the German lion."

When Soviet forces first arrived, many Poles thought they had come to defend them. They soon discovered their error. Red Army planes patrolled the skies and gunned Poles down in fields and on roads. In dozens of cities and towns, Soviet troops embarked on wild, random shooting sprees. In Dubno, Soviet soldiers mounted machine guns on street corners and riddled the surrounding houses with bullets, killing scores of residents.

The Russian aggression was greeted with worldwide condemnation. Yet nothing was done to stop it. In London, the Chamberlain government expressed its "indignation and horror" but failed even to lodge a formal protest. When Chamberlain told Parliament on September 20 that neither Britain nor France had "forgotten their obligations to [Poland] nor weakened in their determination to carry on the struggle," his critics snorted.

The Soviet invasion, meanwhile, meant the collapse of meaningful resistance within Poland. But the government and the military refused to surrender. Just before the war began, three Polish destroyers slipped out of their ports and sailed for Britain; they were later joined by two Polish submarines. On September 17, tens of thousands of Polish soldiers and airmen headed for their country's borders—not to flee but to reorganize and carry on the fight from outside. Most of them escaped to Romania, joined along the way by a flood of civilian refugees, their carts, wagons, bicycles, and baby carriages laden with personal belongings. Some Polish pilots, including Zdzisław Krasnodębski, were able to fly the few remaining air force planes across the frontier as well.

At an airfield near Bucharest, Virginia Cowles, an American journalist working for the London *Sunday Times,* was struck by the "indomitable pride" of the Polish pilots she met and interviewed. They were exhausted and unshaven, their steel-blue uniforms torn and dirty. Many had been wounded or otherwise injured. But, Cowles noted, "there was no plea for pity, no request for help of any kind, only a passionate determination to escape from Romania, to join the French Air Force." One of the pilots, who had lost his entire family in German bombing attacks, exclaimed to the British air attaché accompanying Cowles: "What are they going to do with us? They can't shut us up! We must go *on*!"

A number of fliers and soldiers on foot, not knowing when, if ever, they would return, hesitated before crossing the frontier. "It was a horrible moment," recalled one pilot. "We all had tears in our eyes." Some kissed the red-and-white frontier barriers, while others kissed the ground. Almost everyone picked up a clump of earth, a pebble, or a flower—something, anything, to remind them of home. Said another pilot: "I have never seen so many people weeping."

―――――――

AS THOUSANDS OF Poles left the country, hoping to fight on, the people of Warsaw and their indomitable mayor, as well as the military garrison assigned to defend the capital, continued to resist. When government leaders and ministry officials fled Warsaw on September 7, Mayor Starzyński declared over radio and the citywide wireless loudspeaker system that Warsaw would never surrender. He was ready to sacrifice the city he loved and had nurtured, he told the residents, because there was something more important at stake. Warsaw was no longer just a city; it represented Poland itself. As long as the capital resisted, the nation would survive. It had before. It would again. "Destiny," Starzyński declared, "has committed to us the duty of defending Poland's honor." Władysław Szpilman,* a young Warsaw pianist, saw Starzyński as "the heart and soul of [Warsaw's] defense, the real hero of the city.... Everyone waited eagerly for his speeches and drew courage from them. There was no reason for anyone to lose heart as long as the mayor had no doubts."

Among those who drew courage from Starzyński's broadcasts was

―――――――

* Szpilman, a Jew, was the central character in the movie *The Pianist*, based on his book describing how he spent the duration of the war hiding from the Nazis.

Wanda Krasnodębska, the wife of the Kościuszko Squadron's commander. Wanda had barely escaped from her Warsaw apartment on the first
morning of the war when the Luftwaffe bombed the nearby airfield. Not
knowing if her husband was alive or dead, she moved in with relatives
and threw herself into refugee relief—such as it was, as block after
block of the besieged city was destroyed by German bombs.

After September 7, Warsaw was effectively cut off from the rest of
the country, as more than 100,000 troops continued to defend the city.
Food and ammunition supplies were rapidly diminishing, and long
queues formed outside food shops, with hunger trumping the people's
fear of bombs and bullets. Yet Warsaw strove to maintain a semblance
of normality. Each morning, piles of rubble from the previous night's
bomb attacks were removed and the sidewalks swept. Newspapers were
still published, electricity was still generated, water still flowed from the
taps, and most telephones still worked (thanks to linemen who continued working as bombs burst around them). The defiant, resolute strains
of Chopin's "Military Polonaise" could be heard daily on the radio, and
the cafés remained open, although they now served black bread with
marmalade instead of pastry and cakes, and the coffee was made with
burnt grain.

Faced with Warsaw's resistance, Hitler flew into a frenzy. He had
traveled to the city's outskirts shortly after the invasion, waiting there
for several days in hopes of entering, as William Shirer put it, "like a
conquering Caesar." As the city fought on, Hitler was forced to change
his plans, something he hated to do in the best of circumstances.
Instead of delivering his victory speech in the Polish capital, as he
wanted to, he had to deliver it in Danzig. His face, Shirer reported,
"flamed up in hysterical rage." Warsaw would pay for this humiliation.
Hitler would make it an example for any other city foolish enough to
stand in his way.

Now the German army added heavy artillery barrages to the bombing attacks. The sound of the shelling was "like being in a steel drum,"
recalled one Varsovian. "It shook one to the heart." Each day, it intensified until the whole of Warsaw was enveloped in a grey pall of smoke so
thick that it was sometimes impossible to see across the street. Just
about every pane of glass in every window in every building that was
still standing was shattered. Bodies and body parts were strewn everywhere. Burial details were in danger of being overwhelmed, physically

and emotionally. Formerly flower-bedecked squares and gardens had become makeshift cemeteries. Scores of graves, some of them marked with flowers and candles, also dotted the grassy verges of the main streets and avenues. By now gaiety had been vanquished, if not the Varsovians themselves. Exhausted, terrified, starving, people huddled in their homes or crept into the streets in search of food, their eyes red-rimmed, their faces haggard and haunted. Horses killed by bomb or artillery blasts were set upon by women, who hacked off chunks of meat until nothing was left but skeletons.

In Britain, the government and press bore witness to Poland's suffering with all the windy rhetoric they could muster. "In the agony of their martyred land," *The Times* editorialized, "the Poles will perhaps in some degree be consoled by the knowledge that they have the sympathy, and indeed the reverence, not only of their allies in western Europe but of all civilized people throughout the globe." On September 20, the BBC broadcast a message to the people of Warsaw: "All the world is admiring your courage.... We, your allies, intend to continue the struggle for the restoration of your liberty. Please reply, if you can, to this message."

Stefan Starzyński did reply—by making clear that the words of encouragement, while appreciated, were useless. "When will the effective help of Great Britain and France come to relieve us from this terrible situation?" he demanded of the BBC. "We are waiting for it." Stung, the British Foreign Office argued, in a bit of tortured logic, that the government's declaration of war in itself constituted assistance for Poland. True, the RAF had not yet honored the promise to bomb German targets, but the Poles could rest assured that the mere *threat* of British air strikes would be enough to demoralize the Germans. Understandably, with German bombs and artillery shells raining down on them, the Poles remained unimpressed—all the more so when they realized that the French government was, if anything, even more immobilized than the British.

As the war entered its third week, Warsaw was ringed by 13 German infantry divisions and more than 1,000 guns. In a single day, and on Hitler's personal orders, more than 400 bombers, in wave after wave, pounded the city with both high explosives and incendiaries. On top of that, the Germans were now pouring in 30,000 artillery shells a day, "showering a hot rain of metal over Poland's capital," as one Wehrmacht officer wrote. "Looking to Warsaw, we saw columns of smoke soaring languidly, as if from mighty cigars."

The city had become a gigantic bonfire, the glow of its flames visible for miles. "In the heavens," the Wehrmacht officer reported, "the clouds were as red as blood." The Royal Castle, the opera house, the National Theater, government buildings, old palaces, theaters, cafés—all and more were reduced to twisted, smoking hulks. In a little over two weeks, almost half the city had been totally or partially demolished and more than 60,000 of its citizens killed. Even in the face of such destruction, Varsovians persisted in the hope that British and French help was on the way. People continued to scan the sky, looking for their allies' bombers. "You know the British," an air warden in Warsaw confided to a friend. "They are slow in making up their minds, but now they are definitely coming."

On September 23, a disheveled and unshaven Stefan Starzyński went on the air to talk about the destruction of Warsaw. "Where there were beautiful homes," he said, "rubble now lies. Where there were parks, there are today barricades, thickly covered with bodies." Yet in the ruins Starzyński found courage. "I wanted Warsaw to be great," he said, his hoarse voice thickening with emotion. "Today, Warsaw, defending the honor of Poland, is at the pinnacle of her greatness...." Then there was silence. A bomb had struck the main power plant. Radio Warsaw was off the air, and Starzyński had delivered his last message to the people and the city he cherished.

Somehow, Warsaw managed to hold out for five more days. Only on September 28, when there was no more water, food, medicine, electricity, or ammunition, did the city fall to the Germans. When he entered Warsaw after its capitulation, Walter Schellenberg, chief of Hitler's espionage service, was stunned at "what had become of the beautiful city I had known—ruined and burnt-out houses, starving and grieving people.... Warsaw was a dead city."

On October 5, the last battle of the campaign was fought, and lost, by the Polish army. The end came in Kock, a small town north of Lublin. For thirty-five days, Poland had managed to stave off defeat by an incomparably stronger Germany and its new ally, the Soviet Union. Not even defeat on their own soil persuaded the Poles that the conflict had ended, however. The tens of thousands of military personnel who escaped abroad at the end of September would be joined by more than

Views of the market square in Warsaw's Stare Miasto *before and after German bombing in September 1939. (Library of Congress)*

100,000 others before the war was over—all of them under the command of a government-in-exile that refused to surrender.

While suffering severe military casualties of their own (70,000 killed, 140,000 wounded) in the September campaign, the Poles managed to inflict relatively heavy losses on their enemies as well. Over 16,000 German troops were killed, and some 30,000 wounded. In addition, the Germans lost about a quarter of the tanks and a fifth of the aircraft that participated in the combat. In a cable to the Foreign Office shortly after the Polish campaign, the British ambassador in Yugoslavia said he had learned that the German losses in men and matériel were "immeasurably greater" than the Germans had publicly acknowledged. The bravery of Polish pilots, the ambassador added, was "beyond belief."

Years later, the historian John Lukacs wrote: "Whatever her previous faults, whatever her previous follies, Poland [had] found her soul once again. Unswervingly, proudly, she withstood German threats and Russian encirclement. And when the end came she was to go down in battle with a noble dignity rarely to be found in our century."

Yet, during the war, in most of Europe and in the United States, the idea arose and persisted that the Poles had demonstrated both military ineptness and a lack of will in their fight against the enemy. At best, they were described as rather comic nineteenth-century romantics. When Adrian Carton de Wiart returned to London after Poland's defeat, General Ironside snapped: "Well, your Poles haven't done much!" Carton de Wiart, who had observed Polish forces in combat, snapped back: "Let us see what others will do, sir." After the war, he observed: "No one who had not been there could imagine what the Poles were up against.... It was the armed might of Germany against the weight of human bodies, and if heroism could have saved the Poles, their story would have been a different one."

The idea of Polish incompetence was reinforced by two myths about the campaign—both of which originated with German propagandists but were reported as true in both German and Allied news accounts and, later, in many World War II histories. The first was that the Polish Air Force had been destroyed on the ground in the first twenty-four hours of the war; the second, that Poland's defense consisted mainly of brave but hopeless cavalry charges against German tanks. In fact, the Poles dispatched almost all their front-line aircraft to camouflaged airfields *before* the Germans invaded, which helps explain how Polish pilots managed to shoot down 126 German planes and damage hundreds more before losing most of their own. In the case of the cavalry, there were no suicidal charges, only a couple of instances where isolated cavalry units were surprised by tanks and tried to fight their way out. The legend actually took hold after an incident on the first day of combat, when two Polish cavalry units charged a German infantry battalion. During the battle, several German armored cars arrived and opened fire, killing about two dozen Polish cavalrymen and their horses. The next day, foreign correspondents were taken to the battlefield, shown the corpses of men and horses, and told by the Germans that the charge had been typical of the Polish effort.

ON THE DAY Warsaw fell, Joachim Ribbentrop and Vyacheslav Molotov, the German and Soviet foreign ministers, signed a document officially creating the fourth partition of Poland. Later, in a speech, Molotov crowed: "One swift blow to Poland, first by the Germans and then by the Red Army, and nothing was left of this ugly bastard of the Versailles Treaty."

On October 5, Hitler finally made it to Warsaw. He reviewed his goose-stepping troops from a stand on Aleje Ujazdowskie, not far from the British Embassy, where jubilant crowds had gathered little more than a month before. Still fuming over the Poles' audacity in fighting for their capital, Hitler lectured the foreign correspondents who accompanied the official party: "Gentlemen, you have seen for yourselves what criminal folly it was to try to defend this city.... I only wish that certain statesmen in other countries who seem to want to turn all of Europe into a second Warsaw could have the opportunity to see, as you have, the real meaning of war."

Earlier that day, as clouds of smoke blotted out the sun, the correspondents were given a tour of the city that had been the Paris of the East. "A drive of horror," *Chicago Tribune* correspondent John Raleigh called it. Arms and legs still protruded from mounds of rubbish that once had been houses, and the stench of death hung sickeningly in the air. Huge craters pockmarked the capital's main boulevards. Tram rails were twisted into pretzel shapes. People crawled over the ruins with dazed expressions, stopping to claw through the piles of brick for something of use—a bedstead, a piece of clothing, a household utensil. At one street corner, Raleigh spotted a young boy, his clothes torn and filthy, his cheeks smudged with dirt and tears. The child's arms were wrapped around his chest while great sobs wracked his body. "This is the best thing that ever happened to Poland," the correspondents were told by their Nazi escort. "Now she will become civilized, guided by efficient German methods."

Shortly before the Germans marched in, Polish government leaders in Romania had sent a plane to fly out Mayor Starzyński. He refused to go. Later, the man chiefly responsible for Warsaw's defiance was taken hostage by the Nazis, along with twelve other prominent Warsaw citizens, and held liable for the misbehavior of the city as a whole. In October, Starzyński was sent to Dachau. There, four years later, he was shot.

Even before the fighting ended in Poland, squads of *Einsatzgruppen,* special extermination units, had entered the country. Their mission, in the bizarre words of Reinhard Heydrich, the chief of Reich Security and one of the chief planners of Hitler's "Final Solution," was the "housecleaning of Jews, intelligentsia, clergy, and the nobility." No Poles were safe, regardless of religion, ethnicity, or social standing. On September 4, more than 1,000 residents of the town of Bygdoszcz, including several dozen Boy Scouts between the ages of twelve and sixteen, were taken to the central marketplace, stood up in bunches against a wall, and killed by a firing squad. When Admiral Wilhelm Canaris, chief of Hitler's counterintelligence service, traveled to Poland in early September to see how the campaign was progressing, his intelligence described "an orgy of massacre" around the country. Canaris protested the killings to Field Marshal Wilhelm Keitel, head of the German armed forces, to no avail. Friends said he returned to Berlin "entirely broken" by his country's "brutal conduct."*

Ghastly as those first days of war had been, Poland's torment was only beginning.

---

* On April 9, 1945, Canaris was hanged by the SS for his role in the unsuccessful attempt to assassinate Hitler in July 1944.

CHAPTER FIVE

"Sikorski's Tourists"

As they streamed across the border into Romania, many Polish pilots had the idea that here, finally, was a country they could count on. Poland and Romania had been on good terms since long before busy post–World War I cartographers provided the two countries with a short stretch of shared border (later erased by busy post–World War II cartographers). In 1921, Poland and Romania had signed a mutual defense treaty, which, although it didn't amount to much in geopolitical terms, provided both with a little more security in an ever more insecure Europe. When Germany invaded Poland, no one really expected the Romanian government to send troops, and it didn't. What the government did do—and the pilots were grateful for this—was to agree to accept delivery of new fighter planes that the French and British had shipped, in their own good time, to the Polish Air Force.

Among those who escaped to Romania during this chaotic period, although not all at the same time or to the same place, were the pilots and ground crews of Zdzisław Krasnodębski's two Warsaw defense squadrons and the Dęblin cadets under Witold Urbanowicz's command. Then there was Jan Zumbach, who, broken leg and all, was still trying to catch up with his Kościuszko Squadron buddies.

Flying the unarmed little liaison plane that headquarters had provided him a few days earlier, Zumbach crossed into Romanian airspace on September 17 and landed at an airfield near the town of Cernauti. Shutting down his engine and using his cane to help pry himself out of the cockpit, he expected to be greeted as a comrade-in-arms. Instead,

Romanian soldiers approached and ordered him to surrender any weapons he had. Seeing that the Polish pilots who had arrived ahead of him were already being corralled "like cattle" into two nearby hangars, Zumbach managed to hide his sidearm in a pocket of his jacket. When the soldiers motioned him toward one of the hangars, he asked if he could first move his plane to a safer spot. Moments later, he was airborne again, looking down on the shouting, fist-shaking Romanians.

What neither Zumbach nor any of the others knew before they escaped from their own country was that Romania, having observed the quick work that the Germans and Soviets made of Poland, had nervously declared itself neutral and reneged on its agreement to accept the shipments of French and British planes. From that point on, whenever Polish political and military escapees crossed the Romanian border, they were arrested and hustled off to internment camps. The pilots and crews of the two Warsaw squadrons were sent to a dirt-floor barracks near the village of Babadag. There they slept on lice- and roach-infested straw mats, swatted malaria-carrying mosquitoes, and soon began to despair of ever getting back into the war.

Urbanowicz and his cadets received a similar Romanian welcome. But Urbanowicz, like Zumbach, was having none of it. Shortly before he'd left Poland, he discovered a scrap of paper in his pocket, a message from a young woman friend to whom he had just said good-bye in Warsaw. On the paper was one sentence: "You will have no other aim in your life until your country is free once more." He took that message to heart: if he couldn't fly, he would find some other way to fight, despite having dissuaded the cadets from doing the same thing. They would just have to get along without him, he decided, and he turned them over to another officer. Then, in a white-hot fury, Urbanowicz crossed back into Poland—on foot, heading for Warsaw.

He didn't get far. That same evening, Red Army troops captured him in a forest and took him, with several other Polish military prisoners, to an abandoned school. As he sat there, his hands tied behind his back, Urbanowicz decided he'd rather face a Romanian refugee camp than a Soviet gulag or whatever else the Russians might have in store for him. While a guard dozed, Urbanowicz and a Polish army sergeant sitting next to him spent several hours, back-to-back, trying to work each other's knots loose. When they succeeded, they leaped up, knocking over an oil lamp, and, one after the other, dove through an open

Evacuation Routes, 1939 and 1940

——————▸ 1939   - - - - - -▸ 1940

window into the pitch-dark night. Scrambling to their feet, they bolted in different directions.

Urbanowicz heard shouts, rifle fire, men running. Outside the schoolyard, he came to a dirt road. Sprinting down it, he discovered to his horror that it dead-ended at a deep, icy stream. He had no choice: he plunged in and, as he dove to the bottom, struck his knee hard on a rock. His groan of pain resonated through the black, freezing water. By the time he gasped to the surface, his Russian pursuers were on the bank. With only the top half of his head above the water, he slowly took cover behind a large boulder in midstream. A spray of machine-gun fire chunked at the water on both sides of him and ricocheted off the boulder. Finally, the Russians stopped firing but continued standing on the bank a torturously long time, talking softly. When they gave up and left, Urbanowicz, his teeth chattering, clung to the boulder a while longer. Then he swam to the far bank and crawled out, his injured knee sending jolts of pain through his body. Nearby, he found a fallen branch to use as a walking stick, and finally—wet, hungry, exhausted, and hurting—he started to hobble south. Back to Romania.

He lost track of time and never knew exactly how far he walked. Along the way, he met other escaped Polish military men who shared food with him and knowledge about the whereabouts and movements of the Soviet troops. Finally, Urbanowicz sneaked back across the border and eventually found the cadets at a transit camp. From there, they were marched to an internment barracks. They weren't in the camp long when a Polish courier approached Urbanowicz and slipped him a roll of money and a stack of false identity cards. *Give each cadet some money and a card,* the official said, *then split up into small groups and make your way to Bucharest any way you can. We're going to get you to France.*

Urbanowicz immediately felt better. At last there was a plan. People were making decisions, acting on them. The chaos was ending.

———

A NEW POLISH government had been created and was taking charge. Based in France, it was organized after the collapse of the prewar military junta, many of whose leaders were to spend much of the rest of the war interned in Romania. At the head of the new government, serving as prime minister and commander in chief, was General Władysław Sikorski, a highly respected, ramrod-straight hero of the 1919–20 Polish-Soviet conflict. Sikorski had been prime minister and chief of the General Staff in the early 1920s but had resisted the repressions imposed by Piłsudski and, later, the junta. As a result, his career had gone into eclipse. Only after the German-Soviet onslaught and Poland's collapse was he asked by the new president, Władysław Raczkiewicz, to form a government-in-exile. He chose men for his cabinet representing a broad spectrum of Polish political parties, most of them liberal by inclination and strongly opposed to the former government.

From the moment he took over, the first item on Sikorski's agenda was to get Polish forces out of Romania and the other countries to which they had escaped, and back into combat. Britain and France favored the idea. Both countries had utterly failed Poland in this crisis, but now they were at war with Germany themselves and needed all the extra manpower they could get as they prepared to defend their own soil and skies. Having seen what the Luftwaffe was capable of, the British and French governments ordered their embassies in Bucharest to help with the covert evacuation of Polish military personnel. Top priority, the order stressed, was to go to the well-trained pilots and air crews of the Polish Air Force.

There wasn't much time. At first, security at the Romanian camps had been haphazard; the guards had not paid much attention when Poles tried to escape, especially if bribes were paid in advance. But Berlin was pressuring Bucharest to shape up, reminding Romania's leaders of their obligations as newly fledged neutrals and accusing them of harboring hostile feelings toward the Reich, an accusation that carried with it the implicit threat of invasion. Nor were the Nazis relying solely on warnings from a distance; they made their point even clearer by sending hard-eyed Gestapo agents to Romania. The Poles feared that all avenues of escape might soon be closed.

To expedite matters, the Polish government-in-exile established a clandestine network worthy of the Scarlet Pimpernel. In Bucharest, General Stanisław Ujejski, a top Polish Air Force official, set up a secret evacuation center in a private apartment, using as desks every flat space he could find—the dining-room table, a grand piano, a huge bed, the floor. Meanwhile, in a basement beneath the Polish military attaché's office, Polish embassy employees were busy forging passports and visas, inventing false names for the holders (with the real names sent to Paris in coded dispatches). Many Poles escaped on their own, but others were helped by couriers, among them several young women, who took money, civilian clothing, and the phony identification papers to the camps. Risking arrest or worse, the couriers often bribed camp commanders and guards to look the other way while an escape was in progress.

In a camp at Babadag, a courier arrived one day to give the men of the two Warsaw squadrons the same instructions that the Dęblin cadets had received: *Take the money and papers, form yourselves into small groups, get to Bucharest.* That same night, the first group of pilots melted into the darkness. The following morning, the Romanian camp commander, evidently suspicious, ordered a roll call. Witold Łokuciewski, one of two officers left in command of the rest of the men, explained the absences by saying the missing pilots were working in the fields, helping the local peasants. The commanding officer, greatly displeased, made Łokuciewski sign an affidavit that all squadron members were present and accounted for. The next night, more men slipped away, and the camp commander insisted on yet another roll call. And this time, he warned, every one of the Poles had better be there. Łokuciewski stalled. A short time later, he and the last of the airmen escaped.

Throughout Romania, young Poles were skulking through forests and fields, hitching rides on trucks, stowing away on trains, dodging German agents and military patrols—all trying to get to Romania's dusty capital. Jan Zumbach, having made an emergency landing when his liaison plane ran out of fuel, hopped a freight, while Witold Urbanowicz and some of his cadets eluded the guards at a provincial train station and boarded an express passenger train just as it was pulling out.

When the fliers finally made it to Bucharest, they were given more money and directed by Polish officials to safe hotels and the evacuation center. They were also warned that the city was crawling with Gestapo agents on the lookout for Polish pilots and troops. *Get rid of anything that identifies you with the Polish military,* they were told. Most did, if reluctantly, but others found it difficult to part with the few personal items they had been able to carry out with them. Some kept their pilot's wings; some, their ceremonial daggers. One pilot refused to let go of the wooden propeller he had unbolted from the nose of his aircraft. Before he was through, he would lug the large, wooden propeller from Poland to Romania to France and, finally, to England.*

At the evacuation center, so many Poles lined up to have passport pictures taken that the photographer barely had time all day to pop his

---

* The propeller resides today in a corner of London's Polish Institute and Sikorski Museum, which contains the archives of the Polish armed forces and government-in-exile during World War II.

head out from under the hood. The young women issuing forged pass-ports seemed to take special delight in assigning the most incongruous of professions to their countrymen. Variations on "clergyman" were among the most popular. Thus, the high-flying, skirt-chasing Zumbach became a seminarian, and Urbanowicz—also a ladies' man but with an added touch of urbane, movie-star elegance—a monk.

After Bucharest, many of the airmen headed almost due east to the Black Sea ports of Constanza and Balcic. Hundreds at a time were loaded onto merchant ships under many flags, including a number of Polish ships that had eluded German capture. Urbanowicz and Zum-bach were among 750 Poles packed into a dirty old Greek freighter, the *St. Nicholas*, which, when it wasn't engaged in smuggling of one form or another, had been carrying Jews illegally to Palestine. The ship's most recent cargo had been a flock of sheep, whose lingering reek was over-powering. And that wasn't the worst of it. As the *St. Nicholas* was about to sail, Romanian port officials suddenly and inexplicably decided to deny boarding rights to several airmen. More bribes were paid. As the ship moved away from the pier, the officials did their part by turning their backs, and the airmen did theirs by diving into the oily water. They swam after the ship and were hauled aboard, exhausted but happy, just before it left the harbor.

Psychologically and emotionally, the departure from Romania was a mixed blessing for the fliers on board the *St. Nicholas*. They were finally on their circuitous way to France, which meant, they hoped, that they would soon be flying again against the Germans and thus would be that much closer to the day they could return home. On the other hand, for the first time since the war began, they had time to consider, in all its horror, the cataclysm that had engulfed them and their country—and their failure to prevent it. "We worried about our loved ones in Poland, about our own future," Urbanowicz recalled. "Unending discussions were held. The September campaign was revisited time and again, the same questions were asked, some of which did not invite ready answers." Their only immediate comfort was the thought that soon they would be with their French allies, who would provide them with planes to fly and ammunition to shoot. However indifferent the French may have seemed in the recent crisis, the Poles were sure they would not let them down again.

In all, more than 10,000 Polish Air Force pilots and ground crewmen—assisted by the underground networks of the government-in-exile—managed to escape Poland after the German invasion, along with thousands upon thousands of Polish soldiers and sailors. These were not just refugees but combatants determined to make another stand. For the air force, Romania was a major transshipment point until the Germans finally did manage to force the door closed. Other Poles fled south through Slovakia to Hungary or northeast to Lithuania or Latvia. Wherever the first stop was, it was invariably followed by perilous, exhausting journeys that lasted days, weeks, and sometimes months. There were airmen who traveled by ship from the Baltic to Sweden and on to Denmark, Holland, and Belgium; or from the Black Sea across the Mediterranean to Lebanon and Egypt. Others went by train or auto or on foot through Yugoslavia, Greece, and Italy. Some skied across the Carpathian Mountains in southern Poland, or headed east from Poland to Soviet ports and departed as stowaways on merchant ships. There were even those who passed surreptitiously through parts of Germany on their westward trek or who crossed the Karakum Desert into Iran, and thence to North Africa and France.

This extraordinary epic was unmatched by any other captive country during World War II. In the words of one of the pilots, thousands of Poles moved "as leaves driven by the wind or a ship's wreckage drifting with the tides. All we knew was that we had to get to the only remaining front at any price." He meant they had to get to France. They had to get to the place Urbanowicz called "the country of our dreams."

The Poles felt certain that they could rely on the French people to defend their own nation against a German attack. They had done so in World War I; why not now? The French had a huge army—800,000 men under arms—and what was supposed to be a powerful air force. Surely, they would not allow Hitler to have his way with them. What the Poles did not understand, however, was that the cataclysm of World War I, which had brought Poland its independence, had sent France into a demoralized tailspin. Only twenty-one years had passed since the armistice, scarcely a generation, and the ghosts of Verdun, the Marne, and the Somme still roamed the French landscape.

Witold Łokuciewski and his comrades had their first inkling of this when they arrived in Paris from Romania at the beginning of October

1939. Initially, Łokuciewski was enchanted by the City of Lights, especially by its young women. The handsome pilot quickly acquired a girlfriend, a student at the Sorbonne whose father was an owner of the company that manufactured Renault automobiles. But Łokuciewski's delight soon turned to disappointment and disgust. This was a dream world, not a country at war. Days before, he and his comrades had seen Warsaw burn and their countrymen murdered. Now they were in a place where people whiled away their leisure hours sipping apéritifs on café terraces or betting on the horses at Auteuil. Instead of marching off to war, French soldiers were enjoying themselves in restaurants and nightclubs, while chorus girls sang "We'll Hang Our Washing on the Siegfried Line."

One evening, shortly after their arrival in France, the pilots of Zdzisław Krasnodębski's two Warsaw squadrons gathered for dinner at a Paris restaurant. It was November 11—Independence Day in Poland and Armistice Day in France and Britain, commemorating the end of World War I. Before the pilots began to eat, their commander offered a toast. In a burst of optimism, Krasnodębski declared: "We will be celebrating the next anniversary of Poland's independence back in our country, because we have loyal allies who not only will give us modern planes, but will fight the enemy alongside us. Our victory is certain."

The French would not have disagreed. They, too, believed that victory was certain, but not in the way envisaged by Krasnodębski—not in combat. Rather, they thought victory would come because the Germans would simply wear themselves out attacking France's impregnable defenses. The French did not seem to have learned much from watching the *Blitzkrieg* against Poland; they tended to belittle the Poles and their brave and desperate attempts to resist. Encouraged by false Nazi propaganda, the French thought the Poles had lost their country through incompetence, their air force destroyed on the ground and— *mon Dieu!*—their horse cavalry charging at *tanks*! These canards, coupled with a predisposition to denigrate the Poles in any circumstance, helped lead the French to ignore their own military weaknesses and overestimate the security provided by their Maginot Line, a massively fortified area along the northeastern border that France shared with Germany. When Polish pilots tried to educate their French colleagues about the fury of *Blitzkrieg* and the utter irrelevance of World War I—

style defenses, the French listened with barely concealed disbelief, if not outright contempt.

French military planners, succumbing to the same combination of ennui, self-delusion, and arrogance as the civilian population, were no longer considering even the possibility of waging active, as opposed to purely defensive, war. Between October 1939 and May 1940, they were convinced that any German attack through Belgium would be across the plain north of Namur, not through the much more difficult and dense terrain of the Ardennes Forest, which the French regarded as impassable for tanks. With that in mind the French high command had pulled its troops back into defensive positions, certain that the Maginot Line—a zone 200 miles wide and up to 50 miles deep, consisting of underground forts, barbed wire, pillboxes, tank traps, and guns—would at least slow the Germans enough to allow time for any necessary deployment.

In the event, the high command could not have been more wrong. Not only did the Germans come through the Ardennes, but most French troops were in no mood to fight. General Alan Brooke, who commanded one of the two British Expeditionary Force corps in France, was shocked by the condition of the French soldiers he encountered after his arrival: "Never have I seen anything more slovenly and badly turned out. Men unshaven, horses ungroomed, clothes and saddlery that did not fit, vehicles dirty, and a complete lack of pride in themselves and their units. What shook me most... was the look in the men's faces, disgruntled and insubordinate looks, and although ordered to give 'Eyes left,' hardly a man bothered to do so."

———————

ALTHOUGH FRENCH GOVERNMENT officials had initially encouraged Polish fliers to come to France, they seemed to have changed their minds by the time the Poles arrived. For many of the French, the presence of the airmen was an unpleasant and thus unwelcome reminder of war's reality. The British air attaché in France noted that the French "have received the Poles... without any proper arrangements for them, with the result that they have suffered seriously in morale and in health from the appalling conditions in which they have been kept."

When Urbanowicz and his cadets arrived by ship in Marseilles, they were taken to a base near Istres, where they were housed in a primitive barracks with no heat, no furniture, smashed windows, and only straw on the concrete floor to sleep on. They had to pay for hot showers and meals. French airmen regarded them with condescension, hostility, and suspicion. They heard themselves and their country accused of starting the war, or, at the very least, of having caused it to start. "We did not socialize with the French officers at all," Urbanowicz observed. "They shunned us as if we were enemy prisoners of war." The Poles had expected to be assigned to operational units and to be thrown almost immediately into combat. Instead, while negotiations proceeded between the Polish government-in-exile and the French, the pilots were virtually confined to their slumlike barracks and ignored.

With nothing to do, the homesick, morose Poles, most wearing the civilian clothes they had picked up in Romania, whiled away the days in endless debates about their shortlived fight against the Germans and in speculation about what was happening to their homeland under German and Russian occupation. Some of them did get occasional passes to Marseilles, where they met young women and saw the sights. But the good times paled quickly whenever they saw unmolested Luftwaffe aircraft overhead. "If only we had a couple of good fighters," Urbanowicz complained. In one story, which may be apocryphal but nonetheless illustrates how the Poles viewed their French allies at the time, they heard what sounded like gunfire one night outside the barracks. A pilot shouted that he was sure it was ack-ack. The Poles rushed outside, hoping against hope that war had finally arrived in France—only to discover that the noise was the popping of champagne corks in the French officers' mess.

The frustrated Urbanowicz, for one, had had enough. A call had gone out for Polish pilots to go to England and join the Royal Air Force, and Urbanowicz was put on the list. At the end of 1939, he was part of a small group of Polish pilots and ground staff who crossed the English Channel. But the British, like the French, seemed to be having second thoughts about the Poles, once they were at hand. The Air Ministry said it could accommodate only 300 Polish Air Force pilots to begin with—and they would be relegated to bombers. This was like telling a Formula One race car driver that henceforth he would be circling the track in a bus. Still, as far as Urbanowicz was concerned, if he had to fly

A somber Zdzisław Krasnodębski in the south of France, shortly after he and other Polish pilots escaped from Poland and then Romania in the fall of 1940. (Stanisław Blasiak)

bombers in order to get back into the war, then he would fly bombers. Anything to get out of do-nothing France, his "dream country" only a few weeks earlier. "Leaving France," he said, "was like taking a decent, warm shower."

In early 1940, meanwhile, the French finally got around to the idea of training the Poles in French planes and attaching them to various units. Assigned to a base at Lyon-Bron, they were supposed to spend three months in training. But they proved such skillful pilots that it took most of them only a month to complete the entire course, conducted in mostly obsolete planes. At that, the French were in no great hurry to make the Poles operational. They had hundreds of combat-experienced Polish fighter pilots to choose from, all of them desperate for action, but by the end of March, only one all-Polish squadron had been formed, and only eighteen Polish pilots had been assigned to front-line French units. "For those of us who were burning to pay the Germans back in their own coin, it was a long period of declining morale," Jan Zumbach recalled.

The few Poles assigned to fighter duties found that their joy and relief at being back in the air were spoiled by the laissez-faire attitude of the French pilots they flew with. Sometimes it seemed to the Poles that the French really didn't *care* if the Germans overran their country. Returning from a routine fighter patrol with four Frenchmen, one Polish pilot spotted a German bomber and suggested they go after it. "You can do what you like," the flight leader radioed. "We're going home." The Pole pursued the German plane and shot it down. Back at the base, he found the French pilots drinking champagne in the mess.

Polish fliers assigned to the front-line base of Luxeuil, near the German border, argued for bombing raids across the frontier. They were told that the Germans were too weak to attack and that the war would soon be over anyway. When the Poles at Luxeuil warned the French to camouflage and hide their planes, their advice was simply ignored. Nothing was done, not even when Germany brought the "phony war" to a shattering halt by invading Norway, then Denmark, in early April. When the Germans launched their aerial attack against France early on the morning of May 10, 1940, the planes at Luxeuil were lined up in neat rows on the grass airfield. Nearly all were destroyed on the ground.

Capitalizing on a lovely dry spring throughout Europe and on eight months of Allied inaction, Hitler had sent his Panzers hurtling through Luxembourg, Holland, and Belgium, while the Luftwaffe bombed targets in all three countries. Within hours, most of the Dutch and Belgian air forces were wiped out. Within five days, Holland had surrendered; Belgium was close to capitulation; and the troops of the retreating French army and the British Expeditionary Force were heading for the beaches of Dunkirk. There, over the following two weeks, they would pile up by the hundreds of thousands, desperately looking across the Channel for rescue.

On May 13, France for the first time felt the full force of Hitler's wrath. A German army group, consisting of more than 1.5 million men and 1,500 tanks under Field Marshal Rudolf Gerd von Rundstedt, advanced, against all French expectations, through the Ardennes Forest, outflanking the vaunted Maginot Line and tearing through the least fortified sector of the French frontier.* At the same time, another large German army group was attacking through the Lowlands closer to the coast. After little more than a day of this, French premier Paul Reynaud telephoned Winston Churchill, who on May 10 had succeeded the now disgraced Neville Chamberlain as Britain's prime minister. "We are defeated," Reynaud told Churchill. "We have lost the battle." Although a number of French soldiers stood their ground and fought heroically, many others did not. General Erwin Rommel, commander of the 7th Panzer Division, was guilty of only slight hyperbole later when he said of his sweep through France: "Nowhere was any resistance attempted.... Hundreds upon hundreds of French troops, with their officers, surrendered at our arrival."

To France and the other countries under attack, this was a nightmarish new form of warfare. To the Poles, it was déjà vu: the Panzers slicing through Allied lines almost as if they weren't there; the Luftwaffe forging ahead of the armored columns, bombing bridges, roads, and train stations, strafing troops and civilians alike.

With its losses accelerating and French and British ground forces in full retreat, France begged the RAF to send more squadrons to supplement the ten British squadrons already in the fight. But the French air force still had little use for the Polish pilots in its midst. A few Poles were put in to reinforce French squadrons, while others were assigned to "chimney flights"—air defense of factories and air force bases, mostly far from the front lines. In all, only about 150 Polish pilots, of the more than 1,600 available, took an active part in the battle for France.

Zdzisław Krasnodębski was in command of the first Polish "chimney flight," over the industrial town of Etampes. The flight consisted of several badly maintained planes, most of them old and obsolete. This marginal assignment, and the treatment of Poles as second-class pilots, left Jan Zumbach, who was flying one of the planes, "beside [myself] with rage." To the French commander at Etampes, Zumbach said, "the idea of a good day's work was sending us to 'guard the chimneys' of the local factories, when [all] we wanted [was] a crack at the Stukas that were

---

* Two days earlier, after all the laughter at the Poles' expense, France had dispatched four horsed cavalry divisions into the Ardennes to try to slow down Hitler's tanks. They failed.

having a field day pounding the...forces retreating toward Dunkirk." Zumbach's French colleagues "refused to fight at all, insisting that the war was a '*cause de Polonais*.' "

The continuing apathy of *L'Armée de l'Air* was as astonishing to Zumbach and the rest of the Poles as was its failure to send all available pilots into front-line combat. On June 3, Zumbach, Krasnodębski, and the other French and Polish fliers at Etampes were having their midday meal when a courier burst in to announce that several German planes had been spotted in the area. As the Poles jumped to their feet, air-raid sirens began blaring. "What's the hurry?" the French commander snapped. "We haven't finished eating." But Zumbach, Krasnodębski, and the other Poles were out the door and running for their planes. A Polish mechanic had started Zumbach's engine, and Zumbach, climbing into his plane, yelled at him to take cover. Ignoring the order—the bombs now exploding around him—the mechanic ran to start up another Polish flier's plane. At that moment, a piece of shrapnel ripped off his left arm.

In this fight with twenty-odd German bombers and fighters, the Poles realized that, for all intents and purposes, they were alone. Just one French pilot joined them; the others, having finally taken off, were chasing a lone bomber. Harried by the escorting Messerschmitts, Zumbach made a pass at the bombers, only to find that the machine guns in his Morane fighter had jammed. Later, he learned that they hadn't been cleaned in over a month. For Krasnodębski, the overall situation—the lackadaisical French attitude, the lack of coordination, the failure to fight as a unit—became intolerable. He demanded that, from then on, the French allow his men to fly alone.

Even in some front-line units, the French were maddeningly uncombative. "For them," said one Polish pilot, "a German in the sky was something you need to close your eyes to, in order not to have to gaze at him too long."

Ludwik Paszkiewicz, a pilot in Warsaw's 112 Squadron who later would join the Kościuszko Squadron in Britain, recalled that the French unit to which he was attached "clearly was avoiding the enemy." During the month that Paszkiewicz flew with the French, "I often heard them saying that they had to save their strength until they [received] new aircraft. I found it very strange because it was happening at the critical moments of the German offensive." Just before the fall of France, Paszkiewicz's flight was finally ordered to make a low-level strike on an armored Wehrmacht column in Normandy. The French pilots refused to carry out the order, declaring it was too risky to attack armored vehicles. In the end, Paszkiewicz strafed the column alone.

On June 14, just a month after the invasion, German troops entered Paris. A week later, Marshal Henri-Philippe Pétain, France's great World War I hero, who became its most infamous defeatist in World War II, signed the armistice. It included a secret protocol that barred the evacuation of Polish troops from France. Accordingly, General Maxime Weygand, the French commander in chief, ordered Poles to lay down their arms. But Prime Minister Sikorski rejected the order out of hand. Having refused to surrender in Poland, his men were certainly not going to surrender in France.

During the fighting there, Polish forces amounted to about 85,000 men, of whom about 11 percent were in the air force. The 75,000 men in the Polish army were a motley group that included university professors, coal miners, poets, priests, college boys, and at least one top diplomat. Józef Lipski, Poland's former ambassador to Germany, had left Berlin at the beginning of the war and enlisted in his country's army as a private. "Now I was to face the Germans once more," he recalled, "but this time with a weapon more convincing to the German mentality than a diplomatic note."

The Poles distinguished themselves in heavy fighting, in a number of instances covering French retreats. On June 13, a Polish armored brigade repulsed a German attack near Montbard and mounted a counteroffensive, inflicting heavy casualties. At Belfort, the 2nd Polish Infantry Rifles Division held the Germans at bay for six days, facing an artillery barrage three times stronger than its own. General Weygand remarked that if he had only had a few more Polish divisions, he might have been able to stem the German tide.

When the armistice was signed, Polish airmen and soldiers were almost as distraught as when their own country fell. France, which they and many other Poles had idealized for so long, France, with its world-famous military might, had been brought to its knees. The French air, said Jan Zumbach, "was thick with resignation and defeat." But if news of the surrender left him and the other Poles in tears, on the opposite side of the airfield, in the French officers' mess hall, "the champagne was flowing freely," as Krasnodębski recalled, "because the war was over."

Relatively few Frenchmen, with the notable exceptions of General Charles de Gaulle and his followers, made any attempt to flee the country and continue resisting from outside. Yet the Poles in France were already preparing to move. On June 18, Sikorski flew to London for an urgent meeting with Churchill. He asked if Britain would help rescue Polish forces so that they could fight again. Churchill's response was swift and unequivocal. "Tell your army in France that we are their comrades in life and in death," Churchill declared. "We shall conquer together or we shall die together."

The next day, Sikorski gave notice over the BBC that Poland would continue to resist. He ordered Poles in France to head immediately to ports in the south. British and Polish ships, he said, were already on their way to pick them up.

Once again, "Sikorski's tourists," as Nazi propaganda chief Joseph Goebbels derisively called the Poles in a radio broadcast, were on the move. And, once again, they discovered that their escape was being hindered not only by the Germans but by an erstwhile ally. Polish pilots had been ordered to fly out any planes they could get their hands on, but many French officials kept them from doing so. At Bordeaux, just as Zumbach was about to appropriate a Morane, French authorities seized it and posted sentries around it. Zumbach had no choice but to leave the plane where it was and hitchhike to the nearest port. Witold Łoku- ciewski, who had been posted to a chimney flight in Ramortin and who had shot down a German bomber a few days earlier, plotted with the other Poles in his flight to grab their planes before first light the next morning and fly them to North Africa. When they arrived at the air- field, they discovered that the planes' fuel tanks had been punctured by bullets—the work of French officers, they were told—and so Łoku- ciewski and the others were forced to get to England by ship. Poles at yet another airfield, thwarted in their attempts to take their planes, commandeered French military vehicles at gunpoint and headed for the sea.

Not everyone failed to get French planes, however. One pilot, who would join the Kościuszko Squadron in England, climbed into a Morane, took off, and set his course for French Morocco. He had not refueled and over Majorca realized his tanks were nearly empty. He had few options, and those grim: it was too late to turn back to occupied France, and if he veered west and landed in neutral but Fascist Spain, he would be interned. "Long live Poland!" he said to himself and flew on. His engine stopped just as he crossed over the North African coast. Moments later, drenched in sweat, he glided in for a landing in a vineyard near Algiers.

Meanwhile, the 3,000 men of the Polish army's Carpathian Brigade— who had been unable to get to the west after crossing the Mediterranean and who formed up in French-controlled Syria instead—were ordered by French authorities to lay down their arms. The brigade commander, General Stanisław Kopański, refused. If the French tried to disarm his brigade, Kopański said, the Poles would, with the greatest regret, fight their former allies. Threatened with arrest, Kopański (assisted by a sympathetic French general) managed to move his troops to British-controlled Palestine.

On June 24, two days after the signing of the armistice, the last Polish units in France were rescued from the port of Saint-Jean-de-Luz, with German troops in hot pursuit. Some Poles who could not get to the sea after the surrender headed for Switzerland. One pilot made his way to Geneva, rowed himself across the lake in a borrowed boat, then clung to the underside of a railroad car that was part of a Yugoslavia-bound train. Eventually, the pilot reported to British authorities in Palestine, saluted, and said he was ready to fly again.

In all, more than 75 percent of the Polish Air Force—some 8,000 men—made it from France to Britain. The army was not as fortunate. Most of the Polish ground troops who fought in France were killed, captured by the Germans, or interned in Switzerland; only a remnant—about 20,000—made it across the Channel, many of those thanks to the historic British rescue operation at Dunkirk. With the naval personnel who had come earlier, the number of military Poles now in England had grown to well over 30,000.

They had arrived, the airmen told themselves, at "Last Hope Island."

CHAPTER SIX

"When Will We Start Flying?"

"THE BRITISH HAVE always been the biggest damn fools in the world," Winston Churchill once declared to an American visitor. "They are too easygoing to prepare [for war]. Then at the last minute, they hurry around and scrape together and fight like hell." As Churchill readied his countrymen for the greatest confrontation in their long history, the prospect of fighting like hell clearly exhilarated him. In that respect, he was very much like the Poles.

Indeed, in temperament and outlook, the new prime minister sometimes seemed to have more in common with the exotic foreigners he had welcomed into Britain's midst than with his own phlegmatic countrymen. Like the Poles, Churchill was a deep-dyed romantic. Honor was his ultimate ideal. Before the war, faced with appeasement, he, along with a handful of other MPs, had defied the government by opposing accommodation with Hitler. Churchill simply did not know how to yield. While others saw the world in shades of grey, he saw it— or at least those portions of it dealing with life and death, war and peace—in stark black and white: the forces of absolute good challenging the forces of utter evil. Patriotism and national pride were paramount, even when much of Britain shared the sentiments of the Oxford undergraduates who in 1933 declared that under no circumstances would they fight for king or country.

A direct descendant of the first Duke of Marlborough, Churchill had been born at Blenheim Palace and was, indisputably, a member of England's aristocratic elite. Yet he lacked the social gloss that Britain's upper-class world cultivated and cherished. Again, like many Poles, Churchill was volatile, voluble, passionate, and impetuous—traits generally frowned upon in the polite, emotionally repressed, well-bred society in which he moved.

But the most important trait that the prime minister and the Poles had in common was their determination to fight on in the face of overwhelming odds. In May 1940, when Churchill moved into 10 Downing Street after Neville Chamberlain's fall from power, a determination to fight was still not a characteristic that many Britons shared with him.

Until the invasion of the Low Countries and France, most of the British public had refused to take the conflict very seriously. In London, sandbags and wire barricades shielded the entrances to government buildings and antiaircraft batteries stood guard in the parks. But restaurants, theaters, and nightclubs were bustling; cricket and football matches continued to draw large crowds; some of the gentry still hunted to hounds; and eager debutantes still waltzed at coming-out balls. Seen from the perspective of London, "this seemed like an almost casual war," Edward R. Murrow told his CBS radio listeners. "The British exhausted their vocabulary of condemnation, asserted that right was on their side, and seemed to feel that Germany could be strangled at long range without too much trouble."

That "smug, insular contentedness," as one RAF pilot described it, was finally shattered when France fell. Despite the heroic rescue from Dunkirk's beaches of more than 200,000 British soldiers and thousands of French, Belgian, and Polish troops, Britons faced a future that verged on the calamitous. Their country, obviously already targeted by Hitler, could muster only twenty army divisions, barely a tenth of the forces fielded by Germany. Several hundred of the RAF's most experienced pilots—not to mention armaments, equipment, and more than 20,000 ground troops—had been lost during the defense of the Lowlands and France and then at Dunkirk. In the aftermath, there were only 600,000 rifles and 500 cannon in all of Britain—and most of the cannon were antiques, appropriated from museums. "Never has a great nation been so naked before her foes," Churchill declared. In June 1940, Sir Alexander Cadogan, the starchy permanent undersecretary of the Foreign Office, wrote in his diary: "Certainly everything is as gloomy as can be.... As far as I can see, we are, after years of leisurely preparation, completely unprepared."

Most of the world had already written Britain off. How could this little island, no matter how glorious its military past, resist an invader that had toppled every country in its path like so many duckpins? In Washington, Pentagon officials advised President Franklin Roosevelt to forget about sending military aid to Britain, as Churchill repeatedly and urgently requested. American generals and admirals, military realists all, could see no hope for Britain. "Up till April, [U.S. officials] were so sure the Allies would win that they did not think help necessary. Now they are so sure we shall lose that they do not think it possible ... ," Churchill wrote Lord Lothian, the British ambassador in Washington. "We have really not had any help worth speaking of from the United States so far." Indeed, Roosevelt was already suggesting to an irritated Churchill that, in the event of Britain's defeat, he consider moving the British fleet to Canada, to guarantee its safety and thus its availability, if necessary, to help defend America.

For that matter, the British themselves had little confidence that they could ward off Hitler. In a survey taken after the fall of France, only about half the population thought that their nation would even continue fighting. "Everyone is going around looking as if they want to put their heads in a gas oven," observed one government report.

A number of ardently pro-German British aristocrats were urging the government to make an immediate peace with Hitler. The Duke of Bedford went so far as to launch a personal peace initiative. Even in Churchill's own cabinet, there was serious opposition to prolonging the war. In a May 27 cabinet meeting, Lord Halifax, the foreign secretary, argued that Britain should seriously consider peace negotiations with Germany, "which," he said, "would save the country from avoidable disaster."

Against such defeatism and despair stood the resolve, courage, and Shakespearean eloquence of one sixty-five-year-old man. "You ask, what is our aim?" Churchill said to the House of Commons on May 13, three days after he became prime minister. "I can answer in one word: victory, victory at all costs, victory in spite of all terror, victory, however long and hard the road may be; for without victory, there is no survival." Those words and that sentiment remained his touchstone for the rest of the war, no matter how dark the times. Yet there were also words of promise and optimism. Churchill told his countrymen: "I take up my task with buoyancy and hope.... I feel entitled to claim the aid of all, and I say, 'Come then, let us go forward together with our united strength.' "

In that speech, as in many unforgettable speeches to come, the prime minister's determination to keep his nation free echoed the declaration in Shakespeare's *King John:* "This England never did, nor never shall, lie at the proud foot of a conqueror." As the Poles had done eight months earlier, Churchill made clear that he would risk everything to uphold the honor of his country. He presented the war as a heroic crusade, linking it in British minds to Nelson's victory at Trafalgar, the defeat of the Spanish Armada, and other national triumphs. In his outpourings of hope and inspiration, Churchill almost single-handedly changed the mood of a nation. Shaking the British out of their lethargy, he imposed his "imagination and will upon his countrymen," the British philosopher Isaiah Berlin recalled, investing them "with such intensity that in the end they approached his ideal and began to see themselves as he saw them." In so doing, the prime minister "transformed cowards into brave men."

Somerset Maugham immediately detected the change in his countrymen when he returned to London in June 1940, after a month in France: "The British people had realized at last they were fighting for their existence, and, to defend their freedom, they were prepared for any sacrifice that was demanded of them."

THAT CLIMACTIC SUMMER, London became home to the displaced governments of five Nazi-occupied European countries: Poland, Czechoslovakia, Holland, Belgium, and Norway. Churchill insisted that all such governments-in-exile be welcomed, but he seemed especially fond of the Poles, in whose ostensible defense Britain and France had declared war in the first place. Besides, by heading west, the Poles had voted overwhelmingly with their feet. In the short time since Hitler began gobbling up Europe, more than 30,000 Polish airmen, soldiers, and sailors had made their way to British shores, eager to take up the fight for England and to resume their fight for Poland. By a ratio of some six to one, they were the largest foreign military force in Britain at the time, and among them were no fewer than 8,500 airmen. (Representatives of Czechoslovakia's air force were second, with 1,250.) Before the end of the war, the number of Polish soldiers, sailors, and airmen fighting on the Allied side would grow to more than 200,000.

But, beyond the Poles' numbers and determination to fight, there was something else about them that Churchill found appealing. Ever the romantic, he admired gallantry wherever he found it, and he found it in the Poles. One day, shortly after the battle for France, Churchill remarked to his luncheon guests that the Polish military, despite its lack of modern equipment and the failures of Poland's political and military leadership, had resisted German aggression better than the French and had shown incomparably greater spirit. Shaken by France's ignominious collapse, Churchill was fond of contrasting Sikorski's perseverance with the defeatism of Vichy France's chief of state, Marshal Pétain, who had so easily capitulated to Hitler. The Poles "seem to be our most formidable allies," John Colville, one of Churchill's private secretaries, wrote in his diary.

Not everyone in the British government, however, was quite as smitten with the Poles as Churchill. A number of senior military officers and diplomats who had been instrumental in the decision to withhold aid from Poland when it was under German attack now questioned the usefulness of Polish volunteers. In part, this was British imperial arrogance. "Britain does not solicit alliances," Lord Salisbury once sniffed, "she grants them." Other important Whitehall figures argued that, dire as the situation was in the spring and summer of 1940, Britain did not need the help of some benighted Central European country that, to most Britons, was little more than "a name on the map."

While much of the British public, unlike many officials, welcomed the Poles with great sympathy and friendliness, they did not know a great deal about these foreigners or their origins. Cultural, historical, and religious ties between the two countries were slight, clashes of temperament and understanding inevitable. "Beyond the fact that Poland existed, that it lay between Germany and Russia, that Piłsudski, Paderewski, and Chopin were Poles, the average Englishman knew absolutely nothing," noted Geoffrey Marsh, an RAF officer who served as an English instructor to the men of the Kościuszko Squadron. Marsh's "average Englishman" imagined that Poland "was some hundred years behind" Britain and that "its inhabitants lived in a state of superlative ignorance." These British misconceptions resulted in "naïve

questions like, 'Have you trams in Warsaw?' or 'cinemas in Cracow?' "
and left the Poles exasperated. When Shakespeare wanted to suggest a
shadowy land beyond the pale of British awareness, he wrote into *Hamlet* a reference to the Kingdom of Poland. Nearly 400 years later, Poland
was, for most Englishmen, still "the other Europe"—exotic, unknown, a
bit savage.

Ignorance was, however, a two-way street. Polish pilots "knew about
Shakespeare and Sherlock Holmes," as one of them put it, and "had
heard of the notorious English fog." Beyond that, the Poles had little
knowledge or understanding of Britain. Some arrived convinced that
"the typical Englishman differs little in temperament from a fish." Even
worse for the pilots, they had been told that "you might spend a lifetime
searching, but that you would never find a beautiful woman the length
and breadth of the country." (To their great relief, that stereotype was
soon shattered.)

Beyond general misperceptions, there was the problem of the war
and how to fight it. The Poles, given their experiences to date, tended to
be rather cynical about their British allies. Certainly, the pilots among
them, dazed and angered by what they saw as an endless series of
betrayals by their allies, were in no mood to put up with British breeziness where the Nazi menace was concerned. "My mind was still reeling
from the desperately heroic Polish shambles and the insouciant French
shambles," recalled one flier. "Therefore it was with some apprehension
that I awaited the first symptoms of some third variety of shambles—a
British shambles."

The initial treatment of the Poles by the Air Ministry and the RAF
didn't help. Like the French, the British accepted as truth German propaganda about Polish fecklessness in resisting the Nazi invasion. Senior
RAF officers, already doubtful about the flying skill of Polish pilots,
believed they had lost their nerve in their confrontation with the Luftwaffe. Fighter pilots, indeed! If the Poles wanted to get into the air
again, they would damn well have to be satisfied with their assignment
to Bomber Command. In the meantime, according to an Air Ministry
report, they needed some seasoning, needed to learn some English,
needed to calm down and quit rattling on about the bloody Jerries, and
needed, by God, to adjust to the Royal Air Force's way of doing things.
Above all, they needed to suppress their "inherent individualism and

egotism," show some discipline and good old British team spirit, and "learn by example" from their English counterparts. "If the Polish air units in this country are ever to become efficient," said the report, "their command must never be taken out of British hands."

This kind of condescension, understandable as it may have been, drove the Poles wild. Most of the airmen who arrived in Britain in late 1939 and early 1940 were experienced fighter pilots. The problems they had faced in defending their country had little or nothing to do with their flying skill. Give them modern fighters—Spitfires or at least Hawker Hurricanes—and they would show these Brits a thing or two. The Poles had already agreed to convert to bombers—anything to get back into the fight—but were far from happy about it. Many had been flying at Polish *aeroklubs* since they were youngsters, and most were proud graduates of Dęblin, one of the most difficult and demanding air force training academies in the world. Witold Urbanowicz and several others had even been combat flight instructors there. The Poles had experience against the Luftwaffe, which was more than many of these Englishmen could claim. And, by the way, the Poles had no *intention* of calming down about the bloody Jerries!

Urbanowicz made all of this clear in a face-to-face confrontation with none other than Air Marshal Sir Hugh Dowding, chief of the RAF's Fighter Command, who was, he admitted later, "a little doubtful" at first about the Poles. Dowding—tall, thin, and reticent, the quintessential English gentleman—had journeyed down to the port of Eastchurch in Kent, where the first contingent of Poles was quartered, to welcome them and to explain the virtue of patience. In Eastchurch, the fifty-seven-year-old commander found himself face-to-face with a group of intense, quarrelsome, emotional young men who showed little inclination to pay him the deference his rank and position were due. Dowding, affectionately known as "Stuffy" to his subordinates, delivered a polite, noncommittal speech, which a translator put into Polish. When Dowding asked if there were questions, Urbanowicz jumped to his feet. "When will we start flying?" he demanded. That, said Dowding, will depend on "many circumstances." Urbanowicz pressed on. "When will Polish *fighter* pilots begin their training?" Dowding shot him an icy stare. "The first to receive training will be the Polish bomber crews," the air marshal snapped. In short, the Poles were going to drive buses whether they liked it or not.

During negotiations with the British in early 1940, General Sikorski urged that Polish soldiers, airmen, and sailors serve in independent units, under direct Polish command. Impossible, said the British. Instead, Whitehall decreed that they be integrated into the British armed forces, under British command and subject to King's Regulations.* The Air Ministry's plan for incorporating Polish aviators was even more humiliating: they would not be admitted into the Regular RAF, most of whose pilots were graduates of the RAF College at Cranwell. Instead, the Poles were to be in the Volunteer Reserve, part of a citizen air force formed before the war, whose assignment, along with the RAF Auxiliary, was to create a second line of defense behind the Regulars.

The distinction between the Auxiliary and Volunteer Reserve was largely one of social class. Auxiliary squadrons consisted primarily of wellborn young men, graduates of England's elite public schools, who had learned to fly as a gentleman's hobby on weekends. Many were wealthy enough to own private airplanes; more than a few had peerages. Volunteer Reserve pilots had also been weekend fliers before the war but stood on a lower rung of Britain's largely unclimbable social ladder, tending to be self-made businessmen (or sons of them), shopkeepers, bank clerks, and the like. It was said that a Regular was an officer trying to be a gentleman, an Auxiliary was a gentleman trying to be an officer, and a Volunteer Reserve was some poor sod trying to be both. The Poles, who could be quite touchy on matters of personal dignity, already considered themselves officers *and* gentlemen and resented the implication that they were neither.

For the pilots, the other terms outlined in the preliminary agreement offered still more indignities. All Polish personnel would be required to take an oath of allegiance to the British king as well as to the Polish government-in-exile. A number of Polish fliers, including some of the cadets Urbanowicz had shepherded out of Poland, flatly refused to take the British oath, not because they were anti-British but because the idea of divided loyalty was anathema to them. Furthermore, the Poles would be required to wear RAF uniforms, with the Pol-

* The British informed Sikorski that when the war was over, Poland would be charged for all costs involved in maintaining Polish forces in Britain.

ish Air Force eagle on their cap and a "Poland" flash on the shoulder. Each Polish pilot, regardless of rank, was to begin as a "pilot officer," the RAF's lowest commissioned rank, equivalent to second lieutenant in the Polish Air Force. Only after retraining and posting would anyone be promoted to a higher grade. Finally, all senior Polish officers would be required to have a British counterpart.

As negotiations on these points dragged on, it became clear that the RAF really hadn't the faintest idea what actually to do with the hundreds of young airmen arriving at Eastchurch—2,000 of them by the end of February. "The whole future of the Poles seems extremely nebulous," an Air Ministry official reported on February 29, 1940. The British certainly were more polite to their guests than the French had been, and living conditions at Eastchurch were far superior to those filthy, bleak barracks in France. But the Poles thought they saw the same indifference in the British as in the French, the same unwillingness to let them do what they did best—fly. At Eastchurch, their days were taken up mainly with English lessons, parade ground drills, and being force-fed RAF regulations. Even when some of them were finally assigned to flight training at nearby bases, the prospect of actual combat seemed merely theoretical.

"I am extremely perturbed over the present situation of the Polish Air Force contingent in England," Wing Commander Cyril Porri, an RAF intelligence officer, wrote in a memo to the Air Ministry in late May, as the battle in France reached its peak. "There appears to be no immediate prospect of their being employed to further Allied war efforts in the air for several months at least, although they have been available since late December. I cannot help feeling that there must, in the present crisis, be a growing feeling of impatience and unrest amongst so large a body of men whose aim in coming here was to help the Allied cause."

Porri didn't know the half of it. Driven to distraction by inactivity and by increased concern about the fate of their loved ones back home, the Poles resisted what they saw as British obtuseness, a resistance that served only to confirm the British view of them as a bunch of undisciplined cowboys. The Poles were constantly complaining, constantly quarreling with their British counterparts. Having already been in combat, those who had been assigned to flight training found their lessons tiresome. To relieve the tedium, they would, from time to time, buzz the airfield or perform dangerous aerobatic stunts over the green English countryside or otherwise infuriate their British superiors in any way they could. One irritated station commander posted this notice to his errant Polish charges: "You are here in order to train for battle with the Germans according to our methods, and not in order to fool about or argue with each other.... If you cannot take yourselves in hand in a disciplined way, we cannot make anything of you."

Even the Poles' own leaders found cause for alarm in their men's behavior. "Let us be gentlemen," chided a Polish Air Force newsletter. "Let us look at the English, let us observe them, let us study their better qualities and appropriate them. We are not tourists who do not need to adapt themselves to the manners of the country. We are soldiers of the Polish forces, and the eyes of all Englishmen are upon us."

———————

TIME, OR RATHER the lack of it, was on the Poles' side. By June, the topmost officers in the Royal Air Force, increasingly aware that England was facing the full fury of German power, were finally forced to rethink their position on how best to use the men of the Polish Air Force. Germany was moving more than 2,500 fighters and bombers, in three Luftwaffe air fleets, to bases in northwestern France, as well as in conquered Norway, Denmark, Belgium, and Holland. In the meantime, the German army and navy, under a plan code-named "Operation Sea Lion," were preparing for a possible cross-Channel invasion, to begin after the Luftwaffe had established air superiority. Whatever misgivings the RAF's senior commanders may have had at first, they were finally beginning to realize that they really had no choice: they would have to use the Poles, and they would have to use them as fighter pilots.

The losses in pilots and planes that Britain had suffered in the battle for France and the Dunkirk evacuation were severe. When the Germans launched their invasion of France, six RAF fighter squadrons were based there. Later, over Air Marshal Dowding's impassioned opposition, four more were sent. To Churchill and others in Whitehall, Dowding argued that sending so many squadrons abroad was jeopardizing Britain's own defense. Besides, he believed that France, with its obvious reluctance to fight, was already a lost cause and that RAF pilots were being sacrificed for nothing. That Dowding could not abide, for beneath his unsmiling exterior was a deep paternal concern for the young men whom he fondly called "my fighter boys."

Lacking combat experience and steeped in fly-by-the-book procedures, the young British pilots who had flown over France had no idea what they were getting into. For that matter, neither did their superiors. "From the Royal Air Force point of view," said one British pilot, "the battle for France was a complete and utter shambles. There was no intelligence. Communications were poor. Everything appeared to be *ad hoc.*" In just three weeks, more than 300 RAF fighter pilots were killed or reported missing over France and the Low Countries—close to a third of the Command's overall strength. More than 100 others were taken prisoner. During the Dunkirk operation alone, the RAF lost some 80 pilots and 100 planes.

"Replacements came for the planes we lost in France, and we lost them, too, and more replacements came, and we lost them as well," said RAF squadron leader Ted Donaldson. "I think we must have lost dozens of planes in our squadron alone.... We were in awful shape by the time we finally got pulled back to England." Altogether, almost 1,000 aircraft, about half the RAF's front-line strength, had been destroyed—this at the outset of the German offensive in Western Europe—and with nothing to show for it but the capitulation of France.

As it struggled to rebuild its shattered forces, Fighter Command was about to square off against an enemy that was utterly confident and seemingly invincible. *Reichsmarschall* Hermann Göring, the Luftwaffe commander, assured Hitler that Britain and its empire would be crushed by autumn. With more than 1,400 bombers and dive-bombers and about 1,000 fighters, Göring believed unequivocally that his pilots—veterans of the campaigns against Poland, the Low Countries, and France— would wipe out the RAF. And once that job was done, Germany could proceed to bomb Britain into submission or launch the invasion that Hitler was even now considering.

In mid-July, the Luftwaffe began attacking ship convoys in the Channel and targets on England's southern coast. Britain handled these limited assaults well enough, but, against an all-out German air attack, the RAF could send up a combined total of only about 700 fighters—Hurricanes and the faster Spitfires. Worse, fewer than two pilots per plane were available. It would take a good many more of both for Britain to maintain control of its skies against the Luftwaffe. New Hurricanes and Spitfires were being turned out as fast as possible, and Dowding was doing everything he could to make up the shortfall in men.

Among other things, he was now pirating pilots from Bomber and Coastal commands as well as reaching out for volunteers from such places as Canada, Australia, New Zealand, and the United States. He was even ordering mere trainees into combat—youngsters who, in some cases, had fewer than ten hours of flying time in either Hurricanes or Spitfires. Even at that, he was coming up short. Against his better judgment, Dowding issued a new order: train Poles as fighter pilots and feed them into undermanned RAF squadrons.

Among the Poles chosen was Witold Urbanowicz.

DESPITE URBANOWICZ'S all-but-nonexistent English, it took him less than a week to persuade the British that he knew what he was doing at the controls of a fighter plane. On his first day of training, he and others in his group were put through their paces in a Tiger Moth trainer, an aircraft that Urbanowicz said was "much slower than a Jaguar [automobile]." The next day, he was given basic training in ground control and navigational aids. Then he went up for the first time in a Hurricane—and that was good enough for his instructors. The following weekend, he was in a staff car, heading for Tangmere airfield in Hampshire, just a few miles from the Channel and home base for several RAF squadrons, including the one to which Urbanowicz was now assigned.

He felt at home at once. The yellow roses blooming in profusion on the lawn in front of the officers' mess reminded him of the roses bordering his quarters in Dęblin. When a batman escorted him to his room, Urbanowicz found there a ready-made pet, a sad little dog curled up on a comfortable armchair. His batman said the dog had belonged to the previous occupant of the room, a fellow who had been shot down and killed only a few hours earlier. In fact, Urbanowicz learned, all three previous residents of this same room had died in the space of a week.

Urbanowicz was not one to dwell on the gloomy side, however.

Witold Urbanowicz in front of a Hurricane during the Battle of Britain. (Polish Institute and Sikorski Museum)

Taken to the bar in the officers' mess, he found himself surrounded by a congenial bunch of British pilots. Their warm, if typically reserved, welcome and their obvious taste for the good life—right down to the silver mugs from which they drank their pints of beer—were about as far removed as possible from Urbanowicz's miserable experience in France. Their elegant style of living, which reminded Urbanowicz of life in Dęblin, delighted the man known to his Polish friends as "the Englishman." So did their traditions. When Urbanowicz drained his first mugful of ale, he discovered that the mug had a double bottom, with dice between two layers of crystal. The custom, he learned, was to shake the mugs after each beer: whoever got the highest score bought the next round. This was his kind of place, Urbanowicz decided, and these were his kind of pilots.

His first impression was confirmed later that same evening when he was ushered into the dining room, with its tables of polished oak, tapers flickering in silver candlesticks, and meals served by pretty enlisted representatives of the Women's Auxiliary Air Force (WAAF). After dinner, Urbanowicz and the squadron leader adjourned to a nearby pub and met several more young women, all competing for the honor of serving as English tutor for this blond, slender, hand-kissing Pole in his handsome RAF uniform.

On the next day, August 8, war intruded again. For his first combat mission, Urbanowicz was assigned to be the "tail-end Charlie," flying behind the rest of the squadron to cover its back. This was a new tactic for Urbanowicz—new and not especially welcome, since it was clear that the "tail-end Charlie" could easily be picked off by a Messerschmitt while the rest of the squadron flew on, unaware. Once Urbanowicz and his Hurricane were in the air, though, he began to think that maybe bringing up the rear wasn't so bad after all. His squadron and the others that had taken off from Tangmere were heading toward the Channel in tight V-formations, as if in a ceremonial fly-past. Urbanowicz was astonished. He was accustomed to flying in a loose, fluid configuration. How could RAF pilots scan the sky for enemy aircraft when they had their hands full just trying to avoid colliding with one another? And how could they possibly engage in lightning-quick evasions or attacks when they were virtually wingtip-to-wingtip with other RAF planes?

Now they were at 18,000 feet, over the Channel. Below was the speck of the Isle of Wight. Dazzled by the sun and its reflection off the water, Urbanowicz felt as if he were suspended in a great ball of sparkling crystal. He squinted into the shimmer and searched the sky, as he had been trained. Then he spotted them—a small cloud of Messerschmitts approaching from France, hovering like mother hens above a flight of German bombers. Urbanowicz radioed the squadron leader, who ordered his men to turn and meet the enemy. At long last, Urbanowicz was getting his wish: he was about to meet German pilots on roughly equal terms, in a tough and sturdy modern airplane, flanked by skilled comrades. Now he would find out just how good he really was. His cheeks burned, his heart raced. He checked his eight machine guns and his gunsight, he adjusted his goggles and oxygen mask.

Keeping an eye on the fast-approaching Messerschmitts, Urbanowicz spotted four other planes closing in from the direction of England.
At first, he thought they might be RAF reinforcements but soon identified them as still more Me-109s—returning home and heading directly
at him. With barely a pause, Urbanowicz turned and attacked three of
them head-on. Those three scattered, but a fourth was more persistent.
A dogfight began, the Hurricane and the Messerschmitt dueling in tight
circles. Suddenly, the German fighter veered off and banked into a steep
dive. Urbanowicz followed him down, only to discover that he had been
led straight into a swarm of still more Messerschmitts. He had never
seen so many black crosses in his life. "It was," he recalled, "like finding
myself in an airborne cemetery." He was shaken but nonetheless stayed
close on the tail of his prey, while the other 109s, otherwise occupied in
a maelstrom of combat, ignored him.

The 109 Urbanowicz was chasing turned and dove again toward the
sea, pulling up at the last instant and heading back toward the English
coast, skimming the waves, trying to shake off his pursuer. Just as the
German pulled up to clear the Dover cliffs, Urbanowicz opened fire at
close range. The Messerschmitt flipped, exploded like a bomb, and
slammed into the Channel. Urbanowicz was jolted upward by the con-
cussion. A mixture of oil and seawater splashed across his windshield.

After circling the site of the crash, he headed back to base, still dizzy
from the sharp turns and dives, too exhausted to think much about his
first German kill. Back on the ground, he looked in a mirror and saw
bloodshot eyes with livid red rings around them from the pressure of
his goggles. It was stiflingly hot, but Urbanowicz collapsed onto one of
the cots in the dispersal tent without pulling off his Mae West life vest
or his fur-lined boots. In an instant, he was asleep. Soon enough, it
would be time for his next scramble.

———

ON AUGUST 8, RAF fighter pilots throughout Britain gathered in their
squadrons' operations rooms to hear a momentous Order of the Day:
"The Battle of Britain is about to begin. Members of the Royal Air
Force, the fate of generations lies in your hands." That was to say, the
fate of generations lay in the hands of a group of very young men, many

still teenagers—"little boys," wrote the American journalist Virginia Cowles, "with blond hair and pink cheeks who looked as though they ought to be in school." To Winston Churchill, the fighter pilots of the RAF were "these splendid men, this brilliant youth," the modern equivalents of the Round Table knights or the Crusaders, "who will have the glory of saving their native land, their island home, and all they love, from the most deadly of attacks." That romantic view of aerial warfare was one shared by many of the young fliers themselves, who saw the upcoming confrontation as a grand adventure. In that respect, they were not unlike Polish pilots prior to September 1, 1939.

Before his first days in combat, Geoffrey Page, who was to be badly burned when his plane was shot down during the battle, imagined war in the air "to be Arthurian—about chivalry." He continued: "Paradoxically, death and injury played no part in it. I had not yet seen the other side of the coin, with its images of hideous violence, fear, pain, and death. I did not know then about vengeance." Another Battle of Britain flier, Paddy Barthropp, added: "I am absolutely convinced that people my age hadn't the faintest idea, not a bloody clue, what was going on. It was just beer, women, and Spitfires, a bunch of little John Waynes running about the place."

Many of Air Marshal Dowding's "fighter boys" who were flung into battle after August 8 had never flown a combat sortie in their lives. Barely 10 percent had undergone rigorous gunnery practice. Few knew how to sight their guns: when attacking the enemy, they tended to open fire at ranges of 500 yards or more, then break away just as they were getting close enough to hit something. They learned their lessons quickly in combat, but many were dead before they could put the lessons to use.

Meanwhile, as the Luftwaffe was beginning an all-out assault on British airfields, the RAF's increasingly desperate need for experienced pilots forced the Air Ministry to acknowledge the Poles' concerns and to accede to some of their demands. In early August, the British government and the Polish government-in-exile signed an agreement removing the Polish pilots from the RAF's Volunteer Reserve and formally recognizing them as members of the Polish Air Force. The only allegiance they would have to swear would be to Poland. They would, however, be required to wear RAF uniforms (with Polish Air Force buttons, cap badges, and insignia of rank) and would be subordinate to the

RAF in organization, training, equipment, discipline, promotions, and operations. There was, after all, only so much the Air Ministry could reasonably be expected to give.

But for Polish fighter pilots, all that was overshadowed by another RAF announcement during the summer of 1940. Two new fighter squadrons were to be formed immediately. And their pilots would all be Poles.

CHAPTER SEVEN

The Battle of Northolt

SQUADRON LEADER Ronald Kellett, just assigned to command the RAF's new 303 Squadron, was far from happy about it. Britain was facing the prospect of an all-out German attack, and here he was, with orders to help organize, train, and lead a bunch of damned Poles!

The short, brawny Kellett believed that Britain was better off fighting the Germans on its own, without any aid from its so-called Allies. Although half-French himself, he was particularly contemptuous of France's pusillanimous response to Nazi aggression. As for the Poles, he rather thought that Flight Lieutenant John Kent, one of two RAF flight commanders posted to 303, had it about right when he said: "All I knew about the Polish Air Force was that it had only lasted about three days against the Luftwaffe, and I had no reason to suppose that [it] would shine any more brightly operating from England."

Making matters worse, in Kellett's view, was the assignment of 303 to Northolt, a key RAF sector station only 14 miles from central London, which was under the umbrella of the all-important 11 Fighter Group. The other new Polish squadron, 302, had been handed over to 12 Group and was safely tucked away at Leconfield in Yorkshire, where it couldn't do much harm. But the twenty-one squadrons of 11 Group were on the front line—responsible for protecting London itself, not to mention the rest of southeast England with all its ports, population, and history. The group's squadrons would be crucial to the defense of Britain, and Kellett seriously doubted that the Poles of 303 would be up to it.

No one had bothered to explain to Kellett why he was given command of 303 in the first place. He speculated that it might have been because he spoke French; a number of the Poles also had some knowledge of French, and a squadron leader did, after all, have to be able to communicate with his men. But that didn't change his belief that he was being sidetracked.

A London stockbroker in civilian life, the thirty-one-year-old Kellett had little use for the regular RAF. He was an Auxiliary, one of those wealthy weekend fly-boys whom the Regulars scorned as dilettantes. Born in Durham in the north of England, Kellett was the son of a self-made man who had parlayed ambition and a rough capitalist instinct into ownership of several coal mines. The family was quite well off by the time Ronald was born. He attended Rossall, a public school in Lancashire, and took his holidays in Switzerland, where he skied at Davos in the winter and spent summers at the Chamonix chalet owned by the family of his French-born mother.

Kellett, however, was hardly the stereotypical son of a rich English family. He dropped out of Rossall at the age of fourteen and before long was working as an errand boy on the Liverpool Stock Exchange. When he was only twenty-one, he returned home and stood for Parliament in his hometown—a Tory candidate in one of Labour's strongest constituencies. He lost, of course, but his campaign put him in touch with Harold Macmillan and other rising young Tory politicians of the day. Those connections proved useful over the years. There was, for instance, the time when Kellett, by now a stockbroker, applied to join the Auxiliary's 600 Squadron, also known as the City of London Squadron. His application was turned down at first, and he suspected class prejudice. Unlike most of the young men who belonged to 600, he was not of the landed gentry; he was new money, miles below the salt. But Kellett persisted and, with the help of some of his chums in the Conservative Party (or so his family believed), was finally accepted.

As much as he loved to fly, in the prewar years he regarded his RAF aircraft more as a tool for cracking open English high society than as a weapon for defeating Britain's enemies. Blond and blue-eyed, Kellett was a witty bachelor, a "tremendous flirt," whose nickname was "Boozy" and who, regardless of his nouveau riche status, was a popular houseguest at weekend hunting parties. He often sent his horse ahead by trailer, then, on Friday evenings, flew his plane from 600 Squadron's base at Hendon to join the party. After one such weekend, on his way back to London, he realized he was running low on fuel. Landing on a rural road, he bought some petrol at a nearby garage, and told the proprietor to send the bill to the Air Ministry.

Kellett's playboy days, however, came to an end as World War II approached. He was married now, to the daughter of a prominent surgeon, and his careless approach to both flying and life had vanished. He developed a rather gruff exterior and could go into flaming rages if he thought others were too casual about the threat Hitler posed to Britain. "Father took the war very, very seriously," said his son, Jonathan. "He was older than most of the other pilots, and he was very concerned about whether we would be able to fend off the Germans."

Called to active duty about a week before Britain declared war, Kellett was assigned in May 1940 to help form and train the RAF's 249 Squadron, a new unit of Regulars. He was a strict commander and was furious when some of his pilots failed to approach their training with the proper urgency. One day, several of them showed up late for duty. Kellett considered that "absolutely unforgivable" and ordered the miscreants to run laps around the airfield. "This was totally unheard of— making Regular officers do such a thing," said Jonathan Kellett. "You made the other ranks run around the airfield, never the officers." Kellett was unapologetic: *You can't bloody well expect the Germans to postpone their attacks until you're ready to meet them!*

Two months later, 249 Squadron was flying regular patrols off the Yorkshire coast and encountering the occasional probe by German aircraft when Kellett received his reassignment to Northolt. Already in ill humor because of this new posting, he was further put out when he arrived to find that the Poles allotted to 303 Squadron had not even reported in yet. So far, only a skeleton RAF staff, including John Kent, was on duty. (The second flight commander, Flight Lieutenant Athol Forbes, would report later.) For Kellett, it didn't help that Kent was a Regular and proud of it.

A Canadian, the tall and gangly Kent had grown up on the prairie outside Winnipeg. He had been in love with flying since he was four. At eighteen, he became the youngest Canadian with a commercial pilot's license. He moved to England in 1933 to join the RAF and quickly established himself as one of its hottest pilots. Kent was ambitious and could be arrogant, but everyone acknowledged that the man did know how to fly. He had been a test pilot for the RAF in both Hurricanes and Spitfires. After the German invasion of France, he was desperate to get into the fight, and, like Kellett, was "thoroughly fed up and despondent" when he learned he had been assigned to 303. "It was about the last straw," he later recalled, "to find myself after all my efforts posted to a foreign squadron that had not even been formed." As if that weren't bad enough, he also had to serve under Kellett—an *Auxiliary*.

303 Squadron was off to a most inauspicious beginning.

On August 2, the Poles finally appeared. In their dark blue French aviators' uniforms, a few sporting archly cocked berets, they seemed alien and exotic to Kellett. Most of the Poles had flown in France and since coming to Britain had been quartered in the seedy northern seaside resort of Blackpool. Initially, there were 21 pilots and 135 members of the ground crew. Almost all were from the Warsaw defense squadrons—111 (Kościuszko) and 112. In the next few days, 13 more pilots, including Witold Urbanowicz, would arrive.

On paper, fighter squadrons in the RAF consisted of eighteen to twenty-one aircraft. Twelve were supposed to be air-ready at all times, with up to nine in reserve. Each squadron generally started with about 28 pilots and 130 ground crew members. A squadron was divided into two flights, "A" and "B." Each flight was made up of two sections of three planes—"Red," "Yellow," "Blue," and "Green."

The new Polish squadron was blandly designated "303" by the RAF, but the Poles preferred "Kościuszko Squadron," after the elite unit with the internationalist traditions in which many of them had flown back home. They painted the squadron's emblem—red cap, crossed scythes, stars and stripes—on the fuselage of their Hawker Hurricanes, just below the cockpit, and took great pride in the history it represented.

Under the Anglo-Polish air forces agreement, each senior position in a squadron was to be filled by both a Polish and British officer. Thus, Kellett's counterpart in 303 was "the King"—Zdzisław Krasnodębski. The two Polish flight leaders, counterparts of Kent and Forbes, were Witold Urbanowicz, finally reunited with his former Kościuszko Squadron comrades, and Ludwik Paszkiewicz, who had been with 112 Squadron in Poland.

*Jan Zumbach on the wing of his plane, studying his Donald Duck logo and the Kości-
uszko Squadron emblem. (Polish Institute and Sikorski Museum)*

Then there were the other pilots, an extraordinary group of men
who were determined to fly again, to fight again, to win the war—not
only because the Nazis were unqualifiedly evil but because the Poles
wanted their country, families, and former lives back. Most people in
the anti-Nazi alliance experienced similar emotions at one time or
another, to one degree or another. But few felt them as intensely, or for
as long, as the Poles.

Perhaps the most colorful of the Kościuszko pilots was Jan Zumbach,
whose dry humor, rumbling voice ("our golden-voiced bullhorn,"
Mirosław Ferić affectionately called him), and roguish style ensured
that he would never go unnoticed. As one entry in Ferić's diary noted:
"Zumbach returned from leave yesterday, which means peace and quiet
is now out of the question."

Zumbach was known in Britain by several nicknames. The two most
common were "Johnny," an Anglicization of his first name, and "Donald," because his sloping nose with its oddly upturned tip reminded

A group of Kościuszko Squadron pilots, including (from left) *Witold Łokuciewski, Mirosław Ferić, and John Kent. Jan Zumbach is third from right and Zdzisław Henneberg, extreme right. (Imperial War Museum)*

people of Donald Duck's bill. Zumbach did not seem to be offended by the comparison. He had his ground crew paint a Donald Duck likeness—or as close as the untutored cartoonists in the ground crew could come to a likeness—on every fighter he regularly flew during the war.

Then there was Mirosław Ferić, nicknamed, for reasons lost in time, "Ox." Like Zumbach, Ferić was popular in the squadron, although he began testing his popularity as far back as September 1939, when he came up with the idea of keeping a daily diary of all squadron activities and exploits. This was not an official record but a personal diary, which began with Ferić's thoughts, feelings, and actions during Poland's futile resistance to the German invasion. Soon, however, he began asking his fellow pilots to write entries of their own. Actually, he came closer to demanding. Wrote one pilot in a late-night entry from Poland: "I must stress that I was forced to write this, although I simply *hate* writing. My aversion is compounded by the fact that Ox is lying next to me now and gazing at my fingers."

In France, Ferić kept up the pressure. Writing in the diary one evening, he noted: "I spent the entire day hounding them, and I will continue in my efforts until I succeed and this book starts filling up with their stories and impressions." On the squadron's arrival in Northolt, he made clear he would do the same there, and the other pilots responded predictably. "Why do they keep pelting me with such strong epithets?" a wounded Ferić wrote.

Zumbach and Ferić were two of three pilots in the squadron who, because of their exploits on the ground and in the air, were known as "the Three Musketeers." The third, Witold Łokuciewski, known as "Tolo" (a diminutive form of his first name), was friendly, talkative, and outgoing—and the envy of his colleagues because of his extraordinary, seemingly effortless success with women. With his movie-star looks, charm, and flirtatiousness, Łokuciewski had "women falling all over him," recalled one former Kościuszko pilot. "We thought him a bit conceited. Perhaps we were just jealous."

Witold Łokuciewski in the cockpit of his plane. (Polish Institute and Sikorski Museum)

Another Kościuszko pilot was Jozef František, a remarkable—some thought a little crazy—Czech who flew with a fury that none of the others could match. From his first days in the Czech air force, František was known as much for his lack of discipline as for his exceptional flying. He had fled to Poland after Czechoslovakia capitulated to Hitler in 1938, and from that day on seemed to regard himself as a kind of honorary Pole, determined to even the score with the Nazis.

After retraining at Dęblin, František became a flight instructor, yet still had discipline problems. One hot summer day, shortly before the invasion of Poland, he was flying in formation on a training maneuver when he suddenly veered off. At first, the others in the formation thought his engine might have failed. Then František's plane reappeared in the distance, and he seemed to be diving repeatedly at the banks of the Vistula River. As the other pilots flew closer, they saw what he was really up to: buzzing a group of young women who were sunbathing naked on the banks of the Vistula. As the women scattered into the brush on one pass, František pulled out of his dive at such a low altitude that he came within an ace of colliding with a sailboat. When he finally landed, his superior officer, Witold Urbanowicz, reprimanded him. "A lot of fine pilots have killed themselves through lack of discipline," Urbanowicz snapped. František said he knew that, but, "When I saw those lovely ladies on the sand, my nerves snapped."

His nerves didn't seem to bother him in combat, however. In the days after the German invasion of Poland, František flew reconnaissance missions for the Poles, and on at least two occasions lobbed grenades from his unarmed observer plane at German infantry columns.

KELLETT, KENT, AND the other British officers at Northolt knew little or nothing about what the men under their command had already accomplished and endured. Nor did they seem very curious. They were unknowingly commanding some of the best pilots in the entire Royal Air Force, and yet there was a great reluctance to let them get into the air. Even as German air activity increased markedly over the Channel and the English coast, the RAF insisted that the squadron could not become operational until its personnel learned British tactics and basic English. Group Captain Stanley Vincent, a forty-three-year-old World

War I veteran who was the station commander at Northolt, was especially adamant on the latter point. "I'm not having people crashing round the sky until they understand what they're told to do," he said. It was a perfectly reasonable point, but, to the Poles, it began to seem as if they would *never* get back into the war.

Thus began the Battle of Northolt, a tense month-long conflict of wills between the Poles and the British. It had been almost a year since Germany swept into Poland. In that time, the Polish pilots had experienced nothing but intense frustration, bordering on despair. Hungry for combat, they discovered that, once again, in Zumbach's words, "we were not to be let off the leash." Adding to the torture was the knowledge that at least forty other Polish pilots were already operational. But these other Poles were in squadrons that, except for them, were all-British. In other words, they had minders.

All this underscored another source of Polish discontent: that the Kościuszko Squadron was taking orders from British officers who acted so damned superior. The Poles were in no mood to be lectured on their language abilities or their tactics, least of all from the likes of Kellett, who had never flown a day of combat in his life and didn't speak a word of Polish. As one Polish pilot wrote, "We cannot stand being ordered about—we won't do anything without a fight." When he arrived at Northolt, the famously independent Witold Urbanowicz, who had already shot down two German planes, was particularly upset at having to take orders from the blunt, brusque Kellett, whom Urbanowicz considered "grim," "nervous," and "tactless." After the war, Kellett acknowledged that the tensions between the British officers and the Poles were "sometimes extreme."

The Polish pilots showed their rebelliousness in various ways. They were constantly reproved for rowdiness, for not conforming to regulations in dress (unbuttoned uniform jackets, missing belts, nonregulation shirts and shoes), for sneaking into WAAF housing at night or smuggling WAAFs into their quarters. "They were a complete law unto themselves," recalled a British mechanic.

But since it was their country and their air force, the British prevailed. Language lessons remained a top priority. According to Kent, only one of the Polish pilots knew any English at all, and his knowledge was confined to the phrase, "Come on, boys!" That was not quite true. Several of the pilots had learned a bit of English in their six weeks at

Blackpool. A young woman whom Ferić met on the promenade there had taught him the words to "Roll Out the Barrel" and "It's a Long Way to Tipperary." And Krasnodębski had picked up the phrase "Four whiskeys, please." Still, the Brits did have a point. None of the pilots had the basic English vocabulary of flying.

So, every morning, they boarded a bus and headed for language school at the RAF station at Uxbridge near Northolt. There they learned RAF code words—"angels" for altitude; "pancake" for landing; "bandits" for enemy planes; "tally ho" for launching an attack. They learned how to count to twelve in English, so they could understand the clock-face system for giving bearings—i.e., "bandits at twelve o'clock."

At one point, the RAF came up with what must have seemed an ideal way of training and testing the Poles in tactics without risking any airplanes or lives. They were ordered to ride a fleet of oversized tricycles—each fitted with a radio, compass, and speed indicator—in flying formation around an Uxbridge soccer field. As they rode, they were directed to "interceptions" from an "operations room" at the top of the bleachers. The indignity of it all infuriated the Poles—skilled, veteran pilots being forced to ride around a football field on *trikes*! "Their spirit's magnificent," Vincent said to Kent. "I think they hate my guts now more than they hate the Germans." He wasn't far wrong. Zumbach, for one, fumed about "the British wasting so much of our time with their childish exercises, when all of us had already won our wings."

But the lessons continued. The Poles were taught how to measure speed in miles, not kilometers, and fuel in gallons, not liters. During their early training in Hurricanes, they struggled with the many unfamiliar intricacies of modern aircraft controls. Unaccustomed to having radios in the cockpit, they often violated proper radiotelephone procedures or failed to respond properly. In Polish planes, to accelerate you pulled the throttle back, whereas in British planes you pushed it forward. The British seemed to do everything backward, right down to the side of the road they drove their cars on. Even the toggle to open a parachute was on the wrong side. "We had to reverse all our reflexes," said Zumbach.

There were several instances of overshooting the runway, and—because most of the pilots had also never flown aircraft with retractable landing gears—landings with the wheels still up. "How in hell do you think you are going to fight the Germans if you can't even fly the bloody damn planes?" Kent shouted at František, after the Czech damaged his Hurricane by landing it with the landing gear still retracted. František, who didn't understand what Kent was saying (although he doubtless caught the drift), nodded as if he did, repeating over and over, "*Oui, oui, mon commandant!*" Finally, a member of the ground crew was stationed at the end of the runway with a Very pistol, under instructions to fire a flare as a reminder to any pilot coming in for a wheels-up landing.

As the Polish squadron leader, Krasnodębski was caught in the middle. He understood the importance of the training but thought the RAF was carrying the exercises to ridiculous extremes. It was treating men already blooded in combat like ignorant schoolboys. Feeling a deep responsibility and affection for the headstrong young pilots he had led on a 1,000-mile odyssey, Krasnodębski worked hard to keep their anger in check, while trying to persuade Vincent and Kellett to get on with it.

The Polish commander knew how the inaction was feeding his men's already considerable frustration and guilt about not being able to

A group of Kościuszko Squadron pilots toss their popular commander, Zdzisław Krasnodębski, into the air during a squadron celebration at Northolt. (Stanisław Blasiak)

save Poland, about escaping and leaving their country, especially their own families, to suffer under German and Soviet occupation. "No one can deny the fact that we were defeated so quickly because of our weak air force!" a brooding Ferić wrote in his diary.

However misplaced, the guilt gnawed at Krasnodębski, too. He had too much time on his hands now, too much time to think about his wife and worry about what might have happened to her. Although he had had no direct communication from Wanda, word had filtered out of Poland that she had joined Warsaw's burgeoning resistance movement. As savage as the Nazis were to all Poles, Krasnodębski knew their treatment of captured underground members was particularly barbarous.

———

WHETHER THEY LIKED it or not, the Poles' training continued. So did the friction with their British commanders. Nevertheless, the RAF officers began showing a little more understanding and respect. While the Poles were learning English, Kellett, Kent, and the others picked up a bit of Polish. Kellett mastered the Polish words for critical plane parts like *klapy* for flaps and *podwozie* for landing gear. Kent, more thorough and organized, learned Polish for all the procedures involved in take-off, flying, and landing. He wrote out the Polish words phonetically on his pant leg so that he would have them available when giving instructions in the air. (The Poles, amused by his earnestness, christened him "Kentowski.")

Despite the belly landings and other early problems, it soon became clear to Kellett, Kent, and Forbes that the Kościuszko pilots actually were very, very good. As their training advanced, Kent was impressed with both their flying ability and their unusually quick reaction times, and Kellett even developed into something of an advocate. He was quick to challenge any disparaging remarks by other officers (remarks such as he himself had made in the beginning). He even took on Hugh Dowding when the head of Fighter Command, during a visit to Northolt, asked if he had shown the Poles the "bloody wall where we shoot pilots who kill their own side." Kellett replied that his men were quite able to tell British and German planes apart, thank you very much. Where the Luftwaffe were concerned, Kellett reminded Dowding, the Poles had already seen "the real thing."

On occasion, Kellett expressed his growing admiration in more tangible ways. At the end of August, the Polish enlisted men and noncommissioned officers received their pay, but because of a bureaucratic snafu, the officers did not. The situation was of more than routine concern to the pilots, who had just been fitted for their RAF uniforms and had no money to pay the tailor. So Kellett wrote a check on his personal bank account and gave it to Northolt's accounting officer to cover the Poles' pay until proper paychecks could be cut.

When Northolt officials offered the squadron the use of a battered old truck, instead of the usual car, to transport them from the officers' mess to the airfield, Kellett intervened again. That simply would not do, he declared. If other squadrons had cars—one Canadian squadron even boasted a 1911 Rolls-Royce, complete with liveried English chauffeur—so, by God, would his. He brought in his own Rolls, a roomy 1924 open touring car that could ferry as many as twelve pilots at a time to their planes. The Polish mechanics tended the car almost as lovingly as they did their pilots' Hurricanes, Kellett said. It was an "excellent morale factor."

If Kellett thought the Poles were reconciled to the endless delays in getting them airborne, however, he was mistaken. To them, confining a group of rested, eager, experienced pilots to training exercises while the Luftwaffe moved in for the kill, striking at the heart of Fighter Command itself, was, to say the least, bizarre.

HERMANN GÖRING had designated August 13 as *Adler Tag*—"Eagle Day"—the beginning of the Luftwaffe's all-out air assault on England. From that point on, the Germans launched an aerial *Blitzkrieg*, hitting the airfields where the squadrons of 11 Group were based, as well as radar installations and aircraft factories in the south. "We have reached the decisive point in our air war against England," Göring declared. "Our first aim must be the destruction of the enemy's fighters." Day after day, hundreds of German bombers, closely guarded by swarms of fighters, swept over the Channel with the intent of blasting British defenses into rubble.

Against these massive enemy formations were hurled the 300-plus Hurricanes and Spitfires of 11 Group. The days were clear and hot, and the RAF pilots were scrambling from dawn to dusk, which in England at that time of year amounted to about fifteen hours a day. Their lives had suddenly become a madness of activity—fierce combat, followed by frenzied refueling and rearming on fields that German bombing was turning into lunar landscapes. The stress of several sorties a day took an enormous physical and psychological toll: some fliers were so exhausted after a sortie that as soon as they landed they immediately fell asleep in their cockpits. Nerves were frayed, morale began to slip; more and more mistakes were made, including faulty landings, and accidents occurred.

During this time, both the RAF and the Luftwaffe suffered severe losses of both men and planes. The planes were replaceable—and, in the RAF's case, *were* being replaced by British industry—but the men were another matter. From August 8 to August 18, 154 RAF fliers were killed, seriously wounded, or missing in action—more than twice as many as could be replaced, even with wartime urgency. By the third week of August, Fighter Command was short more than 200 pilots. On August 19, the RAF slashed its training period for new pilots. It had earlier been reduced from six months to one month. Now, it would be cut to two weeks—two weeks to learn to fly, and fight, at speeds in excess of 300 miles an hour.

Among the graduates of this assembly-line training, few had ever fired at a moving target: gunnery practice often consisted of attacking a cloud or a sandbank. Some had never fired their guns at all. Until they experienced it for themselves, they could not really comprehend the *speed* of aerial battle: of being one moment in the middle of a tangle of wheeling, diving aircraft, and the next, dozens of miles away, staring at an empty sky. They had no idea about the breakneck aerobatics they would have to perform just to stay alive. Or the physical and mental pressures and pain. Or the G's they would have to pull. Or the times they would black out during a steep dive—"like being with your eyes open in a dark cellar with no lights on," as one flier described it. The new pilots did not know about the noise and sheer chaos of air combat: the scream of the engines, the chattering roar of the guns, the surprising recoil when the cannon fired, the sight and sound of exploding aircraft, the warnings shouted over the radio by other pilots, the pitiful cries for help when bullets or flames, or both, tore through a cockpit and its occupant.

Yet, in a matter of days, the new boys were fed into the maw of battle. When two novice fliers arrived at Croydon airfield, they were told by the leader of their squadron: "I'm sorry, but I'm afraid you'll have to go in today." An hour later, one of them was dead, the other seriously wounded. Their gear was still unpacked.

"You just took an ignorant young man, stuck him in an aeroplane, and told him, 'Go and fight the Germans,'" said Air Marshal Christopher Foxley-Norris, one of the "ignorant young men" fortunate enough to survive the Battle of Britain. "Most people who went into 11 Group didn't last. They couldn't last. They had no chance at all. But there was no means of stopping it. You had to fill the cockpits." Many years after the battle, another former RAF pilot was paging through a book listing the names of the pilots who had been in his squadron. "Some I couldn't remember," he said. "They passed through and had been shot down before I could get to know them."

During this period of "intense struggle and ceaseless anxiety," as Winston Churchill described it, the Germans were relentless. As August drew to a close, they launched raids in such numbers against RAF airfields and radar stations that the controllers in 11 Group were forced to choose which attacks should get priority attention from their depleted squadrons. It was not uncommon for a section of three RAF fighters, or a flight of six, to be sent aloft to challenge upward of a hundred German planes. "On virtually every occasion that the Germans operated in force, they grossly outnumbered the defending squadrons," noted the official postwar RAF account of the Battle of Britain. Most of the time, individual RAF squadrons were sent unaccompanied into combat, thus sometimes engaging enemy formations that outnumbered them more than tenfold.

Fighter Command was stretched to the limit. Day after day, Luftwaffe bombers hammered Manston, Biggin Hill, Kenley, and the other airfields of 11 Group. In the two weeks beginning August 24, 103 pilots were killed or missing, 124 seriously wounded—nearly a quarter of the command's total pilot strength. "The incidence of casualties became so serious," Dowding recalled, "that a fresh squadron would become depleted and exhausted before any of the resting and re-forming squadrons was ready to take its place. Fighter pilots...could not be turned out in numbers sufficient to fill the widening gaps in the fighting ranks." To Zdzisław Krasnodębski, Ronald Kellett fumed that "the squadrons they're bringing in now are as near valueless as makes no odds."

Despite the growing pilot shortage, the Poles in the Kościuszko Squadron were still being kept far from the action. On August 14, the only other Polish squadron, 302 (known as the Poznań Squadron), was made operational, although, as part of 12 Group, it was assigned to protect the Midlands and thus saw only intermittent combat. Determined to keep in place a defense network for the entire country, Dowding insisted on holding the squadrons of 10, 12, and 13 groups mostly in reserve. They were to patrol the parts of Britain assigned them—10, the southwest; 12, the Midlands; 13, the north. They were also to serve as temporary replacements for overextended 11 Group squadrons and to be called upon during periods of especially intense enemy attack.

On August 19, Air Vice Marshal Keith Park, commander of 11 Group, informed his group controllers and sector commanders that the Kościuszko Squadron could now be used—but only to protect airfields while the group's other squadrons, the ones in actual combat, were refueling on the ground. On August 28 and 29, Kościuszko pilots were ordered to perform gunnery practice, even as the Germans prepared to embark on their most concentrated assault yet. On August 30, Luftwaffe bombing succeeded in cutting the electricity to seven radar stations, knocking them temporarily off the air. Biggin Hill and other air stations were hit as never before. Yet that same day, the pilots of the Kościuszko Squadron were making simulated attacks, using British Blenheim bombers as targets. A disgusted Jan Zumbach called the exercise "playing games with Blenheims."

At about 4:15 p.m. that day, the squadron was flying over the green fields of Hertfordshire, preparing for yet another boring exercise. Suddenly, Flying Officer Ludwik Paszkiewicz spotted a large formation of German bombers and fighters 1,000 feet above him. The formation was being attacked by a handful of RAF fighters. "Hullo, Apany Leader," Paszkiewicz radioed Kellett, "bandits at ten o'clock." Kellett did not bother to answer. The squadron had been ordered to practice, not go after the enemy. According to RAF procedure, if the Luftwaffe happened to appear in the neighborhood, the squadron's job was to guard the Blenheim bombers they were using as dummy targets and escort them safely back to Northolt.

Paszkiewicz had other ideas. Unlike most of the other Poles, he didn't have a flamboyant bone in his body, but his frustration over the lack of combat had reached epic proportions. Although he had been a pilot in Warsaw's 112 Squadron, he'd been on a military purchasing mission to Paris when the Germans invaded Poland and thus did not get a chance to fight for his homeland. He later flew in France, but the French unit to which he was assigned had done everything it could to stay out of battle. After the fall of France, Paszkiewicz had spent six weeks in Blackpool twiddling his thumbs and then four weeks listening to British officers tell him what he already knew. Now, he had the enemy in sight. To hell with RAF procedure!

Paszkiewicz broke formation and, opening his throttle, roared off to meet the Germans at last. Ahead, a Messerschmitt 110 banked and nosed into a steep dive, pursued by another Hurricane. Paszkiewicz followed. When the German fighter pulled out, the two Hurricanes attacked it from close range. Closing almost to the collision point, Paszkiewicz kept firing until he saw the Messerschmitt burst into flames, spiral down, slam into the earth, and explode. Only then did he look around for the rest of his squadron and realize they were gone. After flying back to Northolt, he executed a victory roll over the field to show just how good he felt about helping to knock a German fighter out of the sky.

A summons to the base commander's office came as soon as he climbed out of his cockpit. When he arrived, he was confronted by an angry Group Captain Vincent. "Training flights are just that—training flights!" the commander exploded. "That means that you do not go off gallivanting around the skies, shooting up Germans. The safety of your squadron, as well as the Blenheims, is your *first* consideration!" Vincent's tirade continued for a few moments more, then his voice finally softened and a hint of a smile played over his face. He said he also felt it his duty, however, to congratulate Paszkiewicz—"beyond my better judgment"—for making the squadron's first kill.

Later that evening, Kellett put in a call to Fighter Command headquarters. He explained what had happened and declared: "Under the circumstances, sir, I *do* think we might call them operational." Having lost nearly 100 pilots in the previous week, Fighter Command was in no mood to argue. On the following day, the eve of the first anniversary of Germany's attack on Poland, the Kościuszko Squadron was officially scheduled to fly for the first time against the enemy.

In the officers' mess, meanwhile, an exultant Paszkiewicz ("Paszko" to his comrades) wrote in Ferić's diary: "I have fired at an enemy aircraft for the first time in my life!" That night, in the company of his equally jubilant comrades, he scored another first. The man whose "sobriety," in the words of Jan Zumbach, "was so proverbial that his Polishness was seriously questioned," got himself outrageously, uproariously drunk.

CHAPTER EIGHT

"My God, They *Are* Doing It!"

O N   T H E   H O T , bright morning of August 31, the men of the Kość ciuszko Squadron lounged on deck chairs or sprawled on the grass outside the Northolt dispersal hut. Wearing their yellow Mae Wests, they were tense and impatient as they waited—hoped—for the shrill of the phone and the call to battle. The sun rose higher and hotter. Cigarette butts piled up on the ground beside them. Sweat soaked through their clothing and dampened their faces. And still they waited.

The intensity of the battle had been mounting steadily ever since August 13, but the pilots sensed that something bigger than usual was taking place that day over England. A Canadian squadron, also based at Northolt, had scrambled at 8:00 a.m. and had yet to return. At one point, a group of Poles cornered Squadron Leader Kellett and demanded to know when their turn would come. Kellett stalled. "Soon enough," he growled. "And when it does, I don't want you going off half-cocked, fighting your own private war. We work as a team, and, above all, you obey my instructions until I tell you otherwise."

At midmorning, the Canadians—what was left of them—began limping back to Northolt. Four of their planes had been shot down, and three of their pilots were hospitalized with serious burns. As the minutes wore on, it became obvious that Germany was throwing everything it had at Fighter Command airfields and the all-important radar stations encircling London. On that single, white-hot day, the Luftwaffe flew more than 1,400 sorties and was bombing and strafing almost at will. Biggin Hill, a key sector station south of the Thames, had been heavily damaged again, including a direct hit on its operations center.

Noon came. Two o'clock. Four o'clock. The heat was nothing compared to the frustration and anger the Poles were feeling. What kind of stupid game were the British up to now? Then, shortly before six, with the late-summer sun still fairly high in the sky, the dispersal-room telephone rang. At least another 200 enemy aircraft were on their way across the Channel, and it looked as if they intended to have another go at Biggin Hill. Thirteen RAF squadrons were ordered into the air to meet them. Among them—finally—was the Kościuszko Squadron.

Kościuszko pilots relaxing outside a Northolt dispersal hut. Ludwik Paszkiewicz is on the left, Witold Łokuciewski on the right. (Jacek Kutzner)

The Poles, pilots and ground crews alike, did not need to be told twice. They sprinted for their Hurricanes, the pilots pausing only long enough to clip on their parachutes. They scrambled into their cockpits. The engines were switched on. The planes roared to life. Ground crewmen removed the chocks from under the wheels, ducked away, and watched as the fighters bounced over the uneven turf, gaining speed, and finally lifted into the air and moved into formation. Barely two minutes had elapsed since the phone rang.

The squadron's two flights—Ronald Kellett's A Flight, Athol Forbes's B Flight—were vectored toward Dorking, but Kellett's men were the only ones to see action that day. After about twenty minutes of flying, the six Hurricanes were east of Biggin Hill when they saw a formation of some sixty German Dornier bombers in the distance, guarded by a screen of fighters. As the flight prepared to attack the bombers, one of the Poles spotted several Messerschmitts nearby and pointed them out to Kellett. Kościuszko's British squadron leader said simply: "Pick out your target and go get 'em." It had been one year, almost to the day, since the Luftwaffe had joined in the devastation of Poland—and the humiliation of the Polish Air Force. Now, after twelve months of anguish, anger, and frustration, the time had come to begin settling the score.

Red section, led by Kellett, swooped out of the sun, hurtling down on the surprised enemy like avenging furies. Within moments, three Messerschmitts had plummeted to the ground. When other nearby German fighters turned to take on Kellett and his wingmen, they were attacked from the rear by Kościuszko's Yellow section. On one German's tail, Mirosław Ferić marveled at how easy it seemed to get a Messerschmitt into a Hurricane's sights. "The fuselage now filled the entire diameter of the luminous ring," he wrote in his diary later. He fired a short burst, about twenty rounds, and was "surprised and puzzled at the ease of it—quite different from Poland where you had to scrape and try until you were in a sweat, and then, instead of getting the bastard, he got you." Here, Ferić noted, the result was "immediate and wonderful." In seconds, the German plane was trailing fire and smoke. The pilot scrambled out and jumped, his parachute flaring out above him. As Ferić watched him descend, he thought of Warsaw and what the Germans had done to it, of the Polish women and children slaughtered by German pilots like this one. It crossed his mind that he could start getting even by shooting this now helpless German out of the sky, but he decided against it. It wasn't his scruples that dissuaded him; it was the number of witnesses. He would leave the Jerry to the British Home Guard on the ground.

In less than fifteen minutes, each of the six pilots in A Flight, including Kellett, had shot down a Messerschmitt. By seven o'clock, the entire squadron was back on the ground. In their first all-out fight, they hadn't lost a single pilot or plane, and before they landed, Ferić and several others performed victory rolls over the field.

The squadron was euphoric. After reporting details of the action to the unit's intelligence officer, the pilots found themselves suddenly eager to write entries in Ferić's diary. "If it goes on like this, we shall fill volumes!" Ferić whooped in his own entry. There were congratulations from the RAF's senior command as well. Late that night, the squadron received a message from Sir Cyril Newall, chief of the Air Staff: "Magnificent fighting 303 Squadron. I am delighted. The enemy is shown that Polish pilots definitely on top." And from Stanley Vincent: "Congratulations on magnificent first operational day."

The best-known photo of the Kościuszko Squadron. It—along with others showing Polish pilots in the RAF—was smuggled by the underground into occupied Poland during the war. On the extreme left are Mirosław Ferić and John Kent. Jan Zumbach (goggles atop his head) is in the center. Witold Łokuciewski is fourth from the right in the foreground. (Imperial War Museum)

The Kościuszko Squadron compiled a brilliant overall record in the Battle of Britain. But it is doubtful that its contribution was ever more urgently needed than on that first day of combat. For it was on August 31 that Fighter Command suffered its heaviest losses of the entire battle—thirty-nine fighters destroyed and fourteen pilots killed. But the Germans lost an identical number—and the Kościuszko Squadron's pilots were credited with 15 percent of those kills, with no losses of their own.

Although scrambled the following day, the squadron encountered no enemy planes. It wasn't until late in the afternoon on September 2 that the Poles again saw action, with A and B Flights dispatched to intercept two German formations over Kent. This time, the Luftwaffe was not caught off guard. In a heartbeat, ten or so Me-109s peeled off from the bomber formation and dove out of the sun at the Poles. Spotting the Messerschmitts approach in the glare, Sergeant Jan Rogowski, a baby-faced twenty-year-old, aimed his Hurricane directly at them, scattering the formation and ruining the surprise. As John Kent later remembered it, "a general melee ensued," with the brown and green Hurricanes once again getting the better of the Messerschmitts.

When the German pilots, who had to worry about fuel limitations on their long-range attacks, turned to head back across the Channel, the Poles were in hot pursuit. Most gave up and headed to Northolt as soon as the Germans were out of British airspace, but Ferić and Zdzisław Henneberg, a former Dęblin instructor, continued to pursue two of the Me-109s until they found themselves over the French coast. Just as Ferić closed in on his quarry and fired a short burst from his guns, he felt a sharp jolt, and black oil exploded across his windshield, making it almost impossible for him to see. He'd been hit. Reluctantly, he broke off his attack and turned to head back across the Channel. Opening his canopy so he could reach around and wipe the windshield with his handkerchief, he saw black smoke pouring from his violently shaking engine.

Ferić switched off the still smoking engine and decided to try to glide back across the Channel to home. Trailing smoke, unable to maneuver, he was an easy prey for any German fighter that happened to be returning to France from England. As the seconds ticked by, with nothing below him but water, Ferić saw his altimeter steadily dropping: 8,000 feet...7,200...6,800. Two planes appeared in the hazy distance, and Ferić caught his breath. Then he recognized them as Hurricanes and saw the Kościuszko Squadron insignia on their fuselages. The planes turned and flanked him, flying close enough that he could see Witold Łokuciewski and Ludwik Paszkiewicz in the cockpits. Moments later, Jan Rogowski joined them to see Ferić safely home.

The Dover cliffs began to loom on the horizon, and Ferić wondered if he was closing fast enough to clear them. The altimeter was at 5,000 feet now ... 4,500 ... 4,000. He positioned his Hurricane for maximum lift. Then there was nothing more to do but ride on in—unless he wanted to lose the plane, and possibly his life, by ditching or jumping into the Channel. Ferić listened to the wind whistling past his canopy and stared at the altimeter as the needle approached 2,700 feet. He was so low now he could see individual waves on the water. Nevertheless, he was beginning to think he might actually make it over the cliffs. A few moments later, he did—at 900 feet.

Spotting a large field near the coast, Ferić tightened his safety harness and braced himself for a crash landing. His Hurricane hit the ground with a tremendous jolt, skidded a few hundred feet, and bounced to a stop. The plane was badly damaged—its propeller ruined, its undercarriage jammed, its skin in various places dented and peeled back like an orange's. As for Ferić, he escaped with only scratches and a mild reprimand (directed at Henneberg as well) in the form of a telegram from Air Vice Marshal Keith Park: "The Group Commander appreciates the offensive spirit that carried two Polish pilots (Henneberg and Ferić) over the French coast in pursuit of the enemy today. This practice is not economical or sound now that there is such good shooting within sight of London."

AFTER THE EXCITEMENT and success of the Poles' first two days in combat, the next two days proved a disappointment. On September 3, the Kościuszko Squadron engaged in two brief and mostly inconsequential encounters with enemy planes, although František did record his second kill by downing an Me-109 over the Channel. On the 4th, there was no contact at all with the Germans.

On September 5, however, the Poles more than made up for their inactivity. The Luftwaffe that day was in the process of launching twenty-two separate raids throughout England, striking hard at airfields and factories but also bombing dozens of towns and cities, from

London to Liverpool. Approaching the Thames estuary in midafternoon, Kościuszko's Red section, led by Kellett, spotted a large German formation bombing the London docks. In a repeat of August 31, Kellett and his two wingmen pounced on the formation in a lightning attack. All three Hurricanes claimed a victim within moments. Then Sergeant Stanisław Karubin went after his second Messerschmitt, forcing it to fly lower and lower—Karubin firing all the while—until the two were just above the treetops. When Karubin finally exhausted his ammunition, he flew straight for the 109, missing it by only a yard or two. The unnerved German lost control and crashed.

The squadron's Blue section, led by Athol Forbes, proved just as successful, shooting down three bombers and a fighter. In all, the Poles were credited with destroying eight enemy aircraft—20 percent of that day's RAF kills.

In those first exciting and exhausting days of combat, the Kościuszko Squadron seemed almost invincible. With all its victories, it had not yet lost a single pilot; indeed, its only reported injury had been a fractured shoulder. That happy situation, as everyone knew, could hardly continue.

Shortly before 9:00 a.m. on September 6, the Kościuszko Squadron, along with the rest of 11 Group, scrambled to intercept a vast German air armada—300 or 400 planes, in formations almost 20 miles long. It was a tough assignment in the best of circumstances—all the more tough for the Poles, whose takeoff time was set too late for them to achieve surprise. What they needed to do was gain as much altitude as possible as quickly as possible, so they could scan the sky, pick their targets, and gain a slight advantage over the faster 109s. But that, too, was a problem, because a plane loses speed and maneuverability when it climbs. As the squadron ascended, the pilots, squinting into the milk-white dazzle of the sun, realized, too late, that they were flying straight into a formation of German bombers screened by Messerschmitts. Already committed, the Poles attacked but were quickly set upon and surrounded by a horde of 109s. Bullets and the smoke of tracer bullets crisscrossed the sky.

Zdzisław Krasnodębski, who was leading Yellow section that morning, had just set his sights on a German bomber when he was hit from behind. The glass on his instrument panel shattered, and his fuel tank must have been punctured, too, because he suddenly smelled and saw

Zdzisław Krasnodębski takes a nap between sorties, using sandbags as a pillow, out-side a Northolt dispersal hut during the Battle of Britain. (Stanisław Blasiak)

gasoline sloshing around in the cockpit. When it ignited, Krasnodębski was instantly swathed in flames. He grappled with the straps of his safety harness and, unable to unbuckle them, for a brief moment resigned himself to death. Then the pain of his seared face and hands somehow goaded him, and he began struggling again with the straps. Finally, he freed himself, ripped off his oxygen mask, and pulled open the canopy. Turning the plane on its back, he fell out of the cockpit and into the cold rush of air somewhere over Farnborough, smoke streaming away from his burning flesh and clothing.

As he fell, Krasnodębski remembered, through a fog of pain, his last parachute jump. It had been over Poland, and he had come close to being shot by a Messerschmitt as he descended. He had learned a lesson from that. This time, he would wait to open his chute so that he would not make such a tempting target. Hurtling downward, the icy wind whistling past, he grabbed for the ripcord when he was about 10,000 feet above the ground. He grabbed, and grabbed again. He couldn't find it! With the ground rushing toward him, he frantically moved his burned fingers over the surface of the parachute bag until, finally, he located the handle and gave it a sharp tug. The chute opened and filled, jerking Krasnodębski upward. As he floated down, flames eating into the tough material of his overalls, he heard the rumble of an approaching plane. *My God!* he thought. *Not again!* But it wasn't a Messerschmitt this time. It was a Hurricane, which continued circling him until he was down. Later, Krasnodębski learned that the pilot had been Witold Urbanowicz, who "initially took me for a German and intended to change the direction of my journey—from down towards the ground to straight to heaven. I was saved by my yellow Mae West, which he recognized." For his part, Urbanowicz never acknowledged any such bloodthirsty intent.*

As for Krasnodębski, he was barely conscious when he hit the ground. He was immediately surrounded by members of the local Home Guard, who rushed out of the bushes with their World War I–vintage rifles pointed menacingly in his direction. Despite his dazed mind, his pain, his scorched and blackened face and hands, and his minimal command of the English language, Krasnodębski somehow managed to persuade the Home Guardsmen that he was on their side. Soon he was in an ambulance headed for Farnborough Hospital.

Ronald Kellett also ended up in Farnborough Hospital that day. Kellett's Hurricane had been hit while he was in the process of shooting down a Heinkel. Large chunks had been shot out of both of his wings, the rudder barely worked, the elevator didn't function at all. Unable to bale out because of a jammed canopy, Kellett was left with few options, none of them good. He managed to slow his Hurricane down to about 140 miles per hour and landed at that speed on the bomb-pitted runway at Biggin Hill, careening down the entire length of the runway before his brakes finally brought him to a stop. An airman rushed out of a nearby dugout, hacked off the Hurricane's canopy with an ax, and pulled out the dazed, slightly wounded Kellett. They had just made it to a dugout when German bombers made another pass over the airfield—

---

* Enraged by the Germans' machine-gunning of parachuting Polish and British pilots, the Poles were sometimes guilty of doing the same to Luftwaffe airmen as they descended under parachutes.

and hit the runway on which Kellett had landed. After the raid, he was taken to the hospital, where the wound in his leg was treated and he was released back to Fighter Command for duty.

It had been a very rough day for the Kościuszko Squadron. The unit was credited with shooting down seven more German aircraft—a remarkable score, considering the difficulties it encountered—but four of its men had been wounded and four planes destroyed. Most distressing was the loss of Krasnodębski, the squadron's popular Polish commander. "The King" was the squadron's soul, the man who Urbanowicz said had done the most to meld a group of unruly individualists into a spectacularly successful team. "He didn't score many vic-

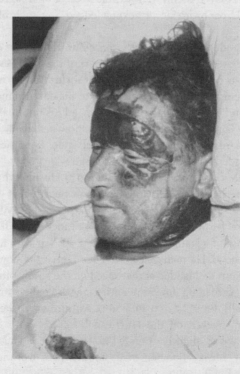

Zdzisław Krasnodębski, his face and hands badly burned, in the hospital after being shot down on September 6, 1940. (Stanisław Blasiak)

tories in the air," said Urbanowicz. "His victory was on the ground—in the training and upbringing of the young officers in his command."

That night, Urbanowicz and the Kościuszko Squadron's doctor went to see Krasnodębski at the hospital. He was in bed and awake, but his burned face, hands, and legs were swathed in bandages. "How did we do today?" he asked weakly. Urbanowicz recounted the day's victories and losses. "I just hope they don't keep me here too long," Krasnodębski said. "I plan to be back as soon as possible." Later, the squadron's doctor learned that Krasnodębski, who had seen only one week of combat in England, would have to spend months, perhaps years, in the hospital. It was unlikely, the British doctors said, that this man who lived for flying would ever fly again.

WHEN THE FIRST wave of German planes swept over the English coast the next afternoon, September 7, there was little indication that the day's raids would be significantly different from the dozens that had preceded them over the previous three weeks. At exactly 3:54 p.m., a WAAF plotter at 11 Group's Uxbridge sector control station set down a marker on the large map table, indicating that radar had picked up twenty-plus enemy aircraft. Less than a minute later, the number had jumped into the hundreds—a flotilla of bombers and fighters even more massive than the one responsible for the previous day's devastation. "I'd never seen so many," marveled an RAF pilot whose squadron was one of eleven immediately ordered into the air. "As far as you could see, there was nothing but German aircraft coming in, wave after wave." Not until the raiders bypassed Biggin Hill, Kenley, Manston, and other hard-hit airfields did it become clear the Germans were altering their strategy once again. Now they had a new primary target: London.

Actually, the Luftwaffe had been hitting London for more than a week. The attacks, though relatively minor and intermittent, had been enough to cause an angry Winston Churchill to order the first British bombing raids on Berlin. Then it became Hitler's turn to be angry, and, as the Führer had already amply demonstrated in Poland, his temper often led to major and irrational tantrums. "If they attack our cities," he thundered, "we will simply *rub out* theirs!"

By this time, too, Hitler and Göring had persuaded themselves that the Luftwaffe had succeeded in neutralizing the RAF and was therefore free to concentrate on London and other cities. It was a spectacular miscalculation—and no less so for being almost true. In two weeks, the RAF had lost 227 fighters, had seen major damage inflicted on its airfields and sector control stations, and was close to being finished. What Fighter Command needed above all was time to regroup, and Hitler was about to provide just that. As Churchill wrote later: "In the fighting between August 24 and September 6, the scales were tilted against Fighter Command. If the enemy had persisted in heavy attacks against [RAF installations and communications], the whole intricate organisation of Fighter Command might have broken down."

But Germany did not persist. Instead it began eight weeks of massive bombing of London—eight weeks that were the most intense chapter in the eight-month reign of terror called the Blitz.

At Northolt, the Kościuszko Squadron pilots had been on standby for hours. They waited in their planes, sweltering in their Mae Wests, as the sun beat down. Four pilots were in Hurricanes on loan from the Canadian squadron, replacing the ones that had been lost the day before. At 4:45 p.m., the pilots' earphones crackled with an urgent call: "303, scramble! 303, scramble!" Red flares shot into the sky. The planes jounced over the field, and in thirty seconds were airborne.

The Poles joined forces with 1 RAF Squadron, also based at Northolt. Both squadrons were ordered to fly east, toward the London docks, where the full wrath of the Luftwaffe was about to be felt. Approaching the outskirts of the capital, Jan Zumbach could see below what looked like wads of cotton wool—the shell bursts of British antiaircraft guns in the vicinity of the docks. Then, off to the right, he saw about forty Dornier bombers, surrounded by Messerschmitts, on their way to drop their bombs. Zumbach waited impatiently for the order to attack, but Athol Forbes, who was leading the squadron that day, continued on course, seemingly oblivious to the enemy's presence. Zumbach was "writhing with frustration." If the squadron didn't strike in the next few seconds, more than 40 tons of bombs would rain down on London.

Then, over the radio, he heard a voice barking in Polish: "Attack! Follow me!" It was Ludwik Paszkiewicz, who was leading Yellow section and once again was taking matters into his own hands. Paszkiewicz rocked his wings and broke formation, turned right and dived. Close behind was the rest of his section, then those commanded by Henneberg and Urbanowicz, and bringing up the rear, the section led by Forbes, who had finally caught on to what was happening. The entire squadron, wheeling around in a great arc, plummeted down, out of the sun. "We gave them all we had," Forbes reported later, "opening fire at 450 yards and only breaking away when we could see the enemy completely filling the gunsight."

Jan Zumbach in front of a Hurricane. (Jacek Kutzner)

When it came Zumbach's time to shoot, he pushed the firing button and nothing happened. Realizing that he had left the safety catch on, he turned the air blue with his swearing as he wrenched his plane into a tight turn, the centrifugal force of the maneuver pushing him back against his seat. Once more, he managed to get a German bomber into his sights. After several bursts from his guns, the Dornier disappeared in a wall of fire. Zumbach dived after another and fixed on him easily. He pressed the firing button, and, moments later, that bomber, too, exploded. Trying to avoid the ball of flame, Zumbach banked so violently that he blacked out. His plane plummeted downward. He regained consciousness and pulled out of the dive only a few hundred feet from the ground.

By this time, nearly a quarter of the German bomber formation had been destroyed. "It was like twelve hounds tearing a boar's body to pieces," Urbanowicz declared. With another hunting simile, Forbes marveled at the sight of "the Dorniers fall[ing] out of the sky like partridges out of a covey, sometimes two at a time." The surviving bombers, after scattering in panic, turned and headed back to France without dropping their bombs. The Poles then focused their attention on the Messerschmitts, which already had come under attack from 1 Squadron.

Marian Pisarek, who had been an infantry officer in Poland before joining the air force, picked off a 109, but was attacked and hit by another German fighter—one of three Kościuszko pilots to be shot down that day. With his plane in flames, Pisarek started to scramble out, but his left foot snagged on the edge of the cockpit. As the burning Hurricane spiraled down, Pisarek, dangling from it, desperately tried to wrench his foot loose. He finally managed to pull his foot out of his boot, fell free, and opened his parachute a few thousand feet from the ground. He landed in the backyard of a suburban cottage, in the middle of the owner's prized rose garden. Rushing out of the house, the owner proceeded to give the dazed young Pole a mild lecture about the importance of not trespassing on private property. But the English passion for privacy soon gave way to English cordiality: the man took Pisarek into his house and brewed him a pot of tea. Limping inside sans boot, the highly embarrassed Pisarek tried hard to conceal the large, ragged hole in his left sock.[*]

Victory roll followed victory roll as the triumphant Hurricanes returned home to Northolt. "Everyone was dancing with excitement," Zumbach said. In less than fifteen minutes of combat, the Poles had shot down fourteen German planes, plus four "probables." Paszkiewicz and Zumbach had a pair of kills each; Urbanowicz had one, plus a "proba-ble." Łokuciewski also had a kill, a German plane that he said "burst like a soap bubble" as soon as he fired at it. Perhaps even more signifi-

---

[*] Pisarek's boot was found in May 1976, when archaeologists excavated part of his crashed Hurricane from a nearby garden.

cant than the number of kills that day was the Kościuszko Squadron's remarkable ability to disperse a German bomber formation before it could hit London. A day already filled with horror on the ground would have been that much worse if all forty Dorniers had made it through.

The Poles' joy at their accomplishments was tempered by their dismay at the damage that the Germans had managed to inflict anyway. In that first raid of the Blitz, hundreds of Londoners were killed, thousands injured and driven from their homes. Seeing the huge columns of smoke and the blood-red glow of the fires in the East End, the men of the Kościuszko Squadron were reminded of the way their own capital had been attacked and set ablaze just a year earlier. But, like Warsaw, London, about to endure fifty-seven straight nights of bombing, would prove indomitable because, like Varsovians, Londoners were willing to risk everything in the name of independence, liberty, and honor. His countrymen, Winston Churchill remarked during the war, were "bred to value freedom far above their lives."

———————

IN ITS FIRST week of combat, the record compiled by the Kościuszko Squadron was so impressive that some people in Fighter Command simply didn't believe it was true. Among the doubters was Northolt's station commander, Stanley Vincent, who wondered if the Poles might be guilty of inflating the numbers in their post-action reports.

Questioned by Vincent, Kellett insisted that he maintained the strictest scoring standards. If anything, he said, the squadron's combat reports had understated its accomplishments. Vincent was not persuaded. He ordered his intelligence officer to "treat these claims with a lot of reserve—go through them with a toothcomb." After a brief investigation, the officer reported back that he could find no discrepancies. Still skeptical, Vincent decided he would find out for himself. On September 11, he was following the squadron in his own Hurricane when the Poles encountered a large enemy bomber formation over Horsham heading for London. Flying above the squadron, Vincent watched as two Hurricanes peeled off and dived almost vertically at the German bombers "with near suicidal impetus." Startled by the ferocity of the attack, the German pilots broke formation, whereupon the Poles began picking off the scattered bombers one by one. Several times during the

combat, the Poles would close almost to a collision point before opening fire on a target. The results were devastating for the Germans.
"Suddenly," Vincent declared, "the air was full of burning aircraft, parachutes, and pieces of disintegrating wings. It was all so rapid that it was
staggering." An experienced fighter pilot himself, Vincent tried to get
into the fight, but every time he started to close on an enemy bomber, a
"diving Pole would cut in between, and I had to pull away to avoid
being hit myself." Remaining prudently on the sidelines, Vincent was
finally persuaded. When he landed at Northolt that afternoon, he told
his intelligence officer, "My God, they *are* doing it!"

The station commander, who from that day on was a staunch supporter of the Poles, was hardly their only admirer. Indeed, by the middle of September, the pilots of the Kościuszko Squadron had become
unofficial heroes of the realm. Government officials, senior RAF officers, private citizens, the prime minister, and the king himself joined at
various times in paying honor to the squadron that shot down nearly
forty planes in a little over a week.* Wrote the BBC's director-general:
"The BBC sends warm greetings to the famous 303 Polish squadron,
with lively congratulations upon its magnificent record and all best
wishes for its future. You use the air for your gallant exploits, and we for
telling the world of them. Long live Poland!"

Most of these tributes were carefully copied by Ferić into his diary.
Throughout the Battle of Britain, he never lost sight of his goal: to document the squadron's achievements in the little book he carried everywhere with him. When his fellow pilots, particularly Zumbach, refused
on occasion to write about their victories, Ferić did it for them. "I am
committed," he wrote, "to preserving all that may be forgotten, all that
is most dear to us right now—the heroic battle deeds of our pilots."

His commitment was still not much appreciated. "Ox has become a
real plague for the pilots," Zumbach growled in mid-September. "The
poor sods are still in their planes when he grabs them by their ties,
pushes the pen and book towards them and hisses ominously into their
combat-deafened ear: 'Start writing—now!' " As his colleagues discovered, it was almost impossible to elude Ferić's pursuit. From his hospital

---

* At one point, Ronald Kellett sent a note to Fighter Command saying that, while all this
recognition was nice, wasn't it time for a more concrete token of appreciation? The hint was
taken, and soon afterward, a case of whiskey arrived at Northolt.

bed, a wounded Kościuszko pilot wrote on September 21: "So he finally got me: I mean Ox, of course. He came here, ostensibly on a visit, but he had the book with him and he ordered me to write."

When he did deign to write in Ferić's diary, Zumbach, who was far less romantic than his friend and had no interest in proclaiming his or anybody else's heroism, would often parody the florid, overheated prose used by some of his compatriots. Writing about the hectic combat on September 7, Zumbach began: "The sun was just like it is today. Its hot rays caused the earth to give off a fragrance, as intoxicating as the scent of your beloved girl's body. Somewhere, hidden in the lilac thicket, a nightingale was warbling its song. This mood was shattered suddenly by the scream of sirens . . ."

Jan Zumbach and Mirosław Ferić with a squadron mascot. (Imperial War Museum)

That, Zumbach noted, was how a writer would begin his account. "Not being one," he went on, "I will tell how things really were. Well, the sun was there all right, but not like it is today, because today, it is raining and the sky is overcast. There are no lilac bushes on the aero-

drome and the nightingale is a beast entirely unknown in England.*
There was no fragrance either.... The one thing that did happen was
the alarm."

While Zumbach played down his and his comrades' victories, the
British, including the prime minister, were doing the opposite. Over
dinner at 10 Downing one September night, a major topic of conversation was the success of the Polish pilots. "It was generally agreed that
they were magnificent fighters," John Colville wrote of the evening's
discussion. There was some debate, however, about just how good the
Poles really were. Winston Churchill averred that one Pole was easily
worth three Frenchmen. Lord Gort, commander of the British Expeditionary Force in France, and Air Chief Marshal Sir Hugh Dowding,
once so skeptical about the Polish fliers, strongly disagreed. The ratio,
in their view, was more like *ten* Frenchmen per Pole.

At Buckingham Palace, George VI's secretary, Alexander Hardinge,
admiringly referred to the Polish pilots as "absolute tigers." In a letter
to Lord Hamilton, Hardinge wrote: "One cannot help feeling that if all
our Allies had been Poles, the course of the war, up till now, would have
been very different." An RAF squadron leader, speaking of the Polish
airmen, was quoted as saying: "They are fantastic—better than any of
us. In every way they've got us beat."

Over and over, the question was asked: what made the Poles so good?
The answer was complex. Generally older than their British counterparts, most Polish pilots had hundreds of hours of flying time in a variety of planes, as well as combat experience in both Poland and France.
Unlike British fliers, they had not been trained to rely on a sophisticated
radio and radar network and had learned to fly in primitive, outdated
planes. As a result, said one British flight instructor, "their understanding and handling of aircraft was exceptional." Although they appreciated the value of tools like radio and radar, the Poles never stopped
using their eyes to locate the Luftwaffe. "Whereas British pilots are
trained...to go exactly where they are told, Polish pilots are always
turning and twisting their heads to spot a distant enemy," an RAF flier
noted. To become a pilot in prewar Poland, one had to have virtually
perfect vision, and Polish airmen worked hard to maintain and even
improve their ability to spot objects at long distances.

* Zumbach was wrong about the nightingale, of course.

A British pilot spoke with awe about two Polish fliers assigned to his squadron. The two Poles would lie on their cots in the dispersal hut and track the progress of flies creeping up and down the wall. Later in the war, Witold Urbanowicz, attached briefly to the fighter group that succeeded the legendary Flying Tigers in China, astonished his young American comrades with his visual acuity. "To me, Colonel Urbanowicz was like a swami or seer—someone who sees all and knows all," said Donald Lopez, a rookie pilot with the group. "I couldn't believe the details he could give you after a fight. He saw everything that happened and everything that everybody did."

The Poles' exceptional concentration was equaled only by their daring. British pilots were taught to fly and fight with caution. They were instructed not to get in too close, to open fire on the enemy at a distance of not less than 150 yards. The Poles, by contrast, had been trained at home to be aggressive, to use their planes the way a cavalryman uses his charger, to crowd and intimidate the enemy, to make him flinch, and then to bring him down. After firing a brief opening burst at a range of 150 to 200 yards, just to get on the enemy's nerves, the Poles would close almost to point-blank range. That was where they did their real work. "When they go tearing into enemy bombers and fighters they get so close you would think they were going to collide," observed Athol Forbes. Only then did the Poles unleash their devastating broadsides, which, as Forbes noted, "will cut chunks out of any part of a German bomber and generally disable it in one attack."

In the airborne war of nerves, Polish pilots, more often than not, were the winners. On several occasions, Forbes reported, crew members of Luftwaffe bombers, seeing that Kościuszko's Hurricanes were about to attack, baled out before their planes were hit. Even allowing for the hyperbole of war, the squadron's ability to break up bomber formations and send them fleeing back to France was just as important in the defense of Britain as its ability to shoot planes out of the sky. Indeed, the Poles' daredevil style proved so effective that Ronald Kellett and John Kent both adopted it on occasion. Kent, when commanding "these intensely brave men" in combat, liked to think of himself as leading a charge of the famed Polish cavalry. "In fact," he said, "the Poles seemed to transport their cavalry tactics, and certainly its élan, from the ground into the air."

Thanks to the Poles, Kellett also cut back on the use of the RAF's tight V-shaped flying formations and the use of outdated, prewar text-book tactics.* The rigid, close formations, with a "tail-end Charlie" or "weaver" behind, were "simply suicidal," said one Polish pilot. He spoke for all the Poles, whether in British or Polish squadrons. They hated flying in close formation, because it forced them to worry about avoiding collisions with their own planes instead of concentrating on finding the enemy. In their view, loose formations, spread out fairly wide, with planes at slightly different altitudes, were far more effective, if for no other reason than that they gave everyone in the squadron a clear view of the sky.

For the Poles, the idea of using set-piece attacks (and expecting the Germans to follow British textbooks) was also ridiculous. The pilots of the Kościuszko Squadron were constantly devising new tactical variations in response to the latest German maneuvers. "It was just common sense, really," Kellett said after the war. "Besides, once you'd gone in to attack, there was no time to worry about what anyone else was doing." In other words, combat rarely, if ever, went by the book. Once the shooting began, it was every pilot for himself.

Up to a point. The Poles also believed in protecting one another as much as possible. They were noted for going to the aid of other pilots under attack, and in many post-action reports, there are references to Kościuszko Squadron pilots shepherding damaged planes or protecting pilots who had baled out from German strafing attacks. During one sortie in early September, John Kent was chasing a German bomber when he realized a 109 was closing in on him from behind. In a flash, Zdzisław Henneberg's Hurricane cut in front of the Messerschmitt and forced him to break off. Henneberg stayed with Kent, acting as his bodyguard, until the British pilot shot down the bomber and gained cloud cover. Back at Northolt, Kent thanked Henneberg for chasing the German fighter off his tail. *No thanks necessary,* the Pole said. *By the way, there were six Messerschmitts chasing you, not just one.*

Ronald Kellett, who also had been protected by the Poles on a number of occasions, credited them with keeping him alive during the Battle of Britain. "Unless the leaders are well supported by those behind them, they fall an easy prey to the enemy fighters," he wrote after the

---

* After the Battle of Britain, Hugh Dowding acknowledged that the close formation flying and complicated combat tactics prescribed by the RAF left much to be desired.

war. "In this connection it is greatly to the credit of the Polish airmen that the three English pilots who commanded the Squadron and flights survived the Battle...."

Another reason, often overlooked, for the squadron's success was the extraordinary skill and dedication of its Polish ground crew members. "I don't believe that any squadron had better... aircraft maintenance than 303," Kellett wrote. From the first days of the campaign in Poland, the mechanics of the Polish Air Force were noted for the fiercely protective care they lavished on their aircraft. In his diary, Mirosław Ferić recalled how, on the second day of the war in Poland, his mechanic presented him with a special brush to clean his P-11's windshield in the air. And when Ferić was shot down two days later, "my mechanic could not console himself after the loss of my machine, which he took such loving care of."

When the squadron was first organized in England, Kellett suggested to members of the ground crew that they keep the same hours as the pilots—in readiness from one half hour before sunrise to one half hour after sunset. But during the frenetic weeks of the Battle of Britain, the

Five Kościuszko Squadron pilots seen behind the wing of a Hurricane (from left): *Mirosław Ferić, unidentified pilot, Jan Zumbach, Zdzisław Henneberg, and John Kent. (Imperial War Museum)*

squadron's mechanics worked round the clock to keep the planes flying. They were such wizards at repairing badly damaged planes that only four times during the battle did the squadron take off with fewer than its full complement of twelve Hurricanes, an accomplishment that obviously increased the squadron's effectiveness.

The climactic day of the Battle of Britain—September 15, 1940—turned out to be the ultimate test of the ground crew's skill. At the end of that day of ferocious fighting, Kellett declared that nine of the squadron's aircraft were good for nothing but the scrap heap. Control fins had been shot off, cables severed, wings and engines punctured with bullets, radiators smashed. But the mechanics were determined to prove the squadron leader wrong.

After working through the night, they had all nine planes on the runway the next morning, ready to sortie.

CHAPTER NINE

"The Credit That Is Their Due"

MORE THAN A month after the Battle of Britain began, the RAF was still flying, and London, after a weeklong battering, was still defiant. Adolf Hitler didn't understand how any of that was possible. The Luftwaffe had hard figures to *prove* that Fighter Command had been decimated. Surely, one more push was all it would take to gain control of British skies and clear the way for the planned German invasion.

Germany wasn't the only country with bad intelligence: British estimates of the number of men and planes lost by the Germans were almost twice the actual figure. But the internal German estimates of British losses were *five* times too high. Hitler, Göring, and others were thus misled into believing they were closer to victory than they were. Although Hitler was having doubts about Operation Sea Lion, he decided to give Göring another chance to make *Götterdämmerung* possible. And so Göring gave the order: all available Luftwaffe aircraft to be unleashed on September 15 in an all-out push to end RAF resistance.

Early that morning, a touch of mist still hung in the air. When it burned off, another hot late-summer day was revealed—perfect for the Luftwaffe. The sun was still arcing upward when British radar began picking up masses of planes forming near French airfields. By noon, the first huge swarm of bombers and fighters had already crossed the coast.

Seventeen fighter squadrons, including the Kościuszko and Poznań squadrons, were ordered into the air to meet that first German wave.

From Northolt, the Kościuszko Squadron joined with the British 229 Squadron to take on an enemy formation of bombers and fighters near South London. While three sections of Poles tore into the bombers, the other section and the British squadron attacked the dozens of Messerschmitt escorts. In seconds, a vicious, chaotic fight was under way. The men who were in it found themselves confronted with "a fearful jumble of [RAF] roundels and [Luftwaffe] black crosses, flame and tracer crossfire, a dance of turning wings and drifting parachutes." Amid all this, Jan Zumbach began a "little polka" of his own with a 109. The Messerschmitt began to bob and weave and otherwise try to shake Zumbach's Hurricane. To "stop [the German pilot] from dreaming and to augment his courage," Zumbach sent several short bursts his way. He hoped that the German would get "tired of this fun and [fly] in a straight line." When he did, Zumbach fired at nearly point-blank range, then veered off as the Messerschmitt exploded.

With all of 11 Group's squadrons now involved, plus much of 12 Group, dozens of dogfights were taking place over the south of England. The air was swarming with planes—dodging, diving, circling, firing, falling. In the underground operations room at 11 Group's headquarters at Uxbridge, an anxious Winston Churchill turned to Air Vice Marshal Keith Park, the commander of 11 Group, who was standing next to him. "What other reserves have we?" the prime minister asked. "There are none," Park answered. Churchill wrote of that day in his memoirs: "The odds were great; our margins small; the stakes infinite."

The RAF more than held its own against the first wave, but the price was steep. Many squadrons lost planes, either destroyed or severely damaged. The Kościuszko Squadron, credited with the destruction of ten German aircraft in its initial sortie, had only nine of its twelve planes in the air by afternoon, although only one pilot had so far been wounded. That was Witold Łokuciewski, who, having shot down a 109, was himself hit by a German fighter. A cannon shell opened a huge hole in the wing of his Hurricane. Shrapnel penetrated the cockpit and tore into Łokuciewski's legs. Bleeding heavily, he struggled to maintain control and somehow managed to make it back to Northolt, where he landed hard and fast, without flaps. He collapsed after climbing out of his plane.

And the day had only begun. The second German wave arrived less than three hours after the first—hundreds of bombers and fighters sweeping over Kentish fields toward London. Refueled and rearmed, every Hurricane and Spitfire available, including those from five squadrons in 12 Group, was sent up again. Over Gravesend, the Kościuszko Squadron's nine Hurricanes faced off against an enormous enemy formation, later estimated by Kellett to have been 400 strong. The line of bombers stretched for miles, with scores of fighter escorts flying above and beside the bombers like so many sheepdogs. Kellett's flight—four planes—attacked one group of bombers in a quarter-frontal approach. The squadron's remaining five Hurricanes, led by Witold Urbanowicz, flew head-on at another bomber formation. As the Messerschmitts rallied to the bombers' defense, a British squadron joined the brawl.

It was a repeat of the morning's fight. Suddenly, everywhere one looked, there were blazing planes and blossoming parachutes. "I have never seen such a party in the air," a Kościuszko pilot later wrote. "If a pilot had to bail out, he just prayed not to get some burning piece of wreckage on his [parachute]. There were so many of us going down that I thought [the Home Guard] would take us for a bloody parachute division and shoot us with duck shot, or catch us on a halberd while we were landing." So many Poles and Germans were parachuting at the same time, the pilot added, "that the Huns did not fire at the parachutes, because too many of them were their own."

In that second action, two Kościuszko Squadron planes were shot down, and one pilot was killed. Five of the seven Hurricanes that made it back to Northolt were badly damaged. The squadron was credited with six more kills, giving it sixteen for the day. Just as important, the pilots had succeeded in breaking up and dispersing the German bombers, forcing many back across the Channel before they could carry out their mission.

IN ALL, NEARLY seventy Poles—members of the Kościuszko and Poznań squadrons, plus those attached to British units—participated in the crucial battles of September 15, making up almost 20 percent of the total RAF force. Winston Churchill would later call that day's fighting "one of the decisive battles of the war."* The Luftwaffe had thrown nearly everything it had at the British but had failed to achieve its main objective—the elimination of the RAF as a defensive force. There would be more German raids in the future, more destruction and death visited on London and other English cities in the months ahead.‡ Nevertheless, the myth of the Luftwaffe's invincibility was forever shattered on September 15. Two days after that, Hitler decided he'd had enough and canceled Operation Sea Lion until further notice.

On September 26, George VI paid a call on the Kościuszko Squadron to congratulate the pilots and ground crews for their outstanding record. When the men had paraded past him at Northolt, His Majesty signed Ferić's diary. The royal visit had been a rousing success, even if there were a few small communications problems. One of the pilots, failing to understand a question put to him by the king, used a phrase he had learned in radiotelephone training: "Say again, sir?" The informality of the response caused quite a stir among the king's staff. Fortunately for the embarrassed young pilot, the alarm to scramble sounded a few moments later.

Vectored to Portsmouth to help break up another German raid, the squadron swooped down out of the sun on an unsuspecting bomber formation. Everything "worked perfectly," Kellett later wrote. "We returned to Northolt delighted with ourselves and the good luck the King had brought us." The squadron was credited with eleven kills and one "probable," with no losses of its own. The Kościuszko Squadron was closing in on its one hundredth kill.

Kellett may have overstated the level of the squadron's delight in all this, however. Fear and fatalism, the strain of almost constant combat, were beginning to take their toll.

---

* When he left 11 Group headquarters late that afternoon, Churchill was "absolutely—totally exhausted," recalled his daughter-in-law, Pamela Churchill, who accompanied him. "It was as if he had personally repulsed the German bombers."
‡ The London Blitz would continue until the following spring, killing a total of 40,553 persons. Still more would die in 1944 when Germany added the V-1 buzz bomb (a forerunner of the cruise missile) and the V-2 rocket (a forerunner of the intercontinental ballistic missile) to the devil's mix of urban terror—a mix to which the Allies also contributed heavily in such places as Dresden, Tokyo, Hiroshima, and Nagasaki.

George VI shakes hands with Mirosław Feric during his Battle of Britain visit to the Kościuszko Squadron at Northolt. Jan Zumbach stands next to Feric. Directly behind the king is Squadron Leader Ronald Kellett, with Witold Urbanowicz behind Kellett. Shortly after this photo was taken, the squadron was scrambled. During the mission it was credited with shooting down eleven enemy planes, with no losses of its own. (Polish Institute and Sikorski Museum)

THE MORNING AFTER the king's visit, the pilots were chatting idly as they waited to scramble again. The conversation turned to past German raids and dogfights, and debates about individual scores. Then, as Witold Urbanowicz recalled it years later, one of the pilots posed a question: What do you want most in the world? There was considerable laughter and joking. Many of the responses, predictably, had to do with women. Only Ludwik Paszkiewicz remained silent. The man whose downing of a Messerschmitt on August 30 had finally persuaded Fighter Command that the Kościuszko Squadron was ready for combat was unusually pensive that day. Another pilot pressed him to answer the question. "All I want," Paszkiewicz said, "is not to waste my last bullet."

Just then the phone rang.

A few moments later, the squadron was flying south, sent to intercept yet another enemy raid aiming for London. Over Horsham, the Poles encountered a formation of about thirty bombers, protected by fifty or sixty Me-109s. The Hurricanes attacked from behind, and, as they closed in for the kill, the Messerschmitts pounced. During the melee, Urbanowicz, having fought off several enemy fighters, noticed three bombers trying to slip away. He dove after them, but before he had a chance to fire, another Hurricane "flashed down like lightning" and attacked the bombers, one of which burst into flame and hurtled earthward. Almost at the same instant, the Hurricane was hit. Gouting fire, it, too, spun down. Urbanowicz watched anxiously but saw no parachute. When the sortie was over and he returned to Northolt, he learned that the pilot had been Paszkiewicz, who had not, as it turned out, wasted his last bullet.

On that same mission, another Kościuszko pilot, Sergeant Tadeusz Andruszkow, was also killed. He and Paszkiewicz were the fifth and sixth squadron fatalities in the Battle of Britain. By RAF standards at the time, this was not a high percentage. The Poles, with their don't-fire-till-you-see-the-whites-of-their-eyes tactics, were often accused of recklessness, but that was unfair. The Kościuszko Squadron's death rate was actually almost 70 percent lower than the rate for other RAF squadrons during the battle.

But statistics were small consolation to the close-knit band of warriors who had endured so much since September 1, 1939. When Paszkiewicz died, the usually cynical Jan Zumbach poured out his anguish in a eulogy in Ferić's diary. "He gave his life high up there, somewhere," wrote Zumbach, "where earthly matters are so distant, the rays of the sun so pure, and God so close."

Each loss also served to remind the survivors that one of them might be next. Late in his life, Urbanowicz remarked: "So many people ask me now, 'Were you afraid to take off and fight?' My answer is: 'Sure, all the time. I was always under tension.' " Yet the emotional strain the Poles were experiencing then, real as it was, was probably less than that felt by many other pilots who had been fighting since the end of July. For many, the worst part wasn't so much the fighting but the *waiting* to fight. "You might be at readiness for a very long time," recalled one British pilot, "and that was enormously stressful, because you were so much on edge. It was apprehension rather than fear." Some RAF pilots developed Pavlovian responses to sounds that merely portended combat. The click of a squadron telephone just before it started to ring, or the buzz of a loudspeaker before the announcement of a scramble, could at times induce the sweats or a bout of helpless retching.

By the end of September, the Kościuszko Squadron pilot who appeared to be suffering most under the strain was Jozef Frantíšek, the Czech, who, with seventeen confirmed kills, was now the RAF's top gun in the battle. At first, unlike many others, Frantíšek had seemed quite fearless. When air-raid sirens had sounded at night, he would remain calmly tucked in his bunk, shouting rude and uncomplimentary remarks at those who ran for the shelters. Lately, however, that had begun to change. Frantíšek was now among the first to bolt at the siren's wail. When asked if he was all right, he confessed that the only place he felt safe anymore was in the air.

Everyone had stories about Frantíšek's steely nerves in combat. Stanley Vincent recalled how, during one sortie, the Czech had seemed to take no notice of a Messerschmitt on his tail. When he returned to Northolt, Vincent reprimanded him.

"You can't ignore a fighter on your tail," Vincent said.

"But he could not fire at me," Frantíšek replied. "I was too close on the tail of a bomber." He explained that he had killed the bomber's rear gunner and was attacking from behind while also using the bomber as a shelter. If a Messerschmitt had fired at him, Frantíšek said, the rounds would have hit the German plane as well.

Frantíšek was audacious and charming. His rather dour appearance—craggy face, high forehead and cheekbones, beetling brows, thin and unsmiling lips—masked an almost childish spirit. In the early going, he was noted for his ebullience and wide-eyed wonderment. In one combat report, he wrote about parachuting from a shot-up Hurricane and landing in a cabbage field. The local constabulary took him to Brighton, where, still clutching his parachute, he caught a train for Northolt. "At the railway station, girls gave me some chocolate, and people photographed me," he wrote. "I am very grateful for the kindness which was shown me by everybody."

Frantíšek's charm could wear thin, though. There was also a certain arrogance about him, a certain obdurateness when he was given an order. He could be passionate at times and he had an anachronistic streak that sometimes even the passionate, anachronistic Poles found

*Jozef František, the only non-Pole in the Kościuszko
Squadron, was the RAF's highest-scoring ace in the Battle of Britain. (Polish Institute and Sikorski Museum)*

irritating. In a wartime book about the Kościuszko Squadron, the Polish
author Arkady Fiedler described František as being "altogether out of
place in modern times, [a man of] romantic exuberance and medieval
fervor; he was like a volcano pouring out its lava in the least expected
direction."

From the day in 1938 when he first arrived at Dęblin, František had
allied himself with Poland not only physically but spiritually. In
England, when asked his nationality, he invariably answered, "I am a
Pole." Proud to be in the Kościuszko Squadron, he refused many invita-

tions to join a Czech unit. Yet when Jozef František flew, it was as if he were alone in the sky, fighting the Nazis all by himself.

Time after time, he would break formation, reducing the squadron's ability to defend itself, and fly to the coast. There, he would lie in wait for German planes heading back to Europe. On these solitary expeditions, František often scored a kill, sometimes two or three. This presented his superiors with a dilemma. Furious as they frequently were at what had come to be known as "František's method," they could not afford to lose a pilot who was so successful. His penchant for hunting alone was "an irresistible instinct, an incurable disease," Fiedler wrote. "It was not merely ambition to put up his score; it was something more deeply imbedded in František's mind and character. In the air, he needed loneliness. There, he could not bear company, he could not stand any restrictions, he burst all bonds."

After one such foray, Urbanowicz, who had been named the squadron's acting Polish commander after Krasnodębski became a casualty, confronted František. The Czech pleaded that he had simply seen a fleeing German plane and pursued it, but Urbanowicz was not convinced. He ordered him never to leave the formation again without permission. Two days later, František disobeyed the order.

Clearly, something had to be done. He was endangering lives and undermining discipline. Worse, other pilots had begun using his "method." Even if the copycats as a rule waited until they had completed the squadron's primary mission before going off on their own, this kind of vigilantism could easily get out of hand. In the end, Kellett and Urbanowicz hit upon a compromise. They formally declared František to be a "guest of the Squadron," which meant they could save face while he continued doing what he was clearly going to do anyway. The next day, František—free at last—shot down three more German planes.

The more he flew, however, and the more success he had, the more he seemed to wither, the more fearful he became, the more his ebullient spirit seemed to drain away, as if someone had left a valve open. Every pilot had his demons, but František's demons seemed to be gaining the upper hand.

On October 8, squadron members, František included this time, went up on a routine patrol. They flew over London a while, found no Germans, and headed back to Northolt. They were landing when František veered off again. The other pilots watched as he turned his plane slowly toward the coast and flew on until the sound of his engine had faded to silence and his plane had disappeared. No one thought much about it. It was just František being František—the knight errant, alone with his demons. He would return when his fuel started running low, probably with another three or four 109s to his credit.

A few hours later, word came that František's plane had crashed near the town of Ewell, in Surrey. He apparently had been trying to make a forced landing in a clearing when his plane flipped in midair and slammed into the ground. His body, the neck broken, was found near the wreckage. There were no bullet holes in the Hurricane, no evidence that František had been in combat. Some thought that he might have crashed while doing a little stunt flying to impress a girlfriend who lived nearby. Others knew better. They were sure Jozef František's demons had finally overwhelmed him.

John Kent declared his death to be not only "a very great loss" but "a very worrying one."

―――――――――

THE KOŚCIUSZKO SQUADRON was pulled out of the front lines three days later and sent to Leconfield, in the middle of England, for a rest. In only six weeks of combat, during the Battle of Britain's most crucial period, the squadron was credited with shooting down 126 enemy aircraft, more than twice as many as any other RAF squadron for that period.* Nine of the squadron's thirty-four pilots qualified as "aces," fliers who have shot down five or more enemy planes. Many years later, a Battle of Britain historian would write: "Even though it was equipped with the Hurricane, the least effective of the…main fighters, 303 Squadron was by most measures the most formidable fighter unit [RAF or Luftwaffe] of the Battle…."

* When Luftwaffe records became available in 1947, the RAF reevaluated its own battle damage claims and those of the Germans. The investigators concluded that 1,733 Luftwaffe aircraft had been shot down during the Battle of Britain, as opposed to the 2,692 claimed by the RAF. Because the Polish Air Force was forced to disband immediately after the war, no official reassessment of Polish claims was ever conducted. But a number of contemporary Polish aviation experts have concluded that those claims should probably be reduced by roughly the same proportion as the RAF's.—Cynk, *The PAF,* p. 193.

Before the Poles left Northolt, Winston Churchill dropped by to add his congratulations to those of King George. Ronald Kellett (whose wife had given birth to a daughter during the height of the battle) took advantage of the prime minister's visit to bring up a delicate matter. After all the squadron had done for Britain, Kellett said, the RAF still had not authorized automatic payment of the officers' salaries. For the second month in a row, he had written a personal check to cover their pay, a procedure the Northolt accounting officer recently declared improper. Kellett asked if Churchill didn't agree that Great Britain had finally moved beyond the days of the Crimean War, when commanding officers had to pay their men out of their own pockets. Yes, Churchill said, "They must be paid." The very next day, the RAF approved automatic payment for the Kościuszko officers.

As he was about to leave Northolt, the prime minister leaned toward Kellett and whispered confidentially: "I value the commander of a fighter squadron today as much as a Cabinet minister, but don't tell."

In December, Air Marshal William Sholto Douglas, who had replaced Hugh Dowding as head of Fighter Command in October, came to Leconfield to award five of the squadron's nine aces the Distinguished Flying Cross (DFC), the RAF's top decoration for achievement and valor by a commissioned officer. Among the recipients was Witold Urbanowicz, who, as a thirty-one-year-old flying instructor at Dęblin, had feared he would never get a chance to fly in combat. In the Battle of Britain, he shot down fifteen German aircraft to become the battle's highest-scoring Polish pilot (as opposed to František, the Czech, who was the highest-scoring pilot regardless of nationality). The squadron's other DFC recipients were Jan Zumbach and Zdzisław Henneberg, both with eight kills; Mirosław Ferić, with seven (and one "probable"); and, posthumously, Ludwik Paszkiewicz, with six. František, who shot down seventeen German aircraft, was a sergeant during the battle and thus, under RAF regulations, ineligible for the DFC. Before he died, he was awarded the Distinguished Flying Medal, the RAF's top decoration for enlisted men.

Four of the Kościuszko Squadron's nine aces—Witold Urbanowicz, Jan Zumbach, Mirosław Ferić, and Zdzisław Henneberg—proudly show off their Distinguished Flying Crosses, awarded by the RAF in December 1940. (Imperial War Museum)

IN LATER YEARS, military historians generally agreed that the Battle of Britain ended on October 31, 1940, although most people in Britain, including the pilots who flew in it, had little sense at the time that the battle was over. Bombing raids on London and other cities and targets continued until mid-May 1941, when Germany was about to invade the Soviet Union. But the battle for air supremacy was over by the end of October 1940, and Britain's ability to defend itself was not further weakened. The RAF, which had lost 915 fighters in air combat,* would grow

---

* The figure does not include aircraft destroyed on the ground.

steadily stronger. In contrast, the Luftwaffe, which lost 1,733 planes, both fighters and bombers, between July 10 and October 31, never fully recovered and would never again be able to mount such a massive air offensive against an enemy.

Another casualty of the battle was the belief in Germany's invincibility. For the preceding four years, since the Wehrmacht's audacious march into the Rhineland, the German military had swept through Western Europe like an inexorable lava flow. Now, the flow had been stopped, and Germany was about to turn its attention to the East—a move that would prove to be Hitler's greatest mistake. The Battle of Britain marked the first time since 1918 that Germany had been defeated after launching a major campaign.

In years to come, even the Germans agreed that the battle had been a turning point. After the war, a group of Russian historians interviewed Field Marshal Gerd von Rundstedt, commander of German forces in the 1940 campaign in France and the Low Countries, who in 1944 commanded German troops at Normandy. The Russians asked von Rundstedt which battle he thought was the most decisive of the war. Without hesitation, he said: the Battle of Britain. If the Luftwaffe had crushed the RAF, Germany would have gone on to defeat Russia. Only the United States, militarily weak as it was then, would have stood in Hitler's way.

Britain's stubborn resistance was also a key factor in ending isolationism in the United States and in building public support for Lend-Lease, the dispatch of U.S. ships and military supplies to the desperately strapped British. From the beginning of the battle, American newspaper and radio correspondents in London, notably Edward R. Murrow and his CBS colleagues, described in vivid detail the heroism of the RAF pilots and the courage of the English under aerial siege. In early September 1940, a Gallup poll showed that only 16 percent of Americans favored providing more U.S. aid to Britain. A month later, as the sound of exploding bombs was carried by radio from London into American living rooms, the number had jumped to 52 percent.

Of the pilots who defended Britain, Winston Churchill declared in August 1940: "Never in the field of human conflict was so much owed by so many to so few." In recent years, the cherished British belief of the "few" against a superior Luftwaffe force has been challenged by some historians, who note, among other things, that the overall number of

RAF fighter pilots available during the battle actually exceeded the number of Luftwaffe fliers. In part, this was because RAF pilots who bailed out during the battle and landed safely in Britain or were rescued by RAF air-sea rescue units in the Channel could usually return to the air. Parachuting German pilots, however, were captured and were thus out of action until the end of the war.

In any event, the number of pilots available is not by itself an especially relevant statistic. Britain was on the defensive, its fighter pilots on call and subject to immediate action from dawn to dark every day, seven days a week. Many of the RAF pilots in the battle's later and most crucial stages were young, undertrained, and more likely than their seasoned predecessors to suffer the deleterious effects of fear and constant tension. As Churchill wrote in his memoirs: "In my talks with Air Marshal Dowding...the sense of Fighter Command being at its utmost strain was evident.... The physical and mental stresses upon pilots are not reflected on the paper charts—there are limits to human endurance." Dowding himself declared that by the end of the campaign, "the majority of the squadrons had been reduced to the status of training units and were fit only for operations against unescorted [bomber] units."

The presence of 142 well-trained, combat-experienced Poles—76 of them in British squadrons, 66 in the two all-Polish squadrons—thus proved critical. "There was no doubt about it," John Kent said years later. "The Poles were playing the game for keeps far more than we were." Of the some 400 fighter pilots who defended London and the critical area to the south at any one time in September and October, 50 to 100 were Polish. At times, Poles flew as many as 20 percent of the planes in combat and accounted for an even greater percentage of downed enemy aircraft. On September 26, for example, the day that George VI visited the Kościuszko Squadron at Northolt, Poles were responsible for 48 percent of the kills. After the war, Wing Commander Thomas Gleave, an RAF pilot during the Battle of Britain and later the commander of Northolt, said of the Poles: "I wonder if mankind is yet aware of the credit that is their due. They fought for English soil with an abandon, tempered with skill and backed by an indomitable courage such that it could never have been surpassed had it been in defense of their own native land."

In the opinion of a number of RAF pilots and commanders, the contribution of the Poles, particularly those in the Kościuszko Squadron, made the difference between victory and defeat in the battle. Ronald Kellett was one who thought so. So did Air Chief Marshal Frederick Rosier, who assumed command of Northolt in early 1943. Said Sir Archibald Sinclair, Britain's air minister: "Our shortage of trained pilots would have made it impossible to defeat the German air force and so win the Battle of Britain, if the ... airmen of Poland had not leapt into the breach." But perhaps the most telling comment came from no less an authority than Sir Hugh Dowding, initially so reluctant to send the Poles aloft. Shortly after the battle, he declared: "Had it not been for the magnificent [work of] the Polish squadrons and their unsurpassed gallantry, I hesitate to say that the outcome of battle would have been the same."

IN THE SPACE of three months, the RAF, once so dismissive of Polish pilots, had completely reversed itself. Now, it clamored for more of them. At the end of 1940, the Polish Air Force had five fighter squadrons and two bomber squadrons operating with the RAF. By the spring of 1941, six more all-Polish fighter squadrons were operational, and the RAF had dropped the requirement that British officers be in command. (Before the war was over, Poles would even command squadrons whose pilots were mostly British.)

Not that the clash of cultures and traditions didn't still cause trouble from time to time. Many RAF officers and pilots, with their stiff British upper lips, remained baffled by the exuberance and stormy emotionalism of the Poles, famous not only for their flying but for their riotous parties and their off-duty pursuit of women. "There were all sorts of discipline problems," the British commander of Poznań Squadron reported. "[The Poles] were very inclined to have ladies in their quarters, which was a bit frowned on in the officers' mess."

For their part, the Poles in the Kościuszko Squadron still found fault with Kellett and their other RAF superiors for not spotting German planes soon enough on sorties and for deficiencies in their methods of attack. Urbanowicz, the acting Polish commander of the squadron, con-

Witold Urbanowicz (center), *who replaced the injured Zdzisław Krasnodębski as Polish squadron leader during the Battle of Britain, enjoys a light moment with other Kościuszko pilots. (Polish Institute and Sikorski Museum)*

tinued to be at odds with Kellett. Urbanowicz "would always speak his mind," one Kościuszko pilot recalled. "He was never reluctant to challenge Kellett. There was constant friction between the two."

Yet when Kellett, Kent, and Forbes left the squadron as ordered at the end of the year, the previous troubles were swept away in goodbyes filled with fondness and respect. "You have given me many headaches during the time we have been together, but I would willingly have them all again," wrote D. A. Upton, the British adjutant of the Kościuszko Squadron, in a farewell entry in Ferić's diary. He signed the entry "Uptonski."

John Kent, who had been so depressed four months earlier at the thought of flying with a bunch of Poles, was now devoted to them. At a nightclub one night, he lunged at a fellow British officer who would not stand when the band played the Polish national anthem, *Jeszcze Polska* *nie zginęła.** Kent hauled the miscreant to attention and bloodied his nose. On his departure from the squadron in late 1940, Kent recalled many years after the war, the squadron threw "a most magnificent party" for him. Before leaving for his new assignment, he wrote in Ferić's diary: "It is with genuine regret and sorrow that I terminate my association with the squadron, the finest the RAF has seen. I can count the time I have spent with you as the most impressive and instructive of my life." In a later diary entry, Kent wrote: "Profound thanks for keeping me alive and teaching me to fight."

The Northolt station commander, Stanley Vincent, showed his fondness for the Poles by writing a delightful piece of doggerel in Ferić's diary to spoof their early problems with Hurricanes and their attractiveness to British women:

> *Whenever a Pole ...*
> *Can ever be seen*
> *He lands his machine*
> *All over the place ...*
> *He's over the edge*
> *He's into the hedge ...*
> *All over the place.*

> *The ladies adore*
> *Nobody more,*
> *Good heavens above!*
> *He'll always make love*
> *All over the place!*

For their part, the men of the Kościuszko Squadron, once so wary of the British, now returned their esteem. They often invited top British officers to their parties and were pleased to note that the starchy higher-ups actually seemed to have a good time. Vincent, who had taken a particular interest in the Poles' welfare and had become a favorite of theirs, was the guest of honor one night at a party celebrating the squadron's

---

* *Jeszcze Polska nie zginęła* might be freely translated "Poland still lives." But the Poles, deeply aware of their tragic history, cling to a more pessimistic, and literal, meaning: "Poland has not yet perished." The first line of the anthem is thus: "Poland has not yet perished as long as we live."

one hundredth enemy kill. As the wine and good fellowship flowed, the Poles introduced him to an old Polish custom—picking someone up and throwing him three times in the air. A delighted Vincent later recalled: "I have never been so high without wings."

At a dinner shortly after the squadron arrived at Leconfield, Air Vice Marshal Trafford Leigh-Mallory, commander of 12 Group, was given the same treatment. Kellett had advised the very proper Leigh-Mallory that he would be honored by the Poles after dinner. First, though, he must take everything out of his pockets. The group commander "had no other warning," Kellett recalled, "but when we sent him into the anteroom, he was duly picked up and thrown to the ceiling three times. He went up like a ramrod and, even if surprised, appeared to enjoy it."

In October 1941, when Kent, Kellett, and Athol Forbes were awarded the *Virtuti Militari*, Poland's highest military award, General Sikorski was the host at a lavish lunch in their honor. Afterward, the men of the Kościuszko Squadron took the three British pilots out for a night on the town in London. Dinner at a posh hotel was followed by stops at various

Ronald Kellett, John Kent, and Athol Forbes beam after receiving Poland's highest military honor, the Virtuti Militari. *(Polish Institute and Sikorski Museum)*

nightclubs. "A few of us ended up at five in the morning in somebody's flat off Park Lane, drinking pink champagne which was being poured out for us by a Polish army officer serving from behind a bar of mirrors," Kent said. "I don't know to this day who the place belonged to, but it was most memorable...."

––––––––––

WHEN THE POLES had arrived in England, fresh from the catastrophe in France, many doubted whether the British would fight. Their fears had proven groundless. British defiance of Hitler easily met Polish standards. Antoni Słonimski, one of Poland's leading writers, remembered how "defeated and betrayed" he and his countrymen had felt when they came to England after Poland fell to the Nazis, and how "England made us feel the strength and righteousness of our common cause." The Poles were grateful to the English for many things, Słonimski wrote. Above all, they were grateful "for our rekindled faith in humanity and in victory.... We shall not forget the ideals and honesty by which this great nation is guided."

CHAPTER TEN

"The Glamor Boys of England"

IN CONTRAST TO the RAF's initial wariness toward the Polish pilots, British civilians welcomed them with unambiguous affection. Here were allies worthy of the name. As the Poles marched through the streets of British port cities on their arrival, they were applauded and cheered by passersby and bathed in shouts of "Long Live Poland!" In London and other cities, bus conductors refused to take their fares, waiters would not let them pay for meals, and pub crawlers stood them to all the pints they could drink. Remembering how badly he had been treated by the French, one delighted Pole declared: "My God, this is a lovely place to be!"

During the Battle of Britain, friendship blossomed into hero worship—for Polish pilots generally and for the men of the Kościuszko Squadron in particular. British and American journalists swarmed to Northolt to learn more about these dashing young fighter pilots. "The Poles flying in the RAF are becoming the legendary heroes of this war," New York Times correspondent Robert Post told his readers in June 1941. "Wherever airmen gather, conversation is likely to shift around to some new exploits of a Polish flier.... The Poles not only are appreciated; they are pretty close to being adored." Quentin Reynolds, one of America's best-known war correspondents, agreed. As he wrote in Collier's: "The Polish aviators are the real Glamor Boys of England now."

Newspaper and magazine articles bore such headlines as POLAND'S AVENGING ANGELS, POLISH CAVALRY OF THE AIR, POLISH DAREDEVILS, and, referring to one of the Kościuszko Squadron's many notable days in the air, THE DEMON POLES DO IT AGAIN! 7–0. In the articles, the pilots' identities were masked by fictitious names or initials ("Squadron Leader K," "Flying Officer Z") so that the German and Soviet occupiers of Poland could not take revenge on their families—an element of mystery that only enhanced the Poles' romantic aura.

As the legend of the Kościuszko Squadron took shape, Jan Zumbach became a poster boy for British war bonds. WAR SAVINGS WILL BRING WINGS FOR VICTORY, proclaimed one poster featuring a color photograph of "Donald" Zumbach, grinning, as he sat in the cockpit of his Hurricane, its Kościuszko Squadron insignia visible on the fuselage. With all this publicity and propaganda, fan mail poured into Northolt. A school in Ruislip, near Northolt, sent a package of 450 cigarettes "for the brave Polish fighters." Students at a school for girls in Glasgow mailed in their pocket money—a total of ten shillings. The London suburb of Willesden collected money to help pay for a Spitfire, on the condition that it be flown only by a Pole.

Letters and gifts arrived from as far away as the United States. In response to an appeal by New York mayor Fiorello LaGuardia, more than 4,000 books, in Polish and English, were sent to the Polish squadrons. A group of British butlers in New York staged a charity ball to raise money for the construction of a Polish airmen's club in London. Perhaps best of all were fan letters sent by two of the Kościuszko Squadron's American founders. The Poles had long cherished their connection to the Yanks who flew in the 1919–20 Soviet-Polish War. So when the letters arrived from Merian Cooper and Cecil Fauntleroy, they were carefully pasted into places of honor in the squadron diary. And when Cooper, now a famous Hollywood producer, arrived at Northolt in March 1941 for a visit to the squadron he had helped create, Zumbach, Mirosław Ferić, and the others were as excited as schoolboys.

After returning to the United States from Poland in 1921, Cooper had gone exploring in Turkey and Laos, and become a successful documentary filmmaker. Then he headed for Hollywood, where in the early 1930s he convinced RKO to make a movie about a giant gorilla. The movie was *King Kong,* and Cooper was its co-director and writer. With that huge money-maker to his credit, he was named RKO's head of production, responsible for *Little Women,* among other classics, and for pairing Fred Astaire with Ginger Rogers. He and director John Ford later formed a partnership and produced some of Ford's most notable

Jan Zumbach is featured in a poster for British war bonds. Note the Kościuszko Squadron emblem on the fuselage. (Polish Institute and Sikorski Museum)

films, including *She Wore a Yellow Ribbon, Fort Apache, The Quiet Man,* and *The Searchers.*

But flying remained Cooper's greatest passion. When the United States entered World War II nine months after his visit to Northolt, he returned, at the age of forty-seven, to the air force and became General Claire Chennault's chief of staff in China. Later, he was named deputy chief of staff for all U.S. Army Air Force units in the Pacific, under General Douglas MacArthur.

Mirosław Ferić, Merian C. Cooper, and Jan Zumbach during Cooper's March 1941 visit to the Kościuszko Squadron at Northolt. (L. Tom Perry Special Collections, Brigham Young University)

For all his accomplishments, Cooper was especially proud of founding the Kościuszko Squadron. During his visit to Northolt in 1941, the pilots, who had formed up to greet him, shouted in unison: "Honor to you, heroes!"—the same acclamation that Cooper, Fauntleroy, and the other Yanks had heard when they had departed Poland in 1921.

Cooper, wearing a rakishly tilted fedora and smoking a briar pipe, was visibly moved. He told the Poles that the accomplishments of the

American pilots of the Kościuszko Squadron had been "but a little thing compared with your present wonderful record." He was particularly touched, he said, by the sight of the Kościuszko insignia—the cap, crossed scythes, and stars and stripes—on the squadron's Hurricanes. He and the other original pilots were proud of that insignia, he said, because it stood for "the friendship of the United States and Poland throughout the pages of history."*

That same year, the movies discovered the Polish pilots. RKO Pictures released a British film entitled *Dangerous Moonlight*, whose hero, a Polish concert pianist, becomes a pilot in the Polish Air Force shortly before Germany invades Poland. He escapes to England and flies in the Battle of Britain. Starring a popular Austrian actor named Anton Walbrook, *Dangerous Moonlight* was a huge hit in Britain, particularly among young women enamored of the soulful Walbrook. It was followed a few months later by Ernst Lubitsch's American-made farce, *To Be or Not to Be*, starring Jack Benny as a third-rate Polish actor and manager of a theater troupe who is married to a renowned actress played by Carole Lombard. In the movie, Lombard has an affair with a handsome Polish pilot, played by Robert Stack. When the Nazis invade Poland, the pilot makes his way to England, followed (after some complicated intrigue) by Benny, Lombard, and the rest of the troupe.

The Polish pilots were bona fide celebrities now. It was the height of chic to have a Pole or two at cocktail parties and formal dinners. In February 1941, a leading socialite, Jean Smith-Bingham, "adopted" the Kościuszko Squadron and threw a splashy dinner-dance in its honor at the Dorchester Hotel. Among the other guests were many society hostesses like Smith-Bingham. "Every other woman was titled," a bemused Kościuszko pilot wrote in the squadron diary, "and many had 'more than their share of years,' although there were also a few young and charming daughters of Albion." Lavishly chronicling the affair in a two-page spread, *The Tatler*, a British society magazine, pronounced it "one of the

---

* Later in the war, Cooper collected money from the other surviving Americans who had flown with him in the Kościuszko Squadron and used the proceeds to buy an engraved silver cigarette box, which he sent to the Poles at Northolt. The inscription read: "From the old guard to the new guard." Engraved beneath were the names of the American pilots who flew in the Soviet-Polish War.

gayest and most amusing that London has seen for many months." Smith-Bingham's social coup started a trend: within days, other women in the upper reaches of London society hastened to adopt Polish squadrons of their own.

Tadeusz Andersz, a fighter pilot attached to the recently formed Polish 315 (Dęblin) Squadron, was at a party in London one night when an

Kościuszko Squadron pilots with their "mother," Jean Smith-Bingham, who hosted a dinner-dance in the Poles' honor at the Dorchester Hotel. Standing at far left is Mirosław Feríc. Witold Łokuciewski is fifth from left, and Jan Zumbach is directly behind Smith-Bingham. (Polish Institute and Sikorski Museum)

attractive blonde asked if his squadron had a mother yet. She turned out to be Virginia Cherrill, a movie actress who, among other starring roles, had appeared opposite Charlie Chaplin in *City Lights*. Once married to Cary Grant, Cherrill was now the wife of the Earl of Jersey. When Andersz informed her that the squadron was still an orphan, Lady Jersey asked if she might have the honor of adopting it. Andersz passed her request to his no-nonsense squadron leader, who exploded, bellowing something along the lines of "Doesn't that silly woman realize we're in the middle of a *war*?" Told of this negative reaction, Lady Jersey never-theless persisted. She began telephoning the squadron commander directly, pestering him until he finally relented.

Once she had what she wanted, Lady Jersey did not rest on her lau-rels. Ever attentive to the airmen's needs, she threw party after party in their honor, sometimes at her London town house, sometimes at her country estate. (She always took care, Andersz recalled, "never to invite girls prettier than herself.") She attended the squadron's Christmas din-ners, mailed parcels to captured pilots in stalags, and gave the others her old silk stockings to wrap around their knees to keep them warm during high-flying missions. Once, when a journalist was interviewing her at her country house, they heard the roar of an airplane overhead. Looking out the window, they saw a Spitfire circling low over the house. "That is one of my Poles," Lady Jersey proclaimed. "I'm their mother."

ALL OVER ENGLAND, citadels of the British class system were falling to the Poles. One Kościuszko Squadron pilot, shot down during the Battle of Britain, parachuted onto an exclusive golf course, landing near the eighth tee. The men playing the hole insisted on carting the dazed flier off to the clubhouse for drinks. Another parachuting pilot drifted into a copse near a private tennis club in the London suburbs. Three club members observed his descent as they awaited the arrival of a fourth for their weekly doubles match. They helped extricate the Pole from the trees and, giving up on their expected fourth, asked if he played. When the young pilot said he did, he was dressed in borrowed white flannels and was soon on the court, borrowed racket in hand. This is how Richard Cobb, a young Oxford-educated historian who served as an English instructor to Polish pilots, was told the story by a member of the foursome: "In the club minutes, you can read: 'August 23rd, Polish officer, introduced by Mr. and Mrs. ———.' That's how a Pole ... entered the English Holy of Holies, a lawn tennis club which was strictly closed to all but 'nice people.' "

Pleasant as these excursions into British high society doubtless were for the Poles, they came at an emotional cost. The pilots (and many Britons as well) were troubled to discover that the upper crust—their country at war, their skies and cities regularly filled with fire and death—could act as if nothing had changed, as if nothing was wrong. The Poles had witnessed the devastation of their own nation and were acutely aware that the families and friends they had been forced to leave behind were now living under German or Soviet occupation. Yet here the pilots were in England, fêted and pampered by the upper echelons of society, glamorized in movies and the press, enjoying themselves in spite of any guilt they may have felt. And here were their hosts and hostesses, with their very British insouciance, acting as if there would always be an England. In one context, this attitude was infuriating; in another, it was one of Britain's greatest strengths. "On the ground, things went on very much as usual, despite the stuff that was falling around," Richard Cobb observed. "The hops had to be picked, the old ladies couldn't interrupt their bridge, the old gentlemen still had to take the sun and rebuild the Empire at the club."

Not that British insouciance was limited to society hostesses, old ladies at bridge, and harrumphing old gentlemen in clubs. Even high government officials, who understood Britain's peril better than most, were able on occasion to divorce themselves from the reality of the war. Indeed, some seemed to regard the dogfights overhead as a form of entertainment and relaxation. There was, for example, Lord Halifax, the British foreign secretary, who found respite from worry and pressure in country weekends with friends, watching from their garden "one of the summer battles in the air and *forgetting the war*" (italics added). And there was John Colville, the young aristocrat who was Churchill's favorite private secretary. Colville wrote in his diary about a weekend in the country, during which he and other guests enjoyed "a grandstand view of a fight"—Stuka dive-bombers screaming down on a nearby airfield and Luftwaffe bombers plummeting to the earth. "When peace was restored," Colville wrote, he and two female guests "sat on the terrace in high spirits, elated by what we had seen." After tea, he and one of the young women, a volunteer nurse, played tennis until she was summoned to the hospital to tend the casualties that resulted from the lunchtime battle.

In London, despite rationing and other material deprivations, those who had money and connections were largely able to maintain their customary standard of living during those early years of the war. "London lives well," noted Henry Channon, a hard-partying member of Parliament, after an evening at the Dorchester in November 1940. "I've never seen more lavishness, more money spent, or more food consumed than tonight, and the dance floor was packed." Top-hatted doormen still graced the entries of the Dorchester, the Savoy, and other posh hotels. Strawberries and cream were still available for afternoon tea at the Connaught. Eight different varieties of oysters were on the menu at Scott's restaurant in Piccadilly. Smoked salmon and champagne were plentiful. In October 1940, Quentin Reynolds noted in his diary that the only material hardship he had encountered in London to that point was the lack of a decent martini. "No French vermouth, of course, has come here since June," he wrote.

Even the nightly German bombardments were often not enough to deter long-established social routines. Harold Macmillan and several other junior government ministers were chatting one evening at the Carlton Club, a Tory bastion on Pall Mall, when, quite literally, the roof caved in. A bomb had smashed into the club, almost completely destroying it, although, to everyone's amazement, only one person was killed. Unhurt themselves, Macmillan and another government minister—their clothes and hair covered with ash, their faces blackened by dirt and smoke—staggered from the rubble and proceeded across the street to the Carlton Hotel for dinner. (They had to tidy themselves up, however, before the maitre d' would admit them.)

———

FOR MOST LONDONERS, of course, life during the Blitz was quite something else again. Fear, loss, pain, and anger were far more prevalent than casual indifference or casual courage. Still, in this period and for most of the war, London was undeniably a place of intoxicating energy and excitement. "You walk through the streets... and everyone you pass seems to be pulsating with life," Quentin Reynolds observed. As in other wars, the threat of death often heightened the exhilaration and romance of survival. The slogan "Live today, for tomorrow we die" may be a war-movie cliché, but it resonated all the same in London's damp streets and tube stations, its chilly flats and crowded bomb shelters, its hotels and restaurants, its pubs and palaces, its situation rooms and its bedrooms. Certainly, the pilots of the RAF—not least the romantic Poles—felt this way, and with good cause, given the steep odds against their survival. "Life?" one of the Polish pilots wrote. "One measured it in days and hours, sometimes even in minutes, and the charm of life made one drunk with its allure and fascinated with its pace and excitement."

London was less than an hour from Northolt by tube, and the men of the Kościuszko Squadron, like other British and Allied servicemen, made the journey as often as their military duties, their wallets, and their stamina permitted. Nightclubs held special appeal—smoky, dark, tempting places like the 400 Club, featuring Tiny Tim Clayton and his Whispering 400 Band, or the Café de Paris, whose bandleader was the fabled Ken "Snakehips" Johnson. On the crowded dance floors, couples swayed to "Night and Day," "A Nightingale Sang in Berkeley Square," "I've Got You Under My Skin," and other wistful hits of the day. Like the cigarette smoke curling to nightclub ceilings, romance and sex hung thick in the air, and conventional morality tended to get packed away for the duration. One Polish pilot left no doubt about what attracted him in the capital: "In London," he confided to his diary, "waited lips red as roses."

It didn't take long for the Poles to acquire a reputation as gallants. John Colville once asked a woman friend, the daughter of an earl, what it was like to serve as a WAAF driver for Polish officers. "Well," she replied, "I have to say 'Yes, sir' all day, and 'No, sir,' all night." The head of a British girls' school made headlines when she admonished the graduating class about the pitfalls of life in the outside world, ending her speech with: "And remember, keep away from gin and Polish airmen."*

Not even the Poles' faulty English slowed them down. One RAF language instructor recalled: "I was never allowed a half-hour's peace without somebody wanting me to write their love-letters for them or translate those received from their English girlfriends." Another instructor, besieged by similar requests, composed a series of form letters for the Poles in the squadron to which he was assigned. The topics ranged from a simple request for a date to a passionate profession of love. "So, depending on what you wanted to do with a girl," said one of the squadron's pilots, "you'd go up to him and say 'Teacher, letter number three please.' "

Not that romance was a one-way street where the Poles were concerned. Their Continental air, their penchant for hand-kissing, their

---

* In the British movie *Hope and Glory* (1987), directed by John Boorman, which takes place during the London Blitz, one character confides to another that his wife has just run off "with a Polish pilot."

belief that no occasion was too insignificant for a gift of flowers, probably would have given them an edge over their rather starchy British
competitors even in peacetime. As it was, in a war in which the Poles
were seen as heroes, it was almost no contest. Young British women,
having sat and sighed through Anton Walbrook's performance in *Dangerous Moonlight,* became the pursuers as much as the pursued. And that
was true not only of British women. At a London cocktail party in her
honor, Martha Gellhorn, Ernest Hemingway's talented and beautiful
wife, then covering the war for *Collier's,* ignored the rest of the guests
and "devoted her entire attention to a couple of Polish pilots."*

In contemporary diaries and letters, and in later recollections, a number of fliers described their wartime romances with some amazement.
"As for the women," one of them wrote in his diary, "one just cannot
shake them off." Others found all the adoring attention a bit unnerving.
"These English girls are quite different from Polish girls," another diarist
noted after a date. " 'Do you love me?' she asked, just like that. She's very
sweet, but that's no way for a girl to win a man." When he was in his eight-
ies, Witold Urbanowicz recalled those days with a chuckle: "I think English women should have some monument, some big monument. They
were wonderful to us."

———————

DURING WORLD WAR II, young British women experienced a heady
new sense of freedom and independence. They had grown up in a society in which few women worked outside the home or went to college.
Before the war, women were expected to remain primly in life's background and to demand little more than the satisfaction of having served
their husbands and raised their children. That staid and predictable
existence, however, began to be shattered in September 1939.

Hundreds of thousands of women signed up for jobs in defense
industries or enlisted in the Women's Auxiliary Air Force and other
military units for women. Even debutantes who had never so much as
boiled an egg went to work in aircraft factories and munitions plants.
"It was a liberation, it set me free," declared one former deb. "If it

———————

* This rather catty observation came from one of the other partygoers, Time-Life journalist
Mary Welsh, another American. Welsh would soon succeed Gellhorn as Mrs. Hemingway.

hadn't been for the war, I would never have had the chance to find out what I could do—or the satisfaction of doing it." Many women discovered what they could do in other areas, too—with or without general approval. They wore slacks. They appeared in public without stockings. They smoked, they drank, and they had sex outside of marriage—more often and with fewer qualms and less guilt than their mothers and grandmothers.

At Northolt, the Kościuszko Squadron pilots experienced firsthand the effects of liberation. A young WAAF, a former actress who served as a driver for the squadron, was known as "Speedy"—and not just for her performance behind the wheel of her white Jaguar. A number of young women who frequented the Orchard, a favorite inn near Northolt, were dubbed "Messerschmitts" by the fliers, for their assertiveness and for their willingness to "escort" the pilots from the dance floor to bed.

One night at the Orchard, Jan Zumbach met an attractive young woman named Ann, who, at first glance, did not seem to fall into the "Messerschmitt" category. A few days later, she invited Zumbach home for dinner, to meet her parents. After the meal, Ann's parents retired, and she invited him to do the same—with her. In her bedroom, she put a record on her gramophone, and they danced. After a breathless bout of kissing, Ann excused herself and disappeared into the bathroom. Not quite sure what was coming next, Zumbach decided to gamble: he undressed and slipped into her bed. While he waited, he picked up a thick notebook lying on Ann's bedside table and began leafing through it. It was her diary. It contained rather detailed reviews of the lovemaking skills of what seemed to Zumbach to be an extraordinary number of men. He saw the names of several of his Kościuszko Squadron comrades and was pleased to note that the Poles had been awarded higher marks than Ann's own countrymen. Soon Zumbach was added to her conquests, although he never learned how he ranked.

However memorable women like Ann were, they were hardly typical. Most British women were seeking more in their relationships with men than just sex, and the Poles were valued for more than their prowess in bed. Charming and highly flirtatious, they were famous for the courtly way they treated women. They paid lavish compliments in broken English and otherwise made women feel adored. "This kissing of hands," noted a rather baffled Ronald Kellett, "seems irresistible to the opposite sex!" After a first date, a woman might well receive roses worth

*The Orchard inn, near Northolt, was the Kościuszko Squadron's
home away from home during the war. (Orchard Restaurant)*

a month's pay. One Polish pilot bewitched a British female journalist
with his "blue eyes, dashing manner and fascinating charm." While she
was interviewing him, he asked if he could borrow her soul on his next
mission, "to take up into the clouds for luck." "Of course, I gave it to
him," she breathlessly confided in her story.

The Poles actually seemed to *enjoy* female company. To the enchant-
ment of the women they dated, they were willing to express their feelings and show their vulnerability. British men of the middle and upper
classes were products of all-male prep schools. For much of their childhood and young adulthood, they had little contact with girls and
women outside their immediate family. Indoctrinated with the idea that
it was unmanly to show emotion or respond to it in others, they often
seemed truly at ease only in the company of like-minded men. "For the
habitually reserved Englishman ... concealment of his emotions is the
first and cardinal rule of gentlemanliness and social grace," one Kościuszko Squadron pilot observed. A former WAAF, recalling her romantic experiences during the war, agreed. "British officers had no idea how
to treat a girl," she said. Ah, but the Poles! They "had that look in their

eye—you knew that the fellow saw you as a woman and wanted you. That was an extraordinarily sexy feeling, quite new for us."*

For their part, British men seemed unable to understand the Poles' appeal. "They notice what the women are wearing," a British pilot remarked. "Seems they know about clothes as well as fighting. Odd, isn't it? But it seems the girls like it." Six other British fliers made their puzzlement public in a letter to the advice column of the *Daily Sketch*. "We are worried because we can't get a woman to even look at us," the letter began. "Why? Because this 'drome is overrun by Polish airmen, and they are commandeering anything that's prim and pretty.... What can you suggest for us to do?"

According to a number of newspaper stories, some enterprising British pilots solved the problem by pretending to be Poles themselves. They adopted phony Slavic accents, kissed hands everywhere they went, even sewed "Poland" flashes on their uniform sleeves before going to a dance. Quentin Reynolds cited one RAF pilot's pickup line, which proved to be very successful: "I am Polish aviator. Please have drink with me. I am very lonely."

ALTHOUGH THE MEN of the Kościuszko Squadron enjoyed their celebrity, they sometimes felt it necessary to draw the line. It wasn't manly— it simply was not pilotlike—to attract too much attention to oneself. During the Battle of Britain, Ferić and several other Kościuszko pilots were at a pub one evening, celebrating the six German planes shot down by their squadron that day. When the pub's other patrons found out about their success, they tried to get the fliers to stand in the middle of the room so that they could toast them. The Poles politely refused: in Ferić's words, "we did not wish to be made a spectacle of."

Among many Poles, there was the feeling that the English, as kind and friendly as most of them were, didn't understand them or their country. Richard Cobb, who after the war became an eminent Oxford historian, concurred, admitting that when he was asked to teach English

---

* Many Poles, among them a number of Kościuszko Squadron veterans, married British women. In one case, a pilot met his future wife when he was shot down during the Battle of Britain and parachuted into her parents' garden.

to Polish fliers, Poland was only "a mental and imaginative idea" to him, "a series of names and treaties and maps and mental tableaux of magnificently dressed exotic Slavs." Once, on a British train, a conversation between two Polish pilots was interrupted by an elderly Englishman, who asked anxiously, "But you are not talking in German, are you?" "No," one of the Poles replied, "we are speaking in our native language." The man nodded in dawning comprehension. "Ah!" he said. "So you have your own language!"

Another Polish flier spent a good deal of his pay on books by Polish writers, which he then gave to English friends. "He had a passionate desire that they should know more about Poland than they thought they did," remarked Alyse Simpson, a writer who was one of those friends. "It was not, he protested with great restraint, a place of snow and bears and ignorant peasants, but a civilized land of much beauty and tradition. It had a great literature."

While helping to create the legend of the Polish pilots, the British and American press had not done much to educate their readers about the complex history of these heroes' homeland. Indeed, in the view of many Poles, the press had gone overboard in sensationalizing the pilots' exploits and perpetuating what the Poles considered to be inaccurate and condescending stereotypes. Writing about the members of the Kościuszko Squadron, Geoffrey Marsh, one of their RAF English instructors, remarked: "Artists came to sketch them, journalists to write about them; but their spirit, like a darting trout, was too elusive to catch. Heroes are too often fleshless creatures, [eulogized] into demi-gods for the sake of an ideal."

In his paean to Polish pilots, Quentin Reynolds was one of those who turned airmen from the Kościuszko Squadron into supermen, claiming they had shot down 126 German planes in one week "without losing one man or one airplane." In other purple-prose stories, the Poles were portrayed as amusing foreigners with a funny way of speaking or as savage romantics who lived only to kill Germans. (One headline managed to include both clichés: BOMBING REICH THRILLS POLES—WE GO TONIGHT, YES?)

Unquestionably, Polish pilots were fiercely determined to avenge the horror visited by the Luftwaffe on their countrymen and country. It is also true that most of them hated the Germans and didn't care who knew it. But they were hardly the maniacal warriors that many articles made them out to be. One story by correspondent Robert Post in the *New York Times Magazine,* for example, described "demoniac fighters" who had "lost practically all spiritual values except hatred of the Germans and the thirst for vengeance.... All their capacity for love has become the channel of hatred for the agency of their destruction and dispersal. If they are reckless, what does it matter? Death is to them unimportant as long as in dying they are able to deal a blow at the cause of their tragedy."

The same stereotype, although less pretentiously presented, found its way into *Flare Path,* a play by Terence Rattigan that opened in the West End in 1942. One RAF pilot says of another major character, a Polish flier: "They're a bit different from us, the Poles, you know. Crazy types, most of them. They're only really happy when they're having a crack at Jerry."

Arkady Fiedler, whose *Squadron 303* was published in Britain in 1943, spent considerable time with the men of the squadron as part of his research. In his book, the Polish author remarked that the best thank-you gift Britain could give the squadron for its invaluable service was "to get to know the Poles better. To know them honestly, intimately, through and through, putting aside prejudices and preconceptions, to know the Poles as they really are...." Then, Fiedler wrote, "the British would no doubt discover that the nation living on the banks of the Vistula is just like all other healthy and civilized nations, neither better nor worse. They would find that the average Pole is not very different from the average Mr. Brown of London.... That is the reward which the Polish airmen desire: a fair and intelligent view of their nation."

Not to mention a better understanding of the airmen themselves, members of the Kościuszko Squadron might have added. As the war progressed, they continued to venture into London, but they preferred the Orchard, a rambling, half-timbered, neo-Tudor inn, with its polished brass, flowered cretonne curtains, pots of geraniums and azaleas in window boxes, and manicured lawn out front. Instead of beautiful society hostesses who smiled more for photographers than for the pilots they were entertaining, the inn had an owner who insisted on hearing every detail of every mission, who opened a bottle of champagne every time a Pole at Northolt shot down an enemy plane, and who sent baskets of fruit to the bedsides of the wounded. Instead of the polished sounds of Tiny Tim Clayton and his Whispering 400 Band, there was a makeshift orchestra, "who made up for a lack of technique with an eagerness to please."

"When we burst in [at night]," Jan Zumbach fondly remembered, "...everything stopped for us. The other customers realized that we weren't just a bunch of randy barbarians speaking a language nobody understood. They felt a genuine friendship for these noisy foreigners who had come so far."

In other words, the Orchard had become home.

PART TWO

BETRAYAL

CHAPTER ELEVEN

"The Cold-Blooded Murder of a Nation"

O NE DAY IN the fall of 1941, a solitary figure stood at the edge of a Northolt runway, watching the Kościuszko Squadron's recently acquired Spitfires take off for France. Zdzisław Krasnodębski had just been posted back to Northolt after spending eleven months in the hospital. To a casual observer, "the King" might have seemed fully recovered from the horrific burns that scorched and nearly killed him when his Hurricane was hit during the Battle of Britain. But he still had scars and infirmities, some of them invisible.

Not that he hadn't received excellent care. Shortly after the squadron leader was shot down, he was taken to Queen Victoria Hospital at East Grinstead in West Sussex. There, he came under the care of a renowned New Zealand–born plastic surgeon, Dr. Archibald McIndoe. Before the war, McIndoe had been known for his fashionable Harley Street practice, where his grateful patients were mostly aging women. Now the affable, bespectacled surgeon was regarded as a miracle worker of an altogether different sort. He had demonstrated a remarkable ability for rebuilding not only the faces and bodies of terribly burned RAF pilots but their psyches and lives as well.

The patients in Queen Victoria's Ward Three—the burn unit—had never seen a place quite like it. One of them fondly compared it to a madhouse; another described it as "a cross between [an] emergency ward..., the Red Lion [pub], and a French bordello." In place of a hospital's normal rules and regulations, there was noise and general chaos—radios blaring; typewriters clacking; bandaged men, on crutches and in wheelchairs, talking and laughing. In one part of the ward was a large Rube Goldberg–like contraption: a saline bath devised by McIndoe for healing burns. In another corner was a beer barrel, to which patients were free to help themselves whenever they liked. Then there were the nurses, known as much for their beauty as for their medical skills and kindness. This was no accident. Nursing applicants for Ward Three had to submit photographs of themselves for McIndoe's approval. He wanted his patients, badly disfigured and racked with intense pain as many of them were, to have the attention and sympathy of the loveliest women he could find.

McIndoe did everything he could to help the burn victims in Ward Three ease back into the world, and they revered him for it. "He was a god," said one. A close bond also developed among his patients, especially the earlier ones who were shot down during the Battle of Britain. In July 1941, they formed the Guinea Pig Club, which, according to Peter Williams and Ted Harrison, authors of *McIndoe's Army*, "immediately became the most exclusive in the country, far harder to join... than any of the ancient and privileged haunts of London clubland." Only RAF or Allied airmen who had been treated in Ward Three could belong. Krasnodębski, known as "Kras" to his fellow patients, was a founding member.

As godlike as McIndoe may have seemed to the men he treated, there were miracles he could not perform. His ability to rebuild a face and restore function to burned limbs was remarkable, but a fair number of his patients were so severely burned that permanent disfigurement and disability—as well as "the terrible despair" that often accompanied the loss of looks and vitality—were inevitable.

Compared to some of the other men in Ward Three, Krasnodębski had been lucky: his face was scarred but, thanks to McIndoe's surgeries, not badly disfigured. His hands were another matter. Although he had regained some use of them, they were so badly burned that he had trouble holding a cigarette between his fingers. As some doctors earlier predicted, Krasnodębski would never fly in combat again. When he came back to Northolt, the pilot who had led and inspired his famous unit from the first days of the war was given a desk job. To Witold Urbanowicz, now co-commander of three Polish squadrons, including Kościuszko, "the King" seemed sad and lonely, haunted by thoughts of

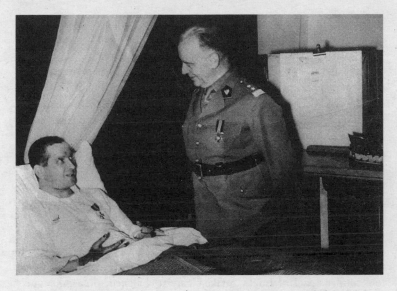

General Władysław Sikorski, prime minister and commander in chief of the Polish government-in-exile, at the bedside of Zdzisław Krasnodębski after awarding the wounded Kościuszko Squadron leader the Virtuti Militari. *(Stanisław Blasiak)*

his wife in Poland, "no longer the same Krasnodębski as before, laughing and overflowing with zeal for the fight."

Krasnodębski found Northolt a very different place from the one he had left almost a year earlier. It was now known as *the* Polish fighter base in Britain, the home of the officially designated First Polish Fighter Wing, composed of the Kościuszko Squadron and two new squadrons, 306 and 308. After the Battle of Britain, wings of two or more fighter squadrons, all now equipped with Spitfires,* began to operate as single formations to carry out offensive operations over France. Although by this time the RAF had agreed to let Polish officers command individual

---

* The Spitfire and the Hurricane were both excellent fighters. The Spitfire was generally regarded as superior, although the Hurricane, flown by the Kościuszko Squadron throughout the Battle of Britain, had its adherents.

squadrons, the new wings were for a time still under joint command. Hence, the First Polish Wing, which had been created at Northolt in April 1941, had Urbanowicz and John Kent as co-commanders.

Kent and Group Captain Theodore McEvoy, who succeeded Stanley Vincent as base commander, were now the most senior RAF officers at Northolt. Most of the other officers, from squadron leaders on down, were Polish. Mass was celebrated every day in a makeshift chapel, and a Polish library was created. The staid hush of the mostly British officers' mess had disappeared. Now the parties tended to be louder and rowdier. In the bar, where a tongue-in-cheek "English Spoken" sign was displayed, rookie pilots who had just scored their first kill were obliged to drink a lethal cocktail called a "Messerschmitt." Devised by Kościuszko pilots, it mixed whiskey, port, sherry, crème de menthe, and whatever other spirits and liqueurs happened to be handy. During one raucous celebration, Jan Zumbach played William Tell and shot an apple off another pilot's head with his pistol. On another occasion, a Polish flier took aim at a pack of Lucky Strike cigarettes balanced on a colleague's head. Luckily, despite the vast amounts of alcohol consumed in both cases, the shooters' aim was true.

The nature of the war had also changed while Krasnodębski was away. As the Germans gradually but unmistakably abandoned the idea of conquering Great Britain in favor of trying to conquer the Soviet Union, the way was open for the British to begin launching offensive operations. The government had no intention of ordering a ground invasion of Europe this early, but it did approve ever more aggressive bombing raids against Germany and German-held territories. This decision changed the nature of Fighter Command's assignment—from defending Britain to escorting bombers and attacking German installations.

As in the Battle of Britain, the Poles played an important role in these sweeps over France, Belgium, and Holland. Polish squadrons took part in the vast majority of the new operations and were credited with nearly 30 percent of the kills scored against the Luftwaffe in 1941.

Low-level fighter sorties with colorful code names like "Rhubarb" and "Mosquito" were launched against German positions. After crossing the Channel, the fighters would disperse and then, singly or in pairs, swoop down over France or the Low Countries, strafing airfields, gun emplacements, railway stations, trucks, troops, or any other tempting military target. "One has to fly very low over the ground, hedgehopping, so that nobody can see the plane approaching until it pops out from behind some trees or houses," the Kościuszko Squadron's Zdzisław Henneberg explained to a reporter. "Before the Germans have time to shoot or take cover, we can give them plenty of bullets." It was this kind of fighting, Henneberg said, that "best suited the Polish temperament" and "the tradition of our cavalry."

Because British bomber crews (and, later, American crews) clamored for the Poles as their escorts, they were also important contributors to operations called "Circuses"—daylight bombing raids over France and the Low Countries, which were also designed to draw German fighters into battle. In effect, the British bombers taking part in the raids were used as bait in the "Circuses," luring Messerschmitts into a destructive web created by the bombers' Spitfire escorts.

The Poles' popularity with bomber pilots stemmed primarily from their unique approach to escort assignments. According to Jan Zumbach, they had developed "a highly effective technique of close escort. We practically glued ourselves to our charges, a pair of us flanking each plane and shielding it from attack, at the risk of being shot down [ourselves].... By making ourselves expendable, we were allowing the other fighter squadrons a free hand to deal with the enemy...." Despite the disadvantage created by "making ourselves expendable," Kościuszko Squadron pilots who flew in "Circuses" managed to rack up more than their share of kills: in one six-week period during the summer of 1941, the squadron destroyed forty-six enemy planes over France—and did so without losing a single bomber.

Many pilots, however, considered "Circuses," "Mosquitoes," and other such operations to be much more dangerous than dogfights during the Battle of Britain. The RAF was facing the same perils (and fuel limitations) in flying over enemy-held territory that the Luftwaffe had encountered earlier. Besides the threat of fighter attacks, German antiaircraft batteries bristled along the coast, and machine-gun nests encircled the airfields. "On the way to France, you could surprise [the coastal defense]," a Polish pilot said: "On the way back, they knew you were there, and they knew you had to cross the coast. They were waiting for you."

If RAF and Allied pilots were shot down over land and survived, they were taken prisoner and, unless they escaped, were out of the war for the duration. If they ran into trouble over the Channel and had to ditch in those always cold and often stormy waters, the chance of rescue could be slim. A pilot who managed to get safely out of his plane might drown or die of hypothermia before a ship could reach him.

As the RAF offensive intensified, squadrons sometimes flew two or more sorties a day; and as the number of sorties increased, so did the number of casualties. In the last six months of 1941, more than 500 RAF fighter planes were shot down, including 17 Spitfires on one day alone. The Kościuszko Squadron lost six of its best fliers in less than two months. Among them was Zdzisław Henneberg, who in September 1940 had joined Mirosław Feric in an unauthorized chase of Messerschmitts over France. Henneberg made it back safely from that adventure. This time, he drowned in the Channel after being forced to ditch.

In the blur of war that engulfed the squadron's survivors, death became a convenient way of measuring time. During an interview with a correspondent, a Kościuszko Squadron pilot tried to recall the exact date of some occurrence during the Battle of Britain. "When was it?" he said. "Let me see.... It was about two days after they had got František.... No, I'm wrong, it must have been two days before Paszko went down."

As the fighting dragged on, the number of grim milestones increased.

———

ON FEBRUARY 14, 1942, Mirosław Feric had just returned to Northolt after a two-month stint in the hospital. No one now knows the reason for this hospital stay, although apparently, on occasion, RAF pilots in combat were sent to the hospital simply to give them a long rest. Whatever the reason, Feric, once back at Northolt, was anxious to get into the air again. The pilot who constantly nagged others to write their flying experiences in his diary and who, as a youngster, used to teeter on the balcony railing of his mother's fourth-floor apartment, his arms outstretched like wings, was never truly happy unless he was flying.

At midmorning on that cold, overcast February day, he took up a Spitfire for a routine practice flight. When the Rolls engine roared to life, Feric grasped the stick and worked the foot pedals. Yes, it was *very* good to be back.

After takeoff, he started putting the Spitfire through its paces. When the aircraft was at about 3,000 feet, part of a wing suddenly broke off and struck the tail, tearing it off as well. The Spitfire started corkscrewing earthward, accelerating as it plummeted. Ferić threw open his canopy and struggled to get out of his safety harness. On the ground, some of his comrades watched, horrified, as the Spitfire screamed down toward them, closer and closer, until it slammed into a runway with a sickening roar. The impact was so violent the plane's nose was buried up to the cockpit in concrete.

Pilots and ground crews raced to the wreckage. They found Ferić's dead body hanging halfway out of the cockpit. Clearly, he had tried to jump before the crash but had been unable to overcome the G's and work himself free. As a mischievous boy and as a dedicated fighter pilot,

Wreckage of the Spitfire in which Mirosław Ferić was killed on February 14, 1942. (Polish Institute and Sikorski Museum)

"Ox" Ferić had had many near misses in his life, but quick wits and good luck had always saved him. This time, he had no chance, and he died knowing it. He was twenty-six years old—the only one of Dęblin's famed, hell-raising "Three Musketeers" to die in the war.

"The Kościuszko Squadron chronicler is killed," wrote squadron language instructor Geoffrey Marsh. "He was a man of extreme sensibility and idealism, and all through his writings, there is revealed the bitterness and courage of the present and the optimism of the future." Ferić was also a man with a fiercely passionate love for his country, as shown in a 1940 diary entry that he wrote while he and the others were still in France: "We know that many of us will die.... But what of it? There is nothing to live for if there is no Poland. It is for her that we are doing all this—not to achieve fame, not to score a certain number of kills, not for the French, not for the English. We are doing this for Poland."

Ferić's diary, so often the subject of more or less good-natured complaints by his Kościuszko Squadron colleagues in the past, now became

Witold Łokuciewski (left) *serves as a pallbearer at the funeral of Mirosław Ferić, his close friend and fellow "Musketeer." (Polish Institute and Sikorski Museum)*

a means of paying tribute to him. The squadron made the diary its own. In it, the pilots, without prodding now, continued to write personal accounts of their missions and to record important events—weddings, funerals, VIP visits—in the squadron's life. When one of them was killed, his photo went into the diary, with a border neatly drawn around it in black ink. This was the kind of thing Ferić had had in mind from the beginning. It was as if the pilots who survived him were seeking to atone for the way many of them had resisted the idea when he was alive.

By 1945, Mirosław Ferić's wartime diary consisted of seven volumes, totaling thousands of pages.

Mirosław Ferić's death is commemorated in the diary begun by him at the beginning of the war and continued by fellow squadron members after he was killed. Beneath his photo are his combat ribbons, including his Distinguished Flying Cross ribbon. "Honor His Memory!" is written at the bottom of the page. (Polish Institute and Sikorski Museum)

It took some time for word of Ferić's death to reach his mother back in Poland. Because of the difficulty in communicating between England and Nazi-occupied Poland, Jadwiga Ferić had had only one letter from her beloved Mika in the years since she had last seen him. Actually, it was just a postcard, saying that life in England was good and that his superiors were pleased with him. But he did arrange for parcels of food—chocolate, sardines, coffee, and other scarce delicacies—to be sent to her through secret channels, and those parcels continued to arrive even after his death. Otherwise, for the rest of the war, Jadwiga had no tangible memento of her son's service in France and England.

After the war, a friend of Ferić's sent her a few of his things: some of his decorations, the Polish Air Force eagle insignia from his uniform, a few small photographs of the Spitfire's wreckage and Mika's grave, a first edition of Arkady Fiedler's book about the Kościuszko Squadron. She memorized the parts of the book about Mika and, in tears, often recited them to herself at night as she tried to sleep. But there was something else in this sad little collection—a small black-and-white photograph of a curly-haired blond toddler, no more than two years old, in the arms of a drably dressed older woman. On the back of the photo were the words: "Philip and his nanny."

Philip was Mika's son, the result of a wartime affair with a young Englishwoman, to whom he was engaged at the time of his death. The young woman was devastated by Ferić's death, recalled one of his colleagues, but she soon slipped from sight, and no one knew what happened to her. The man who sent the photo to Ferić's mother knew nothing about her, not even her name. In years to come, Ferić's brother, in Poland, tried without success to trace the boy. Jadwiga Ferić clung to the fading photograph as the only evidence of her English grandson that she would ever possess. After her death, the photo was kept by Mika's brother and, after his death, by his son, Mika's nephew. The family speculated that Philip's mother probably married after the war and that the child never knew that his father was a young Polish pilot who had once kept a squadron diary and who had helped defend England in its darkest, finest hour.

ON MARCH 13, barely a month after Ferić's death, the Kościuszko Squadron was assigned to escort a formation of Boston bombers to a target in Holland. The night before the mission, several of the pilots, including Witold Łokuciewski, went to see the Charlie Chaplin film *The Gold Rush.* They liked it so much that they bought tickets to see it again the next night, after they had returned from the bombing run. Before climbing into their Spitfires, however, they gave the movie tickets and everything else in their pockets to the squadron's intelligence officer. That was standard procedure. If they were shot down and captured, they didn't want the contents of their pockets to give away any information about the unit or its location.

The flight to the target was uneventful, but on the return, over French territory, a swarm of Me-109s attacked. Locked in a duel with one of the Messerschmitts, Łokuciewski felt a sudden, sharp pain in his left leg. Smoke began pouring from his engine. His controls were immobilized. Looking back, he saw that half his tail fin had been shot away. He prepared for a crash landing, but moments later the engine burst into flames and the cockpit filled with smoke. Barely conscious, his shattered shinbone protruding from his leg, Łokuciewski flipped the Spitfire over and bailed out. He landed hard on a plowed, frozen field, unconscious. Captured by the Germans a few minutes later, he was taken to a hospital in Saint-Omer, where he underwent surgery on his leg, still containing more than thirty shrapnel fragments from a previous engagement.

Not long afterward, Łokuciewski was transferred to a hospital in Germany, and following a short convalescence, was shipped to *Stalag Luft III,* a prisoner-of-war camp near Sagan, in an area of Poland that had been annexed by Germany. By the time of his arrival, the camp's other inmates, most of them RAF and Allied airmen, were deeply involved in the planning of what became famous in later years (in a movie, among other media) as "the Great Escape." It didn't take long for Łokuciewski to join the plotters.

After he had been shot down, Łokuciewski's Kościuszko Squadron comrades flew over the area in a futile attempt to locate him, finally giving him up for dead. That night, a Kościuszko pilot jotted down his bleak, somewhat disjointed thoughts in the Ferić diary: "Dear 'Tolo' is the second of the ... Musketeers to go; a month ago Ox died in an accident. This is bad, you guys. [Y]ou were the backbone of our squadron, of its fame in combat. Now that the two of you are gone, we feel as if an arm is missing.... You had a wild side, and you gave your commanders many headaches, but now, looking back, we would gladly have the trouble you caused all over again.... It is so hard to believe that you are no more, that you will not come back. Tolo, as recently as yesterday, we were together at the cinema, we were happy and having a good time, and today, you are gone.... None of us knows the answer."

———

THE FAMED RAF ace Peter Townsend once described the war as a "charnel house, where most of my friends had now become burnt and mutilated corpses." But for Townsend, as for other British pilots, "this hideous slaughter" was balanced by the fact that they were dying to defend a "country we loved, which had nourished us and breathed its formidable, unconquerable spirit into our souls." The Poles were dying, too, but there did not seem to be any immediate benefit for Poland.

Polish pilots felt anguish and guilt over their inability to help their countrymen, who, thanks to underground radio broadcasts and the Polish resistance's information network, nevertheless knew all about Polish contributions to the Battle of Britain and revered the pilots as heroes. Among the clandestine supplies dropped by parachute into Poland by RAF planes were photographs, stories, and books about the Poles flying in England. One underground leader recalled how he and other members of the resistance once unpacked a canister from the latest parachute drop and found in it a pile of photos of Polish pilots in RAF uniforms: "Everybody grabbed them. We looked at them, deeply moved." One young woman burst into tears. "How wonderful they are," she sobbed. "How handsome!"

Arkady Fiedler's book, *Squadron 303*, was also among the material parachuted into Poland. There, the book was copied on microfilm, then made into a tiny edition the size of a pack of playing cards. This 303 "pack of cards" proved so popular throughout Poland that the resistance publishers could not keep up with the huge demand.

"We left the country to continue the fight, but our hearts are with you," Mika Ferić had declared in a propaganda broadcast to occupied Poland shortly before his death. "In September 1940, our squadron was the best in the entire British empire, shooting down the largest number

Witold Łokuciewski (left) with two Kościuszko Squadron colleagues. (Polish Institute and Sikorski Museum)

of planes in the shortest time. We did this for you, for Poland.... We will not be a disappointment. We will return to Poland, to you.... Rest assured, we will not let you down."

The prospect of transforming those words into direct action remained remote, however, and the Poles, helpless as they were to do anything to liberate their own tortured land, experienced a sense of isolation and increasing melancholy. "Memories of home and religion—these are the only things left to them," wrote a British pilot, "and to these they cling with a tenacity that we, who have never been dispossessed, can barely comprehend. They have no country, but they carry Poland in their hearts." A young British woman who met several Polish fliers at a pub recalled how they came calling one Sunday afternoon, not to see her but to "gather at my grandmother's feet, to tell her about home and family in Craców and Warsaw."

The only reminders of home that most pilots had were a few tattered photos of wives, parents, girlfriends, children. Many had heard little or nothing from their loved ones since they left Poland in 1939, and the news filtering out of there now made them fear the worst. "The Polish airmen are charming," remarked a British education officer. "They have a sense of humor. But most of them have sad eyes. One does not like to ask the Poles about their families."

―――――――

ON NOVEMBER 9, 1939, just a month after Germany had vanquished Poland, the professors of Jagiellonian University in Kraków were summoned, ostensibly for a lecture, to the school's main building, the magnificent Collegium Maius. Founded in 1364 by Kazimierz the Great, the university was the country's oldest and one of the most distinguished centers of higher learning in all of Europe. The Polish astronomer Mikołaj Kopernik (Nicholas Copernicus, as he is known in the non-Polish world) was among its many illustrious alumni; in 1939, its students included Karol Wojtyła, the future Pope John Paul II. The school was the embodiment of intellectual life in Poland, which was why the Nazis decided to begin their mass arrests there.

A few Jagiellonian professors, suspicious of the summons, stayed away on that rainy November morning. But almost 200 others—some of Poland's most notable scholars—crowded into the medieval lecture hall. They were met by a squad of SS storm troopers carrying rifles and machine guns. Hands high, these professors of law, history, biology, and literature, among other disciplines, were marched through the fifteenth-century arcaded courtyard and loaded into trucks and vans, which carried them to Sachsenhausen concentration camp in Germany. After the scholars were gone, the SS ransacked the university, tearing apart its libraries and wrecking its laboratories. At Sachsenhausen, some of the professors were tortured. Many were dead in a matter of months.

"All Poles will disappear from the earth," SS chief Heinrich Himmler, the former chicken farmer turned chief Nazi executioner, had declared at the beginning of the German occupation of Poland. Like the Jews, Poles and other Slavs were regarded by the Nazis as *Untermenschen*, subhumans, who, in Hitler's view, occupied land meant for the expansion of the Aryan "master race." The eradication of the Poles and their nation, the destruction of their culture and identity, would begin with the systematic liquidation of their educated elite, those considered most likely to rise up and challenge Nazi rule. In the first months and years of the war, the slaughter of the country's leadership was the SS's top priority in Poland.

The Holocaust was unique. Under the Nazis, Jews, regardless of country, were to suffer unimaginable horrors. No single group suffered more. But the full, terrible machinery for their mass liquidation would not be in place for another two years. In the meantime, they were herded into ever shrinking, ever more appalling urban ghettos, while the Nazis concentrated on murdering non-Jewish Poles.

The main killing ground was the country's midsection, known by the Germans as the "General Government." This area contained some 13 million people and the country's three major cities—Warsaw, Kraków, and Lublin. The residents now included Polish Christians and Jews who had lived in the western part of the country and who had been uprooted and shipped east when their native regions were absorbed for German *Lebensraum.*

Presiding over the campaign of terror in central Poland as head of the General Government was one Hans Frank. A lawyer and former president of the German Bar Association, Frank was, in other circumstances and other surroundings, a smooth, cultivated man. But he could be, in William Shirer's words, "icy, efficient, ruthless, and bloodthirsty." In Berlin, Shirer wrote in his diary: "My information is that there will be no Polish race left when Dr. Frank and his Nazi thugs get through with them."

Certainly, the Nazi definition of "educated elite" was so broad that a wide swath of Polish society was caught up in the net of the Death's Head Brigade—SS troops who had formerly served as concentration camp guards and who were now turned loose on Poland. Lawyers, doctors, priests, teachers, writers, artists, journalists, and businessmen were among those yanked from their beds or pulled off streetcars or snatched from offices and classrooms, to be executed immediately or transferred to concentration camps.

Eventually, the definition of an intellectual would include anyone with a higher or secondary education. Eventually, no one was safe. The banshee wail of police sirens echoed night and day through Warsaw, Kraków, and other cities. Carloads of men in black shirts and brown ties, their caps and collars adorned with a silver skull and crossbones, careened through the streets, the muzzles of their automatic weapons aimed at passersby. Anyone who caught their interest, for any reason, could be arrested on the spot. The terror was utterly random. Those who were picked up could be shot immediately, or hauled off to jail, probably to be shot or hanged later. But two other fates were also possible, both of which often ended in death: those arrested could be sent as slave laborers to Germany, or they could end up in Auschwitz or one of several work camps.*

The historian John Lukacs has observed of the Poles that "[n]one of Germany's enemies on the continent fought more bravely and more hopelessly; none of Germany's enemies was handled with such a frightful mixture of brutality, torture and truly inhuman contempt."

By 1941, street executions, torture, and large-scale deportations to labor and death camps had become everyday occurrences in Polish cities. In Warsaw, "volleys of shots in the streets were as common as the ringing of church bells elsewhere," declared a Polish resistance leader. In villages and small towns throughout the General Government, there were hundreds of mass killings: 215 people killed in Skłoby; 232 in Borów; 370 in Lipniak. A notorious act of Nazi barbarism—the destruction of the town of Lidice in Czechoslovakia and the murder of almost 200 of its citizens—was multiplied many times over in Poland. Asked about the distinction between Nazi killings in Czechoslovakia and Poland, Hans Frank remarked: "In Prague, large red posters were put up announcing that seven Czechs were shot [in one] day.... If I wanted to put up a poster for every seven Poles shot, the forests of Poland would not suffice to produce the paper for such posters."

To the rest of the world, it had become clear that the decimation of Poles by the Nazis far surpassed the savagery in any other German-occupied country. In London, Winston Churchill used a powerfully graphic figure of speech to underscore the difference: "Every week

---

* Auschwitz is infamous as the extermination site of more than a million Jews. Initially, however, it was intended as an internment center for Poles generally, regardless of religion or ethnicity. On June 14, 1940, the same day German troops marched into Paris, more than 700 Polish men, many of whom had been caught trying to cross the border to join the Polish army in France, were the first prisoners to arrive at Auschwitz. In the course of the war, well over 150,000 Poles would be sent there, and more than half that number would be put to death. Hundreds of thousands more would be taken to Majdanek, Treblinka, Sobibor, and other places in the metastasizing network of Nazi death and slave labor camps in Poland.

Polish women being led to their executions by Nazi troops. (Library of Congress)

[Hitler's] firing parties are busy in a dozen lands. Mondays he shoots Dutchmen. Tuesdays, Norwegians. Wednesdays, French or Belgians stand against the wall. Thursdays, it is the Czechs who must suffer, and now there are the Serbs and the Greeks to fill his repulsive bill of executions. But always, all the days, there are the Poles." Added Seymour Cocks, a Labour member of Parliament: "We are witnessing in Poland the cold-blooded and deliberate murder of a nation."

Poles who escaped execution or the camps (in many cases, a merely temporary condition) were treated by the Nazis as virtual slaves. It was illegal for Poles to stroll in public parks, make calls from public phone booths, ride in taxis, or have their teeth filled with gold. A Pole could be shot for not making way on the sidewalk for a German or for not doffing his hat when a German approached.

Vowing to turn Poland into an "intellectual desert," Hans Frank shut down universities, schools, museums, theaters, and libraries. Poles were to be given a minimal education—"just enough," Himmler said, "to recognize road signs." Books by Polish authors were burned, the playing of musical works by Polish composers was forbidden. Monuments to Kościuszko and other Polish patriots were dynamited. The majestic statue of Chopin in Warsaw's Łazienki Park was pulled down and dismantled for scrap iron. Polish newspaper offices were closed, and all radios were to be turned in to the Nazi authorities. If a Pole was caught listening to a radio or singing the Polish national anthem, the penalty was immediate death.

The American poet and writer Stephen Vincent Benét, writing in a September 1942 issue of *The New Republic*, tried to capture for his readers the enormity of what was happening: "Let us imagine the closing of every college in [America], the deliberate destruction of Mount Vernon, the Statue of Liberty and the Lincoln Memorial ... and the shooting of boys who whistled 'The Star Spangled Banner.' Let us imagine starvation, typhus and death. We shall then get a very faint and feeble idea of what the New Order has meant to Poland and her people."

———————

POLAND OF COURSE was not unfamiliar with the burdens of occupation and partition, nor with devising ways to resist. Centuries of living between Germany and Russia had seen to that. And although no prior atrocities could match the Nazis' barbarism, not even they were able to quench the fire in the Polish spirit. Poland was the only occupied nation in which the Nazis were unable to find quislings to form a puppet government. There were some Poles, particularly in rural areas, who were guilty of more or less unofficial collaboration. The 1941 murder of hundreds of Jews in the village of Jedwabne is perhaps the most notorious example. But there were virtually no prominent Nazi collaborators in Warsaw or any of the other large Polish cities. In that respect, Poland stood alone, undivided, swearing allegiance to no administration but the Polish government-in-exile in London. Its resistance movement began organizing the day before Warsaw fell, and the country's first underground weekly newspaper appeared three weeks later.

Poland's resistance movement, the largest, most sophisticated, and best organized in all of Europe, made clear that it expected Poles to defy the Germans in every way possible, from noncooperation to outright sabotage. Many, if not most, Poles met the resistance's expectations and then some.

Wanda Krasnodębska was typical. The wife of the Kościuszko Squadron commander remained in Warsaw for almost the entire war. By day, she worked for Polish social service organizations, first caring for elderly people, then for children. At night, she was a courier for the resistance, carrying clandestine messages and dispatches and distributing underground literature. She also sheltered Poles who were hiding from the Nazis, including Polish intelligence operatives who had parachuted in from London and, in at least one instance, a fugitive from Auschwitz. If she had been caught in any of these activities, the penalty would have been summary execution at worst, deportation to a camp at best.

Wanda Krasnodębska, wife of the Kościuszko Squadron commander. Krasnodębska was a member of the Polish resistance throughout the war. (Stanisław Blasiak)

Wanda also courted death by listening to the radio. One spring night in 1940, she and other members of the underground were crowded around a secret receiver, listening to the latest news of the German invasion of France, when the announcer read off the names of some of the Polish pilots who were then flying in France's defense. Krasnodębska's heart caught when she heard the name "Zdzisław Krasnodębski." It was the first she had heard of her husband since he had said good-bye to her the previous September.

Millions of Poles mounted the same kind of resistance, creating a remarkable secret society that operated under the noses of their German occupiers. Throughout the country, orchestras and chamber quartets performed behind closed doors, as did troupes of professional and amateur actors. In response to the closure of schools and universities, clandestine classes were held for more than a million children and young adults in apartments and homes across Poland. In Kraków, Jagiellonian University, like other major Polish institutions of higher learning, reorganized itself underground, offering study in all its departments. More than 800 students, including the future pope, Karol Wojtyła, attended the classes.

Although the Polish resistance flourished throughout the country, its greatest strength was in Warsaw, which the Nazis dubbed "the city of bandits." From his Kraków headquarters, Hans Frank declared: "We have in this country one point which is the source of all evil: that is Warsaw. If we had no Warsaw in the General Government, we would not have four-fifths of the difficulties to contend with. Warsaw is, and will continue to be, a hotbed of turbulence, a point from which unrest spreads over the country." Frank probably overstated his case against Warsaw—there was plenty of opposition to the Nazis elsewhere in Poland—but the capital was unquestionably the epicenter of resistance.

Early in the war, the following Nazi notice was posted in Warsaw and other Polish cities: "You are hereby warned that every attempt at rebellion will be drowned in a sea of blood." Varsovians were not deterred. A symbol resembling a large anchor, actually the letters P and W joined together, was splashed in red paint on walls throughout the capital. It stood for *Polska Walczy*—"Poland Fights." And the anti-Nazi graffiti didn't end there. At one point, young resistance members slipped through the city at night, altering a single letter of a ubiquitous Nazi placard, written in German. The placard was supposed to read: "Germany Stands Tall on All Fronts." As altered, it read: "Germany Lies Fallen on All Fronts." On another occasion, the resistance managed to tap into the Nazi loudspeaker system in Warsaw: suddenly, the stirring strains of the Polish national anthem could be heard throughout the city. Almost as one, pedestrians stopped and took off their hats. Many wept.

When the Germans pulled down a monument to Jan Kiliński, a hero of Tadeusz Kościuszko's anti-Russian rebellion in 1794, and placed it in the cellar of the National Museum, a message was scrawled the next day on one of the museum's outside walls: PEOPLE OF WARSAW, I'M IN HERE!—JAN KILINSKI. It was clear that the Poles' sharp wit had survived Nazi barbarity. "Laughter was the redeeming feature that saved us from going mad," said one underground member. "If we had not been able to laugh occasionally, we would not have survived the five frightful years of occupation." One of the most popular underground books published during the occupation, a collection of anti-Nazi jokes, was entitled *The Germans—Laugh at Them.*

More serious books were published as well, along with more than a thousand underground newspapers and journals. Listening posts were set up to monitor radio broadcasts from London, and the news from those broadcasts was printed in widely distributed secret bulletins. In turn, reports of what was happening in Poland—the latest German decrees, arrests, tortures, executions—were sent to the British capital on microfilm smuggled out by couriers or tapped out in code by underground radio operators on transmitters squirreled away in attics or basements. Gestapo communications vans roamed the streets, trying to fix on the locations of the clandestine radio signals, and often succeeding. For the wireless operators, discovery and death were never more than a few moments away.

As the war continued, news of the growing horror of the Holocaust was also transmitted to the West by the Polish underground. Some 3 million Jews—10 percent of the population—had lived in Poland at the beginning of the conflict. After the Germans gained control, they uprooted Jews from all over the country and herded them into ghettos in Warsaw, Kraków, and other cities in the General Government. In Warsaw alone, more than 450,000 Jews were jammed into an area of less than 3 square miles.

As appalling as life was for Polish Christians under Nazi occupation, it was incomparably worse for Jews in the ghettos. Hunger, for instance, was a fact of life for most Poles, but the Jews faced starvation. By 1942, many of the Warsaw Ghetto's inhabitants were little more than walking skeletons, their eyes sunken and glassy. Hundreds were dying daily, and the stench of decomposing corpses filled the air.

As far as Hitler was concerned, however, the Jews weren't dying fast enough. In 1942, the Nazis began building a string of camps in Poland— Majdanek, Treblinka, Bełżec, and Sobibor, among others. Their purpose—their only purpose—was to kill as many people, primarily Jews, in as efficient a manner as possible. The largest of the killing grounds was Birkenau, an extension of Auschwitz, where torture and murder were made a science. Jews from the ghettos of Warsaw and other Polish cities were the first to be sent to the new death camps. As the "Final Solution" reached its full fury, Jews from all over Europe began to arrive in Poland in German freight and cattle cars.

Reports of these "wholesale murders" were passed on by the Polish underground to the government-in-exile in London, which, in turn, sent the news on to the British and U.S. governments. "You Poles in England must be made to believe things it is apparently impossible to believe, and you must try to make the English and Americans believe it," declared one such report in the summer of 1942. "The total number of Jewish victims now exceeds one million and is constantly increasing.... [Yet] the world regards all these crimes, which are more terrible than anything that has ever happened in the history of mankind, with a calm eye. Millions of helpless people are being massacred, and silence is maintained.... This silence cannot be tolerated any longer."

One underground Polish courier, Jan Karski, managed to smuggle himself into a death camp near Izbica, posing as an Estonian camp guard, to witness the killings firsthand. After getting out and then making his way to London, he described what he had seen to Foreign Secretary Anthony Eden and other members of the British government, and later, in Washington, to President Roosevelt. Karski, like General Sikorski and other officials of the Polish government-in-exile, appealed to the Western leaders for a prompt and vigorous response to the Holocaust. The Poles proposed, among other things, that the death camps and the railroad tracks leading to them be bombed, and that civilian centers in Germany be targeted in retaliation.

As it turned out, British and American officials did little more than condemn the slaughter, and that rather belatedly. Only an all-out Allied victory could aid the Jews, they declared. The Poles were quite familiar with such reasoning: Britain had used it about Poland after the German invasion in 1939. How, Poles wondered, could victory help the Jews in their country if the vast majority of them were dead by the time victory was finally won?

But the Polish resistance was not content just to tell the world what was happening to the Jews. It also tried to help them. In the fall of 1942, the underground established the Relief Council for Polish Jews. This organization, whose code name was *Żegota,* found hiding places for Jews outside the ghettos. It also provided them with money, forged identification documents, food, and medical care. After the war, *Żegota* was one of only three organizations singled out by Yad Vashem, the Israeli memorial to the Holocaust, for their work in rescuing Jews.

Of the some 19,000 individuals honored by Yad Vashem, almost six thousand—nearly a third—are Poles. Of the forty countries whose citizens are cited as "the Righteous Among Nations," Poland ranks first, even though only in Poland were citizens and their families immediately executed if caught trying to help Jews.

Israel Gutman, a former Yad Vashem official, estimated that approximately 40,000 Jews were saved by Poles during the war. "This is no doubt a tiny percentage of prewar Jewry," Gutman said, "but nonetheless, it's a glorious human achievement."

CHAPTER TWELVE

"Are There Any Frozen Children?"

IF AUSCHWITZ AND Treblinka were the ultimate expressions of Nazi barbarism, Joseph Stalin's camps in the Kolyma region of northern Siberia were their Soviet counterparts. There were no gas chambers in Kolyma; inmates died more slowly there—of starvation, exposure, and disease.

One of the coldest places on earth, much of Kolyma lies above the Arctic Circle, a land of darkness, howling blizzards, and despair. Temperatures during the long winters commonly fall to 60 degrees below zero. Stalin established more than 100 slave labor camps in the region, part of the infamous Gulag Archipelago. The camps were for "enemies of the people," which is how the Soviet government classified all Poles who resisted the Red Army's 1939 invasion, or who opposed communism, or who in any other way stood for Polish independence and sovereignty.

In the course of World War II, untold thousands of Polish inmates perished in the Kolyma camps. Dressed in rags, they were literally worked to death in mines, scratching through the permafrost for gold and other minerals. Less than a quarter of the prisoners interned in the camps are believed to have survived their first winter. Those who grew too feeble to work were shot. The many who died in accidents had their hands cut off to prove their deaths to ranking officials, and their bodies were thrown away. The few who did manage to survive and eventually return to civilization were little more than skeletons, many having lost noses, ears, fingers, and toes to frostbite.

UNDER THE TERMS of their nonaggression pact with Hitler, the Soviets were entitled to the eastern half of Poland. Like Hitler, Stalin first singled out the educated Polish elite for elimination. Indeed, officers of the NKVD (a forerunner of the KGB) met regularly with representatives of the Nazi SS to coordinate their twin repressions. Local government officials, lawyers, landowners, priests, writers, students, doctors, and teachers—and their families—were among the first to be rounded up by the NKVD. Later, anyone seen as even a theoretical threat to Soviet rule was shipped to the gulags. (Although large numbers of Polish Jews ended up there, the Soviets, unlike the Germans, did not specifically target Jews.)

In these murderous campaigns, Hitler and Stalin were hoping to finish what their predecessors—the tsars, emperors, and kaisers—had begun in the eighteenth and nineteenth centuries: erasing Poland from the face of the earth. "The Polish nation, as a nation, was to be destroyed once and for all... by the selective murder of all its potential leaders," noted the British writer Louis FitzGibbon. "... Poland, one of the great historic nation states of Europe, was to be so destroyed that it could never rise again."

The Poles, of course, weren't the only inmates in the Kolyma camps. There were citizens of the Baltic states, which also had been occupied by the Soviets at the beginning of the war. Hundreds of thousands of Russians and people from other ethnic groups in the vast patchwork quilt of Soviet "nationalities" were in the camps as well—all treated with the same savagery. Stalin had first sanctioned the widespread use of forced labor camps, along with other means of terror and repression, in the late 1920s and early 1930s. He did so in order to achieve collectivization and industrialization in the Soviet Union—then, increasingly, to feed his own power madness and paranoia. Poles who were sent to Soviet camps and jails soon learned a popular adage: "In the Soviet Union, there are only three categories of people—those who were in prison, those who are in prison, and those who will be in prison."

In the late 1930s, at the height of the Great Terror, an estimated 19 million Soviet citizens were arrested on charges of conspiring against their government. Millions were put to death immediately. Many others died in the gulags. On one day alone, in December 1937, Stalin and his chief henchman, Vyacheslav Molotov, personally approved 3,167 death sentences—then adjourned to Stalin's living quarters in the Kremlin to enjoy a movie. Moscow's crematoria were hardpressed to keep up with the production of corpses. "There was this funny ash that fell from the sky every once in a while," a Moscow resident recalled.

The madness reached epic proportions. When the Soviet national census revealed that the frenzy of executions, touching every level of Soviet society, had caused a serious decline in the country's population, Stalin ordered the members of the census board shot. Most senior army, navy, and air force commanders were killed in the purges, among them Mikhail Tukachevsky, the young Soviet general who had overseen the invasion of Poland in 1920. Also murdered were most of the top Soviet political leaders. Their executions followed highly publicized show trials, during which many confessed to "crimes" they clearly did not commit.

———————

DURING THE TWENTY-ONE months that the Soviets occupied eastern Poland, from September 1939 to June 1941, an estimated 1.5 million Polish citizens were taken from their homes and deported in freight trains to Siberia and other Soviet regions. About 52 percent of those deported were ethnic Poles, 30 percent Jewish, and 18 percent Ukrainian and Byelorussian. Three massive waves of deportations took place in the first half of 1940. A fourth occurred in June 1941 and was halted only when Hitler betrayed Stalin and ordered the Wehrmacht to invade the Soviet Union. For the Poles who survived these journeys, which covered thousands of miles and sometimes lasted a month or more, the unspeakable conditions on the train were but a precursor of what was to come.

The terror often began in the middle of the night. First, there was the pounding on the door, then the crash of its being forced open. Red Army soldiers and NKVD agents rushed in with rifles and rousted sleeping families from their beds. The intruders' curses and shouts mingled with the victims' bewildered questions, the wailing of babies, the sobbing of children. As a rule, a family was given no more than half an hour to pack—a panicked, frantic few minutes of throwing clothes, photographs, other family treasures and mementos into suitcases.

Then, prodded and jabbed by Russian rifles, the Poles were hurried out into the darkness and forced onto a peasant cart waiting by the door. As the cart trundled through the grave-silent village or town, it would pass places where patriotic monuments and religious shrines had been torn down. Street signs were now in Russian or Ukrainian (Cyrillic letters) instead of Polish (Latin letters). The cart finally stopped at the square in front of the local train station, where hundreds of other dazed and frightened Poles were milling about. A locomotive coupled to a long string of freight cars stood at the railway platform, waiting.

The Poles were packed like livestock into the cars, with no place to sit or lie down, no toilets, no windows, no heat. Many days, they were given no food or water. "The lack of bread and heat drove people mad," recalled one Polish survivor of the deportations. Another survivor declared: "I can describe this in a few words: it was the murder of babies and children... the death penalty without sentencing or guilt. One lacks words to speak about the horror of this thing, and one who has not lived through it could never believe what happened."

Thousands froze to death along the way, or died of starvation or disease, their corpses remaining in the freight cars until the trains made one of their infrequent stops. At each stop, dozens of bodies, many of them infants and children, were stacked up like cordwood along the tracks. Soviet soldiers went from one car to the next, asking, "Are there any frozen children?"

One of the Poles who perished en route to Russia was Witold Łokuciewski's father. Łokuciewski, the headmaster of a school near Wilno, was dragged from his home so hurriedly late one winter night that he didn't even have time to put on his shoes. Wearing bedroom slippers, he was led away—and never seen again by his wife and family. Later, they heard he had died on the way east.

Of the survivors of these hellish trips, about half ended up in slave labor camps, many in the Kolyma region. The others, at least a quarter of them children, were dumped onto collective farms and other settlements on the Siberian plain or in arid Central Asia. They were left there to survive any way they could. It has been estimated that between a third and a half of all the deported Poles were dead by the time of the Nazi attack on the Soviet Union. Nobody knows for sure. Most of them vanished into Stalin's archipelago and were never heard of again.

HIGH ON THE Soviet list of "enemies of the people" were officers in the Polish military. In this, the Russians differed greatly from the Germans. As savage as the Nazis were to Polish civilians, they generally treated their Polish prisoners of war according to international conventions. The Soviets, in contrast, considered their military captives, among them hundreds of Polish pilots, to be political prisoners, to be dealt with as the Kremlin decreed.

In November 1939, more than 15,000 Polish officers, including many in the army's top field command, were removed by the Russians from prisoner-of-war transit centers and sent to three makeshift prisons in western Russia. About half the prisoners were reservists, mostly civilian professionals, who had been called to active duty shortly before the German invasion. In their ranks were 21 university professors, more than 300 doctors and 200 lawyers, several hundred elementary and high school teachers, journalists, artists, judges, an Olympic athlete, at least one priest, and the chief rabbi of the Polish army.

Early the following year, Lavrenti Beria, head of the NKVD, recommended the executions of all these Polish officers, whom he described as "hardened and uncompromising enemies of Soviet authority." The order to exterminate them was approved on March 5, 1940, by the Politburo and signed by Stalin. In April, as the Russian winter slowly melted into spring, Polish officers at one of the prisons, near Kozelsk, about 200 miles southwest of Moscow, were given to understand that they were to be repatriated in groups to Poland. Joyful at the news, the first group left the prison and was loaded onto a train, greatly envied by those left behind. To the puzzlement of the men in the first group, their train traveled west only a few hours before stopping at a railway siding outside Katyn Forest, near Smolensk. This was in an area, near the Byelorussian border, that Poland, Russia, the Ukraine, and Lithuania had fought over for centuries, and that now belonged to Russia. From the siding, some of the Poles were loaded into black vans and taken to a small clearing in the woods. It was a lovely early-spring day, marked by the pale warmth of the sun and the delicate scent of new grass and wildflowers. Here and there, small patches of snow, the last remnants of winter, lay on the ground.

The Polish officers stepped out of the vans, most wearing the uniforms in which they had been captured, down to their signature black boots of

calf leather, handmade and still lovingly burnished, in spite of their cap-
tors, to a soft sheen. During those final moments of their lives, among the
last things the prisoners saw were dozens of NKVD men armed with pistols and bayonets, and a large pit dug at the side of the clearing. The prisoners were shoved to the edge of the pit and forced to kneel. Then each
was shot in the back of the head. Those who struggled—and there seem to
have been many who did—were stabbed repeatedly with bayonets. Some
had their mouths filled with sawdust. A choke knot was tied around their
necks, and their hands were lashed together behind their backs and
pulled upward, connected by a cord to the knot around their necks. If
they continued to resist, they strangled themselves.

When the killing was finished, the bodies were pitched into the mass
grave "with the precision of machines coming off a production belt," as
Sir Owen O'Malley, British ambassador to the Polish government-in-

*An international delegation
inspects one of the pits at
Katyn, in Russia, in which
more than 4,000 Polish officers
were buried. (Imperial War
Museum)*

exile, later put it. With this first contingent of Poles taken care of, the vans returned to the trains for more. The next bunch "must have seen a monstrous sight," O'Malley speculated. "In the broad deep pit their comrades lay, packed closely round the edge, head to feet, like sardines in a tin.... Up and down on the bodies the executioners tramped, hauling the [corpses] about and treading in the blood like butchers in a stockyard."

For more than five weeks, the convoys of death from the Kozelsk prison to the forest continued. By the middle of May, nearly 4,500 Polish military officers lay buried in eight common graves. The largest of the graves contained twelve layers of bodies. Among the dead were more than 200 air force pilots. Some had been friends and Dęblin classmates of pilots in the Kościuszko Squadron. One of the victims was the brother-in-law of Witold Łokuciewski. Atop the burial ground, the Poles' killers planted a grove of birches, hoping to cover up, literally and figuratively, what they had done.

From intercepted letters that had been sent to the murdered men while in prison, the NKVD compiled a list of their families, many of whom—unaware of the fate of their husbands, fathers, and sons at Katyn—were later rounded up and also shipped east, into the Soviet darkness.

———

ON FEBRUARY 9, 1941, a year after the Soviets began the mass deportations, the *New York Times* reported that Poles were being transported to Siberia and "dumped there to get along as best they can or to perish if they are not strong enough to survive." That brief story was one of the few news accounts to appear during the war about Russia's brutal occupation of eastern Poland. While Nazi atrocities were reported by the Poles themselves, it was virtually impossible for Polish victims of the Soviet terror, held captive deep inside that closed-off country, to get word out about what was happening to them.

Even so, some information did filter out—enough that many British officials, if not the public, were aware of what was going on. In August 1941, John Colville wrote in his diary: "A Pole, Count Zamoyski, dined with me. Also confirmed what I have been told previously, that the Russian occupation of Poland was on the whole more terrible than the

German." By then, however, the British government had no intention of publicizing the frightfulness of Soviet rule over Poland, which the American diplomat and historian George Kennan would later label as "little short of genocide." By then, the Soviet Union, having been invaded by Germany on June 22, was in the Allied camp.

———————

MORE THAN HALF a century after the fact, World War II's "Grand Alliance" of Britain, the Soviet Union, and the United States (after December 7, 1941) seems almost to have been preordained. It was hardly that. The 1939 German-Soviet nonaggression pact may have been a marriage of convenience between two natural antagonists, but the convenience to both was considerable, and the marriage might have lasted a good deal longer had Hitler proved more faithful to his vows. Certainly, in the early going, Stalin did his part. While Fascist Italy protected and expanded Germany's southern flank, the Soviet Union invaded Poland from the east soon after Hitler invaded from the west. Then, as the Wehrmacht prepared to assault Scandinavia and Western Europe, Stalin took the Baltic countries and ordered the Red Army into Finland. Following those successes, he stood quietly by as the Germans rolled up country after country—Norway, Denmark, the Low Countries, France—and attacked Great Britain at sea and from the air.

Nor were these Stalin's only contributions to the German war effort. He also provided oil, grain, cotton, iron ore, and other crucial raw materials—assistance that was, according to the German War Office, "of decisive military importance" in the Nazi offensive, thwarting Britain's attempts to cut off German supplies through a naval blockade. Hitler could hardly have asked for more from an ally. As the Führer himself acknowledged in the fall of 1939, Stalin's support, active and passive, would make it possible for him to attack France and Britain by ensuring that the war would be waged on only one front at a time.

Hitler's betrayal the following summer came as an enormous shock to Stalin, who had ignored warning after warning from Churchill and others of an imminent German attack. In one of the war's great ironies, the Russian dictator found it impossible to believe that Hitler could be so treacherous. "Stalin distrusted [almost] everyone," observed Ivan Maisky, the Soviet ambassador to Britain during much of the war. "The only man he trusted was Hitler." Even after German troops invaded Soviet territory, it took Stalin several crucial days to recover his wits and begin to direct a credible defense.

If Stalin was stunned by Hitler's violent abrogation of the nonaggression treaty, he also had difficulty accepting that his new ally was a Great Britain led by die-hard anti-Communist Winston Churchill. Churchill had always opposed what he called the "sullen, sinister Bolshevik state" and "had tried ... hard to strangle [it] at its birth." As British war minister in 1919, he supported the unsuccessful efforts of the White Russian armies to overturn the Bolshevik government, in which Stalin was then serving under Lenin as (among other things) Commissar of Nationalities. In succeeding years, Churchill continued to regard the Soviet Union as "the mortal foe of civilized freedom." He always understood, he said later, that if the Soviet Union had not been invaded by Germany, Stalin "would have watched us being swept out of existence with indifference and gleefully divided with Hitler our Empire in the East."

In 1941, however, Churchill was the soul of pragmatism. "If Hitler invaded Hell," he declared to John Colville, "I would make at least a favorable reference to the devil in the House of Commons." As much as he despised Stalin's "wicked regime," he was fully prepared to welcome it to the Allied ranks. Churchill needed the Russians to bear the brunt of a new German onslaught, to lift some of the burden of fighting from British shoulders so that he and his country could catch their breath and regroup. As Churchill saw it, the future of Britain, its empire, and his own tenure as prime minister were at stake.

By 1941, the hope and glory of the Battle of Britain had largely faded, replaced by gloom and frustration. Nothing seemed to be going right. British forces were on the defensive everywhere. Defeat had followed defeat in the Middle East, Greece, and Crete, and shipping losses in the Atlantic were skyrocketing, thanks to the depredations of German submarines. In North Africa, early British gains against the army of Italy's Fascist leader, Benito Mussolini, were seriously threatened by Hitler's appointment of the renowned General Erwin Rommel, soon to be known as "the Desert Fox," to command the German *Afrika Korps.* Although the likelihood of a cross-Channel invasion of Britain had subsided, the Luftwaffe continued to inflict considerable damage and death with its bombing raids. Victory was nowhere in sight, and the United States was still officially neutral.

Small wonder that Churchill was excited and encouraged when he learned on June 22, 1941, that Germany had launched "Operation Barbarossa"—the invasion of the Soviet Union along a huge front that stretched from the Black Sea to the Baltic. Without consulting any of his Allies, Churchill went on the radio that same night to promise unconditional support for Stalin and his country. "Any man or state who fights against Nazism will have our aid," Churchill declared. "... It follows therefore that we shall give whatever help we can to Russia and the Russian people." He never stopped to consider the long-term ramifications of so sweeping a promise to a regime so antithetical to his own beliefs and those of his nation. Indeed, he didn't think there would be any long-term ramifications. Churchill was just playing for time, convinced, like almost everyone else in the West, that Germany sooner or later—he hoped later—would crush the Soviets.

That assessment seemed to be borne out in the early weeks and months of battle on the new eastern front. At first, Stalin, in shock, his army already in disarray because of the liquidation of so many senior officers in the purges, locked himself in his study and abdicated control. German Panzers were able to roll over Soviet territory as swiftly as they had in Poland and Western Europe. In the first two days of the German offensive, the Soviet air force lost more than 2,000 aircraft—on the ground. In the first month, more than half a million Russian troops were taken prisoner. By autumn, the Nazis had occupied the Ukraine and the eastern half of Poland that the Soviets had previously held. Soon the Crimea would fall. By September, the siege of Leningrad had begun. By October, the Wehrmacht was only 40 miles from Moscow, and most of the Soviet government was being evacuated to Kuibyshev, 530 miles to the southeast.

When Stalin finally recovered his wits, it didn't take him long to begin acting with his characteristic boldness, arrogance, and deviousness. Russia was now bearing the brunt of the burden against Hitler and was close to collapse, its troops in desperate need of everything from tanks and planes to rifles and boots. Stalin was no fool. He recognized how much the opening of an eastern front benefited Britain, and he sought to take immediate advantage of the situation.

Even as Britain was shipping large amounts of war matériel to him, Stalin upped the ante. He wanted new fronts opened in the Arctic and northern France—now. He even wanted Britain to supply troops to help the Red Army fight in the east. Barely three months after the German invasion, Stalin was demanding that Churchill send 25 to 30 divisions—upward of 400,000 men—to counter the German thrust into the southern part of the Soviet Union. It was an impossible demand. When a British official in Moscow tried sweet reason with him, Stalin replied, "The paucity of your offers clearly shows that you want to see the Soviet Union defeated."

Stalin's charge infuriated the British. In October, writing to Sir Stafford Cripps, the British ambassador in Moscow, Churchill said: "[The Russians] certainly have no right to reproach us. They brought their own fate upon themselves when ... they let Hitler loose on Poland and so started the war. They cut themselves off from an effective Second Front when they let the French Army be destroyed." Anthony Eden, who had replaced Lord Halifax as British foreign secretary in December 1940, later speculated that Soviet badgering of the British government was prompted by "fear that we would stand inactively watching their life-and-death struggle, as they had watched ours."

Angry as he often was over Stalin's tactics, Churchill nonetheless was determined to conciliate the Russian dictator in every way possible. Although Stalin had little alternative but to throw everything he had at the Germans—Hitler was not going to offer him a separate peace—the specter of another Soviet-Nazi pact somehow continued to haunt London, and, later, Washington. Much would be sacrificed in the name of keeping Stalin in the fight—as Poland would soon enough discover.

————

THE FIRST INKLING of what was in store for Poland came in July 1941. Working to improve Russia's public image, the British government did its best to draw a curtain over the Soviets' earlier—and now embarrassing—collaboration with the Nazis. As the chief victim of that collaboration, Poland, Britain's most steadfast ally, was pressured to make peace with the country that had arrested, killed, or deported more than a million of its citizens.* "Whether you wish it or not, [a] treaty must be

---

* The killing of Poles by the Soviets continued even as the Germans invaded. On June 22, soon after German bombs started falling in Lwów, the NKVD herded hundreds of imprisoned Poles into jail cellars, where they were shot.

signed," Eden bluntly informed General Sikorski, prime minister of the Polish government-in-exile. As Churchill and Eden saw it, a treaty was crucial, if only to mollify and reassure the British public, whose sympathies tended to be with the Poles and whose admiration for Polish fighting ability, particularly as demonstrated in the Battle of Britain, could hardly have been greater.

Actually, Sikorski was not averse to the idea of a treaty if it would result in an independent postwar Poland. The day after the German invasion of the Soviet Union, Sikorski made a broadcast to his occupied country, declaring that Poland welcomed Russia into the fight against the Nazis and was willing to put the past aside. Sikorski had two conditions: the release of all Polish prisoners in Russia; and recognition by Stalin of Poland's prewar borders. The latter condition meant, of course, that Stalin would have to renounce all claims to the Polish territory he had grabbed in 1939, most of which was now in German hands.

For his part, Stalin wanted nothing to do with the Poles or the Polish government in London. But because he was on the brink of defeat militarily and in desperate need of British aid, he grudgingly agreed to open treaty negotiations, making it clear from the outset it would be on his terms, not Sikorski's. Moscow was willing to renounce the 1939 nonaggression pact with Hitler, the Soviet ambassador in London told the British and Polish governments, but it would not relinquish its claim to the disputed territory. That and other issues, the ambassador said, should be left to a postwar peace conference.

Under its 1939 treaty with Poland, Britain was committed to defending Polish sovereignty and independence, which, according to international law, if not always in actual practice, meant defending Polish borders as well. But Churchill and Eden were unwilling to pressure Stalin, no matter how weak his military and diplomatic positions. To assuage Polish concerns about leaving open the question of postwar borders, Eden assured Sikorski in an official note that the British government did not and would not recognize changes in Poland's borders that had taken place after August 1939. Eden also declared that Britain would not recognize any territorial changes during the war without the consent of the parties concerned.

Many, if not most, officials of the Polish government-in-exile strongly opposed the idea of postponing specific Soviet territorial guarantees, but they faced a difficult situation. More than a million of their countrymen were in effect being held hostage, under unspeakable conditions, in Soviet camps. With word filtering out that huge numbers of Poles were dying each week, it was imperative to rescue those who survived as soon as possible. Not that the motives of the Sikorski government were entirely altruistic on this point. Nearly 300,000 members of the Polish armed forces had been taken prisoner by the Soviets in September 1939; their release would greatly increase Poland's military strength—and thus its importance in the Allied scheme of things.

Prodded by these incentives and under heavy pressure from the British government, Sikorski gave in. On July 30, in the presence of Churchill and Eden, the Polish prime minister and the Soviet ambassador in London signed a treaty restoring diplomatic relations between the two countries and calling for annulment of the Nazi-Soviet nonaggression pact—without Soviet recognition of Poland's prewar borders. In addition, Polish prisoners taken by the Red Army and the NKVD were to be granted "amnesty," after which they would become part of a Polish army to be formed in the Soviet Union. This last proviso, supplied by the Soviets, was astonishing in its audacity. An implicit justification of the Russian invasion of Poland, it granted "amnesty" to people who, unlike Stalin and his government, were innocent of any crime.

Outraged by what they viewed as Sikorski's capitulation, three members of his cabinet immediately resigned. The rivalries and divisions within the government-in-exile, present from the beginning, were becoming markedly more pronounced.

ON AUGUST 4, 1941, Poland's General Władysław Anders, gaunt and ashen-faced after spending almost two years in Moscow's dread Lubyanka Prison, was released and set up in a four-room apartment, complete with cook and maid. Overnight, Anders had been transformed from an "enemy of the people" to a Soviet ally. Under the treaty that had been negotiated in London between Poland and the Soviet Union, Anders was named commander in chief of the new Polish army to be organized inside the Soviet Union.

Commander of a cavalry brigade in September 1939, the forty-seven-year-old Anders had been wounded twice—shot in the back and hip—before being captured by Soviet troops. Accused by NKVD agents of being a spy, he had been locked up in a vermin-infested Lwów prison, where he was interrogated and beaten for five months before being shipped off to Lubyanka. There, the interrogations and the beatings continued until his release in 1941.

Now, still limping badly because of his injuries, he was faced with the enormous task of assembling an army in a country that was allied to Poland in name only. The problems inherent in that task were obvious from the outset. Anders did not know the whereabouts of most of the Polish officer corps, including members of his own staff, who had been captured by the Soviets in 1939. The cream of Poland's military leadership had for the most part simply vanished. No one had heard from any of them since the spring of 1940. Evading questions about the missing Polish officers, Soviet authorities insisted they would turn up eventually. A deeply worried Anders began his own personal investigation, sending out subordinates to all parts of Russia to make inquiries. They learned nothing.

Although he badly needed the organizational skill and leadership of the missing officers, Anders didn't have time to wait for them to be found. He had an army to organize and lead, even if there weren't enough people to help. The Soviet decree granting amnesty to Polish civilians and prisoners of war had triggered a deluge: from every corner of the immense country, Poles streamed out of prisons, slave labor camps, and collective farms, all heading for several makeshift camps near the Volga River. Suffering from starvation, exhaustion, dysentery, frostbite, and countless other ailments, they journeyed for hundreds, even thousands, of miles over the taiga and steppes, many on foot. A sizable number were women and children—the latter, with their pipe-stem limbs and protruding rib cages, resembling the child survivors of Nazi concentration camps.

Of the more than 20,000 Poles who had been sent to the mines in Kolyma, only about 170 made it to the army camps on the Volga, many missing fingers and toes. From the gulags of Novaya Zemlya, an island in the Barents Sea above the Arctic Circle, several hundred prisoners of war set out for the camps, a journey of more than 3,000 miles. Along the way, all but one died of starvation or exposure, and the lone survivor collapsed and died the day he arrived. There were some slave labor

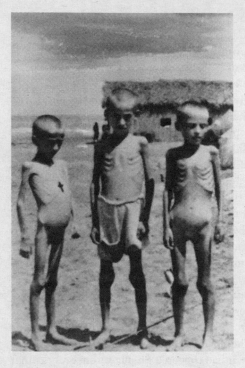

Three emaciated Polish children—survivors of Stalin's massive, brutal deportations of Poles to the Soviet Union—after their evacuation to Iran in 1942. (Corbis)

gulags from which no one at all emerged after the amnesty. Every one of the 3,000 Polish POWs who were sent to work in the lead mines of North Kamchatka, for example, died within a year, mostly from lead poisoning.

Still, there were enough survivors, not counting the many women and children, for General Anders to form his new army. In early September, the first contingents, some 17,000 troops, marched in review at one of the camps near the Volga, their feet wrapped in rags, a number of them wearing tattered old Polish uniforms. Many, Anders later recalled, looked more like corpses than soldiers—emaciated, toothless, their stooped bodies covered with sores. The general was close to despair. How could he mold these sick, starving men into a potent military force? After all they had suffered, how could they ever endure the additional physical and psychological strain of combat? The men themselves, however, seemed to have no doubts about the future. "For the first time in my life, and I hope the last, I took the salute of a march-past of soldiers without boots," Anders wrote. "They had insisted upon it. They wanted to show the Bolsheviks that even in their bare feet, and ill and wounded as many of them were, they could bear themselves like soldiers on their first march towards Poland."

The survivors' unquenchable spirit also made a powerful impression on a number of foreign visitors to the camp, including Ilya Ehrenberg, the noted Russian journalist and writer, who accompanied General Sikorski and several Russian officials on an inspection tour later in the fall. Ehrenberg was struck by the sight of "grey-haired soldiers ... and very young boys kissing the rifles they had just received. They were holding the weapons tight in their hands with radiant happiness—as one holds a beloved woman." During that same visit, Major Victor Cazalet, a British liaison officer to General Sikorski, was deeply touched by the joyous appreciation of life shown by men who "looked half-starved," whose "faces were grey, quite a different colour than those of ordinary people." In a report written on his return to London, Cazalet noted that, despite the horrors endured by the Poles, they were "smiling, laughing, singing. . . . To me, at any rate, remembrance of the Poles is a constant corrective to any thought of irritation in everyday life. It is, no less, an inspiration."

Almost as soon as people started arriving at Anders's camps, the Soviets made clear that, despite the new treaty, they did not want a strong, independent, well-equipped Polish army to be formed on their soil. They drastically cut food rations and arms shipments to Anders's units, and Polish and other foreign relief agencies, including the American Red Cross, were prevented from providing food, medicine, and clothing. As snow began to fall that autumn, and temperatures plunged to well below freezing, the Poles—soldiers and civilians alike—continued to be housed in canvas tents, heated only by primitive brick stoves. A typhoid epidemic swept the encampment. Malaria and hepatitis were rampant. Each day, dozens died from cold and disease. When Anders tried to persuade the Soviets to live up to an agreement they had made to move the army south, they came up with various excuses for delay.

As originally planned, Anders's army was to number about 300,000 men and was to train in Russia, then head west. Its initial assignment was to help the Red Army liberate Nazi-occupied Russia and Poland. Yet, during the first two months of the amnesty, only about 100,000

Poles, including women and children, made it to the camps. There were still hundreds of thousands more throughout the country who either had not been told of the amnesty or had been prevented from leaving their gulags. Anders faced a dilemma. If he pressed for evacuation, the chances were remote that his army would ever be in a position to liberate its homeland. Even worse, the countless Poles not yet freed would probably be condemned to live in Soviet detention for as long as they could survive. Yet if Anders's troops didn't leave, many of *them* would surely die.

In the end, he decided he had no choice. He had to save the lives in front of him and worry about the others later. The Russians began pressing Anders to send individual Polish divisions, under Russian command, to the front as soon as they were organized. The general refused. At the beginning of 1942, he was finally allowed to move his army and the civilians with it 1,200 miles south, to a transit center near Tashkent, in Uzbekistan. Eight months later, more than 75,000 Polish soldiers, plus about 40,000 civilians, would make another exodus of biblical proportions—this time, appropriately enough, to the Holy Land.

In Iran and Iraq, and then in British Palestine, the troops evacuated from Russia began to regain their health and to train in earnest. After a few months, they joined forces with the Carpathian Brigade, a Polish unit based in Palestine, which had already distinguished itself in fighting at Tobruk and in Libya. The new, combined force, which eventually amounted to more than 100,000 men, was called the II Polish Corps. Less than a year after the Poles left Russia, General George S. Patton, commander of the Allied task force that landed in Morocco in November 1942, would describe II Corps as "the best-looking troops, including the British and American, that I have ever seen." By 1944, under Anders's command, the corps would be, in the words of the British historian John Keegan, "one of the great fighting formations of the war."

Not all the Polish exiles ended up in the Middle East. More than 1,000 released prisoners—pilots and air crews who had been captured in September 1939 or had been turned over to the Soviets after escaping to Latvia and Lithuania—left Russia to join Polish Air Force fighter and bomber squadrons in Britain. The first group arrived in Scotland by ship in the late fall of 1941. Fellow fliers who welcomed them at the port were overwhelmed by the sight of the human wreckage shuffling slowly down the gangplank—emaciated, trembling, their faces the color of the sullen grey clouds.

Like the Polish troops in the Middle East, most of these airmen were nursed back to physical health and went on to distinguish themselves in combat. Few, however, fully recovered from the deep psychological scars of their horrific internment in the Russian gulags. One pilot who spent two years in a wind-blasted Kolyma camp insisted on keeping a small suitcase stowed beneath his bed at all times. After he was shot down and killed, his roommate opened the case and found nothing inside but a set of woolen underwear and a supply of dry biscuits.

IN THE SECOND week of August 1941, only a few days after Winston Churchill witnessed the signing of the Soviet-Polish treaty, the prime minister met with Franklin D. Roosevelt in a secret shipboard conference off Newfoundland. Although his country was still officially neutral, Roosevelt joined Churchill at the Placentia Bay meeting to proclaim the goals and principles that, according to the two leaders, should govern a postwar world.

Dubbed the Atlantic Charter, this declaration of war aims, with its pledge of equality and freedom, had a much more powerful impact than its two authors ever envisioned. It captured the imagination and sparked the hopes of people living in occupied countries throughout Europe—and none more than the Poles. In the charter, the United States and Britain committed themselves to "respect the right of all peoples to choose the form of government under which they will live." Churchill and Roosevelt specifically condemned any changes in a country's borders against its people's will and called for the restoration of "sovereign rights and self-government...to those who have been forcibly deprived of them." For almost two centuries, the West had watched in silence as Poland was denied its nationhood. Now, the leaders of the West's two leading democracies were pledging themselves to work to prevent that kind of thing from ever happening again.

It didn't take long for Stalin to puncture the idealistic bubble. In December 1941, Churchill's foreign secretary, Anthony Eden, who had resigned from the same post in 1938 to protest Neville Chamberlain's appeasement policy, traveled to Moscow to negotiate a British-Soviet treaty with Stalin. Recently, and contrary to all expectations, the Red Army had managed to stave off military defeat in the face of the German onslaught. September's near catastrophe had led to October's successful defense of Moscow, forcing a German retreat from the suburbs of the Soviet capital. The Russian victory was Hitler's first major setback on land, and it made Stalin, Britain's already difficult new ally, just that much more determined to have his own way.

Yes, he told Eden, he would be glad to affix his name to a public proclamation of high-minded generalities. But he also wanted Britain to join Russia in a *secret* agreement—in which Britain would recognize Soviet claims to eastern Poland, as well as to the Baltic states and the Finnish and Romanian territories snatched by Russia in 1939. Getting back the lands he had occupied in his days as Hitler's ally was, Stalin matter-of-factly told the British foreign secretary, "the main question for us in the war."

The brazenness of this request, which, among other things, aimed to deprive Poland permanently of half its territory and a third of its citizens, was breathtaking. Stalin was demanding that Britain ratify his aggression against a nation with which he had just concluded a treaty, an ally on whose behalf the British had gone to war in the first place— an ally, moreover, that had played a major role in the defense of Britain and was even now helping carry the fight to the Germans. Although the Soviet Union signed the Atlantic Charter, one of nine Allies to do so, Stalin was urging Churchill to join him in making a mockery of the principles the document espoused.

To justify his claims, Stalin argued that the Soviets needed eastern Poland and the other territory as a buffer to protect them from any future German aggression. The argument had little historical validity: for one thing, Soviet occupation of half of the disputed territory in June 1941 did not even slow the Germans down when they headed for the Russian motherland. But Stalin also wanted a cordon sanitaire for another reason: to keep his country free from the "contamination" of the West and its democratic influence. Like the Russian tsars before him, Stalin was determined to avoid the threat that free, independent, and prosperous neighboring countries would pose to his autocratic rule.

Like the tsars, too, Stalin was anxious to expand his country's empire. In Anthony Eden's view, Stalin "was much more the heir of Peter the Great than of Lenin, quite indifferent to ideological issues but very determined on getting the territory and the strategic frontier he wanted." Actually, in his appetite for Poland, the Soviet dictator was acting more like Catherine the Great, architect of the first three Polish partitions, than Peter.

Just as Catherine had done, Stalin cloaked his territorial ambitions in hypocrisy and guile. Poland, he argued, was entitled only to territory that had a predominantly Polish population. The Polish lands that Stalin was claiming—essentially the eastern border areas over which the Poles, Russians, and Ukrainians had contended for centuries—was populated in large part by Ukrainians and Byelorussians, nationalities that he argued were ethnically and linguistically more Russian than Polish.* Hence, Stalin contended, the Poles had no valid ethnological claim. While the Soviet Union could—and did—have many national minorities within its borders (including Byelorussians and Ukrainians), Poland, according to Stalin, could not.

In fact, Poland had far closer links to the territory than Stalin would admit. Most of the borderlands had been an integral part of the Polish state at the time of the eighteenth-century partitions. Of the area's 12 million inhabitants, roughly a third were ethnically Polish, a third Ukrainian, and the rest primarily split between Byelorussians and Jews. Fewer than 150,000 were ethnic Russians. Although the countryside in eastern Poland was heavily Ukrainian or Byelorussian, the major cities of the area, particularly Lwów, had been Polish since ancient times and were centers of Polish history and culture.

What Stalin claimed as the correct border between Poland and the Soviet Union was essentially the Ribbentrop-Molotov Line. That was the boundary agreed to by the German and Soviet foreign ministers in the 1939 nonaggression treaty under which the Soviets gained all of eastern Poland. But the Soviet leader refused to call the border by that now embarrassing name, redolent as it was of his recent, bloody part-

---

* The point is debatable. It is true, however, that the Byelorussian, Ukrainian, and Russian languages, all three of which use the Cyrillic alphabet, belong to the East Slavic branch of Common Slavic. Polish, which has used the Latin alphabet since the sixteenth century, belongs to the West Slavic branch and is more closely related to Czech, Slovak, and the Sorbian language of eastern Germany.

nership with Hitler. No, said Stalin, the rightful border was, in fact, the Curzon Line.

In truth, no one but Stalin had given much thought to the Curzon Line since it had first been suggested as a temporary demarcation during the Soviet-Polish War of 1919–20 in response to the Red Army's march on Warsaw. Part of an Allied effort to bring about an armistice, the line was based on a temporary boundary suggested several months earlier by the Supreme Allied Council, which had also declared that any interim frontier should not prejudice future Polish rights and claims to the eastern territory that lay beyond it.

In the event, the question had been mooted almost immediately. Confident that they would soon occupy all of Poland, Lenin and his government had rejected the Curzon Line. After the Red Army was turned back from Warsaw and finally defeated by the Poles, the frontier between the two countries, agreed upon by the Treaty of Riga and recognized by both the Soviets and the West, extended about 200 miles *east* of the Curzon Line. It remained Poland's official eastern border, unchallenged by anyone, until the German-Soviet invasions of 1939.

Despite the Curzon Line's lack of legal or historic validity, Stalin saw an advantage in citing it as his authority for drawing a new border. Since it more or less coincided with the Ribbentrop-Molotov Line, its revival would regain eastern Poland for the Soviet Union, giving Stalin essentially the same deal he had had with Hitler. (One exception: the Curzon Line, as originally conceived, would have left Lwów inside Poland.) Moreover, Stalin hoped that citing Lord Curzon's name, as opposed to the Nazi Ribbentrop's, would appeal to British patriotism and self-importance and lend his reborn aggression a flavor of legitimacy.

The ploy worked. Anthony Eden—of whom a government colleague once remarked, "If only there were more strength behind the charm, what a great Foreign Secretary he would be!"—did not challenge Stalin's sophistry. Nor did he reject out of hand the proposed secret protocol. Instead, Eden ducked. He told Stalin he did not have the authority to make such a deal, that he would have to consult not only with London but with Washington, too, now that the United States was in the war. (The Japanese attack on Pearl Harbor had occurred just a few days earlier.) Eden's attempt to stall left Stalin with the impression that it was just a matter of time until he got what he wanted. He told

Eden he would be content, for now, with an agreement giving the Soviets hegemony in the Baltic states—and leave eastern Poland for later.

When he returned to London, the foreign secretary acknowledged to the War Cabinet that the Soviet demands were "amoral" and clearly violated the Atlantic Charter. Yet Eden—the same official who had promised the Poles in writing that the British government did not recognize any post-invasion changes in their borders—now declared: "We shall not succeed in removing Stalin's suspicions of ourselves and the Americans unless we agree to these claims." If Stalin's demands were not met, Eden maintained, the Soviet leader might well refuse any future cooperation with the Allies and might "revert to the pursuit of purely selfish aims."

Stalin, of course, had shown no sign of pursuing anything but selfish aims—a point that Winston Churchill made when he angrily rejected the proposal. The Soviets "are fighting for self preservation and have never had a thought for us," the prime minister exploded. In response to Eden's argument that British approval of Stalin's claims was, for the Soviet leader, "the acid test of our sincerity," Churchill snorted: "I on the contrary regard our sincerity [to be] involved in the maintenance of the principles of the Atlantic Charter."

Churchill was not the only British official to be dismayed by Stalin's demands—and Eden's apparent willingness to yield to them. In his diary, Sir Alexander Cadogan acidly remarked: "How funny A[nthony] is! Because it fits in with his trip he is quite prepared to throw to the winds all principles (the Atlantic Charter) which he has not drafted. This amoral, realpolitik line was never his." Later, Cadogan wrote: "Much better to say to the Russians, 'We can't discuss postwar frontiers; we want to work with you now and later: let's have a mutual guarantee....' I believe, still, it would be better not to crawl to the Russians over the dead bodies of *all* our principles."

Churchill—for a time—seemed to feel the same way. But by the early spring of 1942, principles had once more given way to the harsh realities of war. If 1941 had been a humiliating year militarily for the British, 1942 was proving far worse. Every day, it seemed, there was a new disaster. The shock of multiple British losses in Asia was particularly profound: Britain's proud Asian empire now lay largely in ruins, with the supposedly invincible Singapore, as well as Hong Kong, Malaya, and Burma, falling to the Japanese. In North Africa, Rommel seemed all but unstoppable in his relentless advance across the desert. In the Atlantic, German submarines were taking an ever more devastating toll on British shipping.

As one calamity followed another, the mood in Britain grew progressively fractious and sour. Among the public and in Parliament, there was widespread grumbling about the government's handling of the war, and no amount of Churchillian eloquence could stem the discontent. "You...hear people say that they've had enough of fine oratory," Mollie Panter-Downes wrote in her "Letter from London" for *The New Yorker*. "[W]hat they would like is action and a sign from Mr. Churchill that he understands the profoundly worried temper of the country." Harold Nicolson, a National Labour MP, echoed that feeling, observing in his diary: "The country is too nervous and irritable to be fobbed off with fine phrases."

Along with increasing public doubt about the fighting ability and mettle of British troops (doubts expressed privately by Churchill himself), there was a groundswell of sympathy and admiration for the Russian army, which, after beating back the Germans at Moscow, was mounting an increasingly effective and broader defense against the Wehrmacht. In part, the high esteem for the Red Army stemmed from a sense of gratitude and relief that it was the Russians, not the British, who were now bearing most of the burden of the fight, doubtless with worse to come. (The Battle of Stalingrad still lay ahead, and the frightful siege of Leningrad would not end until 1944.) In London's East End, which had been badly bombed in the Blitz, windows in shops and flats were decorated with pro-Russian signs, one of which read: "They Gave Us Quiet Nights."

With the immediate Nazi danger removed, sentiment was growing in Britain that the government should be doing considerably more to help the Russians. "It's apparently useless to point out [to the public] that the R.A.F. is regularly battering Germany's production bases, that the steady stream of British war material to Russia continues at considerable sacrifice to this country, and that Britain is already fighting on three fronts," Mollie Panter-Downes reported. "From the tone of private conversations and public utterances at mass meetings, it appears that the British people can't or won't recognize the existence of any substitute for a genuine, slap-up opening of a land offensive on the Continent."

The escalating sentiment for a second European front was fueled by an intensive "Second Front Now" campaign in the British press, instigated by Lord Beaverbrook, owner of the *Daily Express* and other newspapers, who had resigned from Churchill's War Cabinet to whip up public support for aid to Russia. "Already the press is clamoring for Churchill to do something to take the pressure off the Russians," wrote Time-Life correspondent Walter Graebner in early 1942. "If he doesn't and if the Russians fall, an anti-Churchill movement might begin to snowball."

In fact, there was already talk in some parliamentary circles of ousting the man who, less than two years earlier, had almost single-handedly rallied his nation to defy Hitler. Facing this threat to his tenure as prime minister and emotionally battered by the seemingly endless string of British military defeats, the sixty-seven-year-old Churchill, at least temporarily, had lost some of his ebullience and bull-dog tenacity. He "is at a very low ebb," his daughter, Mary, wrote in her diary in February. "He is not too well physically, and he is worn down by the continuous crushing pressure of events."

The prime minister strongly opposed the amphibious landing on the mainland of Europe that Stalin and Lord Beaverbrook were demanding. The United States had not yet mobilized enough troops or sufficiently geared up its wartime production capacity to be a potent force, and Churchill knew that the burden of a landing now would fall most heavily on the British, with huge casualties.

If Churchill could not satisfy Stalin's and the British public's increasingly strident demands for a second front, however, he could yield to the Russian leader over what Stalin had called "the most important question for us in the war." Thus, on March 7, 1942, three months after Anthony Eden's discussions with Stalin in Moscow, Churchill, in a somewhat disjointed, rambling cable, informed Roosevelt: "The increasing gravity of the war has led me to feel that the principles of the Atlantic Charter ought not to be construed so as to deny Russia the frontiers she occupied when Germany attacked her." Two days later, the prime minister cabled Stalin: "I have sent a message to President Roosevelt urging him to approve our signing agreements with you about the frontiers of Russia at the end of the war."

There was, however, strong U.S. resistance. State Department officials were not pleased with this attempt to undermine the Atlantic Charter, insisting that settlement of all territorial questions be put off until the war was over. Secretary of State Cordell Hull condemned what he called the "trafficking in the independence of small countries." And Undersecretary of State Sumner Welles declared that Stalin's territorial demands were "indefensible from every moral standpoint and equally indefensible from the standpoint of the future peace and stability of Europe." Later, Welles wrote: "Our acquiescence in [the agreement] would have been interpreted in every quarter of the globe as meaning that the Atlantic Charter was, in fact, no more than a hollow sham, a collection of high sounding phrases designed merely to impress the ingenuous."

Roosevelt supported his State Department team, and, again, Stalin had to wait. When the final draft of the British-Soviet treaty was signed in May, it contained no reference to the Baltic states, eastern Poland, or any of the other territory Stalin demanded, and there were no secret codicils promising he would get them.

Less than a year later, FDR, who had never felt as strongly as Hull and Welles about the issue, would change his mind. Stalin, he decided, must have his way.

CHAPTER THIRTEEN

"I Can Handle Stalin Better"

IN THE FALL of 1942, Witold Urbanowicz arrived in Washington, D.C., as the new assistant air attaché at the Polish Embassy. He was far from enthusiastic about the assignment: flying a desk was not Urbanowicz's idea of patriotism. The war had been going on for three years, and the thirty-four-year-old major, Poland's top ace in the Battle of Britain, had spent two of those years in England, fighting only indirectly for his country—as a Kościuszko Squadron pilot, as commander of the First Polish Fighter Wing, and as a flight instructor. What he wanted to do now was to take a more direct approach. He had heard about a special new RAF squadron that had begun smuggling arms, money, and resistance fighters into and out of Nazi-occupied Europe, including Poland. That, Urbanowicz thought, was just the thing for him.

The Polish government-in-exile disagreed. Urbanowicz, in addition to being a bona fide hero, was handsome (in a refined, Leslie Howard sort of way) and polished—the perfect candidate, his superiors decided, to help promote Poland's cause in the United States. Indeed, he had demonstrated his diplomatic proficiency a year earlier when he and Zdzisław Krasnodębski had been sent on a tour of the United States and Canada to give speeches on Poland's behalf and to lecture on fighter tactics to student pilots. The Polish ambassador to the United States, Jan Ciechanowski, was sufficiently impressed that he requested Urbanowicz's reassignment from Britain to Washington.

A few months later, less than a year after the Japanese attack on Pearl Harbor, Urbanowicz arrived in the U.S. capital. As a veteran of Germany's invasion of Poland, the Battle of Britain, and the London Blitz, he could not help being a bit critical of the city's complacent normalcy. This was the capital of a country at war, and a two-ocean war at that? Even with Washington's characteristic Southern lassitude shrouded beneath the busyness of a mushrooming bureaucracy, the city seemed curiously untouched. Eric Sevareid, who had been posted to Washington by CBS after covering the fighting in Europe, had a similar view. "Life was easy and getting more prosperous every week...," wrote a disillusioned Sevareid. "The nation was encouraged to believe that it could produce its way to victory, or buy its victory by the simple measure of writing a check."

To Sevareid, Washington, unaffected as it was by actual combat, "seemed to be no part of the war, however vast its work for war." Even President Roosevelt grumbled that there was "less realization of the

Zdzisław Krasnodębski, Witold Urbanowicz, and another (unidentified) Polish pilot enjoy the company of several starlets during lunch at the RKO Studio in Hollywood. Krasnodębski and Urbanowicz were on a 1941 lecture tour of the United States to promote the Polish cause. (Stanisław Blasiak)

actual war effort in Washington, D.C., than anywhere else." In the capital, as in the rest of the country, rationing of various essential commodities and products was gradually being imposed. But Washington's lights still glowed brightly at night, and the social life was, if anything, considerably more frenetic than it had been before the war. There were hunt breakfasts, lunches, tea dances, dinners—and, of course, an endless round of cocktail parties and diplomatic receptions.

Urbanowicz's bemusement at all this descended into gloom when he discovered how little interest there was in Poland and the Polish cause among most of the Americans he encountered. "Poland has never loomed large in the American mind or in American foreign policy," the historian and diplomat Edwin O. Reischauer wrote years later. "The tendency in this country has been to ignore Poland in our concern for larger countries and those with which we have been more directly involved either as friend or foe." During World War II, that indifference had major policy implications. In spite of Allied rhetoric about equal rights and freedom for all nations, Poland, like a number of other European and Asian countries, was excluded from any significant role in the management of the war and from discussions about the geopolitical shape that the postwar world would take.

In January 1942, Roosevelt and Churchill stage-managed the signing in Washington of an agreement by the twenty-six nations then in the alliance (dubbed "the United Nations" by Roosevelt). Under the agreement, each country pledged its full resources to the fight and reiterated its commitment to the principles of the Atlantic Charter. Yet only the Soviet Union and China were consulted in advance about the drafting of the document, and only the Soviet and Chinese ambassadors received formal invitations to the White House signing ceremony with Roosevelt and Churchill. Jan Ciechanowski and the ambassadors of other Allied countries were merely informed that they could drop by the White House, at their convenience, to sign the "Declaration by the United Nations."

In a letter to General Sikorski, Ciechanowski noted that "if the concept of the United Nations could still be regarded as an international family concern, it was one definitely composed of rich and poor relations." Despite the contributions to the Allied cause by its army, navy, and air force (especially the last), Poland was forced into a distinctly subservient role when the Soviet Union and the United States entered the war. That was defensible, or at least understandable, in realpolitik terms. Poland's strength lay not in the power of its armaments or in the size of its population. Its strength lay in the will of its people to resist, a factor that somehow accounted for relatively little at various great power negotiating tables.

American indifference was especially difficult for the Poles in exile to bear. Most had looked forward to the day when the United States would enter the war, when, like Kościuszko and Pułaski in the American Revolution, they would once again be comrades-in-arms with a nation that shared their traditions of national independence and individual freedom. Poles held similar feelings about the British and French, but no nation captured the modern Polish imagination more than America. Scarcely a generation earlier, in 1926, Poland had celebrated the 150th anniversary of American independence with an extraordinary gift— 111 bound volumes expressing Poland's gratitude and friendship to the United States and signed by almost 6 million Polish citizens, more than one sixth of the country's total population. "For Poles, America was always something fascinating—the best country in the world," Urbanowicz noted.

But after Pearl Harbor, Poles, for a variety of reasons, felt increasingly isolated and ignored by the United States. For the Kościuszko Squadron pilots, this was made even harder to accept by the warm relationship they had had with American combat pilots in the earliest days of the U.S. involvement.

———

WHEN THE SQUADRON was reconstituted in Britain in 1940, its insignia, incorporating a stylized version of the American flag, was proudly painted on its Hurricanes. The Stars and Stripes were thus carried into combat against Germany long before the United States entered the war—a point of pride to the Polish pilots. After the Yanks formally joined the fight, the Poles did all they could to make them feel welcome.

In 1942, Jan Zumbach, then the squadron commander, and other pilots staged a ceremony "as proof of our deep gratitude for your friendship," in which they bestowed honorary squadron membership on Anthony Drexel Biddle, the U.S. ambassador to the Polish government-in-exile. Not long after that, the pilots of the Kościuszko Squadron provided aerial combat instruction for the U.S. 94th Combat Squadron, recently assigned to the European theater. The Americans came away from this training full of praise for the Poles and their ability in the air. "We owe more to [you] than can be expressed in words," wrote one American pilot. He called the Polish unit "the best damn fighting squadron in the world."

The Polish pilots shepherded their American counterparts on their first seven operational sorties over France. They taught them what they had learned about German tactics and how they had improved on British tactics. They treated the Yanks not as tyros but as colleagues, whom they were welcoming to the fight and with whom they were sharing the experience that had helped them survive and prevail. Nor was this comradely attitude limited to their time in the air. Off duty, the Poles were as impressive to the Americans as they were at the controls of a Spitfire. "In regard to having a good time, we found that [Kościuszko Squadron] has no equals," an American flier wrote in the Polish squadron's diary. Wrote another: "When I left the States, I hoped to meet the finest airmen in the world.... [T]hat end has been realized."

One American pilot, Francis Gabreski, asked his superiors for permission to train with the Kościuszko Squadron on his own. Of Polish ancestry, Gabreski had read everything he could find about the squadron and its heroics. By the time he arrived in Britain, however, it had been taken out of action for a rest, and Gabreski was assigned to another Polish unit, 315 Squadron. flying with them, he wrote later, was "not an honor I took lightly. Some of these guys had been in the war since the first day back in 1939, when I was still a kid marking time on the campus at Notre Dame." Gabreski flew some two dozen missions with the Poles, during which he carefully studied their tactics. The tutorials paid off: before he was through, Gabreski, with thirty-one kills, was the ace of aces among American pilots in Europe.

WHILE AMERICAN FIGHTER pilots were still in training, the Poles joined other RAF fighter units as escorts on "precision bombing" raids by B-17s from the U.S. Eighth Air Force. These missions, conducted in daylight for better target visibility, were the subject of much favorable publicity in the United States but were highly controversial among senior military officers and among the crews who had to fly them. In daylight, bombers were far more vulnerable to German antiaircraft guns and air attacks, especially since the bombers' fighter escorts, from mid-1942 to the end of 1943, did not have the fuel capacity to accompany them all the way to Germany.* B-17 "Flying Fortresses" were built to take a lot of punishment. Their crews were another matter.

It was not surprising, then, that the American bomber crews, like their RAF counterparts before them, became fans of the Poles' ability to keep German fighters away. The Polish pilots had developed a unique formation that put the bombers into a cocoon of close protection. The fighters positioned themselves high and in front, as well as directly overhead, and low and behind. So successful were these tactics that the U.S. Army Air Forces eventually requested that all RAF escort wings employ them. Americans also valued the Poles for the unusual amount of tender loving care they provided bombers in trouble. Several times, Kościuszko Squadron planes, for example, circled in relays above crippled B-17s that had been forced to ditch in the Channel. The Poles attacked any German planes that went after helpless bomber crews in rubber dinghies, and tried to remain on station until the men could be rescued.

Yet, while Kościuszko's escort duties were an important part of the expanding war effort, its fliers—once celebrated as brave knights over the sceptered isle—received scant public attention for what they did in these later stages of the war. Bombers, not fighters, were now the core of the Allied aerial campaign. More and more, fighters were relegated to serving the bombers' needs.

Then, too, there was the sheer enormity of the Allied effort. Despite their quantitative and qualitative contributions, the Poles were increasingly lost in the American-led "crusade." From 1941 to 1943, Polish fighter pilots had been credited with between 15 and 30 percent of the annual losses inflicted on the Luftwaffe. Polish-manned bombers made up one sixth of the RAF's effective bomber force during this period. In 1943, the Polish Air Force (PAF), with its eleven fighter squadrons and three bomber squadrons, was the fourth largest Allied air force, behind only the United States, Britain, and the Soviet Union. It had more men in uni-

---

* This changed in December 1943 with the introduction of the longer-range and faster P-51 Mustang fighter. Although built in the United States, the Mustang was flown by both the RAF (including the Poles) and the U.S. Army Air Forces.

form than the Czechs, Dutch, Free French, Norwegians, and Belgians combined. But, as the massive buildup of U.S. airpower continued, the Polish contribution shrank into relative insignificance.

At the same time, the Poles were suffering appallingly heavy losses, particularly in their bomber squadrons. Only about 40 percent of Polish bomber crews—flying in Liberators, Lancasters, and Wellingtons—lived through their first tour of duty in the war; for a second tour, the figure dropped to 20 percent. The surviving Poles found each new loss extremely painful, for personal and strategic reasons. "A British plane fails to return. Who knows about it? Only the immediate circle of one Allied squadron out of a thousand," a Polish pilot wrote. "A Polish plane is posted missing. Who knows about it? Everyone! Every one of our squadrons, every unit, every Polish base!" Unlike the British and Americans, the PAF had no great pool of reserves ready to replace its casualties. In early 1942, the PAF had been able to replenish its depleted squadrons with men who had come out of the Soviet Union with General Anders. By 1943, its strength was decreasing again. But now there were no replacements.

Acutely aware of their own casualties and diminishing strength, Polish airmen were baffled by the casual, if not careless, attitude some Americans seemed to have about war casualties. One Polish pilot recalled talking to an American colleague about the loss of six U.S. bombers the day before. "For the Poles, it seemed a shame," the pilot said. "But my American friend said, 'Never mind. We'll have twenty planes to replace them tomorrow.' And they did. To me, it was a real American way of thinking."

The "American way of thinking" was about to be experienced by the Poles in other ways as well.

ISAIAH BERLIN, THE noted British intellectual who served in his country's embassy in Washington during the war, observed that the people of Poland and the rest of occupied Europe regarded Franklin D. Roosevelt as "a kind of benevolent demigod who alone could and would save them in the end." The president's "moral authority—the degree of confidence which he inspired outside his own country—has no parallel," Berlin asserted.

In the early years of the war, Roosevelt sent several messages to occupied Poland, calling the country "an inspiration to all nations" and praising "the magnificent and continuing resistance of the Polish armed forces and people...." Poles inside and outside the country treasured those declarations, often citing them as proof that the United States and its president admired and cared about them and would soon rescue their country from foreign domination. One such message was reprinted as a pamphlet entitled *The President Knows* and distributed to General Anders's ragged troops in Russia in early 1942. Reading the president's declaration helped starving men in tattered uniforms recover their courage, Anders later observed.

The soldiers in Russia, like many other Poles, had no way of knowing that the president's expressions of praise for Poland were meant as a sop to General Sikorski, to compensate for the lack of American support for the Polish government-in-exile over the question of the Curzon Line. In fact, Roosevelt—chief architect of the Atlantic Charter, champion of self-determination and freedom for all nations—made clear throughout the war that he had little interest in Poland's fate, except as it affected his alliance with Stalin and his chances in the next presidential election. Unlike Churchill, FDR had no treaty obligations to Poland. As he explained to the Soviet dictator toward the end of the war, he took "a distant view on the Polish question."

Franklin Roosevelt's conduct of the American war effort in general, and his attitude toward Poland in particular, revealed some of the contradictions in his complex character. Although he could be a large-souled idealist, he preferred issuing abstract pronouncements to figuring out how to put them into effect. Even when he proposed means to his lofty ends, as with his call for the creation of the United Nations, he tended to employ vague generalities. Like Woodrow Wilson, with the League of Nations and his notion that World War I would "make the world safe for democracy," Roosevelt thought the United States's World War II mission was to help build a freer and more just postwar world. In his 1941 State of the Union address, he declared that all people, everywhere, had a right to "Four Freedoms": freedom of speech, freedom of worship, freedom from want, freedom from fear. He did not, however, address the issue of how those freedoms were to be guaranteed and defended.

Whatever moral authority Roosevelt enjoyed in the world, he was essentially a pragmatist, a short-term problem solver. As he repeatedly demonstrated in his administration's two great crises—the Depression and World War II—if something worked, fine; if it did not work, he tried something else. He did not bother himself much with the long-term consequences of his actions and promises, and he tended to postpone or duck decisions that were politically difficult or that might limit his options. To some, including officials in his own administration, Roosevelt often seemed cool and devious, a man whose highest priority was his own political success. When Robert Boothby, a Tory MP and one-time close associate of Churchill's, asked a prominent New Dealer (whom he didn't identify) if the president had any deep sense of purpose about anything, the man hesitated, then replied: "Only one. To remain in office."

That was too harsh. But under pressure—and Roosevelt was under constant pressure for more than thirteen years in the most difficult of times—he tended, like a jazz musician, to improvise. His idealistic public rhetoric often diverged from his hardheaded, behind-the-scenes decisions and actions. As FDR biographers James MacGregor Burns and Susan Dunn have noted, there was a "profound gap between Roosevelt's moral code and his day-to-day practice, between his lofty ends and his dubious means, between his magnanimity and his Machiavellianism.... [T]he higher he set his goals and the lower he pitched his improvisations, the more he widened the gap between the existing and the ideal and thus raised people's expectations while failing to fulfill them."

A case in point was the dichotomy between the president's public call for self-determination for all nations and his private belief that the United States and the other major Allies had the right to dictate to smaller or less powerful states, not only during the war but afterward as well. In the spring of 1942, during a meeting with Vyacheslav Molotov, the president sketched a picture of a postwar world very different from the one envisioned in the Atlantic Charter. This Rooseveltian world would be governed not by the ideals of equality and justice but by great power politics. The United States, the Soviet Union, Great Britain, and China would be the police force of this world, and smaller countries like Poland would perforce submit to the police force's will. As the war progressed, Roosevelt continued to champion that idea, even as he also pushed his inchoate vision of an international federation of nations.

Roosevelt did not of course invent the notion that the United States was destined (with its major Allies, more or less) to lead the world. It was part of the American ethos long before Roosevelt and long after him. One of his most prominent political opponents, Henry Luce, the Republican co-founder of *Time* magazine, had very much the same thing in mind when he proclaimed the twentieth century to be "the American century." So did Woodrow Wilson when he declared that God had chosen the United States to "show the way to the nations of the world how they shall walk in the path of liberty." It was America's emergence as *the* global power in World War II, however, that gave the vision new meaning and force—a vision that Roosevelt's brain trusters saw as a mandate. According to Harry Hopkins, FDR's closest adviser, "a more humane and democratic world order [was] plausible"—but only under Roosevelt's leadership and based on the tenets of the New Deal. The president's men, Isaiah Berlin noted wryly, seemed to regard themselves as "divinely inspired to save the world."

Roosevelt had no doubt of his own ability to help create and lead this utopia. A man of supreme confidence, he used his preternatural charm and charisma to bedazzle and captivate everyone he met. Being exposed to Roosevelt's sparkling exuberance, his joie de vivre, was, as Winston Churchill memorably put it, like opening your first bottle of champagne. His optimism and eloquence had helped restore hope and confidence to a country mired in the Great Depression. His innovative leadership—"Hell, Harry, if this isn't the answer, let's try *that*"—had led at least to the beginnings of recovery (although it would take World War II to get to the end). Because of Roosevelt and his administration, the lives of Americans had been transformed forever, largely for the better, and the federal government had assumed vast new power and authority.

Roosevelt's presidency was from the beginning an intensely personal one: he was at the center of everything. In 1936, when an aide asked what his stand on new taxes would be in the upcoming campaign, FDR waved the question aside. "That's a detail," he replied. "There's one issue in this campaign. It's myself, and people must either be for me or against me." Most of them were for him—then and later. He won the 1936 election in an overwhelming landslide, weakening the Republicans almost to the point of extinction. He did it again in 1940 for a precedent-shattering third term, then again in 1944.

His extraordinary triumphs only served to reinforce Roosevelt's confidence, not to mention his determination to be in charge. Henry Wallace, Roosevelt's third-term vice president, wrote in his diary that the key to the president's character was "the desire to be the dominating figure, to demonstrate on all occasions his superiority." Former FDR aide Raymond Moley felt that Roosevelt had yielded to the "intensifying and exhilarating effect of power," which showed itself in a habit of "telling, not asking." According to Moley, FDR's "irritable certitude" in his own beliefs and actions led to a conviction that people who questioned his decisions were guilty of "self-interest or cowardice or subtle corruption or stupidity."

The same combination of charm and "irritable certitude" governed Roosevelt's conduct of foreign affairs. He had an unbounded faith in his ability to win over leaders of other countries. Writing to Churchill in March 1942, Roosevelt remarked: "I know you will not mind my being brutally frank when I tell you that I think I can personally handle Stalin better than either your Foreign Office or my State Department. Stalin hates the guts of all your top people. He thinks he likes me better, and I hope he will continue to do so." This from a man who had not yet even met Stalin, from a man who had never been to the Soviet Union, who did not know much about Soviet history or ideology, and who saw little reason to learn.

Like Churchill, Roosevelt had by this time already pledged unconditional military and economic aid to Stalin and his country, declaring that Russia's survival was vital to U.S. defense. Whether that was true or not is a matter of continuing debate, but Roosevelt certainly believed it at the time. Averell Harriman, the multimillionaire former industrialist and investment banker sent by Roosevelt to discuss the aid question with Stalin in October 1941, told the American people when he returned that they must give unstintingly to keep the Soviets in the war. "To put it bluntly," Harriman said in a radio broadcast, "whatever it costs to keep this war away from our shores... will be a small price to pay."

By early 1942, an astonishing cornucopia of American weapons and supplies—planes, trucks, Jeeps, steel, gas, boots, food, blankets, and more—was beginning to make its long, perilous way across the ocean to Russia. By the end of the war, more than $11 billion worth of Lend-Lease goods had been sent to the Soviet Union, playing a crucial—perhaps decisive—role in the Red Army's ability to stand its ground against the Germans, and then to go on the offensive. The United States provided the Soviets with more than two thirds of their motor vehicles and half of their aircraft. In 1943 alone, more than 5,000 fighter planes were shipped. American communication equipment made it possible for Moscow to keep track of its military's movements, and American explosives were used in Russian bombs and shells. Without U.S.-provided transportation, Soviet troops, after the turning of the tide at Stalingrad, would not have had the mobility to mount paralyzing attacks against the enemy, striking deeply and fast into rear areas. In 1943, even Stalin, who did not like giving credit where it was due, acknowledged that without American Lend-Lease aid, "we would lose this war."

The U.S. government's unqualified largesse was nonetheless often troubling to those few American officials—diplomats and military officers—who had actually spent time in the Soviet Union and were familiar with how Stalin and his government operated. "Virtually without exception," the historian John Lewis Gaddis noted, "subordinate officials responsible for dealing with the Russians from day to day became convinced that the President's open-handed policy was unwise." Those officials included George Kennan, Charles Bohlen, and Loy Henderson, the leading members of a group of young Soviet specialists in the State Department, two of whom—Kennan and Bohlen—were to become U.S. ambassadors to Moscow. The first Foreign Service officers to be trained as Soviet experts, they spoke Russian, had studied Russian and Soviet history and ideology, and had worked in the U.S. Embassy in Moscow.

Kennan, who, according to *New York Times* correspondent Harrison Salisbury, "knew the Russians as no one else in my generation," and the others in his circle did not oppose U.S. aid to Russia per se. What they did question was Roosevelt and Churchill's unwillingness to demand anything from the Soviets in return—a generosity that the Soviet specialists believed was interpreted by Stalin as a sign of weakness. "We all admired the fight the Russians were making," Bohlen remarked. "What we worried about was the future." Kennan thought Churchill and Roosevelt should have said to Stalin: " 'Look here, old boy, our memories are no shorter than yours. We know very well how you tried to arrange your affairs in this war.... If you are interested in receiving our material and military aid, we will give it to you ... precisely so long as this suits our purpose.... You may expect small comfort from us in those of your ambitions which extend beyond the territory that was recognized as yours up to 1938.' "

To Harry Hopkins, however, Roosevelt did not seem "much concerned about the future. His preoccupation [is] with the next few months." As usual, Roosevelt was focused on the task at hand—in this case, winning the war. During World War II, the United States "had no peace aims," *New York Times* military correspondent Hanson Baldwin later wrote. "We had only the vaguest kind of idea, expressed in the vaguest kind of general principles (the Atlantic Charter, the United Nations) of the kind of postwar world we wanted."

When Sumner Welles suggested the creation of a group of Allied representatives in 1942 to begin the planning of peace settlements and postwar international policies, the idea was "summarily turned down" by Roosevelt. In FDR's view, "winning the war was and must remain the foremost objective," Welles later wrote. "No step could be taken politically, however beneficial it might promise to be later on, if it jeopardized or threatened to postpone the victory."

During the war, one of the president's key objectives was to keep Stalin happy while the Allies prepared and planned for the invasion of Western Europe. To that end, the president did not attach strings to U.S. aid—not even a request for the sharing of intelligence or military information (standard operating procedure for an ally) or a requirement to account for how the supplies were being used. Throughout the war, Russia had almost complete autonomy and refused to cooperate with its Western allies. Allied missions, British and American, were even barred from visiting the eastern front. "The truth is that they want to have as little to do with foreigners, Americans included, as possible," General John Deane, head of the U.S. military mission to the Soviet Union, wrote in exasperation to General George C. Marshall. "We never make a request or proposal to the Soviets that is not viewed with suspicion. They simply cannot understand giving without taking, and as a result, even our giving is viewed with suspicion."

William Bullitt, whom Roosevelt appointed in 1933 to serve as America's first ambassador to the Soviet Union, urged the president to demand a pledge by Stalin to keep Soviet hands off Eastern Europe in return for Lend-Lease. Roosevelt refused. "I just have a hunch," FDR wrote Bullitt, "that Stalin doesn't want anything but security for his country, and I think that if I give him everything I possibly can and ask nothing from him in return, *noblesse oblige,* he won't try to annex anything and will work for a world of democracy and peace." Twenty years earlier, Bullitt had admired the Soviet Union.* Now the ambassador was deeply mistrustful of Stalin and appalled by Roosevelt's cheerful naïveté and apparent belief that his own patrician standards were universal. Stalin, Bullitt declared, was nothing more than "a Caucasian bandit whose only thought when he got something for nothing was that the other fellow was an ass." After questioning Roosevelt's policy, Bullitt discovered that he no longer had the president's ear.

But, then, virtually no one who advocated policies and actions contrary to those favored by FDR had his ear. He bypassed his own secretary of state and the entire State Department in the making of foreign policy and used a group of personal emissaries, notably Harry Hopkins and Averell Harriman, to do his bidding and serve as go-betweens with Stalin, Churchill, and other foreign leaders. Later in the war, when Harriman was sent to the Soviet Union as ambassador and started warning Roosevelt about Stalin's plans and intentions, his advice, too, would be ignored.

Wrote Kennan after the war: "The truth is—there is no avoiding it— that Franklin Roosevelt, for all his charm and for all his skill as a political leader, was, when it came to foreign policy, a very superficial man, ignorant, dilettantish, with a severely limited intellectual horizon."

FDR's limited horizon would eventually cause a great deal of grief for a great many people.

———————

ON JANUARY 31, 1943, Field Marshal Friedrich von Paulus, his face haggard and grey-stubbled, led the remnants of his once mighty German Sixth Army out of the snow-covered ruins of Stalingrad and surrendered to the Red Army. Thus ended World War II's most savage battle, an epic turning point in the war, with grave consequences for Poland and the rest of Europe and for the entire Western alliance.

---

* In 1923, Bullitt had married Louise Bryant, widow of American journalist and Communist John Reed, the author of *Ten Days That Shook the World.* Reed had died of typhus in Moscow in 1920 and was entombed in the Kremlin wall.

The Battle of Stalingrad had begun the previous August as a result of a massive German summer offensive on the eastern front. It soon seemed that Hitler was on the verge of defeating the Russians once and for all. Five months later, the Wehrmacht had not only lost the battle but had seen the momentum shift to its enemy. The Germans had finally been checked in their relentless eastern advance, and the Soviets had won their desperate struggle for survival. Now the Red Army was preparing a counteroffensive. It would soon head for Germany— through Eastern and Central Europe.

At the height of the fighting in Stalingrad, Stalin had bombarded Churchill and Roosevelt with near-hysterical accusations of cowardice and bad faith for failing to create a second European front. Nothing could assuage him—not massive amounts of Allied aid, not the invasion of North Africa. There was a reason for Stalin's anger. In 1942, Roosevelt had casually led Molotov to believe that a second front *would* be opened later that year. He had not consulted the other Allies on this, however, and since at that point the United States was hardly in a position to open a new front alone, the vague promise was far more easily made than kept. Roosevelt did not, in any case, keep it, which served to fuel Stalin's anger and suspicions while providing him with leverage for future negotiations. The more he complained about the lack of a second front, the guiltier Roosevelt and Churchill felt about the heavy military load the Soviet Union was carrying and the more like putty they became in Stalin's hands.

After Stalingrad, Stalin made clear to the world that he meant to seize once again the eastern half of Poland and perhaps the western half as well. On January 16, 1943, the Soviet government had informed the Polish government-in-exile that all Poles still held in the Soviet Union would henceforth be considered Soviet citizens. The curt official note meant that the hundreds of thousands of Poles in Soviet territory, many wasting away in gulags, would probably be forced to remain there the rest of their lives. And that wasn't the end of it. Two months later, the Soviets publicly demanded that the Polish government, their ostensible ally, accept the Curzon Line as the new boundary between the Soviet Union and Poland, as well as purge itself of all officials whom Moscow regarded as anti-Soviet.

The United States and Britain responded to Stalin's high-handed move by vaguely reiterating their adherence to the principles of the

Atlantic Charter. At a secret meeting in March, however, Roosevelt and Anthony Eden agreed to let Stalin have his way with eastern Poland and the Baltic states. Despite his administration's repeated insistence that territorial matters were not to be settled until after the war, Roosevelt had indicated even earlier that he had no objections to Stalin's plans. In May 1942, he told Assistant Secretary of State Adolph Berle that he "would not particularly mind about the Russians taking quite a chunk of territory; they might have the Baltic republics and eastern Poland...."

During his meeting with Eden, the president concurred when the British foreign secretary declared that Stalin really wanted "very little" from Poland. How could the Poles possibly object to the Curzon Line, especially if they were compensated after the war with territory taken from Germany? According to Roosevelt, it was up to the United States, the Soviet Union, and Britain to decide Poland's borders, and he, for one, had no intention of "go[ing] to the peace conference and bargain[ing] with Poland or the other small states." Poland was to be organized "in a way that will maintain the peace of the world," Roosevelt said—as if Poland, not Germany, had started the war in the first place. Indeed, Roosevelt went on, the three major powers could help guarantee the peace by forcing *all* smaller nations to give up their armaments after the war, allowing them nothing more dangerous than rifles.

The president "seemed to be ignoring the obvious difficulty of disarming neutral countries," Eden observed later, but "I did not take the idea as a serious proposal, and it passed with little comment." In another gibe at FDR, the foreign secretary remarked: "He seemed to see himself disposing of the fate of many lands, allied no less than enemy. He did all this with so much grace that it was not easy to dissent. Yet it was too like a conjuror, skillfully juggling with balls of dynamite, whose nature he failed to understand." (The criticism might well have been leveled at Eden himself.)

Three months later, Maxim Litvinov, the Soviet ambassador in Washington, assured Stalin in a confidential note that Roosevelt clearly was "accessible to our influence." The ambassador added: "The USA is not at all interested in the economic or foreign political aspects of the Baltic region's problems or in the frontier issue between us and Poland."

That lack of interest, however, remained a closely guarded secret from the public—and even from most members of the president's administration. Roosevelt, a consummate gauger of the public mood, knew that any endorsement of Russia's claims would create severe political problems for him. The Democrats' extraordinary hold on the allegiance of American voters was slipping: in the 1942 congressional elections, the Republicans added forty-four seats in the House and nine in the Senate. Particularly worrisome to the president was the knowledge that a large percentage of Polish-American and other ethnic groups who traditionally voted Democratic had not even cast ballots this time. With the 1944 presidential election coming up, Roosevelt could not afford to alienate some 6 million Polish-American voters, whose ballots conceivably could make the difference.

Publicly, the president and his administration insisted until early 1945 that only a postwar peace conference could settle the question of Polish boundaries. FDR was content to sit back and appear impartial. Such deception did not seem to bother him: he once told an administration official that he was "perfectly willing to mislead and tell untruths if it will help win the war." If the Poles needed to be pressured to accept the Curzon Line and other Soviet demands, he would leave that job— and the political heat—to Churchill. As a result, while the Poles became disillusioned with what they regarded as Britain's betrayal and appeasement, they retained their faith that the United States would eventually come forward to save them.

That hope was strongest in occupied Poland itself, so far away from the political maneuvering in the Allied capitals. When the Germans sealed the gates of the Jewish ghetto in Warsaw, an old resident confidently told a young friend: "Oh, don't you worry! They'll soon let us out. We only need America to know."

IN WASHINGTON, the Kościuszko Squadron's Witold Urbanowicz was developing a rather more cynical view. After five months as a relatively junior diplomat, he had already had enough—enough of Washington's fecklessness, enough of what he viewed as the Roosevelt administration's failure to practice what it preached in terms of international justice and equality, enough of double-talk. It was time to get back to fighting the war.

Urbanowicz was married now—to a young Polish woman, the daughter of a shipping executive, who had lived in Kraków when the war broke out but managed to escape to America with her mother. She had first met Urbanowicz in Poland and then ran into him again during his 1941 lecture tour in the United States. They had been married only a few months when Urbanowicz encountered Merian Cooper at a Washington cocktail party in the spring of 1943. The founder of the Kościuszko Squadron had left his job as Hollywood producer to join General Claire Chennault, now commander of the U.S. Army Air Forces in China, as Chennault's chief of staff. Cooper introduced Urbanowicz to Chennault, who asked the Polish ace if he would be interested in a little temporary duty, joining the Americans in fighting the Japanese. Chennault did not have to ask twice.

By that fall, Urbanowicz, having received permission from Polish Air Force headquarters in London, was flying as a volunteer in southern China, the air intake of his P-40 fighter painted with the characteristic sharp-toothed animal grin of the Flying Tigers. Wearing his Polish uniform, he represented, he later quipped, "the smallest army in World War II—one fighter pilot." At first, the other pilots in the squadron regarded Urbanowicz with some skepticism, but it wasn't long before they realized just how good and daring a pilot he was, especially with his ability "to see the whole sky." "We were an elite outfit in China, and we knew it. To be in the 75th [squadron] was something special," noted Myron Levy, the squadron's adjutant. "We had seen some of these European heroes fall flat on their butts. Not Urbanowicz.... [W]e were proud that he was one of us."

Urbanowicz was simply "outstanding" in the air, added Donald Lopez, then a rookie pilot with the 75th, who many years later would become deputy director of the National Air and Space Museum in Washington. "I had only a few combat missions at the time and was amazed at how much of what occurred in an air battle he was able to report, compared with what the rest of us saw. Later...I was able to see and report a lot more, but I was never able to reach his level of expertise."

On December 11, Urbanowicz shot down a pair of Japanese Zeros, both of which had been on the tail of the squadron's commander, Major Elmer Richardson. The following month, the Polish Air Force summoned Urbanowicz back to Britain. As he was about to leave, Chennault presented him with the U.S. Air Medal for his "courage and fighting skill in the face of the enemy."

Urbanowicz's time with the Americans had been all that he hoped for. When he was alone in the sky, things seemed purer somehow than they did in government offices, where the air was heavy with smoke, the talk laced with betrayal.

CHAPTER FOURTEEN

"Speak of Them Never"

DURING THEIR 1941 tour of the United States to rally support for
Poland, Zdzisław Krasnodębski and Witold Urbanowicz described
to their audiences the horrors inflicted on their homeland by both the
Nazis and the Soviets. The fliers spoke as natives of eastern Poland and
thus with special feeling about the Soviet occupation and the executions
or deportations to Russia of relatives and friends. The handsome, somber
Krasnodębski, with his burn-scarred face and hands, was particularly
effective at conveying the magnitude of the tragedy that had been visited
on occupied Poland after the twin invasions of 1939. Krasnodębski
emphasized that he and other Poles did not blame the German or Russian
people for the crimes against their country. The blame, he declared,
rested solely with the regimes of Adolf Hitler and Joseph Stalin.

The audiences had no trouble believing the pilots' descriptions of
Nazi atrocities in Poland: Hitler's barbarism was common knowledge in
the United States. But some Americans were reluctant to accept a similar indictment of their new friend and ally, the Soviet Union. At first,
this reluctance was mainly among those relatively few on the left who
had not been disillusioned by Stalin's purges and his 1939 nonaggression
pact with Hitler. Over the next two years, however, the tendency of
Americans to think more or less well of Stalin and his government
broadened substantially, thanks in no small part to a vigorous propaganda campaign conducted and encouraged by the U.S. Office of War
Information (OWI).

The OWI, with a staff and contractors that included many brilliant intellectuals, scholars, artists, writers, photographers, journalists, and film directors,* was created in 1942 by merging four federal agencies into one. Its mission was to support the war effort with information and propaganda for both foreign and domestic consumption. Despite hints from the American codebreaking VENONA Project that a number of Soviet agents had penetrated the Washington bureaucracy during World War II, OWI's output seems for the most part to have been reasonably truthful and well meaning. In the context of the times, even the attempt to pretty up Stalin and his government—moral and historical nonsense that it was—had a certain logic behind it.

Essentially, the government wanted to build understanding and support for the role the Soviets were now playing in the war and for the high cost of the U.S. aid they were receiving. To that end, OWI propaganda portrayed Stalin as no longer the unbridled tyrant of yesteryear but a relatively benign leader who was somehow becoming more moderate and democratic all the time. There were still skeptics, but for a while even they tended not to make too much of their skepticism. As the pro-Republican *New York Herald Tribune* put it, the Soviets, after all, were "killing the men who would [otherwise] kill Americans."

At first, Stalin joined in trying to sell the idea that he and his government had mellowed and had abandoned all thoughts of territorial and ideological aggression. To hear Stalin tell it, the Red Army was protecting Mother Russia, and Mother Russia alone, and had no other thought or purpose. In one radio message to his people, Stalin declared: "Comrades, we are fighting for our country! For justice and freedom! We have no desire to seize foreign territories or conquer foreign people." As far as most of his listeners were concerned, that fervent statement of patriotism, untainted by narrow thoughts of undeserved gain, may well have been true. But for Stalin himself, the sentiment lasted only about as long as his army was on the defensive. Soon after the tide had turned at Stalingrad, it became clear that territorial expansion was very much on the dictator's mind—and specifically expansion into Poland.

---

* Among those who worked with and for OWI were: former CBS commentator Elmer Davis, playwright Robert Sherwood, poet Archibald MacLeish, economist Barbara Tuchman, historians Arthur Schlesinger, Jr., and Henry Steele Commager, anthropologist Margaret Mead, photographer Gordon Parks, philosopher Herbert Marcuse, Oscar-winning screenwriter Philip Dunne, film directors William Wyler and Frank Capra, artist Ben Shahn, future educator Milton Eisenhower, future CBS correspondent Richard C. Hottelet, and future U.S. senator Alan Cranston.

His timing could hardly have been better, for back in the United States, the government's pro-Stalin propaganda campaign was now bearing bushels of fruit. Much of the press had begun portraying him as the wise and compassionate "Uncle Joe." *Time* and *Life* magazines, twin flagships of the words-and-photos empire founded by that staunch anti-Communist Republican Henry Luce, could barely contain their enthusiasm. Whereas *Time*'s 1940 Man of the Year cover had portrayed Stalin as glowering and sinister, and the accompanying article had described him as "match[ing] himself with Adolf Hitler as the world's most hated man," he was magically transformed just three years later. Man of the Year once again, he was now an ally whose cover portrait depicted a serene, almost saintly figure, against a snowy backdrop of forbidding Russian winter. In the article, Stalin was hailed for his military acumen and "magnificent will to resist," as if he alone were somehow responsible for the Russians' heroic defense. "Only Joseph Stalin fully knew how close Russia stood to defeat in 1942," said *Time*, "and only Joseph Stalin fully knew how he brought Russia through."

Two months later, *Life* devoted an entire issue to the Soviet Union, which it depicted as a country very much like that of its readers. The Russians, *Life* declared, were "one hell of a people," who "look like Americans, dress like Americans, and think like Americans." The cruelties of Stalin's rule were explained away with breathtaking ease: "Whatever the cost of farm collectivization in terms of human life and individual liberty, the historic fact is that it worked." And the NKVD, the Soviet secret police that was responsible for arresting, torturing, and murdering millions of Russians? In reality, said *Life*, the agency was just "a national police similar to the FBI," whose main job was "tracking down traitors."

Other mass circulation magazines and newspapers, including the *Saturday Evening Post, Collier's*, and *Reader's Digest*, carried similar articles. Even the good, grey *New York Times* waxed eloquent on occasion about how the Soviet Union and the United States were converging, politically and economically. "It is not misrepresenting the situation to say that Marxian thinking in Soviet Russia is out," said one *Times* editorial. "The capitalist system, better described as the competitive system, is back."

Some journalists, however, declined to join the chorus of those who, in *Commonweal*'s words, wanted to depict the Soviet government as "something like a combination of Washington's, Jefferson's, and Lincoln's, and functioning under a similar constitution." Among the naysayers was a small group of correspondents who had actually worked in the Soviet Union. One of them was William Henry Chamberlin, a highly respected correspondent for the *Christian Science Monitor* who had spent thirteen years in Moscow and had written several books about Russia.

In Chamberlin's view, it was one thing to acknowledge the necessity of an alliance with Stalin, to praise the heroism of the Russian people, to appreciate the fact that Russia's wartime sacrifices meant fewer sacrifices for the United States. It was quite another to ignore the obvious facts of Soviet history, to "prettify" a man "whose internal homicide record is even longer than Hitler's" and a government that had "starved its recalcitrant peasants and decimated its pre-revolutionary intelligentsia." In the United States, Chamberlin wrote, there seemed to be "a curious mystical belief that if only we trust Stalin enough, no matter what he does, we will all be happy ever after. The more Stalin does to undermine our confidence, the more our publicists and statesmen insist on a blind, deaf and dumb cultivation of [that] confidence."

Pushed hard by the federal bureaucracy, Hollywood did its part as well to promote the idea of American and Soviet brotherhood. OWI, keenly aware of the movies' potential for mobilizing public opinion, placed a high priority on using the silver screen to sell the new Soviet image. By 1943, the agency had already had a profound influence on Hollywood. It issued guidelines for the studios on how to help the war effort, vetted and rewrote screenplays, and sent its representatives to sit in on story conferences. On occasion, the feds even persuaded studios to abandon movies deemed antagonistic or detrimental to the cause.

In 1943 and 1944, most of the movie studios produced paeans, in one form or another, to the Russians and their spirited defense. MGM made *Song of Russia*, which extolled the virtues of collectivism and starred Robert Taylor (who claimed during the McCarthy era that he made the movie only under protest). Samuel Goldwyn's contribution was *The North Star*, with an original (but heavily rewritten) script by Lillian Hellman. Gregory Peck made his screen debut in 1944 as a gallant Soviet guerrilla in *Days of Glory*. But the best-known and most controversial of these movies—one whose production had been virtually commissioned by OWI and encouraged by Roosevelt himself—was Warner Bros.' *Mission to Moscow*, which seemed more interested in saluting Stalin and his regime than in praising the grit of the Russian people.

Mission was based on a best-selling book by Joseph E. Davies, a friend and campaign contributor of FDR's who served as U.S. ambassador to the Soviet Union in the late 1930s. By most accounts, Davies, who knew little about foreign affairs before being sent to Moscow, had been a disaster as ambassador. Before switching to diplomacy, he'd been a millionaire corporate lawyer and lobbyist for foreign governments in Washington. He became even richer upon marrying the cereal heiress Marjorie Merriweather Post. In 1936, Davies and his wife donated a considerable amount of money to Roosevelt's second presidential campaign. The following year, they were off to Moscow.

Stunned by Davies's appointment, George Kennan and the other young Soviet specialists in the U.S. Embassy held a meeting shortly after his arrival to decide whether they should resign en masse. The professionals in Moscow considered Davies a dilettante, a man whose lack of knowledge about the Soviet Union was exceeded only by his hunger for personal publicity and his arrogance in thinking—and publicly declaring—that he could improve U.S.-Soviet relations where others had failed. "What mortified us most of all," Kennan later remarked, "was the impression that the President himself knew nothing about, or cared nothing for, what we had accomplished in building up the embassy at Moscow, that the post, with all that it stood for...was for him only another political plum, to be handed out in return for campaign contributions." Kennan added: "Had the President wished to slap us down and mock us for our efforts in the development of Soviet-American relations, he could not have done better than with this appointment."

In the end, Kennan and the others decided to stay at their posts, but their apprehensions about Davies proved justified. In a grim, fear-ridden country where uncounted thousands were dying each day at the hands of the NKVD or from famine, Joseph and Marjorie Davies spent much of their time hosting elaborate dinners, spending millions of dollars on Fabergé eggs and other tsarist treasures, and sailing the Baltic on Marjorie's magnificent yacht, *Sea Cloud*. At one point, Secretary of State Cordell Hull felt it necessary to rebuke Davies for spending so much time away from Moscow.

Kennan and his colleagues, on the other hand, fervently wished for Davies to absent himself as often and for as long as possible. At least when he was away, he couldn't play the apologist for Stalin and his government, as he so often did when he was in the Soviet capital. There was the time, for instance, when he attended the show trials of leading Communist Party members and came away announcing to American journalists that the defendants were clearly guilty of plotting to overthrow Stalin. Davies "was much less concerned about the trials, the executions, and the terror than he was at the thought that the purge...might mar the picture of Stalin as a benign, idealistic person that he had been trying to paint for the benefit of the president, the Department of State, and the other readers of his reports," noted Loy Henderson, the embassy's deputy chief of mission. In addition, the ambassador ignored escalating Soviet harassment of U.S. diplomats and reporters, and when his staff wrote reports to the State Department critical of Stalin or his regime, he often appended personal assessments that sought to refute the reports' conclusions. In 1938, Davies was sent to Belgium as ambassador, and in 1940 he was appointed special assistant to Cordell Hull. When Germany invaded the Soviet Union, Roosevelt encouraged his friend, by then out of the government but serving as an unofficial presidential emissary, to write a book about his Moscow experiences that would reassure Americans about Stalin's government.

Ghostwritten quickly and published on December 29, 1941, three weeks after Pearl Harbor, *Mission to Moscow* easily met Roosevelt's expectations. In his panegyric, which sold more than 700,000 copies, Davies praised the "kindness and gentle simplicity" of Stalin, a man so warm and appealing that "a child would like to sit in his lap and a dog would sidle up to him." As Davies saw it, the main aim of the Soviet leadership was to "promote the brotherhood of man and to improve the lot of the common people. They wish to create a society in which men may live as equals, governed by ethical ideals." He expressed some reservations about Stalin's purges, but explained away the show trials and generally justified the executions of top Soviet officials and untold other Russians as a necessary "cleansing and purging" of "measly" and treasonous "anti-Stalinists."

A few months later, the movie version of *Mission to Moscow,* directed by Michael Curtiz and starring Walter Huston as Davies, was in production at Warners. It was released in 1943. Jack and Harry Warner later claimed that Roosevelt himself had asked them to make it during a dinner at the White House; Davies said that the president had merely encouraged the project. However direct or indirect FDR's involvement, the president and OWI played important roles in encouraging the production of a movie that was soon to become notorious for its "wholesale rewriting of history, its use of visual innuendo, and its explicit appeal to facts known to be incorrect."

Presented as a quasi-documentary, *Mission to Moscow* eliminates even the minimal reservations expressed by Davies in his book. It chastises France and Britain for prewar appeasement but portrays the Hitler-Stalin pact as a necessary Soviet time-buying tactic that allowed Russia to prepare secretly for war. At the beginning of the movie, a map of Poland flashes on the screen. Half of it is consumed by Hitler's flames; the other half—the part invaded and occupied by Stalin's army—is depicted as peaceful and untouched. The show trials are portrayed as rooting out Nazi conspirators intent on sabotage and the betrayal of Stalin.

OWI was delighted. "The presentation of the Moscow trials is a high point...," declared one of the office's internal memos, "and should do much to...dispel the fears which many honest persons have felt with regard to our alliance with Russia. MISSION TO MOSCOW pulls no punches; it answers the propaganda lies of the Axis and its sympathizers with the most powerful propaganda of all: the truth."

American scholars and film critics, including several on the left, didn't quite see it that way. Most were appalled. "Shameful rot," snorted James Agee in *The Nation*. Manny Farber, the movie critic of *The New Republic*, awarded *Mission to Moscow* the all-time movie "booby prize." "To a democratic intelligence," he wrote, "it is repulsive and insulting." Dwight Macdonald, a former Marxist, was so outraged that he recruited a number of other prominent leftist writers and intellectuals, including Alfred Kazin, Edmund Wilson, Max Eastman, and Sidney Hook, to sign a letter denouncing the movie in blistering terms, accusing it of, among other things, "glorifying dictatorship."

But it was John Dewey, America's most eminent living philosopher, who issued the most powerful condemnation of all. In 1937, Dewey had chaired an independent inquiry of the Soviet purges, which found that the show trials were ruthless "frame-ups" of men whom Stalin perceived as his personal and political enemies. In a May 1943 letter to the *New York Times,* Dewey blasted *Mission to Moscow* as "the first instance in our country of totalitarian propaganda for mass consumption—a propaganda which falsifies history through distortion, omission or pure invention of facts."*

For his part, Roosevelt seemed unconcerned. He continued to use Joseph Davies as one of his principal Soviet advisers and as a liaison between the White House and the Soviet Embassy in Washington. The arrangement gave Soviet ambassador Maxim Litvinov a direct channel to the president, without the necessity of going through the State Department.

In the spring of 1943, Davies was dispatched to Moscow on a special presidential mission to try to arrange a private, one-on-one meeting between Roosevelt and Stalin. Davies arrived aboard a plane with "Mission to Moscow," in both English and Russian, painted on the nose. In their talks, Davies assured Stalin that FDR was not averse to the Kremlin's claim to Polish territory but that, for political reasons, the president could not say so publicly. Roosevelt "is concerned," Davies told Stalin, "that there should not even be the suspicion that the principles of the Atlantic Charter were not being now sustained by the three Allies."

———

IN GILDING THE Soviet image in the United States, Roosevelt and his administration did their best to mask the Soviets' brutal treatment of the people of eastern Poland—the deportations, the missing Polish officers, the Kremlin's note declaring that Poles in the east were now to be considered Soviet citizens.

Hoping to guarantee the Polish government-in-exile's silence on these and other matters, the White House and State Department played on the Poles' belief that the United States—and the president him-

* In 1947, as the Cold War and McCarthyism gathered force, Warner Bros., concerned about congressional investigations of Hollywood, destroyed all release prints of *Mission to Moscow.* In the late 1940s and early 1950s, Warner Bros. and certain other studios evidently sought to atone for their wartime, pro-Soviet enthusiasm by producing a stream of equally mindless anti-Communist pictures, such as *I Was a Communist for the FBI* and *Big Jim McLain* (starring John Wayne).

self—would, when the time was right, intercede on Poland's behalf. At about the same time that Davies was in Moscow, reassuring Stalin, FDR was telling the Polish ambassador, Jan Ciechanowski, that, much to his regret, his advisers had persuaded him that the time was *not* right—yet. Until a more propitious time arrived, Roosevelt said, the Polish government must not publicize the Soviet demands for Polish territory or the Soviet policy of retaining Poles who were now trapped in the Soviet Union. "I felt this was a mistake...," Ciechanowski later wrote. "To be effective... intervention would have to be immediate, strong, and publicly known. And we were asked to keep everything secret. We were deprived of the possibility of obtaining the support of public opinion. Our lips were sealed."

In Britain, Prime Minister Churchill was doing some arm-twisting of his own. When the exile Polish press—more than twenty newspapers and magazines—became a little too feisty, the Polish government was pressured into vetting all editorials prior to publication. At the same time, the Churchill government demanded that the Polish press not discuss Polish-Soviet differences, particularly in regard to Soviet demands for eastern Poland.

Technically, Britain's wartime censorship was supposed to cover only security matters that might be of assistance to the enemy—troop movements, battle plans, and the like. The government had no authority to censor expressions of opinion. But as the war progressed, Churchill tried to persuade British newspapers, as well as Polish, to keep controversial matters quiet. On occasion, he even tried to sanction publications for publishing stories and opinions of which he did not approve. Lord Francis-Williams, the Ministry of Information official in charge of press censorship, deplored the willingness of much of the British press to give in to an "increasingly autocratic" Churchill and to cover up such ticklish issues as the Soviets' persecution of the Poles. "I am convinced...," Francis-Williams wrote after the war, "that, even in the special circumstances of war, more damage was done when the newspapers accepted, as they often did, Government directives on policy outside the strict and narrow limitations of security censorship than when they ignored them."

With the silencing of the Polish press and the government-in-exile and with the co-opting of much of the British press, the Kremlin was free to disseminate, virtually unchallenged, its views on Poland and its future. Moscow's chief instrument in Britain was *Soviet War News,* a weekly journal published by the Soviet Embassy in London and sent to British newspapers and to government officials and other prominent public figures. Later, it was sold to the public, its circulation reaching a peak of 50,000 copies.

With an eye to discrediting any potential rival for power in Warsaw once the war was over, *Soviet War News* frequently attacked the government-in-exile. The mostly liberal London Poles—who, unlike the Kremlin, had never made a deal with Hitler and had been fighting him since 1939—were accused of being, among other things, conservative reactionaries, unrepresentative of the Polish people, and "accomplices of the cannibal Hitler." So vitriolic were these assaults that Churchill himself felt compelled more than once to protest to the Soviet ambassador. His complaints had little effect.

By 1943, such British publications as the *Manchester Guardian,* the *New Statesman,* the *News Chronicle,* and the *Daily Express* were also inveighing against the Poles. Echoing some of the Soviets' milder accusations, the papers claimed that Polish hatred of Russia was at the core of the Polish-Soviet dispute, that the Poles, in refusing to give up some of their territory, were behaving with a suicidal lack of common sense.

By this time, the Polish-British romance was clearly over. The Poles, because of their opposition to Soviet demands, were now regarded by a growing number of Britons as troublemaking nuisances rather than as valued allies. Polish airmen were no longer the darlings of the press and the public. Lady Jersey, for one, had given up her duties as "mother" to Squadron 315 and started throwing parties instead for the U.S. Army and Air Force officers flooding into Britain.

In a gloomy mood, the Polish ambassador to Great Britain, Edward Raczyński, wrote in his diary: "The Polish Government and people have at the moment nothing to offer except what they have already thrown into the scale—a cause worthy of support by all free nations, the steadfastness of our countrymen oppressed by the invader, and the courage of our fighting men, especially sailors and airmen. These things, however, are no substitute for material strength in a life-and-death struggle, and we have no political freedom of manoeuvre which would enable us to 'put up our price.' "

The Poles' steep decline in popularity in Britain was matched by a dizzying rise in popular regard for the Russians, aided, as in the United States, by a vigorous government public relations campaign. In movies, books, lectures, magazine and newspaper articles, the Soviet government was portrayed as popular, strong, and increasingly liberal. The Soviet example was frequently offered as something for the British to follow. A Ministry of Labor poster, for instance, urged British female factory workers to emulate their Soviet counterparts. And, as Mollie Panter-Downes noted with amusement in *The New Yorker,* British farmers were encouraged to "study the success of the Russian scorched-earth policy, with a view to repeating in Sussex villages what has been found to work so admirably in the Ukraine grain fields." The Soviet ambassador in London, Ivan Maisky, once a pariah, now was deluged with party invitations, requests for lectures and press interviews, and summons to meetings with Churchill and other government officials. This former revolutionary was even given honorary membership in the exclusive Athenaeum Club.

As the war progressed, there was less and less tolerance in Britain for anyone who dissented from the prevailing jolly view of Stalin and his government. A. P. Herbert, an independent member of Parliament and iconoclastic writer for *Punch,* discovered this for himself when he wrote a poem called "Less Nonsense," tweaking Stalin's British admirers who were now calling for a second front:

> *Let's have less nonsense from the friends of Joe;*
> *We laud, we love him, but the nonsense—NO!*
> *In 1940, when we bore the brunt,*
> *WE could have done, boys, with a second front.*
> *A continent went down a cataract,*
> *But Russia did not think it right to act . . .*

Herbert's doggerel touched off a firestorm of protest among British leftists. A colleague of Herbert's declared in the House of Commons that the poem was "offensive to the Soviet Union and calculated to injure our friendship toward that country." Noting that copies of the poem had been circulating among some British army units, the MP demanded that such "political activity" be stopped immediately and that lectures praising the Soviet Union be given to the soldiers "to counteract the effects of this propaganda."

When George Orwell submitted *Animal Farm,* his biting satire on Soviet totalitarianism, to British publishers in 1943, it was rejected by every editor who saw it. One publisher, who initially accepted it, had second thoughts after receiving a warning from the Ministry of Information that the book would damage Britain's relationship with Russia. "If the fable were addressed generally to dictators and dictatorships at large, then publication would be all right," the publisher wrote Orwell's agent. "But the fable does follow, as I see now, so completely the progress of the Russian Soviets and their two dictators [Lenin and Stalin], that it can apply only to Russia.... Another thing: it would be less offensive if the predominant caste in the fable were not pigs. I think the choice of pigs as the ruling caste will no doubt give offence to many people, and particularly to anyone who is a bit touchy, as undoubtedly the Russians are."

Orwell was furious. England's most prominent political writer was already an outspoken critic of what he saw as a whitewashing of Soviet behavior by left-wing British intellectuals and the press. Called "the conscience of his generation" by V. S. Pritchett, Orwell was a militant socialist and, at the same time, an uncompromising champion of democracy and individual liberties. He had no patience for political hypocrisy and deceit, and spoke out against "this nation-wide conspiracy to flatter our ally," this "fog of lies and misinformation."

"Any serious criticism of the Soviet regime, any disclosure of facts which the Soviet government would prefer to keep hidden, is next door to unprintable...," Orwell later wrote. "These people [in the press and the government] don't see that if you encourage totalitarian methods, the time may come when they will be used against you instead of for you.... If liberty means anything at all, it means the right to tell people what they do not want to hear."

Despite Orwell's warnings, uncritical British and American admiration of all things Soviet continued. In the spring of 1943, elation over the Russian victory at Stalingrad was fresh, *Mission to Moscow* had just been released, *Life* had published its adulatory issue on the Soviet Union, Britain had celebrated Red Army Day with speeches, parades, and parties throughout the country. And, on top of all that, the U.S. and British governments were continuing to promote the idea of a happy, trouble-free alliance with the Soviets. There was no mention of Stalin's ever-increasing demands, of the escalating Polish-Soviet crisis.

No mention at all—until Katyn.

ON APRIL 13, 1943, German radio made a stunning announcement: Wehrmacht troops had just found the bodies of more than 4,000 Polish officers packed in mass graves in Katyn Forest, in German-occupied western Russia. According to the Nazis, the murderers were Russian.

News of the massacre struck Poles everywhere like a hammer blow. For twenty months, from the time General Anders began forming his army in Russia, the Polish government had been searching for those officers and 11,000 others—all of whom had vanished during the spring of 1940. Ever since, in notes and letters, in official and unofficial visits, Polish leaders, including Sikorski and Anders, had repeatedly pressed the Soviets for information about the missing men. Again and again, the Soviets denied any knowledge of their whereabouts; in 1941, Stalin himself suggested that they might have escaped to Manchuria. After the bodies were found in Soviet territory, the Kremlin insisted it had no information on the matter. Soviet officials speculated that the officers must have fallen into German hands and been killed when the Nazis invaded Russia in 1941.

This crossfire of accusations left the Poles in an excruciating dilemma. At first, knowing that the Nazis were quite capable of committing the murders, they were reluctant to credit German accusations against the Soviets. Indeed, they suspected—again, not unreasonably—that the Germans might simply be using the case to create dissension among the Allies. Still, the wealth of detail supplied by the Germans, supplemented by information gathered by the Polish underground, unequivocally pointed toward Russian culpability. What to do? If the Polish government accused the Russians directly, there would be trouble among the Allies, and the Germans would have achieved the propaganda victory they desired. Yet the savage murder of thousands from Poland's military and civilian elite cried out for justice. Messages from the Warsaw underground to London made clear that the country, shaken with horror and grief, was demanding nothing less.

On April 15, General Sikorski formally requested that the International Red Cross conduct an independent investigation. "We Poles ... are trying to refrain from proclaiming a premature verdict...," said an official. "We are awaiting conclusive evidence and we repeat to the world: We know nothing." About Sikorski's request to the Red Cross,

George Kennan would later write: "It is hard to see how [he] could have done less."

Yet Churchill and others in the British government were dismayed when they learned what the Poles were asking. The prime minister, so solicitous about Polish suffering in the past, now offered little sympathy and no condolences. Churchill had little doubt about Soviet guilt but was concerned about Stalin's reaction to Sikorski's proposal. He had already said to Sikorski: "Alas, the German accusations are probably true. The Bolsheviks can be very cruel." But he and Anthony Eden warned the Polish leader not to make an issue of the atrocity and urged him to withdraw his request to the Red Cross.

Sikorski refused. "Force is on Russia's side, justice on ours," he declared. "I do not advise the British people to cast their lot with brute force and to stampede justice before the eyes of all nations." Churchill and Eden, however, were far less concerned with justice at that point than with Allied unity, or at least a semblance of it. Under continuing pressure, Sikorski reluctantly agreed to stand mute and take no further action.

As it turned out, the Red Cross declined to conduct an investigation of the Katyn murders because the Soviet Union, the other party in the dispute, refused to cooperate. On April 26, the Soviets, using the Red Cross appeal as a pretext for taking a step it had been planning for months, formally severed diplomatic relations with Poland.

In a top-secret cable, the British Foreign Office informed the U.S. State Department that it believed the "Soviet Government had broken with the Poles . . . to cover up their guilt." Nonetheless, when Churchill sent a message to Stalin urging him to reconsider the break, the British prime minister placed all the blame for the rupture on the Poles. "Eden and I have pointed out to the Polish Government," Churchill wrote, "that no resumption of friendly or working relations with Soviet Russia is possible while they make charges of an insulting character against the Soviet Government and thus seem to countenance the atrocious Nazi propaganda." He also promised to gag the Polish press in Britain—those "miserable rags," he called them—if they persisted in printing anti-Soviet material.

Meanwhile, the Soviets kept up their drumbeat of what Alexander Cadogan described in his diary as "savage and disgraceful" attacks against the Poles, accusing them, above all, of colluding with the Nazis. Much of the British press followed their own government's lead, charging the Polish government-in-exile with seeking to subvert the alliance. Until the Katyn graves were found, most Westerners, thanks to the tactics of the United States and Britain, had heard nothing about the missing officers or the attempts to find them. Even when the graves were opened and the bodies exhumed, many in the West, misled by Polish silence and the whitewashing of the murders by the British and the United States, still sided with the Soviets.

In most British publications, there were no calls for investigations of Katyn, no reference to the ideals and moral principles on which the anti-Axis alliance was based. Instead, the emphasis was on power politics and winning the war, on soothing the Soviets and preserving the alliance. In condemning the Poles for appealing to the Red Cross, the *New Statesman* acknowledged that Polish officers might indeed have been shot by the Soviet secret police. But, in a chilling aside, the publication justified such an action, saying it was understandable that "the Soviet Government, often with reason, would regard the landed aristocracy and the officer class of Poland in the light of Fascists and class enemies." In another criticism of the Poles' appeal, the *Spectator* declared: "There is more to be said for leaving the dead to their sleep. No amount of investigation will bring them to life."

While British officials and editors tried to draw a curtain over the Katyn affair as swiftly as possible, one member of Churchill's government did the opposite. Sir Owen O'Malley, the British ambassador to the Polish government-in-exile, conducted his own investigation of the murders, examining dozens of documents and interviewing a number of Polish sources. From his research, he reconstructed the story of the officers' imprisonment and executions in, as it turned out, an extraordinarily accurate manner. The result—a report sent to George VI, Churchill, and the War Cabinet in June 1943—was a meticulously detailed, passionately written confirmation of Soviet guilt.

In his report, O'Malley described the camp where the Poles had been imprisoned, their scribbled messages on the walls of the train that took them to their deaths, the mouths of those who resisted stuffed with sawdust, the bullets in the back of their skulls, the bodies stacked like so much firewood in the pit. "When it was all over and the last shot had been fired and the last Polish head had been punctured," the ambassador wrote, "the butchers—perhaps trained in youth to husbandry—seem to have turned their hands to one of the most innocent of occupations: smoothing the clods and planting little conifers all over what had been a shambles."

O'Malley's report did not stop at an indictment of the Soviets, however. Profoundly shaken by the Katyn killings and by his government's whitewash of them, the career diplomat jettisoned all diplomatic detachment. He acknowledged the political considerations that made the British government believe that silence and dissembling were, in this case, necessary evils. But he also pondered the moral and ethical costs. "We have been obliged to ... distort the normal and healthy operation of our intellectual and moral judgements," he wrote. "We have been obliged to give undue prominence to the tactlessness or impulsiveness of the Poles, to restrain the Poles from putting their case clearly before the public, to discourage any attempt by the public and the press to probe the ugly story to the bottom.... We have, in fact, used the good name of England to cover up a massacre." What, O'Malley wondered, would "this dislocation between our public attitude and our private feelings" portend for Britain's future dealings with both the Poles and the Russians?

Deeply unsettled by O'Malley's "brilliant, unorthodox and disquieting dispatch," as one top official described it, Churchill and his government decided to keep it secret. "Of course, it would be only honest to circulate it," acknowledged Alexander Cadogan. "But as we know that the knowledge of this evidence cannot affect the course of action, or policy, is there any advantage in exposing more individuals than necessary to the spiritual conflict that a reading of this dispatch excites?" And Churchill cautioned Anthony Eden: "We should, none of us, ever speak a word about it."

Still, Churchill did see fit to send a copy of the O'Malley report to President Roosevelt, describing it in an accompanying letter as "a grim, well-written story ... perhaps a little too well-written." "Nevertheless," Churchill added, "if you have time to read it, it would repay the trouble. I should like to have it back when you have finished with it, as we are not circulating it officially in any way."

If Roosevelt ever bothered to read the O'Malley dispatch, he apparently never said so, in public or private. Nor does he seem to have discussed it with anyone at the White House or circulated it among his cabinet or other government officials. He had already received his own report on the Katyn tragedy, researched and written by an army officer serving as U.S. military liaison with the Polish army in Britain. That report also concluded that the Soviets were guilty of the murders—and was stashed away in a government warehouse, by order of the White House.

Roosevelt's principal response to Katyn seems to have been annoyance. The "graves question," he fumed, "wasn't worth such a fuss." "Wow," he added, "what fools [the London Poles] are! I've no patience with them." In a cable to Stalin, the president said he "fully understood [the Soviet leader's] problem." He thought the Poles "misguided" but hoped Stalin would not break off relations with them. Noting in his cable the large number of Polish-Americans in the United States, the president was obviously thinking of his own standing with Polish-American voters when he added that "the situation would not be helped by the knowledge of a complete diplomatic break between yourself and Sikorski."

Behind the scenes, the president did ask John F. Carter, who was leading a small research team that worked directly for the president, to investigate Katyn and to prepare a report. Roosevelt told Carter he thought the Russians were probably guilty. Yet when Carter and his team presented that very conclusion to FDR, the memo was suppressed. So were two other U.S. indictments of the Soviets, one written by a U.S. Army colonel, a German prisoner of war, who was present at the exhumation of some of the Polish officers' bodies and who concluded that the Soviets had indeed murdered the Poles. Classified "top secret" at the time by army intelligence in Washington, no trace of the colonel's report has ever been found. After the war, an army intelligence official acknowledged that the report had been classified and jettisoned because of its "great possibilities of [causing] embarrassment.... The [Russians] would have gotten mad."

The only report on Katyn that the Roosevelt administration did not suppress was written in early 1944 by Kathleen Harriman, the daughter of U.S. ambassador to Moscow Averell Harriman. After the Soviets recaptured western Russia, they invited Miss Harriman, among other Americans, on a "fact-finding" tour of the Katyn gravesite. Afterward, she wrote that the Germans, in all likelihood, had killed the Polish officers. Years later, she acknowledged that, at the time, she actually believed the Russians to be the guilty party but could not dispute the "evidence" they had produced.

Denied knowledge of the details of Katyn, most American newspapers and magazines, like the British press, took the Soviets' side. In Berlin, Joseph Goebbels wrote in his diary: "The Poles are given a brush-off by the English and the Americans as though they were enemies." A number of U.S. publications flatly declared that the Russians were innocent of the killings and that the Poles were irresponsible troublemakers intent on wrecking the Western-Soviet alliance. *Newsweek* attributed what it called "the Poles' mistaken tactics" to "that curious trait of unrealism that led Polish lancers to charge German tanks and that still permeates Polish politics." *Life* said Poles were "the most chip-shouldered chauvinists in Europe," and, in a candid expression of realpolitik, added: "The important thing for us to remember is that no vital U.S. interest is involved in the Russo-Polish dispute.... Since our major self-interest lies with Russia, our diplomats ought not to get too huffy in backing up the Poles."

For Witold Urbanowicz, who was based in Washington at the time of the Katyn revelations, this cynical attitude was impossible to understand. His pain and outrage over Katyn was heightened by the fact that he knew a number of the victims—and by the knowledge that, if he hadn't escaped from the Soviets in late September 1939, he might well have ended up in one of those mass graves, too.

In the matter of Katyn, Stalin and his government, with a great deal of help from London and Washington, had pulled off a public relations coup—turning a hideous crime into a diplomatic and propaganda victory. Like Urbanowicz, Jan Nowak, a young Polish resistance fighter, noted with stunned disbelief the Western Allies' anger at the Poles for "demanding that the truth be established." Nowak was a courier with the Polish underground who slipped in and out of Poland to bring vital intelligence information to the British government and the Polish government-in-exile. As was true of many of his countrymen in occupied Poland, he had been looking to Britain and the United States as beacons of hope in an otherwise dark world. Surreptitiously listening in Warsaw to Polish-language broadcasts from the BBC and from the government-in-exile, Nowak and many other Poles had come to believe that the attention of the entire world was focused on their country, that Poland, because its people had fought so long and so bravely, was widely admired by its powerful Allies.

Occupied Poland "lived by faith in the Allies, in Churchill [and] Roosevelt...," Nowak later recalled. "Trying to forget the daily reality of arrests and executions, of death camps—it lived with a vision of a sunny future." Above all, nothing could shake the Poles' belief that Britain and the United States, with their "ideals of justice, truth, and freedom," would help to liberate their country.

After Katyn, Nowak realized he and his fellow Poles had been living a dream. Rather than admiring Poland, the Western Allies seemed to regard it as little more than an embarrassing nuisance. They failed to grasp that Poles could not simply write off thousands of murdered men as if they were numbers in a ledger, that there was a limit to the price a country should have to pay in the name of Allied harmony. Like other Poles, Nowak wondered how the British and Americans would have reacted had thousands of their officers been found dumped into mass graves. A year later, shortly before the Warsaw uprising, Nowak tried to convince his compatriots that they should not place so much faith in Britain and the United States. He did not succeed.

In London, meanwhile, the government-in-exile had learned its lesson from Katyn. When the Soviet government report exonerating itself of the murders was issued in early 1944, a bitter Owen O'Malley assured Anthony Eden that the British government had nothing to worry about in terms of Polish reaction. "Let us think of these things always and speak of them never," O'Malley wrote in a memo to Eden. "To speak of them never is the advice which I have been giving to the Polish Government, but it has been unnecessary. They have received the Russian report in silence. Affliction and residence in this country seem to be teaching them how much better it is in political life to leave unsaid those things about which one feels most passionately."

CHAPTER FIFTEEN

"The War Is in Poland"

For a few months in the midst of the war, an exquisitely embroidered, hand-stitched banner was on display at Northolt. Under the care of the Kościuszko Squadron for that period, the banner was the official standard of the Polish Air Force in Britain. It had been secretly sewn in 1940 by women in the city of Wilno, which was occupied then by the Soviets. From Wilno, the banner had been smuggled into England by the Polish underground.

Bearing an image of the Virgin Mary and the words "Love Demands Sacrifice," the banner was designed in late 1939 by a young Polish fighter pilot who, with thousands of his countrymen, had just arrived in France. Another pilot, a native of Wilno, arranged through underground contacts to have the standard made in his hometown. A search began for scarlet and white damask and for gold and silver embroidery thread, which were finally found in Berlin, of all places, and brought to Wilno by neutral diplomats. For more than three months, Polish women throughout the city risked their lives to work on the banner. It was completed in June 1940, but France had fallen by then and the problem of getting it to the Polish Air Force in England seemed insuperable. Once again, a diplomat—Wilno's Japanese consul, whose country was still nominally neutral at that point—came to the rescue by sending it out in a diplomatic pouch. The standard finally reached London in the spring of 1941. Most of the women who had sewn it never knew that: they, like hundreds of thousands of others in eastern Poland, had vanished—deported to the gulags and collectives of the Soviet Union.

That July, General Sikorski handed over the standard, which symbolized the connection between the Polish Air Force and the people of Poland, to 300 Bomber Squadron. Every three months, Sikorski declared, the standard would be sent on to another Polish squadron—until the fliers could carry it back to its rightful home in Poland.

A Kościuszko Squadron pilot hands over the official Polish Air Force standard to a pilot of 304 (Silesia) Squadron in March 1942. The standard was secretly sewn in 1940 by women in Wilno, then under Soviet occupation, and smuggled to London. (Polish Institute and Sikorski Museum)

From his first days in London, Sikorski had been making plans for the liberation of Poland. He was counting on the Polish armed forces abroad, particularly the air force, to play a key role. Polish infantrymen, pilots, and sailors took part in every major Allied campaign in Europe and North Africa. They helped defend Britain and liberate France, Belgium, and other European countries. To the Polish military, however, those were but means to an end. Their motto was "For Your Freedom and Ours." Once they had fulfilled the first part of the pledge, they planned to fulfill the second—by freeing their own land.

Under Sikorski's plan, when the tide of the war finally turned, Poland's huge underground fighting force, the Home Army (the *Armia Krajowa*, or *AK*), was to rise up, harassing the Germans as they retreated. Eventually, the Home Army was to link up with Polish and other Allied troops for the final push to freedom. But before all this happened, the air force was to drop arms and supplies to the Home Army. As early as 1941, these missions had already begun, albeit on an irregular basis, and Poles were making clandestine trips from London to Poland, behind German lines, to discuss with Home Army leaders the logistics of liberation.

BY 1943, THE Poles, with well over 150,000 men in arms, were an important element in Allied planning for future campaigns. Two large Polish armies were winding up their training, preparing for impending assaults on Europe. In Palestine, more than 60,000 soldiers of II Polish Corps, commanded by General Władysław Anders, were drilling daily under the hot desert sun, waiting for word to head for Italy. Observing these bronzed, tough, disciplined soldiers, visitors found it difficult to believe that many of them had been little more than walking skeletons in Russia less than two years before. A correspondent for *The Times* predicted: "This is going to be an army to be reckoned with." During his own visit to II Corps, Harold Macmillan, then the British government liaison to the Allied forces in North Africa, was also impressed—less by the Poles' toughness and discipline than by their spirit, which Macmillan described as "an extraordinary sense of romance—not gaiety, exactly, but chivalry, poetry, adventure."

In Scotland, more than 30,000 troops of I Polish Corps continued their training as well, awaiting the cross-Channel invasion of Europe. Many of them had come to Britain in 1940 after fighting in France and had spent much of the previous three years guarding British shores from German invasion. They were joined in 1941 by several thousand troops evacuated from the Soviet Union. Among the corps' premier units was the 1st Armored Division, soon to make its mark in Normandy and beyond.

Winston Churchill, accompanied by General Władysław Sikorski, inspects Polish troops in Scotland. (Imperial War Museum)

Also undergoing intensive training in Scotland was the 1st Independent Polish Parachute Brigade, organized by General Stanisław Sosabowski for the purpose of parachuting into occupied Poland when the planned Home Army uprising began. Sosabowski's men were the only Polish troops whose sole objective was to fight for the liberation of their homeland. By Polish-British agreement, the parachute brigade, unlike all other Polish military units, was to be under complete Polish control.

Of course, the Polish Air Force, numbering more than 11,000 men by mid-1943, had already been in action in Britain for three years and continued to fly bombing, escort, and strafing missions over the Continent. The Polish pilots were still distinguishing themselves in action. During the Dieppe raid in August 1942, the Kościuszko Squadron, now under the command of Jan Zumbach, had demonstrated once again why it was one of the top Allied fighter units of the war. On Kościuszko's second sortie during the raid, Zumbach—together with Stanisław Skalski, his Dęblin classmate and the commander of 317 (Wilno) Squadron—laid a trap for German fighters attacking the small force of Allied commandos trying desperately (and futilely) to gain a beachhead on the French coast. Skalski's pilots, weaving and wobbling in the air like the rankest of aerial amateurs, were the bait. Spying these seemingly luckless novices, a swarm of Luftwaffe planes pounced, only to be ambushed themselves by Zumbach and his squadron, who had been flying above and behind the Wilno Squadron. The Kościuszko Squadron accounted for ten kills during the raid, while Wilno downed five—making up almost 20 percent of the total Allied score.

Since 1940, the Polish navy, albeit a considerably smaller force than its sister services, had played a not unimportant role in the Allied effort as well. Escaping from Poland with three destroyers and two submarines, the navy eventually received seven more destroyers, five submarines, and two cruisers from the Allies. During the war, it helped cover the evacuation of British forces from Dunkirk, took part in the Dieppe raid, escorted supply convoys to Malta and Russia, and patrolled the North Atlantic with both ships and submarines. By war's end, Polish naval personnel were credited with sinking at least thirty-one enemy warships and some fifty other vessels, and with downing nearly a hundred enemy planes.

Meanwhile, in occupied Poland, the Home Army was also in the fight, using sabotage and intelligence gathering as its main weapons. More than 350,000 strong, it was the largest resistance force in any occupied European nation and, according to a British military staff report, "the strongest, best organized and most determined."

The Home Army, however, was just one element of a highly sophisticated underground Polish government, complete with a bureaucracy, courts, parliament, and a countrywide network of clandestine schools. The Polish underground recognized the government-in-exile in London as the country's supreme political and legal authority, while making clear that it would not sanction any decision that seemed to interfere with the goal of regaining Poland's freedom. Communication between London and Poland was constant: couriers and others regularly slipped in and out of the country, despite extreme danger, and coded radio traffic was frequent.

In most other German-occupied countries, the resistance movements were largely organized and populated by leftists, from Christian democrats and democratic socialists to Communists. In Poland, virtually the entire nation—left, right, and center—had joined the conspiracy. Major General Colin Gubbins, who headed the British agency charged with inciting sabotage and subversion in occupied Europe, observed after the war that of all the European countries overrun by the Nazis, "only the Poles, toughened by centuries of oppression, were spiritually uncrushed."

Ordered to hand over their grain harvests to the Germans, Polish peasants abided by the maxim "as little, as late, and as bad as possible." In Nazi-run factories that produced goods for the German war economy, Polish workers sabotaged machinery and deliberately turned out defective products. Perhaps the most important sabotage, however, was carried out by the country's railway workers, who, together with members of the Home Army, were responsible for massive delays and disruptions of German rail transports through Poland.

The main supply and communications route from Germany to the eastern front lay through Poland, and the Poles were spectacularly successful in sabotaging it, slowing down and occasionally halting the movement of troops and materials to the front. Between 1941 and 1944, more than 7,000 German trains were destroyed, damaged, or derailed. Dozens of railroad bridges were blown up. The electricity grid at the Warsaw railroad center was shut down more than 600 times. At one point, 43 percent of all the locomotives in the General Government were inoperable.

After the war, Sir Douglas Savory, a member of Parliament from 1940 to 1955 and a staunch supporter of the Poles, argued that by interrupting the flow of matériel to the eastern front, the Polish resistance had contributed greatly "to the collapse of the German offensive in Russia." A Polish underground newspaper claimed that although 80 percent of the Soviet victory at Stalingrad was attributable to Russian effort, 20 percent belonged to the Poles, because of the delays they caused in the transport of German reinforcements and supplies. In an implicit acknowledgment of this, Germany operated trains through Poland only under increasingly heavy guard or diverted them away from Poland altogether, which caused more delays.

Inside Poland, German officials and troops discovered that they could never feel completely safe. The Polish underground assassinated thousands of them, including many members of the SS and Gestapo, during the six years of the war. In response, German government head-quarters in Warsaw and other major cities were barricaded, and Germans were forbidden to go into the countryside and forests where Polish partisan units were known to operate. Despite savage reprisals, the Polish resistance continued unabated. In September 1943, Joseph Goebbels noted in his diary that "acts of sabotage and terrorism have increased enormously in the General Government of Poland." According to one Polish resistance leader, the sabotage activities of his countrymen contributed as much to the Allied war effort as "several divisions fighting at the front."

As important as Polish sabotage was to the Allied cause, however, the underground's intelligence gathering, inside and outside Poland, proved even more vital. The young Polish cryptologists who broke Germany's Enigma cipher, for example, escaped to France after the fall of Poland and helped French radio intelligence operatives decipher traffic from the German military and from Nazi agents operating inside France. When France capitulated in 1940, the Poles worked at a clandestine center in southern France set up by Major Gustave Bertrand, head of French radio intelligence. With the crucial assistance of Polish cryptologists, and in defiance of the new Vichy government, Bertrand continued to supply Britain with information on German army, air force, and naval operations.

A number of Polish army officers who fought in France also stayed behind after the armistice and organized some of the French resistance movement's first major intelligence networks. One of those officers became a double agent and, in his spurious reports to the Reich, informed German authorities that Pas de Calais, not Normandy, would be the landing site for the Allied cross-Channel invasion in 1944. This was part of a much larger intelligence operation run out of London, aimed at persuading the Germans that Pas de Calais was to be the eventual landing point. The Polish officer's accounts strengthened the case and contributed to Hitler's decision to shift troops away from Normandy.

In the Swiss capital of Bern, a Polish female operative, under cover as a typist in the Polish legation, served as the link between British intelligence and Admiral Wilhelm Canaris, the disaffected head of Hitler's counterintelligence service. Determined to topple Hitler because of, among other things, his atrocities in Poland, Canaris passed on classified military information to the Polish woman, a friend of his before the war, who in turn handed the material over to the British Secret Intelligence Service.

Another woman working for British intelligence was perhaps the most spectacular Polish spy of all during the war. Known as Christine Granville, she was actually Countess Krystyna Gizycka (née Skarbek), the young and beautiful scion of a Polish aristocratic family. A legend in intelligence circles for her daring, Granville smuggled British prisoners of war out of Poland and transmitted intelligence from German-occupied Hungary and Romania. Later in the war, she rescued three French resistance leaders from prison the night before they were to be executed by the Germans. Sir Owen O'Malley, who worked with Granville while serving as British ambassador to Hungary early in the war, called her "the bravest person I ever knew." He added: "She could do anything with dynamite except eat it."*

In Poland itself, the underground operated a highly developed intelligence network that extended into every part of the country, even into Auschwitz and other Nazi camps. The Home Army intelligence service was the Allies' chief source of information about German involvement on the eastern front, including the German forces' order of battle, troop and ship movements, armament and industrial production, Nazi secret weapon testing, and the morale of German troops. "We cannot over-emphasize the importance and value attaching to the very excellent services which have been rendered by this magnificent organization...," a British military intelligence report declared in July 1942.

In 1943, thanks in large part to intelligence received from Poland, the RAF was able to locate and bomb a major German rocket-testing site at

---

* Polish women played an important part both in the resistance and in the work of the armed forces abroad. In the underground, women performed a variety of roles, including the highly dangerous job of carrying messages and correspondence from one underground cell to another. Hundreds of these so-called liaison girls were caught and executed immediately or sent to concentration camps. A number of operatives wound up at Ravensbruck, where they were injected with bacilli and otherwise treated as medical guinea pigs by Nazi doctors. The results usually were fatal.

In Britain, several Polish women, including Jadwiga Piłsudska, the daughter of Marshal Piłsudski, were ferry pilots in the Polish Air Force, delivering new and repaired Hurricanes, Spitfires, and other planes to RAF stations around the country. More than 1,400 other women, many of whom had been deported to the Soviet Union and left with General Anders's army in 1942, joined the Polish Women's Auxiliary Air Service in Britain, equivalent to the British WAAFs. A similar women's auxiliary organization was created by Anders in the Middle East: its members, attached to the II Polish Corps, drove trucks, worked in hospitals and canteens, operated radios, and provided other essential support services.

Peenemünde—an action that served to delay Germany's launching of the V-1 and V-2 missiles against Britain until after D-Day. If the rockets had rained down on southern England before the Allies invaded the Continent, the result could well have been disruption of the military buildup and postponement or cancellation of the attack. In 1944, a V-2 missile that misfired from a range in Poland was recovered by members of the Polish underground, who dismantled it and smuggled it to London.

There was one other vital service that the Polish underground performed for its Western allies: sheltering scores of British and American prisoners of war who had escaped from German camps, as well as Allied airmen shot down over Poland. In late 1944, seven crew members of a B-17 downed over eastern Poland described in the *Saturday Evening Post* how they had been rescued and protected by a large band of Polish partisans operating near Brest-Litovsk. The American fliers spent more than a month with the Poles, who, on July 4, 1944, staged a makeshift parade in honor of their guests' Independence Day, complete with patriotic speeches. "That parade made a lasting impression on all of us," said the B-17's co-pilot. The Poles "were trying to give us a little hunk of home—and to do it, they risked surprise by the Germans, who were always nearby." Eventually, the resistance was able to spirit the Americans out of the country. After returning to their base in England, one of them declared: "If we worked all our lives for the Poles, regardless of the dangers and hazards involved, we should never be able to repay what they did for us."

NOTWITHSTANDING all these contributions, the primary objective of the Polish underground movement from its inception was the planning and carrying out of a full-scale national uprising against the Germans. In the early days of the war, a number of British officials approved of that priority. In 1940, a secret British agency, the Special Operations Executive (SOE), was set up at Winston Churchill's behest to foment sabotage, subversion, and resistance in occupied Europe. The SOE saw its main job, at least in the beginning, as the supplying of underground armies in German-occupied countries. At the right moment, according to the SOE plan, the armies would rise up against the Germans and capture such key local targets as military headquarters, broadcasting stations, and other communication centers. Together with Allied sea and air invasion forces, the resistance armies would destroy German forces and thus help liberate their own countries.

As the ally with the strongest and most effective resistance movement, the Poles were highly regarded by the SOE and were given special privileges. The Polish government was granted autonomy in communicating with its own resistance movement, using its own ciphers. The Poles, not the SOE, planned supply drops and clandestine sorties into and out of Poland and chose the agents for the missions. The SOE served merely as a supply agency, providing the aircraft and other means to carry out the operations.

The problem was, the SOE did not have the freedom to assign planes on its own. The agency was subordinate to the British chiefs of staff, who looked with jaundiced eye on the SOE's unconventional ventures and resisted the sharing of scarce resources, particularly aircraft. Bombers were the only planes suitable for dropping men, arms, and supplies into Poland and other occupied countries, and the RAF's Bomber Command was strongly opposed to lending out any aircraft that could be used in its bombing offensive against Germany. More often than not, the SOE did not get the bombers it requested.

Making matters worse for the Polish Home Army, the British military command decided in the fall of 1941 that national uprisings by secret armies were no longer a necessary prerequisite to the Allied liberation of Europe. As a result, while resistance movements were still encouraged and would receive money and supplies for sabotage activities, there would be no massive arms drops in preparation for an uprising.

Even the limited supply missions to Poland proved more sporadic and less frequent than the British had promised—a source of serious concern for the underground, which relied on the flights to bring in vitally needed agents, money, ammunition, and other matériel. The British military insisted that difficult logistical problems were the main reason for the small number of flights. Making the 1,000-mile trip from Britain to Poland was unquestionably a highly dangerous undertaking: the crews of 138 Special Duties Squadron, the bomber unit assigned to the drop operations, had to cross German-occupied territory to reach their destination, braving antiaircraft fire and enemy fighter planes along the entire route. Another significant obstacle was the weather. Even if skies were clear in England and over the North Sea when the bombers took off, there were often clouds or rain over Poland, making drops or landings highly problematic. The round-trip flight could take up to fourteen hours, and the bombers' fuel reserves were so limited that even the slightest navigational mistake could be disastrous.

The Poles acknowledged the difficulties, but they and a number of Britons in the SOE were nonetheless convinced that military and political considerations also restricted the number of missions. As planning for a cross-Channel invasion progressed, aid to resistance movements in France, Belgium, and Holland received a much higher priority from the British and Americans, as did assistance to resistance fighters in Italy, Greece, and Yugoslavia. Throughout the war, Poland, despite the strength and effectiveness of its underground, received a tenth of the supplies that were dropped to Greece, and barely one twentieth of those dropped to France and Yugoslavia. Since Poland was so far from future Allied theaters of operation in Europe, there was little strategic value for Britain and the United States in coming to its aid.

In the last two months of 1942, for example, the RAF, despite good weather conditions, suspended all scheduled flights to Poland. Bomber crews were reassigned to what were considered operations of higher priority—drop missions over France and Norway and providing cover for the Allied landings in North Africa. Such last-minute changes, giving short shrift to the Poles, were not uncommon and were a source of great irritation to SOE officials and to Lord Selborne, the minister of economic warfare, whose portfolio included the SOE.

In one angry memo to Air Ministry officials, Selborne declared that those responsible for delaying or postponing the missions to Poland seemed to have no idea of the "enormous preparation" that members of the Polish underground had to make to receive the drops on designated nights without the Germans' finding out. Reception parties lay in hiding near the drop zones and waited days and nights that sometimes turned into weeks. The delays imposed a considerable hardship on them and only added to the already great risk of capture and death.

In a memo to Churchill about the Polish government's bitterness over the scarcity of supply operations to Poland, Selborne wrote: "I confess to great sympathy with the Polish standpoint. They braved Hitler in 1939 on Britain's guaranteed support. They have been crucified. They have not winced. Alone among our occupied Allies, they have no Quisling. They have incurred considerable casualties in very successfully attacking German communications to Russia at our request. They have an organized army of 250,000 in Poland which only needs equipment.... To the Poles the war is in Poland and this is their best chance of fighting there."

But to Britain and the United States, the war in Poland had little significance, and on this issue, the Poles had no leverage over their two larger Allies. The British and Americans well knew that the Polish armed forces would remain loyal to the Allied cause, even if little help was given to the Home Army. A Joint Planning Staff memo from a 1943 conference between Roosevelt and Churchill in Quebec observed: "It is assumed that Polish forces will continue to fight with the British, and they need not be considered as sacrificed by non-support of the Polish 'Secret Army.'..."

The Soviets, on the other hand, were always a question mark in terms of loyalty to the Allied cause. Britain and the United States never stopped worrying that Stalin might sign a separate peace with Hitler. The Poles in London therefore continued to believe that the most important reason for the Western Allies' failure to provide significant aid for the Home Army was not logistical problems or the distance of Poland from future fronts. Rather, they were convinced, it was the reluctance of Churchill and Roosevelt to annoy the Soviet leader.

The Poles' suspicions were confirmed in the summer of 1943 when, after the Katyn controversy, the government-in-exile made a last-ditch request to British and American military leaders for a substantial increase in support for its underground movement. The Poles held firm to their plans for a national uprising: under their blueprint, the Home Army would seize control of central Poland as part of the upcoming Allied offensive in Europe, with the army's strength reinforced by the transfer to Poland of units of the Polish Air Force and 1st Parachute Brigade. The Home Army would then link up with Allied forces advancing from the west.

The combined British and American military chiefs of staff rejected the Polish government's request. They could not provide the arms and other supplies, they said, because they lacked aircraft to deliver them and because they believed the Home Army could not stage a successful uprising without the immediate support of Allied troops. A Polish colonel attached to the Washington headquarters of the Combined Chiefs of Staff asked an American counterpart if "these arguments put forward were actually the main reason for the decision or whether the crux of the question lay elsewhere." Off the record, the American acknowledged, the "crux of the question was connected with the Soviet problem."

The Combined Chiefs had been advised in a top-secret memo by their intelligence staff that "in the present circumstances, the Russian reaction to any attempt to equip fully the secret army in Poland would be violently hostile." This, of course, was because the Kremlin was already planning a Soviet takeover of postwar Poland. In a report to London, the British military mission in Washington noted that the rejection of the Poles' request was meant to avoid friction with the Soviet Union.

In an attempt to soften the blow of their veto, the British and American military chiefs did promise that they would increase aid to the Polish Home Army for sabotage purposes. In November 1943, the six Polish crews attached to 138 Special Duties Squadron in Britain were sent to Brindisi, Italy, and re-formed as the 1586 Polish Special Duties Flight. On paper, their primary task was to fly supply operations to Poland.

But even this latest promise of limited military support met with Soviet disapproval. In October, at a Big Three foreign ministers' meeting in Moscow, Vyacheslav Molotov made clear to Anthony Eden that the Russians did not take kindly to the idea of *any* arms for the Poles. The following month, Stalin, Churchill, and Roosevelt were to travel to Tehran for their first face-to-face meeting, and the British and Americans were particularly anxious not to do anything that might cause problems at the conference.

Despite the Combined Chiefs' promises and the transfer of the Poles to Italy, Allied supply missions to Poland were almost completely curtailed for the next five months. Of the 301 flights originally planned to Poland from October 1943 to March 1944, only 28 were actually made.

As the end of the war came nearer, as the Germans increasingly lost ground and the Red Army once again approached Poland's borders, the Home Army, largely deprived of its lifeline to the West, found itself desperately short of money, communications equipment, ammunition, and arms. Still, in their determination to mount an uprising against the Germans, the Poles were unshakable.

The stage was set for disaster.

CHAPTER SIXTEEN

A Question of Honor

IN THE FALL of 1943, Franklin Roosevelt and Winston Churchill set out separately on a lengthy wartime odyssey. They were bound first for Cairo, where they were to discuss with China's Generalissimo Chiang Kai-shek the progress of the war in the Pacific. Then the president and the prime minister were to fly on to Tehran for the main event—their first Big Three conference with Joseph Stalin. Boarding the battleship USS *Iowa* in the Chesapeake Bay on November 12, Roosevelt anticipated his first meeting with Stalin "with the enthusiasm of a boy." Churchill, who left Plymouth aboard the battleship HMS *Renown* the day before, was hopeful but apprehensive. And what was Stalin thinking as he prepared for his own journey from Moscow to Tehran? Well, one never quite knew what the inscrutable Georgian had on his mind.

During the five days of the Cairo Conference, Roosevelt, Churchill, and Chiang agreed to pursue all-out war against Japan until they had achieved an unconditional surrender. Afterward, Roosevelt and Churchill proceeded to Iran's dusty capital, sprawled beneath the snow-covered peaks of the Elburz Mountains, for their meeting with Stalin, set to begin on November 28. As they made their way to Tehran, Roosevelt and Churchill could take considerable satisfaction in the way the European war seemed to be going. After repeated setbacks, Anglo-American forces were finally and firmly on the offensive. Rommel had been vanquished in North Africa. Sicily had been captured. Mussolini had been overthrown, and his Fascist government had surrendered. Allied troops were now slogging their way up the Italian boot, trying to reclaim it from the Germans. Rome was within the Allies' grasp, or so British and American military leaders believed (they were soon proven wrong). And on the eastern front, the Red Army was close to pushing the Germans completely out of Russia.

The war's political and diplomatic aspects, however, were an altogether different matter. Eighteen months before, Stalin had managed to wangle a pledge from Roosevelt that a western front would soon be opened. That had not happened—and would not happen for another six months. Stalin, who regarded the North African and Italian campaigns as mere sideshows, was boiling with anger—so much so that the previous summer he had recalled his ambassadors from London and Washington.

Nor was the western front issue the alliance's only irritant. Stalin was also furious when British convoys carrying arms and other supplies to the USSR were temporarily suspended in May 1943 because of the extreme danger to the convoys' ships. Convoy duty to northern Russian ports was among the most brutal assignments of the war: German U-boats constantly patrolled the North and Norwegian seas and so far had managed to sink almost a fourth of all Allied shipping to the area.

Churchill had assured Stalin in September that the convoys would soon resume, although he demanded better treatment of British seamen once they reached Russian ports. Seamen in previous convoys had been forbidden by the Soviets to leave their ships without special passes, and a number of sailors who had gone ashore had been thrown indefinitely into Russian jails on charges of drunkenness. Stalin countered with a message of shrill fury: the British had an "obligation" to send the convoys, British sailors were nothing but idlers and spies, and Churchill's demands could only be seen as a "threat." The prime minister's response demonstrated that Stalin wasn't the only one who could be imperious. Churchill sent the message back to the Soviet Embassy with word that he refused to accept delivery.

On the eve of the Tehran Conference, it was clear to Churchill, at least, that the Western Allies' relationship with the Soviet Union was in considerable trouble, despite the image of a happy, problem-free alliance that he and Roosevelt had so strenuously promoted. Churchill's fear that Stalin would seek a separate peace with Hitler had been augmented by new worries about the Soviets' postwar intentions in

Europe, now that the Red Army had taken the offensive. The prime minister's concerns appeared, to those closest to him, to be wearing him down.

Churchill had been waging war for more than three years now, and the physical and emotional strain, compounded by the demands of his frequent trips to visit British troops and Allied statesmen, had left him gloomy and exhausted. Sir Alan Brooke, the wartime chief of the Imperial General Staff, and others in the British government were concerned about their chief's abrupt change of moods and positions on strategy and tactics, his "inability to finish one subject before taking up another," and an occasional "instability of judgment." More and more, Churchill's views on Stalin and the Soviets seesawed between hope and optimism, on the one hand, and an anxiety that approached outright despair on the other.

Looking toward the end of the war, he was determined to do whatever was necessary to protect long-term British interests in Europe. In the case at hand, that meant preventing, if possible, Soviet encroachment into such countries as Italy, Greece, and Turkey. For some time, Churchill had been urging Roosevelt to delay further the planned invasion of France and to mount instead an offensive through the Balkans, Europe's "soft underbelly," as Churchill saw it. During World War I, when he was First Lord of the Admiralty, Churchill helped devise a similar operation at Gallipoli—with utterly disastrous results. There were differences between the two plans. The first was in support of the Russians; the second meant to thwart them. Still, there were sound objections to the latest one—military as well as political—and Roosevelt in the end rejected it.

As things stood now, once the Red Army had the Germans decisively on the run, it would be poised to occupy most or all of Eastern Europe. Seeing that he was losing his "soft underbelly" argument, Churchill tried a diplomatic tack. He and Anthony Eden attempted to sell the idea of creating a confederation of democratic Eastern and Central European states, including Poland, which they hoped would act as a check against postwar Soviet power. The British also proposed that the United States and Britain join with the Soviets in deciding the future of Eastern Europe. For those plans to have any chance of success, they would need strong U.S. support. They did not get it. At a Moscow conference of foreign ministers in October, Soviet foreign minister Vyacheslav Molotov flatly (and not surprisingly) rejected the British ideas, while Secretary of State Cordell Hull declined to side with Eden, referring to questions over Eastern Europe as "these piddling little things."

Faced with this new strategic setback, Churchill struggled hard to convince himself that Stalin really meant it when he said he was in favor of a free and independent (if truncated) Poland. In that case, perhaps receiving the long-disputed parts of eastern Poland would be enough to satisfy the dictator's expansionist appetite. But Churchill's exercise in self-delusion was simply an example of a proud and principled man trying to rationalize something incapable of being rationalized. In the final analysis, it came down to a question of honor—whether promises were to be kept or broken, whether trust was to be justified or betrayed. Britain, as Churchill so often reminded others, had gone to war in the first place for Poland's independence. Churchill had pledged repeatedly to help recover that independence. Now he was searching for a way to break his pledge, yet keep his honor.

SHORTLY BEFORE THE Tehran Conference, Churchill (in spite of his qualms) and Eden effectively began the process of ceding eastern Poland to the USSR by putting direct pressure on the Polish government in-exile to accept the Curzon Line. The Poles refused. Even had they been inclined to accept, which they emphatically were not, Polish tradition and their own democratic principles prevented their surrendering any part of the country without agreement by the Polish people. The leaders of the Polish underground had already made clear their opposition to the idea. Furthermore, the Polish government argued that handing over eastern Poland to Stalin would only encourage, not deter, him from what they were convinced was his second goal: the establishment of a puppet Communist government for the entire country. From their unhappy experience during the nineteenth-century partitions, Poles knew only too well that loss of territory often leads to loss of independence.

This was an extremely difficult time for the Poles in London. They were being pressed by the Soviets and British at the same time that they were facing an uncertain future without their respected leader, General Władysław Sikorski. The Polish prime minister and commander in chief had been killed in a plane crash off Gibraltar in July; many Poles suspected sabotage, although an investigation by the British government concluded that the crash was an accident. Sikorski's successor was Stanisław Mikołajczyk, the leader of the influential, left-of-center Peasant Party and a member of the government-in-exile's cabinet.

The son of a farmer, the stocky, balding Mikołajczyk, who had led a strike in the 1930s against the repressive prewar Polish government, had a reputation as a tough liberal. Pledging to continue Sikorski's policies, he soon gained Churchill's and Roosevelt's respect for his intelligence, quiet dignity, and stubborn courage. Even so, the forty-nine-year-old prime minister did not have Sikorski's influence with the U.S. and British leaders, limited though that had been. He also lacked Sikorski's ability to hold together the numerous feuding factions in the Polish government and to withstand right-wing demands for a harder line against Stalin.

As he struggled to keep peace within the Polish coalition, Mikołajczyk worked desperately that summer and fall to counter what he viewed as a growing tendency on the part of his leading Allies to use Poland as a pacifier for Stalin. On the eve of Tehran, Mikołajczyk asked for an appointment with Churchill and was turned down. He then asked Anthony Drexel Biddle to arrange a one-on-one meeting with Roosevelt. Again, his request was denied. Convinced by now that Poland would be a major topic of discussion at the summit and that Roosevelt and Churchill were in an appeasing mood, the Polish leader was beside himself with concern. "Even a man condemned to death is granted a last word before the court," he protested to Biddle.

The Americans and British told Mikołajczyk he was overreacting. Just before leaving London, Eden promised that he and Churchill would not "commit the British government, or, more important, the Polish government, to any decisions without first allowing the Polish government to get an opinion and agreement from its people in Poland." The duplicity and lies were multiplying.

HAVING EVADED MIKOŁAJCZYK during this period, Roosevelt was also dodging Churchill. In the past, the two men had spent Christmas and other holidays together. They had fished together, joked, sung, drunk together. Now, suddenly, Roosevelt seemed to want to have as little as possible to do with his British friend and ally. Churchill, who knew a cold shoulder when he received one, was beginning to understand how Mikołajczyk felt. With the help of the Poles and other Allies, Britain had managed to hold Germany at bay through 1942 but, lacking the economic resources and manpower to win the war on its own, had been forced to yield pride of place to the stronger, richer United States. After the huge 1943 buildup of U.S. forces in Great Britain and North Africa, Churchill, to his considerable pain and alarm, found himself and his country being treated as junior partners in the Anglo-American alliance.

By this time, Roosevelt was far more interested in wooing Stalin, whom he saw as a potential future partner for America, than in pleasing Churchill, whom he viewed as a figure from the past. "Our relations with Russia are of paramount importance," FDR cabled Churchill in early October. Just before the Tehran Conference began, Harry Hopkins warned Lord Moran, Churchill's personal physician: "You will find us lining up with the Russians." The doctor later wrote in his diary: "What I find so shocking is that to the Americans the P.M. is the villain of the piece; they are far more skeptical of him than they are of Stalin."

As he had told Churchill already, Roosevelt was convinced he could handle Stalin far better than could the prime minister—or, for that matter, than could any other British or American official. The president believed that to win Stalin over, all he had to do was meet with him face-to-face and ply him with his patented Hyde Park charm. Roosevelt (and Churchill) often referred to Stalin as "Uncle Joe" or "UJ," as if the old Bolshevik were some crotchety relative who could be jollied out of his habitual sulks.

For two years, FDR had delayed making important and difficult decisions involving the Soviet Union. Those and other matters would be taken care of, he said, when he and Stalin finally met. Roosevelt had made three formal requests for such a meeting. Each time, Stalin put him off, just as he had spurned previous suggestions of a three-way meeting with Roosevelt and Churchill. Increasingly concerned about the fraying of the "Grand Alliance" and the imagined threat of a separate peace between Stalin and Hitler, the president was delighted when Stalin finally agreed to the Big Three conference in Tehran. Now, finally, the chance for a personal meeting with Stalin had come, and

FDR planned to make the most of it. His plan, according to Cordell Hull, was to "talk Mr. Stalin out of his shell, so to speak, away from his aloofness, secretiveness and suspiciousness until he broadens his views, visualizes a more practical international cooperation in the future, and indicates Russia's intention both in the East and in the West."

In Tehran, Roosevelt rejected Churchill's invitation to stay with him at the British legation and—after the Russians claimed to have uncovered an assassination plot against him and promised to ensure his safety—took up residence at the Soviet legation. Later, during the four-day conference, Churchill invited the president to have a private lunch with him, and Roosevelt declined. Harry Hopkins was reported to have explained that Roosevelt did not want "the impression to get abroad that he and Winston [were] putting their heads together in order to plan Stalin's discomfiture."

Instead, Roosevelt joined forces with Stalin to discomfit Churchill. At a three-way dinner early in the proceedings, the Soviet leader persisted in needling the British prime minister, while FDR, according to his interpreter, State Department official Charles Bohlen, "not only backed Stalin but seemed to enjoy the Churchill-Stalin exchanges." Dismayed, Bohlen later remarked that the president "should have come to the defense of a close friend and ally, who was really being put upon by Stalin."

A couple of days later, Roosevelt upped the ante. Thus far in the conference, his attempts to charm Stalin had met with little success. The president was plainly disconcerted. "I had done everything he asked me to do," Roosevelt later told Labor Secretary Frances Perkins. "I had stayed at his embassy, gone to his dinners, been introduced to his ministers and generals. He was correct, stiff, solemn, not smiling, nothing human to get hold of. I felt pretty discouraged."

He decided to try another tactic: mocking Churchill as Stalin had done earlier. At the next session, FDR began by whispering to Stalin, "Winston is cranky this morning. He got up on the wrong side of the bed." Encouraged by Stalin's slight smile, the president twitted Churchill directly, chaffing him about "his Britishness, about John Bull, about his cigars, about his habits." The more Churchill reddened and scowled, the more Stalin smiled, until he finally broke out into a loud laugh. "[F]or the first time in three days I saw light," Roosevelt exulted.

"From that time on, our relations were personal. We talked like men and brothers."

With these schoolboy gibes, meant to inspire Stalin's trust and friendship, Roosevelt had belittled his closest ally, a man who greatly admired him. In the process, the president sent a very different message than he intended. How could the ever suspicious Stalin be expected to trust these men when they showed no loyalty to each other? And what did he have to fear from them if they were so obviously divided? In Bohlen's view, Roosevelt's ganging up on Churchill was "a basic error. . . . Russian leaders always expected and realized that Britain and the United States were bound to be much closer in their thinking and in their opinions than either could conceivably be with the Soviet Union. In his rather transparent attempt to disassociate himself from Churchill, the President was not fooling anybody and in all probability aroused the secret amusement of Stalin." Bohlen's State Department colleague George Kennan later wrote that Roosevelt's attempt to achieve a special relationship with Stalin through the demeaning of Churchill was "one of the saddest manifestations of the almost childish failure on FDR's part to understand the personality of Stalin himself and the nature of his regime."

Later in the war, Stalin told a group of Yugoslav Communists: "Churchill is the kind of man who will pick your pocket of a kopek if you don't watch him. Yes, pick your pocket of a kopek! . . . Roosevelt is not like that. He dips in his hand only for bigger coins."

ALTHOUGH ROOSEVELT AND Churchill were largely responsible for initiating the Tehran summit, they made minimal formal preparations for it. There was no official agenda, and no minutes were kept. Before the summit, Averell Harriman told Molotov that Roosevelt, who would act as chairman, envisaged the meeting merely as an informal "get together." For the president, the main purpose of the Tehran meeting was to establish a close personal relationship with Stalin, rather than to reach definite decisions about the war. FDR wanted to sound out Stalin on broad Allied strategy for the defeat of Germany and then to open the meeting "to anybody to discuss whatever they liked and to leave undiscussed whatever they did not like," Harriman told Molotov. FDR's fondness for improvisation extended to his refusal to use State Department briefing books and position papers on the various issues to be considered at the conference. A few years after the war, Sumner Welles acknowledged that Roosevelt and his men often embarked on discussions of postwar territorial and political problems "in a singularly haphazard fashion, and without full consideration or preparation."

By all accounts, Stalin, who was both prepared and well organized, was easily the best negotiator of the three leaders. American and British officials marveled at his mastery of the details of military operations and diplomatic issues. Indeed, many years later, Anthony Eden wrote: "If I had to pick a team for going into a conference room, Stalin would be my first choice." His sullen, bullying side was nowhere in sight at Tehran. He was "hooded" and "calm," Eden remembered. Occasionally flashing a brief, practiced smile, he never raised his voice, never wasted a word. He made no specific commitments—and received many in return. At Tehran, and later at Yalta, British and American diplomats and military authorities shared the "uneasy feeling," in the words of

Marshal Joseph Stalin, President Franklin D. Roosevelt, and Prime Minister Winston Churchill during the Tehran Conference, 1943. (Library of Congress)

one British official, that "the immediate gains had always gone to Russia; the vague promises about the future to the United States and Britain."

At the Tehran Conference, Roosevelt's still hazy dream of a postwar international peacekeeping organization was discussed, but nothing concrete was decided. The same was true of the postwar role of France and the Allies' treatment of a defeated Germany. Nonetheless, there were some important decisions reached at Tehran. Stalin finally received a firm commitment for "Operation Overlord," the long-awaited invasion of mainland Europe, and a tentative date—May 1944 (later pushed back a month). In return, Stalin agreed to an eastern offensive to coincide with the invasion. He also secretly promised to go to war against Japan after the defeat of Germany. With Roosevelt's help, the Soviet leader stymied Churchill's proposal for expanded Allied operations in the Mediterranean and the Balkans. The Big Three also guaranteed the postwar independence and territorial integrity of Iran.

Poland, "the principal object of [Stalin's] passion and the center of his policy," was not discussed at length until the final session of the conference. But by then, Stalin had already got his way on that issue—and without so much as lifting a finger.

After dinner on the summit's first day, Churchill had pulled the Soviet leader aside for a private chat about several issues, including Poland. He made clear that while the fate of the Poles was important to Britain, "[n]othing was more important than the security of the Russian western frontier." In other words, Churchill was agreeing with Stalin's contention that the USSR needed eastern Poland as a security buffer against future invasions. Poland, Churchill said, could simply "move westwards, like soldiers taking two steps 'left close' "—that is, making up for the loss of its eastern borderlands by adding part of Germany to its territory in the west.

The prime minister acknowledged that he had no authority from Parliament to redraw Poland's frontiers. That in itself was a gross misstatement. The fact was that neither Churchill nor Parliament had any legal say in the matter at all. As a sovereign Allied country, Poland alone could agree to a change in its borders—a right that Churchill's government had affirmed in 1941, assuring the Polish government-in-exile that Britain recognized no changes in its country's borders made after August 1939. While Britain couldn't force Poland to accept the revised boundary, Churchill told Stalin he thought he could persuade the Poles to do so after the Big Three informally settled the matter. In this brief discussion, he never asked Stalin for a quid pro quo, not even a verbal pledge to respect Poland's independence.

Stalin responded by subtly underscoring the sharp difference between his Western Allies' public statements of lofty ideals and their private willingness to betray their comrades-in-arms. Would this redrawing of frontier boundaries, he asked, be accomplished without the participation of the Poles? Yes, said Churchill.

Then it was Roosevelt's turn. Hours before the conference's last formal session, he and Stalin sat down for a meeting, with only Averell Harriman, Vyacheslav Molotov, and the two leaders' interpreters also present. FDR said he wanted Stalin to know he was in full agreement with him on moving Poland's frontiers to the west. But for political reasons, he could not take part in the Big Three's discussions on Poland later that evening. A presidential election was coming up in 1944, and, although reluctant, he probably would run again. If he did, he did not want to risk losing the votes of some 6 to 7 million Polish-Americans. The subject of the Curzon Line, as Harry Hopkins later explained to Eden, was "political dynamite" in the United States.

Charles Bohlen was stunned as he translated the president's words. In secret, Roosevelt was reversing his administration's long-held public position that all territorial decisions must be delayed until after the war. He was signaling to Stalin that the Soviet premier could have his way on the Curzon Line, but that under no circumstances could the president's complicity in that deal leak out. What was more, this was the first that Bohlen—or virtually anyone else in the U.S. government—had heard of the president's intention to run for a fourth term. If Stalin was as surprised as Bohlen, he didn't show it. Inscrutable as ever, he merely said he understood.

True to his word, Roosevelt refrained from any further substantive discussion of Poland at Tehran. He opened the final plenary meeting by saying only that he hoped the Polish government-in-exile and the Soviets would soon resume diplomatic ties. That seemingly innocuous statement touched off an explosion from Stalin, who hurled accusation after accusation at the London Poles, calling them cowards, Hitler's accomplices, and murderers. Neither Churchill nor Roosevelt spoke up in the Poles' defense, and Churchill quickly changed the subject to the Curzon Line. With that, he, Stalin, and their subordinates gathered around two maps and began to carve up Poland.

During that same session, Anthony Eden made a brief, belated attempt to salvage something for the Poles. He argued that Lwów should remain inside Poland, that the Curzon Line, as originally drawn, did not give that indisputably Polish city to the Bolsheviks. Stalin and Molotov rejected the appeal, even though Lwów lay only a few miles beyond what was generally accepted to be ethnic Poland. Eden stood his ground but lost the argument when Churchill failed to support him. "I was not prepared to make a great squawk about [Lwów]," the prime minister acknowledged in his memoirs.

As the statesmen traced on the maps their ideas for the Curzon Line in the east and a new German-Polish border in the west, little or no attention was paid to the human consequences inherent in such sweeping, arbitrary border shifts. The statesmen were operating in a vacuum of power politics. They did not pause to consider the uprooting of millions of people from their native soil, nor the searing pain of losing part of one's country, which, for most Poles, was like losing part of oneself. The German territory to be given to Poland, Churchill argued, was industrial and therefore much more valuable than Poland's Pripet Marshes, which were to be handed over to the Soviets. He said he would tell the Poles that they "had been given a fine place to live in" and that they would have "a much better Poland" now. Stalin agreed that Poland would now be a large industrial state. "And friendly to Russia," Churchill added.

When the Poles stood up to Germany in 1939, when they poured out of Poland to fight on, when they tried to defend France, and when they flew against the Luftwaffe in the Battle of Britain, they could not have imagined that their country would be disposed of—by their *allies*—in so casual and callous a way. General Władysław Anders would later remark that Poland "was certainly entitled to full independence without paying half her territory to Russia for it."

In retrospect, it is clear that the Big Three conference at Tehran—not the more commonly cited Yalta Conference in February 1945—was the turning point for Poland. While the country's fate would continue to be a major issue for the three leaders until the end of the war, its postwar future as a Soviet satellite, under an imposed Communist system, was essentially settled at Tehran. Churchill and Roosevelt had given in so completely on the Curzon Line, asking for nothing but secrecy in return, that Stalin might be forgiven for thinking they would not resist him much in the future over anything he might demand in Poland or elsewhere in Eastern Europe.

Where Poland was concerned, "we didn't hold any high cards" to begin with, Lord Vansittart, the former Foreign Office undersecretary, said later. "But in poker you can win, even with nothing in your hand, provided your opponents do not see your cards." Churchill, he said, had made the "unforgivable mistake" of showing Stalin, a master poker player, all his cards.

———————

THE LID OF secrecy that was imposed during the four days of the Tehran Conference was kept tightly in place thereafter. Reporters had not been permitted to cover it (or any of the other major conferences of the war), and there were no communiqués, no details about what had been agreed upon or discussed. When Roosevelt and Churchill returned home, they confined themselves to praising the summit meeting as a triumph in which the Big Three had become "friends in fact, in spirit, and in purpose." They did not mention Poland and did not inform the Polish government-in-exile about what they had done. "Any pronouncement on the topic might have disastrous effects in the United States in the election year," Churchill warned Eden in a memo, "and there is no doubt that we should ourselves be subject to embarrassing attacks in the House of Commons...."

Roosevelt had initially planned to address Congress on Tehran but had second thoughts and canceled. He similarly decided against providing any further information to journalists. The State Department's Charles Bohlen dutifully forwarded his notes on the conference to the White House. No one else at State, including Secretary Cordell Hull (who had not been present at Tehran), received any official information about what had been decided about Poland; four months after the conference, Hull complained to William Bullitt that he "still did not know what had happened at Teheran...." When Polish ambassador Jan

Ciechanowski later asked for details, Hull told him—on what authority is unclear—that Roosevelt had tried "time after time" to plead Poland's case but that Stalin had been recalcitrant.

In his memoirs, Anthony Eden said he "began to fear greatly for the Poles" following Tehran. Yet, shortly after his return to London, he went before the House of Commons to assuage a growing concern among some of its members over possible secret understandings. "I can...tell the House, lest there is any uneasiness about it, that we have not entered into any kind of secret engagement or treaty or anything which can cause anyone a sleepless night or a sleepless hour...," the foreign secretary declared. To this obvious misstatement, Eden added another. Asked by Conservative MP Kenneth Pickthorn if the government stood by the Atlantic Charter and Eden's own 1941 assurance to Poland that Britain did not recognize any post–August 1939 territorial changes, Eden answered: "His Majesty's Government [does] not recognize any territorial changes which have been effected in Poland since August 1939. This remains the position."

At the very least, this was casuistry. Eden and Churchill had not formally recognized Stalin's claims to the Curzon Line, but they had left no doubt in the Soviet leader's mind that he would get his way.

Secure in the knowledge of Roosevelt's and Churchill's concessions at Tehran, the Soviets made abundantly clear to the world in early 1944 that they planned to have Poland. Having pushed the Germans out of western Russia, the Russians crossed Poland's legal frontier in January and claimed the country's eastern borderlands as rightfully theirs. Poland would be compensated by German territory in the west, the Kremlin said, echoing the informal agreement at Tehran.

In an official note, the Soviets demanded that the Polish government-in-exile accept this loss of territory and get rid of several of its top officials who were regarded as anti-Soviet. A couple of weeks later, the Kremlin announced the formation of the Union of Polish Patriots, a group of Polish Communists who had lived in Moscow since the beginning of the war. At the same time, the Soviet government escalated its public assault on the Polish leaders in London, calling them "fascists" and accusing them of treason to the Allied cause. Of a particularly vitriolic attack by *Pravda*, the official newspaper of the Soviet Communist

Party, Reuters news agency noted: "If [this] were not a newspaper article but an official accusation drawn up by a Soviet public prosecutor, all Polish leaders incriminated therein would be liable to arrest if they ever set foot in Poland again."

Most of the British press accepted the Soviet demands as legitimate and showed little concern about the abuse heaped on the Poles. The notion of the Curzon Line as the new official boundary between Poland and the Soviet Union quickly took hold. As Stalin had foreseen months earlier, the name of the proposed boundary itself worked to its favor in Britain. The British "have the idea from the name that it must be something respectable, an honest Conservative view given by an honest Conservative statesman, as to where a line of demarcation between Poland and Russia should be drawn," noted Tory MP Victor Petherick.

At the BBC, a censor deleted a reference to Lwów and Wilno as Polish cities in a speech broadcast to Poland by a member of the Polish government-in-exile. *The Times* and other newspapers began referring to "the old Polish frontier" and the "1939 frontier" when referring to Poland's eastern border. *The Times* launched a pro–Curzon Line campaign, urging Poland to accede to Russian demands and thereby "gain their friendship." To that argument, a Polish newspaper in Britain replied: "It is impossible for anyone to gain the friendship of another by allowing him to cut off his hand and leg.... Three times has Poland's body been subjected to similar amputations during the 18th century, and it has not contributed in any way towards changing Russia's hostile attitude to one of friendliness towards Poland."

When another Polish publication criticized the British government's censorship of the mention of Lwów and Wilno as Polish cities, Brendan Bracken, the minister of information, ordered the paper's newsprint ration stopped, thereby shutting it down. Called to account in the House of Commons for this de facto censorship, Bracken declared: "I don't believe that British sailors should have to cart paper across the ocean to provide opportunities for foreigners in this country to help German propagandists and sow discord among the Allies."

A disheartened Edward Raczyński wrote in his diary about the "dense fog of mendacity" in Britain that now shrouded Soviet-Polish relations: "Every statement is divorced from reality, and every argument distorted." The Polish ambassador added: "We hear less and less...of Britain's 'moral obligation' [to Poland]; or rather we hear nothing at all about it...."

By early 1944, people in London and the rest of Britain were profoundly tired of war. The energy and excitement of life in the English capital had ebbed considerably; the city and its residents looked increasingly shabby and down-at-the-heels. "Everybody's nerves are frayed," *The New Yorker*'s Mollie Panter-Downes reported from London in January. Eric Sevareid, who spent several months in London in 1944, likened the capital in a broadcast to "a once-smart hotel gone seamy and threadbare after an interminable convention of businessmen.... The exaltation of danger is gone."

Although many Britons retained at least some sympathy for the Poles, a growing number now regarded them with resentment and anger, viewing their resistance to Soviet demands as a deliberate obstacle to ending the war. The hostility was sometimes expressed in overt ways. On a streetcar in Blackpool, several passengers shouted, "Go home, you dirty Pole!" to a Polish pilot and his wife. At the RAF's training base at Cranwell, someone wrote "Poles, Go Home!" on a bulletin board.

"The common view is that the Poles have outlived their usefulness and deserve to be kicked from time to time, or at least given cold douches of more or less justified reproach," Raczyński gloomily noted in his diary. The goal seems to be "to vilify us and hustle us off the stage, like [actors] at the end of a bad play."

Winston Churchill, meanwhile, intensified his pressure on Mikołajczyk and other Polish officials to accede to Soviet terms that, unbeknownst to the Poles, had essentially been agreed upon at Tehran. Churchill's arm-twisting was relentless, ruthless, and at times almost frantic. After one particularly tense session, Edward Raczyński noted Churchill's "hectoring tone, to which he resorts when unsure of himself." Whether the prime minister actually still believed in Stalin's pledges to honor Poland's independence or not, he needed the Poles' agreement to the Curzon Line to get him out of the various legal, ethical, and political dilemmas in which he now found himself.

The Poles "must back the [Tehran] settlement to the hilt," Churchill wrote Roosevelt, who, as he had stipulated at Tehran, remained comfortably out of the controversy. "This will be their duty to the powers of Europe who will twice have rescued them." In a memo to Eden, the prime minister made the same point: "Nations who are found incapable of defending their country must accept a reasonable measure of guidance from those who have rescued them and who offer them the prospect of a sure freedom and independence."

Had the Poles known about these blustering, rather arrogant declarations of Churchill's, they might have been excused for wondering just when the rescues he spoke of took place. Certainly not in 1939, when Britain and France declared war over Poland—and then did nothing to stop Germany from overrunning the country. In fact, if any rescuing had been done, it had been done by the Polish pilots who helped stave off German invasion during the Battle of Britain.

In response to Churchill's browbeating, Mikołajczyk did make several significant concessions. To the dismay and anger of several members of his government, he said he was ready to negotiate with the Russians on all matters, including frontiers. He even agreed to consider the idea of creating a temporary boundary between Poland's prewar border and the Curzon Line, keeping Lwów and Wilno in Poland. A permanent border could be settled after the war, he said. But he adamantly refused to accept the Soviet version of the Curzon Line as the fixed border now. Nor would he agree to get rid of members of his government whom the Soviets considered hostile. In his discussions with Churchill and Eden, Mikołajczyk pointed out that Britain was asking his government to give up half of its country's territory without offering in return any formal guarantee to protect the independence of the rest of Poland.

In any event, Mikołajczyk's concessions had no effect. The Kremlin rejected them outright, declaring that the Poles in London would have to agree to all Soviet demands before any negotiations could take place. With the British-Polish discussions at an impasse, Churchill wrote to Roosevelt: "We doubt very much whether we can push [the Poles] any further and we should feel alarmed about the effect upon opinion here and in the USA...of a Soviet refusal to give sympathetic consideration to the present proposals."

Yet, instead of pressing Stalin to consider Mikołajczyk's compromises, an annoyed Churchill told the Poles that the deadlock was their fault and that, because of their intransigence, he would go public with the British government's support of Soviet demands. Although Polish troops, and particularly Polish pilots, "had made themselves both loved and respected" in Britain, Churchill said, their government, with no power of its own, must accede to British wishes. If Polish leaders did not, he and the Soviets would "certainly make the agreement without them."

The Polish prime minister begged his British counterpart not to say anything in public about the controversy, pointing out it would further undermine the Poles' position. Nonetheless, on February 22, 1944, Churchill rose in the House of Commons to declare his government's support for the Curzon Line as the new boundary between the Soviet Union and Poland. It was, said Churchill, a border that the Polish government-in-exile should accept. "Here I may remind the House that we ourselves have never in the past guaranteed, on behalf of His Majesty's Government, any particular frontier line to Poland...," the prime minister declared. "I cannot feel that the Russian demand for reassurance about her Western frontiers goes beyond the limits of what is reasonable or just." The Soviet Union needed to feel secure from future invasion, he added. He did not mention Poland's need for security, and he gave no hint at all of the secret concessions that were made at Tehran.

Sitting in the House gallery, Jan Nowak, the young Polish underground courier from Warsaw who had spent the last several months in London, was devastated by Churchill's announcement. Despite the prime minister's disclaimer of support for any particular Polish frontier, his backing of Soviet demands was in direct contradiction to Eden's 1941 pledge not to recognize changes in Polish territory made after August 1939. As news of the prime minister's speech spread, Nowak's shock and sense of betrayal were shared by many of his colleagues in the Polish underground and by compatriots in the Polish armed forces, most of whom had no idea of the behind-the-scenes maneuvering over the Curzon Line that had been going on for more than two years. Churchill's speech made clear that "Stalin had been given the green light," Nowak later remarked. "The way to Poland was open. He would be able to do what he wanted with us with no risk of conflict with the Allies."

The Poles' disquiet was echoed by several members of Parliament in a debate over the prime minister's speech. "When does aggression cease to be aggression?" John McGovern, an Independent Labour MP, demanded of Eden, who spoke for the government during the debate. "Is it aggression only when perpetrated by Hitler and the Nazi party, or does it cease to be aggression when it is perpetrated by Stalin?" In a later confrontation on the House floor, McGovern told the foreign secretary: "In my opinion, you are marching towards a showdown. You are evading the issues of the present moment, but they are coming faster and hotter on your trail as the war comes to a conclusion."

In the days to come, to Churchill and Eden's dismay, the dreaded word "Munich" was increasingly bandied about by some MPs, even by several members of their own government. Churchill, the staunchest opponent of Neville Chamberlain's appeasement of Hitler over Czechoslovakia, was now seen by some to be doing the same with Stalin over Poland. To his critics, Churchill's argument that the Poles must give up the eastern part of their country to retain their independence was suspiciously reminiscent of Chamberlain's insistence prior to Munich that the Czechs cede the Sudetenland to Hitler. "I am determinedly opposed to an Anglo-Soviet agreement giving the latter what the Poles won't give," Alexander Cadogan wrote in his diary on March 6. "What *won't* be said about 'another Munich'!"

In a note to Eden, Sir Owen O'Malley raised the same questions about Poland that Churchill had raised about Czechoslovakia in 1938—questions about the British government's complicity in the annexation of another country's territory, about whether "the basis of international law is to be law or an exhibition of power politics." On this point, the British ambassador to the Polish government-in-exile was as uncompromisingly blunt in his language as he'd been in his report on the Soviet massacre at Katyn. "The real choice before us...," he wrote, is either "selling the corpse of Poland to Russia and finding an alibi to be used in evidence when we are indicted for abetting a murder," or "putting the points of principle to Stalin in the clearest possible way."

In private, Churchill anguished over the morality of the position he and Roosevelt had taken. "What are we to say to our Parliaments and nations about modifications in the Atlantic Charter?" he wrote to Eden in late March. "We are being blamed today for departing from idealistic principles," all for the sake of a country that is determined to "take what she wishes from Poland...."

Following Churchill's speech, Stalin took pains to underscore that point in several hostile, bullying notes to the prime minister that sharpened his demands for changes in the Polish government. After receiving one such message, a "much perturbed" Churchill phoned Eden. "I share his anxiety," Eden wrote in his diary, "and truly don't know what course to advise...."

CHURCHILL'S SPEECH AND Stalin's demands over Poland prompted growing anxiety in the United States, too. From November 1943 to January 1944, the number of Americans who believed that Russia could be trusted to cooperate with the United States after the war dropped from 54 percent to 42 percent. Americans of Polish descent made clear their displeasure over Churchill's support of the Curzon Line, and the fifteen Polish-American members of Congress sent a message of protest to the prime minister and the House of Commons. "Nobody can wipe out Britain's obligations to Poland from the conscience of the British people...," the congressmen declared. "No one can do this as long as the graves of Polish fliers killed in action over England are not removed from British soil."

Although the American press, for the most part, hailed the Tehran Conference as a rousing success, some journalists, foreign policy experts, and diplomats began expressing concern about what was done there—and about Roosevelt's role in it. A memo from the State Department's Division of European Affairs warned that any American collusion in forcing the Poles to accept the Soviets' territorial demands "would expose this Government to the justifiable charge of violating the principles for which this war is fought."

In January 1944, Anthony Drexel Biddle, the U.S. ambassador to the Polish government-in-exile in London, resigned in protest over what he suspected was the president's secret abandonment of Poland. Biddle, who had been the American ambassador in Warsaw when the Germans invaded in 1939 and who himself had come under repeated bombing attacks from the Luftwaffe then, had no direct knowledge of what had happened in Tehran. But, from his Foreign Office and State Department contacts, he surmised enough to conclude that, at the very least, Roosevelt had done nothing to defend Poland's territorial integrity and sovereignty. The reason for his resignation was kept secret, however, and Biddle joined the army as an expert on Eastern Europe.

In the March 1944 issue of the *American Mercury*, the journalist and author William Henry Chamberlin voiced his own suspicions about the Tehran meeting—and raised the specter of Munich. "As in the Munich days, the explanation...is that the aggressor is too strong to be stopped," Chamberlin wrote. "That is perhaps true, although Britain and the United States are probably underrating their own diplomatic and economic leverage. But even if the Soviet grab cannot be prevented, there is no excuse for concealing the picture from the American people, or worse, presenting...Tehran as a great and noble achievement in this respect.... Even if Stalin attains his East European objectives, there is no reason why Americans should pretend to be happy about it."

President Roosevelt, meanwhile, did his best to stay aloof from the controversy. He voiced none of Churchill's moral qualms about Tehran and seemed to regard the Polish issue as little more than a nuisance—a potential obstacle to closer U.S.-Soviet relations and the founding of a new world order. Unlike Churchill, FDR showed little concern about a pro-Soviet government taking control in Poland after the war. Indeed, in the spring of 1944, he told Averell Harriman, the U.S. ambassador to Moscow, that he "didn't care whether the countries bordering Russia became communized."

After Churchill's speech in February, Stanisław Mikołajczyk, clinging to the hope that the United States, at least, would support the Poles in resisting Soviet demands, made several urgent attempts to see FDR. On March 23, in a long, passionate appeal for a meeting with Roosevelt, the Polish prime minister wrote that "the Polish people...still believe that the rights of the weak will be respected by the powerful.... Mr. President, your name is revered by every Pole. The Polish nation looks upon you as the champion of the principles which you have proclaimed with such deep faith and conviction, presenting to mankind a vision of human freedom in a better world.... I am convinced that [its] faith will be justified."

Two weeks later, Mikołajczyk received a laconic presidential note in reply. Unfortunately, Roosevelt wrote, he had come down with a "slight case" of bronchitis and couldn't see the Polish leader at the present time. In a bit of noncommittal boilerplate, he added: "I wish to thank you for your courtesy in explaining in such a frank manner your position and that of your colleagues on various problems confronting your cabinet at this time." In truth, wrote Secretary of State Cordell Hull years later, the Pole's request for a meeting was turned down because D-Day was imminent and "we could not afford to become partisan in the Polish question to the extent of alienating Russia at that critical moment."

For Roosevelt, however, there would soon be an even bigger worry, one that would eclipse his concern over Stalin's reaction to a Washington visit by Mikołajczyk. Despite the president's best efforts to calm the fears of Polish-American voters, there were growing signs of disaffection over his lack of all-out support for the territorial integrity of Poland. Both the Democratic and Republican parties believed that, in the 1944 election, Polish-Americans potentially held the balance of power in such battleground states as Illinois, Michigan, Pennsylvania, Ohio, New Jersey, and New York. Even worse, warned one of Roosevelt's political advisers, if Polish-American voters began jumping the Democratic ship, they could "start enough of a rumpus to swing over other groups before November. . ."

In the spring of 1944, the heads of dozens of Polish-American fraternal, church, and professional organizations, whose membership totaled more than 6 million people, came together in Buffalo, New York, to form an umbrella group called the Polish-American Congress. The purpose of the new federation, its leaders made clear, was to put political pressure on the Roosevelt administration and Congress to support Poland's territorial integrity and independence. It didn't take long for the pressure to surface. The White House was bombarded with thousands of letters, telegrams, and postcards urging the president to oppose another partition of Poland. On May 3, Poland's Constitution Day, more than 140 members of Congress made speeches and inserted comments into the *Congressional Record* calling for support of Poland against Soviet demands.

In response to this pressure, Roosevelt's political advisers and others in his administration prodded him to extend an invitation to Mikołajczyk. Such a visit "would help dispel the undesirable impression created . . . among Americans of Polish descent that the President and the United States Government had lost all interest in the fate of Poland," observed William J. Donovan, director of the Office of Strategic Services, America's wartime intelligence agency. Roosevelt finally agreed. He invited the Polish leader to Washington for a visit beginning June 6, the day that hundreds of thousands of Allied troops finally landed at

Normandy to open the long-awaited second front. Two Polish fighter wings, numbering six squadrons, were among the Allied units providing air cover for the landing forces and for the paratroopers landing inland. In the first days of the invasion, the Poles shot down thirty German planes, while also bombing and strafing German troops.

In Washington, meanwhile, Mikołajczyk was exposed to the full-megawatt force of Roosevelt's warmth and charm during several sessions with him, and came away bedazzled. FDR assured the prime minister of his deep understanding and sympathy for Poland. But he said he knew that Mikołajczyk, as a "politician," would understand that in this "political year," the president could not officially intervene with Stalin over Poland.

While putting Mikołajczyk on notice that neither the United States nor Britain would ever consider going to war with the Soviets over Poland and that the Poles probably would have to make some concessions, Roosevelt said he agreed with the Polish position deferring settlement of the territorial question until after the war. He told the prime minister that it was Churchill who suggested adoption of the Curzon Line at the Tehran Conference and that Stalin, not surprisingly, had agreed to it. Then, in an obvious fabrication, the president assured Mikołajczyk that he himself was "still opposed to dividing Poland with this line." In due course, he said, "I will act as a moderator in this problem and effect a settlement.... I will see to it that Poland does not come out of this war injured."

Mikołajczyk returned to London upset at what Roosevelt had told him about Churchill but greatly heartened by the president's pledges of support. When Anthony Eden heard of the conversation between FDR and the Polish prime minister, he wrote in a Foreign Office memorandum: "The President will do nothing for the Poles.... [They] are sadly deluding themselves if they place any faith in these vague and generous promises. The President will not be embarrassed by them hereafter."

During Mikołajczyk's visit, Roosevelt sent an apologetic message to Stalin via Averell Harriman, explaining that he had been forced to see the Pole for political reasons. And, he assured the Soviet premier, he still held firm on the understandings reached at Tehran.

CHAPTER SEVENTEEN

"People of Warsaw! To Arms!"

I N THE WINTER and spring of 1944, the Red Army surged west like a great, cresting wave. German divisions were routed, then swept aside. By May 1, the Soviets had captured nearly all of eastern Poland.

One Allied force was paying particularly close attention to the Russians' progress. Three years before, most of the 60,000 men of II Polish Corps had been ragged, starving inmates in Stalin's frozen gulags. They had made their way down from Siberia and then, as part of a new Polish army, crossed through Central Asia and the Middle East before landing in Italy in February 1944. Their hegira, Harold Macmillan said, was a "classic of military prowess and courage." Now II Corps was a key element in Britain's Eighth Army, struggling up the Italian boot.

Most of the troops were natives of eastern Poland, with homes and families still there, and they huddled around radios at night to follow reports of the Russian advance with what *Collier's* correspondent Martha Gellhorn described as "agonized interest." Gellhorn, who spent several days with the soldiers of II Corps that spring in Italy, wrote of them: "They fight an enemy in front of them and fight him superbly. And with their whole hearts they fear an ally, who is already in their homeland." Gellhorn tried to assure the Poles that their fears were misplaced, that the world would honor their bravery and suffering by restoring their country's freedom and helping them rebuild. She told them she could not believe that a war fought to "maintain the rights of man will end by ignoring the rights of Poles." They looked at her with weary, jaundiced eyes, and she realized how she must have appeared to them: "I am not a

Pole; I belong to a large free country, and I speak with the optimism of those who are forever safe."*

The Poles possessed an intense, ardent patriotism that Gellhorn and others, including the Poles' British and American comrades, found impressive but difficult to understand. II Corps was "more than a military formation," Macmillan remarked. "It was a crusade." Of the differences that distinguished Poles from Britons, one Polish infantryman wrote: "We Poles have a completely different attitude to fighting. What the British soldier does is prompted by duty, whilst we respond to our sense of commitment and the need for heroism."

The men of II Corps and their commander, General Władysław Anders, were particularly determined to put the lie to the barrage of Soviet propaganda in the West variously condemning the Poles as traitors, Nazi collaborators, and cowards who had been afraid to face the Germans in combat. Time and again, the Soviets singled out Anders and his men in their violent attacks, accusing them of refusing to join forces with the Red Army and of deserting the USSR in 1941, because they had been afraid to fight the Nazis. Obsessed with refuting those charges, the Poles in Italy vowed to defend their honor—and that of their nation.

They would do that in one of the most ferocious battles of what was arguably the most misguided and wasteful major campaign of the war. When the vanguard of Allied troops landed in Italy the previous autumn, their commanding generals had averred that routing the enemy would be relatively easy. But after the Italians surrendered, the Germans dug in. They occupied the mountains and hills of southern Italy behind the formidable Gustav Line, stretching across the Italian peninsula from the Tyrrhenian Sea to the Adriatic. From those heights, studded with pillboxes, barricades, and minefields, the Germans mowed down Allied infantrymen as they tried to ford raging rivers, wade through knee-high mud, and fight uphill in blinding snowstorms.

The linchpin of the Gustav Line was the Benedictine abbey atop Monte Cassino, blocking the way to Rome. All winter long, Allied attempts to capture the peak had been worse than futile: they had been a bloodbath. U.S. bombers were called in to demolish the abbey, even

---

* *Collier's* declined to publish Gellhorn's story about the Poles. She was never told why but later speculated that the editors found her article to be "too critical of our popular allies, the Russians."—Gellhorn, *Face of War*, p. 121.

though it contained priceless collections of art and artifacts. But the Germans weren't in the abbey; they were in the area surrounding it. After the bombing, they quickly fortified the ruins and set to work decimating the thousands of Americans, Britons, Indians, and New Zealanders who clawed their way up the Cassino slopes in successive assaults.

Stymied at Cassino and trapped below on their Anzio beachhead, the Allies planned a major offensive in May to break the stalemate. II Corps was asked to take on the most difficult challenge: capturing Monte Cassino itself. From the moment they set foot on those rocky hills, the Poles would be under constant artillery and mortar fire from the strongly fortified German positions around and atop the summit. Their only cover would be makeshift shelters of sandbags and boulders. Yet bloody as the battle was certain to be, General Anders and his commanders seemed enthusiastic about fighting it. Once and for all, they would answer Soviet lies about Polish cowardice. Just as important, in Anders's view, a victory at Cassino would give "new courage" to the resistance movement in Poland.

As they took up their positions on the hills, the Poles found themselves in a surreal landscape of beauty and horror. Above loomed the smoke-shrouded mountain and the gaunt skeleton of the bombed-out abbey. In the valley below, red poppies covered the ground like a vast, deep carpet, and birds twittered under the hot spring sun. Up ahead, huge rats darted among hundreds of blackened, decaying bodies scattered on the blasted, treeless hillside—corpses of those who had tried and failed to take the mountain before. The bodies lay there, rotting in the sun, unretrieved and unburied, because of the withering German bombardment from above. The stench of death on the way up the slopes of Monte Cassino was overpowering.

On the night of May 11, 1944, the thunder of Allied artillery shattered the quiet from coast to coast as the massive Allied offensive began. In the darkness shortly before midnight, Polish gunners on the foothills poured fire on German positions, and at one o'clock on the morning of May 12, two Polish infantry divisions began scrabbling up the slopes. They were met, from the first, with such devastating mortar, artillery, and small-arms fire that the leading battalions were all but wiped out.

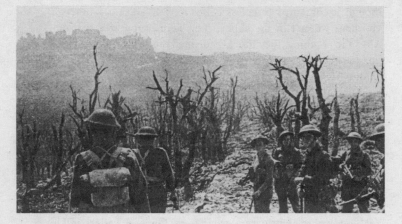

Soldiers of II Polish Corps prepare to fight for Monte Cassino in May 1944. (Imperial War Museum)

Still, the Poles pressed on. They fought all that day and well into the night before they were finally ordered to fall back.

So enormous were their losses on the first assault that it took them five days to regroup. On May 17, Anders told them: "May your hearts be like those of lions." That night, they launched the second attack, a savage sweep up the mountainside that at times brought them into hand-to-hand combat with the Germans. Early the next morning, the word came: the Germans had abandoned their positions. After five months of deadly futility, the Poles, on their second try, had taken Monte Cassino, and the road to Rome was open.

Nearly 1,000 Poles were killed and more than 3,000 wounded in those two assaults. Among the dead were diplomats, writers, artists, the former chief of the Polish intelligence service, several former members of the *Sejm*—and the brother of Witold Urbanowicz. The survivors were so exhausted, so battered, after the second attempt that it took some time to find men with enough strength to climb the few hundred yards to the summit and the monastic ruins. A patrol of the 12th Podolski Lancers finally made it to the heights. There, in the drifting smoke, amid fragments of shattered frescoes and broken statues, they raised a homemade regimental pennant.

*Polish soldiers remove their dead from the battlefield at Monte Cassino.
(Imperial War Museum)*

As the standard gently fluttered atop the mountain, the sound of a
bugle suddenly pierced the air. An unseen lancer was playing the
Kraków Hejnal, a famous call celebrating a thirteenth-century trumpeter
in Kraków, whose throat had been pierced by an arrow as he summoned
his fellow citizens to battle against the Tatars. Commemorating the
trumpeter's interrupted call to arms, the *Hejnal* breaks off abruptly, in
the middle of a note. At the sound of the trumpet, one Polish officer
recalled, thousands of hardened infantrymen wept like children. After
their years of wandering and exile, they were hearing, from a supposedly impregnable German fortress, the "voice of Poland."

BY THE END of June 1944, the Allies in the West had at last firmly
established their beachhead in France, and the Russians had taken all of

eastern Poland. But the Red Army did not stop or even slow down. It crossed the Curzon Line and headed into territory that no one, not even Stalin, could contend was anything but Polish. The Poles, British, and Americans watched with mounting anxiety: would Stalin abide by his repeated pledge to honor the freedom and independence of ethnic Poland?

Of course, the Soviet leader replied. His army was just passing through western Poland on its way to Germany. He and his regime would never interfere in Poland's internal affairs or claim land that didn't rightfully belong to them. Instead, the Kremlin announced in July the organization of the Committee of National Liberation—the Polish Communists handpicked by Stalin—and proclaimed it the legitimate interim civil government in Polish territories recaptured from the Germans. The committee would set up shop in Lublin, the first major Polish city to be freed from German control west of the Curzon Line. It was possible, said Stalin, that the committee might, in time, become the nucleus of a new, provisional Polish government.

For Poles in areas still occupied by the Germans, this was calamitous news. As they saw it, they had two options: do nothing and let the Soviets take over Poland through their puppet government; or rise up against the Nazis and try to establish control themselves. Britain and the United States recently had been pushing them to assist Russian troops in vanquishing the Germans. Now, encouraged by the D-Day landings in France and determined to show their good faith, the Home Army (AK) did just that. When Soviet troops first crossed the Polish border, the AK joined and supported their attacks on German outposts.

But that was just a beginning. Since 1939, the underground's primary goal had been to launch an uprising when the moment was right. In July 1944, that moment had arrived. The lightning-fast Soviet advance across Poland had made a national uprising impossible, but there was hope that the Home Army could drive the Germans out of Warsaw and at least take control of the capital before the Russians arrived.

No city in Europe had suffered as much or as long under Nazi occupation. But despite five years of savagery, the Germans still saw Warsaw as what it had been in September 1939 under Mayor Stefan Starzyński—a "city of bandits" and the main bastion of Polish resistance. The underground's political and military headquarters were in Warsaw, as were some 35,000 officers and troops of the Home Army, all of them eager to fight for Poland in this critical hour. "National dignity and pride required that the capital should be liberated by the Poles themselves," said a top underground official, "and that was accepted without any discussion.... What kind of an army would it be, what sort of a government, that, being in the capital, failed to take part in the battle for the liberation of the city?"

The resolve to fight stemmed from the Poles' centuries-old tradition of uncompromising resistance to invaders. But it was also fueled, like the courage of General Anders's II Corps, by a determination to disprove Russian charges of Polish ineffectuality and cowardice. After meeting with Home Army courier Jan Karski in London, a British government official reported to his superiors that the Polish underground seemed "almost morbidly afraid of being suspected abroad of passivity and resignation."

As General Anders had hoped, Varsovians had been inspired by II Corps' triumph in Italy. Shortly after the victory, the words MONTE CASSINO were proudly splashed on walls and the sides of buildings throughout the city. But there was another example of courage, much closer to home: the uprising in the Warsaw Ghetto.

IT HAD BEGUN in late 1942 as Jews organized against mass deportation from the ghetto to the Treblinka extermination camp. Between July and September of that year, 265,000 Jews had been deported—a little more than half of those whom the Nazis had originally crammed into the 840-acre walled ghetto in the center of Warsaw. By the end of 1942, the cumulative effects of deportations, starvation, and disease had reduced the ghetto's population to only about 55,000. So effective was the forming resistance, however, that the Nazis had to suspend the deportations for a time. Then, on April 19, 1943, the first night of Passover that year, 2,000 SS and German army troops, with tanks and artillery, moved into the ghetto under orders from SS chief Himmler to put down the resistance once and for all, and to resume the deportations.

During four weeks of street fighting, some 1,500 Jewish guerrillas, armed with only a few machine guns, grenades, and homemade bomb

The bodies of Jewish resistance fighters, shot by the SS during suppression of the Warsaw Ghetto uprising, lie in front of the ruins of a building in the ghetto. (U.S. Holocaust Memorial Museum)

launchers, held off everything the Nazis could throw at them. At one point, the frustrated German command was forced to relieve the officer in charge of the operation. When the new commander brought in flame-throwers and ordered the systematic torching of ghetto tenements and houses, defeat became only a matter of time for the guerrillas. Nevertheless, their resistance continued sporadically into July, when their ammunition ran out. Before the fighting ended, the insurgents had killed or wounded hundreds of German troops, while some 40,000 Jews had been killed or deported. The ghetto—including the Great Synagogue of Warsaw—was razed to the ground. Although most of the surviving Jews were either sent to Treblinka or took their own lives, several dozen guerrillas did manage to escape into Warsaw itself or the forests around the city, where they continued to harass the Germans for as long as they occupied Poland. It says something about Poles in general, Jews and non-Jews alike, that two of the three greatest urban uprisings in the entire history of World War II took place in Poland—first in the Jewish ghetto, then in all of Warsaw.

IN THE SUMMER of 1944, the Home Army prepared for an insurgency of its own. Its plans were based on an assumption that it would receive adequate supplies from Allied airlifts. The assumption was invalid. The general Warsaw uprising was to be almost as ill-equipped with guns and ammunition as the ghetto uprising had been. This was due, in no small part, to Britain's decision to ban RAF supply missions for an uprising— a decision of which the Home Army (living, as an underground official later put it, "in a world of illusion") was hopelessly unaware. *AK* leaders were sure that Britain and the United States, despite previous reluctance to provide adequate support, would rush arms to them once the uprising broke out. Furthermore, they were convinced that their Western allies would pressure the Soviets to do the same.

In late July, underground leaders received word that Soviet troops were nearing the capital. They did not need to be told. Russian bombers had already begun hitting German military targets on the outskirts, and *AK* troops could hear the *whoosh* of incoming Russian artillery rounds. A few miles from the city, advance Red Army patrols had been spotted. The German evacuation from Warsaw had begun, and, as the Russians drew nearer, it turned into a panicky, headlong retreat. Nazi newspapers suddenly ceased publication. Chimneys belched the black smoke of burning German documents. High-ranking Nazis made their quick, awkward exits. And German civilians crowded the railway stations, demanding immediate passage home. Wehrmacht soldiers, in the classic, demoralized posture of the defeated, trudged through Warsaw streets, heading west, their uniforms ripped and disheveled, their faces dirty and streaked with sweat, their rifles hanging from their shoulders or carried limply at their sides.

But the Germans still were not finished with Warsaw. Even in the midst of their retreat, they ordered all male Varsovians between the ages of seventeen and sixty-five to dig trenches outside the city. *AK* leaders suspected a trap. They feared that once the SS had rounded up all able-bodied men in the capital, they would not be put to work but would be deported to labor or death camps. It was now or never for the great uprising.

On July 26, General Tadeusz Bór-Komorowski, commander of the Home Army, radioed the government-in-exile in London: "We are ready to fight for Warsaw at any moment. I will report the date and hour of the beginning of the fight." In his message, Bór-Komorowski asked that the 1st Polish Parachute Brigade and Polish fighter squadrons be dispatched to Warsaw; that German airfields near the capital be subjected to bombing attacks; and that supplies of arms, ammunition, and other equipment be airlifted to the insurgents. The British military command, focused now on post–D-Day operations in Western Europe, was appalled by Bór-Komorowski's urgent request, which it considered "completely impossible." Why hadn't the government-in-exile made clear to the Home Army that it couldn't rely on Britain for help? Didn't the Poles realize yet how dangerous it was to make *any* flights to Poland, let alone embark on the kind of large-scale air operations they were asking for now? The losses would be astronomical. Besides, there was no strategic benefit for Britain.

Another objection was left unstated by the British: the probable Soviet outburst in response to any Allied military support for the uprising. In effect, that probability gave the Kremlin a veto. "It would be politically unacceptable to undertake any such measures without the approval and cooperation of the Russians," advised a secret British Chiefs of Staff report. The report went on to caution—guiltily, it seemed—against repeating that argument to the Poles, "who might read into [it] an intention on our part to abandon them just at a time when they need and have been promised our moral support."

Although the Home Army had specifically asked only for Polish military units to be directly involved, Britain had the power to deny such requests, because it had operational control over all Polish forces. Currently, that control extended even to the Parachute Brigade, which had earlier been under exclusive Polish command. Organized in 1941 specifically to parachute into Poland when the uprising began, the brigade soon won such renown for its toughness and skill that British commanders began casting covetous eyes its way. In March 1944, General Bernard Law Montgomery, who was then preparing to lead U.S. and British ground forces in the invasion of Europe, reviewed the Polish paratroopers and told their commander, General Stanisław Sosabowski: "You have first-class soldiers."

Soon afterward, the British army command pressured the Polish government-in-exile to deploy the brigade in Western Europe after the D-Day landings—under Montgomery's command. If the Poles agreed, the British promised that "every effort would be made" to find aircraft to transport the brigade to Poland in the event of an uprising. Over Sosabowski's strong objections, the Polish government finally yielded to British pressure. Four months later, with the uprising just days away, British officials refused to grant permission for redeployment of the Parachute Brigade to Poland. There were insufficient aircraft for transport, the British insisted, but even if enough planes were available, the mission would be suicidal for crews and paratroopers alike.

The British command also denied Bór-Komorowski's request that the thirteen Polish bomber and fighter squadrons under RAF control be sent in support of the uprising. There were good reasons for the denial. Only a few of the fighter squadrons had aircraft specially fitted for long-distance flights. Even if those fighters—and the bombers—managed to make it safely to Poland (a doubtful proposition in itself), the Germans were still in control of the area around Warsaw. There were no landing fields where Polish airmen could land and refuel, no facilities where their aircraft could be repaired and maintained.

But it was also true that the RAF considered the Polish squadrons important to the Allied advance in the West and was loath to spare them for a campaign that was vital only to Poland and that would, in any case, rile the Russians. The bomber squadrons were involved in the offensive over Germany, and the fighter squadrons, now equipped with Spitfires and P-51 Mustangs, were escorting bombers and ship convoys, providing support for Allied troops in Normandy, strafing and dive-bombing enemy ground targets, and shooting down V-1 missiles.

As for Bór-Komorowski's final request, the dropping of arms and other supplies into Warsaw, the British could offer little or no encouragement on that score, either. According to Air Marshal Sir John Slessor, the RAF commander in chief in the Mediterranean, only two units—1586 Polish Special Duties Flight and the RAF's 148 Squadron, both based in Italy—had the ability to fly such missions. Both, however, had suffered particularly heavy casualties in the previous few months as the result of stiffened German air defenses, and were at their lowest levels of operational strength. The surviving crews, several of which had already completed two tours of duty, were exhausted, and their bombers were plagued with mechanical problems.

While the British fumed about what they viewed as the Poles' unrealistic attitude and lack of common sense (Slessor called the Poles "tragically unwise" and "too often their own worst enemy"), the leaders of the Home Army continued to lay plans for the upcoming struggle. Between London and Warsaw, there was an enormous chasm of understanding. In Whitehall offices, coolness and rationality reigned. In Warsaw, there was only desperate passion. For five years, Varsovians had suffered hunger, cold, humiliation, terror, and death. For five years, they had awaited the chance to regain their freedom. Now their chance had come, and they were not going to be stayed by cold British logic.

"We have no choice," a top underground leader declared at the time. "I ask you to imagine a man who had been gathering speed for five years in order to leap over a wall. He runs faster and faster, and then, one step before the obstacle, the command is given to stop! By then he is running so fast that he cannot stop: if he does not jump, he will hit the wall. Thus it is with us. In a day or two, Warsaw will be at the front." Throughout the city, men, women, and children were retrieving revolvers, rifles, grenades, and other arms from all the places in which they had been hidden—cellars, attics, gardens, cemeteries—since 1939. Then the weapons were cleaned and surreptitiously distributed to members of the Home Army.

While the Poles armed themselves, the Red Army drew ever closer to Warsaw. On July 29, Soviet artillery began shelling the Warsaw suburb of Praga. All that day and the next, Soviet radio broadcasts, declaring that the "guns of liberation" were now within hearing, made impassioned appeals to Varsovians to join Russian troops in combat. "Warsaw trembles from the roar of guns," one broadcast proclaimed. "The Soviet armies are pushing forward and are near Praga! People of Warsaw, to arms!...Attack the Germans!" A similar urgent appeal, signed by Vyacheslav Molotov, was contained in leaflets dropped by Russian planes over Warsaw. "Poles! The time of liberation is at hand!" the leaflets declared. "There is not a moment to lose!"

As Averell Harriman later observed, these Soviet slogans strengthened Varsovians' determination. "To remain in hiding," said the U.S. ambassador to Moscow, "would only have confirmed Stalin's taunts that the Home Army existed chiefly in Mikołajczyk's imagination, or that it collaborated willingly with the Nazis."

On July 29, Bór-Komorowski and his chief lieutenants met to discuss final plans for the uprising. Also present was Jan Nowak, the Home Army courier, who, after several months in London, had just been flown secretly back to Poland. Nowak warned Bór-Komorowski and the others not to expect any help from the Allies—no Parachute Brigade, no Polish Air Force relief operations, no supplies. Based on Nowak's report, a number of people at the meeting called on Bór-Komorowski to delay the uprising.

Others felt differently. "I have no illusions about what awaits us here after . . . we come into the open," said one underground leader. "But even if the worst fate should befall me, I would prefer that to giving up without a fight. We must do our duty to the end."

On July 31, Bór-Komorowski made his decision. The uprising would begin the next day at 5:00 p.m.

On August 1, a Tuesday, scores of Warsaw residents—adults and children, male and female—left their homes, shops, factories, and offices in late morning and early afternoon. Emerging in small groups, many carrying heavy briefcases and packages, they walked as casually as possible along the streets, trying not to attract the attention of German patrols. When they arrived at prearranged destinations, they drew rifles, pistols, and grenades from their packages. Then some of them changed into what passed for fighting clothes in their ragtag army—faded old Polish uniforms, stolen Wehrmacht tunics and helmets, bits and pieces of other military regalia. Those who didn't have some semblance of a uniform remained in their civvies. Those who didn't have weapons grabbed rocks. The only standard military item worn by every Home Army soldier was a red-and-white armband, the first symbol of Polish nationhood to be worn overtly in Warsaw since the German occupation began five years earlier.

At precisely five o'clock that afternoon, thousands of windows and doors were flung open all over the city, and the Home Army's attack began. From balconies and windows, underground soldiers cut down passing German troops with a cascade of rifle and small-arms fire. Rushing to capture key military objectives, other Poles lobbed grenades at Nazi headquarters and hurled Molotov cocktails at ammunition dumps and troop transports. They ambushed tanks, which, once captured, were immediately painted with the underground symbol—the anchor formed by the letters PW: "Poland Fights!"

In dozens of neighborhoods, citizens—housewives, workmen, university professors, shopkeepers—dragged tables, chests, desks, sofas, cupboards into the street to build barricades against German tanks and troops. Others dug trenches and tore up pavement for the same purpose. In one neighborhood, an apartment building janitor emerged with a Polish flag that he had kept hidden in his cellar for five years. To an exultant roar from his neighbors, he raised the flag on a pole outside the building. As the red-and-white standard unfurled, the crowd stopped digging and lugging furniture to the barricade. They stood at attention and, as if obeying an unseen command, began singing the *Warszawianka,* a Polish anthem commemorating the 1831 uprising in Warsaw. The music swelled as other people, tears streaming down their faces, joined in from their windows and balconies. The *Warszawianka* was sung in many other neighborhoods that evening, and Polish flags were defiantly waved. Soon, Warsaw was a sea of red and white. Although German soldiers were still very much present, someone even managed to get atop

The broad smile on the face of this pretty young Home Army soldier reflects the joy of freedom felt by Varsovians in the early, hopeful days of the Warsaw uprising. (Jerzy Tomaszewski)

Home Army soldiers during the Warsaw uprising. Having no regular uniform of their own, many wore captured German helmets. (S. Braun, Historical Museum of Warsaw)

the sixteen-story Prudential Building—Warsaw's tallest—and hoist a giant Polish flag.

By nightfall, virtually every visible trace of the German occupation had vanished. Varsovians had torn down German street signs and shop signs, posters, inscriptions, announcements, flags. Portraits of Hitler and other prominent Nazis were yanked from their places of honor in German offices and affixed to the barricades so that, if the Germans counterattacked, they would have to fire at images of their own leaders. The people of Warsaw were bent on taking back their city and their country.

During the first three days of the uprising, the Home Army—only some 2,500 of which were well armed—gained control of most of Warsaw. The *AK* failed, however, to take several key military targets, including German airfields and the bridges over the Vistula River, in that critical first stage of the fight. The insurgents were already overextended and in desperate need of help. But no help of any kind came from the Red Army, which was camped on the outskirts of the capital. In fact, nothing at all had been heard from the Soviets since the start of the uprising. Their bombers had stopped flying over the city, and their radio, which had so urgently called on the Poles to rebel, had fallen silent. Nor was there any sign of aid from Britain or the United States.

On their own, at least for now, the Poles were discovering that their insurgency, instead of hastening the German retreat, appeared to be having the opposite effect: the Nazis were bringing up reinforcements and preparing to counterattack. Adolf Hitler clearly was not going to permit this city that had flagrantly defied him in 1939, and again in the ghetto uprising, to win back its freedom now. He would teach these upstart Poles a final lesson. He had destroyed the ghetto and the Jews in it; now he would destroy *all* Varsovians and their precious capital, too.

"Every inhabitant of Warsaw must be killed, and there shall be no taking of prisoners," declared Heinrich Himmler, whom Hitler had placed in charge of Warsaw's ruin. Himmler, in turn, assigned General Erich von dem Bach-Zelewski, a specialist in tracking down and killing partisans, to command a force of SS troops and police, made up in part of convicted criminals, to put down the uprising. Once they had carried out that task, they were to flatten whatever was left of Warsaw. "From the historical point of view, this insurrection is a blessing," the SS chief crowed to Hitler. "Warsaw will be eradicated—the capital, the center, the flower of a nation of Poles. That nation which for seven hundred years has...stood in our way...shall no longer be a problem for our children or even for ourselves."

STANISŁAW MIKOŁAJCZYK, WHO was in Moscow when the uprising began, appealed to Stalin to provide Soviet support for the *AK*, reminding him that the Kremlin's official radio station had called for the insurgency. Stalin assured Mikołajczyk that the Soviets would provide arms to the insurgents. He added that the Soviet army, which had hoped to take Warsaw by August 6, was facing an unexpectedly strong German defense on the outskirts.

Mikołajczyk had gone to Moscow at the urging of Churchill and Roosevelt, who wanted him to work out a compromise with Stalin over the makeup of the postwar Polish government. But George Kennan, who had become minister-counselor at the U.S. Embassy in Moscow, believed there was little chance for the establishment of a government in Poland that was not under the Kremlin's thumb—and no hope at all for Warsaw and its defenders. Mikołajczyk and his party were, in Kennan's view, "the doomed representatives of a doomed regime...." "I knew," he wrote, "that...the Russians would be no more inclined at present than they were a hundred years ago to accept...the grant of [democratic rights to the Poles] which were not yet given in Russia."

Invited to a dinner in Mikołajczyk's honor at the British Embassy, Kennan found the evening "a hard one." Overall, he reflected, there was "something frivolous" about the British and American treatment of Poland, a casual "lightheartedness" in the way the two great powers had gone about giving advice to this intrepid nation regarding its most vital interests. "I was sorry to find myself, for the moment, a part of this," Kennan observed. "And I wished that instead of mumbling words of official optimism, we had had the judgment and the good taste to bow our heads in silence before the tragedy of a people who have been our allies...."

AS HIMMLER'S SS and police units surged into Warsaw, Home Army radio operators sent out desperate appeals to London, requesting ammunition, antitank weapons, guns, and other arms, as well as help from the Polish Parachute Brigade and Air Force. As the hours ticked by, the *AK* felt more and more ignored and cut off from the world—a sense of isolation that was only heightened by reports of new Allied advances on the Normandy front and the liberation of a growing number of French cities and towns. What the fighters in Warsaw didn't know, however, was that their appeals were beginning to have an effect. On August 2, Churchill and Anthony Eden, under pressure from Polish civilian and military leaders, urged their reluctant chiefs of staff to come to the Home Army's assistance with "maximum effort."

Air Marshal Slessor was asked by the chiefs if supply flights from Italy to Warsaw over the next few nights were feasible. Slessor was emphatically opposed to the idea. "I was never one to shrink from casualties if they were really justified," he later recalled. "In this case, however, I was convinced that a prohibitive rate of loss to the Air Force could not conceivably affect the fate of the Polish Underground Army in Warsaw." Even if the planes made it through the 750-mile gauntlet of German fighters and antiaircraft fire, Slessor argued, only a small fraction of the arms and other equipment they dropped would get to the Home Army. "It was one thing to drop supplies to pre-arranged dropping-zones...in open country behind the lines.... It was quite another thing to bring a big aircraft down to a thousand feet, flaps and wheels down to reduce speed, over a great city, itself the scene of a desperate battle and consequently a mass of fires and flashes from guns and bursting shells...."

With his superiors not persuaded, Slessor authorized fourteen bomber crews, seven of them from 1586 Polish Special Duties Flight, to fly supply sorties to Poland on the night of August 4—but not to Warsaw itself. Instead, they were to make their drops at Home Army sites elsewhere, including Kraków and Lublin. Four of the Polish crews, however, disregarded their orders and flew to Warsaw anyway. Although three of them managed to make accurate drops over Home Army positions, in other respects the night's mission was a disaster. Four RAF bombers were shot down, and one of the Polish-manned planes, damaged by a German fighter, was forced to crash-land.

Furious at the Poles' unauthorized flights to Warsaw and the heavy losses, Slessor canceled all future supply flights to Poland.

———

IN WARSAW, THE SS and police units dispatched by Himmler took full advantage of their license to kill. After pushing the Home Army out of the eastern suburb of Wola on August 5, they went from house to house on a wild rampage of looting, rape, and murder. In one neighborhood after another, residents were herded into courtyards and streets to be executed by machine-gun fire. On a side street, a German trooper spotted a baby carriage containing six-month-old twins. He walked up to the carriage, drew his pistol, and shot the babies dead. By day's end on August 5, more than 10,000 civilians had been slaughtered in Wola alone. Over the next several days, the orgy of killing swept through many of the city's other suburbs, with the Germans claiming more than 30,000 new victims. Hospitals were favorite targets.

Wanda Krasnodębska was working as a nurse at the Hospital of the St. Elizabeth Nuns, one of the hospitals captured by the Germans. When it was set afire, the nurses and doctors pleaded with the SS to allow them to carry the patients outside. The request was denied, and everyone, including Krasnodębska, was ordered to the basement. "It was night," she recalled. "The hospital was burning. There was fire all around. The Germans were all drunk, and on the street, you could hear them yelling and young girls screaming. I said to myself, 'You will not be taking me out of here alive.'" A German put a gun to her head and ordered her to come with him outside. She said no. He threatened to shoot. A doctor, an elderly woman, told him in German, "Let her be. Can't you see she is dying?" He leaned close to Krasnodębska, the gun still pointed at her head. Terror-stricken, she held her breath. The soldier apparently believed the old doctor. Kicking Krasnodębska hard, he stalked away.

The hospital's patients had been carried to a long, narrow, bunkerlike room in the basement, where they were joined by Krasnodębska and other medical personnel. Once all were assembled, three German military policemen entered, pistols drawn. "Bandits," they shouted, as they went from bed to bed, shooting each patient. "Bandits, bandits, bandits, bandits..." The doctors and nurses could only watch. "We could do nothing to save the patients," Krasnodębska recalled. "We were utterly helpless." In the chaos, she managed to escape.

THE SS BUTCHERY in Warsaw was so extreme that even General Bach-Zelewski, no shrinking violet when it came to murder, was appalled. In defiance of Himmler's order, he ordered all killing of women and children to cease. After that, the slaughter of Warsaw civilians lessened but never completely stopped.

Once the Germans had pushed the Home Army from the city's outer districts, they targeted the insurgents' central-city stronghold. The Poles were steadily losing ground. Armed with rifles, pistols, Molotov cocktails, and a small number of machine guns, they were defending themselves against Nazi forces that were constantly being reinforced and that had armored cars and tanks, long-range artillery, dive-bombers, and other heavy weapons at their disposal.

By the middle of August, the Germans were shelling and bombing the city twenty-four hours a day. No part of Warsaw was out of artillery range, and much of the downtown area was on fire. Bricks were falling like rain, blazing timbers flew through the air, dust and smoke blanketed everything. Sidewalks and streets were littered with bodies, and many more corpses were buried in the rubble of collapsed buildings. Thousands of wounded were crammed into makeshift hospitals. Food and water were running out; the threat of a typhoid epidemic was growing.

Still, the Poles fought on. The combat was most savage in Warsaw's *Stare Miasto* (Old Town), just north of the city center, with its narrow, winding cobblestone streets and tall, beautifully restored medieval houses. There, in extremely close quarters, Poles took on Nazis in hand-to-hand combat so intense that it reminded some Germans of the last days of the Battle of Stalingrad.

From the cellars of bombed-out buildings, Home Army radio operators continued to tap out urgent pleas for Western aid, just as other Polish radio operators had done during the German siege in September 1939. At one point, General Bór-Komorowski sent a personal message to Churchill and Roosevelt: "In the name of the Atlantic Charter and of the Four Freedoms … [and] confident of the part we have played in the war effort of the Anglo-Americans, we have the full right to address to you, Mr. President and Mr. Prime Minister, this ardent appeal for immediate help to be sent to wounded Warsaw."

———

MOVED BY THE insurgents' passionate resistance and stunned by the Germans' barbarity, Winston Churchill, at least, was increasingly eager to help. From all sides, he was bombarded by entreaties—from the underground in Warsaw, from the government-in-exile, from General Anders in Italy, from the Polish pilots in Britain. Even General Sikorski's widow weighed in with a plea to Churchill's wife, Clementine, and to Eleanor Roosevelt.

Like others in the British government, Churchill was receiving much of his information about the latest events in Warsaw from a most unlikely source: an RAF pilot who had escaped from a German prisoner-of-war camp in Poland and now was a member of the Home Army. Flying Officer John Ward was one of hundreds of British and American escaped POWs who had been sheltered by the Polish underground as they tried to make their way back to safety. Ward, who had escaped two years earlier, had joined the resistance and now spoke fluent if heavily accented Polish.

When the uprising broke out, underground leaders suggested that Ward make regular reports to London on what was happening. He roamed the stricken city for hours each day, dodging shrapnel and rifle fire to interview Home Army soldiers and to observe the fighting for himself. His reports were sent by short-wave radio in Morse code—descriptions of the most recent combat, of current positions held in the city by the Germans and Poles, of the latest Nazi atrocities. He told the British government and the world, for instance, of the German practice of binding Polish women and children to the fronts of tanks, or tying them to ladders and forcing them to walk ahead of German troops to discourage the Home Army from firing.

Ward's accounts were believed where others' might not have been. "The Allies gave full credit to Polish sources of information only after they had been endorsed by a Britisher," remarked one underground leader. "If we ourselves reported these incidents, so inconceivable to civilized men, the Allies would not believe us, and might think it was exaggerated Polish propaganda."

Stirred by Ward's reports and influenced by the crescendo of Polish pleas for help, Churchill insisted on more aid for Warsaw. In Italy, Air Marshal Slessor felt the heat. After canceling all future flights to Poland on August 5, he was pressured two days later to order resumption of limited missions by Polish crews only.

On the nights of August 8 and 9, seven planes from 1586 Flight were authorized to make supply runs to Warsaw. There, in downtown squares and other predetermined drop sites, women bearing hurricane lamps braved heavy German artillery fire to lie on the ground and form themselves into the shape of crosses, marking the drop spots. The Liberators and Halifaxes came in at rooftop altitudes. As the parachutes floated down, crowds of shouting, cheering Varsovians, many waving handkerchiefs at the departing planes, rushed into the streets to collect the supplies.

When most of the drops reported successful results, pressure on Slessor to continue them grew stronger. Over the next week, he dispatched more than ninety Polish, British, and South African crews to the Warsaw area. In the course of this all-out effort, Slessor's initial misgivings proved entirely justified. The Germans had reinforced their antiair-craft defenses along the bombers' routes. The flak was murderous as the planes neared and flew over Warsaw. The Allied crews, their vision impaired by crisscrossing German searchlights and by the smoke and fire shrouding the embattled city, had to evade enemy fighters and ground fire while trying to make accurate drops over the rapidly shrink-ing areas held by the Home Army. Seventeen of the ninety-odd planes that were sent to Warsaw that week—each with crews of at least six men—were shot out of the sky. Most of the others were damaged, three so badly that they crashed on landing back in Italy. To make matters even worse, the Germans recovered many of the dropped supply containers.

By late September, after more heavy casualties, a furious Slessor told his superiors that "it was useless to continue this effort, which by then had cost us twenty-five crews and achieved practically nothing." He managed to prevent British and South African airmen from going on most future relief missions. Even so, Polish military authorities con-vinced the British to allow Polish crews to keep on flying. The missions grew more and more deadly, with fewer supplies actually reaching the Home Army. In less than three weeks, 1586 Flight had lost a total of twelve crews, or 120 percent of its established strength. As replacement crews from Polish bomber squadrons in Britain were transferred to 1586 Flight, they were fed into the maw—with similar results. One top Pol-ish Air Force officer called the missions "a suicidal waste of airmen."

Despite the extreme danger and apparent futility, many other Polish pilots clamored to get into the action. Their requests were always denied. They had flown in defense of France and Britain. Since D-Day, they had helped liberate Western Europe from German occupation. The four squadrons of 133 Polish Fighter Wing, under the command of Jan Zumbach, were protecting London once again that summer by inter-cepting and bringing down the Germans' fearsome new weapon—the V-1 buzz bomb. Zumbach called such missions "a kind of aerial shooting gallery—but highly dangerous, as several of my pilots learned to their cost." The sorties, which required the pilots to fire at the flying missiles at close range or to tip them over with their plane's wing, claimed the lives of several Polish fliers. Nonetheless, the four squadrons were cred-ited with downing almost 200 V-1s by war's end.

When their own country most needed their help, however, the Poles could only go to their base mess and listen to BBC radio accounts of the deteriorating situation. As the Home Army's supplies and ability to fight ran out, the Polish pilots in Britain were overwhelmed by feelings of impotence, guilt, and futility. They had to sit there, listening to the news of defeat and "dying a little," as one of them said, "during each of those sixty-three days of the Rising."

In a broadcast to occupied Poland, one fighter pilot revealed his deep frustration: "My God, to be with you! To fly over Warsaw with the armament we have now.... The Palace, the Main Post Office, the Old City—I know how they look from the air. I know every back street, almost every building. I would know how to shoot without hitting you. I could help you. I would be able to win with you. But I must wait. Well-armed, strong, ready to fight—I must await the order."

During the uprising, a number of desperate Polish fighter squadrons, the Kościuszko Squadron among them, pressed the RAF to let them fly to Warsaw to attack German positions. The RAF turned them down for the excellent reason that their planes did not carry enough fuel for the round trip. Unpersuaded and irrationally determined, the pilots were willing to sacrifice their planes and themselves for Warsaw (which was to say, for Poland). The Kościuszko Squadron's pilots even went so far as to send a blunt telegram to the queen:

EVERY NIGHT, FROM THIS GREAT ISLAND, THOUSANDS OF AIRCRAFT TAKE OFF FOR THE CONTINENT. A FEW OF THEM COULD SAVE WARSAW. WHEN IN 1940, THE FATE OF GREAT BRITAIN WAS IN THE BALANCE, BELIEVE US, YOUR MAJESTY, WE POLISH AIRMEN NEVER THOUGHT OF ECONOMIZING OUR BLOOD OR OUR LIVES.... AT THAT TIME, OVER BURNING LONDON, THERE WAS NO DEARTH OF POLISH OR BRITISH AIRMEN. ARE THEY TO BE LACKING NOW OVER BURNING WARSAW? IS THE CITY TO PERISH ON THE EVE OF VICTORY, AFTER YEARNING FOR LIBERATION FOR FIVE YEARS?... SHALL FAITH IN GREAT BRITAIN BE DESTROYED IN THE FLAMES WHICH NOW ENVELOP OUR CAPITAL? WE BEG YOU TO PARDON US AS SOLDIERS, YOUR MAJESTY, FOR OUR OUTSPOKENNESS AND SINCERITY. WE CAN, HOWEVER, NO LONGER REMAIN SILENT WHILE OUR WOMEN AND CHILDREN ARE DYING. WE FIRMLY BELIEVE, YOUR MAJESTY, THAT YOU ARE NOT INDIFFERENT TO THEIR FATE.

As far as anyone knows, the queen never answered. As commander of one of the Polish fighter wings, Jan Zumbach continued to plead the pilots' case. RAF officials regarded his lobbying, he wrote later, as a "show of indiscipline which was not merely sentimental, but, worse still, impolitic." Already cynical about the Allies' treatment of Poland, Zumbach became even more jaundiced when, a short time later, RAF officials, for unknown reasons, withdrew an earlier recommendation that he be awarded one of the British military's highest honors, the Distinguished Service Order.

WHILE HUNDREDS OF Polish, British, and South African airmen risked—and in many cases lost—their lives on long-distance missions in support of the Warsaw uprising, Soviet troops waited less than a dozen miles away from the heart of the Polish capital, and did...nothing. Despite Stalin's assurances to Mikołajczyk in early August that Soviet troops would aid the insurgents, the Red Army had suddenly stopped its headlong advance just short of Warsaw. No Soviet planes flew in supplies. Soviet long-range artillery went suddenly quiet. What's more, Radio Moscow, which just a few weeks before had implored the Poles to rise up against the Germans, now was condemning the uprising and its leaders.

"It is difficult to resist the conviction that the Russian failure to supply Warsaw is deliberate," Air Marshal Slessor cabled the chief of the Air Staff shortly after the uprising began. That same suspicion was also gnawing at Churchill, who told Anthony Eden: "It certainly is very curious that at the moment when the Underground Army has revolted, the Russian armies should have halted their attack against Warsaw and withdrawn some distance." On August 12, Churchill urged Stalin to airlift supplies to the Home Army from the liberated East, noting the extreme hazards that RAF flights from Italy were facing as they flew over territory still occupied by the Germans.

Washington, meanwhile, was making its own appeals to Stalin on behalf of the Polish insurgents. Immediately after the uprising began, Office of Strategic Services (OSS) director William J. Donovan urged President Roosevelt and his top military advisers to allow the OSS to mount large-scale supply operations to the Poles. Senior U.S. Army Air

Forces officers were not necessarily opposed to such missions. But, they said, U.S. bombers flying supplies from England to Warsaw would have to land on Soviet airfields in the Ukraine so that the planes could be refueled and the crews could rest before making the return flight.

At first glance, that did not seem to pose much of a problem. The Soviets had already granted landing rights at three airfields to U.S. planes on bombing missions over Germany and Romania. But when U.S. officials requested similar permission for supply flights to Warsaw, the Soviets replied with a curt *nyet.* The uprising was a foolhardy affair, the Kremlin said, and "the Soviet Government could not lend its hand to it."

Averell Harriman and British ambassador Archibald Clark Kerr pleaded with the Soviets to reconsider, declaring that it was "in the interests of the [Allied] cause and of humanity to support" the Poles. The United States wasn't asking the Soviets to participate directly in the operation, said Harriman, who could not understand how the Soviets could possibly object. Andrei Vyshinsky, the deputy foreign minister, contemptuously dismissed Harriman. The Kremlin would not encourage any "adventuristic actions" that might later be turned against the Soviet Union, he snapped.

Two days later, Harriman renewed his appeal, this time with Vyshinsky's boss, Vyacheslav Molotov. The Soviet foreign minister responded by threatening to cut off *all* U.S. access to the Soviet bases if the Americans kept up these absurd requests. George Kennan recalled that Harriman returned to the embassy "shattered." It had become clear to both of them that the Soviets, guided by "ruthless political considerations," as Harriman later noted in a report to Washington, wanted the Warsaw uprising crushed and would not brook any attempt by the Allies to support it.

Molotov's rejection of Harriman's plea was "a gauntlet thrown down, in a spirit of malicious glee, before the Western powers," Kennan wrote. "What it meant to imply was: 'We intend to have Poland, lock, stock and barrel. We don't care a fig for those Polish underground fighters who have not accepted Communist authority. To us they are no better than the Germans.... It is a matter of indifference to us what you Americans think of all this. You are going to have no part in determining the affairs of Poland from here on out, and it is time you realized this.' "

As Kennan saw it, this was the point of no return in Western-Soviet relations, the time when the United States and Britain should have had a "full-fledged and realistic political showdown" with the Kremlin. There was no reason for further conciliation: D-Day had established the second front demanded by Stalin; Allied forces were on the Continent in massive numbers; the Soviet Union had expelled the German invaders. What now was at stake was the freedom of Poland and other countries that were about to be overrun by Soviet forces. It was time, Kennan believed, to tell Stalin: we will no longer support you, materially or otherwise, if you insist on subjugating these lands.

Heavily influenced by Kennan, Harriman had also come to the conclusion that the United States must get tough with the Russians. Once a strong advocate of unconditional aid to the Soviet Union, he now wrote despairingly of its leaders: "These men are bloated with power and expect they can force acceptance of their decisions upon us and all countries without question." The Poles had every right to stage an uprising and every right to expect help from the Allies, including Russia, Harriman declared to Roosevelt and Secretary of State Cordell Hull.

The ambassador urged FDR to send "a strong message" to Stalin, pressing him to authorize use of Soviet landing bases for American relief missions. Roosevelt had already authorized Harriman to ask Stalin to reconsider the Soviet refusal. But the president declined to send a message on his own. And Hull cautioned Harriman to proceed cautiously, lest the Soviets follow through on their threat to deny all U.S. access to bases in the Ukraine.

Harriman was nonplussed. He wrote to Harry Hopkins: "[The Soviets] have misinterpreted our generous attitude toward them as a sign of weakness and an acceptance of their policies. The time has come when we must make clear what we expect of them as the price of our goodwill. Unless we take issue with [them], there is every indication the Soviet Union will become a world bully wherever their interests are involved."

Winston Churchill was coming to the same conclusion. Indeed, according to Lord Moran, his doctor, the prime minister was consumed during the Warsaw uprising with fears of Soviet aggression. "Winston never talks of Hitler these days; he is always harping on the dangers of Communism," Moran wrote in his diary. "He dreams of the Red Army spreading like a cancer from one country to another. It has become an obsession...."

Churchill was also personally caught up in the epic David-and-Goliath struggle taking place in Warsaw. The Poles' resistance won the prime minister's esteem, and the searing eyewitness accounts of German atrocities committed against Polish civilians left him enraged. "I am most painfully affected by this Polish [uprising]," he wrote to his wife on August 18. More than fifty years later, Churchill's grandson, also named Winston Churchill, remarked: "My grandfather was beside himself in desperation to secure help for the Poles."

Churchill's emotional involvement in the uprising was reinforced by a late August meeting with General Anders in Italy. The prime minister much admired the commander of the II Polish Corps, whose men had acquitted themselves so heroically at Monte Cassino. And just days before, another Polish army unit, the 1st Polish Armored Division, had played a pivotal role in sealing the Allied victory in Normandy by cut-

Winston Churchill and General Władysław Anders, commander of the II Polish Corps, meet in Italy in August 1944. Churchill assured Anders at this meeting that he and President Roosevelt would never abandon Poland. (Imperial War Museum)

ting off the withdrawal of tens of thousands of German forces trapped at Falaise.

Churchill promised Anders that Britain would never let Poland down. "[We] entered this war in defense of the principle of your independence, and I can assure you that we will never desert you," he said. Over and over again, Churchill repeated the pledge, as if he were trying to convince himself as well as Anders. "I and my friend President Roosevelt, who will again be elected President, will never abandon Poland," the prime minister said. "Put your trust in us."

Having made that promise, Churchill now had to try to keep it. Earlier in August, he had persuaded a reluctant Roosevelt to send a joint telegram to Stalin, asking the Soviet leader to dispatch aid to Warsaw or to allow the Americans and British to do so by giving them access to his air bases. Failure to provide such help would upset world public opinion, Churchill and Roosevelt suggested. The telegram was couched in mild language, but it caused Stalin to throw a tantrum. He called the Warsaw insurgents "a band of power-seeking criminals" and again rejected the idea of helping them. He did not even acknowledge his Allies' appeal to use the Soviet bases.

After that, Roosevelt declined to put any further pressure on the Soviet premier. When Churchill sent the president a wrenching eyewitness account of Nazi mass killings in Warsaw, including the wholesale murder of hospital patients, FDR coolly replied: "Thank you for the information in regard to the appalling situation of the Poles in Warsaw and the inhuman behavior of the Nazis.... I do not see that we can take any additional steps at the present time that promise results."

Churchill continued to press. Urging FDR to join him in sending yet another appeal to Stalin, he declared that if the effort failed, "we ought to send the planes [anyway] and see what happens." Roosevelt declined. "I do not consider it... advantageous to the long-range general war prospect for me to join with you in the proposed message to Stalin," he said. "But I have no objection to your sending such a message if you consider it advisable...."

The message was not sent.

CHAPTER EIGHTEEN

"A Tale of Two Cities"

A T THE HEIGHT of the Warsaw uprising in late August, a Home Army radio operator handed General Bór-Komorowski an urgent message, just relayed from London: Paris had been liberated. "Lucky Paris," Bór-Komorowski muttered.

Except for the Allied response, the parallels between recent events in Paris and Warsaw were striking. Like the Home Army and the occupants of the Warsaw Ghetto, members of the French resistance in Paris had risen up against the Germans. And, as with the Warsaw uprising, this one came as a surprise to the Allies. Until it began, General Dwight Eisenhower and other Allied military leaders had had no intention of liberating Paris, which they considered of little strategic importance to their accelerating dash across France to Germany.

But the French pleaded that if the Allies did not come to the insurgents' aid, hundreds of thousands of Parisians would be killed and— under new orders issued by Hitler—the city destroyed. At that, Eisenhower relented, and the parallels with Warsaw's situation ended. On August 25, only four days after the Paris uprising began, the Allies, led by a French armored division under Major General Jacques LeClerc and loyal to the London-based government of Charles de Gaulle, reclaimed a delirious Paris. "No one blamed the Parisians for having tried, with their own forces, to cooperate in the liberation of the capital," Bór-Komorowski reflected on hearing the news. "How different would [be] the fate of Warsaw had American and British armies been standing at her gates."

Instead, it was the Russians who were standing there, unmoved and unmoving.

The following week, while the people of Paris were still toasting their liberators with champagne, thousands of Polish resistance fighters and civilians slipped down manholes and disappeared into Warsaw's stinking, night-black sewers. Since the beginning of the uprising, couriers and others in the Home Army had used the far-flung sewer network as a means of getting around the city. Now it became the Poles' only means of escape from the shelled and bombed-out ruin that *Stare Miasto* had become. Against all odds, elements of the Home Army had held out for almost a month in *Stare Miasto*, the nerve center of the uprising, still battling the Germans as the rubble smoldered. Now, cut off from ammunition, food, and water, they were on the verge of annihilation, and Bór-Komorowski gave the order to evacuate.

In early September, more than 1,500 soldiers and 3,000 civilians, many of them wounded, vanished below ground, setting out on an agonizing, snail-slow trek through the Stygian labyrinth. For many, it would be the most hellish experience of a hellish war. Struggling to keep their balance on the curved tunnel floors, they slogged through thick ooze that occasionally reached as high as their shoulders. Some of the fighters became lost in the subterranean maze and disappeared; others slipped and drowned in the muck. The stench was overpowering: Bór-Komorowski recalled that "it made me sick and brought tears to my eyes."

The sewer's total blackness and tight spaces sometimes produced a profound claustrophobia. The reverberating moans from the wounded and the cries from the terrified served to heighten the sense of impending doom. The slightest sounds were amplified in the tunnels, rolling through them in ghastly echoes and frequently alerting the Germans on the streets above. Dozens of Poles were killed when the Nazis threw grenades down sewer manholes or poured in gasoline and ignited it to create an underground inferno. The one-mile journey from *Stare Miasto* to the center of the city took up to nine hours for those who survived it. After climbing into daylight, many, perhaps most, collapsed.

In Berlin, Heinrich Himmler, the SS chief, remarked to his lieutenants: "For five weeks we have been fighting the battle for Warsaw. This is the most bitter struggle of all we have had since the start of the war."

A Home Army soldier being helped out of a sewer. During the uprising, Warsaw's sewers served as the Home Army's main escape route. (Jerzy Tomaszewski)

AN RAF BOMBER pilot who flew over Warsaw during the uprising later remarked that if Dante could have seen the Polish capital then, he would have had a realistic picture of his Inferno. Yet few people in the West had any idea of Warsaw's anguish. Except for some slim news accounts and a few editorials about how unfortunately premature it all was, the drama, the heroism, the tragedy of the uprising went largely unnoticed in Britain and the United States. The liberation of glamorous, romantic Paris and the Allied advance toward Germany were dominating newspaper headlines and radio broadcasts. Understandable as this was, Win-

Warsaw in ruins after the uprising. The skeletal remains of the Prudential Building are on the left. (S. Braun, Historical Museum of Warsaw)

ston Churchill and others couldn't help wondering if news of the Warsaw insurgency was being deliberately silenced. "Is there any stop on publicity for the facts about the agony of Warsaw, which seem from the papers to have been practically suppressed?" an indignant Churchill cabled Brendan Bracken, his minister of information, from Italy on August 23. No, Bracken replied. With all the good news from Paris, the press simply had little interest in what was going on in Poland—including the Russians' refusal to support the uprising.

Churchill thus found himself in a dilemma of his own making. For some months, he and his government had tended to portray the Poles as reckless troublemakers, an image echoed in the British press. At the same time, the Soviets were lauded as the large-hearted, magnanimous saviours of Eastern Europe, all contrary evidence having been covered up. Now, the prime minister searched frantically for a way to publicize the fighting in Warsaw, the insurgents' heroism, and their desperate need for help—without, somehow, indicting the Soviets. "There is no need to mention the strange and sinister behavior of the Russians, but is there any reason why the consequences of such behavior should not be made public?" Churchill asked Bracken.

How that might be accomplished, the prime minister never made clear. In any event, Bracken, Anthony Eden, and other British officials remained determined to conceal Soviet intransigence from the press and public. More than once, they lied outright. After Stalin barred American planes from landing at Soviet air bases, the Foreign Office assured the BBC that both the Soviets and the British were eager to send help to the Poles by air. Eden cautioned the War Cabinet that the Poles in Britain must not learn about the Soviet rebuff. The foreign secretary even asked the Americans to inform the Polish government-in-exile that the USAAF was still awaiting landing clearance from the Russians.

News of the Russians' refusal to aid the Home Army nevertheless began to leak out. According to the British government's home intelligence reports, the British public by the end of August was starting to have renewed sympathy for the Poles and considerable concern about the Soviets' unwillingness to help them. A number of MPs pressed the government to reconvene Parliament for a full-scale debate on the matter. Sixteen MPs issued a statement urging all possible aid for Warsaw and demanding that the government make public immediately all problems involved in providing such aid: "It should be known beyond any doubt what limitations, if any, have been imposed upon [the government's] activities and by whom."

In a letter to the *Daily Mail*, Lord Vansittart, the former Foreign Office undersecretary, declared: "A tragedy is being enacted before an insufficiently attentive world. The British and Russians stimulated the Polish patriots to revolt in order to assist the oncoming Russian army. The Poles did so; then the Russian advance was halted.... The unsupported Poles are being slaughtered and Warsaw is being obliterated. Is humanity going to allow this tragedy to be consummated?"

And George Orwell, still the scourge of leftist intellectuals and their support for most things Soviet, lambasted the "mean and cowardly attitude" of the British press for criticizing the Poles and turning a blind eye to the Russians. From reading the papers, Orwell wrote, "one [is] left with the general impression that the Poles deserved to have their bottoms smacked for doing what all the Allied wirelesses had been urging them to do for years past, and that they ... did not deserve to be given any help from the outside."

Yet, although most newspapers were loath to focus on the Poles' need for assistance, a few, including several left-leaning publications that previously had been uncritically pro-Soviet, began to report how the Kremlin had initially encouraged the uprising, then withheld support once it began. "No doubt there are good reasons why the Russians paused; why no arms were sent...," declared the then left-wing *Daily Mirror*. "But they will have to be the best reasons, for the crumbling walls of Warsaw and the broken bodies of her children demand an explanation of why the help was delayed."

The Economist, in the leader of its August 26 issue, published what was perhaps the toughest critique of all. Called "A Tale of Two Cities," the weekly's piece offered a grim, "heartbreaking" comparison between the relatively easy liberation of Paris and Warsaw's cruel struggle for survival. Almost exactly five years earlier, *The Economist* pointed out, just three nations—France, Britain, and Poland—had gone to war against Germany in defense of liberty. Since that time, the British, with help from their Allies, prominently including the Poles, had managed to hold on to their freedom, and the French, with even more Allied help, were recovering theirs. But now the Poles were trying to drive out the Germans, and in this "vastly bloodier and more desperate battle," they have been "almost unsupported by their Allies, materially or even morally."

The Russians' refusal to provide military support or to allow their allies the use of their air bases was "intolerable," *The Economist* leader added. "The rising in Warsaw is a glorious contribution to the Allied cause, and it cannot be refused. Talks are now going on about aid to Warsaw.... In honour and expediency alike, they should have only one result, and that speedily. But, incredibly, the present prospect is said to be precisely the opposite. To our joy in victory, it seems that the Allies may have to add the ultimate shame of desertion."

An agitated Churchill was trying to forestall that outcome. He had already given in to Stalin on the question of eastern Poland; now the Soviet dictator's guarantee of a free and independent Poland was clearly in jeopardy. As Anthony Eden remarked: "[T]he conclusion seems inescapable that Stalin, surprised by the vigor and success of the rising, was content to see the underground and remaining political and intellectual leaders of Poland destroyed." In other words, if Warsaw were ruined and the Home Army wiped out, Stalin would have a much easier time installing a regime of his own creation. Churchill concluded that the Kremlin "did not mean to let the spirit of Poland rise again at Warsaw."

On September 3, the prime minister received a copy of a message sent by women in Warsaw to Pope Pius XII, begging his intercession. "Holy Father, no one is helping us," the women declared. "The Russian armies...have not advanced a step. The aid coming to us from Great Britain is insufficient. The world is ignorant of our fight. God alone is with us." This latest appeal threw Churchill into even more of a rage at the Russians' cold-bloodedness.

The next day, the prime minister, though suffering from a fever, met with members of his War Cabinet, who were as furious as he was. "I do not remember any occasion when such deep anger was shown by all our members, Tory, Labour, Liberal alike," he later wrote. Deeply concerned about the reaction of the British public if they found out the full story of Soviet perfidy in Poland, Britain's top officials seriously considered sending bombers to help Warsaw and having them land on Soviet airfields without permission. If Stalin took it badly, Churchill would immediately halt all convoys to the Soviet Union.

As in the past, however, the prime minister and his government decided against taking unilateral action against Moscow. It was, Churchill wrote after the war, another in the "terrible and even humbling submissions [that] must at times be made to the general aim." In the end, the British settled for cabling a rather mild rebuke to Molotov: "[We] find it hard to understand your Government's refusal to take account of the obligation of the British and American Governments to help the Poles in Warsaw. Your Government's action in preventing this help...seems to us at variance with the spirit of Allied cooperation to which you and we attach so much importance both for the present and the future."

Churchill also passed the Polish women's message to Franklin Roosevelt and urged the president to support the plan to send large-scale relief to Warsaw and, if need be, "gate-crash" Soviet airfields. "In view of our great successes in the West," Churchill said in an accompanying note, "I cannot think that the Russians could reject this *fait accompli*."

Roosevelt was well aware of what the Kremlin was up to. A State Department report to the White House had advised the president that the refusal to support the Poles "appears to indicate Stalin's determination that the Soviet-sponsored committee [of Polish Communists] gain as full control as possible of the country." All other things being equal, Stalin's motives in this matter might have been of some interest to Roosevelt, but all other things were not equal. The president was facing an election in two months and wanted no hint of dissension within the alliance to harm his chances. Roosevelt was still unwilling, despite the war's dramatically altered circumstances, to confront Stalin. In his response to Churchill, Roosevelt said he had been informed by intelligence sources that the Germans were now in full control of Warsaw: "The problem of relief for the Poles...has therefore unfortunately been solved by delay and by German action, and there now appears to be nothing we can do to assist them."*

As in Britain, the press in the United States gave very little coverage to Warsaw. The president held nine press conferences during the uprising, and neither he nor the reporters in attendance mentioned it once. Not until October 3, when the insurgency finally ended, did it finally figure in a reporter's question to FDR, which he offhandedly parried: "I think that I had better set a good example. I suppose I know as much about that particular thing as any American, and I don't know enough to talk about it."

──────────

FROM THE BEGINNING of the uprising, the Soviets held bridgeheads on the western bank of the Vistula River south of Warsaw. By the second week of September, Russian troops had captured the Warsaw suburb of Praga, a mile from the city's center. Only the Vistula, shrunken by a lack of rain, lay between the Russians and the insurgents, who were now just barely holding out. And still the Soviets stayed put.

One Red Army unit, however, decided it could wait no longer. A division of Poles, pressed into service by the Soviets after being stranded in the Soviet Union when General Anders left with his forces in 1942, included a large number of Varsovians. Having wangled permission from its Soviet commanders, a battalion from the division crossed the Vistula in mid-September and briefly joined the fight.

By the time the Polish battalion crossed the river, the city was little

───────

* The president's intelligence was obviously faulty. The uprising would continue for another month.

more than a giant cemetery. Countless rows of unmarked graves lay in the squares and in the courtyards of blasted buildings; thousands of other bodies were interred in the rubble. Some parts of the city were so covered with debris that it was impossible to tell where streets and avenues had been. The Varsovians still alive were close to starvation. "All the horses had long been consumed, and the turn of the dogs had come," an underground leader recalled. Newborn babies were dying because of lack of milk.

At that late stage in the uprising, the Polish arrivals from the Red Army could be of little help. They were too few, and the Germans were too many and too strong. Unsupported by Soviet forces or artillery, the battalion suffered heavy casualties and was forced to withdraw back across the Vistula.

Another unit from the Polish division was charged with picking up Home Army members trapped by the Germans near the river and ferrying them to safety across the Vistula. One of the soldiers in the unit was a twenty-year-old future Communist prime minister of Poland named Wojciech Jaruzelski. Many Polish soldiers died in that operation, and Jaruzelski himself was slightly wounded. Still haunted years later by the sight of Warsaw burning and by the odor of smoke and death that permeated his uniform, Jaruzelski commented carefully and rather defensively: "It was possible to take Warsaw.... But the [Kremlin's] decision not to try was reasonable, given the Soviets' logic: 'Why begin such an operation, pay such a price, when in any event the Warsaw Uprising is not in our interests?' "

Six weeks after the uprising began, Stalin finally decided to make the Soviets' presence felt in Warsaw. He still refused to act in direct military support of the Home Army, but Soviet artillery shells were fired at parts of the city, while Soviet planes dropped canisters of food and other supplies. (Most of the canisters were pushed from the planes without parachutes and were smashed to bits on landing.) It was "as if they wanted to mock us...," said one resistance leader. "It was obvious that these were purely propaganda drops, which would enable the Soviets to tell the West that they were helping the Rising, while in fact they were not." Knowing by that point that the Home Army was doomed, Stalin then sought to score another propaganda coup by withdrawing his objections to the use of Soviet bases by American bombers.

On September 18, Varsovians heard a low-pitched thrumming from the sky. They rushed from their shattered buildings, looked up, and saw rank after rank of B-17s high above the city. Then multicolored dots blossomed beneath them. "Parachutes!" people shouted. "It's our Parachute Brigade!" Crying and cheering, exhausted civilians and Home Army soldiers ran into the streets.

It soon became clear that the American bombers were dropping containers, not men—more than a thousand large capsules filled with submachine and machine guns, pistols, grenades, medical equipment, and food rations. Swallowing their disappointment that the Parachute Brigade had not arrived, Warsaw's residents celebrated anyway. Minutes later, their celebration turned to horror when they saw most of the containers drifting beyond Home Army barricades into parts of the city that the Nazis had recaptured from the Poles. "Had the... containers been dropped in the first days, when two-thirds of the city was in our hands, they would certainly all have been collected by us and might then have decided the outcome of the battle," General Bór-Komorowski recalled. "Unfortunately, help had come when we retained only small patches of the city. We could merely witness the massive exhibition of power and think of what might have been...."

Only about 20 percent of the supplies dropped on September 18 were actually recovered by the Poles, and no additional large-scale airlifts were conducted. Stalin, having scored propaganda points by allowing the bombers to land and refuel in his territory, thereafter rejected American requests for a repeat performance. Yet British and American journalists treated the September 18 operation as a major success. Particular praise went to the Soviets for allowing the use of their airfields. Stalin's refusal to allow any more missions was kept secret by both the U.S. and British governments.

Churchill and his top officials quickly forgot their anger at Stalin and declared the crisis over. On September 26, the prime minister went before the House of Commons to explain that the Soviets had sent supplies to the uprising as soon as they reasonably could and that no blame should attach to them for the delay. As far as the Churchill government was concerned, it was back to business as usual. As a Foreign Office memo put it: "Nothing should be done to antagonize the Russians."

Not everyone agreed. Air Marshal John Slessor, who had lost some 250 airmen in the harrowing early supply sorties, found it incomprehensible after Warsaw that anyone could place even a minimal faith in Stalin. "The gallantry and self-sacrifice on the part of our air crews— R.A.F., South African, and, above all, Polish" was in stark contrast to "the blackest-hearted, coldest-blooded treachery on the part of the Russians," Slessor later wrote. "I am not a naturally vindictive man; but I hope there may be some very special hell reserved for the brutes in the Kremlin who betrayed Bór[-Komorowski]'s army and led to the fruitless sacrifice of [my men]."

In Slessor's view, Stalin had made clear in the summer and fall of 1944 that the Soviets meant to have full control of Poland—all of it. "How, after the fall of Warsaw, any responsible statesman could trust any Russian Communist further than he could kick him," the RAF Mediterranean commander said, "passes the comprehension of ordinary men."

———————

ON THE DAY of the one great U.S. airlift to Warsaw, the 2,500 men of the Polish Parachute Brigade sat disconsolately at their base at Easton-on-the-Hill, listening to the latest radio reports from their besieged capital. As painful as it was for Polish pilots to be prevented from fighting for Warsaw, it was doubly hard for the paratroopers. Their brigade had been created specifically for this moment—only to find itself handed over to British command two months earlier for use in the Allied advance across Western Europe.

Eight days after the uprising began, Polish officials appealed again to the British to allow at least part of the brigade to parachute into Warsaw. Again, the British denied the request. No air transports could be spared, they said. The following day, men from the brigade, angry and frustrated, refused to enter the mess hall for their evening meal as a sign of protest. Among them was Richard Tice, an American who had joined the Polish unit as a volunteer before the United States entered the war. Tice had learned in school about the roles of Kościuszko and Pułaski in winning independence for America, and, like Merian Cooper after World War I, he wanted to return the favor.

If anything, General Sosabowski was even angrier than his men. The British kept harping on what they saw as the Poles' unsound plans to aid Warsaw, but Sosabowski found the upcoming Allied operation in which his forces were to play a major part even more flawed and unrealistic. Called "Operation Market-Garden," it was the brainchild of Field Marshal Montgomery and was to be the largest Allied airborne assault of the war. Aimed at clearing the way for General Montgomery's army to cross the Rhine and advance into Germany, the plan called for the U.S. 82nd and 101st Airborne divisions and the British 1st Airborne, supported by the Polish Parachute Brigade, to seize a series of bridges and canal crossings in Holland and establish bridgeheads. The last bridge to be captured, by the British 1st Airborne, spanned the Rhine at Arnhem.

Sosabowski protested against what he saw as the casual, slipshod planning of Market-Garden. He was particularly distressed by the offhand way in which the British dismissed the likely strength of Nazi defenses as they contemplated "a powerful, full-blooded thrust to the heart of Germany." Did they really believe that the Germans would allow their sacred Rhine to be crossed without a stiff fight?

From the outset, the fiery Sosabowski insisted that the mission had no chance of success. Regarded by the British as a troublemaker with a grudge, Sosabowski focused primarily on the likely German defenses. But there were many other potential problems. The weather was iffy, and trying to bring up supplies over narrow, easily choked lowland roads was an invitation to disaster. At one of the last planning sessions, the commander of the British airborne division, Major General R. E. Urquhart, asked for questions. There were none. "Everyone sat nonchalantly, legs crossed, looking bored," Sosabowski recalled. "I wanted to say something about this impossible plan, but I just couldn't. I was unpopular as it was, and, anyway, who would have listened?"

On September 21, as Warsaw blazed, the men of the Polish brigade boarded RAF transport planes, after a two-day postponement because of inclement weather, and headed for Arnhem. Operation Market-Garden was in its fifth day—and already in desperate trouble. Sosabowski had been right in his assessment of German resistance: from the first, it proved savage and overwhelmingly tenacious. The U.S. 101st and 82nd Airborne divisions had taken most of their objectives, but the Germans had isolated the British 1st Airborne at Arnhem. The Poles' assignment was to reinforce the British.

As their transports approached Arnhem Bridge, Sosabowski looked down and was stunned to see German tanks crossing it. There were also enemy tanks and antiaircraft guns clustered near the Poles' drop site, patiently waiting. Just as Sosabowski had feared and predicted, he and his men were about to enter an inferno. As they prepared to jump, Messerschmitts suddenly appeared and slashed through the RAF airborne formation, blasting a number of the unarmed transports out of the sky. Many of the Polish paratroopers who made it out of their aircraft were riddled with machine-gun fire and AA flak as they glided helplessly to earth. One recalled seeing so many tracer bullets flashing around him that "every gun on the ground seemed to be aimed at me." A British officer who witnessed the bloodbath described how bodies of Poles "tumbled through the air, inert forms drifting slowly down, dead before they hit the ground." Of those who survived, a large number were killed a few hours later, raked by German fire as they set out in rubber rafts across the Rhine, 400 yards wide, trying to reach the beleaguered 1st Airborne bridgehead at the northern end of the bridge.

More than a fifth of the Polish brigade lost their lives in Operation Marker-Garden. Among the dead was Richard Tice. Worse, somehow, than the appallingly high casualties suffered by the Poles and the British 1st Airborne was the knowledge that the operation was an utter failure: the Germans, were, for the moment, able to hang on to Arnhem and the Rhine.

In the witch-hunt that followed, the British commanders responsible for planning and organizing the fiasco tried to pin some of the blame on Sosabowski, who subsequently was relieved of his command. In fact, wrote the American military historians Williamson Murray and Allan R. Millett, the Pole's "only mistake had been to warn his superiors against overconfidence."

WHEN THE COMMANDERS of the Home Army launched the Warsaw uprising on August 1, they believed they would have to hold out only four or five days before being reinforced by Soviet or Allied troops. As it turned out, the Home Army and other residents of Warsaw held out—with no reinforcements at all—for sixty-three days. It was an astonishing display of tenacity and courage. As SS troops pushed the Poles into smaller and smaller areas of the city, hope still flickered that outside help would arrive in time to save what was left of them and of Warsaw. But the help never came, and in early October, even hope died.

Food, water, and ammunition were gone. Disease was rampant. In the few districts still held by the Home Army, dozens of people were crammed into every basement and cellar, many on the verge of death. Faced with the total annihilation of the city's population, General Bór-Komorowski and his subordinates decided they had no choice but to capitulate. At 8:00 p.m. on October 2, Bór-Komorowski signed the surrender agreement at German headquarters—the second time in five years that Warsaw, after desperate resistance, was forced to submit to the enemy.

But many Varsovians found this defeat even harder to accept than the first. In September 1939, the Allies had been weak and the Germans at the apex of their power. It was painful but understandable that the West did not help. Now, with the Germans on the defensive and the Allies at *their* peak, the failure to rescue a city and a people who had given everything to reclaim their freedom was beyond understanding.

The Americans and British did grant one request made by the Polish underground during the uprising: they recognized the Home Army as a legitimate part of the Allied armed forces. This entitled the army's survivors, including some 2,000 women, to be treated as prisoners of war under international conventions—a distinction that the German commander, General Bach-Zelewski, agreed to observe despite his earlier cruelties.

On October 3, the Polish underground radio station, which had broadcast so many appeals for help in the previous few weeks, sent a farewell message to London. The announcer's voice cracked with emotion as he said: "We have been free for two months. Today, once more, we must go into captivity...."

After the surrender, the Germans ordered all Varsovians to evacuate the city. A staggering 200,000-plus people, about a quarter of the residents who had survived to that point in the war, were killed in the uprising. On the morning of October 5, the still-living, their eyes sunken and red-rimmed, emerged from cellars and shelters, most of them soon to begin an existence in German POW, concentration, or labor camps. After so many days and nights of artillery and mortar fire, a strange silence hovered over Warsaw, broken only by the thud of plodding feet. The wounded were carried on stretchers, the elderly supported by friends and family members. Young mothers cradled toddlers in their arms. As they trudged through their still-smoking city, Varsovians gazed at the desolation—at the corpses sprawled in the streets, at the hospital where bodies of patients and nurses, hanged by the SS, swung from the windows; at the uprooted lampposts, the smashed tanks and tramcars, the hulks of bombed and burned-out buildings.

In the center of the city, Bór-Komorowski and his Home Army troops formed several columns, followed by thousands of civilians. A

The surviving residents of Warsaw, many of them wounded and starving, are expelled from the city by Nazi troops after the uprising. (Hulton Archive)

phalanx of SS men awaited them several hundred yards away. As the Poles moved forward, Bór-Komorowski began singing the Polish national anthem. Tears in their eyes, his men and the civilians behind them joined in the hymn. Their voices swelling in intensity, they sang "Poland Has Not Yet Perished as Long as We Live," as they marched toward the waiting Germans.

Hitler did not massacre the survivors of Warsaw, as he had earlier vowed, but he made life as hellish for them as possible. Many thousands died in

German captivity before the war was over, although the approximately 14,000 surviving members of the Home Army, as POWs, received relatively more lenient treatment than most of the civilians.

Some of the Home Army soldiers and some civilians—among them, Wanda Krasnodębska—managed to avoid the camps by slipping away, in the confusion of the exodus, and heading for other parts of Poland. Although they suffered great privations for the rest of the war, their fate was far better than that of the hundreds of thousands of Warsaw residents who were shipped off to Germany as slave laborers or dispatched to Auschwitz, Ravensbruck, or other concentration camps.

Auschwitz, that ultimate symbol of Nazi savagery, was the destination for more than 6,000 Varsovians, mostly women and girls, a number of whom were Jews who had been hidden by Polish Christians in Warsaw and whose real identities remained secret. The new Auschwitz inmates ranged in age from newborns to people over ninety. They were not sent to the gas chambers, but many died before the end of the war from cold, starvation, disease, and physical abuse. According to Helena Kubicka, an Auschwitz historian, a few others found the idea of just *being* in Auschwitz so terrifying that they went insane shortly after their arrival.

When the uprising was over and the survivors were evacuated, Hitler did follow through on his pledge to raze the former "Paris of the East" to the ground. Nazi sappers divided the city into districts, each given a date for destruction. House by house, block by block, district by district, the remnants of the Polish capital were systematically and methodically burned and dynamited. All that was left when Russian troops at last "liberated" the city in January 1945 were ruins. And the unburied dead.

———

ON OCTOBER 3, a Polish bomber crew had just returned to their British base after a mission over Germany when a mechanic told them that Warsaw had surrendered. Hearing the news, the bomber's tail gunner, a Varsovian, dropped his parachute on the ground and stood stock-still, his face a mask of misery, his eyes darting "this way and that as if seeking enlightenment." Later, in the operations room, he approached the pilot of his aircraft. "Sir, what's the use?" he asked hoarsely. "Warsaw's gone. Live? In such a world? What's the use, sir?"

Turning abruptly, the young Pole walked over to the window. He pressed his face against the glass and stared out—into rain and darkness.

CHAPTER NINETEEN

"A Distant View
on the Polish Question"

L ESS THAN A week after the surrender of Warsaw, Churchill arrived in Moscow for a meeting with Stalin. It was clear to those around him that the prime minister was experiencing another of his mood swings where the Soviets were concerned. Gone was the man who had agonized over the Poles' hopeless fight and raged at the Russians' refusal to help them. In his place was a Churchill who seemed pleased that the Polish underground was out of commission, who assured Stalin that "no serious persons" in Britain believed that the Soviet Union had deliberately withheld military support from the Poles.

"All this havering, these conflicting and contradictory policies are, I am sure, due to Winston's exhaustion," Lord Moran wrote in his diary. "He seems torn between two lines of action.... At one moment he will plead with [Roosevelt] for a common front against Communism and the next he will make a bid for Stalin's friendship. Sometimes the two policies alternate with bewildering rapidity."

The ostensible reason for Churchill's meeting with Stalin was to discuss the Polish situation. At the moment, however, the prime minister was more concerned with the Red Army's push toward the Balkans and the threat of a Communist takeover in Greece, where a civil war between Communist and non-Communist guerrilla forces seemed likely once the Germans withdrew. By the time Churchill arrived in Moscow, he was already planning to send British troops into Greece in hopes of thwarting the Moscow-backed Communists. He wanted to hammer out a spheres-of-influence agreement with Stalin that would allow him a free hand in Greece in return for ... well, Churchill was eager to learn just what Stalin might want in return.

At their opening session on October 9, they did manage to spend the first few minutes on Poland. Churchill noted that General Bór-Komorowski would no longer bother Stalin since "the Germans were looking after him" and conceded that the Poles could be awfully nettlesome at times. When Stalin joked that if only one Pole existed anywhere on earth, "he would begin to quarrel with himself through sheer boredom," Churchill didn't disagree. And when Stalin declared that the London government-in-exile must negotiate with the Soviet-backed Poles, who were then in Moscow, Churchill promptly summoned Stanisław Mikołajczyk to the Soviet capital, threatening "dire" consequences if he did not come. Then Churchill and Stalin got down to the real business at hand.

"Let us settle our affairs in the Balkans," Churchill said. "... So far as Britain and Russia are concerned, how would it do for you to have ninety per cent predominance in Rumania, for us to have ninety per cent of the say in Greece, and go fifty/fifty about Yugoslavia?" He jotted down the percentages on a sheet of paper, along with additional figures for Hungary (also 50/50) and Bulgaria (the Soviets, 75/the British, 25). He pushed the paper across the table to Stalin, who took out a blue pencil, made a large checkmark on it, and returned it to Churchill. The carving up of much of southeastern Europe, Churchill said in his memoirs, "was all settled in no more time than it takes to [write it] down."

At that point, the co-author of the Atlantic Charter suggested that they get rid of what he archly referred to as this "naughty document." If it fell into the wrong hands, Churchill asked rhetorically, "might it not be thought rather cynical if it seemed we had disposed of these issues, so fateful to millions of people, in such an offhand manner?" So he suggested a cover-up. "Let us burn the paper," he said. Doubtless bemused by the fear democracy can engender in its public figures, Stalin replied, "No, you keep it." Later, in a note that was never sent, Churchill again cautioned Stalin that their work that evening might seem "crude" and "callous" to others and therefore should not be made public.

Crude and callous behavior was increasingly in evidence as the complex of wartime deals and understandings approached payoff time. "In saving Greece," the Oxford historian G. F. Hudson wrote, "Churchill had in effect written off the rest of Eastern Europe." When the Polish prime minister arrived in Moscow, as bidden, on October 12, he was treated by Soviet officials and Churchill almost as if he were an enemy. Now that Stalin had agreed to Churchill's proposal for a British sphere of influence in Greece, Churchill would become a batsman for Stalin on the question of Poland. From the start, Prime Minister Mikołajczyk found himself in what seemed like a courtroom dock. Stalin was "judge and jury," and Churchill, who had repeatedly promised the Poles that he would never abandon them, was "public prosecutor." In Stalin's presence, Churchill relentlessly pressured Mikołajczyk to give in to the Soviets' territorial demands and to negotiate with the Lublin Poles (as the Moscow-based, pro-Soviet "Committee of National Liberation"— which was beginning to look more and more like a government—was called).

The Polish leader outlined the concessions he was prepared to make. He would acknowledge the Curzon Line as a temporary boundary, provided that Lwów and Wilno remained inside Poland; and he would agree to a postwar Polish government based on equal representation for each of Poland's leading prewar parties, plus the Communists. This meant that the Communists would get a fifth of Poland's postwar ministries, even though they had never been a major Polish party.

These were important concessions, but Stalin was having none of it. The Curzon Line, with Lwów and Wilno going to the Soviets, must be the *permanent* border, he insisted. And the Lublin Poles, not the London government-in-exile and Polish underground, must be the dominant force in any postwar Polish government. On the question of boundaries, Churchill pressed Stalin's case. It would be unfortunate if the British and Poles split over this issue, the prime minister said. He added that Britain had "the right to ask the Poles for a great gesture in the interests of European peace."

This "great gesture" that Churchill wanted, Mikołajczyk said, was tantamount to national suicide. Churchill was asking him to turn his back on his country's democratic constitution and the right of the Polish nation to determine its own fate—something the British prime minister would never countenance if the same were asked of him in regard to his own country. The decision lay with the Polish nation, Mikołajczyk insisted. "If I agreed, everyone would have the right to say, 'It was for this that the Polish soldiers fought—a politician's sellout.' "

Stalin's foreign minister, Vyacheslav Molotov, who'd been watching the confrontation in silence, abruptly intervened. Why were they still wrangling over the Curzon Line? Hadn't the Big Three already agreed to it at Tehran? Hadn't even President Roosevelt said he regarded the line as a just solution to the border question (while asking that his endorsement not be made public)? Then Molotov turned to Churchill and Averell Harriman, who was present at the session as Roosevelt's observer. The foreign minister challenged the two of them to deny the accuracy of what he had said. "It appears to me," he snapped, "that Mr. Mikołajczyk is not aware of this fact."

There was a long pause. The Polish leader looked as if the earth had dropped from under his feet. He stared at Churchill and Harriman, "silently begging them," as he recalled later, "to call this damnable deal a lie." Like the rest of the world, Mikołajczyk was still in the dark about much of what had transpired at Tehran. That Churchill personally favored the Curzon Line was no great surprise; he had been urging Mikołajczyk to go along with it for some time. But there had been no suggestion that the Big Three—let alone Roosevelt—had already essentially *agreed* to the line. Time and again, the president of the United States had publicly rejected the idea of territorial settlements before the end of the war. Time and again, he had promised to come to Poland's aid when the moment was right. And four months earlier, at the White House, he had assured Mikołajczyk that he had not agreed to the Curzon Line at the Tehran summit.

Harriman stared at the floor. Churchill gazed back at Mikołajczyk. "I confirm this," he said softly.*

The Polish prime minister was devastated by this betrayal, and the British prime minister was both deeply embarrassed and furious at

---

* Churchill likely was talking about his own involvement in the deal at Tehran. He did not know at that point about Roosevelt's private exchange with Stalin on the issue of the Curzon Line. Churchill later wrote to the president, describing what had happened in Moscow and assuring FDR that word of his secret endorsement would not leak out to harm his reelection chances. In his own letter to Roosevelt, Harriman wrote: "I intend to tell Molotov privately at the next opportunity that I am sure you will wish that your name not [be] brought into the discussions again in regard to the boundary question."—U.S. Department of State, *FRUS, Vol. III, 1944,* p. 1323.

being found out. The following day, during two private meetings with Mikołajczyk, a highly emotional Churchill lashed out as if trying to convince himself that he and Britain—not Mikołajczyk and Poland— were the victims. When Mikołajczyk reminded Churchill of his "gloriously worded" speeches early in the war, in which he condemned the taking of territory by force, Churchill's anger only deepened. Unless Mikołajczyk accepted the Curzon Line, he threatened, the Poles were "out of business forever." "The Russians will sweep through your country and your people will be liquidated! You are on the verge of annihilation!"

"We are losing everything!" Mikołajczyk cried. Churchill snorted derisively—"the Pripet marshes and five million people...." When Mikołajczyk argued that the Big Three might just as well have gone ahead and announced that Poland's postwar frontiers had been unilaterally drawn, Churchill waved the point aside as if it were unworthy of an answer. "We will be sick and tired of you if you go on arguing," he threatened.

During their second meeting that day, Churchill continued his browbeating of the Polish prime minister. "You are a callous people who want to wreck Europe!" he shouted at a man who had just lost nearly a quarter of a million of his countrymen in the Warsaw uprising alone, whose country and people had been brutalized by the Germans for five years, whose capital lay in ruins. "You have only your own miserable, selfish interests in mind!...It is a criminal attempt on your part to wreck...the agreement between the Allies. It is cowardice on your part!...I shall leave you to your own troubles.... You have only your own miserable, selfish interests in mind!"

Mikołajczyk was stunned by this bullying but refused to be cowed. At one point he asked Churchill what *he* would do in Mikołajczyk's place. The British leader didn't answer that one either. He told Mikołajczyk he was "absolutely crazy."

Finally, the Polish prime minister had had enough—of Churchill's abuse, of his demands, of broken promises, of endless humiliations. Above all, he had had enough of the delusion that giving half of Poland's territory to the Russians would guarantee its freedom and independence. His voice shaking with pain and anger, he demanded to be parachuted into Poland, so that he could join what remained of the Home

Army. "I prefer to die fighting for the independence of my country," he declared, "than be hanged later by the Russians in full view of your British ambassador!"

The next morning, Churchill was morose; his doctor noted that "it is plain that the P.M. has got the Poles on his conscience." "I was pretty rough with Mikołajczyk," Churchill admitted to Lord Moran. "He was obstinate and I lost my temper." In his diary, Lord Moran mused: "Perhaps the P.M. was thinking of his own indignation when Chamberlain pressed Czechoslovakia to surrender a great part of her country in the interests of peace."

Despite the revelations about what was agreed to in Tehran and his furious quarrel with Churchill, Mikołajczyk stayed on in Moscow for several days and continued talks with the Soviets and two representatives from the Lublin committee. The result was a stalemate. At that point, Churchill and Mikołajczyk returned to London, and Churchill resumed his arm-twisting. Ever since Mikołajczyk succeeded Sikorski sixteen months earlier, he had been under pressure to accept Stalin's version of the Curzon Line. Many in his government were furious over the concessions he had made, and yet those concessions hadn't come close to satisfying the Soviets or, for that matter, his allies. "We were becoming increasingly isolated," he wrote. "The Big Three regarded us either openly or privately as saboteurs of their unity because of our refusal to yield on all points."

Profoundly discouraged, Mikołajczyk resigned as prime minister on November 24. In a speech shortly afterward, he said that "many well-meaning people" had pressured him to reach a compromise with Russia. He had looked up the word "compromise" in the dictionary and found that it meant "an adjustment of differences by mutual concessions." But there was nothing mutual, he observed, about the agreement he and his country were being told to accept.

Tomasz Arciszewski was named Mikołajczyk's successor. He was head of Poland's Socialist Party and had spent most of the war as a top underground official in Warsaw before being smuggled to London four months earlier. His credentials for the post of prime minister were unchallenged. Nevertheless, Churchill and his government, while recognizing the new Polish administration, refused to have any direct dealings with it. For the rest of the war, the prime minister of Britain declined to exchange so much as a word with the prime minister of Britain's most loyal ally. Yet Mikołajczyk and the other Poles in London, despite their anger and frustration, kept quiet about the secret arrangements Churchill and Roosevelt had made at Tehran.

———————

BY EARLY FALL, with just a few weeks to go before the 1944 presidential election in the United States, opinion polls showed an increase in support for Roosevelt's Republican opponent, New York governor Thomas Dewey, while the president himself was steadily losing ground. *Time* predicted a narrow Roosevelt victory, but a number of political experts interviewed by *Newsweek* said the race was too close to call. There were growing questions about Roosevelt's health—recent photos showed him haggard and hollow-eyed—and deepening worries about the Soviets' intentions toward Poland and the rest of Europe. In a cable to Averell Harriman, Cordell Hull noted "a mounting concern and apprehension [on the part of the American press and public], amounting in many cases to suspicion, as to the real motives of the Soviet Government."

Pollster Hadley Cantril reported to the White House that the American people were particularly upset about Soviet behavior during the Warsaw uprising. In private, Harry Hopkins worried that the president had "possibly oversold Russia to the American people." He had done such a good job of it, Hopkins believed, that with the election just weeks away, it would be politically dangerous to express any doubts now about the future of Soviet-American collaboration. If the president needed votes—and he did—he would have to find other ways to attract them.

In late September, as the end of the Warsaw uprising approached, Roosevelt announced his appointment of a successor to Anthony Drexel Biddle, the American ambassador to the Polish government-in-exile, who had resigned the previous January. For eight months, Mikołajczyk and other Polish officials had unsuccessfully urged the president to fill Biddle's position in order to show the United States's commitment to the Polish government in London. Now, barely a month before the election, FDR made public his choice of Arthur Bliss Lane, most recently the U.S. ambassador to Colombia. White House staffers told Polish ambassador Jan Ciechanowski they hoped the appointment of Lane would help win the Polish vote.*

Alarmed at the possibility of political fallout from the uprising, prominent Democrats urged Roosevelt to do even more. Chicago mayor Edward Kelly, who had many Polish-American voters in his city, told the president it was "absolutely imperative" that he meet with leaders of the new Polish-American Congress, who had repeatedly sought such a session to discuss their fears about Poland.

On October 11, a little more than a week after Warsaw's capitulation to the Germans, Roosevelt played host to nine Polish-American leaders at the White House. He avoided saying anything specific about Poland's future government or boundaries, confining himself to expressing the hope that the country would be "reconstituted as a great nation." Next to Roosevelt's desk, prominently displayed and photographed as a backdrop for the meeting, was a large prewar map of Poland, its eastern boundary conspicuously marked not along the Curzon Line but along the Riga Line, the border established after the 1919–20 Soviet-Polish War. The photo of the map did the job it was surely placed there to do. Widely reproduced in Polish-American newspapers and other publications, it reassured voters that Roosevelt supported reestablishment of the prewar Polish boundary.

Then, two weeks before the election, Roosevelt invited Charles Rozmarek, the president of the Polish-American Congress, to a meeting in his private railroad car during a final campaign swing through Illinois. The president assured Rozmarek that he would not abandon the principles of the Atlantic Charter and the Four Freedoms in regard to Poland. He further pledged that he would make sure "Poland is treated justly at the [postwar] peace conference." On the basis of those promises, Rozmarek endorsed FDR for president, an endorsement that the Democrats widely publicized in Polish-American precincts around the country.

On November 7, 1944, Franklin Roosevelt was elected to his fourth term as president. His popular vote victory over Thomas Dewey, while

---

* Having appointed Lane, Roosevelt then refused to let him go to London to take up his post. Angry and embarrassed, Lane stayed on in Washington until July 1945, when he was dispatched to Warsaw as ambassador to the new Soviet-backed government in Poland. —Lukas, *Strange Allies*, pp. 84–85.

substantial, was much narrower than he was accustomed to—53.7 percent to Dewey's 46.2 percent, which made it the closest presidential election since 1916.* FDR's margin might well have been narrower still had he not swept more than 90 percent of Polish-American ballots from Chicago to New York and many cities in between.

THREE MONTHS AFTER the presidential election, on February 5, 1945, Roosevelt joined Churchill and Stalin at the Crimean resort town of Yalta for the second, and final, Big Three conference of the war. Churchill had been pressing hard for the meeting since the previous fall. By the time it finally occurred, the agenda had grown long and difficult.

Hitler's war machine, having failed with a massive counteroffensive in Belgium, was close to collapse, but no Allied decision had yet been made on the specifics of dealing with a defeated Germany. Beyond that, there was the final push against the Japanese to be coordinated, and the functions of the United Nations to consider. (Although the UN's broad outlines had been sketched the previous September at the Dumbarton Oaks Conference in Washington, major differences still existed between the Soviets, on the one hand, and the British and Americans, on the other, over how the organization should actually work.) And then there was the question of the extent of Soviet domination and influence in postwar Eastern and Central Europe, a matter that Churchill, at least, regarded as the most important of all.

By the time of the Yalta Conference, the Red Army had swept the Germans out of most of Poland, Hungary, and Yugoslavia, and was in effective control of Bulgaria and Romania. It had marched into Czechoslovakia and Austria and was advancing deep into Germany. What did Stalin propose to do with the lands he had "liberated"? What were his intentions toward the rest of Europe? For Churchill, as ever, the touchstone was Poland.

The indications were ominous. The Soviets, having established their military domination in Poland, were now tightening their political grip

---

* Roosevelt's Electoral College vote victory—432 to 99—was much more impressive, but still narrower than in any of his three previous presidential elections.

there, too. In January 1945, Moscow formally recognized the Kremlin-spawned Lublin committee as Poland's provisional government.

Chilling reports were also reaching London about Russian brutality toward Home Army troops who had rallied to the Red Army's side during its advance. For the past several months, thousands of Polish resistance fighters had been emerging into the open, as instructed by their government in London. Polish troops had helped the Russians capture Lwów, Wilno, Lublin, and a number of other Polish cities and towns. In Lublin, the Home Army actually drove the Germans out in advance of the Russians' arrival. For their pains, many Poles were arrested. Some were tortured, some shot, some hanged. Others—more than 10,000—were marched off to gulags. One Polish underground communiqué described how the Soviets seized and incarcerated a Home Army detachment that "only an hour before, had blown up a German munitions train to safeguard those same Soviet soldiers from German fire."

Faced with this latest evidence of Stalin's true intentions, Churchill insisted that Britain would recognize no Polish regime but the government-in-exile—"the legal government of Poland and the authority to which the large Polish forces fighting under British command owe allegiance."

FDR, however, was reluctant to follow the prime minister's lead. According to Averell Harriman, Roosevelt believed that "European questions were so impossible that he wanted to stay out of them as far as practicable, except for the problems involving Germany." Beyond that, the president's overriding concerns were the building of a strong United Nations and enlisting Stalin's help to bring the war in the Pacific to a swift conclusion. Still, Roosevelt clearly had to register at least token resistance to Moscow's recognition of the Lublin Poles, if only to reassure the British and the American electorate, who were expressing mounting uneasiness about Soviet expansionism.

In a December 1944 memo, the president's new secretary of state, Edward Stettinius, warned the White House of "increased public confusion and disillusionment... as a result of events in Europe." Stettinius added that while Americans did not necessarily oppose the Russians' acquisition of Polish territory, they definitely would oppose any Soviet seizure of Polish lands without the Poles' consent. It went without saying that they would also be hostile to Soviet imposition of a puppet government.

In mid-December, Roosevelt had appealed to Stalin to delay diplomatic recognition of the Lublin Poles as the provisional government, citing the "great political implications which such a step would entail." When Stalin refused, the president fired off a telegram that, for him, was surprisingly sharp in tone. Neither the American people nor their government, Roosevelt said, had seen any evidence to "justify the conclusion that the Lublin Committee as presently constituted represents the people of Poland.... It is an unquestioned truth that the people of Poland have had no opportunity to express themselves in regard to the Lublin Committee."

Having made his disapproval known, however, Roosevelt took no other action before Yalta on the question of Poland. When the president and prime minister and their aides met briefly on the island of Malta before proceeding to the Big Three meeting, Roosevelt was unwilling to coordinate strategy with the British on Poland or any other issue facing the conference. As at Tehran, he did not want Stalin to think that he and Churchill were conspiring against him.

Anthony Eden, for one, was greatly upset by what he saw as the latest display of Roosevelt's vagueness and naïveté. Here the Western Allies were, "going into a decisive conference," with no plan for "what we would discuss nor how to handle matters with a Bear [Stalin] who would certainly know his mind." To Eden, the president didn't seem to understand that his dream of a strong international organization to prevent future aggression would be frustrated if one of its principal members were allowed to commit aggression even as the organization was being created. "[U]nless the Russians can be persuaded or compelled to treat Poland with some decency, there will not be a [United Nations] that is worth much," noted the British foreign secretary, who seemed to have forgotten his own earlier willingness to capitulate to Stalin over Poland.

The concern about Roosevelt among British officials was heightened by his marked physical deterioration since they had seen him last. The jaunty Roosevelt of old was gone. In his place was a frail, exhausted old man with sunken and glassy eyes. Churchill, who was exhausted himself, worried that the president was no longer able "to take an intelligent interest in the war." The British—as well as most of the Americans who accompanied the president—were unaware that he had been diagnosed ten months earlier with congestive heart failure and that his condition had only deteriorated since then. Before setting out for Yalta, the president met with his old friend, Labor Secretary Frances Perkins. "He was in a pitiable state," she recalled, "appalled at the magnitude of the tasks ahead of him and not knowing whether he had the strength to see himself through." Roosevelt had only ten weeks more to live.

———————

THE QUESTION OF Poland dominated Yalta, taking up more time and causing more friction among the Big Three than any of the other subjects on the agenda. For Churchill and Roosevelt, the discussions were an exercise in futility. As much as Churchill tried to convince himself otherwise, Poland's fate had already been settled. Soviet troops now occupied most of the country, and Stalin made quite clear that his puppet government was there to stay.

As at Tehran, American and British officials were struck by Stalin's apparent command of every detail under discussion, as well as his virtuoso skills in argument. In contrast, most accounts agree that both Churchill and Roosevelt—particularly Roosevelt—seemed ill-prepared, weak on details, and ineffective in debate. "I must say I think Uncle Joe much the most impressive of the three men . . . ," Sir Alexander Cadogan wrote in his diary midway through the conference. "The President flapped about and the P.M. boomed, but Joe just sat, taking it all in and being rather amused."

The summit's first major session began February 5, 1945, in Tsar Nicholas II's Livadia Palace, overlooking the Black Sea. From the beginning, Roosevelt, who acted as moderator, signaled that the United States was not interested in continuing its heavy involvement in Europe after the war. Indeed, he said, he planned to pull all American troops out of Europe, including occupied Germany, after two years.* Still convinced that he and Stalin shared the same vision of the postwar world, Roosevelt did not seem concerned about leaving the Soviet Union as the continent's dominant military and political power.

That scenario, however, was Winston Churchill's worst nightmare. Determined to prevent it, he "fought like a tiger" at Yalta to make sure

* That, of course, did not happen.

France's postwar role in Europe was as strong as possible. That way, he thought, both Britain and France could serve—to some extent, at least—as counterweights to Russia. Under heavy pressure from Churchill, Roosevelt and Stalin reluctantly agreed to a French occupation zone in Germany following a victory by the Allies and to a French seat on the Allied Control Commission that was intended to serve as an interim German government. Thus was France, which had capitulated to Germany in 1940 with barely a whimper, restored to the status of a great European power.

However, when the discussion turned to the question of creating an independent government in Poland, Churchill did not put up the same kind of fight as he had for France. True, his position had been undercut earlier in the summit when Roosevelt declared that "coming from America," he had "a distant view on the Polish question" and made plain that his interest in it was essentially limited to its effect on his own political fortunes. While noting (incorrectly) that most Polish-Americans favored the Curzon Line as Poland's eastern border, he said "it would make it easier for me at home" if Stalin would be magnanimous and give up Lwów and the nearby oil fields. On the question of Poland's government, Roosevelt said that American public opinion was against recognizing the Lublin Poles and that he hoped a more representative government could be created.

Although Churchill's initial appeal was considerably more passionate and emotional than Roosevelt's, he, too, indicated that he did not regard Poland's future to be of vital strategic interest. Rather, he said, it was a question of honor. "Honour was the sole reason why we had drawn the sword to help Poland against Hitler's brutal onslaught," Churchill said, "and we could never accept any settlement which did not leave her free, independent and sovereign. Poland must be mistress in her own house and captain of her own soul."

Stalin had no patience with this sort of high-flown rhetoric. Poland was a question of honor for Russia, too, he retorted. Even more, it was a question of security. Twice in the past thirty years Poland had served as a corridor through which Germany had attacked Russia. The motherland needed to secure that corridor. As they listened, neither Churchill nor Roosevelt saw fit to point out that when Germany invaded the USSR in 1941, the Soviets were in control of the entire eastern half of

Poland, thanks to their pact with Hitler. Yet the Red Army had been unable even to retard the German invasion, let alone stop it.

At Yalta as at Tehran, Stalin seemed to take particular pleasure in twitting Churchill and Roosevelt for espousing lofty moral ideals in public and then abandoning them in private. He subtly noted his Allies' habit of excluding the London government-in-exile from decisions about its country's future by pointing out that *he* could not make decisions about changing the Lublin government without consulting its leaders. "I am called a dictator and not a democrat," Stalin declared, "but I have enough democratic feeling to refuse to create a Polish government without the Poles being consulted."

Stung, Churchill tried to argue the point. The Lublin government was not representative, he said, and most of the Polish people, given a chance to express their opinion, would not support it. At that point, Roosevelt interrupted. As Churchill recalled it, the president seemed "anxious to end the discussion." Poland, Roosevelt complained, "has been a source of trouble for over five hundred years." That was hardly an original view. Poland and its people had vexed many a world leader—from Frederick the Great to Hitler, from Catherine the Great to Stalin, from David Lloyd George to Winston Spencer Churchill. Sitting on strategically important real estate in the heart of Europe, and having endured two centuries of oppression, the Poles *still* had the temerity to insist that they alone, and not whatever great powers happened at the time to be ruling the world, should decide their own destiny.

Like his counterparts on the European stage, Roosevelt disdained such presumption. That evening, he sent a note to Stalin. "I hope I do not have to assure you," it said in part, "that the United States will never lend its support in any way to any provisional government in Poland that would be inimical to your interests." At the next day's session, Roosevelt proclaimed that "there hasn't really been any Polish government since 1939...," and therefore, "I discard the ideal of continuity." With that astonishing statement, FDR contradicted the policy of his own government (and that of every other Ally, except the USSR), which recognized the London government-in-exile as the legitimate, linear successor to Poland's prewar government. "It is entirely in the province of the three of us," Roosevelt continued, "to help set up a government—something to last until the Polish people choose." Then he suggested: "I think we want something new and drastic—like a breath of fresh air."

Roosevelt's idea was to disband the two competing Polish governments and create a new interim body by drawing from officials in the Lublin government and from non-Communist Poles inside and outside of Poland. This was a pivotal moment for Churchill. As recently as a month earlier, he had publicly renewed his support for the Polish government-in-exile. To General Anders during the Warsaw uprising, he said, "Britain will never desert you.... Put your trust in us." That, indeed, had been his mantra to the Poles for the past five years. Now, however, he abandoned the cause of the London-based government and supported Roosevelt's plan. "If we give up the Poles in London, it should be for a new start on both sides, more or less on equal terms," he declared.

That was not, to put it mildly, what Stalin had in mind, but he decided to stage a show of reasonableness anyway. He had Molotov present a plan that called for the Lublin government to take control, but he added a little window dressing. The government would be enlarged to include several leaders from "Polish émigré circles." Free elections for a permanent government, Molotov said, would be held as soon as possible.

Churchill demurred but no longer mentioned honor. His main concern now seemed to be the possibility that his own public image, and the Big Three's facade of unity, might be damaged if "the conference is to brush aside the existing London Government and lend all its weight to the Lublin Government...." The Polish forces under British command would see that as a betrayal, Churchill said, and there would be the "gravest criticism" in Britain and the rest of the world. He and his government "would be charged in Parliament with having altogether forsaken the cause of Poland."

Stalin, as usual, gave little. Communists must dominate the new government, he insisted. Molotov would be glad to consult with the American and British ambassadors in Moscow on adding a few "émigré" Poles to the existing regime, but that was as much compromise as the Soviet Union was prepared to offer.

Faced with this foreign policy disaster in the making, Roosevelt and Churchill seized on the question of elections. When would they be held? Roosevelt asked. "Within a month," Stalin answered, "—unless there is some catastrophe on the front, which is improbable." In that case, Churchill said, his mind was at rest, and he "could wholeheartedly support a freely elected government which would supersede everything else."

The Russians rejected a U.S. plan for supervision of the elections by British and American officials, and Churchill and Roosevelt gave in. They were willing to take Stalin's word that the balloting would be free of coercion—an "incredible" assumption, one British historian wrote later, "in view of the violence and terror which then already prevailed in Poland." "The elections," said Roosevelt, "must be above criticism, like Caesar's wife.... I don't want anybody to be able to question their purity. It is a matter of good politics rather than principle."

With that, the Big Three turned their attention to cloaking the agreement in language that would make it seem consistent with the principles of the Atlantic Charter. In their final communiqué, the three leaders reaffirmed their common commitment to a "strong, free, independent, and democratic Poland." They declared that the Curzon Line would be Poland's eastern frontier but did not mention that the Soviets would keep Lwów. The Lublin government would be "reorganized on a broader democratic basis, with the inclusion of democratic leaders from Poland itself and from Poles abroad." There would be "free and unfettered elections as soon as possible on the basis of universal suffrage and secret ballot." Later, a disgusted George Kennan described the Yalta communiqué as "the shabbiest sort of equivocation...."

As for the Big Three, Stalin and Roosevelt declared themselves satisfied, while Churchill expressed some lingering unease. The agreement on Poland, he glumly told the other two leaders, would be "very heavily attacked in England.... They will say [we] have completely swept away the only constitutional government of Poland. However, I will defend it to the best of my ability."

The Polish government-in-exile was never mentioned in the communiqué. Indeed, as *The Tablet,* a Catholic newspaper in Britain, would later point out, the Yalta report "entirely disregards the existence of the Polish State, with its legal continuity, Government, territory, citizens and armed forces...." For Churchill and Roosevelt, Poland's sovereignty, in the final analysis, was nothing more than "a diplomatic trading asset," in the words of historian G. F. Hudson. Poland, the first ally, the country that had fought so hard against Nazi aggression, was to be treated like a defeated enemy, losing much of its territory and being forced to accept an imposed government. In many ways, Germany— the *real* defeated enemy—received better treatment: it lost, for example, only about 20 percent of its territory after the war. Poland lost half to the Russians.

Another Yalta document, the brainchild of the U.S. delegation, entitled the "Declaration on Liberated Europe," reaffirmed the provisions of the Atlantic Charter and called for, among other things, the restoration of self-determination and sovereignty to all nations freed from German occupation. Specifically, the document demanded that "broadly representative" interim governments take office in those countries until free elections could be held.

When Vyacheslav Molotov first laid eyes on this statement of principles, he was alarmed, thinking it might actually mean what it said. In an aside to Stalin, Molotov said: "This is going too far!"

"Don't worry...," said Stalin. "We can deal with it in our own way later."

SEVERAL OTHER KEY decisions taken at Yalta, including the division of Germany into four occupation zones and the formulation of operating procedures for the new United Nations, were not made public in the communiqué. Also classified was Stalin's promise to enter the war against Japan in exchange for the return of the Kurile Islands between Hokkaido and the Kamchatka Peninsula,* as well as possession of Port Arthur and other parts of Chinese territory held by the Japanese. China was never consulted about the latter. When the details of the deal finally emerged amid a storm of protest, Secretary of State Edward Stettinius shrugged off the criticism, suggesting that the China agreement, like that for Poland, only ratified the inevitable. "What," he asked, "... did the Soviet Union receive at Yalta which she might not have taken without any agreement?"

This question was realpolitik at its baldest, but there was a large element of truth in it. Similarly, where Poland was concerned, even if

---

* Russia and Japan both had claims to the islands but had negotiated an agreement in 1875 that gave them to Japan.

Churchill and Roosevelt had truly subscribed to the principles of the Atlantic Charter and had stood up to Stalin in support of Polish sovereignty and independence, it is quite possible, even probable, that the result would have been essentially the same. As the historian Sarah Meiklejohn Terry has noted: "With the benefit of hindsight, it is clear that, given the power to do so, the Soviets were determined to retain the territories that they had seized... under the terms of the Nazi-Soviet pact. It is also clear that Stalin viewed a truly independent Poland, of whatever political persuasion, as a barrier to the expansion of Soviet influence in Europe...."

The fact remains, however, that Britain and the United States, for all their "Crusade in Europe" rhetoric about democracy and freedom, never put the slightest obstacle in Joseph Stalin's way.

CHAPTER TWENTY

Light and Darkness

FEBRUARY 13, 1945, was a drizzly, bone-chilling day in most of Britain. But melancholy weather could not dampen the spirits of the Polish and British fighter pilots relaxing in the officers' mess at Andrews Field in Essex. The war was almost over, and everyone knew it. For the Poles in the room, the approaching peace signaled the end of a long nightmare. They were anxious about the Soviet Union's intentions toward their country but were counting on British and American pledges that Poland's liberation was nearly at hand. The pilots would be on their way home, they hoped, in no more than a few months.

A few of them sat in large green armchairs, reading newspapers and magazines. Others leaned against the polished mahogany bar, laughing, talking, and drinking tankards of beer served by a corporal in a white tunic. At some point, a radio was turned on. And it was then, on that grey and wintry afternoon, that a bulletin read by a BBC announcer ended the dreams of the Polish airmen. At Yalta, Prime Minister Winston Churchill and President Franklin D. Roosevelt had formally ceded eastern Poland to Stalin and had handed over control of the rest of the country to a provisional, Soviet-bred Communist government.

The radio droned on, but there was only stunned silence in the mess. One of the Polish pilots glanced around the room. Most of his British comrades just stared at the floor. Only one of them met the Pole's anguished gaze. That Englishman's face was streaked with tears.

At the RAF station at Faldingworth in Lincolnshire, the men of 300 Bomber Squadron heard the news just before the operational briefing for that night's mission over Germany. The 300 was the first all-Polish squadron created in Britain, back in the summer of 1940. It had been in action longer than any other Polish squadron and had participated in every major British bombing raid over Germany. Its losses between 1940 and 1945 were appalling—more than 450 men killed, captured, or missing.

By the time the briefing began, the Poles were already in a mutinous mood, but their mutterings turned to angry shouts when they learned what their target was to be that night: Dresden, in support of the advancing Red Army. "Why should we go when we've been betrayed?" one pilot yelled. A chorus of agreement followed. The squadron leader quieted the room with a sharp, short response. They would go because it was their duty to go, he said. A few hours later, the men of 300 Squadron took off for Dresden.

Before climbing into his Lancaster, a young Polish navigator, a native of Lwów who had been a prisoner in one of Stalin's gulags, sat down in despair to write a letter to a friend. "Just think, I and so many others knocked about the world, fleeing like criminals, starving, hiding in forests—all only in order to fight for... what? For this—that we shall not be able to return to our native town, because it has simply ceased to be." He was flying that night, he wrote. "[I]t's the proper thing to do, they say, although anger and despair are in our hearts. It's a funny feeling, but sometimes I wonder if all this makes any sense. If the Germans get me now, I won't even know what I am dying for. For Poland? For Britain? Or for Russia?" Ten days later, on another mission over Germany, he was killed.

For Polish pilots, as for millions of Poles everywhere, the most shattering aspect of Yalta was the complicity of Britain and the United States. As the Polish government-in-exile noted, Poland's fifth partition had just taken place—this one "accomplished by her Allies, instead of, as formerly, by her enemies." Calling the Yalta agreement a basic violation of the Atlantic Charter and the other principles for which the Allies fought, the government-in-exile refused to accept it. The government did, however, instruct Polish forces to continue fighting, to "keep peace, dignity and solidarity, as well as to maintain brotherhood in arms with the soldiers of Great Britain, Canada, the United States, and France."

In Italy, General Anders and the men of II Polish Corps were inclined, at first, to lay down their arms. As calamitous as the news of Yalta was for the rest of the Polish armed forces, it was particularly crushing for these former inmates of the gulags, most of them natives of eastern Poland. It was unlikely that they would ever be able to go home again. So devastating was this thought that some thirty officers and men of II Corps committed suicide on receiving the news from Yalta, and Anders requested permission from his British superiors to withdraw the rest of his troops from battle. "I cannot in conscience demand at present any sacrifice of [my] soldiers' blood," he said.

At that point, Anders was called back to London for consultations with his government. While there, he was summoned to a meeting with Churchill. The prime minister tried to defend the Yalta decision, but Anders was having none of it. "The Polish nation did not deserve to see matters settled the way they have been, and we who have fought on the Allied side had no reason to expect it," he said to the prime minister.

Churchill exploded in indignation. "We have never guaranteed your eastern frontiers!" he shouted. "We have enough troops today, and we do not need your help! You can take away your divisions! We shall do without them!" Even in the heat of anger, it was an astonishing thing for Churchill to say, in light of the Poles' contributions and sacrifices in the Battle of Britain and at Monte Cassino, Falaise, and Arnhem, to name just the best known of the campaigns in which they participated. Anders's reply was cool. "That is not what you said during the last few years," he said.

The British high command at any rate denied Anders permission to withdraw his men. II Corps, regarded as among the best units in the British Eighth Army, was playing far too important a role in the Italian campaign to be taken out of the line now. After Monte Cassino, the Poles had captured the town of Piedimonte. After that, they took Ancona, a key port and supply base on the Adriatic coast, collecting more than 3,000 German prisoners in the process. Now they were engaged in heavy fighting against elite Nazi units in the mountains of northern Italy. After the war, Field Marshal Viscount Alanbrooke, chief of the Imperial General Staff, would declare that, without II Corps, "the series of offensives carried out [in Italy] from Cassino onwards would hardly have been possible."

Following orders, Anders instructed his men to "maintain discipline and dignity" and to continue fighting. Despite this, the Poles' loyalty and dedication remained in doubt for a number of Allied officers and officials, including Harold Macmillan, the British government's liaison to the Allied headquarters in Italy. "At the worst, they will disintegrate into a rabble of refugees," Macmillan fretted in his diary. "At the best, they will be kept enough together to hold a sector of line, without attacks or counter-attacks. I do not think they can now be used offensively."

II Corps proved the skeptics quite wrong. The Polish corps contin-ued its drive, storming and capturing Bologna a few weeks before the end of the war. "I had underestimated the marvelous dignity and devo-tion of Anders and his comrades," Macmillan admitted afterward. "They fought with distinction, in the front of the attack, in the last bat-tles of [the war]. They had lost their country but they kept their honour."

In their sweep north, as the men of II Corps liberated one small Ital-ian town after another, they were surrounded by crowds of smiling, cheering people, many of them shouting: "*Viva Polonia!*" Women threw flowers, men handed them glasses of wine, girls hugged and kissed them. For the Poles, it was a bittersweet time. "On the one hand, I was happy that I could bring freedom to these people who were welcoming me at that moment," recalled one soldier. "But on the other hand, I was disappointed that this was not a Polish street that I was walking on, that I wasn't bringing freedom to my people and my nation, that this was not the fulfillment of our dreams...."

The commander of another Polish army learned about the Yalta agree-ment while he and his troops were inmates at Colditz, a POW camp in Germany. General Tadeusz Bór-Komorowski and thousands of his Home Army fighters had been prisoners since the end of the Warsaw uprising four months earlier. They knew from bitter experience of Stalin's determination to wipe out all opposition and to control their country. What was "incomprehensible" to them, Bór-Komorowski remarked later, was "why the Allies were giving up to slavery and partition their most faithful and oldest ally of the war." The blow, "so heavy and unexpected," he said, "shook us to the core."

———————

IN THEIR DESPONDENCY over Yalta, the Poles were a distinct minority among the Allies. In Britain and the United States, the immediate pub-lic reaction to news of the agreement was euphoria. Londoners, Mollie

Panter-Downes reported in *The New Yorker,* were beaming. "The success of the conference," she wrote, "seemed the most encouraging omen for the postwar world that people here, wearied by the present and frightened by the future, have yet laid eyes on."

The British, like the Americans, were basing their optimism on avowals of unity by Roosevelt, Churchill, and Stalin on every major postwar issue, as well as their renewed declaration of support for the independence and freedom of all nations. All remaining "doubts about the Big Three's ability to cooperate in peace as well as war seemed now to have been swept away," *Time* declared.

In both Britain and America, there was impatience with the Poles for their outspoken attacks on the Yalta accords. Hadn't the Big Three specifically guaranteed their country's independence? Hadn't they promised that the upcoming elections would be free and democratic? With peace on the horizon, why were the Poles behaving like spoilers? According to the *Manchester Guardian,* Stalin had made "generous concessions" to the Poles and deserved their thanks. *The Times* declared that the Yalta agreement was "firmly rooted in both common sense and equity" where Poland was concerned.

In a speech to Congress on March 1, Roosevelt put a new gloss on his vision of a shining postwar future. The decisions reached at Yalta, he said, had cleared the way for "a world of peace...based on the sound and just principles of the Atlantic Charter, on the concept of the dignity of the human being." The new brotherhood of nations, he added, would exist without "the unilateral action, the exclusive alliances, the spheres of influence, the balances of power...that have been tried for centuries—and always failed."

On the agreement's provisions about Poland, the president interjected a slight note of distress. The decision on the boundaries was "a compromise," he said, adding: "Frankly, I did not agree with all of it by any means." That was the extent of any official presidential expression of concern. In the buoyancy of the moment, few of the president's listeners, other than Poles and Americans of Polish descent, appeared to pay much attention.

Winston Churchill also appeared before his country's legislature to discuss the Yalta accords, but a much greater sense of drama surrounded his speech. Notwithstanding broad approval of the agreement among the public and the press in Britain, there was a rising swell of restiveness and discontent in the House of Commons over the treatment of Poland. Conservative MPs were the most outspoken in their criticism, but a number of Labour members expressed their disapproval as well.

This wasn't the first time, of course, that members of Parliament had spoken out against what they saw as Churchill's appeasement of Stalin over Poland. There had been criticism and expressions of concern after disclosure of the Katyn massacre, after Tehran, after the prime minister's February 1944 speech on the Curzon Line, and during the Warsaw uprising. Much of the debate on those occasions had centered not only on Britain's moral and legal obligations to Poland but on the crucial contribution made to the Allied effort by Polish forces, particularly by the men of the Kościuszko Squadron and other Polish pilots in the Battle of Britain. "If it had not been for the Polish airmen who fought in the Battle of Britain, we might have gone under in 1940, for the margin was very narrow," declared Labour MP Ivor Thomas in December 1944.

In those previous debates, however, the MPs' faultfinding tended to be muted and relatively low key. As the Conservative MP and Cambridge don Kenneth Pickthorn noted during one of the sessions, the parliamentary restraint stemmed in part from repeated warnings by the prime minister and his men that criticism of the Allied treatment of Poland could be detrimental to the war effort. "I think...that we have been so careful not to say things that might do harm," Pickthorn argued, "that we have slipped into the opposite error...the error of keeping quiet about things that will do more harm through public ignorance."

By the time of the Yalta agreement, however, there was such intensity of feeling about Poland that Churchill, realizing government admonitions alone would no longer suffice, decided on an old parliamentary gambit. In late February, he opened a three-day House debate on Yalta by requesting a formal vote of confidence—up or down—on the Big Three's declaration. "A strong expression of support," he said, "will strengthen the Government's position" among its Allies.

Churchill had successfully used this tactic several times before, turning specific criticism of his government into the broader issue of confidence, always with a threat of resignation if the vote did not go his way, as it invariably did. But the prime minister went further this time. He asked not only for a confidence vote but also for House approval of his, Roosevelt's, and Stalin's "determination to maintain unity of action not only in achieving the final defeat of the common enemy, but thereafter, in peace as in war."

The resolution was carefully worded: a vote against it, or even an abstention, might jeopardize an MP's political future amid charges of disloyalty and lack of patriotism. Nonetheless, an "exceptional number" of MPs made clear that they planned to speak during the debate, which *The Times* described as "quite the most important...since the war began." When Churchill rose to begin it on the morning of February 27, the visitors' gallery was packed, the members' benches crowded, the sense of anticipation palpable.

After reporting on the occupation of Germany and other aspects of the agreement, the prime minister, his voice increasing in volume and emphasis, turned to Poland. He had agreed to Russia's seizure of eastern Poland, he said, not because "I bow to force" but because the Soviet claim to the territory was "just and right." According to Churchill, Poland owed a huge debt to Russia: the smaller country would have been completely destroyed by the Germans if the Red Army had not marched in. Indeed, he contended, the Russians had been "received with great joy" in many areas of Poland (a statement based on Stalin's assurance and at considerable variance with reports Churchill had received from the Polish government-in-exile). As for Stalin's promise of free elections in Poland, Churchill urged the House to put its faith, as he had done, in the Soviet leader and his government. "I feel...that their word is their bond," he said. "I know of no government which stands to its obligations...more solidly than the Russian Soviet government."

That ringing declaration of faith in Soviet steadfastness was belied by Churchill's certain knowledge that Moscow was already reneging on the Yalta agreement as it pertained to Poland. Four days earlier, the prime minister had received word that the Soviet-backed provisional government in Poland refused to invite to coalition talks in Moscow most of the non-Communist Polish leaders whose names had been put forth by the British and American ambassadors. Churchill, depressed by the news, worried aloud to John Colville and others about the Russians "one day turning against us" and nervously compared himself to Neville Chamberlain. Chamberlain had trusted Hitler as Churchill was now trusting Stalin—albeit, the prime minister was quick to add, "in different circumstances."

Perhaps it was this latest word from Poland that caused Churchill to insert in his speech a discordant note of doubt and anxiety, one that was much stronger than that expressed by Roosevelt in his address to Congress. Now that Poland's frontiers had been settled, Churchill wondered, would the Poles be allowed to be "masters in their own house?...Are their sovereignty and their independence to be untrammeled, or are they to become a mere projection of the Soviet state, forced against their will by an armed minority to adopt a Communist or totalitarian system?" Churchill provided no answers.

He did, however, betray even more anxiety by proposing that members of the Polish armed forces then serving under British command be permitted to become British citizens if they felt they could not return home after the war. MP Harold Nicolson, a strong supporter of Churchill, and many of his colleagues were bemused by the prime minister's contradictory message. As Nicolson wrote in his diary: "[The prime minister] makes an extremely good case for arguing that Poland in her new frontiers will enjoy an independent and prosperous existence. But in his closing words...he rather destroys all this by saying that we will offer British citizenship to those Polish soldiers who are too frightened to return."

When Churchill finished his two-hour speech, Arthur Greenwood, deputy leader of the Labour Party, was first to respond. More than five years earlier, he had confronted Neville Chamberlain on the floor of the House about the government's failure to abide by its treaty with Poland and declare war against Germany. Now he was confronting Chamberlain's successor over *his* government's treatment of Poland. Greenwood, who had served in Churchill's coalition cabinet early in the war, strongly disagreed with the prime minister's defense of the Yalta accords on the grounds of justice. In fact, he declared, deciding "the fate of a nation...in its absence and behind its back" was the very opposite of British justice.

It was not Greenwood, however, who galvanized the House during the first day of the Yalta debate. That distinction went to a tall, thin, bespectacled Scottish aristocrat, a quiet Tory backbencher not normally given to dramatic gestures. His name was Lord Dunglass.* Diag-

---

*Lord Dunglass became prime minister himself eighteen years later, when, having renounced his peerage, he went by his given name, Alec Douglas-Home.

nosed early in the war with tuberculosis of the spine, Dunglass, most of his body encased in a plaster cast, had spent more than two years in bed at his ancestral home. During that period, units of the 1st Polish Armored Division had been quartered at his estate, and he became close friends with a Polish tank gunner who was a minor member of Poland's nobility. Dunglass and the aristocratic Polish gunner spent many hours in conversation, much of it about the long history of German and Russian occupation of Poland. Thanks to these discussions, the Scottish laird became a staunch supporter of the Polish cause.

After he recovered his health and returned to Parliament, Lord Dunglass became concerned about what he saw as the British government's penchant for conciliating Russia at Poland's expense. Just before Churchill left for Moscow and his meeting with Stalin in October 1944, Dunglass rose in the House to caution him: "Russia must not be allowed to settle matters as she wishes.... We must honour our legal and moral commitments to restore Poland...."

In his view, the Yalta agreement made a mockery of those commitments. When Churchill asked the House to show its support not only for the agreement but for the justice of the agreement, the irony almost became more than the forty-one-year-old Dunglass could bear. He rose slowly to his feet, still frail and stooped from the lingering effects of his illness. "As far as Poland is concerned," he said, "there is no country which by reason of its opposition to tyranny has earned a greater right to independence. There is no country to which independence has been more specifically pledged in treaty and declaration...." He glanced around the hushed chamber. "When the Prime Minister says that he accepts this as an act of justice, I must take a fundamentally opposite view. We have, dozens of times in our history, accepted this kind of arrangement as a fact of power." His voice grew in intensity. "I accept it as a fact of power, but I cannot be asked to underwrite it as an act of justice."

The following day, twenty-five opponents of the Yalta agreement's handling of the Polish question decided to do more than merely register their dissent. They introduced an amendment to the confidence vote, regretting the government's "decision to transfer to another power the territory of an ally" and to fail to give liberated nations "the full right to choose their own Government free from the influence of any other power." In other words, the amendment politely indicted Churchill and his government for violating the Atlantic Charter.

This was highly unusual and highly explosive. The dissidents, mostly members of the Conservative Party, were formally challenging the conduct of a Conservative prime minister and his coalition government during wartime. In the debate that followed, those who supported the amendment made clear they realized the gravity of their action. There was a deep sense of sadness, even anguish, in many of the speeches, along with an uncommon passion. "It was magnificent," Tory MP Henry Channon wrote. It was "the supreme debate," "the conscience of the gentlemen of England" on display.

Commander Sir Archibald Southby, one of the amendment's two main sponsors, told his colleagues that this was the most difficult speech of his career. As much as he wanted to support the prime minister, he said, "if our foreign policy is to be based upon expediency and not upon principles then it is bound to fail, and I cannot in honour express my confidence in it, no matter what the consequences of my decision may be to me personally. I hold that there is a greater loyalty than that which we owe to any one man, government, or party—the loyalty to those fundamental ideals of justice, liberty and honour... which we have twice in our lifetime seen the British sword drawn to uphold."

Southby's speech—and several that followed—sounded remarkably like those made by Churchill in the days of Munich, a point that Lord James Willoughby d'Eresby made when he rose to address the House. Having just returned to Parliament after five years at the front, Willoughby d'Eresby, an army major and regimental commander, observed that members' roles seemed to have changed dramatically in the years he had been away. For example, in the late 1930s, he said, it had been Churchill and Eden who "spoke up in this House" on "questions of British honour."

Willoughby d'Eresby had lost his leg in combat at Normandy. His men had fought alongside the 1st Polish Armored Division, and several Polish officers had been attached to his unit. He was, he acknowledged to the House, "violently prejudiced" in favor of the Poles. When he talked to the men in his command about why Britain was fighting the war, he said, he gave the reasons put forth by the prime minister, among them, to safeguard the freedom and independence of all nations, but above all, to restore the independence of Poland. Now, he said, the Yalta agreement had made a "sham" of such talk.

Willoughby d'Eresby's comments must have deeply wounded Churchill. So must have the speech of Victor Raikes, a high-principled Tory from southeast Essex who, as his *Times* obituary pointed out years later, "put causes before career." Raikes noted that the last time he had defied a sitting government in a vote of confidence, it had been 1935, and he had followed the government's chief critic, Winston Churchill, into the lobby in opposition. He voted against the government then because he believed Churchill was right, he said. "Because I differ from him today, I do it," Raikes added, "not because I am 'anti' the Prime Minister—I have stood by him in days when he was far less popular than he is today—but because I believe that, for all his greatness today and insignificant as I am, I speak with the voice of my country."

When the debate was over, the members of Parliament, in deciding how to vote, struggled, as Alastair Forbes wrote in the *Daily Mail*, to "reconcile their troubled consciences [over Poland] with their political duties, which... they interpret as the support and retention in office of Mr. Churchill's government." For most, political duties won out. The amendment was defeated by 396 votes to 25, with eleven members abstaining. A number of the MPs who voted for the amendment were, like Lord Willoughby d'Eresby, on active military duty during the war. Among them were several RAF pilots who had flown with the Poles.

On the vote of confidence itself, the government won a unanimous victory, 413–0. The Tory parliamentary whips had put massive pressure on members to fall into line. In the end, even some of the most outspoken critics of the Polish settlement, like Lord Dunglass, did not feel that they could vote against the government unless they were prepared to see it fall, which they were not. Thirty members, however, did show their opposition by abstaining. One of them, a junior minister in Churchill's government named Henry Strauss, resigned his post the following day. He explained in a letter to the prime minister that he found it "impossible to approve of the treatment of the Polish people by the Crimean [i.e., Yalta] Conference."

Although he had scored what seemed to be an overwhelming parliamentary victory, Churchill knew that in this case appearances were deceiving. Despite their vote of confidence, many MPs, along with their constituents, remained deeply concerned about the threat of Poland's domination by the USSR. As Churchill wrote to Roosevelt, on the Polish question "Labour men were as keen as Conservatives, and Socialists as keen as Catholics."

In private, and contrary to what he had told the House, Churchill expressed his mistrust of the Soviets. The day after his speech, when he received word that the Soviets had just installed a puppet government in Romania, he told John Colville: "I have not the slightest intention of being cheated over Poland, not even if we go to the verge of war with Russia." Churchill was "trying to persuade himself that all is well," Colville wrote in his diary, "but in his heart I think he is worried about Poland and not convinced of the strength of our moral position."

Scarcely a month after signing the Yalta agreement, Stalin made clear he had no intention of abiding by it where Poland was concerned. Big Three unity, prayed for and lavishly publicized, was crumbling fast. Eden noted in his diary: "Altogether, our foreign policy seems a sad wreck." After Molotov had rejected virtually all the non-Communist Polish leaders proposed by the American and British ambassadors as participants in the talks on creation of a new Polish government, Churchill remarked that the Soviet foreign minister "clearly wanted to make a farce of consulting the 'non-Lublin' Poles."

Reports were also reaching London of mass Soviet arrests of Poles in Kraków and other major cities. One of those arrested was Mrs. Tomasz Arciszewska, the wife of the new prime minister of the Polish government-in-exile, who had been working for the Polish Red Cross. There were reports that thousands of Poles who lived in the former General Government area had already been shipped off to Soviet gulags, while others, mostly Home Army officers and men, were accused by the NKVD of spying for Britain and the London Poles. The Home Army troops "are starved, beaten, and tortured," according to one account from the Polish underground. "There are many deaths."

The Soviets had also gone back on their pledge at Yalta to allow foreign observers into Poland, including Anglo-American military teams who were to help in the repatriation of American and British prisoners of war imprisoned in German camps there. Many POWs, once liberated by the Red Army, remained under temporary Soviet detention; others were released but had to find their own way to Anglo-American lines, with no transportation or any other aid from the Russians. The only help they received, a number of British and American POWs later said, came from the Poles, who shared their meager food with them, housed them, and sometimes accompanied them part of the way. "Our men would have starved if it had not been for the generosity and hospitality of the Polish people," Averell Harriman wrote to FDR. Harriman added that the liberated POWs had "nothing but resentment for the treatment they received from the Russians."

To Winston Churchill and others in his government, it became increasingly apparent that the Soviet government wanted to delay for as long as possible the circulation of British and American eyewitness accounts of its persecution of the Poles and its tightening grip over the country. "There is no doubt in my mind," the prime minister told Roosevelt, "that the Soviets fear very much our seeing what is going on in Poland."

In their clash over the Yalta accords, Churchill and his parliamentary opponents were in agreement on at least one point: Poland was to be the measure of the postwar alliance's success or failure. In a letter to Roosevelt on March 8, Churchill called the Polish question "the test case between us and the Russians of the meaning which is to be attached to such terms as democracy, sovereignty, independence, representative government...." For the next month, until Roosevelt's death, the clearly conflicted British prime minister bombarded the American president with urgent cables, proposing that the two of them join forces to intervene forcefully with Stalin over Poland. "If we do not get things right now," Churchill wrote March 8, "it will soon be seen by the world that you and I, by putting our signatures to the Crimea settlement, have underwritten a fraudulent prospectus."

The drumbeat of Churchill's messages was reminiscent of his pressure on Roosevelt during the Warsaw uprising. Now as then, the president's response was to hold off taking any action that Stalin might interpret as a threat. Under the best of circumstances, Roosevelt's tendency was to delay difficult, controversial decisions. Frail and weak as he was in March 1945, he was even more inclined toward postponement. He thought it best, he told Churchill, to go slow on personal intervention and, instead, to persuade the London government-in-exile and the Soviet-backed government in Poland to declare "a general political truce."

Churchill, his alarm growing by the day, sharply—if all too belatedly—disagreed. Poland was on the brink of total Soviet domination; his repeated personal promises of independence to the Poles were about to turn to ash. There was no time to waste. "I do not wish to reveal a divergence between the British and the U.S. Governments," he wrote Roosevelt March 13, "but it would certainly be necessary for me to make it clear that we are in the presence of a great failure and an utter breakdown of what was settled at Yalta...." If he were forced to do that, he implied, he would also have to make clear that the United States was dragging its feet on the issue, and that "we British have not the necessary strength to carry the matter further...."

The intensity of Churchill's rhetoric escalated in late March, when he was jolted to learn that sixteen prominent leaders of the Polish underground had disappeared after being invited to a meeting with Soviet military commanders. Although weakened by the collapse of the Warsaw uprising and the imprisonment by the Germans of several major resistance leaders, the underground still wielded considerable influence in the country. A number of the missing men, as Eden later noted, would have been prime candidates for top positions in a broad-based postwar Polish government. They included General Leopold Okulicki, who had replaced Tadeusz Bór-Komorowski as commander of the Home Army, and the heads of the four major political parties in the underground government.

Anxiety among British officials over the disappearance of the sixteen men was heightened by their realization that they had been unwitting accessories in bringing it about. In early March, at Eden's request, the Polish government-in-exile had given the Foreign Office the names of the underground's key officials. Eden, in turn, handed over the names to the Soviets, declaring that if any harm came to them, the British would consider it a serious violation of the Yalta agreement.

Armed with the names, the NKVD tracked down the men, most of whom were in hiding, and invited them to a meeting with Soviet military officials to discuss possible cooperation between the Red Army and the underground. Promised safe-conduct, they agreed. None of them returned from the meeting place outside of Warsaw, and for the next six weeks, the Soviets ignored repeated British inquiries.

———

PRESSED HARD BY Churchill, Roosevelt, in the last weeks of his life, finally began to express concern about the fate of the Yalta accords. He was indignant over the shabby treatment of American POWs, as well as

Soviet exclusion of most of the non-Communist Poles suggested by the United States and Britain from the Polish government. But he was even more upset when Stalin announced that Molotov would not travel, as planned, to San Francisco in May for ceremonies marking the birth of FDR's dream, the United Nations.

On April 1, Roosevelt sent a reproving note to Stalin that, at its end, revealed how little he really understood the Soviet leader. "I must make it quite plain to you," FDR wrote, that Soviet attempts to bar non-Communists from the new Polish government were "unacceptable and would cause the people of the United States to regard the Yalta agreement as having failed." The Russians, he said, must stop their persecution of the Poles and must allow foreign observers into the country. Then he added: "You are, I am sure, aware that genuine public support in the United States is required to carry out any Government policy foreign or domestic. The American people make up their own mind.... [I] wonder whether you give full weight to this factor."

Whether he gave full weight or not, Stalin obviously didn't care. In a return message, he blamed Britain and the United States for the difficulties in creating a new Polish government and made clear he would brook no interference from his Allies in deciding the government's members. But it was another cable from Stalin, sent a few days earlier, that drove the president into a real fury. The Soviet premier had just learned of a meeting in Switzerland between a German general and American and British officials to discuss the possible surrender to the Western Allies of SS forces in Italy. In his cable, Stalin, an expert double-dealer who always suspected others of the same tendency, accused Roosevelt and Churchill of conspiring with the Germans against him.

Roosevelt was deeply wounded. He had done everything he could to create a close personal relationship with Stalin—humored him, placated him, appeased him. And this insult, this abuse, was what he got in return. He fired off the sharpest message he had ever sent to the Soviet leader, expressing his "feeling of bitter resentment" for "such vile misrepresentations of my actions or those of my trusted subordinates."

Startled, Stalin immediately backed off, pleading that he never doubted Roosevelt's trustworthiness and integrity. His response raises the question of what might have happened had Roosevelt stood up to Stalin earlier on other issues. In the event, the Soviet leader's placating message had its hoped-for result: it put Roosevelt in a much more conciliatory mood. On April 11, he wrote Churchill that he planned "to minimize the general Soviet problem as much as possible, because these problems, in one form or another, seem to arise every day, and most of them straighten out."

The next day, at his vacation retreat in Warm Springs, Georgia, Franklin D. Roosevelt looked up after signing a pile of letters and documents. He raised his hand to his head. His face was contorted in pain. "I have a terrible pain in the back of my head," he said. Then he collapsed. Two hours later he was dead, of a massive cerebral hemorrhage.

BY MID-APRIL 1945, Allied armies were hurtling across Germany—the Americans, British, Canadians, and Poles from the west, the Russians from the east. Polish fighter squadrons, including the Kościuszko Squadron, were among the RAF units supporting the ground troops' advance.

On April 25, the same day as the historic link-up of U.S. and Soviet infantrymen at the Elbe River, members of the Kościuszko Squadron, flying U.S.-built P-51 Mustangs, took part in their last combat mission of the war. With four other Polish squadrons, they were among the escorts for the huge Allied bombing raid on Berchtesgaden, Hitler's cherished hideaway in the mountains of Bavaria. For the Poles, there was a special satisfaction in seeing that final target demolished. For it was at Berchtesgaden that Hitler had planned his invasion of Poland, and it was from there that he had ordered the destruction of the Polish people.

The elation arising from that moment of vengeance passed quickly, however. Having helped rid the world of Hitler, the Poles and their country had nothing to look forward to now except more years under another dictator's control. Among the fliers of the Kościuszko Squadron, "a strangely hollow silence descended as peace approached," one of them later wrote. "We, the Poles, were not experiencing joy...but rather a profound pain."

At the time of the Berchtesgaden raid, none of the Kościuszko pilots who flew in the Battle of Britain was still attached to the squadron.

Most of the early members were dead: of the thirty-four in the original group, only thirteen survived the war. But just before the Germans surrendered, one of the battle's heroes rejoined the squadron. On a beautiful May morning, Witold Łokuciewski, who had been shot down over France in March 1942, climbed out of a transport plane at Andrews Field, where the Kościuszko Squadron now was stationed. He was immediately surrounded by a crowd of beaming pilots, many of whom he had never met but who, nonetheless, were anxious to welcome back one of Dęblin's famed "Three Musketeers" after his three years in German captivity.

For most of that time, Łokuciewski had been held in the infamous *Stalag Luft III*, a camp for RAF and other Allied fliers in Sagan, Germany. Like most of his fellow inmates, he had spent much of his time figuring out ways to escape. In 1943, he and several other airmen— American, British, and Polish—had indeed escaped from the camp and hopped a train, only to be arrested by the Gestapo at the next station. Returned to the stalag, Łokuciewski promptly threw himself into the planning for "the Great Escape," a highly sophisticated breakout scheme involving the participation of hundreds of prisoners, who surreptitiously dug several tunnels, acquired German uniforms and civilian clothes, and prepared maps and false personal documents.

Some 600 POWs drew lots to see who would leave in the first group of escapees. Having drawn a high number, Łokuciewski was left behind during the initial breakout on March 24, 1944. As it turned out, he was lucky. Of the seventy-eight escapees who actually got away, at least fifty were quickly captured by the Germans—and just as quickly shot. Six of those executed were Polish pilots, among them the former aide-de-camp to General Sikorski.

On returning to England, Łokuciewski was soon reunited with Jan Zumbach, the other surviving Musketeer. By this time, Zumbach, like Zdzisław Krasnodębski, Witold Urbanowicz, and other Battle of Britain heroes, had been taken off active flying duty and "kicked upstairs"—to a series of high-ranking desk jobs. Now a wing commander, Zumbach had led the Kościuszko Squadron from May to December 1942, and later was given command of the 133 Polish Fighter Wing. In June 1944, the wing's four squadrons strafed the beaches and countryside of Normandy in support of the Allied landings. Despite his outstanding record as a fighter pilot, Zumbach himself didn't see much of the action. "[A]ll my time was devoted to command duties, and I had to leave the fighting to others," he recalled ruefully many years later. "That was the price I paid for status."

A man who thrived on excitement and danger, Zumbach had become jaded and cynical about the British and U.S. abandonment of Poland. In late 1944, now a liaison officer between the RAF and several Polish squadrons sent to Belgium and Holland, he discovered new ways of living life on the edge. Like a number of other Polish (and British) pilots in the last stages of the war, Zumbach became a smuggler, transporting contraband goods to and from the continent in RAF planes. His specialty was diamonds. Recruited by a Polish diamond dealer in London, he carried small packets of the stones to Antwerp dealers on his frequent flights to Belgium. It was a career he was to pursue even after the war was over.

Meanwhile, Witold Urbanowicz was back in Washington, living a far more staid life than his raffish Polish comrade. After his adrenaline-charged time with the 75th Squadron in China, he had gone back to London for a few months and then, in August 1944, had returned to the Polish Embassy in Washington as air attaché. He was delighted to be reunited with his wife and to get to know the baby son who had been born while he was in China. But there was great frustration and anger, too, as he observed the Roosevelt administration's acquiescence in the Soviet takeover of Poland. "It was horrible," he said many years later. "Just a horrible, horrible situation."

The original commander of the Kościuszko Squadron, Zdzisław Krasnodębski, had been confined to a desk since 1941 because of the severe burns to his hands. Occasionally, he'd take a Spitfire or a trainer plane up for an hour or two, but he never again flew in combat. Ending the war with the rank of group captain, he served as commander of the RAF station at Heston and, later, of the 131 Polish Airfield. In 1944, he was attached to the Polish Air Force headquarters in London.

As the war approached its end, Krasnodębski still did not know if his wife, Wanda, was alive or dead, and he was deeply depressed over what was happening to Poland. In 1944, he and Urbanowicz had dinner and talked about the future. Krasnodębski was sure that he and his former deputy would never be able to return to their native country. More the optimist, Urbanowicz disagreed. Surely, he said, the Russians would soon throw off Soviet dictatorship, and Poland would be liberated. Krasnodębski shook his head. "Not in *our* lifetime," he said.

———

IN LATE APRIL 1945, with Harry S. Truman now the president of the United States, delegates from forty-four countries gathered in San Francisco to take part in the founding conference of the United Nations. Among the nations represented were several of Hitler's former allies, including Italy, which had switched sides in October 1943, and Romania, which had done the same in late 1944—just in time to be declared a belligerent against Germany and thus eligible for UN membership. Poland—the first country to resist Hitler; the only country to fight the Nazis from the first day of the war to the last; the one country defeated by Germany that neither surrendered nor collaborated—was not on the list of invitees. Once again, the British and Americans, who still officially recognized the London government-in-exile as the legal government of Poland, did not want to alienate the Russians by snubbing the Soviet-backed regime.

One evening during the conference, the renowned concert pianist Artur Rubinstein, a native of Poland, performed at the San Francisco Opera House, where the meetings were taking place. After opening his concert with the American national anthem, Rubinstein stood up and told the audience that he did not see the flag of his own country among the dozens displayed in the Opera House. His next selection, he announced, would therefore be the Polish national anthem. As he played the stirring notes of "Poland Has Not Yet Perished as Long as We Live," the audience burst out in loud, sustained applause.

Aside from Rubinstein's symbolic gesture, the issue of independence for Poland received scant public support at the conference. The Russians used the occasion to drive home the message that *they* now controlled Poland, lest anybody still harbor any illusions to the contrary. At a cocktail party hosted by Anthony Eden at the Mark Hopkins Hotel, Vyacheslav Molotov swept in, accompanied by his interpreter and bodyguards. Having announced in March that the Soviet foreign minister would not attend the conference, Stalin changed his mind and decided to send him after all. But Molotov made clear that his presence did not signify any new interest in Allied cooperation.

Drink in hand, he pushed through the crowd toward Eden, who was talking to Secretary of State Edward Stettinius. Molotov bowed slightly to the British foreign secretary and complimented him on the party. Then, turning to include Stettinius in the conversation, he said just as casually: "By the way, those Poles you are interested in? We have arrested them." Before the other two men had time to reply, the Soviet foreign minister and his entourage walked away.

Eden and Stettinius were thunderstruck. The Poles Molotov was referring to were the sixteen underground leaders who had disappeared six weeks earlier, the leaders whose names had been given by Eden to the Soviets with the warning that if any harm came to them, it would be considered a grave violation of the Yalta accords. According to a British official who witnessed the encounter between the foreign ministers, Molotov clearly meant his announcement as "a deliberate affront," "a calculated rudeness." He was thumbing his nose at his British and American counterparts, letting them know that his government would not be bound by the principles embodied by this new international organization.

Later in the evening, Eden and Stettinius, with several aides, adjourned to the secretary of state's hotel room to decide how to respond. After an hour or so of weighing alternatives, Stettinius said, "Perhaps we should just say that we are anxious." Eden, who had far more at stake than his American counterpart where the Poles were concerned, lost his temper. "Perhaps," he exploded, "we should just say we are bloody *angry*!" Unfazed, Stettinius took off his tie, lay down on the bed, and said: "I'm going to sleep. If you want to issue anything, do it on your own."

Eden was not prepared to do that, and he apologized to Stettinius for blowing up. Once again, in the face of American indifference, British anger over the Soviet treatment of Poland had ebbed quickly, replaced by a spirit of mild compromise. In the end, the British and American governments settled for a note to Stalin condemning the arrests. The Soviet leader ignored it.

The cocktail party incident was a profoundly troubling omen: the United Nations had barely been born and already its future effectiveness was seriously threatened. Reporting from San Francisco, CBS correspondent Eric Sevareid talked about the growing foreboding among Western statesmen regarding the shape of the postwar world. "They do their work in a curiously mechanical spirit," Sevareid said. "One has the feeling they dread the moment when they must lift their eyes and face an incoming tidal wave of human problems, social, economic and political, which will not wait."

THAT UNCERTAIN FUTURE was now at hand. On May 7, 1945, at 2:41 a.m., General Alfred Jodl, chief of the German armed forces, sat down at a scarred wooden desk in a little French schoolhouse and signed Germany's formal declaration of surrender. All fighting was to cease at midnight. The war in Europe—which began in Poland five years, eight months, and eight days earlier—was now officially over.

The following day in London, hundreds of thousands of people jammed Piccadilly Circus, Trafalgar Square, the streets surrounding Parliament and Whitehall, and the parks around Buckingham Palace, awaiting the official announcement. It was a glorious spring day, and the joyful, exuberant crowds reveled in the warm sun. Mothers adorned their babies' hair with red, white, and blue ribbons, and dogs sported red, white, and blue bows. Children raced through the parks waving Union Jacks. Soldiers kissed laughing young girls as they strolled by. In Piccadilly, American sailors formed a conga line, with everyone around joining in. Church bells pealed. From tugboats on the Thames, horns blared in celebration.

Early that afternoon, vast throngs cheered Winston Churchill as he drove to Buckingham Palace, then to Parliament, to announce the German surrender. Later, from a balcony on Whitehall, the prime minister, his voice choked with emotion, told the thousands of people massed below him: "God bless you all, this is your victory!" "No," the crowd roared back. "It's yours!" In fact, the prime minister continued, it was "a victory for the cause of freedom in every land."

Churchill knew better. In a speech to the British people broadcast that night, he alluded to the fate of Poland and other Soviet-dominated countries when he said: "On the continent of Europe, we have yet to make sure that the simple and honorable purposes for which we entered the war are not brushed aside ... and that the words 'freedom,' 'democracy,' and 'liberation' are not distorted from their true meaning...." At the same time, in a cable to his wife, Clementine, Churchill admitted to a profound discouragement in the face of the "poisonous politics and deadly international rivalries" that underlay the Allied triumph.

There were few, if any, Polish pilots, soldiers, or sailors in the jubilant London crowds that May 8. The defeat of Germany had been Poland's goal since September 1, 1939. Now that it was here, with such bitter consequences, the Poles could not bring themselves to join in the celebration. "The word 'Victory!' is devoid of meaning, power and any sense today only for the Poles," a disillusioned Polish pilot wrote in his diary.

That evening, London, liberated from more than four years of blackout, glowed with light. Buckingham Palace, Parliament, St. Paul's Cathedral, and other bomb-damaged public buildings were floodlit. The face of Big Ben, illuminated once again, could be seen for miles.

In other European capitals—Paris, Rome, Copenhagen, Amsterdam, Oslo, Prague—lights also blazed brightly, as people sang, kissed, and danced in the streets.

In the graveyard that was Warsaw, there was only darkness and silence.

CHAPTER TWENTY-ONE

"For Your Freedom and Ours"

SHORTLY AFTER THE war in Europe ended, Sir Archibald Sinclair, the British air minister, sent a letter of thanks to Polish airmen for their service to the Allied cause. "[We] do not forget that you were the first to resist the aggressor," he wrote, "neither do [we] forget that you came after manifold trials to our aid when we most needed your help. Your valiant squadrons fighting alongside our own were in the forefront of the Battle of Britain and so helped to restore the fortunes of the Allies throughout the years of struggle. In good times and bad you have stood by us and shared with the RAF their losses and their victories."

In the postwar period, Polish loyalty was very little reciprocated by either the British government (with the notable exception of the RAF) or by many of the British people. This was all the more painful for the Poles in Britain as they learned about developments at home. Stalin, far from honoring his pledge to hold early elections, quickly moved his puppet regime from Lublin to Warsaw and draped it in all the trappings of Soviet-backed power. On April 23, 1945, Secretary of State Stettinius had told America's new president, Harry Truman, that the Warsaw government "was not representative of the Polish people and that . . . the Soviet Government intended to try to enforce upon the United States and British Governments this puppet government of Poland and obtain its acceptance as the legal government. . . ."

The Soviet ploy worked. On July 5, Britain and the United States, still chasing the chimera of "Allied unity," withdrew formal recognition from the Polish government-in-exile and bestowed it on the Communists in

Warsaw.* While military units from countries such as Norway, France, and the Netherlands were able to return home in triumph, more than 200,000 Polish military men and women became, in the words of a British judge, "the largest illegal private army ever known in this country."

Near the end of July, Britain held its first general election since 1935. When the votes were tallied, Winston Churchill, so inspirational in wartime, had been unceremoniously turned out of office by weary, warsick voters who decided that they preferred the Labour Party to manage their crippled economy. The war had cost the lives of 357,000 British military and civilians and had bled away a quarter of Britain's national wealth. A country of some 46 million people had seen more than 4 million of its dwellings destroyed or heavily damaged. The resultant housing shortage became a full-blown crisis as the military began to demobilize. Food, petrol, and other basic commodities were also in extremely short supply—so much so that the government was forced to continue, then expand, rationing. Unemployment was beginning to soar, and for the first time in its long history Britain had become a debtor nation.

The voters seemed to think that Churchill, having spent almost his entire life dealing one way or another with foreign affairs, wasn't up to these new challenges. They had a point. Now seventy years old, he was still looking mainly abroad, more and more concerned about growing Soviet dominion over most of Central and Eastern Europe and the need for strengthening Britain's alliance with the United States. The situation in Poland especially haunted him. The country was being "denied all free expression of her national will," he said from his unaccustomed seat in the minority benches. Overlooking the part he played in creating that situation, he urged the British not to turn their backs on the Poles who had fought so hard on Britain's behalf.

The new prime minister, Clement Attlee, and his Labour government felt rather differently. If anything, they were more eager than Churchill had been to establish and maintain good relations with Moscow and were disinclined to do anything that might jeopardize that objective. In early 1946, a few months after two U.S. atomic bombs

---

* Churchill had originally suggested to U.S. officials that their two countries recognize the new Communist regime on July 4. The Americans replied that severing ties with the Polish government-in-exile on the United States's Independence Day was hardly a good idea and suggested July 5 instead.—Ulam, *The Rivals,* p. 7.

forced Japan to surrender and end the war, Attlee's foreign secretary, Ernest Bevin, warned the cabinet that the Polish military in Britain was a "source of increasing political embarrassment in our relations with the Soviet Union and [Communist] Poland." What's more, with the British economy in shambles, the continuing presence of so many foreigners—competing with Britons for housing, jobs, ration books, and the like—was bound to cause friction. In this atmosphere, an internal government report proposed that "everything should be done to ensure that as few Poles as possible remain in this country."

But what did that mean? The government couldn't force the Poles to return to a country dominated by a foreign power they feared and hated and that equally feared and hated them. It would be contrary to every principle the nation stood for, and bad for Britain's public image. After considering its options, the Labour government finally decided to try to *scare* the Poles into going home. In a variety of forums, government officials painted the bleakest possible picture of the Poles' future prospects if they chose to remain in Britain. The hope was that, upon hearing the bad news, they would simply pack up and leave.

At this point, the RAF's incensed high command intervened. While understanding the rationale behind the government's "cold and dispassionate attitude," the RAF brass made very clear that they, at least, would not turn their back on the "strongest, the most loyal and faithful, and the most persistent European ally of all...." An Air Ministry report declared in January 1946 that the Poles "are part and parcel of the RAF, they have fought with us during the whole of the war, they were with us in the Battle of Britain, and with us from D-Day onwards to 'the kill' in Germany. To contemplate, in their tragic hour, anything short of sympathetic and generous treatment is unthinkable."

The report was the clearest indication yet of how dramatically the RAF's attitude toward the Poles had changed in the course of the war. When Polish pilots arrived in England six years earlier, they had been treated with disdain by many of their British counterparts. But their courage, tenacity, and skill—and, above all, their crucial help in the Battle of Britain—had swept away most of the prejudice and replaced it with gratitude and friendship. As Air Chief Marshal William Sholto Douglas put it, "Together, we have formed a brotherhood."

The RAF appealed to the Attlee government to give preferential treatment to the 14,000 Polish pilots and ground crew in Britain. Among other steps, the RAF urged a shorter waiting time for British citizenship for Polish airmen. The great debt owed the Poles by Britain, the Air Ministry argued in a paper to the cabinet, could "only be satisfactorily repaid by giving them special and generous consideration at a time when their Air Force, of which they were intensely proud, and which they had built up with such hopes for the future, crashes to the ground."

The Labour government, insisting that it would be wrong to give preferential treatment to the Polish Air Force over units of the Polish army and navy that were also still in Britain, rejected the RAF's appeal. In March 1946, all Polish military personnel, regardless of service, were ordered to assemble at their bases and stations. There, they were handed two letters. The first, from Poland's Communist government, demanded that they return home. The second, from Ernest Bevin, announced the imminent demobilization of all Polish armed forces under British command. It was the Poles' "duty," Bevin declared, to "return to their home country without further delay" in order to assist in its reconstruction. If any felt they absolutely could not return, the foreign secretary added, the British government would help them "as far as our resources permit." But there was no guarantee that they would be allowed to settle in Britain or any other part of the British Empire.

Polish airmen and many of their British comrades were shattered by this action. Recalled RAF pilot Thomas Johnson, who was with several Polish pilots as they read the letters: "To all intents and purposes, [Bevin's letter] said, 'Thank you for your contribution to our victory. I am sorry you cannot come to England. You are forthwith released from duty....' It is the only time in my life that 'politics' in its stark inhumanity caused me an anguish I have no desire to experience again. I was twenty-three years old. Can you imagine what I felt? I stood by the side of my brothers-in-arms and cursed my government."

Less than three months later, on June 8, 1946, Britain staged its grand Victory Parade. The Labour government invited Communist Poland to take part—and, to avoid annoying Stalin, barred the hundreds of thousands of Poles who had fought under British command. This latest insult was too much for the RAF, which insisted that at least a token delegation of Polish airmen be included. In the end, the government relented on that point. A few Polish fliers were belatedly and grudgingly invited to march, but they declined the invitation to protest the exclusion of their army and navy compatriots. In the event, not one Pole marched in the parade. The Polish provisional government in Warsaw and the Soviet Union refused to send delegations.*

The Attlee government's decision to cast aside men and women who had fought so long and so courageously under British command prompted an outpouring of sadness and anger from a number of British political and military leaders. In the House of Commons, Winston Churchill said he profoundly regretted the exclusion of the Poles, adding: "They will be in our hearts on that day...." "Have we lost all sense of decency and gratitude?" sputtered Air Marshal Philip Joubert de Ferté, assistant chief of the Air Staff during the Battle of Britain. "Are we too feeble to stand up to those who attempt to bully us?"

In a June 7 letter to General Władysław Anders, a deeply distressed Harold Macmillan told his close friend that his thoughts would be with II Polish Corps the following day. "I tell you this frankly," Macmillan added. "With all the legitimate joy and pride in every British heart will be mingled much sorrow and even shame."

FOR THE THOUSANDS of Polish pilots and other Polish Air Force personnel in Britain, the spring and summer of 1946 was an agonizing time. Most of them, like the rest of the Polish armed forces, wanted desperately to return to their homes and families in Poland. But they did not want to go back to a Poland controlled by a Communist government. A sizable number, having been inmates of Stalin's gulags, already had firsthand knowledge of what it was like to live under Soviet domination. But if they chose to remain in Britain, what would happen to them? They faced a highly uncertain future as stateless aliens, without money, jobs, or prospects.

"We are all struggling with one dilemma, tormented by the same fears: Should we go back or not?" one Kościuszko Squadron pilot wrote. "There is a lot of bickering, back-stabbing and animosity among the

---

* Czech military units that fought with the British were allowed to march in the parade. The Czech government-in-exile under Eduard Beneš had already returned to Prague and was trying to achieve a constructive relationship with Moscow-backed Communists in the government. The attempt failed. In 1948, Beneš resigned, a broken man (he died a short time later), and the Communists gained complete control.

Poles nowadays." As their anxiety and cynicism increased, Polish airmen began quarreling with one another and lashing out in anger at the British. There was no organized resistance, however, and no mutiny. As hurt and angry as the Poles were by British behavior, they continued to follow orders—to patrol German airspace and carry out their other postwar duties. Adding to their anguish was the knowledge that, having already lost their country and in many cases their loved ones, they were also about to lose their squadrons, which had been their surrogate families for more than half a decade. "Friendships and memories," said Jan Zumbach, "were about to be scattered to the four winds."

On September 18, the Kościuszko Squadron and other Polish units began a series of emotionally wrenching farewells. At a somber ceremony at the RAF station at Coltishall in Norfolk, Air Marshal Sir James Robb told the Polish fighter pilots who paraded before him: "You are men of courage, truth, honour, and proven worth." Their exploits, he said, would live in "undying memory." Robb presented the squadrons with the RAF's official standard as acknowledgment of a debt that "we will never be able to repay." Then, as he and thousands of other onlookers watched, the Poles took off in their Mustangs and roared overhead in tight formation—the last time they would fly together as a unit.

Two months later, on November 27, the Kościuszko Squadron, the most illustrious group of Polish fliers to take to the air during World War II, was officially disbanded. Presiding over the ceremony at Hethel airfield was Witold Łokuciewski, who ten months earlier had been named the squadron's last commander. Many of those who had flown with the unit over the past six years were present for what Zdzisław Krasnodębski, its first wartime commander, called "the most painful day in the history of our squadron." In an impromptu speech, Krasnodębski declared: "Our wings are being taken away from us ... but we remain united in the belief that there will come a day when our machines, bearing the silver scythes of Kościuszko, will touch down in a free [Warsaw]."

With that, Łokuciewski climbed onto the port wing of a Mustang and carefully removed from its fuselage the insignia that had been designed by one of the squadron's American founders—the circle with the U.S. stars and bars and the Polish cap and scythes. Łokuciewski held it high for the assembled pilots to see.

No one spoke. A grand and glorious adventure was over.

Witold Łokuciewski, the Kościuszko Squadron's last commander, removes the Kościuszko insignia from a Mustang at November 1946 ceremonies marking the disbanding of the squadron. (Jacek Kutzner)

The other surviving member of the "Three Musketeers" was not on hand at Hethel to witness his squadron's deactivation. Two weeks earlier, Jan Zumbach, having decided that his future lay elsewhere, left England. Because his paternal grandfather was Swiss, he held Swiss citizenship and hence was issued a Swiss passport, along with a combined train and boat ticket from British military authorities, valid as far as the Swiss frontier. Attached to the ticket was a notice: "British territory must be vacated within three days." Zumbach protested against so peremptory an ejection. "I've been in England for six years," he told an official. "I've got friends here. Do you want to prevent me from saying goodbye?" The official replied: "Of course not. That is the reason for your three days' notice."

After three nights of hard partying with old comrades, Zumbach turned in his pistol, parachute, and other RAF-issue gear, and headed for Switzerland. He would eventually settle in Paris. From there, he began a raffish new career that would violate every RAF regulation there ever was.

IN THE END, less than 20 percent of the Polish military in Britain—about 30,000 people in all—decided to return to Poland. Resigned to the reality that most Poles would be staying in Britain, the British government in mid-1946 set up a Polish Resettlement Corps, which offered them temporary jobs until they could find permanent work.

Establishing the resettlement agency, however, was not a popular move among Britons, suffering as they were from material and emotional exhaustion and focused on their own problems. For many, the Poles and their contributions during the war had become irrelevant, and the fact that Britain had entered the war in the first place in hopes of protecting Polish independence was becoming, at best, a dim memory. At a society wedding in London in January 1946, Tory MP Henry Channon, closing his eyes to the chaos in the lives of so many of his countrymen, remarked to socialite Emerald Cunard how satisfying it was that life in London had returned so quickly to normal. "After all," he said, glancing around at the other well-dressed guests sipping their champagne, "this is what we've been fighting for." Known for her sharp tongue and quick wit, Cunard couldn't resist a jab at such fatuousness. "What?" she cooed, looking around, too. "Are they all Poles?"

In June 1946, 56 percent of Britons polled in a nationwide survey favored sending the Poles back to Poland. Only 30 percent said they should be allowed to remain if they chose. Shortly after the end of the war, anti-Polish graffiti—"England for the English"—began appearing on walls near the air stations where Poles were based. "Who do you think will give you a job, while English lads are looking for work?" an Englishman shouted at one Polish pilot. "Go home!"

Before venturing off their bases and into the civilian community, many fliers now took off their Polish Air Force badges. Those badges had once been magnets to an adoring British public, but now, all too often, they elicited jeers and confrontations. "I don't think official quarters...realize the amount of persecution which [the Poles] have suffered during the last few weeks," a member of Parliament wrote the Foreign Office in the fall of 1945. "...[T]he men are pestered wherever they go." Years later, a Polish pilot who remained in Britain recalled "choking with bitterness" at the change in British attitude. "Not so long before, I had enjoyed the exaggerated prestige of a fighter pilot and the hysterical adulation that surrounded him. Suddenly I turned into slag that everybody wanted to be rid of—a thing useless, burdensome, even noxious. It was very hard to bear."

Although the Air Ministry had been unable to persuade the government to give favored treatment to Polish pilots, the RAF came to their aid in another way, inviting more than 500 Poles to join its ranks. Others took posts as commercial and test pilots and as technical experts for aircraft manufacturers. Relatively few of the 8,000-plus Polish airmen who stayed in Britain were able to find flying-related occupations, however. For the most part, given the job shortage, they tried (with varying degrees of success) self-employment or entrepreneurship of one kind or another, including farming. For many, the trauma of having to remain in a country that no longer wanted them was compounded by not knowing what had happened to their loved ones back in Poland. There, as elsewhere in occupied Europe, millions had been uprooted from their homes and displaced. But, with the Soviet Union now in control of the entire Polish state, getting word about the fate of families was extraordinarily difficult.

Zdzisław Krasnodębski was one of the lucky ones. He had been trying to trace his wife, Wanda, for months before the war ended. Soon after the German surrender, he learned she was still alive. From that moment on, his overriding goal was to get her out.

———————

FOLLOWING THE WARSAW uprising, Wanda Krasnodębska's life was "very, very hard." After she and others in the resistance were taken into custody by the Germans, she managed to slip away and head south, then west, on foot. Sometimes she slept in fields. Sometimes she managed to gain a roof over her head by helping peasants with their farm chores and other odd jobs. For food, she recalled, "I was happy if I could go to a marketplace and get a little cup of hot water and a piece of bread to last me all day. That was a great meal for me in those days."

With the help of friends she encountered along the way, she eventually reached Kutno, west of Warsaw, where she worked for the Red Cross. After the war ended, an NKVD official summoned her to his office. Where was her husband? he asked. She said she hadn't heard from him since the war began, whereupon the secret police agent pulled out a photograph of Krasnodębski in his RAF uniform, thrust it at her, and accused her of being a British spy. Terrified, Krasnodębska nevertheless managed to keep her voice under control as she denied the charge. "I wouldn't even know what a spy is supposed to do," she said. "I have never been a spy, and I never met any spies." The police official laughed. "It doesn't matter what spies do," he said. "What matters is what we do with spies."

He let her go, but from then on, she was followed by plainclothes agents wherever she went. Then, not long after her meeting with the NKVD official, a man came to her apartment and said he had been sent by her husband to get her out of Poland. He told her to go to a certain address in Warsaw. Despite her doubts, she agreed to go. The next night, members of the Home Army helped smuggle her out of Kutno, placing her aboard a freight train to the capital. From there, she made her way to Kraków, where, with other fugitive refugees, she was hidden in the back of a truck heading for the Czech border. When they arrived, bribes were paid, and the truck was allowed to cross Czechoslovakia.

In February 1946, Wanda Krasnodębska was sleeping in a Red Cross billet in British-occupied Germany when she was awakened by the sound of footsteps outside. A familiar voice was calling her name. She ran to the door—and straight into her husband's arms. They hadn't seen each other in more than six years, not since the day in August 1939 when he left to fight the Germans and assured her that he would be right back.

Krasnodębski stayed with the Polish Air Force command in England until it was disbanded in 1948. He was offered a number of jobs in Britain and the United States, his wife later said, but he refused to settle permanently in either country because of his bitterness over what he saw as Churchill and Roosevelt's betrayal of Poland. At the urging of friends who had earlier moved to South Africa, the couple finally decided to emigrate to Cape Town.

In all, some 2,500 Polish pilots left Britain to live in countries whose governments had agreed to accept Polish refugee servicemen and their families. Most went to South America, Australia, New Zealand, Canada, and the United States. South Africa reluctantly accepted about a hundred.

OF THE SURVIVING original members of the Kościuszko Squadron in Britain, only two returned to Poland. One of them was Witold Łokuciewski. As was true of many of the 3,000 other Polish airmen who repatriated, his yearning to return to family and country proved stronger than his fear of a future under Soviet rule. Łokuciewski's father had died during the Soviet deportations early in the war, and his brother-in-law was murdered at Katyn, but his mother, sister, and brother, now living in Lublin, all wrote him letters begging him to return. Also back in Poland was an old girlfriend, whom Łokuciewski told friends in England he wanted to marry. When he arrived home in 1947, however, he discovered that his girlfriend had married someone else, and that his own future was bleak at best, perilous at worst.

In Poland, as in the Soviet Union and the rest of the Soviet bloc, xenophobia now ruled. Any previous contact with the West was equated with treachery. Innocent men and women who had such contact were frequently tried and convicted as traitors and spies. The stage had been set as early as June 1945, when the Soviets tried the sixteen Polish resistance leaders who had been kidnapped the previous March. In a breathtakingly cynical mockery of justice, men who had battled the Nazis from the first day of the war (and throughout the period of the Stalin-Hitler partnership) were herded into a crude wooden dock in a Moscow courtroom, guarded by two NKVD guards with fixed bayonets, and charged with German collaboration, subversion, and espionage. All but three were found guilty and sentenced to terms in prison. Four, including General Leopold Okulicki, the head of the Home Army after Bór-Komorowski, died there.

As the trial of the sixteen proceeded to its cruel conclusion, Poland's World War II Allies, including Britain and the United States, looked on and did nothing. Having considered attending the trial, the American and British ambassadors decided against it, for fear their presence, in the words of Averell Harriman, would "be interpreted as casting doubts on Soviet good faith." "Of all the moral surrenders of the Western democracies, none was more obscene than this," asserted Norman Davies. "[An] act which publicly disgraced and humiliated some of the founding members of the anti-Nazi alliance in the interests of political revenge, places a blot on the conscience of everyone who watched in silence."

At Yalta, Stalin had told Churchill and Roosevelt that "free and unfettered elections" would probably be held in Poland within a month. Almost two years later, on January 19, 1947, elections were finally held, amid brutal police intimidation of voters, arrests, and a number of murders. Despite the pressure on Polish voters, Stanisław Mikołaj-czyk—who, alone among former top officials of the Polish government-in-exile, had returned to Poland after the war—declared that his non-Communist Peasant Party had captured more than 70 percent of the vote. The Communists, however, claimed an overwhelming victory, and the government promptly certified the Communist claims. Not long afterward, Mikołajczyk, facing imminent arrest, was smuggled out of Warsaw and back to London.

To this latest violation of the Yalta accords, the U.S. and British governments responded with mild expressions of regret. Angered by the Truman administration's lukewarm reaction to what he called a "farce" of an election, U.S. ambassador Arthur Bliss Lane quit his post on January 23.

Having firmly established themselves as the indisputable rulers of Poland, the Communists intensified their crackdown. Thousands of Poles who had fought the Germans, both resistance fighters and members of the returning Polish armed forces, were arrested and imprisoned. By 1947, well over 100,000 had been taken into custody by Soviet and Polish secret police, according to Lane. Prisons in Kraków, Poznań, and Lublin were overflowing. The Communist government even used Auschwitz and several other abandoned German concentration camps as Polish detention centers. On occasion, Polish resistance leaders found themselves sharing prison cells with high-ranking Nazis. In the most notorious case, Kazimierz Moczarski, a Home Army intelligence officer, was thrown into the same cell as Jürgen Stroop, the SS brigade commander in charge of liquidating the Warsaw Ghetto in 1943.

Among those arrested in the postwar period were a number of pilots who had flown in Britain, including Stanisław Skalski. A Dęblin classmate of "the Three Musketeers," Skalski, with eighteen kills, was the ace of aces among Polish pilots who had flown with the RAF. Accused in 1948 of spying for "American and British imperialists," he was kept locked in a tiny underground prison cell for two years and periodically underwent interrogation and torture. In 1950, he was sentenced to death for espionage. The sentence was commuted to life after Stalin's death in 1953, but Skalski was not informed of the commutation. He remained in prison, never free of the thought that each day could be his last, until a general amnesty was declared for Polish political prisoners in 1956. Skalski emerged from his cell a bitter and deeply resentful man, changed utterly from the person his fellow pilots remembered. At that, he could perhaps count himself lucky. Dozens of other pilots arrested at about the same time *were* executed on trumped-up espionage charges.

Although most of the pilots who returned to Poland managed to escape imprisonment, they were subjected to various forms of harassment and persecution. "I was made to feel like some sort of criminal, a bandit," said one. Many had trouble finding steady work. When they did, it often involved unskilled labor.

On his arrival back in Poland, Łokuciewski managed to get a job as a flying instructor at a Lublin airport. He was fired, however, when two fellow pilots defected to the West. Branded politically suspect after that, Łokuciewski could find no work of any kind for months. During this period, he met a pretty young student at the Catholic University in Lublin. "It was love at first sight," Wanda Łokuciewska recalled years later. "When he proposed to me, he said, 'I am poor, but I am a decent man.'" After they married, Łokuciewski worked briefly as a messenger in his father-in-law's law office. For several years in the early 1950s, the only job he could get was as a common laborer at a soft drink plant.

———

AS WESTERN EUROPE began to recover from the war and the United States headed into an era of extraordinary prosperity, as European colonies in Asia and Africa launched drives for independence, a beggared Poland was thrust back into the shadows of history.

Having spent most of the war pacifying the Soviets, the U.S. government was now trying to contain them. Soon after the conflict ended, massive amounts of U.S. economic aid began pouring into West Germany and Japan, helping to jump-start astonishingly rapid economic recoveries in both countries. By the mid-1950s, West Germany had been rearmed and admitted to NATO, and the Japanese economy was primed for explosive growth. In response, the Soviets tried many counter-strategies—some successful, some colossally unsuccessful. Beginning almost immediately after the war and continuing through the 1980s, they sank ever larger portions of their GDP into conventional and nuclear armaments and later the space program. In 1948, they tried to blockade Berlin. In 1949, they formed the Council for Mutual Economic Assistance (COMECON) with the Communist countries of Eastern Europe, including Poland. In 1955, they. created the Warsaw Pact military alliance. The two great powers were now, in effect, shielded from one another, with allies in both camps fearful that *they* might soon become nuclear battlefields. The main difference was that while Western Europe and Japan thrived, both economically and politically, the Soviet bloc, under Moscow's feudal imperium, sank into varying degrees of Stalinist and post-Stalinist repression and poverty.

In the process, Poland, despite having been a prominent member of the victorious wartime coalition, continued to suffer. It had been ripped apart, and nobody, least of all the Soviets, was helping to put it back together again. Warsaw still lay in ruins. Most of Poland's industrial infrastructure had been looted and dismantled—first by the Germans, then by the Soviets. After the war, much of the country's coal and other raw materials were extracted (without even token environmental protection) and shipped to the USSR. As if that weren't bad enough, Stalin refused to let Poland, or any other Soviet bloc country, accept aid under the U.S. Marshall Plan. Such basic assistance as did get through—blankets, clothing, food, and other emergency supplies—came from organizations like the United Nations Rescue and Relief Association (UNRRA) and often went to the Communist Party faithful.

For the next forty-five years, the economic lives of ordinary Poles, like those of citizens throughout the Soviet bloc (not to mention Communist China), were dominated by shortages and queues. The mere rumor of a shipment of bread or shoes was often enough to create a line of would-be consumers several blocks long. After a visit to Poland in 1960, Martha Gellhorn wrote in *The Atlantic Monthly:* "Young Poles have never known even rudimentary ease; for twenty years the main problem has been [finding enough] to eat." To Gellhorn, Poland, on the surface at least, was synonymous with "dirt and neglect; bad food and scruffy rooms; broken plumbing...filthy, slow, overloaded trains; shoddy goods at absurd prices."

But the shortage felt most keenly in Poland was the shortage of people. More than 6 million Poles, about equally divided between Jews and non-Jews, died in the war. No other country in Europe suffered, proportionately, more damage and casualties. Poland lost about 20 percent of its population, compared to 11 percent for the Soviet Union, 7 percent for Germany, and less than 1 percent for both the United States and Britain. More people died in Warsaw alone during the war than did Americans in both European and Pacific combat theaters.

The deaths of so many was a particularly staggering blow for Poland because they included not only massive numbers of young people, who would have been the country's future, but also most of Poland's prewar educated and professional elite—doctors, lawyers, writers, teachers, judges, professors, engineers, civil servants, business leaders. "This gaping wound in the living flesh and blood of the nation," observed Norman Davies, "...took three decades to heal, and has left permanent scars and disfigurations." Adding to the pain of the Poles' sense of loss was the feeling that once again they had been severed from the West, at least geographically. Their country now shared no borders with a nation not dominated by the Soviet Union. Poles also sensed that relatively few in the West knew—or cared—what had happened to them.

Despite their many contributions to the Allied victory, Poles were not even permitted a place at the table where their own history was written. Once again, they and their nation were defined by others—notably Russia, which had a long record of distorting Polish history, but now also by the West. "History will be kind to me, for I intend to write it," Winston Churchill once said. In his magisterial six-volume history of World War II, he tended to gloss over his policy failures, especially where Poland was concerned. While praising the gallantry of Polish pilots and troops, Churchill suggested that the Poles bore much of the blame for what had happened to their country. "[T]hey doomed themselves by their follies" to suffer these "awful slaughters and miseries," he wrote. Later historians—British and American, Soviet and German—tended to agree.

In many of the most prominent memoirs and histories, Poland, the catalyst of World War II, was treated at best as a rather pitiful victim and at worst as little more than a footnote. In a comprehensive account of the war, A. J. P. Taylor, one of Britain's most noted historians, remarked on how "the devastated cities of Europe—London and Coventry, Berlin, Hamburg and Dresden—became the symbols" of the conflict. There was no mention of Warsaw, the most devastated European city of all.

The repeated failures of the Allies to come to Poland's assistance, despite promises and treaty obligations, were also minimized. So was the important contribution of the Polish armed forces to winning the war. The key part played by Poles in obtaining the Germans' Enigma coding machine and of Polish cryptographers in helping to break the ciphers was not made public until the mid-1970s, and, once revealed, was soon ignored.

In the United States, the fate of Poland was of little interest, except for use as a political weapon by McCarthyites seeking Soviet spies and fellow travelers in and around the Roosevelt administration. Spies and fellow travelers there certainly were, but there is no indication that they had any significant influence on U.S. policy toward Poland. In truth, the abandonment of Poland and the rest of Eastern Europe can be traced to a complex of very human traits exhibited at critical times by Roosevelt, Churchill, and their advisers—fear, insensitivity, naïveté, ignorance, political calculation and ambition, and physical exhaustion.

"When it comes to political disasters, Americans are strangely unwilling to accept an error of judgment as an explanation," the scholar of Soviet history Adam Ulam has observed. "They tend to seek an answer in moral guilt.... The American people were unwilling to recognize themselves as having been naïve and historically unsophisticated, but they were ready to accept that they had been intentionally deceived. Their officials, especially those entrusted with foreign affairs, were accused, in turn, not so much of being misinformed ... as being guilty of virtual treason."

As Poland became a Cold War symbol, enshrouded in a fog of ideology and recrimination, the Poles themselves were forgotten once more.

———————

UNDER SOVIET DOMINATION, the Poles could only watch as Stalin and his men proceeded not only to rewrite their history but to turn justice on its head. No Soviets were ever put on trial or otherwise held accountable for wartime crimes committed in Poland or any of the other countries they occupied. At the Nuremberg War Crimes Trials, Soviet prosecutors even tried—in the end, unsuccessfully—to pin the Katyn massacre of Polish officers on the Germans. It wasn't until 1990, fifty years after the atrocity, that the cover-up ended, and Soviet premier Mikhail Gorbachev finally admitted that the Poles in that forest near Smolensk had indeed been murdered by NKVD and Red Army soldiers.*

Until the late 1970s, it was risky for a Pole to make public mention of Katyn or the 1939 Soviet invasion of Poland. Transgressors could lose their jobs or their place in school. Noted one Polish historian: "The Russian crimes have not only gone unpunished, but we have not even been permitted properly to mourn our dead at their hands." For more than a decade after the war, writing or speaking in public about Prime Minister Sikorski, General Anders, the Kościuszko Squadron pilots, and other Polish World War II heroes was generally considered taboo. Until the fall of communism, schoolchildren were taught a highly distorted, Russocentric version of World War II and its aftermath. One elementary school chronicle declared: "Unfortunately, the Polish reactionary regime [before the war] did not permit our fatherland to become free. Only after the hard experiences of World War Two did the Soviet Union lift up our fatherland from defeat and poverty. For twenty-three years now we have been free ... we owe this to our friends from the east."

Any tombstone or obituary noting that the deceased had served in the Home Army or Polish armed forces in the West was forbidden. War memorials, scattered throughout the country, honored the Red Army and the Poles in its ranks—but not the Poles who fought and died defending their homeland in 1939. In Lwów, the memorial to the three American pilots of Kościuszko Squadron who died during the Soviet-Polish War was vandalized and all reference to their being Americans was obliterated.

---

* The Soviets also admitted to the murders of 11,000 other missing Polish officers during the same period. Those bodies, however, have never been found.

Yet a stubborn, defiant Poland—"that great garden of rampant individualism," as the Polish writer Tadeusz Konwicki has called it—continually resisted Soviet efforts to subjugate it. Popular uprisings and various forms of passive resistance were a regular feature of Polish life under the Communists, and Marxist atheism never had a chance. The Catholic Church's hierarchy and members clung to their faith despite government decrees closing all parochial schools and requiring supervision of appointments to the clergy. Peasants, who after the war still constituted more than half the population, rebelled against collectivization so strenuously that most Polish farms remained private. In trying to govern, Polish Communists were always nervously aware that another uprising could be just around the corner. Stalin himself had it right, back in 1920, when he advised Lenin that "introducing Communism into Poland is like fitting a cow with a saddle."

Just as they had done under the tsars, the Poles clung tightly to their Polishness—their language, music, literature, art, religion, and, above all, their history. At school, children read Communist history textbooks. At home, like their parents and grandparents before them, they read—and reread—Henryk Sienkiewicz's *The Trilogy,* a sweeping nineteenth-century romantic epic about Polish heroes of the past. "Sienkiewicz taught different values and a different code: courage, honor, gentlemanly conduct," said a former Solidarity activist who grew up in the 1960s. "He took my imagination back to a time when Poles, even in adversity, could be confident and proud." *The Trilogy* was "a holy book, a bible of Polish patriotism. Every Polish teenager secretly identified with one of *The Trilogy*'s heroes...."

To the chagrin of the Communist bureaucrats who ruled the country, the Poles proved to be amazingly inventive subversives. They employed gestures great and small to establish their intractability. Instead of calling each other "comrade," for instance, many continued using the traditional forms of address—*pan* and *pani* ("sir" and "madam"). A large number of Polish men also offended Communist etiquette by insisting on the bourgeois custom of kissing women's hands. And the Poles rarely missed an opportunity to make fun of their Soviet masters with characteristic insouciance and dry wit. "Roaring with laughter at Russians is a Polish specialty," wrote Martha Gellhorn, who marveled at the "lionhearted gaiety of these people."

When the rebuilding of Warsaw began, Poles were helpless to prevent the springing up of hundreds of shoddy, ugly, grey-concrete apartment and office blocks that were the hallmark of Stalinist architecture. Nor could they stop the building of the Palace of Science and Culture, a grandiose monstrosity that looms still over the center of the city. But they could, and did, insist that the Polish government support the reconstruction and restoration of *Stare Miasto*, the medieval Old Town that for centuries had been the heart of Warsaw.

In the immediate postwar years, hundreds of Varsovians came after work or on their days off to pick through the rubble of *Stare Miasto* and salvage precious remnants of shattered buildings, including seventeenth-century door frames, fragments of pediments, the heads of plaster angels, the fluted pedestals of statues. These bits and pieces of the past were carefully catalogued and stored, while conservators, using old maps, paintings, and photographs, drew up meticulous plans for the rebuilding of *Stare Miasto*. The actual reconstruction began in 1949. Six years later, this little urban jewel—an area of winding cobblestone streets, Gothic and Baroque churches, and houses with gilded window sashes, intricate carvings, and richly painted facades—once again took its place as the showpiece of Warsaw.

Honoring the past took other forms as well. On numerous street corners in Warsaw (and in other towns and cities throughout Poland), red and white flowers and candles adorned small makeshift shrines to Poles who were executed on those spots by the Nazis. In Powązki Cemetery, Warsaw's oldest, flowers and wreaths were placed daily on a little cobblestone square, unmarked by a plaque or any other identification. The square, according to the British journalist Stewart Steven, was "for many years one of the best-kept secrets in Poland.... [I]t was simply known as Katyn square—a memorial adopted by a people who were officially forbidden one."

In another part of the cemetery, thousands of people gathered each August 1 to commemorate the anniversary of the beginning of the Warsaw uprising and to pay tribute to the Home Army soldiers and other participants who are buried there, their graves marked with simple crosses of white birch. For the Poles, the Warsaw uprising had become the latest cherished legend in their centuries-long history of fighting for their freedom against foreign occupiers. It would prove a vital source of inspiration for the next generation of insurgents in the late 1970s.

———————

AFTER THE BRITISH government's withdrawal of recognition from the Polish government-in-exile, Ambassador Edward Raczyński offered defiant words: "The Polish nation will never give up its right to an independent existence and will never cease to struggle for it."

Over the next thirty-five years, Poles were as good as Raczyński's words. In 1956, workers in Poznań rose up, and the government had to call in the army to restore control. During the "Prague Spring" of 1968, students in Warsaw, Poznań, Lublin, and Kraków demonstrated in support of Czechoslovakia's doomed attempt to create "socialism with a human face." This time the government responded with a campaign against Jews. In 1970, there were mass strikes and demonstrations in opposition to a sharp increase in food prices. Again, the army was brought in, and dozens of demonstrators were killed. A few years after that, a movement of intellectual dissidents sprang up, publishing and distributing underground publications and encouraging workers to organize independent trade unions. Among the labor organizations formed during this period was a union of Gdańsk shipworkers, one of whose members was an electrician by the name of Lech Wałęsa.

The election of Karol Wojtyła, the cardinal of Kraków, as pope in 1978 set off an explosion of Polish nationalism that would have enormous consequences in the years to come. The morning after Wojtyła's election, a young Pole recalled looking around him at the other passengers on a bus. "I felt for the first time the division between 'us,' the people, and 'them,' our rulers," he said. " 'We' were the majority of the people on the normally dreary bus, who were smiling, chatting to strangers, sharing our delight. 'They' were a few morose faces in the back seats...." When millions of Poles turned out in 1979 for John Paul II's first visit to his native land since becoming pope, that same young Pole realized "for the first time that 'we' were more numerous than 'them.' " It was a realization whose time had come in Poland.

The following year, Lech Wałęsa led a shipworkers' strike in Gdańsk that eventually ignited the first mass revolt against a Communist regime in history. This was the uprising that the authorities had always feared: Poles had joined forces under the *Solidarność* banner and were mounting direct, nonviolent resistance to the government. At its peak, Solidarity had more than 10 million members, more than a quarter of the country's population, representing nearly every family in the land. It was a national crusade. Succumbing to Soviet pressure and fearing invasion by the Red Army, the Polish prime minister, General Wojciech Jaruzelski, imposed martial law in December 1981. He ordered Solidarity suppressed; many of its leaders were arrested and thrown in prison.

But the ferment continued. Solidarity went underground, and opposition to the regime gathered force. In the spring of 1989, faced with the threat of new strikes, the Jaruzelski regime in effect admitted defeat and entered into negotiations with opposition leaders. Solidarity was legalized and allowed to participate in that year's parliamentary election. In the first democratic vote in Poland since before World War II, the non-Communist opposition swept virtually every contested seat.* Days later, Tadeusz Mazowiecki, a Catholic intellectual and adviser to Solidarity, became prime minister of Poland, the first non-Communist head of a Soviet-bloc country in more than forty years. Like the tsars before him, and a line of Soviet leaders after him, Stalin had been right to fear a free and democratic Poland. There had been various kinds of rebellions and reforms in other Communist countries, of course—notably in Hungary, Yugoslavia, Czechoslovakia, and even the Soviet Union itself—but nothing quite like this. The rise of Solidarity helped spark a chain reaction. By the early 1990s, totalitarian communism in Europe and Russia had collapsed.

The long night of Poland's soul was over. The people had reclaimed their nation. There would be many difficulties ahead, but the Poles—resilient as ever, forgiving as ever of past betrayals—looked to the West again for friendship and assistance. And this time, the West responded. On July 9, 1997, Poland was admitted to NATO, along with Hungary and the Czech Republic. The following day, the president of the United States, William Jefferson Clinton, arrived in Warsaw to mark the occa-

---

* In 2001, with the country's economy stagnant and considerable corruption in government, the Polish left, including former Communists, gained a parliamentary majority. The change, however, had only marginal effects on either domestic or foreign policy.

sion. In the center of *Stare Miasto*'s cobblestoned Castle Square, he declared: "Together, we will work to secure the future of an undivided Europe—for your freedom and ours."

For your freedom and ours. Time and again, in the course of two full centuries, Poles had carried those words with them into desperate battle and, time and again, had heard them drowned out in the clash of steel and the roar of self-interest. Now an American president was speaking them, and the centuries of steel and self-interest melted away. Thousands of jubilant Poles, packed into the square and surrounding streets, waved their Polish and American flags and cheered. Clinton paused, then continued. "Never again," he said, "will your fate be decided by others. Never again will the birthright of freedom be denied you.

"Poland," he said, "is coming home."

Epilogue

IN A SENSE, World War II did not end in 1945. It ended when the Soviet Union's reformist president, Mikhail Gorbachev, relinquished Soviet control over Poland and the rest of Central and Eastern Europe. When Gorbachev finally curtailed the cruel and ruthless policies of his predecessors and helped precipitate the collapse of the Soviet Empire, the territorial and human rights issues over which World War II was fought were finally resolved.

The end came too late, however, to be of much benefit to those Polish men and women who fought abroad during the war for their country's independence. Many had already died by 1989, and those who were still living often found themselves in bittersweet confusion. The exiles among them had put down roots elsewhere, had lived and worked in other countries, had married and raised children and now were watching their grandchildren grow up. Even so, their hearts remained in Poland. Trapped as they were between two worlds, they had an aura of sadness about them that could not be dispelled, not even by the news that Poland's independence had at last been achieved.

Nor was the exiles' situation that much different from the situation of those who returned to Poland after the war and paid the heavy price exacted by their Soviet-dominated government. For them, too, there was a sense of melancholy. After their return, some had been forced to make significant moral compromises—and had been struggling ever since with the consequences.

IN THE AFTERMATH of Stalin's death in 1953, the Polish government began to soften its attitude toward returnees who had fought with the British. In 1956, Witold Łokuciewski and several other pilots were asked to rejoin the Polish Air Force. Łokuciewski, who lived to fly, did not have to be asked twice. He and a number of other ex-RAF pilots were sent for retraining in modern, Soviet-built aircraft. When Łokuciewski first flew a MiG jet, he so impressed his instructors with his skill that he was pronounced ready for active duty on the spot. Over the next twelve years, he managed to move upward in the Polish Air Force's hierarchy.

Witold Łokuciewski after he rejoined the Polish Air Force in 1956. (Wanda Łokuciewska)

In 1969, Łokuciewski, by this time a full colonel, returned to London as a military attaché for Poland's Communist government. The posting shocked and angered most of the Poles he had flown with during the war, especially those who had remained in exile. In their eyes, Łokuciewski had sold his soul by openly allying himself with the Communists and, through them, the Soviets. "I told him, 'Tolo, you are a bastard, a real bastard. You have no right to come here—to a place where you had a lovely time, a lovely life,' " recalled Ludwik Martel, a fighter pilot who had flown in the Battle of Britain and had settled in London after the war. "He was allowing himself to be used by the Communists. There was no excuse for that."

Witold Łokuciewski, as Polish military attaché, with his wife in London in the early 1970s. Łokuciewski was ostracized by other Polish ex-pilots for accepting a diplomatic post under the Communist regime. (Wanda Łokuciewska)

Other former close friends of Łokuciewski's, people he had flown with, laughed and partied with, treated him as a pariah. They excluded him from gatherings of Polish ex-pilots and shunned him whenever they happened to encounter him on the London social circuit. During one reception, Łokuciewski spotted Tadeusz Andersz, who had been a year behind him at Dęblin and was a member of 315 Squadron during the war. Striding toward Andersz, Łokuciewski thrust out his hand. "I looked at him," Andersz recalled, "turned 180 degrees, and walked away."

Łokuciewski, who by most accounts was hardly a political sophisticate, offered little explanation or justification for accepting a diplomatic post under the Communist regime. When Martel confronted him, his only response was: "They made me do it." In any case, a great fissure had opened between the pilots in England and their former brothers-in-arms in Poland. According to Ignacy Olszewski, one of the former RAF pilots who rejoined the Polish Air Force in 1956, "the boys who stayed in England" looked down on those who went back to Poland. They accused the returnees of being Communists, even when they were not, and the rift was never mended.

In Łokuciewski's case, his non-Communist friends in Poland, though they also deplored what he had done, had a far better understanding of how things were, of how difficult it was to maintain one's moral balance in the environment in which they were forced to live. Polish Nobel laureate Czesław Miłosz, who spent time as a diplomat under the Communist government, has noted how easy it is for someone in a free society to condemn the moral compromises of someone forced to live under totalitarianism. "Those people . . . who showed a more or less open disgust toward us," Miłosz wrote, "did not see the extent of the moral problem."

As for Łokuciewski, when he completed his London tour as military attaché in 1972, he returned to Warsaw, and two years after that, retired from the air force. The ostracism by so many former colleagues was a deep and lasting wound—the "greatest pain" he would suffer until the end of his life, said one friend.

On April 17, 1990, in Warsaw, Witold Łokuciewski died. He was seventy-three years old.

ONE NIGHT IN the mid-1960s, a number of the pilots who had flown in Britain and who now lived in Poland gathered for a party at Warsaw's Bristol Hotel. Their host was Jan Zumbach, visiting from his home in Paris. Zumbach ordered a bottle of cognac for each man, and when all those had been drunk, he ordered a second round of bottles. "It was such a good party," remarked a Polish aviation historian, "that the hotel staff was spinning stories about it for years afterward."

Gregarious, friendly, and charming as ever, Zumbach had no time for rifts, rivalries, or partisanship. He stayed on good terms with his wartime buddies in Poland as well as with his chums in England. Witold Łokuciewski, for instance, remained one of his closest friends. Tolo's assignment as air attaché in London never seemed to bother "Johnny" Zumbach, who knew a bit about what it felt like to be a black sheep.

Shortly after the war, Zumbach and two other former RAF pilots started a charter air transport company that became a cover for a bank-note-smuggling operation. Its activities soon expanded to include the shipping of Swiss watches to London, gold bars from Tangier to France, Israeli agents to Palestine, and various kinds of weapons to various kinds of countries.

After several years of this, having stayed one step ahead of the law the whole time, Zumbach retired from smuggling and went more or less straight. With the money he had made, he opened a discothèque in Paris. In time, he married a French woman less than half his age and fathered a son. But life eventually became a little too sedate for Johnny Zumbach. In 1962, he went into the mercenary business, setting up a primitive air force for Katanga, the breakaway Congolese province. Five years later, using the alias "Johnny Brown," he performed the same ser-vice for Biafra during its war with Nigeria. On bombing raids, Zumbach was the pilot of Biafra's only aircraft, a World War II–vintage B-26, while his bombardier, an Ibo tribesman, dropped homemade explosives on Nigerian targets.

Many of Zumbach's former Polish Air Force colleagues were scan-dalized by his postwar pursuits. Still, he managed, with his abundance of easy charm and generosity, to retain their affection and friendship. More than fifty years after the war, the mere mention of his name would invariably bring a smile to the faces of old friends. "Ah, *Johnny*!" they would sigh, remembering.

Even at seventy, an age when most men are firmly retired, Zumbach was still living on the edge. "Trouble comes naturally to some men," he once wrote. In late 1985, he told Ludwik Martel in London that he was involved in a hush-hush deal that was going to make him a lot of money. "It was clear," Martel said, "that something fishy was going on." A cou-ple of weeks later, Zumbach phoned Tolo Łokuciewski in Warsaw and talked vaguely about some "buying and selling" he was doing.

The next day—January 3, 1986—Łokuciewski received another phone call, with a message that left him in shock: seventy-one-year-old "Johnny" Zumbach had been found dead in Paris. No cause of death was ever announced, but many of his friends were certain he had met with foul play.

———————

ZDZISŁAW AND WANDA Krasnodębski emigrated to Cape Town, South Africa, in 1948, and lived there for more than two years before picking up stakes again. For the most part, Krasnodębski's life as an exile was a sad and unhappy one. Of all the Kościuszko Squadron veterans, he was perhaps the least well equipped for the postwar world. He was older than the others—forty-one when the war ended. He had no real skills, except for flying, and couldn't do that for a living because his hands had been so badly burned during the Battle of Britain.

This proud man, the former commander his men called "the King," could find no other job in Cape Town but driving a taxi. The local cabbies, furious that foreigners like Krasnodębski were muscling in and robbing them of fares, sabotaged his cab and otherwise made his life miserable. By 1951, he had had enough. He and Wanda left for Canada, where he held a number of blue-collar jobs, including one as an inspector on a television set assembly line.

In their later years, the Krasnodębskis, who were childless, lived a rather spartan life in a small Toronto apartment. As an old man, the former Kościuszko Squadron commander took considerable pleasure in reminiscing about that terrible yet somehow golden summer and fall of 1940 when he and his men helped defeat the vaunted Luftwaffe in the Battle of Britain. For the British author Richard Collier, who interviewed him for a book on the battle, Krasnodębski painted word pictures of those days, describing, among other things, "the electric excitement of young [Ludwik] Paszkiewicz's first combat, and the comradeship of those...nights at The Orchard restaurant." After listening to Krasnodębski's vivid stories, Collier wrote, "you sense how infinitely precious life was then."

Above all, in those final years, Krasnodębski thought about his country. Most émigré Poles could hardly do otherwise. Eva Hoffman, who emigrated as a child, wrote that "[t]he largest presence within me is the welling up of absence, of what I have lost." Krasnodębski, too, was filled with longing.

A historian in Warsaw who corresponded with him in the 1970s

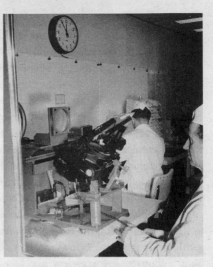

Zdzisław Krasnodębski working as a technical inspector at a television factory in Canada after the war. (Stanisław Blasiak)

recalled that "you could feel the nostalgia in his letters. He was bitter about the way he had been cast off. But more important than that, he missed Poland very, very much. And he knew he could never come back. The bitterness, the way he missed his country—that's what finally killed him."

Krasnodębski died in Toronto on July 3, 1980, when he was seventy-six years old.

––––––––––

FOR WITOLD URBANOWICZ, the adjustment to postwar life was also traumatic. Like the others in his famous squadron, Urbanowicz, who lived in the United States, had gone from being a hero to being a nonentity. The adrenaline-filled excitement of the war had vanished, replaced by the routine of daily life.

Urbanowicz and other Poles were not alone in facing that adjustment, of course. Regardless of country, many World War II veterans found it difficult to resume their former lives after a period in which, dreadful as it often was, they had never felt more alive. But, unlike the Poles, many veterans could more or less pick up where they left off before the war, and those returning to the increasingly prosperous United States could look forward to a bright future: marriage, kids, college on the G.I. Bill, a well-paying job, a house in the suburbs. "Life was good," recalled Francis Gabreski, the top U.S. fighter ace in Europe, who married his childhood sweetheart shortly after returning home, fathered nine children, and eventually became president of the Long Island Railroad. "I was a lucky guy." The Poles Gabreski flew with, however, were on a "different road," he said. "They were dispossessed of everything; they had to find their own homes, their own futures. Nobody said to them, 'I'm going to take care of you, son.' "

After the war, Urbanowicz and his family moved to New York, where he worked in a series of low-level marketing and production control positions for Eastern and American Airlines and Republic Aviation. For many years, he was a disappointed, bitter, and unhappy man, recalled his son, also named Witold. This new life—a little house in a blue-collar Queens neighborhood, a low-paying, unrewarding desk job—was not at all what Urbanowicz had in mind when he'd started out as an ambitious young fighter pilot in Poland. "He had done all these amazing things," said his son. "Then it all just fell apart. He went through these long, long periods of loneliness and depression."

To the younger Urbanowicz, his father was a distant figure—difficult to know, impossible to understand. They didn't spend much time together. Urbanowicz often worked at night and had little interest in baseball or any of his son's other pastimes. But there was another, more profound gap between them. Young Witold was a typical American kid growing up in the 1950s. He watched television, participated in sports, and formed his own rhythm-and-blues band. His father had grown up in a completely different world. As a child, he had shot wolves from his grandfather's sleigh as the old Polish revolutionary traveled about the country at night, distributing anti-Russian literature. As a young man, Urbanowicz had watched Warsaw burn, had engineered a hair-raising escape from the Russians, had seen family and close friends die, had lost his country.

In the 1960s, as the Vietnam War escalated and student revolts erupted, the Urbanowiczes, father and son, also had little in common politically: young Witold was a liberal; his father, very much a conservative. But the son, by now a student at New York University, also felt the pull of his family's long, illustrious military history. He told his father that he was "really torn" about whether to serve in Vietnam. The father, conservative though he was, unhesitatingly advised against it. "This family has given enough to war," he said. "You're the last Urbanowicz. We've given enough." His son took the advice and obtained a student deferment.

His father, meanwhile, still yearning for his country, found solace in certain new interests and pursuits. He started to write and found he was good at it. He turned out several books in Polish, among them accounts of his days of combat flying in Poland, in Britain with the RAF, and in China with the 75th Squadron. Ironically, the only publisher he could find was in Poland, at that point still under Communist rule, and his books were heavily censored. Even so, he took great pride in them.

He took even more pride in the accomplishments of his son, who became an executive at Chase Manhattan Bank. "When I was made vice president..., my father couldn't stop talking about it," the younger Urbanowicz recalled. "He was so thrilled, because I was able to do in this society what he was unable to do—succeed." After young Witold married and had two children, his father became a doting grandfather.

And there was another important comfort in Urbanowicz's middle and old age—ten acres of land that he bought on Martha's Vineyard, many years before that island off the Massachusetts coast became so fashionable and expensive. Urbanowicz never built on his marshy, windswept parcel, which reminded him of his native eastern Poland. He was content just to walk it, to stand on it, to gaze eastward from it toward the Atlantic—and home. "To him, it was '*moja ziemia*,'" his son recalled. "He meant, 'My land here,' but he also meant, 'My land there, in Europe...Poland.'"

The younger Urbanowicz didn't realize how much the land meant to his father until years later, when he suggested that it be sold. "Martha's Vineyard was very, very hot by then, and I thought he could make a big profit on the property and invest the money. Well, he went ballistic. He was furious that I would even suggest such a thing. I understood then what the land symbolized to him. It was his anchor. He needed it desperately."

In June 1991, Witold Urbanowicz, at the age of eighty-three, was finally invited back to his real *ziemia*—back to Poland. After more than fifty years in exile, the Kościuszko Squadron's leading Polish ace returned in a kind of delayed triumph. Everywhere he went, this tall, thin, elegant man with the white mustache he had grown in his later years—still looking very much the "Englishman," as he was known to his cadets—was mobbed. Visiting Dęblin, where he was a flight instructor when the Germans attacked in 1939, he leaned on his walking stick and wandered through the lovely eighteenth-century manor house which still serves as the school's headquarters. He saw the ballroom where he had danced at glittering formal balls, the underground nightclub where he had partied with his fellow instructors. The war's bomb damage had been repaired, and the school seemed much the same as in the 1930s. Urbanowicz felt fifty years younger, he said, and tears shone in his eyes.

He returned to Warsaw the following year as part of a large delegation of Polish pilots who had flown with the RAF. The old veterans were deeply moved as the official standard of the Polish Air Force in Britain, embroidered with an image of the Virgin Mary and the motto, "Love Demands Sacrifice," was at long last established in its rightful place by émigré Polish pilots and several high-ranking RAF officers. They and the standard had flown from London aboard the official aircraft of the president of Poland, Lech Wałęsa. In Wałęsa's presence, the standard was solemnly transferred to the Polish Air Force and later moved to Dęblin, where it remains today, in a place of honor.

Urbanowicz "came back glowing" from these trips, his son recalled. "He was absolutely in heaven." He went back several more times in succeeding years, once to accept a promotion to general in the Polish Air Force. During his last visit to Poland, a few weeks before he died in 1996, he spoke to a group of young fighter pilots in Warsaw, urging them to uphold the honor and rich tradition of those who had gone before them.

That tradition was gradually reshaped into some semblance of its former self during Poland's post-Communist years. Schoolchildren learned the truth about the pilots who flew with the RAF in World War II, many of whom were officially honored as national heroes. Some became local heroes, too. In the town of Ostrów Wielpolski, the elementary school attended by Mirosław ("Ox") Ferić is now named for him. The school's 600 students are taught about Ferić's exploits during the war, about his diary, about his love of country. The school newspaper, published every two months, is called *Ox*. On the sixtieth anniversary of his death, the children sent flowers for Mika Ferić's grave in distant England.

Polish pilots who flew under British command in World War II return the official Polish Air Force standard to their native country in 1992, three years after the fall of the Communist regime. The commander in chief of the Polish Air Force receives the standard while Lech Wałęsa, president of Poland, looks on. (Polish Institute and Sikorski Museum)

SOME TWENTY YEARS after the war, Kościuszko Squadron flight leader John Kent wrote about the Polish pilots: "We who were privileged to fly and fight with them will never forget, and Britain must never forget, how much she owes to the loyalty, indomitable spirit and sacrifice of these Polish fliers." Yet, in Britain and elsewhere, there has been little official recognition of the vital role played by the pilots and the rest of the Polish armed forces during the war or of the Poles' wartime and postwar anguish. Even during the 1980s and 1990s, when the fortieth and fiftieth anniversaries of various events connected with the war were celebrated, recognition somehow bypassed the Poles. In June 1984, during the fortieth anniversary celebrations of D-Day, the beaches at Normandy were lined with the flags of Britain, the United States, Norway, the Netherlands, and a host of other wartime Allies. But the Polish flag was missing. Again, when the British commemorated the fabled Enigma codebreakers at Bletchley Park, there was scant reference to the Polish cryptographers who helped make the breakthrough possible. And although the Allied liberation of Paris was remembered in many forums, the Warsaw uprising was all but forgotten.

In 1993, an imposing monument was unveiled by Britain's Queen Mother on the cliffs of Dover in honor of the RAF fighter squadrons that took part in the Battle of Britain. The memorial was adorned with the insignia of sixty-six squadrons—but those of the Poznań and Kościuszko squadrons, the only all-Polish units at the time, were missing, even though the latter was responsible for more German kills than any other squadron in the RAF. The exclusion was a "resounding *faux pas*," declared the *Financial Times*. The highly embarrassed people responsible for the monument insisted that the omission was an oversight and the two missing insignia were quickly added.

The forgetfulness has not been universal, however. As the twenty-first century began, several former Polish pilots living in Britain said they had noted a resurgence of interest among the British people. Franciszek Kornicki, who commanded a couple of Polish squadrons during the war, observed that a young English doctor whom he had recently consulted told him: "We owe a great debt to you." Schools and other organizations, Kornicki said, were now inviting him and his colleagues to speak on their efforts to help defend Britain.

At the Orchard restaurant near Northolt, some 14 miles outside central London, black-and-white photographs of young men in RAF uniforms, wearing Polish eagle badges, decorate the walls. They are there today, kneeling beside their Hurricanes and Spitfires, petting their mascots, lounging in deck chairs on the lawn waiting for the call to action, playing chess, smoking, talking, laughing.

The Poles' wartime hangout has been modernized a bit under its current owners, the Beefeater Gin people. The dance floor and orchestra are gone. Customers are no longer greeted by a maitre d' in tailcoat and gloves. But the Orchard remembers its past—and the dashing young foreigners who once considered it a second home. Outside, on the lawn in front of the restaurant, is a plaque: "In thankful memory of the gallant Polish airmen who gave their lives in the defence of the United Kingdom in World War II."

A few miles away, there is a memorial of another sort. In a corner of Northwood Cemetery, five neat rows of identical white headstones mark the graves of more than fifty Northolt-based Polish pilots killed during the Battle of Britain and afterward. Here, during the height of the war, their bodies were brought, the simple wooden coffins borne shoulder-high by members of their squadrons, a Catholic priest officiating at the rites. Mika Ferić lies in one of these graves. In the next row are Jozef František, the Czech who called himself a Pole, and Ludwik Paszkiewicz.

Polish pilots and air crew killed in World War II are buried in 139 cemeteries throughout Britain, from the hills of Devon to the Scottish Highlands. The largest number of Poles—346, most of them from bomber crews—are interred in the cemetery in the pretty little town of Newark-upon-Trent, in Nottinghamshire. A large stone cross stands over their graves, engraved with the words *Za Wolność* ("For Freedom"). On the other side of the cross is inscribed a quotation from St. Paul, which could stand as the credo of the nearly 2,000 Polish airmen who died while fighting under British command in World War II:

> *I have fought a good fight,*
> *I have finished my course,*
> *I have kept the faith.*

Notes

PROLOGUE

3 They marched: *Daily Telegraph* and *The Times,* June 9, 1946.

4 Standing along the parade route: Witold Urbanowicz, *Początek Jutra* (Kraków: Znak, 1966).

4 Writing in *Collier's:* M. Lisiewicz et al., eds., *Destiny Can Wait: The Polish Air Force in the Second World War* (Nashville, Tenn.: Battery Press, 1949), p. 77.

5 A week earlier: *Daily Telegraph,* June 5, 1946, p. 4.

5 "If Poland had not": Speech by Queen Elizabeth II to Polish *Sejm* and Senate, Warsaw, March 26, 1996.

6 "If it had been given": Quoted in Władysław Anders, *An Army in Exile: The Story of the Second Polish Corps* (New York and London: Macmillan, 1949), p. 183.

6 "We wanted Poland back": Witold Urbanowicz speech, National Air and Space Museum, Washington, D.C., Nov. 17, 1981.

6 "We shall conquer": Jan Ciechanowski, *Defeat in Victory* (Garden City, N.Y.: Doubleday, 1947), p. 15.

6 "the Glamor Boys": Quentin Reynolds, *A London Diary* (New York: Random House, 1941), p. 73.

6 "Why are you crying": Adam Zamoyski, *The Forgotten Few: The Polish Air Force in the Second World War* (New York: Hippocrene, 1995), p. 4.

PART ONE

CHAPTER ONE

9 The night before the barnstormers: Jan Zumbach, *On Wings of War* (London: André Deutsch, 1975), p. 35.

10 "swore by all the saints": Ibid., p. 36.

10 At just about this same time: Interviews with Edward Idzior and Irena Rothkael.

11 Of particular renown: Adam Zamoyski, *The Polish Way: A Thousand-Year History of the Poles and Their Culture* (London: John Murray, 1987), p. 3.
11 Sitting on the restaurant terrace: Witold Urbanowicz, "Blaski I Cieni," *Tygodnik Powszechny* 14 (1961).
12 Among the teenagers: Interview with Jadwiga Piłsudska.
12 "Yet, try as she might": Zumbach, *On Wings*, p. 12.
13 The new cadets came: Zamoyski, *Forgotten Few*, p. 12.
13 "Remember": Cadet's Code, Dęblin Archives.
13 To show off for girlfriends: Zamoyski, *Forgotten Few*, p. 14.
13 Łokuciewski, who came from: Untitled MS by Tadeusz Dalecki.
14 In the class of 1938: Class rankings, Dęblin Archives.
14 According to a Polish Air Force historian: Interview with official historian, Dęblin.
14 "We were trained to scan": Interview with Tadeusz Anderz.
14 In one exercise: Zumbach, *On Wings*, p. 46.
15 Among the Yank volunteers: Robert F. Karolevitz and Ross S. Fenn, *Flight of Eagles: The Story of the American Kosciuszko Squadron in the Polish-Russian War 1919–1920* (Sioux Falls, S.D.: Brevet Press, 1974), p. 23.

CHAPTER TWO

16 Growing up in Jacksonville: Merian Cooper biographical sketch, Cooper Papers, Special Collections, Harold B. Lee Library, Brigham Young University (BYU).
18 Young Merian Cooper: Ibid.
19 The resultant American victory: James S. Pula, *Thaddeus Kościuszko: The Purest Son of Liberty* (New York: Hippocrene, 1999), p. 99.
19 "Let us be honest": Ibid., p. 100.
20 Catherine did not think much: Ibid., p. 217.
21 In 1794, he led: Ibid., p. 227.
22 In a separate, earlier will: Ibid., p. 252.
22 "as pure a son of liberty": Ibid., p. 248.
23 "Poland might be": Zamoyski, *Polish Way*, p. 4.
23 The Polish flag, national anthem: Norman Davies, *Heart of Europe: A Short History of Poland* (Oxford: Oxford University Press, 1984), p. 269.
23 Prussian forces melted down: Zamoyski, *Polish Way*, p. 5.
23 Wiped out were the centuries: Ibid.
25 "I am the happiest": Merian Cooper, letter to his father, undated, Cooper Papers, BYU.
25 "The only thing": Merian Cooper, letter to his father, Jan. 23, 1919, Cooper Papers, BYU.
26 "stubborn as a mule": Marguerite Harrison, *There's Always Tomorrow* (New York: Farrar & Rinehart, 1936), p. 230.
26 Nearly half a million of its people: Richard M. Watt, *Bitter Glory: Poland and Its Fate, 1918 to 1939* (New York: Simon & Schuster, 1979), p. 80.
27 In dirty, dilapidated Warsaw: Harrison, *There's Always*, p. 224.

27 "Rarely had I experienced": Arthur Bliss Lane, *I Saw Poland Betrayed* (Indianapolis: Bobbs-Merrill, 1948), p. 29.

28 The conquest of Wilno: Watt, *Bitter Glory,* p. 98.

28 Convinced that the Bolshevik leader: Ibid., p. 108.

28 Lenin ordered his troops: Norman Davies, *White Eagle, Red Star* (London: Macdonald, 1972), p. 140.

28 "It is easier to saddle": Davies, *Heart of Europe,* p. 3.

28 "to probe Europe": Watt, *Bitter Glory,* p. 134.

29 "There is romance to the word 'Poland' ": Merian Cooper autobiography (unpublished), Cooper Papers, BYU.

30 He had grown up: Fauntleroy obituary, newspaper clipping, December 1963, Cooper Papers, BYU.

30 The Kościuszko Squadron and three Polish squadrons: Jerzy B. Cynk, *The Polish Air Force at War: The Official History, 1939–1943* (Atglen, Pa.: Schiffer, 1998), p. 35; cited hereafter as *The PAF.*

30 From an altitude of about 600 feet: Cooper autobiography, Cooper Papers, BYU.

31 General Antoni Listowski: Rosme Curtis, *Winged Tenacity* (London: Kingston Hill, 1944), p. 6.

31 given most of the credit. Cynk, *The PAF,* p. 35.

32 According to the British historian: Quoted in Davies, *White Eagle,* p. ix.

32 He had been the political commissar attached to: Robert Conquest, *Stalin: Breaker of Nations* (New York: Viking Press, 1991), p. 87.

32 Stalin countermanded the order: Robert Payne, *The Rise and Fall of Stalin* (New York: Avon Books, 1966), p. 295.

32 When the divided Soviet armies: Davies, *White Eagle,* pp. 218–19.

32 It was from a man: Harrison, *There's Always,* p. 349.

CHAPTER THREE

35 "Poland's existence is intolerable": Cynk, *The PAF,* p. 58.

35 "may safely count": Ibid.

36 The future prime minister Harold Macmillan: William Manchester, *The Last Lion: Winston Spencer Churchill: Alone, 1932–1940* (New York: Dell, 1988), p. 468.

36 So did more than a few: Ibid., p. 88.

36 "The Poles have completely": Davies, *White Eagle,* p. 243.

37 "Peace is a valuable": Watt, *Bitter Glory,* p. 40.

37 "will fight": Ibid., p. 396.

37 "While Poland": Philip Cannistraro, Edward D. Wynot, and Theodore P. Kovaleff, eds., *Poland and the Coming of the Second World War: The Diplomatic Papers of A. J. Drexel Biddle Jr.* (Columbus: Ohio State University Press, 1976), p. 62.

37 On March 31, Prime Minister Chamberlain: Cynk, *The PAF,* p. 62.

37 In later talks: Jan Karski, *The Great Powers and Poland, 1919–1945* (Lanham, Md.: University Press of America, 1985), p. 331.

38 "This time, at least": Edward Raczyński, *In Allied London* (London: Weidenfeld & Nicolson, 1962), p. 20.

38 A *New York Times* correspondent: Robert Kee, *1939: The World We Left Behind* (Boston: Little, Brown, 1984), p. 189.

38 Hugh Dalton: Waclaw Jedrzejewicz, ed., *Poland and the British Parliament, 1939–1945*, vol. 1 (New York: Piłsudski Institute, 1946), pp. 125–26.

38 Finally, in August: Anthony Read and David Fisher, *The Deadly Embrace* (London: Michael Joseph, 1988), p. 108.

38 That July, while the aid: David Kahn, *Seizing the Enigma: The Race to Break the German U-Boat Codes, 1939–1943* (Boston: Houghton Mifflin, 1991), pp. 79–80.

39 Many years after the war: Gordon Welchman, *The Hut Six Story* (New York: McGraw-Hill, 1982), p. 289.

39 In a memoir of the period: Rulka Langer, *The Mermaid and the Messerschmitt* (New York: Roy, 1942), p. 20.

40 By the early 1930s: Watt, *Bitter Glory*, p. 292.

40 "Old Town": Maria and Andrzej Szypowski, *As You Enter the Old Town . . .* (Warsaw: Artibus Foundation, 2001), p. 109.

40 Every evening at twilight: Dorothy Adams, *We Stood Alone* (New York: Longmans, Green, 1944), p. 66.

40 A popular posting for foreign diplomats: Watt, *Bitter Glory*, p. 293.

41 Since taking office in 1934: Langer, *Mermaid*, p. 196.

41 The worldwide Great Depression: Watt, *Bitter Glory*, p. 293.

41 Anti-Semitism in this once most tolerant: Zamoyski, *Polish Way*, p. 347.

42 "Even admitting the defects": Raymond Leslie Buell, *Poland: Key to Europe* (New York: Knopf, 1939), p. i.

42 Also in 1938: "Hoover Predicts Poland's Rebirth," *New York Times*, Oct. 12, 1939.

44 On August 22, 1939: Quoted in Alan Bullock, *Hitler and Stalin: Parallel Lives* (New York: Knopf, 1991), p. 622.

44 When Starzyński called for volunteers: Alexander Polonius, *I Saw the Siege of Warsaw* (Glasgow: W. Hodge, 1941), p. 18.

44 During the warm, clear: Clare Hollingworth, *The Three Weeks' War in Poland* (London: Duckworth, 1940), p. 9.

44 At a late-night supper: Virgilia Sapieha, *Polish Profile* (London: Heinemann, 1940), p. 294.

44 "The Poles are a delightful": William L. Shirer, *Berlin Diary* (New York: Knopf, 1941), p. 153.

45 "For good or ill": Walter Duranty, "Poland," *The Atlantic Monthly* (September 1939), p. 393.

45 "my dream come true": Zdzisław Krasnodębski, "History of the Kościuszko Squadron," May 1973, Polish Institute, London.

46 If his wife, Wanda: Witold Urbanowicz, "Zdzisław Krasnodębski," *Skrzydła*, 122/608.

46 They had met: Interview with Wanda Krasnodębska (Stanisław Blasiak).

46 In a diary he began: Ferić diary, Lot A V 49/34/1, Polish Institute, London.

46 Germany had at its disposal: Cynk, *The PAF*, p. 70.

47 The Polish fighters' undercarriages: Zamoyski, *Forgotten Few*, p. 25.

47 "Pitiful": William L. Shirer, *The Nightmare Years* (Boston: Little, Brown, 1984), p. 386.

48 The elder Urbanowicz: Interview with Witold Urbanowicz (son).

49 "Right afterward": Tadeusz Malinowski, "Witold Urbanowicz w Polsce," *Lotnictwo* (July 1991).

49 On another occasion: Witold Urbanowicz speech, National Air and Space Museum, Washington, D.C., Nov. 17, 1981.

50 Krasnodębski "was wrong": Ibid.

50 Later, in a nightclub: Ibid.

50 On August 29: Anthony Drexel Biddle cable to Cordell Hall, Aug. 30, 1939, Diplomatic Correspondence Files, FDR Library.

50 It was the fourth largest: "Poland's Might," *Newsweek*, July 31, 1939, p. 16.

50 There were thirty-nine infantry: Andrzej Suchcitz, "Poland's Contribution to the Allied Victory in the Second World War," Polish Institute, London.

51 CBS's William Shirer: Shirer, *Nightmare Years*, p. 386.

51 No longer relying solely: David T. Zabecki, "Invasion of Poland," *World War II* (September 1999), p. 28.

51 Dawn had just broken: Urbanowicz, *Początek Jutra.*

51 called "the Englishman": Interview with Tadeusz Anderz.

52 "You're alive": Interview with Witold Urbanowicz, TV documentary *White Eagles in Borrowed Skies.*

52 In the first wave of the attack: Cynk, *The PAF,* p. 73.

53 The Germans: Ibid.

53 But the Luftwaffe: Lisiewicz et al., eds., *Destiny,* p. 11.

53 The odds against a Polish victory: Ferić diary, Lot A V 49/34/1, Polish Institute, London.

53 "The lovely Polish autumn": Ibid.

53 The Warsaw Pursuit Brigade: Cynk, *The PAF,* p. 79.

54 "Each of us was taught": Urbanowicz, *Początek Jutra.*

54 In the first days of the war: Zamoyski, *Forgotten Few,* p. 23.

54 On September 3: Zdzisław Krasnodębski, "Playing with Fire," *Guinea Pig* (Summer 1973).

54 On the first day of the war: Julien Bryan, *Siege* (Garden City, N.Y.: Doubleday, 1940), p. 10.

54 But in a secret message: Richard C. Lukas, *The Forgotten Holocaust: The Poles Under German Occupation, 1939–1944* (New York: Hippocrene, 1997), p. 3.

55 The Führer commanded his men: Quoted in Cynk, *The PAF,* p. 61.

55 "Everything around us": Urbanowicz, *Początek Jutra.*

55 They strafed toddlers: Anders, *Army in Exile,* p. 3.

55 During one raid: Stephen Baley, *Two Septembers* (London: Allen & Unwin, 1941), p. 26.

55 In the town of Sulejów: Martin Gilbert, *The Second World War: A Complete History* (New York: Henry Holt, 1987), p. 4.

CHAPTER FOUR

56 During World War I, he had lost: Davies, *White Eagle,* p. 94.

56 "I saw": Adrian Carton de Wiart, *Happy Odyssey* (London: Jonathan Cape, 1950), p. 156.

56 From the outset, Chamberlain: Nicholas Bethell, *The War Hitler Won: The Fall of Poland, September 1939* (London: Allen Lane, 1972), p. 12.

57 "I had never seen": Sir Edward Spears, *Assignment to Catastrophe* (London: Heinemann, 1954), p. 18.

57 "For two whole days": L. S. Amery, *My Political Life*, vol. 3: *The Unforgiving Years, 1929–1940* (London: Hutchinson, 1955), p. 324.

57 "I am gravely disturbed": Adrian Ball, *The Last Day of the Old World* (Garden City, N.Y.: Doubleday, 1963), pp. 15–16.

57 Late on the night: Raczyński, *In Allied London*, p. 29.

58 "The time has passed": William L. Shirer, *Collapse of the Third Republic* (New York: Simon & Schuster, 1969), p. 499.

58 "It isn't right!": Ball, *The Last Day*, pp. 27–28.

58 By early afternoon, more than 100,000: Polonius, *I Saw the Siege*, p. 34.

58 Waving improvised: Langer, *Mermaid*, pp. 81–82.

58 Playfully, they threw: Polonius, *I Saw the Siege*, p. 35.

59 "the West is": Davies, *Heart of Europe*, p. 345.

59 the "last hours": Ball, *The Last Day*, p. 153.

59 a British novelist, Margery Allingham: Brian Gardner, *Churchill in His Time: A Study in a Reputation, 1939–1945* (London: Methuen, 1968), p. 20.

59 "didn't really translate into": Eric Sevareid, *Not So Wild a Dream* (New York: Atheneum, 1976), p. 109.

59 "conviction that": Ibid., p. 110.

59 On September 4: Kee, *1939*, p. 304.

59 only "military objectives": Amery, *My Political Life*, p. 329.

59 "Loathing war": Ibid., p. 328.

60 In one of his cables: Kennard telegram to Foreign Office, Sept. 13, 1939, FO 371/22882, Public Records Office (PRO).

60 A young officer: Bethell, *The War Hitler Won*, p. 166.

60 "this tacit bargain": Hollingworth, *Three Weeks' War*, p. 72.

60 At a meeting of the War Cabinet: Manchester, *Last Lion*, p. 576.

60 "not have the means": Kee, *1939*, p. 308.

61 "the Leaflet-of-the-Month Club": Mollie Panter-Downes, *London War Notes, 1939–1945* (New York: Farrar, Straus & Giroux, 1973), p. 6.

61 "What are you": Virginia Cowles, *Looking for Trouble* (New York: Harper, 1941), p. 275.

61 It was "ignominious": Spears, *Assignment to Catastrophe*, p. 31.

61 "Are you aware": Ibid., p. 32.

61 "Smigły-Rydz will never": Carton de Wiart, *Happy Odyssey*, p. 159.

61 The day before the exodus: Cynk, *The PAF*, p. 79.

62 "There was so much": Ferić diary, Lot A V 49/34/1, Polish Institute, London.

62 In Lublin, the brigade encountered: Cynk, *The PAF*, p. 89.

62 As soon as he heard: Zumbach, *On Wings*, p. 48.

63 "They wanted to fight": Urbanowicz, *Początek Jutra*.

63 "miserable machines": Ibid.

63 Dejected, he returned: Ibid.

63 For three days, they drove: Zabecki, "Invasion of Poland," p. 32.

63 "They did not come forward": Gilbert, *Second World War,* p. 7.

64 "We must have": John McCutcheon Raleigh, *Behind the Nazi Front* (New York: Dodd, Mead, 1940), p. 9.

64 "Nothing had been prepared": Ball, *The Last Day,* p. 85.

65 "Germany having killed": *New York Times,* Sept. 18, 1939.

65 In Dubno, Soviet soldiers: Jan T. Gross, *Revolution from Abroad: The Soviet Conquest of Poland's Western Ukraine and Western Belorussia* (Princeton: Princeton University Press, 1988), p. 40.

65 "indignation and horror": John Coutouvidis and Jaime Reynolds, *Poland, 1939–1947* (New York: Holmes & Meier, 1986), p. 22.

65 "forgotten their obligations": Jedrzejewicz, *Poland and the British Parliament,* p. 273.

65 the "indomitable pride": Cowles, *Looking for Trouble,* p. 270.

66 "It was a horrible moment": Zamoyski, *Forgotten Few,* p. 33.

66 "Destiny": Baley, *Two Septembers,* p. 31.

66 "the heart and soul": Władysław Szpilman, *The Pianist: The Exraordinary True Story of One Man's Survival in Warsaw, 1939–45* (New York: Picador, 1999), p. 38.

67 Not knowing if her husband: Interview with Wanda Krasnodębska (Stanisław Blasiak).

67 Newspapers were still published: Bryan, *Siege,* p. 28.

67 "like a conquering Caesar": Shirer, *Berlin Diary,* p. 216.

67 "like being in a steel drum": Hollingworth, *Three Weeks' War,* p. 130.

67 a grey pall of smoke: Baley, *Two Septembers,* p. 42.

68 "In the agony": Kee, *1939,* pp. 315–16.

68 "All the world": Ibid., p. 316.

68 "When will the effective": Ibid.

68 but the Poles could rest assured that: Anita Prażmowska, *Britain and Poland, 1939–1943: The Betrayed Ally* (Cambridge: Cambridge University Press, 1995), p. 36.

68 As the war entered: Tadeusz Bielecki and Leszek Szymanski, *Warsaw Aflame: The 1939–1945 Years* (Los Angeles: Polamerica Press, 1973), pp. 16–17.

68 "showering a hot rain": Bethell, *The War Hitler Won,* p. 139.

69 In a little over two weeks: Baley, *Two Septembers,* p. 52.

69 "Where there were": Bielecki and Szymanski, *Warsaw Aflame,* p. 16.

69 "what had become": C. L. Sulzberger, *The American Heritage Picture History of World War II* (New York: American Heritage, 1966), p. 58.

71 While suffering severe: Cynk, *The PAF,* p. 87.

71 In addition, the Germans: Stephen Bungay, *The Most Dangerous Enemy: A History of the Battle of Britain* (London: Aurum Press, 2000), p. 104.

71 "immeasurably greater": Cable from British Embassy in Yugoslavia to Foreign Office, Oct. 16, 1939, FO 371/23092, PRO.

71 "Whatever her previous faults": John A. Lukacs, *The Great Powers and Eastern Europe* (New York: American Book Co., 1953), p. 222.

71 "Well, your Poles": Carton de Wiart, *Happy Odyssey,* p. 160.

71 In fact, the Poles dispatched: Cynk, *The PAF,* p. 79.

72 The legend actually took hold: Watt, *Bitter Glory,* p. 422.

72 The next day: Zabecki, "Invasion of Poland," p. 31.

72 "Gentlemen, you have seen": Raleigh, *Behind the Nazi Front*, p. 210.

72 "A drive of horror": Ibid., p. 200.

73 "This is the best thing": Ibid., p. 239.

73 Shortly before the Germans: Bielecki and Szymanski, *Warsaw Aflame*, p. 18.

73 Their mission: Allen Paul, *Katyn: The Untold Story of Stalin's Polish Massacre* (New York: Scribner's, 1991), p. 63.

73 On September 4: Gilbert, *Second World War*, p. 5.

73 "an orgy of massacre": Ibid., p. 8.

CHAPTER FIVE

74 Zumbach crossed into Romanian airspace: Zumbach, *On Wings*, p. 52.

75 he discovered a scrap of paper: Urbanowicz, *Początek Jutra*.

75 Red Army troops captured: Ibid.

75 While a guard dozed: Urbanowicz speech at National Air and Space Museum.

77 Sikorski had been prime minister: Davies, *Heart of Europe*, p. 84.

78 Britain and France favored: Zamoyski, *Forgotten Few*, p. 38.

78 But Berlin was pressuring Bucharest: Lisiewicz et al., eds., *Destiny*, p. 17.

78 Nor were the Nazis: Cynk, *The PAF*, p. 95.

78 In Bucharest, General Stanisław Ujejski: Ibid., p. 94.

79 In a camp at Babadag: Dalecki MS.

79 *Get rid of anything:* Zamoyski, *Forgotten Few*, p. 39.

80 the high-flying, skirt-chasing: Zumbach, *On Wings*, p. 54.

80 Urbanowicz and Zumbach were among: Urbanowicz, *Początek Jutra*.

80 As the ship moved away: Zamoyski, *Forgotten Few*, p. 41.

80 "We worried": Urbanowicz, *Początek Jutra*.

81 There were even those who passed: Zamoyski, *Forgotten Few*, p. 43.

81 "as leaves driven": Lisiewicz et al., eds., *Destiny*, p. 35.

81 "the country of our dreams": Urbanowicz, *Początek Jutra*.

81 Witold Łokuciewski and his comrades: Dalecki MS.

82 "We will be celebrating": Ibid.

83 "Never have I seen": Quoted in Robert Leckie, *Delivered from Evil: The Saga of World War II* (New York: Harper & Row, 1987), p. 126.

83 "have received the Poles": Alan Brown, *Airmen in Exile: The Allied Air Forces in the Second World War* (Phoenix Mills, U.K.: Sutton, 2000), p. 28.

84 "We did not socialize": Witold Urbanowicz, *Świt Zwycięstwa* (Kraków: Znak, 1971).

84 "If only we had": Urbanowicz, *Początek Jutra*.

84 The Air Ministry said it could: Cynk, *The PAF*, p. 150.

85 "Leaving France": Urbanowicz, *Początek Jutra*.

85 but by the end of March: Cynk, *The PAF*, p. 111.

85 "For those of us": Zumbach, *On Wings*, p. 58.

86 "You can do": Zamoyski, *Forgotten Few*, p. 51.

86 Polish fliers assigned: Ibid.

87 "We are defeated": Winston Churchill, *Their Finest Hour* (Boston: Houghton Mifflin, 1949), p. 42.

87 "Nowhere was any resistance": Williamson Murray and Allan R. Millett, *A War to Be Won: Fighting the Second World War* (Cambridge, Mass.: Belknap/Harvard University Press, 2000), p. 71.

87 "the idea of a good day's work": Zumbach, *On Wings,* p. 58.

88 "What's the hurry?": Ibid., p. 59.

88 A Polish mechanic: Grzegorz Śliżewski, *The Lost Hopes: Polish Fighters over France in 1940* (Koszalin: Panda, 2000), p. 139.

88 Just one French pilot joined: Cynk, *The PAF,* p. 130.

88 For Krasnodębski, the overall situation: Śliżewski, *Lost Hopes,* p. 139.

88 "For them": Jerzy Radomski, Ferić diary, Lot A V 49/34/2, Polish Institute, London.

88 "clearly was avoiding": Śliżewski, *Lost Hopes,* p. 103.

88 Just before the fall of France: Cynk, *The PAF,* p. 128.

89 "Now I was to face": F. B. Czarnomski, *They Fight for Poland* (London: Allen & Unwin, 1941), p. 164.

89 General Weygand remarked: War Cabinet minutes, June 19, 1940, CAB 65/70, PRO.

89 "was thick with resignation": Zumbach, *On Wings,* p. 61.

90 "Tell your army": Ciechanowski, *Defeat in Victory,* p. 15.

90 "Sikorski's tourists": Zamoyski, *Forgotten Few,* pp. 54–55.

90 At Bordeaux: Zumbach, *On Wings,* p. 62.

90 Witold Łokuciewski, who had been posted: Dalecki MS.

90 Poles at yet another airfield: Interview with Ignacy Olszewski.

90 One pilot: Wojciech Januszewicz, Ferić diary, Lot A V 49/34/2, Polish Institute, London.

91 The brigade commander: Margaret Brodniewicz-Stawicki, *For Your Freedom and Ours: The Polish Armed Forces in the Second World War* (St. Catharine's, Ontario: Vanwell, 1999), p. 93.

91 One pilot made his way: Zamoyski, *Forgotten Few,* p. 53.

CHAPTER SIX

92 "The British have always": W. Averell Harriman and Elie Abel, *Special Envoy to Churchill and Stalin, 1941–1946* (New York: Random House, 1975), p. 113.

93 Seen from the perspective: Norman Gelb, *Scramble: A Narrative History of the Battle of Britain* (San Diego: Harcourt Brace Jovanovich, 1985), pp. 18–19.

93 That "smug, insular": Richard Hough and Denis Richards, *The Battle of Britain* (London: Hodder & Stoughton, 1989), p. 100.

93 In the aftermath: Gilbert, *Second World War,* p. 261.

93 "Never has a great nation": Churchill, *Their Finest Hour,* p. 145.

93 "Certainly everything": David Dilks, ed., *The Diaries of Sir Alexander Cadogan, 1938–1945* (New York: Putnam, 1971), p. 308.

94 "Up till April": Churchill, *Their Finest Hour,* pp. 228–29.

94 "Everyone is going around": Richard Collier, *1940: The Avalanche* (London: Hamish Hamilton, 1979), p. 113.

94 The Duke of Bedford went so far: David Cannadine, *The Decline and Fall of the British Aristocracy* (New Haven: Yale University Press, 1990), p. 623.

94 In a May 27 cabinet meeting: Murray and Millett, *War to Be Won,* p. 83.

94 "You ask": Churchill, *Their Finest Hour,* p. 26.

95 Shaking the British: Berlin quoted in Manchester, *Last Lion,* p. 682.

95 "The British people": Brian Gardner, *Churchill,* p. 66.

95 By a ratio of some six to one: Brown, *Airmen in Exile,* p. 143.

96 One day, shortly after: John Colville, *The Fringes of Power: 10 Downing Street Diaries, 1939–1955* (New York: W. W. Norton, 1985), p. 238.

96 "seem to be our most": Ibid., p. 171.

96 "Britain does not solicit": Brown, *Airmen in Exile,* p. 35.

96 "Beyond the fact": Flying Officer Geoffrey Marsh, "The Collaboration with the English: Squadron 303, Kosciuszko," *Skrzydła,* Sept. 1–14, 1942.

97 "knew about Shakespeare": Bohdan Arct, *Polish Wings in the West* (Warsaw: Interpress, 1971), p. 18.

97 "the typical Englishman": Zamoyski, *Forgotten Few,* p. 57.

97 "My mind was still": Ibid.

97 In the meantime, according to: Air Ministry report on Polish Air Force, March 29, 1940, AIR 2/4213, PRO.

98 "a little doubtful": Quoted in Arct, *Polish Wings,* p. 40.

98 When Dowding asked: Urbanowicz, *Świt Zwycięstwa.*

98 The distinction between the Auxiliary: Gelb, *Scramble,* p. 51.

99 A number of Polish fliers: Urbanowicz, *Świt Zwycięstwa.*

100 "The whole future": Air Ministry memo, Feb. 29, 1940, AIR 14/333, PRO.

100 "I am extremely perturbed": Porri report, May 24, 1940, AIR 2/7196, PRO.

101 One irritated station commander: Zamoyski, *Forgotten Few,* p. 64.

101 "Let us be gentlemen": Ibid., p. 60.

101 Germany was moving more than: Cynk, *The PAF,* p. 171.

102 "From the Royal Air Force": Gelb, *Scramble,* p. 10.

102 In just three weeks: Ibid., p. 23.

102 "Replacements came": Ibid., p. 10.

102 Altogether, almost 1,000 aircraft: Ibid., p. 23.

102 Britain handled these limited: Ibid., p. 53.

103 On his first day of training: Witold Urbanowicz interview, TV documentary, *The Polish Air Force with the Allied Forces.*

103 The yellow roses: Urbanowicz, *Świt Zwycięstwa.*

105 For his first combat mission: Ibid.

106 On August 8, RAF fighter pilots: John Willis, *Churchill's Few: The Battle of Britain Remembered* (London: Michael Joseph, 1985), p. 87.

107 "little boys": Cowles, *Looking for Trouble,* p. 406.

107 To Winston Churchill: Drew Middleton, *The Sky Suspended* (New York: Longmans, Green, 1960), p. 8.

107 Before his first days: Quoted in Willis, *Churchill's Few,* p. 46.

107 Another Battle of Britain flier: Gelb, *Scramble,* p. 77.

107 In early August, the British government: Cynk, *The PAF,* p. 152.

CHAPTER SEVEN

109 Squadron Leader: Ronald Kellett, "303 Squadron," *Skrzydła*, 106/592.

109 "All I knew": John Kent, *One of the Few* (London: Kimber, 1971), p. 100.

109 Making matters worse: Kellett, "303 Squadron."

110 A London stockbroker in civilian life: Interviews with Victor Kellett, Jonathan Kellett, Louise Pemberton, and Judy Williams.

110 a "tremendous flirt": Interview with Louise Pemberton.

111 After one such weekend: Interview with Judy Williams.

111 "Father took the war": Interview with Jonathan Kellett.

111 Kellett considered: Ibid.

111 A Canadian, the tall: Kent, *One of the Few*, p. 13.

112 "thoroughly fed up": Ibid., p. 100.

112 Initially, there were: 303 Squadron Operation Records Book, Aug. 2, 1940, AIR 27/1663, PRO.

113 "our golden-voiced bullhorn": Ferić diary, Sept. 28, 1940, Lot A V 49/34/2, Polish Institute, London.

113 "Zumbach returned": Ibid., Oct. 13, 1940, Lot A V 49/34/2, Polish Institute, London.

114 Wrote one pilot: Ibid., Lot A V 49/34/1, Polish Institute, London.

115 "I spent the entire": Ibid., Lot A V 49/34/2, Polish Institute, London.

115 "Why do they keep": Ibid., Sept. 28, 1940, Lot A V 49/34/2, Polish Institute, London.

115 "women falling all over": Interview with Franciszek Kornicki.

116 One hot summer day: Urbanowicz, *Świt Zwycięstwa*.

117 "I'm not having": Richard Collier, *Eagle Day: The Battle of Britain* (New York: Dutton, 1966), p. 22.

117 "we were not to be let off": Zumbach, *On Wings*, p. 65.

117 "We cannot stand": Zamoyski, *Forgotten Few*, p. 100.

117 "grim," "nervous": Urbanowicz, *Świt Zwycięstwa*.

117 The Polish pilots showed: Daily Orders of 303 Squadron, Polish Institute, London.

117 "They were a complete": Zamoyski, *Forgotten Few*, p. 79.

117 According to Kent: Kent, *One of the Few*, p. 102.

118 A young woman: Ferić diary, Lot A V 49/34/2, Polish Institute, London.

118 They were ordered to ride: Anthony Robinson, *RAF Fighter Squadrons in the Battle of Britain* (London: Brockhampton Press, 1999), p. 249.

118 "Their spirit's magnificent": Collier, *Eagle Day*, p. 22.

118 "the British wasting": Zumbach, *On Wings*, p. 66.

118 "We had to reverse": Ibid., p. 65.

118 "How in hell": Kent, *One of the Few*, p. 103.

120 "No one can deny": Ferić diary, Lot A V 49/34/1, Polish Institute, London.

120 Although he had: Interview with Wanda Krasnodębska (Stanisław Blasiak).

120 Kellett mastered the Polish: Kellett, "303 Squadron."

120 Kent, more thorough: Kent, *One of the Few*, p. 103.

120 He even took on: Kellett, "303 Squadron."
121 On occasion, Kellett expressed: Ibid.
121 one Canadian squadron even boasted: Collier, *Eagle Day,* p. 89.
121 He brought in: Kellett, "303 Squadron."
121 "We have reached": Ronald Clark, *Battle for Britain* (New York: Franklin Watts, 1966), p. 114.
122 "like being with your eyes open": Gelb, *Scramble,* p. 197.
123 When two novice fliers: Ibid., p. 168.
123 "You just took": *Daily Telegraph,* July 25, 2000.
123 "Some I couldn't remember": Gelb, *Scramble,* p. 219.
123 "intense struggle and ceaseless anxiety": Churchill, *Their Finest Hour,* p. 325.
123 It was not uncommon: Gelb, *Scramble,* p. 209.
123 "On virtually every occasion": Hough and Richards, *Battle of Britain,* p. 221.
123 In the two weeks: Gelb, *Scramble,* p. 209.
123 "The incidence of casualties": Quoted in ibid., p. 210.
123 To Zdzisław Krasnodębski: Collier, *Eagle Day,* p. 215.
124 "playing games": Zumbach, *On Wings,* p. 67.
124 Suddenly, Flying Officer: Paszkiewicz combat report, Aug. 30, 1940, AIR 50/117, PRO.
125 "Training flights": Battle of Britain Historical Society, online report.
126 "I have fired at": Ferić diary, Aug. 30, 1940, Lot A V 49/34/2, Polish Institute, London.
126 The man whose "sobriety": Zumbach, *On Wings,* p. 68.

CHAPTER EIGHT

127 "Soon enough": "The Tenacity of the Courageous 303," Battle of Britain Historical Society, online report (www.battleofbritain.net/bobhsoc).
128 At least another 200: Cynk, *The PAF,* p. 75.
129 "Pick out your target": Battle of Britain Historical Society, online report (www.battleofbritain.net/bobhsoc).
129 "The fuselage now filled": Ferić diary, Aug. 31, 1940, Lot A V 49/34/2, Polish Institute, London.
129 In less than fifteen minutes: Cynk, *The PAF,* p. 176.
130 "If it goes on": Ferić diary, Aug. 31, 1940, Lot A V 49/34/2, Polish Institute, London.
130 "Magnificent fighting 303 Squadron": Ibid., undated, Lot A V 49/34/3, Polish Institute, London.
130 For it was on August 31: Cynk, *The PAF,* p. 176.
131 "a general melee": Kent, *One of the Few,* p. 106.
131 Just as Ferić closed in: Arkady Fiedler, *Squadron 303: The Polish Fighter Squadron with the RAF* (New York: Roy, 1943), p. 33.
131 Two planes appeared: Ibid., p. 35.
132 "The Group Commander appreciates": Ferić diary, Lot A V 49/34/3, Polish Institute, London.

133 Shortly before 9:00 a.m. on September 6: Kellett combat report, Sept. 6, 1940, AIR 50/117, PRO.

133 Zdzisław Krasnodębski, who was leading: Krasnodębski, *Guinea Pig* (Summer 1973).

134 He grappled: Ferić diary, undated, Lot A V 49/34/2, Polish Institute, London.

134 As he fell: Krasnodębski, *Guinea Pig* (Summer 1973).

135 "initially took me": Ferić diary, undated, Lot A V 49/34/2, Polish Institute, London.

135 Ronald Kellett also ended up: Kellett, "303 Squadron."

136 The unit was credited: Cynk, *The PAF*, p. 179.

136 "He didn't score": Urbanowicz, *Skrzydła*.

137 Later, the squadron's doctor: Urbanowicz, *Świt Zwycięstwa*.

137 "I'd never seen so many": Gelb, *Scramble*, p. 276.

137 "If they attack": Sulzberger, *World War II*, p. 99.

138 "In the fighting": Churchill, *Their Finest Hour*, p. 330.

138 "writhing with frustration": Zumbach, *On Wings*, p. 70.

139 Close behind was the rest: Cynk, *The PAF*, p. 180.

139 When it came Zumbach's time: Zumbach, *On Wings*, p. 70.

140 "the Dorniers fall[ing]": Zamoyski, *Forgotten Few*, p. 82.

140 Marian Pisarek: Zumbach, *On Wings*, pp. 71–72.

140 "Everyone was dancing": Ibid., p. 71.

141 "bred to value freedom": Quoted in Gelb, *Scramble*, p. 290.

141 Questioned by Vincent: Kellett, "303 Squadron."

141 "treat these claims": Collier, *Eagle Day*, p. 216.

142 "Suddenly": S. F. Vincent, *Flying Fever* (London: Jarrolds, 1972), p. 96.

142 "My God": Collier, *Eagle Day*, p. 217.

142 "The BBC sends": Ferić diary, undated, Lot A V 49/34/3, Polish Institute, London.

142 "I am committed": Ferić diary, Sept. 12, 1940, Lot A V 49/34/2, Polish Institute, London.

142 "Ox has become": Ibid., Sept. 14, 1940.

143 "So he finally": Ibid., Sept. 21, 1940.

143 "The sun was just": Ibid., Sept. 7, 1940.

144 "It was generally agreed": Colville, *Fringes*, p. 245.

144 At Buckingham Palace: Raczyński, *In Allied London*, p. 70.

144 An RAF squadron leader: Curtis, *Winged Tenacity*, p. 7.

144 "their understanding": Zamoyski, *Forgotten Few*, p. 93.

144 "Whereas British pilots": Ibid., p. 94.

145 The two Poles would lie: Philip Kaplan and Richard Collier, *Their Finest Hour: The Battle of Britain Remembered* (New York: Abbeville Press, 1989), p. 180.

145 "To me": Donald Lopez, lecture, National Air and Space Museum, Washington, D.C., Nov. 17, 1981.

145 "When they go tearing": Zamoyski, *Forgotten Few*, p. 90.

145 "will cut chunks": Forbes combat report, Sept. 7, 1940, AIR 50/117, PRO.

145 On several occasions: Forbes combat report, Sept. 11, 1940, AIR 50/117, PRO.

145 "these intensely brave men": John Kent letter in booklet for Polish Airmen's Week, 1965.

146 "simply suicidal": Zamoyski, *Forgotten Few,* p. 72.

146 "It was just common sense": Ibid., p. 90.

146 In a flash: Kent, *One of the Few,* p. 114.

146 "Unless the leaders": Kellett letter, *Daily Telegraph,* June 24, 1946.

147 "I don't believe": Kellett, "303 Squadron."

147 "my mechanic could not": Ferić diary, undated, Lot A V 49/34/1, Polish Institute, London.

147 When the squadron was first: Kellett, "303 Squadron."

148 Control fins had been shot off: Fiedler, *Squadron 303,* p. 125.

CHAPTER NINE

150 While three sections of Poles: Kent combat report, Sept. 15, 1940, AIR 50/117, PRO.

150 "a fearful jumble": Zumbach, *On Wings,* p. 73.

150 a "little polka": Ferić diary, Sept. 15, 1940, Lot A V 49/34/2, Polish Institute, London.

150 "What other reserves have we?": Churchill, *Their Finest Hour,* p. 336.

151 Over Gravesend: Kellett combat report, Sept. 15, 1940, AIR 50/117, PRO.

151 "I have never seen": Tadeusz Andruszkow combat report, Sept. 15, 1940, AIR 50/117, PRO.

151 The squadron was credited: Cynk, *The PAF,* p. 184.

152 One of the pilots: Zumbach, *On Wings,* p. 76.

152 Everything "worked perfectly": Kellett, "303 Squadron."

153 Then, as Witold Urbanowicz: Xavier Pruszynski, *Poland Fights Back* (New York: Roy, 1944), p. 85.

154 Over Horsham: Cynk, *The PAF,* p. 187.

154 "flashed down": Pruszynski, *Poland Fights Back,* p. 87.

154 The Kościuszko Squadron's death rate: Zamoyski, *Forgotten Few,* p. 92.

154 "He gave his life": Ferić diary, Sept. 29, 1940, Lot A V 49/34/2, Polish Institute, London.

154 "So many people": Urbanowicz speech, National Air and Space Museum.

154 "You might be": *Daily Telegraph,* Sept. 25, 2000.

155 Jozef František: Fiedler, *Squadron 303,* p. 118.

155 Stanley Vincent recalled: Vincent, *Flying Fever,* p. 97.

155 "At the railway station": František combat report, Sept. 9, 1940, AIR 50/117, PRO.

156 "altogether out of place": Fiedler, *Squadron 303,* p. 110.

157 "an irresistible instinct": Ibid., p. 115.

157 The Czech pleaded: Ibid., p. 114.

157 They formally declared: Ibid., p. 115.

158 The other pilots watched: Kent, *One of the Few,* p. 126.

158 "a very great loss": Ibid.

158 In only six weeks of combat: Cynk, *The PAF,* p. 193.

158 "Even though it was equipped": Bungay, *Most Dangerous*, p. 346.

159 Kellett asked if Churchill: Kellett, "303 Squadron."

160 The RAF, which had lost: Cynk, *The PAF*, p. 194.

161 After the war, a group: Kaplan and Collier, *Their Finest Hour*, p. 206.

161 In early September 1940: Stanley Cloud and Lynne Olson, *The Murrow Boys: Pioneers on the Front Lines of Broadcast Journalism* (Boston: Houghton Mifflin, 1996), p. 92.

162 "In my talks": Churchill, *Their Finest Hour*, p. 456.

162 Dowding himself: Quoted in Lisiewicz et al., eds., *Destiny*, p. 68.

162 "There was no doubt": Kent, *One of the Few*, p. 121.

162 Of the some 400 fighter pilots: Zamoyski, *Forgotten Few*, p. 97.

162 On September 26, for example: Ibid.

162 "I wonder if": Thomas Gleave, *Skrzydła*, May 15, 1946, 9/482.

163 Ronald Kellett was one: Interview with Victor Kellett.

163 "Our shortage of trained pilots": Cynk, *The PAF*, p. 194.

163 "Had it not been": Zamoyski, *Forgotten Few*, p. 97.

163 "There were all sorts": Gelb, *Scramble*, p. 48.

164 "would always speak": Interview with Franciszek Kornicki.

164 "You have given me": Feriç diary, Jan. 6, 1941, Lot A V 49/34/3, Polish Institute, London.

164 At a nightclub: Collier, *Eagle Day*, p. 177.

165 "a most magnificent party": Kent, *One of the Few*, p. 127.

165 "It is with genuine regret": Feriç diary, undated, Lot A V 49/34/3, Polish Institute, London.

165 "Profound thanks": Ibid., April 7, 1941.

165 *Whenever a Pole:* Ibid., March 19, 1941.

166 "I have never been": Stanley Vincent letter in Polish Airmen's Week booklet, 1965.

166 "had no other warning": Kellett, "303 Squadron."

167 "A few of us": Kent, *One of the Few*, p. 147.

167 "defeated and betrayed": Quoted in Czarnomski, *They Fight for Poland*, p. 287.

CHAPTER TEN

168 Remembering how badly: Interview with Ludwik Martel.

168 "The Poles flying": Robert Post, "Poland's Avenging Angels," *New York Times Magazine,* June 29, 1941.

168 "The Polish aviators": Reynolds, *London Diary,* p. 73.

168 Newspaper and magazine articles: See Zamoyski, *Forgotten Few*, p. 109.

171 "Honor to you": *Skrzydła,* Oct. 1–14, 1942, 19/396.

172 "but a little thing": Feriç diary, March 14, 1941, Lot A V 49/34/3, Polish Institute, London.

172 "Every other woman": Feriç diary, undated, Lot A V 49/34/3, Polish Institute, London.

172 "one of the gayest": *The Tatler,* March 5, 1941.

173 Tadeusz Andersz: Interview with Tadeusz Andersz.

174 Looking out the window: Zamoyski, *Forgotten Few*, p. 110.

174 The men playing the hole: Ibid., p. 84.

174 This is how Richard Cobb: *Skrzydła*, May 1–14, 1942, 9/386.

175 "On the ground": Ibid.

175 "one of the summer battles": Quoted in Hough and Richards, *Battle of Britain*, p. 212.

175 "a grandstand view": Colville, *Fringes*, p. 225.

175 "London lives well": Robert Rhodes James, ed., "*Chips*": *The Diaries of Sir Henry Channon* (London: Phoenix, 1999), p. 272.

176 "No French vermouth": Reynolds, *London Diary*, p. 124.

176 Harold Macmillan and several: Harold Macmillan, *The Blast of War: 1939–1945* (New York: Harper & Row, 1968), p. 86.

176 "You walk through": Reynolds, *London Diary*, p. 65.

176 "Life?": *Skrzydła*, Jan. 15, 1946.

177 "In London": Zamoyski, *Forgotten Few*, p. 119.

177 "Well," she replied: Colville, *Fringes*, p. 296.

177 The head of a British girls' school: Zamoyski, *Forgotten Few*, p. 173.

177 "I was never allowed": Ibid., p. 63.

178 "devoted her entire attention": Nancy Caldwell Sorel, *The Women Who Wrote the War* (New York: Arcade, 1999), p. 220.

178 "As for the women": Zamoyski, *Forgotten Few*, p. 69.

178 "These English girls": Ibid., p. 173.

178 "I think English women should have": Urbanowicz speech, National Air and Space Museum, Nov. 17, 1981.

178 "It was a liberation": Angela Lambert, *1939: The Last Season of Peace* (London: Weidenfeld & Nicolson, 1989), p. 211.

179 A young WAAF: Urbanowicz, *Świt Zycięstwa*.

179 A number of young women: Ibid.

179 One night at the Orchard: Zumbach, *On Wings*, pp. 80–81.

179 "This kissing of hands": Kellett, "303 Squadron."

180 "blue eyes": Zamoyski, *Forgotten Few*, p. 176.

180 "For the habitually reserved": Ibid., p. 169.

180 "British officers had no idea": Ibid., p. 177.

181 "They notice what": Ibid.

181 "We are worried": Ibid., p. 176.

181 According to a number of newspaper stories: Arct, *Polish Wings*, p. 113.

181 "I am Polish aviator": Reynolds, *London Diary*, p. 75.

181 During the Battle of Britain: Ferić diary, Sept. 1, 1940, Lot A V 49/34/2, Polish Institute, London.

182 "a mental and imaginative": *Skrzydła*, Nov. 15–30, 1942.

182 "But you are not": *Skrzydła*, 133/375.

182 "He had a passionate": *Skrzydła*, Sept. 15–30, 1942.

182 "Artists came to sketch": Marsh, "Collaboration with the English."

182 "without losing one": Reynolds, *London Diary*, p. 73.

182 One headline managed: Zamoyski, *Forgotten Few*, p. 116.

183 "demoniac fighters": *New York Times Magazine*, June 29, 1941.

183 "to get to know": Fiedler, *Squadron 303*, p. 181.
183 Instead of beautiful society: Zumbach, *On Wings*, pp. 78–79.

PART TWO
CHAPTER ELEVEN

187 One of them: Peter Williams and Ted Harrison, *McIndoe's Army* (London: Pelham, 1979), p. 31.
188 "He was a god": Ibid., p. 15.
188 "immediately became": Ibid., p. 14.
188 "the terrible despair": Ibid., p. 29.
189 "no longer the same": Urbanowicz, *Skrzydła*.
190 Hence, the First Polish Wing: Cynk, *The PAF*, p. 205.
190 The staid hush: Zamoyski, *Forgotten Few*, p. 118.
190 During one raucous celebration: Interview with Ignacy Olszewski.
190 On another occasion: Zamoyski, *Forgotten Few*, p. 120.
190 Polish squadrons took part: Ibid., p. 108.
190 "One has to fly": Pruszynski, *Poland Fights Back*, p. 152.
191 "a highly effective technique": Zumbach, *On Wings*, p. 83.
191 Despite the disadvantage: Ibid., p. 107.
191 "On the way to France": Tadeusz Andersz, TV documentary, *White Eagles in Borrowed Skies*.
192 In the last six months of 1941: David Oliver, *Fighter Command, 1939–1945* (London: HarperCollins, 2000), p. 179.
192 During an interview with a correspondent: Pruszynski, *Poland Fights Back*, p. 148.
194 "The Kościuszko Squadron chronicler": Marsh, *Skrzydła*.
194 "We know that many": Ferić diary, undated, Lot A V 49/34/2, Polish Institute, London.
196 It took some time: Interview with Krzysztof Ferić.
196 After the war: "Jeden z Dywizjonu," *Rozen* (weekly), 1981.
196 a small black-and-white photograph: Interview with Krzysztof Ferić.
196 The young woman: Interview with Franciszek Kornicki.
197 The night before the mission: Dalecki MS.
197 "Dear 'Tolo' ": Ferić diary, undated, Lot A V 49/34/3, Polish Institute, London.
198 "Everybody grabbed them": Stefan Korbonski, *Fighting Warsaw* (New York: Funk & Wagnalls, 1968), p. 345.
198 "We left the country": Ferić broadcast, 303 Squadron history, Polish Institute, London.
199 "Memories of home": *Skrzydła*, May 15–31, 1942.
199 A young British woman: Zamoyski, *Forgotten Few*, p. 174.
200 "The Polish airmen": Ibid., p. 116.
200 On November 9, 1939: Lukas, *Forgotten Holocaust*, pp. 8–9.
200 A few Jagiellonian professors: George Weigel, *Witness to Hope: The Biography of Pope John Paul II* (New York: HarperCollins, 1999), p. 54.
200 "All Poles": Lukas, *Forgotten Holocaust*, p. 4.

201 In the first months and years: Gitta Sereny, *Albert Speer: His Battle with Truth* (New York: Knopf, 1995), p. 246.

201 "icy, efficient": Shirer, *Berlin Diary,* p. 566.

201 Eventually, the definition: Neal Ascherson, *The Struggles for Poland* (London: Michael Joseph, 1987), p. 100.

202 "[n]one of Germany's enemies": Lukacs, *Great Powers,* pp. 388–89.

202 "volleys of shots": Korbonski, *Fighting Warsaw,* p. 173.

202 215 people killed: Lukas, *Forgotten Holocaust,* p. 37.

202 "In Prague, large": Bielecki and Szymanski, *Warsaw Aflame,* p. 32.

202 "Every week": Quoted in Watt, *Bitter Glory,* p. 444.

203 Added Seymour Cocks: Jedrzejewicz, ed., *Poland and the British Parliament,* vol. 2, p. 3.

203 It was illegal for Poles: Paul, *Katyn,* p. 63.

203 A Pole could be shot: Lukas, *Forgotten Holocaust,* p. 10.

203 Vowing to turn: Ibid.

204 "Let us imagine": Stephen Vincent Benét, "Blueprint for Slaves," *The New Republic,* Sept. 21, 1942.

204 Its resistance movement began: Ascherson, *Struggles for Poland,* p. 100.

204 Poland's resistance movement: Korbonski, *Fighting Warsaw,* p. 117.

205 By day, she worked: Interview with Wanda Krasnodębska (Stanisław Blasiak).

206 In response to the closure: Ascherson, *Struggles,* p. 104.

206 "We have in this country": Bielecki and Szymanski, *Warsaw Aflame,* p. 30.

206 "You are hereby": Tadeusz Bór-Komorowski, *The Secret Army* (London: Victor Gollancz, 1950), p. 35.

206 At one point: E. Thomas Wood and Stanisław M. Jankowski, *Karski: How One Man Tried to Stop the Holocaust* (New York: John Wiley, 1994), p. 97.

206 On another occasion: Bielecki and Szymanski, *Warsaw Aflame,* p. 110.

206 When the Germans pulled down: Ibid., p. 65.

207 "If we had not been able": Korbonski, *Fighting Warsaw,* p. 227.

208 "You Poles in England must be": Polish underground report, July 10, 1942, John Franklin Carter files, FDR Library.

208 One underground Polish courier: Wood and Jankowski, *Karski,* p. 128.

209 Of the same 19,000 individuals: Yad Vashem Web site (www.yadvashem.org).

209 "This is no doubt": Speech by Israel Gutman, U.S. Holocaust Memorial Museum, Dec. 10, 2002.

CHAPTER TWELVE

210 One of the coldest places on earth: Adam Hochschild, *The Unquiet Ghost: Russians Remember Stalin* (New York: Viking Press, 1994), p. xxxiv.

210 The few who did manage: Paul, *Katyn,* p. 181.

211 Indeed, officers of the NKVD: Ibid., p. 65.

211 "The Polish nation": Louis FitzGibbon, *Katyn Massacre* (London: Corgi Books, 1977), p. 14.

211 "In the Soviet Union": Gross, *Revolution,* p. 144.

211 In the late 1930s: Hochschild, *Unquiet Ghost,* p. xvi.

211 On one day alone: Robert Conquest, *Stalin: Breaker of Nations* (New York: Viking Press, 1991), p. 203.

212 "There was this funny ash": Hochschild, *Unquiet Ghost*, p. 128.

212 When the Soviet national census: Ibid., p. xv.

212 During the twenty-one months: Anders, *Army in Exile*, p. 69.

212 About 52 percent: Paul, *Katyn*, p. 65.

212 The terror often began: Ryszard Kapuściński, *Imperium* (New York: Vintage Books, 1995), p. 10.

213 "The lack of bread": Irena Grudzinska-Gross and Jan T. Gross, *War Through Children's Eyes* (Palo Alto, Calif.: Hoover Institution Press, 1981), p. 66.

213 Another survivor declared: Gross, *Revolution*, p. 222.

213 Soviet soldiers went: Ibid., pp. 217–18.

213 It has been estimated: Ascherson, *Struggles for Poland*, p. 93.

214 As savage as the Nazis: Lisiewicz et al., eds., *Destiny*, p. 28.

214 About half the prisoners: Paul, *Katyn*, p. 70.

214 Early the following year: Joseph Persico, *Roosevelt's Secret War: FDR and World War II Espionage* (New York: Random House, 2001), p. 263.

214 The order to exterminate: Michael Parrish, *The Lesser Terror: Soviet State Security, 1939–1953* (Westport, Conn.: Praeger, 1996), p. 54.

214 It was a lovely early-spring day: FitzGibbon, *Katyn Massacre*, p. 67.

215 Some had their mouths: Paul, *Katyn*, p. 110.

215 "with the precision": "Disappearance of Polish Officers in the Union of Soviet Socialist Republics," Sir Owen O'Malley, FO 371/34577, PRO.

216 For more than five weeks: Paul, *Katyn*, p. 112.

216 From intercepted letters: Ibid., p. 82.

216 On February 9, 1941: *New York Times*, Feb. 9, 1941.

216 "A Pole": Colville, *Fringes*, pp. 425–26.

217 "little short of genocide": George Kennan and John Lukacs, *George F. Kennan and the Origins of Containment, 1944–1946* (Columbia: University of Missouri Press, 1997), p. 28.

217 "of decisive military importance": Murray and Millett, *War to Be Won*, p. 110.

217 As the Führer himself acknowledged: Gilbert, *Second World War*, p. 20.

217 "Stalin distrusted": Harrison Salisbury, *A Journey for Our Time: A Memoir* (New York: Harper & Row, 1983), p. 188.

218 "sullen, sinister": Quoted in Louis Fischer, *The Road to Yalta: Soviet Foreign Relations, 1941–1945* (New York: Harper & Row, 1972), p. 57.

218 "If Hitler invaded Hell": Colville, *Fringes*, p. 404.

219 "Any man or state": Dilks, ed., *Diaries*, p. 389.

220 Barely three months after the German invasion: Payne, *Rise and Fall*, p. 622.

220 "The paucity": Anne Chisholm and Michael Davie, *Lord Beaverbrook: A Life* (New York: Knopf, 1993), p. 415.

220 "[The Russians] certainly": Winston Churchill, *The Grand Alliance* (Boston: Houghton Mifflin, 1950), p. 420.

220 "fear that we would": Anthony Eden, *The Reckoning* (Boston: Houghton Mifflin, 1965), p. 313.

220 "Whether you wish it or not": Paul, *Katyn*, p. 159.

221 The day after the German invasion: Ibid., p. 157.

221 Eden also declared: Richard C. Lukas, *The Strange Allies: United States and Poland, 1941–1945* (Knoxville: University of Tennessee Press, 1978), p. 8.

222 Nearly 300,000 members: R. Umiastowski, *Poland, Russia and Great Britain, 1941–1945* (London: Hollis & Carter, 1946), p. 27.

222 On August 4, 1941: Anders, *Army in Exile*, pp. 44–45.

223 Of the more than 20,000 Poles: Lisiewicz et al., eds., *Destiny*, p. 29.

224 "For the first time": Anders, *Army in Exile*, p. 247.

225 "grey-haired soldiers": Quoted in Umiastowski, *Poland*, p. 36.

225 During that same visit: Quoted in Lisiewicz et al., eds., *Destiny*, p. 30.

225 "smiling, laughing": Robert Rhodes James, *Victor Cazalet: A Portrait* (London: Hamish Hamilton, 1976), p. 272.

225 Almost as soon as people: Anders, *Army in Exile*, p. 119.

226 The Russians began pressing Anders: Ibid., p. 96.

226 Less than a year after the Poles: Michael Alfred Peszke, "Polish Armed Forces in Exile—Part 2," *Polish Review* (1987), p. 61.

226 By 1944: John Keegan, *Six Armies in Normandy: From D-Day to the Liberation of Paris* (New York: Viking Press, 1982), p. 262.

226 The first group arrived in Scotland: Umiastowski, *Poland*, pp. 90–91.

227 After he was shot down: Zamoyski, *Forgotten Few*, p. 161.

228 Yes, he told Eden: Conquest, *Stalin*, p. 250.

228 "the main question for us": David Dutton, *Anthony Eden: A Life and Reputation* (London: Edward Arnold, 1997), p. 201.

229 In Anthony Eden's view: Ibid., p. 190.

229 Of the area's 12 million inhabitants: Umiastowski, *Poland*, p. 218.

230 Part of an Allied effort: William Henry Chamberlin, "Will Stalin Dictate an Eastern Munich?" *American Mercury* (March 1944), p. 265.

230 "If only there were": Lord Francis-Williams, *Nothing So Strange* (New York: American Heritage, 1970), pp. 206–7.

230 Eden's attempt: Dutton, *Anthony Eden*, p. 189.

231 When he returned to London: Conquest, *Stalin*, p. 250.

231 If Stalin's demands were not met: Ibid., p. 251.

231 "are fighting for self preservation": Churchill, *Grand Alliance*, p. 616.

231 In response to Eden's argument: Elisabeth Barker, *Churchill and Eden at War* (New York: St. Martin's Press, 1978), p. 236.

231 In his diary: Dilks, ed., *Diaries*, p. 437.

232 "You...hear people": Panter-Downes, *London War Notes*, p. 205.

232 In London's East End: Salisbury, *Journey for Our Time*, p. 211.

232 "It's apparently useless": Panter-Downes, *London War Notes*, p. 228.

233 The escalating sentiment: P. M. H. Bell, *John Bull and the Bear: British Public Opinion, Foreign Policy and the Soviet Union, 1941–1945* (London: Edward Arnold, 1990), p. 77.

233 "Already the press": Gardner, *Churchill*, p. 149.

233 He "is at a very low ebb": Mary Soames, *Clementine Churchill: The Biography of a Marriage* (Boston: Houghton Mifflin, 1979), p. 415.

233 Thus, on March 7, 1942: Winston Churchill, *The Hinge of Fate* (Boston: Houghton Mifflin, 1950), p. 327.

233 Two days later: Ibid., p. 328.

234 "trafficking in the independence": U.S. Department of State, *FRUS, Vol. III, 1942*, p. 511.

234 "indefensible from every moral standpoint": Ibid., p. 541.

234 "Our acquiescence in": Sumner Welles, *Seven Decisions That Shaped History* (New York: Harper & Brothers, 1950), p. 129.

CHAPTER THIRTEEN

235 He was far from enthusiastic: Urbanowicz, *Świt Zwycięstwa*.

236 "Life was easy": Sevareid, *Not So Wild*, p. 215.

236 "less realization of the actual": David Brinkley, *Washington Goes to War* (New York: Knopf, 1988), p. 106.

237 "Poland has never loomed": Piotr S. Wandycz, *The United States and Poland* (Cambridge, Mass.: Harvard University Press, 1980), p. vii.

237 Yet only the Soviet Union: Ciechanowski, *Defeat in Victory*, p. 90.

237 "if the concept": Ibid., p. 128.

238 "For Poles": Urbanowicz interview, TV documentary, *The Polish Air Force with the Allied Forces in World War II*.

238 In 1942, Jan Zumbach: Cynk, *The PAF*, p. 233.

239 "We owe more": Ferić diary, Aug. 23, 1942, Lot A V 49/34/3, Polish Institute, London.

239 "In regard to having": Ibid.

239 "not an honor I took": Francis Gabreski, *Gabby: A Fighter Pilot's Life* (New York: Orion, 1991), p. 37.

240 The fighters positioned themselves: Zamoyski, *Forgotten Few*, p. 113.

240 From 1941 to 1943, Polish fighter pilots: Ibid., p. 136.

241 Only about 40 percent: Cynk, *The PAF*, p. 327.

241 "A British plane fails": Zamoyski, *Forgotten Few*, p. 142.

241 One Polish pilot recalled: Interview with Ignacy Olszewski.

241 "a kind of benevolent demigod": Isaiah Berlin, *The Proper Study of Mankind* (London: Chatto & Windus, 1997), p. 631.

242 "the magnificent and continuing": U.S. Department of State, *FRUS, Vol. III, 1943*, p. 320.

242 One such message: Anders, *Army in Exile*, p. 93

242 "a distant view on the Polish question": Churchill, *Triumph and Tragedy* (Boston: Houghton Mifflin, 1953), p. 367.

243 When Robert Boothby: Robert Boothby, *Boothby: Recollections of a Rebel* (London: Hutchinson, 1978), p. 90.

243 a "profound gap between": James MacGregor Burns and Susan Dunn, *The Three Roosevelts: Patrician Leaders Who Transformed America* (New York: Atlantic Monthly Press, 2001), p. 472.

243 In the spring of 1942: U.S. Department of State, *FRUS, Vol. III, 1942*, pp. 568–69.

244 "a more humane and democratic": Quoted in Thomas Fleming, *The New Deal-*

ers' War: F.D.R. and the War Within World War II (New York: Basic Books, 2001), p. 85.

244 "divinely inspired": Ibid., p. 124.

244 Being exposed to Roosevelt's: Doris Kearns Goodwin, *No Ordinary Time: Franklin and Eleanor Roosevelt: The Home Front in World War II* (New York: Simon & Schuster, 1994), p. 606.

244 "That's a detail": Robert Shogan, *Hard Bargain: How FDR Twisted Churchill's Arm, Evaded the Law, and Changed the Role of the American Presidency* (New York: Scribner's, 1995), p. 29.

245 "the desire to be": Fleming, *New Dealers' War,* pp. 92–93.

245 Former FDR aide: Goodwin, *No Ordinary Time,* p. 202.

245 "I know you will not mind": Quoted in Harriman and Abel, *Special Envoy,* p. 134.

245 "To put it bluntly": Ibid., p. 108.

245 By the end of the war: John R. Deane, *The Strange Alliance* (New York: Viking Press, 1947), p. 95.

246 The United States provided: Goodwin, *No Ordinary Time,* p. 477.

246 Without U.S.-provided transportation: Murray and Millett, *War to Be Won,* p. 450.

246 In 1943, even Stalin: U.S. Department of State, *FRUS, Conferences at Cairo and Tehran,* p. 469.

246 "Virtually without exception": John Lewis Gaddis, *The United States and the Origins of the Cold War, 1941–1947* (New York: Columbia University Press, 1973), p. 81.

246 "knew the Russians": Salisbury, *Journey for Our Time,* p. 242.

246 "We all admired": Charles Bohlen, *Witness to History: 1929–1969* (New York: W. W. Norton, 1973), p. 121.

246 " 'Look here' ": George Kennan, *Russia and the West Under Lenin and Stalin* (Boston: Atlantic Monthly Press, 1960), pp. 353–54.

247 "much concerned about": Colville, *Fringes,* p. 347.

247 "had no peace aims": Hanson W. Baldwin, *Great Mistakes of the War* (New York: Harper & Brothers, 1949), p. 3.

247 When Sumner Welles: Welles, *Seven Decisions,* p. 133.

247 "The truth is": Deane, *Strange Alliance,* pp. 84–85.

247 "I just have a hunch": Quoted in Barker, *Churchill and Eden,* p. 227.

247 "a Caucasian bandit": Gaddis, *The United States,* p. 64.

248 "The truth is": George F. Kennan, "Comment," *Survey: A Journal of East & West Studies* (Winter–Spring 1975), p. 31.

249 In 1942, Roosevelt had casually: James MacGregor Burns, *Roosevelt: The Soldier of Freedom* (New York: Harcourt Brace Jovanovich, 1970), p. 233.

249 On January 16, 1943, the Soviet government: U.S. Department of State, *FRUS, Vol. III, 1943,* p. 323.

250 "would not particularly mind": Persico, *Roosevelt's Secret,* p. 195.

250 During his meeting: U.S. Department of State, *FRUS, Vol. III, 1943,* p. 14.

250 According to Roosevelt: Ibid., p. 15.

250 "seemed to be ignoring": Eden, *The Reckoning,* p. 431.

250 "He seemed to see": Ibid., p. 433.

250 Three months later: Amos Perlmutter, *FDR & Stalin: A Not So Grand Alliance, 1943–1945* (Columbia: University of Missouri Press, 1993), p. 90.

251 Publicly, the president: Francis L. Loewenheim, Harold D. Langley, and Manfred Jonas, eds., *Roosevelt and Churchill: Their Secret Wartime Correspondence* (New York: Saturday Review Press, 1975), p. 66.

251 "perfectly willing to mislead": Fleming, *New Dealers' War*, p. 26.

251 When the Germans sealed: Szpilman, *The Pianist*, p. 60.

252 Wearing his Polish uniform: Jerzy B. Cynk, *The Polish Air Force at War: The Official History, 1943–1945* (Atglen, Pa.: Schiffer, 1998), p. 363; cited hereafter as *PAF 1943–1945*.

252 "We were an elite": Zamoyski, *Forgotten Few*, pp. 150–51.

252 "I had only a few": Robert Gretzyngier and Wojtek Matusiak, *Polish Aces of World War 2* (London: Osprey Press, 1998), p. 79.

CHAPTER FOURTEEN

254 The handsome, somber: Urbanowicz, *Skrzydła*.

255 were "killing the men": Ralph B. Levering, *American Opinion and the Russian Alliance, 1939–1945* (Chapel Hill: University of North Carolina Press, 1976), p. 89.

255 "Comrades, we are fighting": Umiastowski, *Poland*, p. 82.

256 Whereas *Time*'s 1940: *Time*, Jan. 1, 1940, p. 15.

256 In the article: *Time*, Jan. 4, 1943, p. 21.

256 The Russians, *Life* declared: Clayton Koppes and Gregory D. Black, *Hollywood Goes to War: How Politics, Profits and Propaganda Shaped World War II Movies* (New York: Free Press, 1987), p. 219.

256 "It is not misrepresenting": Gaddis, *The United States*, p. 38.

257 "something like a combination": Lukas, *Strange Allies*, p. 91.

257 It was quite another: Gaddis, *The United States*, p. 43.

257 "a curious mystical belief": Chamberlin, *American Mercury* (March 1944), p. 271.

257 By 1943, the agency: Koppes and Black, *Hollywood*, p. vii.

258 Davies, who knew little: Rudy Abramson, *Spanning the Century: The Life of W. Averell Harriman* (New York: Morrow, 1992), p. 347.

258 Stunned by Davies's appointment: George Kennan, *Memoirs (1925–1950)* (New York: Bantam Books, 1969), p. 86.

258 "What mortified us most": Ibid.

258 In a grim, fear-ridden country: Abramson, *Spanning*, p. 347.

259 "was much less concerned": George W. Baer, ed., *A Question of Trust: The Origins of U.S.-Soviet Diplomatic Relations: The Memoirs of Loy W. Henderson* (Palo Alto, Calif.: Hoover Institution Press, 1986), p. 455.

259 In addition, the ambassador: William Wright, *Heiress: The Rich Life of Marjorie Merriweather Post* (New York: New Republic, 1978), p. 136.

259 "kindness and gentle simplicity": Joseph Davies, *Mission to Moscow* (New York: Simon & Schuster, 1941), pp. 356–57.

260 Jack and Harry Warner later claimed: Koppes and Black, *Hollywood*, p. 191.

260 "wholesale rewriting": David Culbert, ed., *Mission to Moscow* (Madison: University of Wisconsin Press, 1980), p. 11.

260 "The presentation of the Moscow trials": Ibid., p. 256.

260 "Shameful rot": Quoted in Koppes and Black, *Hollywood*, p. 207.

260 Dwight Macdonald: Culbert, ed., *Mission*, p. 33.

261 In a May 1943 letter: Ibid., p. 31.

261 The arrangement gave Soviet: Martin Weil, *A Pretty Good Club: The Founding Fathers of the U.S. Foreign Service* (New York: W. W. Norton, 1978), p. 108.

261 Roosevelt "is concerned": Elizabeth Kimball MacLean, "Joseph E. Davies and Soviet-American Relations, 1941–43," *Diplomatic History* (1980), p. 89.

262 Until a more propitious time: Ciechanowski, *Defeat in Victory*, p. 147.

262 When the exile Polish press: Umiastowski, *Poland*, p. 93.

262 Lord Francis-Williams: Francis-Williams, *Nothing So Strange*, p. 169.

262 "I am convinced": Lord Francis-Williams, *Press, Parliament and People* (London: Heinemann, 1946), p. 17.

263 Its chief instrument in Britain: Bell, *John Bull*, p. 121.

263 Lady Jersey, for one: Zamoyski, *Forgotten Few*, p. 170.

263 "The Polish Government": Raczyński, *In Allied London*, p. 84.

264 The Soviet example: Ian McLaine, *Ministry of Morale: Home Front Morale and the Ministry of Information in World War Two* (London: Allen & Unwin, 1979), p. 203.

264 to "study the success": Panter-Downes, *London War Notes*, p. 166.

264 This former revolutionary: Chisholm and Davie, *Lord Beaverbrook*, p. 422.

264 A. P. Herbert: Alan Herbert, *A.P.H.: His Life and Times* (London: Heinemann, 1970), p. 59.

264 A colleague of Herbert's: Ibid.

265 "If the fable were addressed": George Orwell, *The Complete Works of George Orwell*, vol. 17: *I Belong to the Left, 1945* (London: Secker & Warburg, 1998), p. 254.

265 "the conscience of his generation": Quoted in David Morgan Zehr, "George Orwell," *Dictionary of Literary Biography* 15, p. 407.

265 "this nation-wide conspiracy": Orwell, *I Belong*, p. 255.

265 "Any serious criticism": Ibid., p. 258.

266 "We Poles": Umiastowski, *Poland*, p. 123.

267 "It is hard to see": Kennan, *Memoirs*, p. 213.

267 "Alas, the German accusations": Martin Gilbert, *Winston S. Churchill*, vol. VII: *Road to Victory, 1941–45* (Boston: Houghton Mifflin, 1986), p. 385.

267 "Force is on Russia's side": Paul, *Katyn*, p. 222.

267 In a top-secret cable: U.S. Department of State, *FRUS, Vol. III, 1943*, p. 396.

267 "Eden and I": Loewenheim, Langley, and Jonas, eds., *Roosevelt and Churchill*, p. 329.

267 "savage and disgraceful": Dilks, ed., *Diaries*, p. 528.

268 In condemning the Poles: Bell, *John Bull*, p. 124.

268 In another criticism: Umiastowski, *Poland*, p. 126.

268 The result: Bell, *John Bull*, p. 116.

268 "When it was all over": O'Malley memo, FO 371/34577, PRO.

269 "We have been obliged": Ibid.

269 "brilliant, unorthodox": Official minute attached to O'Malley memo.

269 "Of course, it would be": Cadogan minute attached to O'Malley memo.

269 "We should, none of us": Paul, *Katyn*, p. 304.

269 "a grim, well-written": Warren F. Kimball, ed., *Churchill and Roosevelt: The Complete Correspondence*, vol. 3 (Princeton: Princeton University Press, 1984), p. 389.

269 Nor does he seem to have discussed it: Fleming, *New Dealers' War*, p. 303.

270 That report also concluded: Paul, *Katyn*, p. 308.

270 The "graves question": Lloyd C. Gardner, *Spheres of Influence* (Chicago: Dee, 1993), p. 209.

270 In a cable to Stalin: U.S. Department of State, *FRUS, Vol. III, 1943*, p. 395.

270 "the situation would not": Ibid., p. 396.

270 Yet when Carter and his team: J. K. Zawodny, *Death in the Forest* (Notre Dame, Ind.: University of Notre Dame Press, 1962), p. 179.

270 Classified "top secret": Paul, *Katyn*, p. 308.

270 After the war, an army: Zawodny, *Death in the Forest*, p. 186.

271 Years later, she acknowledged: Abramson, *Spanning*, p. 363.

271 "The Poles are given": Louis Lochner, ed. and trans., *The Goebbels Diaries, 1942–43* (New York: Popular Library, 1948), p. 347.

271 *Newsweek* attributed: "Poles vs. Reds," *Newsweek*, May 10, 1943, p. 29.

271 *Life* said Poles: "The Soviet-Polish Break," *Life*, May 10, 1943, p. 30.

271 Jan Nowak: Jan Nowak, *Courier from Warsaw* (Detroit: Wayne State University Press, 1982), p. 131.

272 Occupied Poland "lived by faith": Ibid., pp. 104–5.

272 "Let us think": Quoted in FitzGibbon, *Katyn Massacre*, p. 78.

CHAPTER FIFTEEN

273 Bearing an image: Lisiewicz et al., eds., *Destiny*, p. xv.

275 Under Sikorski's plan: Cynk, *PAF, 1943–1945*, p. 483.

275 As early as 1941: Zamoyski, *Forgotten Few*, p. 185.

275 "This is going to be": Brodniewicz-Stawicki, *For Your Freedom*, p. 163.

275 During his own visit: Anders, *Army in Exile*, p. xiv.

277 Meanwhile, in occupied Poland: Bór-Komorowski, *Secret Army*, p. 143.

277 "the strongest, best organized": David Stafford, *Britain and European Resistance, 1940–1945* (Toronto: University of Toronto Press, 1980), p. 133.

278 In Poland, virtually the entire: Lukas, *Forgotten Holocaust*, p. 95.

278 "only the Poles": Stafford, *Britain*, p. 31.

278 Ordered to hand over: Lukas, *Forgotten Holocaust*, p. 66.

278 The main supply and communications route: Bielecki and Szymanski, *Warsaw Aflame*, p. 136.

278 Between 1941 and 1944: Bór-Komorowski, *Secret Army*, pp. 152–53.

278 At one point, 43 percent: Lukas, *Forgotten Holocaust*, p. 64.

278 "to the collapse of the German": Sir Douglas Savory, "The Forgotten Allies," *Dziennik Polski* (1967).

278 A Polish underground newspaper: Umiastowski, *Poland*, p. 76.

279 "acts of sabotage": Lochner, ed., *Goebbels Diaries*, p. 456.

279 "several divisions fighting": Lukas, *Forgotten Holocaust*, p. 66.

279 The young Polish cryptologists: Kahn, *Seizing*, pp. 91, 115.

279 A number of Polish army officers: E. H. Cookridge, *Inside SOE* (London: Frederick Barker, 1966), p. 128.

279 One of those officers: Lukas, *Forgotten Holocaust*, p. 86.

280 Later in the war, she rescued: Cookridge, *Inside SOE*, p. 186.

280 "the bravest person": Owen O'Malley, *The Phantom Caravan* (London: John Murray, 1954), p. 209.

280 The Home Army intelligence service: Andrzej Suchcitz, "The Home Army Intelligence Service," at www.polishresistance-ak.org.

280 In 1943, thanks: Lukas, *Forgotten Holocaust*, pp. 87–88.

281 In late 1944: "Seven Fighting Guests of the Polish Underground," *Saturday Evening Post*, Dec. 30, 1944, p. 20.

282 The Polish government was granted autonomy: Stafford, *Britain*, p. 32.

282 Making matters worse: Ibid., pp. 63–64.

283 Throughout the war, Poland: Józef Garliński, *Poland, SOE and the Allies* (London: Allen & Unwin, 1969), p. 147.

283 In the last two months of 1942: Cynk, *PAF, 1943–1945*, p. 458.

283 the "enormous preparation": Selborne memo, Dec. 3, 1943, AIR 19/8/5, PRO.

283 In a memo to Churchill: Selborne memo to Churchill, Oct. 21, 1943, AIR 19/8/5, PRO.

284 "It is assumed that": Coutouvidis and Reynolds, *Poland*, p. 90.

284 The Poles' suspicions: Stafford, *Britain*, p. 133.

284 A Polish colonel attached: Coutouvidis and Reynolds, *Poland*, p. 91.

285 The Combined Chiefs had been advised: Stafford, *Britain*, p. 134.

285 In October, at a Big Three: Eden, *The Reckoning*, p. 482.

285 Despite the Combined Chiefs' promises: Jan M. Ciechanowski, *The Warsaw Uprising of 1944* (Cambridge: Cambridge University Press, 1974), p. 46.

285 Still, in their determination: U.S. Department of State, *FRUS, Vol. III, 1943*, p. 489.

CHAPTER SIXTEEN

286 "with the enthusiasm of a boy": Quoted in Kimball, ed., *Churchill and Roosevelt*, vol. II, p. 572.

287 Stalin countered with a message: Winston Churchill, *Closing the Ring* (Boston: Houghton Mifflin, 1951), p. 238.

287 Churchill sent the message back: Roy Jenkins, *Churchill: A Biography* (New York: Farrar, Straus & Giroux, 2001), p. 718.

288 "inability to finish one subject": Lord Moran, *Churchill: The Struggle for Survival, 1940–1965* (Boston: Houghton Mifflin, 1966), p. 118.

289 "these piddling little things": Harriman and Abel, *Special Envoy*, p. 236.

290 On the eve of Tehran: Stanisław Mikołajczyk, *The Rape of Poland* (New York: McGraw-Hill, 1948), pp. 45–46.

290 "Even a man condemned": U.S. Department of State, *FRUS, Vol. III, 1943*, p. 485.

290 "commit the British government": Jedrzejewicz, ed., *Poland and the British Parliament*, vol. 2, p. 290.

291 "Our relations with Russia": Keith Sainsbury, *Churchill and Roosevelt at War* (New York: New York University Press, 1994), p. 77.

291 Just before the Tehran Conference: Moran, *Churchill*, p. 142.

292 "talk Mr. Stalin out": Harriman and Abel, *Special Envoy*, p. 216.

292 "the impression to get abroad": Moran, *Churchill*, p. 146.

292 At a three-way dinner: Bohlen, *Witness*, p. 146.

292 "I had done everything": Goodwin, *No Ordinary Time*, p. 476.

292 At the next session: Ibid.

293 "a basic error": Bohlen, *Witness*, p. 146.

293 "one of the saddest": Kennan and Lukacs, *George F. Kennan*, pp. 34–35.

293 "Churchill is the kind": Conquest, *Stalin*, p. 267.

293 There was no official agenda: Bohlen, *Witness*, p. 136.

293 Before the summit: Keith Sainsbury, *The Turning Point: The Moscow, Cairo and Teheran Conferences* (Oxford: Oxford University Press, 1985), p. 219.

293 "to anybody to discuss": Churchill, *Closing the Ring*, p. 307.

294 FDR's fondness for improvisation: Bohlen, *Witness*, p. 136.

294 "in a singularly haphazard fashion": Welles, *Seven Decisions*, p. 138.

294 "If I had to pick": Eden, *The Reckoning*, p. 595.

294 the "uneasy feeling": Sir Robert Bruce Lockhart, *Comes the Reckoning* (London: Putnam, 1947), p. 335.

295 He made clear that while: Churchill, *Closing the Ring*, p. 319.

295 "move westwards": Ibid.

296 Stalin responded by subtly: Ibid., p. 320.

296 Hours before the conference's: Bohlen, *Witness*, p. 151.

296 The subject of the Curzon Line: Eden, *The Reckoning*, p. 495.

296 Charles Bohlen was stunned: Bohlen, *Witness*, p. 151.

296 True to his word: Ibid.

296 He opened the final: Churchill, *Closing the Ring*, p. 348.

297 During that same session: Ibid., p. 350.

297 "I was not prepared": Ibid., p. 351.

297 "had been given a fine place": Ibid.

297 "was certainly entitled": Anders, *Army in Exile*, p. 193.

298 "we didn't hold": Nowak, *Courier from Moscow*, p. 278.

298 "Any pronouncement": Gilbert, *Road to Victory*, p. 652.

298 Roosevelt had initially planned: Ciechanowski, *Defeat in Victory*, p. 244.

298 The State Department's: Fischer, *Road to Yalta*, p. 196.

298 No one else at State: Robert Beitzell, *The Uneasy Alliance: America, Britain, and Russia, 1941–1943* (New York: Knopf, 1972), p. 347.

298 When Polish ambassador: Ciechanowski, *Defeat in Victory*, p. 260.

299 "began to fear greatly": Eden, *The Reckoning*, p. 497.

299 "I can . . . tell": Umiastowski, *Poland*, p. 232.

299 "His Majesty's Government": Jedrzejewicz, ed., *Poland and the British Parliament*, vol. 2, p. 306.

299 Of a particularly vitriolic attack: Umiastowski, *Poland*, p. 228.

300 The British "have the idea": Jedrzejewicz, ed., *Poland and the British Parliament*, vol. 3, p. 217.

300 At the BBC: Edward J. Rozek, *Allied Wartime Diplomacy: A Pattern in Poland* (New York: John Wiley, 1958), p. 163.

300 *The Times* and other newspapers: Umiastowski, *Poland*, p. 161.

300 *The Times* launched: Ibid., p. 219.

300 When another Polish publication: Jedrzejewicz, ed., *Poland and the British Parliament*, vol. 2, p. 309.

300 "I don't believe that": Ibid., p. 310.

300 "dense fog of mendacity": Raczyński, *In Allied London*, pp. 183–84.

300 "We hear less": Ibid., p. 175.

301 "Everybody's nerves": Panter-Downes, *London War Notes*, p. 310.

301 "a once-smart hotel": Cloud and Olson, *Murrow Boys*, p. 233.

301 On a streetcar in Blackpool: Zamoyski, *Forgotten Few*, p. 193.

301 "The common view": Raczyński, *In Allied London*, p. 217.

301 "to vilify us": Ibid., p. 253.

301 "hectoring tone": Ibid., p. 193.

301 The Poles "must back": Kimball, ed., *Churchill and Roosevelt*, vol. II, p. 651.

302 In a memo to Eden: Gilbert, *Winston Churchill, 1941–45*, p. 642.

302 He even agreed to consider: Umiastowski, *Poland*, p. 229.

302 "We doubt very much": Loewenheim, Langley, and Jonas, eds., *Roosevelt and Churchill*, p. 447.

302 Although Polish troops: Kimball, ed., *Churchill and Roosevelt*, vol. II, p. 720.

303 "Here I may remind": Jedrzejewicz, ed., *Poland and the British Parliament*, vol. 2, pp. 341–42.

303 Churchill's speech made clear: Nowak, *Courier*, p. 268.

303 "When does aggression": Jedrzejewicz, ed., *Poland and the British Parliament*, vol. 2, p. 352.

304 In a later confrontation: Ibid., p. 513.

304 "I am determinedly opposed": Dilks, ed., *Diaries*, p. 609.

304 In a note to Eden: O'Malley note to Eden, Jan. 22, 1944, FO 954/20A, PRO.

304 "What are we to say": Barker, *Churchill and Eden*, p. 244.

304 After receiving one such message: Eden, *The Reckoning*, p. 509.

305 "Nobody can wipe out": Umiastowski, *Poland*, p. 239.

305 "would expose this Government": Lukas, *Strange Allies*, p. 52.

305 In January 1944: Ciechanowski, *Defeat in Victory*, p. 259.

305 In the March 1944 issue: Chamberlin, *American Mercury* (March 1944), pp. 271, 274.

306 he "didn't care": Anna M. Ciencala, "Great Britain and Poland Before and After Yalta (1943–1945): A Reassessment," *Polish Review* 3 (1995), p. 283.

306 "the Polish people": Ciechanowski, *Defeat in Victory*, p. 280.

306 Unfortunately, Roosevelt: Ibid., p. 282.

306 In truth: Fischer, *Road to Yalta*, p. 164.

307 Even worse, warned one: Gaddis, *The United States*, p. 143.

307 In the spring of 1944: Lukas, *Strange Allies*, p. 107.

307 On May 3: Gaddis, *The United States*, p. 143.

307 "would help dispel": FDR Office Files, Part 4, Subject Files, FDR Library.

308 But he said he knew that: Ciechanowski, *Defeat in Victory,* p. 294.

308 He told the prime minister: Ibid., p. 293.

308 "still opposed to dividing": Mikołajczyk, *Rape of Poland,* p. 59.

308 "I will act as a moderator": Ibid., p. 60.

308 "The president will do nothing": Eden, *The Reckoning,* pp. 539–40.

308 During Mikołajczyk's visit: Harriman and Abel, *Special Envoy,* pp. 329–30.

CHAPTER SEVENTEEN

309 "classic of military prowess": Anders, *Army in Exile,* p. xiii.

309 "agonized interest": Martha Gellhorn, *The Face of War* (New York: Atlantic Monthly Press, 1988), pp. 124–25.

309 "more than a military formation": Anders, *Army in Exile,* p. xiv.

309 "We Poles have": John Ellis, *Cassino: The Hollow Victory* (New York: McGraw-Hill, 1984), p. 318.

309 Once and for all: Anders, *Army in Exile,* p. 163.

312 "May your hearts": Raczyński, *In Allied London,* p. 213.

312 The survivors were so exhausted: Ellis, *Cassino,* p. 336.

313 At the sound of the trumpet: Ibid, p. 337.

315 "National dignity and pride": Korbonski, *Fighting Warsaw,* pp. 347–48.

315 After meeting with: Wood and Jankowski, *Karski,* p. 160.

317 "in a world of illusion": Jedrzejewicz, ed., *Poland and the British Parliament,* vol. 2, p. 498.

317 Nazi newspapers suddenly ceased: Bór-Komorowski, *Secret Army,* p. 206.

317 "We are ready to fight": Ibid., p. 208.

318 In his message: Cynk, *PAF, 1943–1945,* p. 472.

318 "It would be politically": COS Joint Planning Staff report, July 31, 1944, AIR 8/1757, PRO.

318 In March 1944: Stanisław Sosabowski, *Parachute General* (London: Kimber, 1961), p. 87.

319 But it was also true: COS Joint Planning Staff report, July 31, 1944.

319 Both, however, had suffered: Cynk, *PAF, 1943–1945,* p. 473.

320 "tragically unwise": Sir John Slessor, *The Central Blue* (New York: Praeger, 1957), p. 611.

320 "We have no choice": Nowak, *Courier,* p. 339.

320 Throughout the city, men: Bór-Komorowski, *Secret Army,* p. 209.

320 All that day and the next: Lukas, *Strange Allies,* p. 63.

320 A similar urgent appeal: Bór-Komorowski, *Secret Army,* p. 213.

320 "To remain in hiding": Harriman and Abel, *Special Envoy,* p. 336.

321 Nowak warned Bór-Komorowski: Nowak, *Courier,* p. 333.

321 "I have no illusions": Ibid., p. 335.

321 At precisely five o'clock: Bór-Komorowski, *Secret Army,* p. 216.

321 In dozens of neighborhoods: Ibid., p. 233.

322 In one neighborhood: Nowak, *Courier,* p. 347.

323 Varsovians had torn down: Bór-Komorowski, *Secret Army,* p. 234.

323 But no help of any kind: Ibid., p. 236.
324 "Every inhabitant": Bielecki and Szymanski, *Warsaw Aflame,* p. 137.
324 "From the historical": Ibid., p. 175.
324 Stalin assured Mikołajczyk: Mikołajczyk, *Rape of Poland,* p. 74.
325 "the doomed representatives": Kennan, *Memoirs,* p. 220.
325 "a hard one": Ibid., p. 219.
325 "I was sorry": Ibid., p. 220.
325 On August 2: Barker, *Churchill and Eden,* p. 253.
325 "I was never one": Slessor, *Central Blue,* p. 615.
326 With his superiors not persuaded: Cynk, *PAF, 1943–1945,* p. 473.
326 On a side street: Bielecki and Szymanski, *Warsaw Aflame,* p. 140.
326 By day's end on August 5: Lukas, *Forgotten Holocaust,* p. 199.
326 Wanda Krasnodębska: Interview with Wanda Krasnodębska (Stanisław Blasiak).
327 The SS butchery in Warsaw: Lukas, *Forgotten Holocaust,* p. 204.
328 At one point, General Bór-Komorowski: Bór-Komorowski, *Secret Army,* p. 263.
328 Flying Officer John Ward: Nowak, *Courier,* p. 357.
329 "The Allies gave": Korbonski, *Fighting Warsaw,* p. 360.
329 "If we ourselves": Ibid., p. 359.
329 There, in downtown squares: Bór-Komorowski, *Secret Army,* p. 265.
330 Seventeen of the ninety-odd: Slessor, *Central Blue,* p. 617.
330 "it was useless": Ibid., p. 618.
330 In less than three weeks: Cynk, *PAF, 1943–1945,* p. 478.
330 "a kind of aerial shooting gallery": Zumbach, *On Wings,* p. 85.
331 "dying a little": Zamoyski, *Forgotten Few,* p. 195.
331 "My God": *Skrzydla,* September 1944.
331 "EVERY NIGHT": Quoted in Raczyński, *In Allied London,* p. 334.
332 RAF officials regarded: Zumbach, *On Wings,* p. 99.
332 "It is difficult": Slessor cable to Chief of Air Staff, Aug. 16, 1944, AIR 8/1757, PRO.
332 That same suspicion: Churchill, *Triumph and Tragedy,* p. 133.
332 Immediately after the uprising began: Anthony Cave Brown, *Wild Bill Donovan: The Last Hero* (New York: Times Books, 1982), p. 621.
333 The uprising was a foolhardy: U.S. Department of State, *FRUS, Vol. III, 1944,* p. 1374.
333 Averell Harriman and British ambassador: Ibid., p. 1375.
333 Two days later: Abramson, *Spanning,* p. 382.
333 "shattered": Kennan, *Memoirs,* p. 221.
333 It had become clear: Harriman and Abel, *Special Envoy,* p. 340.
333 "a gauntlet thrown down": Kennan, *Memoirs,* p. 221.
334 "full-fledged and realistic": Ibid., p. 222.
334 Once a strong advocate: Harriman and Abel, *Special Envoy,* p. 341.
334 The Poles had every right: U.S. Department of State, *FRUS, Vol. III, 1944,* p. 1383.
334 The ambassador urged FDR: Ibid., p. 1378.
334 He wrote to Harry Hopkins: U.S. Department of State, *FRUS, Vol. IV, 1944,* p. 989.
334 "Winston never talks": Moran, *Churchill,* pp. 185–86.

335 "I am most painfully": Mary Soames, ed., *Winston and Clementine: The Personal Letters of the Churchills* (Boston: Houghton Mifflin, 1999), p. 503.

335 "My grandfather": Winston Churchill speech, Jan. 28, 2001, American Institute for Polish Culture, Miami.

336 "[We] entered this war": Anders, *Army in Exile*, p. 211.

336 "I and my friend": Ibid., p. 213.

336 Earlier in August, he had persuaded: Churchill, *Triumph and Tragedy*, p. 135.

336 "a band of power-seeking criminals": Lukas, *Strange Allies*, p. 74.

336 "Thank you for the information": Kimball, ed., *Churchill and Roosevelt*, vol. III, p. 294.

336 "we ought to send": Churchill, *Triumph and Tragedy*, p. 140.

CHAPTER EIGHTEEN

337 "Lucky Paris": Bór-Komorowski, *Secret Army*, p. 292.

337 "No one blamed": Ibid.

338 In early September: Bielecki and Szymanski, *Warsaw Aflame*, p. 150.

338 "it made me sick": Bór-Komorowski, *Secret Army*, p. 306.

338 The reverberating moans: Ibid., p. 302.

338 In Berlin, Heinrich Himmler: Bielecki and Szymanski, *Warsaw Aflame*, p. 175.

339 An RAF bomber pilot: *Skryzdla*, Feb. 15, 1945.

340 "Is there any stop": Churchill, *Triumph and Tragedy*, p. 139.

341 After Stalin barred American planes: Bell, *John Bull*, p. 146.

341 Eden cautioned: War Cabinet minutes, Aug. 16, 1944, AIR 8/1757, PRO.

341 "It should be known": Bell, *John Bull*, p. 164.

341 "A tragedy is being enacted": Umiastowski, *Poland*, p. 297.

341 "mean and cowardly attitude": Ibid., p. 298.

342 "No doubt there are": Bell, *John Bull*, p. 139.

342 *The Economist:* "A Tale of Two Cities," *Economist*, Aug. 26, 1944.

342 "[T]he conclusion seems": Eden, *The Reckoning*, p. 548.

343 "Holy Father": Churchill, *Triumph and Tragedy*, p. 143.

343 "I do not remember": Ibid., p. 141.

343 "terrible and even humbling": Ibid.

343 "[We] find it hard": Ibid., p. 143.

343 "In view of our great": Ibid., p. 142.

343 A State Department report: Lukas, *Strange Allies*, p. 81.

344 "The problem of relief": Churchill, *Triumph and Tragedy*, pp. 143–44.

344 Not until October 3: Lukas, *Strange Allies*, p. 100.

344 Having wangled permission: Bielecki and Szymanski, *Warsaw Aflame*, p. 153.

345 "All the horses": Korbonski, *Fighting Warsaw*, p. 390.

345 "It was possible to take": Tina Rosenberg, *The Haunted Land: Facing Europe's Ghosts After Communism* (New York: Random House, 1995), p. 143.

345 "as if they wanted": Korbonski, *Fighting Warsaw*, p. 388.

346 On September 18: Bór-Komorowski, *Secret Army*, p. 350.

346 "Had the … containers": Ibid.

346 Churchill and his top officials: Umiastowski, *Poland*, p. 325.

346 "The gallantry and self-sacrifice": Slessor, *Central Blue*, p. 612.

346 "How, after the fall": Ibid.

347 Eight days after the uprising: Gilbert, *Second World War*, p. 566.

347 The following day: Keegan, *Six Armies*, p. 267.

347 Among them was Richard Tice: Sosabowski, *Parachute General*, p. 94.

348 Sosabowski protested against: Ibid., p. 108.

348 "Everyone sat nonchalantly": Cornelius Ryan, *A Bridge Too Far* (New York: Simon & Schuster, 1974), p. 142.

348 As their transports approached: Ibid., p. 502.

349 "every gun on the ground": Ibid, p. 503.

349 "only mistake had been": Murray and Millett, *War to Be Won*, p. 443.

350 But many Varsovians: Bór-Komorowski, *Secret Army*, p. 401.

350 "We have been free": Ibid., p. 376.

351 As the Poles moved forward: Ibid., p. 378.

352 According to Helena Kubicka: Interview with Helena Kubicka.

352 On October 3: Lisiewicz et al., eds., *Destiny*, pp. 221–22.

CHAPTER NINETEEN

354 In his place was a Churchill: Warren F. Kimball, "Naked Reverse Right: Roosevelt, Churchill, and Eastern Europe from TOLSTOY to Yalta—and a Little Beyond," *Diplomatic History* (1985), p. 5.

354 "All this havering": Moran, *Churchill*, p. 221.

355 "dire" consequences: Churchill, *Triumph and Tragedy*, p. 230.

355 "Let us settle our affairs": Ibid., p. 227.

355 "was all settled": Ibid.

355 this "naughty document": Ibid., p. 228.

355 "crude" and "callous": Ibid., p. 231.

355 "In saving Greece": G. F. Hudson, "The Lesson of Yalta," *Commentary*, April 1954, p. 376.

356 "judge and jury": "The Fruits of Teheran," *Time*, Dec. 25, 1944, p. 28.

356 He would acknowledge: Mikołajczyk, *Rape of Poland*, p. 92.

356 "the right to ask the Poles": Rozek, *Allied Wartime*, p. 274.

356 The decision lay with the Polish: Mikołajczyk, *Rape of Poland*, p. 95.

357 Hadn't the Big Three: Ibid., p. 96.

357 "silently begging them": Ibid.

357 "I confirm this": Ibid.

358 his "gloriously worded" speeches: Ibid., p. 98.

358 Unless Mikołajczyk accepted: Rozek, *Allied Wartime*, p. 280.

358 "We are losing everything!": Ibid. All quotes from this conversation from Rozek.

359 "I prefer to die": Mikołajczyk, *Rape of Poland*, p. 99.

359 "I was pretty rough": Moran, *Churchill*, p. 215.

359 "We were becoming": Mikołajczyk, *Rape of Poland*, pp. 104–5.

359 "many well-meaning people": Ciechanowski, *Defeat in Victory*, p. 343.

359 He was head of Poland's: Mikołajczyk, *Rape of Poland*, p. 106.

360 By early fall: Goodwin, *No Ordinary Time*, p. 547.

360 *Time* predicted a narrow: Fleming, *New Dealers*', p. 459.

360 In a cable to Averell Harriman: U.S. Department of State, *FRUS, Vol. IV, 1944*, p. 825.

360 Pollster Hadley Cantril: Ibid., p. 470.

360 "possibly oversold Russia": Ciechanowski, *Defeat in Victory*, p. 347.

361 He avoided saying anything: Lane, *I Saw*, p. 60.

361 Next to Roosevelt's desk: Ibid.

361 "Poland is treated justly": Ibid.

362 Churchill had been pressing hard: Bohlen, *Witness*, p. 161.

363 "only an hour before": Umiastowski, *Poland*, p. 328.

363 "the legal government": Loewenheim, Langley, and Jonas, eds., *Roosevelt and Churchill*, p. 633.

363 "European questions were": Harriman and Abel, *Special Envoy*, p. 369.

363 "increased public confusion": Loewenheim, Langley, and Jonas, eds., *Roosevelt and Churchill*, p. 69.

364 "great political implications": Ibid., p. 634.

364 "justify the conclusion": Churchill, *Triumph and Tragedy*, p. 335.

364 "going into a decisive conference": Loewenheim, Langley, and Jonas, eds., *Roosevelt and Churchill*, p. 654.

364 "[U]nless the Russians can be": Eden, *The Reckoning*, pp. 590–91.

364 "to take an intelligent interest": Moran, *Churchill*, p. 243.

365 "He was in a pitiable state": Martin Weil, *A Pretty Good Club: The Founding Fathers of the U.S. Foreign Service* (New York: W. W. Norton, 1978), p. 89.

365 "I must say": Dilks, ed., *Diaries*, p. 706.

365 Indeed, he said, he planned: Churchill, *Triumph and Tragedy*, p. 353.

365 "fought like a tiger": Payne, *Rise and Fall*, p. 665.

366 "coming from America": Churchill, *Triumph and Tragedy*, p. 367.

366 "it would make it easier": U.S. Department of State, *FRUS, Conferences at Malta and Yalta*, p. 677.

366 "Honour was the sole reason": Churchill, *Triumph and Tragedy*, p. 368.

366 Poland was a question of honor: Ibid., p. 369.

367 "I am called a dictator": U.S. Department of State, *FRUS, Conferences at Malta and Yalta*, p. 718.

367 The Lublin government: Churchill, *Triumph and Tragedy*, p. 371.

367 "anxious to end": Ibid., p. 372.

367 "I hope I do not have": Bohlen, *Witness*, p. 189.

367 "there hasn't really been": U.S. Department of State, *FRUS, Conferences at Malta and Yalta*, p. 718.

367 "It is entirely in the province": Ibid.

368 "If we give up": Ibid., p. 788.

368 "the conference is to brush": Churchill, *Triumph and Tragedy*, p. 378.

368 "would be charged": Ibid., p. 379.

368 "Within a month": Ibid., p. 381.

369 In that case: Ibid., p. 382.

369 "The elections": Ibid., p. 384.

369 "reorganized on a broader": Ibid., p. 387.

369 "the shabbiest sort": Kennan, *Memoirs,* p. 222.

369 "very heavily attacked": Remi Nadeau, *Stalin, Churchill and Roosevelt Divide Europe* (New York: Frederick Praeger, 1990), p. 145.

369 "entirely disregards the existence": Umiastowski, *Poland,* p. 430.

370 "broadly representative" interim governments: Loewenheim, Langley, and Jonas, eds., *Roosevelt and Churchill,* p. 655.

370 "This is going too far!": Ciencala, "Great Britain," p. 303.

370 Also classified: Leckie, *Delivered,* pp. 846–47.

370 "What," he asked: Ibid., pp. 847–48.

371 "With the benefit": Sarah Meiklejohn Terry, *Poland's Place in Europe* (Princeton: Princeton University Press, 1983), pp. 357–58.

CHAPTER TWENTY

372 A few of them sat: Zamoyski, *Forgotten Few,* p. 4.

372 Its losses between 1940 and 1945: Cynk, *PAF, 1943–1945,* p. 440.

372 By the time the briefing began: Zamoyski, *Forgotten Few,* p. 198.

372 "Just think": Lisiewicz et al., eds., *Destiny Can Wait,* pp. 168–69.

372 "accomplished by her Allies": Jedrzejewicz, ed., *Poland and the British Parliament,* vol. 3, p. 369.

374 So devastating was this thought: Lukas, *Strange Allies,* p. 204.

374 "I cannot in conscience": Anders, *Army in Exile,* p. 251.

374 "The Polish nation": Ibid., p. 256.

374 "We have never guaranteed": Jedrzejewicz, ed., *Poland and the British Parliament,* vol. 3, p. 373.

374 "the series of offensives": Alanbrooke memo to Chiefs of Staff, Jan. 18, 1946, PRO.

374 "maintain discipline": Lockhart, *Comes the Reckoning,* p. 338.

375 "At the worst": Macmillan, *Blast of War,* p. 572.

375 "I had underestimated": Ibid., pp. 572–73.

375 "On the one hand": Romuald Lipinski, Memoirs, Polish Combatants Association (www.execulink.com/~jferenc).

375 "incomprehensible" to them: Bór-Komorowski, *Secret Army,* p. 385.

376 "The success of the conference": Panter-Downes, *London War Notes,* p. 359.

376 "doubts about": Levering, *American Opinion,* p. 189.

376 "generous concessions": Bell, *John Bull,* p. 175.

376 "firmly rooted": Ibid.

376 "a world of peace": Burns, *Soldier of Freedom,* p. 582.

376 "a compromise": Jedrzejewicz, ed., *Poland and the British Parliament,* vol. 3, p. 371.

377 "I think … that we have been": Ibid., p. 173.

377 "A strong expression": "Mr. Churchill Champions Decisions on Poland," *Daily Telegraph,* Feb. 28, 1945.

378 "determination to maintain": Bell, *John Bull*, p. 176.

378 "I bow to force": Umiastowski, *Poland*, p. 444.

378 "I feel that...their word": Churchill, *Triumph and Tragedy*, p. 401.

378 "one day turning against us": Colville, *Fringes*, p. 562.

379 "masters in their own house": *Daily Telegraph*, Feb. 28, 1945.

379 As Nicolson wrote: Quoted in Gilbert, *Churchill, 1941–45*, p. 1233.

379 "the fate of a nation": Loewenheim, Langley, and Jonas, eds. *Roosevelt and Churchill*, p. 658.

380 Diagnosed early in the war: Alec Douglas-Home, *The Way the Wind Blows* (New York: Times Books, 1976), pp. 88–89.

380 "Russia must not be": Kenneth Young, *Sir Alec Douglas-Home* (Teaneck, N.J.: Fairleigh Dickinson University Press, 1972), p. 67.

380 "As far as Poland": Jedrzejewicz, ed., *Poland and the British Parliament*, vol. 3, p. 388.

380 "decision to transfer": Bell, *John Bull*, p. 177.

381 "It was magnificent": James, ed., *"Chips,"* p. 398.

381 "if our foreign policy": Jedrzejewicz, ed., *Poland and the British Parliament*, vol. 3, p. 436.

381 "spoke up": Ibid., p. 470.

381 "violently prejudiced": Ibid., p. 468.

382 "Because I differ": Ibid., p. 501.

382 "reconcile their troubled consciences": Umiastowski, *Poland*, p. 457.

382 "impossible to approve": Ibid., p. 462.

382 "Labour men were as keen": Loewenheim, Langley, and Jonas, eds., *Roosevelt and Churchill*, p. 662.

383 "I have not the slightest": Colville, *Fringes*, p. 566.

383 "trying to persuade": Ibid., p. 565.

383 "Altogether, our foreign policy": Nadeau, *Stalin*, p. 144.

383 "clearly wanted to make": Churchill, *Triumph and Tragedy*, p. 421.

383 One of those arrested: Brodniewicz-Stawicki, *For Your Freedom*, p. 242.

383 "are starved": Gilbert, *Churchill, 1941–1945*, p. 1243.

383 The only help they received: Deane, *Strange Alliance*, pp. 193–94.

383 "Our men would have": U.S. Department of State, *FRUS, Vol. V, 1945*, pp. 1085–86.

384 "There is no doubt": Loewenheim, Langley, and Jonas, eds., *Roosevelt and Churchill*, p. 676.

384 "the test case between us": Ibid., p. 662.

384 He thought it best: Ibid., p. 667.

384 "I do not wish": Ibid., p. 671.

385 In early March, at Eden's request: Jedrzejewicz, ed., *Poland and the British Parliament*, vol. 3, pp. 642–43.

386 "I must make it": U.S. Department of State, *FRUS, Vol. V, 1945*, p. 195.

386 "feeling of bitter resentment": Abramson, *Spanning*, p. 394.

387 "to minimize the general": Gaddis, *The United States*, p. 172.

387 On April 25: Cynk, *PAF, 1943–1945*, p. 439.

387 "a strangely hollow": 303 Squadron History, Polish Institute, London.

388 On a beautiful May morning: Dalecki MS.

388 Like most of his fellow inmates: Ibid.
388 Some 600 POWs: Lisiewicz et al., eds., *Destiny,* p. 249.
389 "[A]ll my time was": Zumbach, *On Wings,* p. 82.
389 His specialty was diamonds: Ibid., pp. 102–3.
389 "It was horrible": Urbanowicz interview, "Polish Air Force with the Allied Forces."
389 In 1944, he was attached: Urbanowicz, "Zdisław Krasnodębski," *Skrzydła,* 122/608.
390 One evening during the conference: Bielecki and Szymanski, *Warsaw Aflame,* p. 182.
391 Drink in hand: Francis-Williams, *Nothing So Strange,* pp. 201–2.
391 "a deliberate affront": Ibid., p. 203.
391 "Perhaps we should": Ibid.
392 "They do their work": Cloud and Olson, *Murrow Boys,* p. 239.
392 The following day in London: Panter-Downes, *London War Notes,* pp. 374–77.
392 "God bless you all": John Charmley, *Churchill: The End of Glory* (New York: Harcourt Brace, 1993), p. 637.
392 "On the continent of Europe": Churchill, *Triumph and Tragedy,* p. 549.
393 "poisonous politics": Soames, *Winston and Clementine,* p. 530.
393 "The word 'Victory!' ": Zamoyski, *Forgotten Few,* p. 200.

CHAPTER TWENTY-ONE

394 "[We] do not forget": Zamoyski, *Forgotten Few,* p. 200.
394 On April 23, 1945: U.S. Department of State, *FRUS, Vol. V, 1945,* p. 252.
395 "the largest illegal private army": Zamoyski, *Forgotten Few,* p. 203.
395 "denied all free expression": *Daily Telegraph,* June 6, 1946.
396 "a source of increasing political": Cabinet minutes, Jan. 22, 1946, AIR 8/1157, PRO.
396 "everything should be done": Zamoyski, *Forgotten Few,* p. 204.
396 In a variety of forums: Brown, *Airmen in Exile,* p. 71.
396 "cold and dispassionate attitude": Air Ministry memo, Jan. 17, 1946, FO 371/115, PRO.
396 "Together, we have formed": Lisiewicz et al., eds., *Destiny,* p. 343.
397 It was the Poles' "duty": Ernest Bevin message, AIR 55/126, PRO.
397 "To all intents and purposes": Gretzyngier and Matusiak, *Polish Aces,* p. 76.
398 "They will be in our hearts": Anders, *Army in Exile,* p. 300.
398 "Have we lost": *Skrzydła,* March 15, 1946, 5/478.
398 "I tell you this frankly": Anders, *Army in Exile,* p. 300.
398 "We are all struggling": 303 Squadron History, Polish Institute, London.
399 "Friendships and memories": Zumbach, *On Wings,* p. 100.
399 At a somber ceremony: *Skryzdła,* Oct. 1, 1946.
399 "the most painful day": Dalecki MS.
400 "I've been in England": Zumbach, *On Wings,* pp. 100–101.
401 At a society wedding: James, ed., *"Chips,"* p. 414.

401 In June 1946, 56 percent: Zamoyski, *Forgotten Few*, p. 204.

401 "Who do you think": Interview with Franciszek Kornicki.

401 "I don't think official": Brown, *Airmen in Exile*, p. 66.

401 "choking with bitterness": Zamoyski, *Forgotten Few*, p. 207.

402 "very, very hard": Interview with Wanda Krasnodębska (Stanisław Blasiak).

404 As was true of many: Lisiewicz et al., eds., *Destiny*, p. 348.

404 Łokuciewski's father had died: Interview with Wanda Łokuciewski (Andrzej Lewandowski).

404 Also back in Poland: Interview with Tadeusz Andersz.

404 "Of all the moral surrenders": Davies, *Heart of Europe*, p. 97.

405 Despite the pressure on Polish: Mikołajczyk, *Rape of Poland*, p. 200.

405 Angered by the Truman: Lane, *I Saw*, p. 301.

405 By 1947, well over 100,000: Ibid., p. 209.

406 Accused in 1948 of spying: Zamoyski, *Forgotten Few*, p. 212.

406 "I was made to feel": Ibid.

406 On his arrival back in Poland: Interview with Jacek Kutzner.

406 "It was love": Interview with Wanda Łokuciewski.

407 After the war, much of the country's coal: Davies, *Heart of Europe*, p. 81.

407 "Young Poles have never": Martha Gellhorn, *The View from the Ground* (New York: Atlantic Monthly Press, 1988), p. 170.

407 "dirt and neglect": Ibid., p. 177.

408 Poland lost about 20 percent: Davies, *Heart of Europe*, p. 64.

408 "This gaping wound": Ibid., pp. 100–101.

408 "History will be kind": Rosenberg, *Haunted Land*, p. xv.

408 "[T]hey doomed themselves": Winston Churchill, *The Gathering Storm* (Boston: Houghton Mifflin, 1948), p. 323.

409 "the devastated cities": Taylor, *The Second World War*, p. 129.

409 "When it comes to political disasters": Ulam, *The Rivals*, p. 93.

410 "The Russian crimes": Stewart Steven, *The Poles* (New York: Macmillan, 1982) p. 137.

410 writing or speaking in public: Davies, *Heart of Europe*, p. 106.

410 "Unfortunately, the Polish reactionary regime": Radek Sikorski, *Full Circle* (New York: Simon & Schuster, 1997), p. 41.

410 Any tombstone or obituary: Davies, *Heart of Europe*, p. 106.

411 "that great garden": Tadeusz Konwicki, *The Polish Complex* (Normal, Ill.: Dalkey Archive Press, 1998), p. 137.

411 "Sienkiewicz taught different values": Sikorski, *Full Circle*, p. 59.

411 "Roaring with laughter": Gellhorn, *View from the Ground*, p. 150.

412 In the immediate postwar years: Alicia Nitecki, *Recovered Land* (Amherst: University of Massachusetts Press, 1995), p. 8.

412 "for many years one of": Steven, *Poles*, p. 135.

412 In another part of the cemetery: Andrzej Chmielarz, "Warsaw Fought Alone: Reflections on Aid to and the Fall of the 1944 Uprising," *Polish Review* 4 (1994), p. 432.

413 "The Polish nation will never": Raczyński, *In Allied London*, p. 366.

413 "I felt for the first time": Sikorski, *Full Circle*, p. 66.
415 At its peak, Solidarity: Davies, *Heart of Europe*, p. 19.
415 "Together, we will": *New York Times,* July 10, 1997.

EPILOGUE

417 When Łokuciewski first flew: Interview with Jacek Kutzner.
418 "I told him": Interview with Ludwik Martel.
418 "I looked at him": Interview with Tadeusz Andersz.
419 "the boys who stayed": Interview with Ignacy Olszewski.
419 "Those people...who showed": Czeław Miłosz, *To Begin Where I Am* (New York: Farrar, Straus & Giroux, 2001), p. 152.
419 the "greatest pain": Interview with anonymous source.
419 "It was such a good party": Interview with Jacek Kutzner.
420 Shortly after the war: Zumbach, *On Wings,* p. 106.
420 Five years later, using the alias: Ibid., p. 10.
420 "Trouble comes naturally": Ibid.
420 "It was clear": Interview with Ludwik Martel.
420 "buying and selling": Interview with Wanda Łokuciewska.
421 The local cabbies: Interview with anonymous source.
421 "the electric excitement": Collier, *Eagle Day,* p. 276.
421 "[t]he largest presence": Eva Hoffman, *Lost in Translation: A Life in a New Language* (New York: Penguin, 1990), p. 115.
422 "you could feel": Interview with anonymous source.
423 "Life was good": Interview with Francis Gabreski (Andrzej Lewandowski).
423 "He had done all these": Interview with Witold Urbanowicz (son).
424 "This family has given": Ibid.
424 "When I was made": Ibid.
424 "To him, it was": Ibid.
425 "came back glowing: Ibid.
426 In June 1984, during the: Michael Alfred Peszke, "The Polish Armed Forces in Exile, Part 2, July 1941–May 1945," *Polish Review* 2 (1987), p. 168.
427 The memorial was adorned: *Financial Times,* July 13, 1993.
427 Franciszek Kornicki: Interview with Franciszek Kornicki.

Bibliography

Abramson, Rudy. *Spanning the Century: The Life of W. Averell Harriman.* New York: William Morrow, 1992.

Adams, Dorothy. *We Stood Alone.* New York: Longmans, Green, 1944.

Amery, L. S. *My Political Life.* Vol. 3: *The Unforgiving Years, 1929–1940.* London: Hutchinson, 1955.

Anders, Władysław. *An Army in Exile: The Story of the Second Polish Corps.* New York and London: Macmillan, 1949.

Arct, Bohdan. *Polish Wings in the West.* Warsaw: Interpress, 1971.

Ascherson, Neal. *The Struggles for Poland.* London: Michael Joseph, 1987.

Baer, George W., ed. *A Question of Trust: The Origins of U.S.-Soviet Diplomatic Relations: The Memoirs of Loy W. Henderson.* Palo Alto, Calif.: Hoover Institution Press, 1986.

Baldwin, Hanson W. *Great Mistakes of the War.* New York: Harper & Brothers, 1949.

Baley, Stephen. *Two Septembers.* London: Allen & Unwin, 1941.

Ball, Adrian. *The Last Day of the Old World.* Garden City, N.Y.: Doubleday, 1963.

Barker, Elisabeth. *Churchill and Eden at War.* New York: St. Martin's Press, 1978.

Beitzell, Robert. *The Uneasy Alliance: America, Britain, and Russia, 1941–1943.* New York: Knopf, 1972.

Bell, P. M. H. *John Bull and the Bear: British Public Opinion, Foreign Policy and the Soviet Union, 1941–1945.* London: Edward Arnold, 1990.

Berlin, Isaiah. *The Proper Study of Mankind.* London: Chatto & Windus, 1977.

Bethell, Nicholas. *The War Hitler Won: The Fall of Poland, September 1939.* London: Allen Lane, 1972.

Bickers, Richard Townshend. *The Battle of Britain.* London: Salamander, 1999.

Bielecki, Tadeusz, and Leszek Szymanski. *Warsaw Aflame: The 1939–1945 Years.* Los Angeles: Polamerica Press, 1973.

Bohlen, Charles. *Witness to History: 1929–1969.* New York: W. W. Norton, 1973.

Boothby, Robert. *Boothby: Recollections of a Rebel.* London: Hutchinson, 1978.

Bór-Komorowski, Tadeusz. *The Secret Army.* London: Victor Gollancz, 1950.

Brinkley, David. *Washington Goes to War.* New York: Knopf, 1988.

Brodniewicz-Stawicki, Margaret. *For Your Freedom and Ours: The Polish Armed Forces in the Second World War.* St. Catharine's, Ontario: Vanwell, 1999.

Brown, Alan. *Airmen in Exile: The Allied Air Forces in the Second World War.* Phoenix Mills, U.K.: Sutton, 2000.

Brown, Anthony Cave. *Wild Bill Donovan: The Last Hero.* New York: Times Books, 1982.

Bryan, Julien. *Siege.* Garden City, N.Y.: Doubleday, 1940.

Buell, Raymond Leslie. *Poland: Key to Europe.* New York: Knopf, 1939.

Bullock, Alan. *Hitler and Stalin: Parallel Lives.* New York: Knopf, 1991.

Bungay, Stephen. *The Most Dangerous Enemy: A History of the Battle of Britain.* London: Aurum Press, 2000.

Burns, James MacGregor. *Roosevelt: The Soldier of Freedom.* New York: Harcourt Brace Jovanovich, 1970.

———, and Susan Dunn. *The Three Roosevelts: Patrician Leaders Who Transformed America.* New York: Atlantic Monthly Press, 2001.

Cannadine, David. *The Decline and Fall of the British Aristocracy.* New Haven: Yale University Press, 1990.

Cannistraro, Philip, Edward D. Wynot, and Theodore P. Kovaleff, eds. *Poland and the Coming of the Second World War: The Diplomatic Papers of A. J. Drexel Biddle Jr.* Columbus: Ohio State University Press, 1976.

Carton de Wiart, Adrian. *Happy Odyssey.* London: Jonathan Cape, 1950.

Charmley, John. *Churchill: The End of Glory.* New York: Harcourt Brace, 1993.

Chisholm, Anne, and Michael Davie. *Lord Beaverbrook: A Life.* New York: Knopf, 1993.

Cholewczynski, George F. *Poles Apart: The Polish Airborne at the Battle of Arnhem.* New York: Sarpedon, 1993.

Churchill, Winston. *Closing the Ring.* Boston: Houghton Mifflin, 1951.

———. *The Gathering Storm.* Boston: Houghton Mifflin, 1948.

———. *The Grand Alliance.* Boston: Houghton Mifflin, 1950.

———. *The Hinge of Fate.* Boston: Houghton Mifflin, 1950.

———. *Their Finest Hour.* Boston: Houghton Mifflin, 1949.

———. *Triumph and Tragedy.* Boston: Houghton Mifflin, 1953.

Ciechanowski, Jan. *Defeat in Victory.* Garden City, N.Y.: Doubleday, 1947.

Ciechanowski, Jan M. *The Warsaw Uprising of 1944.* Cambridge: Cambridge University Press, 1974.

Clark, Ronald. *Battle for Britain.* New York: Franklin Watts, 1966.

Clayton, Tim, and Phil Craig. *Finest Hour: The Battle of Britain.* New York: Simon & Schuster, 2002.

Cloud, Stanley, and Lynne Olson. *The Murrow Boys: Pioneers on the Front Lines of Broadcast Journalism.* Boston: Houghton Mifflin, 1996.

Collier, Richard. *Eagle Day: The Battle of Britain.* New York: Dutton, 1966.

———. *1940: The Avalanche.* London: Hamish Hamilton, 1979.

Colville, John. *The Fringes of Power: 10 Downing Street Diaries, 1939–1955.* New York: W. W. Norton, 1985.

Conquest, Robert. *Stalin: Breaker of Nations.* New York: Viking Press, 1991.

Cookridge, E. H. *Inside SOE.* London: Frederick Barker, 1966.

Coutouvidis, John, and Jaime Reynolds. *Poland, 1939–1947*. New York: Holmes & Meier, 1986.

Cowles, Virginia. *Looking for Trouble*. New York: Harper, 1941.

Crook, D. M. *Spitfire Pilot*. London: Faber & Faber, 1942.

Culbert, David, ed. *Mission to Moscow*. Madison: University of Wisconsin Press, 1980.

Curtis, Rosme. *Winged Tenacity*. London: Kingston Hill, 1944.

Cynk, Jerzy B. *The Polish Air Force at War: The Official History, 1939–1943*. Atglen, Pa.: Schiffer, 1998.

———. *The Polish Air Force at War: The Official History, 1943–1945*. Atglen, Pa.: Schiffer, 1998.

Czarnomski, F. B. *They Fight for Poland*. London: Allen & Unwin, 1941.

Davies, Joseph. *Message to Moscow*. New York: Simon & Schuster, 1941.

Davies, Norman. *God's Playground: A History of Poland*. New York: Columbia University Press, 1982.

———. *Heart of Europe: A Short History of Poland*. Oxford: Oxford University Press, 1984.

———. *White Eagle, Red Star*. London: Macdonald, 1972.

Davis, Kenneth S. *FDR: The War President 1940–1943*. New York: Random House, 2000.

Deane, John R. *The Strange Alliance*. New York: Viking Press, 1947.

Dilks, David, ed. *The Diaries of Sir Alexander Cadogan, 1938–1945*. New York: Putnam, 1971.

Douglas-Home, Alec. *The Way the Wind Blows*. New York: Times Books, 1976.

Dutton, David. *Anthony Eden: A Life and Reputation*. London: Edward Arnold, 1997.

Eden, Anthony. *The Reckoning*. Boston: Houghton Mifflin, 1965.

Ellis, John. *Cassino: The Hollow Victory*. New York: McGraw-Hill, 1984.

Eubank, Keith. *Summit at Teheran*. New York: William Morrow, 1985.

Fiedler, Arkady. *Squadron 303: The Polish Fighter Squadron with the RAF*. New York: Roy, 1943.

Fischer, Louis. *The Road to Yalta: Soviet Foreign Relations, 1941–1945*. New York: Harper & Row, 1972.

FitzGibbon, Louis. *Katyn Massacre*. London: Corgi Books, 1977.

Fleming, Thomas. *The New Dealers' War: F.D.R. and the War Within World War II*. New York: Basic Books, 2001.

Francis-Williams, Lord. *Nothing So Strange*. New York: American Heritage, 1970.

———. *Press, Parliament and People*. London: Heinemann, 1946.

Gabreski, Francis. *Gabby: A Fighter Pilot's Life*. London: Orion, 1991.

Gaddis, John Lewis. *The United States and the Origins of the Cold War, 1941–1947*. New York: Columbia University Press, 1973.

Gardner, Brian. *Churchill in His Time: A Study in a Reputation, 1939–1945*. London: Methuen, 1968.

Gardner, Lloyd C. *Spheres of Influence*. Chicago: Dee, 1993.

Garlinski, Józef. *Poland, SOE and the Allies*. London: Allen & Unwin, 1969.

Gelb, Norman. *Scramble: A Narrative History of the Battle of Britain*. San Diego: Harcourt Brace Jovanovich, 1985.

Gellhorn, Martha. *The Face of War.* New York: Atlantic Monthly Press, 1988.

————. *The View from the Ground.* New York: Atlantic Monthly Press, 1988.

Gilbert, Martin. *The Second World War: A Complete History.* New York: Henry Holt, 1987.

————. *Winston S. Churchill.* Vol. VI: *Finest Hour, 1939–44.* Boston: Houghton Mifflin, 1983.

————. *Winston S. Churchill.* Vol. VII: *Road to Victory, 1941–45.* Boston: Houghton Mifflin, 1986.

Goodwin, Doris Kearns. *No Ordinary Time: Franklin and Eleanor Roosevelt: The Home Front in World War II.* New York: Simon & Schuster, 1994.

Gretzyngier, Robert. *Poles in Defence of Britain.* London: Grub Street, 2001.

————, and Wojtek Matusiak. *Polish Aces of World War 2.* London: Osprey Press, 1998.

Gross, Jan T. *Revolution from Abroad: The Soviet Conquest of Poland's Western Ukraine and Western Belorussia.* Princeton: Princeton University Press, 1988.

Grudzinska-Gross, Irena, and Jan T. Gross, *War Through Children's Eyes.* Palo Alto, Calif.: Hoover Institution Press, 1981.

Harriman, W. Averell, and Elie Abel. *Special Envoy to Churchill and Stalin, 1941–1946.* New York: Random House, 1975.

Harrison, Marguerite. *There's Always Tomorrow.* New York: Farrar & Rinehart, 1936.

Herbert, Alan. *A.P.H.: His Life and Times.* London: Heinemann, 1970.

Hochschild, Adam. *The Unquiet Ghost: Russians Remember Stalin.* New York: Viking Press, 1994.

Hoffman, Eva. *Lost in Translation: A Life in a New Language.* New York: Penguin, 1990.

Hollingworth, Clare. *The Three Weeks' War in Poland.* London: Duckworth, 1940.

Hough, Richard, and Denis Richards. *The Battle of Britain.* London: Hodder & Stoughton, 1989.

James, Robert Rhodes. *Victor Cazalet: A Portrait.* London: Hamish Hamilton, 1976.

————, ed. *"Chips": The Diaries of Sir Henry Channon.* London: Phoenix, 1999.

Jedrzejewicz, Waclaw, ed. *Poland and the British Parliament, 1939–1945.* Vols. 1–3. New York: Piłsudski Institute, 1946.

Jenkins, Roy. *Churchill: A Biography.* New York: Farrar, Straus & Giroux, 2001.

Johnson, Brian. *The Secret War.* London: Methuen, 1978.

Kacewicz, George V. *Great Britain, the Soviet Union and the Polish Government in Exile (1939–1945).* The Hague and Boston: M. Nijhoff, 1979.

Kahn, David. *Seizing the Enigma: The Race to Break the German U-Boat Codes, 1939–1943.* Boston: Houghton Mifflin, 1991.

Kaplan, Philip, and Richard Collier. *Their Finest Hour: The Battle of Britain Remembered.* New York: Abbeville Press, 1989.

Kapuściński, Ryszard. *Imperium.* New York: Vintage Books, 1995.

Karolevitz, Robert F., and Ross S. Fenn. *Flight of Eagles: The Story of the American Kosciuszko Squadron in the Polish-Russian War, 1919–1920.* Sioux Falls, S.D.: Brevet Press, 1974.

Karski, Jan. *The Great Powers and Poland, 1919–1945.* Lanham, Md.: University Press of America, 1985.

Kaufman, Michael. *Mad Dreams, Saving Graces: Poland, a Nation in Conspiracy.* New York: Random House, 1989.

Kee, Robert. *1939: The World We Left Behind.* Boston: Little, Brown, 1984.

Keegan, John. *Six Armies in Normandy: From D-Day to the Liberation of Paris.* New York: Viking Press, 1982.

Kennan, George F. *Memoirs (1925–1950).* New York: Bantam Books, 1969.

————. *Russia and the West Under Lenin and Stalin.* New York: Atlantic Monthly Press, 1960.

————, and John Lukacs. *George F. Kennan and the Origins of Containment, 1944–1946.* Columbia: University of Missouri Press, 1997.

Kent, John. *One of the Few.* London: Kimber, 1971.

Kimball, Warren F., ed. *Churchill and Roosevelt: The Complete Correspondence.* Vols. II–III. Princeton: Princeton University Press, 1984.

Knapp, Stefan. *The Square Sun.* London: Museum Press, 1956.

Konwicki, Tadeusz. *The Polish Complex.* Normal, Ill.: Dalkey Archive Press, 1998.

Koppes, Clayton, and Gregory D. Black. *Hollywood Goes to War: How Politics, Profits and Propaganda Shaped World War II Movies.* New York: Free Press, 1987.

Korbonski, Stefan. *Fighting Warsaw.* New York: Funk & Wagnalls, 1968.

Kozaczuk, Władysław. *Enigma: How the German Machine Cipher Was Broken, and How It Was Read by the Allies in World War Two.* Frederick, Md.: University Publications of America, 1984.

Kulski, Julian. *Dying, We Live.* New York: Holt, Rinehart & Winston, 1979.

Lambert, Angela. *1939: The Last Season of Peace.* London: Weidenfeld & Nicolson, 1989.

Lane, Arthur Bliss. *I Saw Poland Betrayed.* Indianapolis: Bobbs-Merrill, 1948.

Langer, Rulka. *The Mermaid and the Messerschmitt.* New York: Roy, 1942.

Leckie, Robert. *Delivered from Evil: The Saga of World War II.* New York: Harper & Row, 1987.

Levering, Ralph B. *American Opinion and the Russian Alliance, 1939–1945.* Chapel Hill: University of North Carolina Press, 1976.

Lisiewicz, M., et al., eds. *Destiny Can Wait: The Polish Air Force in the Second World War.* Nashville, Tenn.: Battery Press, 1949.

Lochner, Louis, ed. and trans. *The Goebbels Diaries, 1942–1943.* New York: Popular Library, 1948.

Lockhart, Sir Robert Bruce. *Comes the Reckoning.* London: Putnam, 1947.

Loewenheim, Francis L., Harold D. Langley, and Manfred Jonas, eds. *Roosevelt and Churchill: Their Secret Wartime Correspondence.* New York: Saturday Review Press, 1975.

Lukacs, John A. *The Great Powers and Eastern Europe.* New York: American Book Co., 1953.

Lukas, Richard C. *The Forgotten Holocaust: The Poles Under German Occupation, 1939–1944.* London: Hippocrene, 1997.

————. *The Strange Allies: The United States and Poland, 1941–1945.* Knoxville: University of Tennessee Press, 1978.

Macmillan, Harold. *The Blast of War: 1939–1945.* New York: Harper & Row, 1968.

Manchester, William. *The Last Lion: Winston Spencer Churchill: Alone, 1932–1940.* New York: Dell, 1988.

Marsh, L. G. *Polish Wings over Britain, for Your Freedom and Ours.* London: Max Love, 1943.

Mason, Francis K. *Battle over Britain*. London: McWhirter Twins Ltd., 1969.

McLaine, Ian. *Ministry of Morale: Home Front Morale and the Ministry of Information in World War Two*. London: Allen & Unwin, 1979.

Middleton, Drew. *The Sky Suspended*. New York: Longmans, Green, 1960.

Mikołajczyk, Stanisław. *The Rape of Poland*. New York: McGraw-Hill, 1948.

Miłosz, Czesław. *To Begin Where I Am*. New York: Farrar, Straus & Giroux, 2001.

Moran, Lord. *Churchill: The Struggle for Survival, 1940–1965*. Boston: Houghton Mifflin, 1966.

Murray, Williamson, and Allan R. Millett. *A War to Be Won: Fighting the Second World War*. Cambridge, Mass.: Belknap/Harvard University Press, 2000.

Nadeau, Remi. *Stalin, Churchill and Roosevelt Divide Europe*. New York: Frederick Praeger, 1990.

Nitecki, Alicia. *Recovered Land*. Amherst: University of Massachusetts Press, 1995.

Nowak, Jan. *Courier from Warsaw*. Detroit: Wayne State University Press, 1982.

Oliver, David. *Fighter Command, 1939–1945*. London: HarperCollins, 2000.

O'Malley, Owen. *The Phantom Caravan*. London: John Murray, 1954.

Orpen, Neil. *Airlift to Warsaw: The Rising of 1944*. Norman: University of Oklahoma Press, 1984.

Orwell, George. *The Complete Works of George Orwell*. Vol. 16: *I Have Tried to Tell the Truth, 1943–1944*. London: Secker & Warburg, 1998.

———. *The Complete Works of George Orwell*. Vol. 17: *I Belong to the Left, 1945*. London: Secker & Warburg, 1998.

Overy, Richard. *The Battle of Britain*. London: Penguin, 2000.

Panter-Downes, Mollie. *London War Notes, 1939–1945*. New York: Farrar, Straus & Giroux, 1973.

Parker, Matthew. *The Battle of Britain*. London: Hodder Headline, 2000.

Parrish, Michael. *The Lesser Terror: Soviet State Security, 1939–1953*. Westport, Conn.: Praeger, 1996.

Paul, Allen. *Katyn: The Untold Story of Stalin's Polish Massacre*. New York: Scribner's, 1991.

Payne, Robert. *The Rise and Fall of Stalin*. New York: Avon Books, 1966.

Perlmutter, Amos. *FDR & Stalin: A Not So Grand Alliance, 1943–1945*. Columbia: University of Missouri Press, 1993.

Persico, Joseph E. *Roosevelt's Secret War: FDR and World War II Espionage*. New York: Random House, 2001.

Polonius, Alexander. *I Saw the Siege of Warsaw*. Glasgow: W. Hodge, 1941.

Prażmowska, Anita. *Britain and Poland, 1939–1943: The Betrayed Ally*. Cambridge: Cambridge University Press, 1995.

Pruszynski, Xavier. *Poland Fights Back*. New York: Roy, 1944.

Pula, James S. *Thaddeus Kościuszko: The Purest Son of Liberty*. New York: Hippocrene, 1999.

Raczyński, Edward. *In Allied London*. London: Weidenfeld & Nicolson, 1962.

Raleigh, John McCutcheon. *Behind the Nazi Front*. New York: Dodd, Mead, 1940.

Ramsey, Winston G., ed. *The Battle of Britain: Then and Now*. London: After the Battle, 2000.

Read, Anthony, and David Fisher. *The Deadly Embrace*. London: Michael Joseph, 1988.

Reynolds, Quentin. *A London Diary.* New York: Random House, 1941.

Robinson, Anthony. *RAF Fighter Squadrons in the Battle of Britain.* London: Brockhampton Press, 1999.

Rosenberg, Tina. *The Haunted Land: Facing Europe's Ghosts After Communism.* New York: Random House, 1995.

Rothwell, Victor. *Anthony Eden: A Political Biography.* Manchester, U.K.: University of Manchester Press, 1992.

Rozek, Edward J. *Allied Wartime Diplomacy: A Pattern in Poland.* New York: John Wiley, 1958.

Ryan, Cornelius. *A Bridge Too Far.* New York: Simon & Schuster, 1974.

Sainsbury, Keith. *Churchill and Roosevelt at War.* New York: New York University Press, 1994.

———. *The Turning Point: The Moscow, Cairo and Teheran Conferences.* Oxford: Oxford University Press, 1985.

Salisbury, Harrison. *A Journey for Our Time: A Memoir.* New York: Harper & Row, 1983.

Sapieha, Virgilia. *Polish Profile.* London: Heinemann, 1940.

Sereny, Gitta. *Albert Speer: His Battle with Truth.* New York: Knopf, 1995.

Sevareid, Eric. *Not So Wild a Dream.* New York: Atheneum, 1976.

Sherwood, Robert. *Roosevelt and Hopkins.* New York: Harper, 1948.

Shirer, William. *Berlin Diary.* New York: Knopf, 1941.

———. *Collapse of the Third Republic.* New York: Simon & Schuster, 1969.

———. *The Nightmare Years.* Boston: Little, Brown, 1984.

Shogan, Robert. *Hard Bargain: How FDR Twisted Churchill's Arm, Evaded the Law, and Changed the Role of the American Presidency.* New York: Scribner's, 1995.

Sikorski, Radek. *Full Circle.* New York: Simon & Schuster, 1997.

Slessor, Sir John. *The Central Blue.* New York: Frederick Praeger, 1957.

Śliżewski, Grzegorz. *The Lost Hopes: Polish Fighters over France in 1940.* Koszalin: Panda, 2000.

Smith, Gene. *The Dark Summer.* New York: Collier, 1989.

Soames, Mary. *Clementine Churchill: The Biography of a Marriage.* Boston: Houghton Mifflin, 1979.

———, ed. *Winston and Clementine: The Personal Letters of the Churchills.* Boston: Houghton Mifflin, 1999.

Sorel, Nancy Caldwell. *The Women Who Wrote the War.* New York: Arcade, 1999.

Sosabowski, Stanisław. *Parachute General.* London: Kimber, 1961.

Spears, Sir Edward. *Assignment to Catastrophe.* London: Heinemann, 1954.

Stafford, David. *Britain and European Resistance, 1940–1945.* Toronto: University of Toronto Press, 1980.

Stallings, Laurence. *The Doughboys.* New York: Harper & Row, 1963.

Steven, Stewart. *The Poles.* New York: Macmillan, 1982.

Sulzberger, C. L. *The American Heritage Picture History of World War II.* New York: American Heritage, 1966.

Szpilman, Władysław. *The Pianist: The Extraordinary True Story of One Man's Survival in Warsaw, 1939–45.* New York: Picador, 1999.

Szypowski, Maria and Andrzej. *As You Enter the Old Town . . .* Warsaw: Artibus Foundation, 2001.

Taylor, A. J. P. *The Second World War: An Illustrated History.* London: Penguin, 1975.

Terry, Sarah Meiklejohn. *Poland's Place in Europe*. Princeton: Princeton University Press, 1983.

Townsend, Peter. *Duel of Eagles*. New York: Simon & Schuster, 1970.

Ulam, Adam. *Expansion and Coexistence*. London: Secker & Warburg, 1968.

———. *The Rivals: America and Russia Since World War II*. New York: Penguin, 1976.

Umiastowski, R. *Poland, Russia and Great Britain, 1941–1945*. London: Hollis & Carter, 1946.

United States. Department of State. *Foreign Relations of the United States (FRUS) Diplomatic Papers*. Washington, D.C.: U.S. Government Printing Office.

    1942: Vol. III, Europe. 1961.

    1943: Vol. III, Europe. 1963.

    1944: Vol. III, The British Commonwealth and Europe. 1966.

    1944: Vol. IV, Europe. 1966.

    1945: Vol. V, Europe. 1967.

    Conferences at Cairo and Tehran, 1943. 1961.

    Conferences at Malta and Yalta, 1945. 1955.

Urbanowicz, Witold. *Początek Jutra*. Kraków: Znak, 1966.

———. *Świt Zwycięstwa*. Krakow: Znak, 1971.

Vincent, S. F. *Flying Fever*. London: Jarrolds, 1972.

Wandycz, Piotr S. *The United States and Poland*. Cambridge, Mass.: Harvard University Press, 1980.

Watt, Richard M. *Bitter Glory: Poland and Its Fate, 1918 to 1939*. New York: Simon & Schuster, 1979.

Weigel, George. *Witness to Hope: The Biography of Pope John Paul II*. New York: Harper-Collins, 1999.

Weil, Martin. *A Pretty Good Club: The Founding Fathers of the U.S. Foreign Service*. New York: W. W. Norton, 1978.

Welchman, Gordon. *The Hut Six Story*. New York: McGraw-Hill, 1982.

Welles, Sumner. *Seven Decisions That Shaped History*. New York: Harper & Brothers, 1950.

Williams, Peter, and Ted Harrison. *McIndoe's Army*. London: Pelham, 1979.

Willis, John. *Churchill's Few: The Battle of Britain Remembered*. London: Michael Joseph, 1985.

Wood, Derek, with Derek Dempster. *The Narrow Margin: The Battle of Britain and the Rise of Air Power 1939–1940*. Washington, D.C.: Smithsonian Institution Press, 1961.

Wood, E. Thomas, and Stanisław M. Jankowski. *Karski: How One Man Tried to Stop the Holocaust*. New York: John Wiley, 1994.

Woodward, Sir Llewellyn. *British Foreign Policy in the Second World War: Vols. 1–2*. London: Her Majesty's Stationery Office, 1970.

Wright, Robert. *The Man Who Won the Battle of Britain*. New York: Scribner's, 1970.

Wright, William. *Heiress: The Rich Life of Marjorie Merriweather Post*. New York: New Republic, 1978.

Young, Kenneth. *Sir Alec Douglas-Home*. Teaneck, N.J.: Fairleigh Dickinson University Press, 1972.

Zamoyski, Adam. *The Forgotten Few: The Polish Air Force in the Second World War*. London: Hippocrene, 1995.

————. *The Polish Way: A Thousand-Year History of the Poles and Their Culture.* London: John Murray, 1987.

Zawodny, J. K. *Death in the Forest.* Notre Dame, Ind.: University of Notre Dame Press, 1962.

Zumbach, Jan. *On Wings of War.* London: André Deutsch, 1975.

Acknowledgments

On our first research trip to Warsaw for *A Question of Honor,* we found the following passage in an article in the LOT Polish Airlines magazine: "What does the world know and think about Poland? The Americans wonder whether Poland is really in Europe, and if perhaps polar bears prowl the streets of Warsaw. . . . Knowledge about Poland isn't that deep in Europe itself."

The extent of American misconceptions about Poland may not extend quite to polar bears, but there is a certain truth in the article's complaint: many people in the United States and Europe have only a limited knowledge—if that—of this Central European country with its heroic, tortured history. Myths about Poles and Poland abound—from tasteless Polish jokes to the preposterous notion that Poland in some way collaborated with the Nazis in World War II. In fact, Poland was the only European country invaded and defeated by the Germans that neither surrendered *nor* collaborated. Moreover, Poles made extraordinary—and extraordinarily heroic—contributions to the Allied victory in the war. Nonetheless, despite a spate of books, articles, and movies about World War II over the past decade, the story of the scores of thousands of Poles who streamed out of their country in 1939 to fight the Nazis (as well as those who stayed behind to do the same thing) has been all but ignored. Yet it is one of the war's great epics, filled with adventure and glory, betrayal and tragedy.

We ourselves had only a superficial understanding of the Polish contribution when we first began to think about writing the book. The idea came initially during a Washington dinner party. Lynne was seated next to an international aid consultant named Danuta Lockett. While other conversations at the table focused on the latest doings on Capitol Hill and at the White House, Danuta talked about her father, a Polish pilot who had flown with the RAF during World War II. Some years before, we had learned that Polish fliers were among the fabled "few" who had saved Britain from the Germans in the summer and fall of 1940. Danuta's vivid accounts of her father and his compatriots made clear that Polish pilots played a vital role not only during the Battle of Britain but throughout the war. Their story, played out against the tragic backdrop of wartime Poland, was one that we felt richly deserved telling. Although it took several years for the idea to come to fruition, we thank Danuta for planting the seed.

Assisting us in our research in Poland (and once in England) was the inimitable and invaluable journalist, linguist, and sometime philosopher Andrzej Lewandowski. It is commonplace in book acknowledgments to say that without so-and-so, this book could not have been written. Sometimes, it may actually be true. In the case of Andrzej, it is absolutely true. Far more than a researcher and translator, he was a partner, tolerant of our ignorance and Stan's pitiful attempt to turn his knowledge of Russian into a knowledge of Polish, and gentle and witty as he guided us through the labyrinth of Polish history, military life, and politics. In the course of his work with us, assiduously tracking down information and sources, Andrzej became an expert on the Polish Air Force and the pilots on whom we focus in this book. During the many conversations we had with him in Warsaw and other parts of Poland, and in the countless e-mails we exchanged, we learned not only about Poland and the Poles but also about friendship. We thank him for that and for his dedication, his commitment to the truth, his support, and his sense of humor. Any errors in this book are certainly ours and not his. Nor should they be foisted on any of the many others who assisted us.

Although none of the five Kościuszko Squadron pilots whom we write about were still alive at the time of our research, we talked at length to members of their families, who gave us considerable insight into these dashing, heroic men. We particularly appreciate the many hours of help and hospitality provided by Witold Urbanowicz and his wife, Eliane. We also thank Wanda Łokuciewska, Marek Łokuciewski, Krzysztof Ferić, and the children of Ronald Kellett—Victor Kellett, Jonathan Kellett, Louise Pemberton, and Judy Williams. We're very grateful, too, to Stanisław Blasiak for making available to us his interviews with Wanda Krasnodębska.

Our thanks to the Polish, British, and American pilots who shared with us and Andrzej their own wartime experiences, as well as their memories of the Kościuszko Squadron and the five fliers. They include Tadeusz Andersz, Francis Gabreski, Franciszek Kornicki, Donald Lopez, Jan Maliński, Ludwik Martel (who introduced us to the fine restaurant at the Polish Centre in Hammersmith), Ignacy Olszewski, Tadeusz Sawicz, Stanisław Skalski, and John Young (who gave us a tour of Oxford). We owe a debt of gratitude, as well, to others who helped shed light on our subject, among them Robert Gretzyngier, Edward Idzior, Dr. Jan Koniarek, Tadeusz Konwicki, Helena Kubica, Jacek Kutzner, Wojtek Matusiak, Jerzy Pelc, and Irena Rothkael.

One of our more memorable experiences in writing this book was a dinner at the Warsaw residence of the British ambassador to Poland, Michael Pakenham, and his wife, Mimi. Among the guests for predinner cocktails that night was Jadwiga Piłsudska Jaraczewska, daughter of the legendary Polish leader Jozef Piłsudski. The beautiful and elegant Mrs. Jaraczewska told us and the other guests about her experiences as a Polish Air Force transport pilot during the war, ferrying Hurricanes, Spitfires, and other aircraft around Britain. Thanks to the Pakenhams for their most generous hospitality and for introducing us to Mrs. Jaraczewska, and to the American ambassador, Christopher Hill, and his wife, Patty Whitelaw-Hill.

In the course of our research, we were fortunate to have the assistance of librarians and archivists in Poland, Britain, and the United States. The Polish Institute and Sikorski Museum in London is a particular trove of primary source material for the activities of the Polish Air Force and the Polish armed forces generally during World War II. It is there that the Ferić/Kościuszko Squadron diaries are kept. The institute is also a repository for back issues of *Skrzydła* (*Wings*), a Polish Air Force magazine that began publication in 1941 and whose articles, many written by the pilots themselves, give a unique understanding of their thoughts and feelings during the war. We are grateful to Andrzej Suchcitz, the extraordinarily hardworking head of the Sikorski archives, for all he did during our several visits there.

Our appreciation also goes to officials at the Polish Air Force training academy at Dęblin, who spent a day showing us around that beautiful place and providing us with valuable information and insights about the prewar activities of the Kościuszko Squadron pilots who are at the book's center.

Thanks to the staff of the Public Records Office in Kew, outside London, who helped us locate relevant wartime papers of the British Foreign Office, Air Ministry, and War Cabinet; and to the librarians in the manuscript division of the Library of Congress for providing microfilm copies of documents from the Franklin D. Roosevelt Library. We are grateful, too, for the assistance of James D'Arc and other staffers of the L. Tom Perry Special Collections at the Brigham Young University library, which holds the personal papers of Merian C. Cooper.

A word of appreciation to the writers and scholars whose groundbreaking work on Poland, its history, and its military—especially its air force—was of great assistance to us in writing *A Question of Honor*. We would like to single out Norman Davies, Adam Zamoyski, and Jerzy Cynk.

Working on this book has been a joy from beginning to end, in large part because of the enthusiasm and commitment shown to us and our subject by our editor, Ann Close, and her colleagues at Alfred A. Knopf. Ann is a wonderful editor, and we consider ourselves truly fortunate to have had her support and guidance. We also thank Ann's assistant, Ilana Kurshan, and copy editor Ann Adelman for their help. Our British editor, Ravi Mirchandani, at William Heinemann, was similarly supportive. Our agent, Gail Ross, as always, has been an invaluable friend and counselor.

For their advice and encouragement, we are indebted to a number of other good friends, especially Brian and Lucy Conboy; Barbara, Andrew, and Ola Kapusto; Pat and Cassie Furgurson; Murray and Jeanne Gart; Peter and Marta Richardson; Sandy and Karen Gilmour; Greg and Marie Schneiders; and Rick and Sue Hornik.

And then there are our children and children-in-law (and their children), as always, to thank—Carly, Matthew (and Barnaby), David and Jenni (and Joey), and Michael and Danielle. They bless us with their lives and love.

Permissions Acknowledgments

Grateful acknowledgment is made to the following for permission to reprint previously published material.

A. P. Watt Ltd.: Excerpt from the poem "Less Nonsense" from *A.P.H.: His Life and Times* by Alan Herbert. Reprinted by permission of A. P. Watt Ltd. on behalf of Jocelyn Herbert and Teresa Elizabeth Perkins.

Houghton Mifflin Company and Cassell: Excerpts from *Triumph and Tragedy* by Winston S. Churchill. Copyright © 1953 by Houghton Mifflin Company, renewed 1981 by The Honourable Lady Sarah Audley and The Honourable Lady Soames. All rights reserved. Reprinted by permission of Houghton Mifflin Company and Cassell.

John Murray Publishers Ltd.: Excerpts from *Forgotten Few* by Adam Zamoyski.

Index

Page numbers in *italics* refer to illustrations.

ABOUT THE AUTHORS

Lynne Olson and Stanley Cloud are co-authors of *The Murrow Boys*, a highly acclaimed biography of the correspondents whom Edward R. Murrow hired before and during World War II to help create CBS News. Olson is also the author of *Freedom's Daughters*, the first comprehensive history of the role played by women in the civil rights movement. Cloud was a Moscow correspondent, White House correspondent, and Washington and Saigon bureau chief for *Time*. Olson was a Moscow correspondent for the Associated Press and covered the White House and politics for the *Baltimore Sun*. They are married and live in Washington, D.C.

A NOTE ON THE TYPE

This book was set in Janson, a typeface long thought to have been made by the Dutchman Anton Janson, who was a practicing typefounder in Leipzig during the years 1668–1687. However, it has been conclusively demonstrated that these types are actually the work of Nicholas Kis (1650–1702), a Hungarian, who most probably learned his trade from the master Dutch typefounder Dirk Voskens. The type is an excellent example of the influential and sturdy Dutch types that prevailed in England up to the time William Caslon (1692–1766) developed his own incomparable designs from them.

Composed by North Market Street Graphics, Lancaster, Pennsylvania

Printed and bound by Berryville Graphics, Berryville, Virginia

Designed by Robert C. Olsson

Maps by David Lindroth, Inc.

Voices in the Air 1939–1945

Incredible Stories of the World War II Airmen in Their Own Words

Laddie Lucas (Ed.)

A fascinating collection of stories from the men who took part in the great air battles of WWII

A unique and enthralling anthology compiled by WWII flying ace, Laddie Lucas, *Voices in the Air* tells the story of the air battles of the Second World War in the voices of those who took part. Drawn largely on the writings of the combatants themselves from all sides of the conflict, this book offers a vivid and highly individual account of the great aerial campaigns of WWII.

From a thrilling account of the first sustained dogfight between Spitfire and Messerschmitt in 1940, to an eighteen-year-old Japanese suicide pilot's last letter home and the Luftwaffe leaders' analysis of 'what went wrong' after the Battle of Britain, the book dramatically deals with every aspect of the war.

Full of stories of astonishing escapades, incredible bravery, dogged persistence and moving feats of arms, *Voices in the Air* honours both the sung and the unsung heroes of the war.

arrow books

THE POWER OF READING

Visit the Random House website and get connected with information on all our books and authors

EXTRACTS from our recently published books and selected backlist titles

COMPETITIONS AND PRIZE DRAWS Win signed books, audiobooks and more

AUTHOR EVENTS Find out which of our authors are on tour and where you can meet them

LATEST NEWS on bestsellers, awards and new publications

MINISITES with exclusive special features dedicated to our authors and their titles

READING GROUPS Reading guides, special features and all the information you need for your reading group

LISTEN to extracts from the latest audiobook publications

WATCH video clips of interviews and readings with our authors

RANDOM HOUSE INFORMATION including advice for writers, job vacancies and all your general queries answered

Come home to Random House

www.randomhouse.co.uk